THE APOCALYPSE

A LITERARY AND THEOLOGICAL COMMENTARY

THE APOCALYPSE

A LITERARY AND THEOLOGICAL COMMENTARY

JOHN CHRISTOPHER THOMAS

CPT Press
Cleveland, Tennessee

The Apocalypse
A Literary and Theological Commentary

Published by CPT Press
900 Walker ST NE
Cleveland, TN 37311
USA
email: cptpress@pentecostaltheology.org
website: www.cptpress.com

Library of Congress Control Number: 2012931481

ISBN-10: 193593127X
ISBN-13: 9781935931270

Copyright © 2012 CPT Press

All rights reserved. No part of this book may be reproduced or translated in any form, by print, photoprint, microfilm, microfiche, electronic database, internet database, or any other means without written permission from the publisher.

The Graeca font used to print this work is available from Linguist's Software, Inc., PO Box 580, Edmonds, WA 98020-0580 USA tel (425) 775-1130 www.linguistsoftware.com.

BWHEBB, BWHEBL, BWTRANSH [Hebrew], BWGRKL, BWGRKN, and BWGRKI [Greek] Postscript® Type 1 and TrueTypeT fonts Copyright © 1994-2009 BibleWorks, LLC. All rights reserved. These Biblical Greek and Hebrew fonts are used with permission and are from BibleWorks, software for Biblical exegesis and research.

This book is dedicated to the memory of my father J.D. Thomas (1935-1956), whom I hardly knew, and to the memory of my grandparents John Daniel Thomas (1899-1983), Dollie Christine Phillips Thomas (1895-1978), Charley Walter King (1906-1973), and Lena Irene Tucker King (1908-1974), who loved me more than I deserved and taught me more than they could ever know.

– 'Blessed are those who die in the Lord from now on ... for their works follow them' (Rev. 14.13).

Contents

Preface ix
List of Illustrations xv
Abbreviations xvi
Introduction 1
    Structure and Nature of the Book 2
    The Apocalypse as Visionary Drama 8
    The Apocalypse as Christian Prophecy 11
    The Apocalypse and the Apocalyptic Tradition 13
    The Apocalypse as Intertext 16
    The Canonical Location and Function of the Apocalypse 17
    Audience (Implied by the Text) 20
    Date 30
    Authorship 41
    The Apocalypse and Its Streams of Influence: The
        History of Effects 51

1.1-8 – Prologue 87
1.9-3.22 – 'In the Spirit on the Lord's Day' 97
    1.9-20 – Inaugural Vision of Jesus 97
    2.1-3.22 – The Seven Prophetic Messages to the Seven
        Churches of Asia 108

4.1-16.21 – 'In the Spirit' – In Heaven 201
    4.1-5.14 – Inaugural Vision of Heaven, the One Who Sits
        on the Throne, the Lamb, and the Scroll Sealed with
        Seven Seals 201
    6.1-8.5 – The Opening of the Scroll Sealed with Seven Seals . 238
        6.1-17 – The Opening of the First Six Seals 238
        7.1-17 – The 144,000 and the Great Multitude 258
        8.1-5 – The Opening of the Seventh Seal and
            the Golden Altar 278

8.6-11.19 – Seven Angels with Seven Trumpets 285
  8.7-9.21 – The Sounding of the First Six Trumpets............ 286
  10.1-11.14 – Prophetic Witness.. 308
  11.15-19 – The Sounding of the Seventh Trumpet................ 343
  12.1-14.20 – Redemptive History in Cosmic Perspective........ 351
    12.1-18 – Signs in Heaven: The Woman Clothed with
    the Sun and the Dragon... 352
    13.1-18 – The Two Beasts.. 382
    14.1-20 – The Lamb and the 144,000, the Harvest and
    the Winepress.. 417
  15.1-16.21 – Seven Angels with Seven Bowls of Plagues........ 448
    15.1-8 – Another Great Sign in Heaven: The
    Seven Angels... 448
    16.1-21 – The Pouring Out of the Seven Bowls................ 465

17.1-21.8 – 'In the Spirit' – Carried to a Wilderness............... 490
  17.1-18 – The Woman on the Beast: Babylon the Whore....... 490
  18.1-24 – The Destruction of Babylon.................................... 518
  19.1-21.8 – From Babylon to the New Jerusalem – From
  the Last Judgment to the New Creation 552
    19.1-10 - Rejoicing in Heaven and on Earth and
    the Marriage Supper of the Lamb................................ 552
    19.11-21 – The King of Kings and Lord of Lords:
    Victorious over All... 573
    20.1-10 – The Thousand-Year Reign 592
    20.11-15 – The Final Judgment..................................... 613
    21.1-8 – The Descent of the New Jerusalem 618

21.9-22.5 – 'In the Spirit' – On a High Mountain 634

22.6-21 – Conclusion and Epilogue 666

Bibliography... 689
Index of Biblical (and Other Ancient) References 696
Index of Names 713

Preface

Every book has a story and this book has a particularly long and winding one. I should perhaps confess from the outset that I had never intended to write a commentary on the Apocalypse. Having grown up in the apocalyptic tradition of Pentecostal spirituality, where the return of Jesus comprised a not insignificant place in the theological heart of the movement as part of the five-fold gospel that proclaims Jesus is Savior, Sanctifier, Holy Spirit Baptizer, Healer, and Soon Coming King, I was keenly attuned to the importance of eschatology and the unrivaled role played in it by the book of Revelation. Numerous sermons, lessons, lectures, and prophecy talks were encountered, not to mention films, books, tracts, and larger than life charts! All of these combined to create within me, and numerous others, a robust respect for those who could divine their way through current events by means of biblical prophecy. Rumors about government checks mistakenly sent to unsuspecting citizens that bore the number 666 circulated with a surprising degree of regularity, the naming of world leaders who seemed to fit what was thought to be characteristics of the 'antichrist', the relationship between the ten kings of Revelation 17 and the European Common Market (as it was known in those days), as well as fears with regard to bar codes, etc. all combined to create a heightened sense of interest in signs of the coming end of the world.

But despite my interest and sympathy with such attempts to understand end-time prophecy, problems with 'the script' began to emerge. Too many prophetic predictions and pronouncements by those 'in the know' proved to be off the mark, with little acknowledgement of such mistaken notions and little to no reflection about the significance of such missteps. As I began my interpretive and spiritual journey further into biblical studies I discovered that a straight-forward reading of Scripture often proved not to fit 'the script'; rather it became apparent that Scripture had to be forced into a pre-existing template in order for it to make sense. Eventually

I learned that some specific words essential to 'the script', like 'antichrist', were found not to appear in Revelation at all nor elsewhere in Scripture with the meaning assigned by 'the script'. At the same time, I found certain academic approaches to Revelation were often beholden to their own 'scripts', discounting portions of or emphases in the text that did not fit with their own more nuanced interpretations. Needless to say, the Apocalypse remained for me a closed book, about which I thought it best simply to steer clear.

It was Rick Moore, as I recall, who first mentioned to me that I should or would one day turn my attention to the Apocalypse; a suggestion I laughingly dismissed. But as I look back, Rick's words proved to be a catalyst in helping me to discern that God was calling me to this fascinating part of Scripture. Other encouragements would follow. One day in chapel at the seminary where I teach, a student from the former Soviet Union gave a testimony about his life and ministry. This student, Vladimir Mourashkine, who had experienced imprisonment and other forms of persecution at the hands of the communist government for being a Pentecostal Christian, began to rehearse the history of Russia by means of the story line found in the Apocalypse. Although there were aspects of the story that did not seem to fit for me as well as they did for him, I was enraptured by his words and began to think more deeply about how the book sounds and what it means in parts of the world where people do not have the luxury of spending large amounts of time speculating about end-time events. The other event, which had a significant impact on me, was reading Richard Bauckham's *The Theology of the Book of Revelation*. This was far and away the best thing I had ever read on the Apocalypse, and it gave me reason to ponder the book more intently from a literary and theological vantage point. The cumulative effect of these events caused me to be open to the possibility of working on this distinctive book of the NT.

The very first person to whom I verbalized the conviction that the Lord was preparing me to do something on the Apocalypse was my friend Max Turner, who (along with Joel Green) promptly offered me the opportunity to contribute a volume to the Two Horizons Commentary Series. But the offer was not to write on the Apocalypse (which had already been assigned!). Not long after agreeing to work with the THC project on the other volume, I was asked to consider writing the volume on the Apocalypse instead, as earlier plans had fallen through. As I began work on the commentary I soon enlisted the help of my good friend, Pentecostal theologian Frank Macchia, to join me in the endeavor – a partnership that has been an enjoyable and enriching one from the beginning. When it became clear that the draft of the commentary Frank and I produced was too far over the word limits to be included in the THC series, Eerdmans graciously consented to allow me to publish this longer CPT Press version, without Frank's theological essays, to be followed by the THC version which, along with Frank's fine theological contributions, would fit better within the size envisioned for the THC volumes. I am grateful to THC series editors Joel Green and Max Turner as well as others at Eerdmans for their consent and support.

The completion of this commentary, written over the course of about a decade, would not have been possible without the generous provision of periodic study leaves offered by the Pentecostal Theological Seminary as part of the research provisions attached to the Clarence J. Abbott Chair of Biblical Studies, which has been my privilege to hold since its inception. I would especially like to thank Dr Steven Jack Land, who has been the President during this period, as well as Dr James P. Bowers, who served as Dean during a good portion of this period, for their support.

For the most part the commentary was written at Tyndale House in Cambridge and at the Centre for Pentecostal Theology on the grounds of the Pentecostal Theological Seminary in Cleveland, TN. Both of these research facilities are ideal places for such work. The writing process itself has been the most exhilarating and exhausting experience of my life; perhaps some readers will have similar experiences in working through the volume! At so many points I have simply been overwhelmed by the literary artistry and theological depth found in the Apocalypse. I found it to be an overpowering vision that subverts any temptation to make it manageable or to tame its contents. My own attempt has been to offer a literary and theological reading of the text that seeks to discern the effect of the text on its 'hearers', both implied and actual. Happily, a large amount of art devoted to the Apocalypse is now in the public domain and is able to be included. The reader should note that unless otherwise indicated all citations of Scripture are my own translation.

This work has taken place within the local communities of which I am part. At my local church, the Woodward Church of God in Athens, TN, I have experienced extended and numerous times of prayer for this and the various research projects with which I am involved, dialogue with those in the community about the process and results, and times of interaction where insights from a variety of sources have been processed. Here, I have had the opportunity to teach and preach through the Apocalypse on several occasions. Just as it is difficult to put into words the effects one's family has upon one's scholarship, so it is difficult for me to describe the community's role. For I have learned that the Spirit can and does speak in and through a variety of unexpected contexts and individuals. It has amazed me over the years that in my local church, a congregation where there is a place for many of those on society's margins (the poor, the severely mentally challenged, ex-convicts, ex-addicts, those who have suffered racial discrimination, etc.), the Spirit speaks about certain issues that, while not always directly related to my scholarly work, often have a profound impact upon it. At the seminary the project has been helped along by careful readings of the developing drafts by my students over the years as well as the resulting intensive conversations about the meaning of the Apocalypse and the hearing here proposed. Such dialogue has taken place in the Apocalypse seminar that has been offered on a yearly basis as well as the Abbott lectures and various Ministers Week seminar presentations.

It has also been my happy privilege to have been invited to share portions of my work at a variety of venues both academic and popular including the Society for Pentecostal Studies, the Society of Biblical Literature, Bangor University, Institutul Teologic Penticostal Bucuresti (Romania), Regent University, Southeastern University, and Renovatus (Charlotte, NC). These opportunities have also improved the text. Special thanks are due to Deo Publishing, Wipf & Stock, and Erdmans for the use here of portions of the text that have previously appeared elsewhere in print, specifically:

'Pneumatic Discernment: The Image of the Beast and his Number', in S.J. Land, R.D. Moore, J.C. Thomas (eds.), *Passover, Pentecost, and Parousia: Studies in Celebration of the Life and Ministry of R. Hollis Gause* (JPTSup 35; Blandford Forum, UK: Deo, 2010), pp. 106-24.

'The Mystery of the Great Whore – Pneumatic Discernment in Revelation 17', in P. Althouse and R. Waddell (eds.), *Perspectives in Pentecostal Eschatologies: World without End* (Eugene, OR: Pickwick, 2010), pp. 111-36.

'New Jerusalem and the Conversion of the Nations: An Exercise in Pneumatic Discernment – Revelation 21.1-22.5', in I.H. Marshall, V. Rabens, C. Bennema (eds.), *The Spirit and Christ in the New Testament and Christian Theology – Essays in Honour of Max Turner* (Grand Rapids: Eerdmans, 2012), pp. 228-45.

Finally, I should like to thank a variety of people for their assistance along the way. My colleagues at the Pentecostal Theological Seminary, where I have served full-time since 1982, have contributed to the creation of a wonderful environment in which to pursue constructive Pentecostal theology. Students of my Apocalypse seminar have been energetic dialogue partners, spotting all manner of errors in the drafts, questioning points of interpretation, offering helpful suggestions, as well as prodding me to rethink certain conclusions. Their contributions are hard to overestimate and I thank them here for their dialogue. Special mention should be made of Steven Spears and Trina Sills who meticulously read the manuscript, calling my attention to the many aspects in need of revision, as well as Steffen Schumacher for his careful read of parts of the manuscript. Thanks are also due to two graduate assistants, Rev Larry Flickner and Christopher Brewer, for preparing the indices for this project. My partner on the THC volume Frank Macchia has contributed very much indeed to this commentary. He has read the manuscript carefully on more than one occasion, has engaged me in constructive dialogue all along the way, and graciously encouraged me at every phase of the journey. Frank is my dear friend, brother in the Lord, and model constructive Pentecostal theologian. My friend and colleague, Lee Roy Martin, is also worthy of special mention. He has been my dialogue partner on this and many other projects – always cheerful, always constructive, always dependable, and always ready with a helpful comment. In fact, he created an exquisite stained glass of the Apocalypse for me, the image of which appears on the back cover of the commentary. He has also contributed to the project in many ways less visible and I am indebted to him very much indeed. I have often thought that everyone needs a friend like Lee Roy. I have been blessed by our partnership in this and many other endeavors and I want to offer my heartfelt, public thanks here.

Of course, the greatest debt of thanks is due my family. My parents, Wayne and Betty Fritts, have been a constant source of encouragement to me and my family, offering spiritual, emotional, and financial support without which my academic study of Scripture would not have been possible. Their lives have been models of the best of Pentecostal spirituality and they will never know how deeply their living testimonies have impacted me, my brother Mark, and our extended family, who rise up and call them blessed. The role of my wife, Barbara, to this project has been enormous. She is strong, industrious, hardworking, athletic, independent, beautiful, and deeply spiritual. Barb has sacrificed a great deal for this and many other projects without complaint, creating a home environment that has freed me to pursue the research and writing to which I have felt called. I thank her for all she has done and for what she means to me in our thirty-fourth year of married life together. I should also like to thank our children Paige, Lori, and David (Paige's husband) for bringing great joy to our lives, taking interest in my Apocalypse work, living with our frequent separations, and celebrating the completion of the work with me. Barb and I love them more than life itself and thank God for them daily as they continue their journey through life. We could not be prouder of their professional accomplishments and their spiritual development.

My prayer is that this reading of the Apocalypse will assist the Pentecostal church and those beyond to rediscover and reappropriate this most important book in the canon of Scripture. May the Lord use it as he sees fit.

LIST OF ILLUSTRATIONS

Front Cover: Hans Memling, *Saint John the Evangelist on Patmos* (Memling Museum, Saint John's Hospital, Bruges, Belgium)

Figure 1 *Christ the Judge* (*Coemeterium Maius*, Rome)

Figure 2 *Worship of the Beast and War with the Beast* (*Trinity Apocalypse*, Trinity College Library, Cambridge, England)

Figure 3 *The Fifth Angel Empties His Bowl on the Throne of the Beast* (*Beatus of Liébana, Commentary on the Apocalypse [Morgan Beatus]* The Pierpont Morgan Library, NY)

Figure 4 Albrecht Dürer, *John Devours the Scroll* (State Art Gallery in Karlsruhe, Germany)

Figure 5 Jan van Eyck, *Adoration of the Lamb* (Ghent Altar Piece, Saint Bavo, Ghent, the Netherlands)

Figure 6 Hieronymus Bosch, *John on Patmos*

Figure 7 Albrecht Dürer, *Christ Among the Lampstands* (State Art Gallery in Karlsruhe, Germany)

Figure 8 *The Adoration of the Lamb* (Golden Codex of St Emmeran, Ratisbon, Munich, Bayrische Staatsbibliothek)

Figure 9 Facundus, *The Four Horsemen, Rev. 6* (Madrid, Biblioteca Nacional)

Figure 10 William Blake, *The Angel of Revelation* (Metropolitan Museum of Art, NY)

Figure 11 *The Woman Clothed with the Sun* (*Hortus Deliciarum of Herrad*)

Figure 12 Albrecht Dürer, *The Beasts* (State Art Gallery in Karlsruhe, Germany)

Figure 13 William Blake, *The Whore of Babylon* (British Museum, London)

Figure 14 *Christ the Conqueror, Beatus* at Osma (Burgo de Osma, Archivo de la catedral)

Figure 15 Albrecht Dürer, *Satan Cast into the Abyss* (State Art Gallery in Karlsruhe, Germany)

Figure 16 *The River of Life, Bamberg Apocalypse* (Bamberg, Staatsbibliothek, 140 [olim A ii 42, f. 57r.])

ABBREVIATIONS

ACCS	Ancient Commentary of Christian Scripture
ATR	*Anglican Theological Review*
BAGD	Walter Bauer, William F. Arndt, F. William Gingrich, and Frederick W. Danker, *A Greek-English Lexicon of the New Testament and Other Early Christian Literature* (Chicago: University of Chicago Press, 2nd edition, 1958)
BD	Beloved Disciple
BDF	Friedrich Blass, Albert Debrunner, and Robert Walter Funk, *A Greek Grammar of the New Testament and Other Early Christian Literature* (Chicago: University of Chicago Press, 1961)
BCOT	Baker Commentary on the Old Testament
BZNW	Beihefte zur Zeitschrift für die neutestamentliche Wissenschaft
CBQ	*Catholic Biblical Quarterly*
CNT	Commentaire du Nouveau Testament
CTJ	*Calvin Theological Journal*
CTM	Calwer theologische Monographien
ECNT	Exegetical Commentary of the New Testament
EDNT	Horst Balz and Gerhard Schneider (eds.), *Exegetical Dictionary of the New Testament* (3 vols.; Grand Rapids: Eerdmans, 1990-1993).
EUSST	European University Studies
FG	Fourth Gospel
HTR	*Harvard Theological Review*
Int	*Interpretation*
JBL	*Journal of Biblical Literature*
JETS	*Journal of the Evangelical Theological Society*
JPTSup	Journal of Pentecostal Theology Supplement Series
JSNT	*Journal for the Study of the New Testament*
JSNTS	Journal for the Study of the New Testament Supplement Series

MBPS	Mellen Biblical Press Series
NCCS	New Covenant Commentary Series
NIDNT	Colin Brown (ed.), *New International Dictionary of New Testament Theology* (3 vols.; Grand Rapids: Zondervan, 1975-78)
NIGNT	New International Greek New Testament
NovT	*Novum Testamentum*
NRT	*La nouvelle revue théologique*
NTD	Das Neue Testament deutsch
NTS	*New Testament Studies*
PTR	*Princeton Theological Review*
SBL	*Society of Biblical Literature*
SNTSMS	Society for New Testament Studies Monograph Series
TDNT	Gerhard Kittel and Gerhard Friedrich (eds.), *Theological Dictionary of the New Testament* (trans. Geoffrey W. Bromiley; 10 vols; Grand Rapids: Eerdmans, 1964-1976)
TynB	*Tyndale Bulletin*
WUNT	Wissenschaftliche Untersuchungen zum Neuen Testament
ZNW	*Zeitschrift für die neutestamentliche Wissenschaft*

INTRODUCTION

The Book of Revelation is the most sensual document in the NT, filled with references to things seen, heard, smelt, touched, and even tasted! Its holistic sensory invitation has proven to be an embrace hard to resist for many, whether they be artists, musicians, preachers, film-makers, visionaries, revolutionaries, ascetics, or religious enthusiasts. Yet, its wide appeal, particularly on a popular level, is met with a skeptical response on the part of many with academic training in theology, who often write the book off as the domain of the lunatic fringe. For it is at one and the same time a book which purports to reveal those things which shall soon take place, but its message is conveyed in such symbolic and cosmic language that there are nearly as many interpretations of the book as there are interpreters!

The purpose of this introduction is to aid one in his or her reading of the text of the Apocalypse and the commentary that follows. As a result, it is constructed in such a way so that primacy of place is given to the text of the book and the introductory issues that arise from the text. Thus, the introduction begins with a section devoted to the structure and nature of the Apocalypse. This gives way to an examination of what can be known about the audience of this book, and then on to issues of date and authorship. Owing to the effect of this text upon a wide variety of individuals, the introduction concludes with a section which identifies some of the major streams of influence that can be traced back to the Apocalypse.

Structure and Nature of the Book

The Apocalypse is perhaps the most literarily complex and sophisticated document in the NT. A close reading reveals a vast array of extraordinarily impressive literary devices, which testify to the intricate design and brilliance of the work.[1] When discussing the literary character and structure of the Apocalypse it is important to remember that apparently the document was written to be heard while it was being read aloud (1.3). Part of the genius of the work is that the clues as to its structure seem to communicate at a couple of different levels. On the one hand, some of the literary devices are apparent on one's first exposure to the document, while on the other hand many of these dimensions emerge slowly as the book is repeatedly read and heard over a prolonged period of time. Like so many other aspects of the text of the Apocalypse, the blessing promised to those who hear the words of this prophecy promises more than meets the eye (or ear in this case). It is not an overstatement to say that each hearing or reading of the Apocalypse brings discoveries of connections and nuances previously unnoticed. Given the breadth and depth of its imagery, little wonder that it has fueled the imagination of so many interpreters.

Literary Markers Recognized by a First-Time Hearer of the Apocalypse

Several aspects of the structure emerge after an initial encounter with the text of the Apocalypse. It is clear from an initial hearing of the book that the Apocalypse begins with a prologue. From this prologue the hearer learns that this Apocalypse of Jesus Christ, given by God to John, is a prophecy which results in a blessing for those who read, hear, and keep the things written in it (1.3). After these initial words, the prologue proceeds with a formula normally found at the beginning of an epistle. Here the standard A (author)

---

[1] The most extensive study of the structure of the Apocalypse is that of R. Bauckham, *The Climax of Prophecy: Studies on the Book of Revelation* (Edinburgh: T&T Clark, 1993), pp. 1-37. As will be apparent, much of what follows in this section is informed by this excellent essay. For a critique of Bauckham's work cf. P. Prigent, *L'Apocalypse de Saint Jean* (CNT 14; Geneve: Labor et Fides, 2000), pp. 71-74. For additional discussions on the structure of the Apocalypse cf. F.D. Mazzaferri, *The Genre of the Book of Revelation from a Source-Critical Perspective* (Berlin: Walter de Gruyter, 1989), pp. 330-65; and D.E. Aune, *Revelation 1-5* (WBC 52a; Dallas: Word, 1997), pp. xc-cv.

to B (recipient) greeting occurs, where John is identified as the author and the seven churches in Asia are identified as the recipients. The greeting continues in expanded Christian fashion with the bestowal of grace and peace upon the readers. The prologue moves to a doxology and concludes with two prophetic words.

Another feature of the book's structure, apparent from an initial encounter with the text, is the role and prominence of the Spirit. Soon after mention of the Seven Spirits before the throne (1.4), a pattern begins to emerge in which the Spirit plays a significant role. At four strategic locations (1.10; 4.2; 17.3; 21.10) the phrase ἐν πνεύματι ('in the Spirit') occurs. Each occurrence stands at the beginning of a new section of the book and together act as the major structural markers in the Apocalypse. Significantly, this phrase appears for the first time immediately after the close of the prologue.

Other major structural components one encounters in an initial hearing of the Apocalypse are several series of sevens. There are seven prophetic messages to the seven churches of Asia (2.1-3.22), seven seals (6.1-8.5), seven trumpets (8.2-11.19), and seven plagues (15.1-16.21).[2] Obviously, these series are an important dimension of the text and contribute something to the overall structure of the book. In this regard, the first series of seven (messages) are un-numbered in their delineation and are not formally connected to the other series of sevens. It is also significant that this first series of sevens is followed immediately by the second occurrence of the phrase ἐν πνεύματι ('in the Spirit'), indicating the beginning of a new section of the Apocalypse. The other three series of sevens are each individually enumerated in their description (first, second, third, etc.) and each of these series is formally connected to the others. To illustrate by means of computer software language, when one clicks on the icon of the seventh seal, the seven trumpets appear (8.1-2). Likewise, though not quite as explicit, when one clicks on the icon of the seventh trumpet (11.15-19), following the interlude of chapters 12-14, the seven bowls emerge (15.1). Thus, it would appear that these three series of sevens stand together structurally in the book. Confirming this idea is the fact that immediately after the seventh bowl of plagues is poured out, the phrase ἐν

---

[2] Reference is also made to seven thunders (10.3-4), but unlike the others mentioned they are sealed up and not written down.

πνεύματι ('in the Spirit') occurs for a third time, indicating the onset of the next major section in the Apocalypse.

Additional structural markers for the first-time hearer of the Apocalypse come in the form of the interludes that appear between the sixth and seventh seals (7.1-17), and the sixth and seventh trumpets (10.1-11.14). In each case, the appearance of these interludes seems to interrupt the flow of the document, at the least delaying the action being described. At the same time, such interludes draw attention to significant theological aspects of the text.[3] Similarly, chapters 12-14 appear to interrupt the flow of the document, dividing the description of the seven trumpets (8.2-11.19) from that of the seven bowls (15.1-16.21). While chapters 12-14 do interrupt the flow of the document, they are not without structural significance for they are connected thematically to the first two interludes and the story line of 12-14 converges in 15.1 with the story line left off at 11.19. Suffice it to say at this point, that these interludes would also make a structural impression upon first-time hearers of the Apocalypse.

Near the end of the book the hearer encounters a contrast between two cities; Babylon, the Great Whore (17.1-21.8), and New Jerusalem, the Bride of Christ (21.9-22.9). These sections are each marked by one of the seven angels with bowls of plagues speaking to John (17.1; 21.9), the phrase ἐν πνεύματι ('in the Spirit') (17.3; 21.10), and near identical introductory statements (17.1-3; 21.9-10). Thus, the climax of the book is reached with a description of the destruction of Babylon and the descent from heaven and description of the New Jerusalem.

A final structural dimension of the Apocalypse readily distinguishable to the first-time hearer is the book's concluding epilogue (22.6-21). Not only does the epilogue serve as a balance to the opening prologue, but numerous terms and themes found in the prologue also reappear in the epilogue offering an inclusio effect for the hearer.

---

[3] J.L. Resseguie, *The Revelation of John: A Narrative Commentary* (Grand Rapids: Baker, 2009), p. 53.

The following structure emerges from the above clues available to first-time hearers:

1.1-8 – Prologue

1.9-3.22 – 'In the Spirit on the Lord's Day'

    1.9-20 – Inaugural Vision of Jesus
    2.1-3.22 – The Seven Prophetic Messages to the Seven Churches of Asia

4.1-16.21 – 'In the Spirit' – In Heaven

    4.1-5.14 – Inaugural Vision of Heaven, the One Who Sits on the Throne, the Lamb, and the Scroll Sealed with Seven Seals
    6.1-8.5 – The Opening of the Scroll Sealed with Seven Seals
        6.1-17 – The Opening of the First Six Seals
        7.1-17 – The Interlude of the 144,000 and the Great Multitude
        8.1-5 – The Opening of the Seventh Seal and the Golden Altar
    8.6-11.19 – Seven Angels with Seven Trumpets
        8.6-9.21 – The Sounding of the First Six Trumpets
        10.1-11.14 – Prophetic Witness
        11.15-19 – The Sounding of the Seventh Trumpet
    12.1-14.20 – Redemptive History in Cosmic Perspective
        12.1-18 – Signs in Heaven: The Woman Clothed with the Sun and the Dragon
        13.1-18 – The Two Beasts
        14.1-20 – The Lamb and the 144,000, the Harvest and the Winepress
    15.1-16.21 – Seven Angels with Seven Bowls of Plagues
        15.1-8 – Another Great Sign in Heaven: The Seven Angels
        16.1-21 – The Pouring Out of the Seven Bowls

17.1-21.8 – 'In the Spirit' – Carried to a Wilderness

    17.1-18 – The Woman on the Beast: Babylon the Whore
    18.1-24 – The Destruction of Babylon
    19.1-21.8 – From Babylon to the New Jerusalem – From the Last Judgment to the New Creation

- 19.1-10 – Rejoicing in Heaven and on Earth and the Marriage Supper of the Lamb
- 19.11-21 – The King of Kings and Lord of Lords: Victorious over All
- 20.1-10 – The Thousand-Year Reign
- 20.11-15 – The Final Judgment
- 21.1-8 – The Descent of the New Jerusalem

21.9-22.5 – 'In the Spirit' – On a High Mountain

22.6-21 – Conclusion and Epilogue

If this is the basic structure that emerges from an initial exposure to the Apocalypse, what other significant elements may be discerned from a more intensive engagement with the text? In addition to this broad structure are a number of places where the whole document, large sections, or smaller sections are connected to one another by means of similar or, in some cases, identical vocabulary or themes. For example, a comparison of the language of 1.1-3 with that of 22.6-7 reveals that these verses constitute an inclusio which bounds the entire book.

> The revelation of Jesus Christ, which God gave him to show his servants what must soon take place. He made it known by sending his angel to his servant John, who testifies to everything he saw – that is, the word of God and the testimony of Jesus. Blessed is the one who reads the words of this prophecy, and blessed are those who hear it and take to heart what is written in it, because the time is near (1.1-3).

> The angel said to me, 'These words are trustworthy and true. The Lord the God of the spirits of the prophets, sent his angel to show his servants the things that must soon take place'. 'Behold, I am coming soon! Blessed is he who keeps the words of the prophecy in this book' (22.6-7).

A variety of terms used to describe Christ at various places near the beginning of the book – 'his eyes were like flames of fire' (1.14; 2.18), 'from his mouth came a sharp two-edged sword' (1.16; 2.12, 16), he will rule 'with an iron scepter' (2.26-27), he is 'faithful and true witness' (3.14) – converge in one passage near its end in describing the 'King of Kings and Lord of Lords' (19.11-16). A final example of a literary device that serves to hold the entire book together is the occurrence of seven beatitudes found at various places throughout the book (1.3; 14.13; 16.15; 19.9; 20.6; 22.7, 14).

Not only does one find techniques that help knit the entire book together, one also sees a similar phenomenon within a major section of the book. An example of this occurs in 4.1-16.21. This section, which is devoted primarily to the three series of sevens, is held together in part by a recurring phrase that expands in intensity as the section unfolds. Specifically, the 'flashes, sounds, and thunder' which come from the throne in 4.5, become the 'thunder, sounds, flashes, and earthquake' that come to earth from heaven when the angel casts fire from the altar down in 8.5. When God's temple in heaven opens in 11.19 there come 'flashes, sounds, thunder, earthquake, and great hail'. This recurring theme culminates in 16.18-21 when, after a voice from the throne says 'It is done', there come 'flashes, sounds, thunder', an earthquake greater than any experienced on earth before and hail stones that weigh 100 pounds (ταλαντιαία) each. Significantly, these phenomena do not occur together elsewhere in the book. Similarly, the interlude of chapters 12-14 is bounded on either side by great signs in the heavens. The interlude begins with 'a great sign was seen in heaven' (12.1) and its conclusion gives way to 'And I saw another great and marvelous sign in heaven' (15.1). In like fashion the ending of one section and beginning of another section can be conveyed by the occurrence of the same phrase on two separate occasions. The close of the central major section (4.1-16.21) and beginning of the next section (17.1-21.8) is signaled by the appearance of 'It is done' in 16.17, while the close of the latter (17.1-21.8) and beginning of the final major section in the book (21.9-22.9) is signaled by 'It is done' in 21.6. Additionally, the same term can occur in a given section to convey a sense of movement from one ultimate domain to another. On seven occasions beginning with 13.1 through 15.2, the term εἶδον ('I saw') occurs and is used to convey a sense of movement from the sea, beside which the dragon stood, to the sea of glass, beside which stood those who had been victorious over the beast. The text says:

And I saw a beast coming *out of the sea* (13.1) ...
And I saw another beast coming *out of the earth* (13.11) ...
And I saw ... the Lamb standing *upon Mt Zion* (14.1) ...
And I saw another angel flying *in mid-air* (14.6) ...
And I saw ... one like the Son of Man sitting *upon a cloud* (14.14)
...
And I saw another great and marvelous sign *in heaven* (15.1) ...
And I saw what looked like *a sea of glass beside which* were standing those who had been victorious over the beast (15.2) ....

Another characteristic of the literary structure of the Apocalypse is the fact that on at least three occasions, two sections that come together at a transition point in the book overlap with one another. This is the case where the seven seals give way to the seven trumpets (8.1-5), where the story line of the cosmic interlude converges with the story line of the seven bowls of plagues (15.1-4), and where the description of the New Jerusalem gives way to the epilogue (22.6-11). Such phenomena remind the hearer that while major movements within the book may be discerned, the document stands together as a single visionary drama.

The Apocalypse as Visionary Drama

If this is the understanding of the structure of the Apocalypse which emerges through repeated hearings and readings of the book, what would be conveyed to its hearers with regard to the kind of literature that is being heard and read? While differing aspects of this question receive more extensive treatment below, it is important initially to gain a sense of the way in which a hearer may have understood the document as a whole.

One of the first things evident to the hearer about the literary nature of the Apocalypse is that it is designed for 'oral enactment'.[4] While it is legitimate to note that the document had to be read publicly owing to John's absence on Patmos, such an explanation of the act of reading does not take into sufficient account the dramatic characteristics of the Apocalypse. For at every turn, there are indi-

---

[4] For this designation cf. D.L. Barr, 'The Apocalypse of John as Oral Enactment', *Int* 40 (1986), pp. 243-56.

cations that the book is designed for 'oral enactment'.⁵ Evidence for this observation includes many of the literary features noted in the discussion with regard to the book's structure, but is not confined to them. In addition to the utilization of various numbered series (sevens, threes, and twos), the multiple use of the ἐν πνεύματι ('in the Spirit') phrase, and the employment of periodic interludes, there are numerous other indicators. For example, the images and places used to convey the message of the book are at one and the same time intriguing and memorable. To this might be added the first person address of both John and Jesus, the generous use of hymns, and the fact that at each stage of the Apocalypse more is revealed about Jesus. The liberal use of colors in the Apocalypse tends to confirm that the work is designed for 'oral enactment'. By way of illustration, the relative colorless FG, which makes mention only of white and purple, pales in comparison with the colors of the Apocalypse, which include gold or yellow, white, scarlet, red, purple, silver, green, and black. Given the dramatic characteristics of the Apocalypse, some interpreters have gone so far as to argue that it was constructed to be staged in ways not unlike the Greek tragedies.⁶

The point of these observations is to underscore the fact that, first and foremost, the hearers and readers of the Apocalypse would have experienced this document as the 'oral enactment' of a visionary drama. It is important to take up the issue at this point for discussions which attempt to ascertain the literary genre of the Apocalypse sometimes lose sight of this rather basic understanding of the document.

Part of the power of this visionary drama is that it creates for its hearers and readers a symbolic world offering an alternate version of reality to that experienced by the Asian churches in the Roman

---

⁵ The following observations are based in large part on the work of Barr, 'The Apocalypse of John as Oral Enactment', and S.S. Smalley, *Thunder and Love: John's Revelation and John's Community* (Milton Keynes, UK: Word, 1994), cf. esp. pp. 103-10.

⁶ In addition to the work of Smalley cf. E. Dansk, *The Drama of the Apocalypse* (London: T. Fisher Unwin, 1894); E.W. Benson, *The Apocalypse: an Introductory Study of the Revelation of St John the Divine* (New York: Macmillan, 1900), pp. 4-41; R.R. Brewer, 'The Influence of Greek Drama on the Apocalypse of John', *ATR* 18 (1935-36), pp. 74-92; and J.W. Bowman, 'The Revelation to John: Its Dramatic Structure and Message', *Int* 9 (1955), pp. 436-53.

world.[7] This alternate reality offers heaven as the vantage point from which to assess the reality of this world and its powers. The significance of such an alternate reality is difficult to overestimate, for it empowers its hearers and readers to confront their present reality as faithful witnesses who have an active role to play in the conversion of the nations which lies before them. But this is not all. The hearers and readers are not only invited to hear or view this symbolic world, but also to experience it by means of participation. For throughout this 'oral enactment', the hearers and readers find themselves responding vicariously along with John as he turns, sees, hears, and looks. As the visions of the One who sits on the throne and of the Lamb unfold, the hearers and readers find themselves in the spontaneous acts of worship which erupt on numerous occasions.

The logical place for such 'oral enactment' is the context of worship within the community. Not only would this be consistent with the common practice found across early Christianity of reading significant communiqués before the entire community (1 Thess. 5.27; Eph. 6.21; Col. 4.16; Phlm. 2), but would also be the most appropriate context for hearing, testing, and discerning prophetic utterances. This would be true both of prophetic utterances of a spontaneous nature as well as those prophetic messages (including visions) which, while experienced outside the context of the community's worship, would be brought to it for the appropriate response.[8]

This phenomenological understanding of the Apocalypse, as orally enacted visionary drama, would go a long way toward defining for the hearers and readers the kind of literature the Apocalypse is. It is within this understanding of how the hearers and readers would experience the Apocalypse as visionary drama that other questions with regard to the issue of the literary genre of the book may be pursued.

Technically, this visionary drama takes the form of a circular letter to the seven churches of Asia (1.4, 11; 22.16). The book bears the marks of the standard A (author) to B (recipient) greeting near

---

[7] On this cf. R. Bauckham, *The Theology of the Book of Revelation* (Cambridge: Cambridge University Press, 1993), p. 10.

[8] On the liturgical context of the Apocalypse cf. J.-P. Ruiz, *Ezekiel in the Apocalypse: The Transformation of Prophetic Language in Revelation 16,17-19,10* (EUSST 23; Frankfurt am Main: Lang, 1989), pp. 184-89.

the beginning of the book (1.4) and concludes with the epistolary formula, 'May the grace of the Lord Jesus be with you all' (22.21). Although the content of Revelation 2-3 is sometimes described as the seven letters to the seven churches, in point of fact, the Apocalypse is one circular letter that includes seven prophetic messages to the seven churches of Asia. This literary device means that while each church is informed by the specificity of the message addressed to it, at the same time they are all informed by the fact that all the prophetic messages are to be read by all the churches. The theological reason that such a visionary drama takes the form of an epistle is owing to the command received by John in his inaugural vision.

> That which you see, write in a book and send it to the seven churches, in Ephesus and in Smyrna and to Pergamum and to Thyatira and to Sardis and to Philadelphia and to Laodicea (1.11).

Among other things, the epistolary form, as does the command to write in a book everything seen, serves to re-enforce the idea that this Visionary Drama stands together and is to be heard and read as a whole. That John is told at the beginning to write down in a book all the things he sees, conveys to the hearers and readers that John is to embark on a journey. Perhaps his book will give the impression of being a travelogue[9] for those who care to join him in this journey.

The Apocalypse as Christian Prophecy

A number of indicators in the text reveal that this visionary drama, which takes the form of a circular letter, is a piece of early Christian prophecy. Such an identification comes very early in the book where John describes the volume as 'the words of this prophecy' (1.3). This description is repeated near the close of the book as well, where again the Apocalypse is referred to as 'the words of this prophecy' (22.8). These phrases form an inclusio that bounds the book on either side, indicating that the entire epistle is to be heard and read as 'a book of prophecy'. This identification of the Apoca-

---

[9] For this idea cf. R.W. Wall, *Revelation* (NIBC, NTS 18; Peabody, MA: Hendrickson, 1991), p. 13.

lypse as a prophecy is also confirmed by the words of the angel who instructs John, 'Do not seal up the words of this prophecy' (22.10). Finally, the book closes with a set of warnings that further underscore the fact that this book describes itself as a book of prophecy.

> I witness (to) all who hear the words of the prophecy of this book: if anyone adds unto them, God will add upon them the plagues written (described) in this book. And if anyone takes away from the words of the book of this prophecy, God will take away his part of the tree of life and the city of the saints (holy ones), which are written (described) in this book (22.18-19).

Not only does the book describe itself as prophecy, but also a number of passages in the book look very much to be individual prophetic utterances. These include, but are not limited to: the words of God in 1.8 – 'I am the Alpha and Omega ... who is, and who was, and who is to come'; the prophetic messages of Jesus to the seven churches in 2.1-3.22; the words of Jesus in 16.15 – 'Behold, I come as a thief! Blessed is the one who stays awake and keeps one's garments (pure), in order that he might not walk naked and they see his private parts'; the words of the Spirit in 14.13 – '"Yes", says the Spirit, "in order that they might rest from their labor; for their works follow after them"'; and the numerous words of Jesus in 22.7-20.[10]

In addition to the overt descriptions of the book as prophecy and examples of prophetic utterances in the book, several textual indicators suggest that the context from which the book originates is itself a prophetic one. Mention is made in the book of at least one rival prophet(ess) (2.20). There are also statements which make clear that John does not function alone in his prophetic activity, for he and others are addressed near the end of the Apocalypse by an angel who says, 'I am a fellow servant with you and your brothers the prophets' (22.9). This same group (possibly including the OT prophets) may well be in view a few verses earlier when the angel makes reference to 'The Lord, the God of the spirits of the proph-

---

[10] Another possible prophetic utterance from the risen Jesus is found in 13.9-10, while 2.21 is sometimes taken as reference to an earlier (unrecorded) prophetic word given by John.

ets' (22.6). Other references to these prophets in the Apocalypse include: 11.18; 16.6; 18.20, 24 (cf. also references to prophets in 10.7 and 11.10). Taken together this textual evidence makes one thing very clear; the prophecy that is the Apocalypse comes from a prophetic community. This fact, in and of itself, would add some understanding to the public reading of 'the words of this prophecy' to the community.

Before closing this section it should also be noted that this prophecy has a number of affinities with OT prophecy. Not only does the Apocalypse resemble a number of OT prophetic books in formal ways, i.e. by inclusion of call narratives and the emphasis upon the Word of God and the visions,[11] but it also exhibits a similar prophetic consciousness on the part of the author.[12] In fact, it appears that John so sees himself as heir to the OT prophetic tradition that he, as the OT prophets before him, inherits earlier prophecies the reinterpretation of which figures prominently in his own prophecy. This may be illustrated by the way in which the prophecy concerning Babylon in Rev. 18.1-19.8 echoes every message against Babylon found in the OT, as well as two messages against Tyre.[13] Owing to the many similarities between the Apocalypse and the OT Prophetic tradition, John's own sense of prophetic consciousness, and the scope and magnitude of the Apocalypse, one writer has described the book as 'The Climax of Prophecy'.[14]

The Apocalypse and the Apocalyptic Tradition

It is also clear from several aspects of the text of the Apocalypse that there is some kind of relationship between the Apocalypse and the apocalyptic tradition. In fact, for some interpreters the evidence for this is so strong that it is not uncommon to find commentaries

---

[11] On this cf. esp. Mazzaferri, *The Genre of the Book of Revelation from a Source-Critical Perspective*, pp. 259-378.

[12] On the issue of prophetic consciousness cf. the very helpful works by A.J. Heschel, *The Prophets* 2 vols. (Peabody, MA: Hendrickson, 2003) and R.D. Moore, *The Spirit of the Old Testament* (JPTSup 35; Blandford Forum: Deo Publishing, 2011), pp. 56-68.

[13] Bauckham, *The Theology of the Book of Revelation*, p. 5.

[14] Cf. Bauckham, *The Climax of Prophecy*.

that address the issue of apocalyptic as its first order of business.[15] What is the nature of the evidence for seeing a relationship between the two and what is the nature of the relationship?

Perhaps one of the most significant clues that the Apocalypse has strong connections to the apocalyptic tradition is the fact that this book is the first extant document to use the word ἀποκάλυψις ('revelation') as part of its title. Whatever the relationship between this book of prophecy and the apocalyptic tradition may be, many later documents follow the Apocalypse in using the word ἀποκάλυψις ('revelation') as part of its title. While there is some debate as to the precise meaning of the phrase, 'An apocalypse of Jesus Christ', an issue that will be addressed later, it should be noted that there is some degree of circularity in assuming that this document, from which an entire genre of literature takes its name, is an apocalyptic document owing to the fact that the word Apocalypse is part of its title.[16]

Assessing the nature of the relationship between the Apocalypse and the apocalyptic tradition is complicated by the fact that the broad boundaries and specific characteristics of the apocalyptic genre are anything but fixed and still greatly debated within the scholarly community.[17] Despite the inherent obstacles involved in ascertaining the relationship between the Apocalypse and the apocalyptic tradition, perhaps the following observations will be of some assistance in sorting out this difficult issue.

It should be noted, first of all, that the Apocalypse is similar to the apocalyptic tradition in several respects. The fantastic imagery employed in the Apocalypse, among other things, reminds one of the imagery of a number of other apocalyptic documents. This similarity suggests, at the least, that the Apocalypse and a variety of apocalyptic documents draw from the same conceptual well.[18] Like

---

[15] Cf. for example J. Sweet, *Revelation* (London: SCM Press, 1990), pp. 1-5.

[16] For a similar point cf. G. Linton, 'Reading the Apocalypse as an Apocalypse', *SBL Seminar Papers* (Atlanta: Scholars Press, 1991), pp. 174-82.

[17] Perhaps the most widely used set of criteria utilized in defining the genre are those proposed by J.J. Collins, 'Toward the Morphology of a Genre', *Semeia* 14 (1979), pp. 1-20. Cf. also the perceptive comments of Linton, 'Reading the Apocalypse as an Apocalypse', pp. 178-85.

[18] E. Schüssler Fiorenza [*Revelation: Vision of a Just World* (Minneapolis: Fortress, 1991), p. 23] notes, 'Revelation employs stock images, conventional *topoi* or

the broader apocalyptic tradition, the Apocalypse conveys a transcendent perspective about this world and its history allowing hearers and readers the opportunity to view this world and its history from the perspective of heaven. The Apocalypse also shares with other apocalyptic documents an interest in the question, 'who is Lord over the world?'[19] In addition, the Apocalypse is decidedly eschatological in orientation.[20]

At the same time, there are decided differences between the Apocalypse and what has come to be known as the apocalyptic tradition. One of the best-known differences is that the author of the Apocalypse writes in his own name, unlike the documents normally considered as part of the apocalyptic tradition which are pseudonymous with regard to authorship. If the Apocalypse is to be considered as part of the apocalyptic tradition, it stands virtually alone in this regard.[21] Perhaps this anomaly is to be explained by the fact that John considers his work to be a book of prophecy, or perhaps it has something to do with his closer temporal proximity to the time of Jesus' earthly ministry. Another difference between the Apocalypse and the apocalyptic tradition is evident in the use of visual symbolism. Generally speaking, there is more visual symbolism in the Apocalypse than (other) apocalyptic texts. At the same time, there is a virtual absence of angelic interpretation present in the Apocalypse as opposed to other apocalypses. Additionally, the generally short and self-contained vision normally found in only one part of an apocalyptic document virtually encompasses the whole of this Apocalypse. A final difference to be mentioned is that, unlike the Book of Daniel, where Daniel is instructed by the angel to 'close up and seal up the words of the scroll until the time of the end … go your way, Daniel, because the words are closed up and sealed until the end of time', John is instructed, 'Do not seal up the words of the prophecy of this book, because the time is near'.[22] The Apocalypse is an open book rather than a closed one.

---

places, scriptural figures, and proofs, as well as literary techniques developed in apocalyptic literature'.

[19] Bauckham, *The Theology of the Book of Revelation*, pp. 7-9.

[20] Schüssler Fiorenza, *Revelation: Vision of a Just World*, pp. 24-25.

[21] The other possible exception to this practice also comes from a Christian writer, the Shepherd of Hermas.

[22] Bauckham, *The Theology of the Book of Revelation*, pp. 9-12.

Given the differences and similarities of the Apocalypse to the apocalyptic tradition, what might be concluded about the nature of their relationship? It is important to remember that the hearers and readers of this book would not make the kind of hard and fast distinctions between the prophetic and apocalyptic genre that contemporary students of Scripture sometimes do.[23] It is clear that John and his hearers would be familiar with a number of the symbols, imagery, and language found in apocalyptic documents of the time. However, the use of similar imagery does not necessarily imply a literary dependency but suggests that these ideas were in the air breathed by John and his audience. They often draw from the same conceptual well, but utilize the concepts to suit their own purposes. In other words, regardless of the ambiguity surrounding the relationship of the Apocalypse to the apocalyptic tradition, it appears that the hearers of the Apocalypse would move easily in this apocalyptic conceptual world.[24]

The Apocalypse as Intertext

If there are questions about the extent of the relationship of the Apocalypse to the apocalyptic tradition, there are no such questions with regard to its relationship to the OT. The Apocalypse is literally full of OT imagery, ideas, and vocabulary. Yet, unlike many NT documents, by most reckonings, there is not a single direct quotation of the OT in this book. A reading of the Apocalypse reveals that its utilization of the OT is not primarily concerned with respecting the OT context of a given idea, thought, or term.[25] At the same time, the hearer of the Apocalypse soon discovers that the OT is more than a language arsenal from which the writer constructs his own theological statement or prophetic vision.[26]

---

[23] G.K. Beale, *The Book of Revelation: A Commentary on the Greek Text* (NIGNT; Grand Rapids: Eerdmans, 1999), p. 37.

[24] Bauckham, *The Climax of Prophecy*, pp. 38-91. On the relationship between prophecy and apocalyptic, cf. the helpful comments by R.D. Moore, 'Joel', *The Book of the Twelve* (ed. J.C. Thomas; Blandford Forum: Deo, forthcoming).

[25] Contra Beale, *The Book of Revelation*, pp. 76-99.

[26] Contra E. Schüssler Fiorenza, *Revelation: Justice and Judgment* (Philadelphia: Fortress, 1985), p. 135.

Rather, the relationship between the Apocalypse and the OT is a much more dynamic phenomenon. The Apocalypse is better seen as an intertext where a variety of texts (including the writer, John!) converge and/or intersect. The intersection of OT texts, ideas, imagery, and vocabulary with John's visionary experience results in an intertext where echoes and allusions to the OT (among other things) provide shape and definition of meaning to the vision that is the Apocalypse. Sometimes these allusions are like loud voices calling out to the hearers, while at other times they are no more than mere whispers to which the hearers' ears must be attuned or they will be missed altogether. Such a dynamic understanding of the relationship between the Apocalypse and the OT means that no mere listing of allusions or echoes to the OT does justice to this dimension of the Apocalypse. For everything found in the Apocalypse is influenced, in one way or another, by the OT.[27] Specifically, one must ask how the OT context interacts with the NT context?[28] Discernment of these echoes and allusions is called for here, perhaps in ways not unlike the discernment called for in the receiving and recording of this prophecy by John and the task of the circle of prophets mentioned earlier. However, it is safe to say that any hearers or readers of the Apocalypse who neglect the voice of the OT do so at his or her own peril.

The Canonical Location and Function of the Apocalypse

Whatever the historical events that resulted in the current NT canon, it is clear that the structure of the canon is not without significance with regard to a particular book's interpretive role and influence. The goal of this section is to offer certain observations with regard to the role and function of the Apocalypse in the NT canon.

Before proceeding to these considerations, it is important to note that not all groups of Christians include the Apocalypse as part of their canon.[29] It should also be observed that while the Apoca-

---

[27] On this cf. the helpful comments by F.J. Murphy, *Fallen Is Babylon: The Revelation to John* (Harrisburg, PA: Trinity Press International, 1998), p. 28.

[28] S. Moyise, *The Old Testament in the Book of Revelation* (JSNTS 115; Sheffield: Sheffield Academic Press, 1995), p. 19.

[29] R.W. Wall and E.E. Lemcio, *The New Testament as Canon: A Reader in Canonical Criticism* (JSNTS 76; Sheffield: JSOT Press, 1992), p. 276] observes, 'Today,

lypse stands last in the vast preponderance of canonical lists, the book follows the Gospels in a few listings.[30] Two reasons may account for such a location. First, it may be that since the Apocalypse contained so many words of the resurrected Jesus, it made some sense to locate the book after those documents that give careful attention to his 'pre-ascension' words.[31] At the same time, the natural affinity that exists between the FG and the Apocalypse may also account for its location in these witnesses. In this case, it would seem that their affinities drew the latter to a position in closer canonical proximity to the former.[32]

Owing to its unique standing as the last book in the biblical canon, the Apocalypse functions on several canonical levels. It would appear that the best way to approach this topic is to structure these canonical reflections in a way that moves from the Apocalypse's function in connection with those books in closest canonical proximity to its broader function in the meta-narrative of the Bible.

The Apocalypse is quite obviously connected canonically to those documents that precede it in the NT (the epistles), for, as noted earlier, it too takes the form of an epistle. In this regard, the Apocalypse furthers a number of concerns and themes found both among the letters of Paul and those that come from the Other NT Voices. Of the specific concerns addressed, the Apocalypse continues the theme of false teaching that is of more than passing interest in a large number of the epistles. Among other things, the Apocalypse makes clear that false teaching is both dangerous to the Christian community and that any one who identifies with it will share in the destruction that awaits the evil triumvirate of Satan, the beast, and the false prophet. The Apocalypse also continues the emphasis of several of the epistles on the return of Jesus.

The canonical function of the Apocalypse may also be seen in its connections to the Johannine literature that precedes in the NT. Of the many examples that could be cited, two observations will be

---

there are still some non-Chalcedon (i.e. Nestorian) Christian communions who reject the canonicity of Revelation and follow the Peshitta, an ancient Syriac version of the Bible, which excludes Revelation along with 2 Peter, 2-3 John and Jude'.

[30] B.M. Metzger, *The Canon of the New Testament: Its Origin, Development, and Significance* (Oxford: Clarendon Press, 1987), p. 295.

[31] Metzger, *The Canon of the New Testament*, p. 295.

[32] A suggestion made by John Painter in private conversation.

offered. First, one of the great points of both continuity and development is the presentation of Jesus. On the one hand, continuity is provided by the fact that the image of Jesus as the (paschal) Lamb of God found in the FG (1.29), also appears in the Apocalypse (5.6). On the other hand, the revelation of Jesus in the Apocalypse includes a development of this image to such an extent that it is not uncommon for students of Scripture to speak of the Wrath of the Lamb as a way of describing the Lamb's identity in this book.[33] Second, the pneumatology of the FG, which places a great deal of emphasis upon the role of the coming Paraclete,[34] and that of 1 John, where the Spirit's role in prophetic activity comes into focus,[35] gives way to a more full-blown prophetic pneumatology in the Apocalypse.[36]

The canonical function of the Apocalypse also extends to its relationship with the Gospels that are located at the other end of the NT. The major sections devoted to the return of Jesus in Matthew (24-25), Mark (13), and Luke (21) in some ways serve to anticipate the more extended discussion of this topic in the Apocalypse. Here too, the full implications of the Messiah's coming for both the Jewish people and the nations, announced in Matthew 1, are made explicit in the imagery of the Apocalypse (cf. especially the relationship between the 144,000 and the innumerable multitude in Revelation 7).

In addition, the canonical function of the Apocalypse can also be seen at the meta-narrative level of the Bible. First, the book serves as a fitting conclusion to the story of humanity's rebellion against God. This story, which began so long ago in Genesis, is completed by a vision of God's reign and rule established completely. Second, in the Apocalypse a number of God's purposes for his creation are redeemed, especially through the one thousand year reign. Third, in many ways the Apocalypse functions as the fulfillment and completion of all biblical prophecy that came before it.

---

[33] Sweet, *Revelation*, pp. 50-52.

[34] Cf. J.C. Thomas, *The Spirit of the New Testament* (Leiderdorp, The Netherlands: Deo Publishing, 2004), pp. 157-74.

[35] Cf. J.C. Thomas, *1 John, 2 John, 3 John* (London: T & T Clark International, 2004), pp. 13-14, 123-41, 197-214, 249-64.

[36] Cf. R.C. Waddell, *The Spirit of the Book of Revelation* (JPTSup 30; Blandford Forum: Deo Publishing, 2006).

20 The Apocalypse

Finally, through this book it becomes apparent that many of the judgments of God, which were desired for so long by his people, will not ultimately take place until the end of time.[37]

Audience (Implied by the Text)

What might be known of the audience to whom these words of prophecy were written? Unlike a number of other NT letters (both circular and specific), the text of the Apocalypse gives some specific information as to the identity of its intended audience. This information includes the names of the cities in Asia (Minor) where the churches are located to whom the seven prophetic messages are addressed in chapters 2-3.

Geographical Location – Asia Minor

Thus, the interpreter of the Apocalypse has good reason to believe that the prophecy's intended audience includes churches in the cities of Ephesus, Smyrna, Pergamum, Thyatira, Sardis, Philadelphia, and Laodicea. This geographical location is confirmed by the fact that John writes from the Island of Patmos, which is just off the coast of Asia Minor in the Aegean Sea.

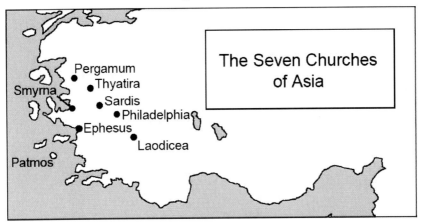

This listing of these specific cities informs the interpreter of the Apocalypse in several ways. When these seven cities are located on

---

[37] For some of these ideas about the Apocalypse's canonical function on the level of meta-narrative cf. Wall and Lemcio, *The New Testament as Canon*, pp. 280-82.

a map of Asia Minor, one discovers that in their textual order they are not haphazardly arranged but take on a certain shape. One who follows the textual order of these cities on a map of Asia Minor would begin with Ephesus in the south, go north to Smyrna, and then on due north to Pergamum. From Pergamum, the northern most point in the list, one would go southeast to Thyatira, south southeast to Sardis, east southeast to Philadelphia, and then southeast to Laodicea. While there may be literary and theological reasons for this particular order, an issue to be taken up later, it is often noted that the textual order of these cities is owing to their location on an ancient trade and postal route.[38]

This list of churches found in the Apocalypse is informative in other ways as well. On the one hand, an examination of this list reveals that several of these cities are also known from other early Christian writings. Paul writes a (circular) letter to the church at Ephesus and indicates that he has written the church at Laodicea, instructing the church at Colossae to exchange letters with this congregation (Col. 4.16). Ignatius is known to have written letters to the churches at Ephesus, Smyrna, and Philadelphia. Polycarp served as the Bishop of Smyrna, while Melito functioned in that capacity at Sardis. On the other hand, there are at least two other Christian churches in Asia Minor which were located in cities not mentioned in the Apocalypse. For example, Paul makes reference to the church in Hierapolis (Col. 4.13), where Papias later serves as Bishop, while Ignatius wrote letters to the churches in Tralles and Magnesia.[39]

The fact that John makes no mention of certain prominent churches and cities (Colossae, Hierapolis), while including others which seem to be less prominent within early Christian circles (Thyatira), suggests that the seven churches listed in the Apocalypse should not be taken to imply that he knows of these seven and no more. Rather, such selectivity suggests that these seven churches serve as representatives of other (unnamed) churches. Owing to the fact that seven is a sign of completion in the Apocalypse, it appears

---

[38] Cf. the work of W. Ramsay [*The Seven Letters to the Seven Churches of Asia and their Place in the Plan of the Apocalypse* (London: Hodder & Stoughton, 1904), pp. 183-96] that has influenced a number of scholars on this topic.

[39] J.R. Michaels, *Interpreting the Book of Revelation* (Grand Rapids: Baker, 1992), pp. 35-36.

that these seven churches represent all (Johannine) churches. Consequently, the mention of these seven churches suggests that the Apocalypse is intended to be heard by all the churches of Asia Minor.

The Johannine Community
Not only do the seven cities listed in the Apocalypse reveal something about the book's intended audience, but the identity of the audience is also brought into sharper focus by enquiring as to the relationship of the Apocalypse to other Johannine documents found in the NT. Specifically, the question may be asked, how is the Apocalypse connected to what most scholars describe as the Johannine Community?

Few NT works are more similar in expression than 1 John and the FG.[40] Thus, it appears likely from the close literary and theological affinities which exist between the FG and the Johannine Epistles that these documents come from the same community or circle, if not the same hand. In the case of the FG, the BD is identified as the one who wrote these things, though it is clear from the third person language used that other hands were involved. In the case of 2 and 3 John, the author explicitly identifies himself as 'The Elder', clearly an (if not *the*) authoritative leader in the community. It is likely that 1 John is also the result of the Elder's literary activity.[41] To speak of the Johannine community, then, is to speak of the individuals and congregations over which the BD and/or the Elder offered spiritual oversight.[42]

Several pieces of evidence suggest that the Apocalypse and its audience(es) are part of this Johannine community. This connection may be observed in at least three ways. First, a careful comparison of the language of the Apocalypse with that of the FG reveals that while a number of linguistic differences exist between the two documents, they exhibit so many kinds of similarities that it is more

---

[40] According to R.E. Brown, *The Epistles of John* (AB 30; Garden City, NY: Doubleday, 1982), p. 21, not even Luke and Acts are as similar to one another as are 1 John and the FG!

[41] For my thoughts on this issue cf. Thomas, *1 John, 2 John, 3 John*, pp. 4-10.

[42] The most helpful work on this topic is M. Hengel's *The Johannine Question* (London; Philadelphia: SCM Press; Trinity Press International, 1989). Cf. also his more extensive treatment *Die johanneische Frage: Ein Lösungsversuch* (Tübingen: J.C.B. Mohr [Paul Siebeck], 1993).

than safe to assume these documents come from the same family or community.[43] Second, there are a number of points at which one can detect certain theological affinities between the Apocalypse and the Johannine literature.[44] As noted earlier, both the FG and the Apocalypse regard Jesus as the (paschal) Lamb of God. Though differently nuanced, the issue of witness or testimony is another point of theological affinity as it is prominent in the FG, as well as the Apocalypse.[45] There are also certain similarities of thought in these major Johannine documents reflected in the understanding of the unity and diversity of God. Third, an obvious indicator that the Apocalypse is part of the Johannine community is the fact that all of these documents are either directly or indirectly tied to the name John, though the Apocalypse is the only document in which the name appears in the text itself.[46]

OT Literature (Intertextuality)

The intertextual nature of the document also reveals something about the audience implied by the Apocalypse. The frequency with which OT imagery and allusions appear within the book suggests that the hearers and readers are not only well versed in the OT (being expected at times to pick up on some very faint allusions), but also suggests that the Jewish Scriptures were revered as authoritative within the community. Such familiarity and respect suggest that the heritage of Israel is regarded in some sense as the heritage of the community as well.

---

[43] Cf. esp. the carefully detailed analysis by J. Frey, 'Erwägungen zum Verhältnis der Johannesapokalypse zu den übrigen Schriften des Corpus Johanneum', in Hengel, *Die johanneische Frage*, pp. 326-429. Prigent [*L'Apocalypse de Saint Jean*, p. 26] describes Frey's work as follows, 'L'étude, remarquablement documentée, bénéficie d'instruments de travail, notamment d'ordre statistique, qui manquaient à ses grands devanciers. Ses résultats sont donc plus précis, plus objectifs et donc plus fiables'.

[44] Y. Simoens, *Apocalypse de Jean: Apocalypse de Jésus Christ* (Paris: Éditions Facultés Jésuites de Paris, 2008), p. xii and S.S. Smalley, *The Revelation to John* (Downers Grove, IL: IVP, 2005), p. 4.

[45] This important Johannine theme is also found in 1 Jn 1.2, 5.6-12 and 3 Jn 3, 6, 12.

[46] On the significance of titles in NT documents cf. M. Hengel, *Studies in the Gospel of Mark* (trans. by J. Bowden; Philadelphia: Fortress Press, 1985), pp. 64-84.

People of the Spirit

In addition to being people of the OT, the text suggests that the hearers are people of the Spirit as well. This aspect of the hearers' identity is supported by two pieces of textual evidence. It is clear that the hearers implied by the text have some understanding of the Spirit's activity. Such an understanding includes both the affinity the hearers appear to have with John's experiences of being 'in the Spirit' at various points and the ability to discern pneumatic speech (2.7, 11, 17, 29; 3.6, 13, 22)[47] and enter into 'pneumatic (πνευματικῶς) interpretation' (11.8). Not unrelated to this awareness of the Spirit's activity is the prophetic activity that permeates the document. For not only is the audience aware of prophetic figures in its midst, but there are also indications that the hearers themselves are viewed as participants in such prophetic activity. Whether or not the text implies a belief in the 'prophethood of all believers', it does suggest a deep level of participation within the community of a variety of (if not all) individuals.[48]

Women

Another dimension of the audience's identity appears to be revealed by the significant role which women play in the Apocalypse. The first of four references to women in this book occurs early on in Rev. 2.20, where reference is made to a woman named 'Jezebel', who speaks of herself as a prophetess, but actually teaches and deceives 'my servants' to commit sexual immorality and eat food sacrificed to idols. That she represents a real person within the community is suggested by the fact that she is given opportunity to repent but has refused. This is confirmed by the judgment that awaits her and her children. Despite the symbolic nature of her name (what the resurrected Jesus calls her, 'Jezebel', as opposed to what she calls herself, 'prophetess'), her existence reveals that among the prophetic figures in this prophetic community are some women. For she is not condemned owing to her gender, but rather owing to her deception. The next reference to a female occurs in Revelation

---

[47] On this cf. Ruiz (*Ezekiel in the Apocalypse*, pp. 195-99) who goes on to suggest that 13.9-10, 18; 17.9, and 1.20; 10.7; 17.5, 7 are also evidence for this phenomenon (pp. 200-14).

[48] Cf. esp. the helpful discussion by D. Hill, *New Testament Prophecy* (Atlanta: John Knox Press, 1979), pp. 87-93 and P. Poucouta, 'La mission prophétique de l'Église dans l'Apocalypse johannique', NRT 110 (1988), pp. 38-57.

12 where one finds reference to a woman clothed with the sun. While her identity is debated, her strategic location in salvation history is clear. Somewhat like psychedelic imagery, this woman changes forms as she conveys characteristics of a variety of female figures to include Eve, Israel, Mary, and the Church. The third female image to appear in the Apocalypse is found in Revelation 17-18, Babylon the Great Whore. This image gives way in Revelation 19 and following to the Bride of Christ, New Jerusalem.

Such depictions indicate that women are included within the audience implied by this text, confirming the picture of the role of women within the Johannine community that emerges from an examination of the FG, where every female character serves as an exemplary model of belief. Though the Apocalypse includes negative images of women, women are never denigrated owing to their gender, but assessed on the basis of their behavior and relationship to God.[49]

Witness and Persecution
The prominence of the theme of witness or testimony against the backdrop of a hostile environment implies that at least certain parts of the intended audience of the Apocalypse are familiar with the necessity of bearing witness in the face of opposition and the distinct possibility that such activity could lead to various forms of persecution, including death. While it might be going too far to say that the entire community experienced persecution, and while the external evidence for the extent of such persecution is very much debated, the text makes clear that the audience is familiar with persecution owing to their witness. One of the primary pieces of evidence for this conclusion is the way in which the prominent witnesses within the Apocalypse all experience death. This theme begins in 1.5 with the description of Jesus Christ, who is called ὁ μάρτυς ὁ πιστός ('the faithful witness'). The fact that being a 'faithful witness' involves death is made clear in the next phrase where he is described as 'the firstborn of the dead'. That such 'faithful witness' is not confined to the work of Jesus, but extends to his followers as well, is confirmed in 2.13 by mention of Antipas, ὁ μάρτυς μου ὁ πιστός μου ('my faithful witness'). In order that

---

[49] The reference to those 'not defiled by women' in 14.4 is taken up in detail in the commentary below.

the point not be missed, the relationship between 'faithful witness' and death is again underscored in the text, where the reference to Antipas is followed by the words, 'who was put to death among you'. Lest it be thought that Antipas' 'faithful witness' was a one off event, Rev. 11.1-13 speaks of two witnesses who are protected by God until their witness is completed, at which point the Beast overcomes and kills them (v. 7). They, like their lord, are vindicated by being raised from the dead and taken up to heaven whilst their enemies look on (vv. 11-13). This theme of the cost of faithful witness may also be found in the poetic words about believers found in 14.4, where it is said, 'These follow the Lamb wherever he leads'.

In addition to the connection between faithful witness and death is the fact that John himself appears to have been on Patmos owing to 'the word of God and the testimony of Jesus'. Several times in the seven prophetic messages of chapters 2-3, there are indications that the hearers have experienced or will experience opposition owing to their belief. This includes hardships (2.3), afflictions, slander, imprisonment (2.8-10), death (2.13), and little strength (3.8). To this evidence might be joined the admonitions to 'overcome' found at the end of each prophetic message (2.7, 11, 17, 26-28; 3.5, 12, 21), the words of encouragement to the hearers found at various points throughout the book (13.9; 14.13; 16.15), and the frequent reference to those who have given their lives, shed their blood, or were 'warred against' for the sake of the Lamb (6.9-11; 7.14-17; 12.17; 14.12; 16.6; 17.6; 18.24; 19.2; 20.4-6). While questions remain about the extent of the community's acquaintance with persecution, the audience envisioned by the text appears to understand that their identification with the testimony of Jesus could and perhaps would lead to persecution.

Opponents and Opposition

If the text of the Apocalypse suggests that persecution and suffering is part of the audience's horizon, what does it reveal about the source of this opposition? This question must be answered in two parts for the text envisions the antagonists in cosmic terms that take concrete expression in the world of the audience.

Cosmic Opposition

On the cosmic level the opposition faced by the community is primarily the evil triumvirate of Satan, the beast, and the false prophet (the other beast). At many points this evil trinity parodies what is said of the One who sits on the throne, the Lamb, and the Seven Spirits of God. The ultimate figure standing behind the opposition to the believers is Satan. In two texts (12.9; 20.2) he is identified more fully as the great dragon, the ancient serpent, the devil, or Satan. He orchestrates religious opposition by means of 'the synagogue of Satan' in Smyrna (2.9) and Philadelphia (3.9). Not only is he able to cause the church to suffer by having some of them imprisoned (2.10), but also, in a parody of God, he has a throne and where he lives is where 'my faithful witness' Antipas died (2.13). Apparently, his 'deep secrets' are the source of false teaching (2.24). Satan is the one who opposes and seeks to destroy the woman clothed with the sun, her male child, and the rest of her seed (12.1-13). However, he loses his place in heaven at the hands of Michael (12.7-12), an event which fills him with fury to oppose more completely the church (12.12). As a result, the Dragon gives his power and throne and great authority to the beast (13.2), which results in worship of the Dragon and the beast (13.4). The relationship between the Dragon and the other beast is indicated by the fact that he spoke like a dragon (13.11). The unity of the Dragon, the beast, and the false prophet is underscored by the fact that demon spirits come from each of their mouths performing miraculous signs (16.13). Satan's work is that of deceiving the nations (20.3, 7-8). However, he is thrown into the Abyss for 1,000 years (20.2) and ultimately into the Lake of Fire (20.7-20).

Satan is joined in opposing God and his people by the beast whose very first mention is in connection with killing the two witnesses who prophesy in 11.7. There the beast comes up from the Abyss, but in 13.1 he comes up out of the sea. Receiving his power from the Dragon, he parodies the Lamb by his fatal head wound that is healed (13.3) and like the Dragon is worshipped (13.4), a practice facilitated by the other beast (13.11-17). The number of the beast is 666 (13.18), but those who receive his mark will be punished by God (14.9-11; 16.2) as will the beast himself (16.10). By way of contrast, the beast, his image, and his number are overcome by those standing beside the sea of glass (15.2). The relationship of the beast to Babylon the Great, the Mother of Whores is made clear in chapter 17, where the woman is found riding the back of the beast (vv. 3, 7). The astonishment he causes is owing to the fact that, in a parody of God, he is described with the words 'he was, he is, and he comes' (vv. 8, 11). His close relationship with the ten kings who have not yet received a kingdom is also underscored (vv. 11-14, 16-17). However, the beast's opposition to the Lamb is futile as he is thrown into the Lake of Fire (19.19), sharing Satan's fate (20.10), while those put to death by him 'live and reign' (20.4).

The third member of the evil triumvirate, the 'other beast', comes up out of the earth. Looking like a lamb and sounding like a dragon, his authority comes from the first beast, which is used to cause all the earth's inhabitants to worship the first beast, going so far as to set up an image of the beast which he causes to speak (13.11-15). He performs great signs, causing fire to fall from heaven, deceiving the inhabitants of the earth (v. 14). His efforts result in a complete control of economic activity, so that anyone wishing to buy or sell must have the mark of the beast in one's hand or on one's forehead (vv. 16-17). Along with the Dragon and the beast, demon spirits come from the mouth of 'the false prophet' (16.13) and he shares their fate in the Lake of Fire (19.20; 20.10).

Joining the evil triumvirate as the other major cosmic opponent in the Apocalypse is Babylon the Great, who is identified as ἡ μήτηρ τῶν πορνῶν ('the Mother of Sexual Immorality'). She sits upon many waters (peoples, multitudes, nations, and languages). Elaborately dressed (17.4), she is drunk on the blood of the saints (v. 5), committing sexual immorality with the nations and kings of the earth (18.3), though she is eventually betrayed by her 'partners' (17.16-17). She is the great city that rules over the kings of the earth. Her destruction and the mourning it causes are described in some detail in chapter 18.

Concrete Expressions of Opposition

The opposition faced by the audience also takes concrete expression in the text of the Apocalypse. While all opposition is understood to have a cosmic explanation, at numerous points it is possible to discern certain concrete expressions of the opposition faced by the church. These primarily take three forms. First, at certain places it appears that the image of Rome is discernible. Perhaps the most likely example of such a reference comes in chapter 17 where the seven heads of the beast upon which the woman, Babylon the Great, sits are seven hills. The reference to the seven hills of Rome may well be present. The mention that these seven hills are seven kings may also be a possible allusion to Roman rulers, especially with the mysterious words that five have fallen, one is and the other is yet to come (17.9-11). The relationship between the beast and Nero, both who suffer fatal head wounds, may also direct the hearers' attention to Rome and the opposition it offers to the church.[50] Finally, there also appears to be a rather direct (and scathing) economic critique of Rome and its power in chapter 18.[51]

There are also hints that the audience of the Apocalypse faced concrete opposition in the form of its relationship with the Jewish community. As already noted, the audience of the Apocalypse appears to be one with a clear appreciation for its Jewish heritage. Not only does its presumed familiarity with the OT point in this direction, but also the way in which certain 'Christian' details are grounded in Jewish roots. At the same time, there is clear tension reflected in the book with the broader Jewish community. The pejorative description, 'the synagogue of Satan', found twice in chapters two and three, carries with it the accusation that there were those who claimed to be Jews but were not (2.9; 3.9). By this 'Jewish' community, the church at Smyrna is slandered (2.9). This group may even have been regarded as having the power to cause the imprisonment of members of the church (v. 10). The opposition offered the church at Philadelphia by this 'Jewish' community is such that vindication before their adversaries is spoken by the risen Christ (3.9). While it might be going too far to argue that the audience as a whole, envisioned in the Apocalypse, is in a struggle with the Jewish community, it does appear reasonable to suggest this envisioned audience is one in some conflict with the broader Jewish community. It would seem that this conflict revolves around the issue of identity.

A final concrete expression of opposition to the audience is perhaps the clearest of the three, for it is obvious that the audience envisioned by the Apocalypse is one faced by the threat of false teaching, false prophet(esse)s, false apostles, and immoral behavior. In point of fact, from the seven prophetic messages in Revelation 2-3 it appears that the churches are more often beset by these problems

---

[50] Cf. Bauckham, *The Climax of Prophecy*, pp. 384-452.
[51] Cf. Bauckham, *The Climax of Prophecy*, pp. 338-83.

than any other opposition. The church at Ephesus is praised for not tolerating evil individuals, testing those who claimed to be apostles but were not (2.2), and hating the works of the Nicolaitans (2.6). Conversely, the church at Pergamum is rebuked for having some in its midst who keep the teaching of Balak (idolatry and sexual immorality) and the teaching of the Nicolaitans (2.14-15). The church at Thyatira struggles with the woman who calls herself a prophetess, but whom the risen Jesus calls 'Jezebel' (2.20-25). Her works include sexual immorality and eating food sacrificed to idols. Those who commit sexual immorality with her will be punished with her. The theme of false teaching and false prophecy, of course, continues as the Apocalypse describes the activities of the Dragon, the beast, the false prophet, and the Great Whore. The temptation of the church to capitulate to these activities is conveyed in part by John's astonishment at the appearance of Babylon the Great (17.6). When the inhabitants of the world saw the healing of the beast's wounded head they were astonished, and in turn worshipped the beast (13.3-4). When John saw the Great Whore he was astonished, and was immediately rebuked by the Angel, asking, 'Why are you astonished at her?', explaining the mystery of the woman (17.6-7). Clearly, such opponents were an on-going part of the reality faced by the audience of the Apocalypse.

Date

The date of the Apocalypse is a notoriously difficult issue to sort out, for the evidence may be read in at least three different ways. The dominant view for the better part of eighteen centuries is that the document was written sometime during the reign of Domitian (81-96 CE). In the last century a not insignificant number of scholars have held that the book emerged at the time of the emperor Nero (sometime between 64-70 CE). A still more recent proposal has sought to combine the evidence for both of these views, arguing that the vision was experienced sometime during the time of Nero but was written down much later during the time of Domitian. What accounts for such wide divergence of dates among interpreters? Part of the answer to this question is the uncertainty that accompanies most every piece of relevant evidence. What one soon discovers is that the interpretive challenges one faces as with so many other aspects of the Apocalypse are no less great here.

Internal Indicators

Given its similarities at a number of points to the OT prophetic literature, it is somewhat surprising to find that in the Apocalypse there is an absence of any internal dates, unlike some of the prophetic literature. This is all the more surprising in the light of the fact that John names himself as the author, rather than using a pseudonym, an unusual if not unique phenomenon among apocalyptic documents. Yet despite this lack of internal references to date several texts within the Apocalypse could provide textual clues that may reveal something about the date of the document. While more extensive exploration of the verses in question must await discussion in the commentary proper, owing to limitations of space, each clue is surveyed briefly here. Some of the more prominent include: the mention of seven kings in Rev. 17.9-11, the present tense reference to the Temple in Jerusalem in Revelation 11.1, the use of the term Babylon to refer to Rome, the relationship between the beast with the wounded head and the legend that Nero would return, the relationship of the worship of the beast and emperor worship in Revelation 13, the use of the language 'the Twelve Apostles' in Rev. 21.14, the identity of the persecutor of the church, and the Sitz-im-Leben of the seven churches in Revelation 2-3.

On the face of it, one of the clearest internal indicators with regard to date is the mention of seven kings in Rev. 17.9-11. Of the seven kings, who are the seven hills upon which the Great Whore sits, five have fallen, one now is, the other is not yet, and when this one comes it is necessary for him to remain a little while. The Beast, who was and is not, is eighth, being one of the seven. Since this list may be thought to have reference to Roman leaders (i.e. the seven hills), theoretically, all one has to do is count down the list of Roman Emperors until one arrives at the number six and the date of composition is revealed. However, a number of complications face the interpreter as the chart on the next page[52] reveals:

---

[52] This chart is a slight modification of one by D.E. Aune, 'Notes to "Revelation to John (Apocalypse)",' in *Harper Collins Study Bible* (New York: HarperCollins, 1993), p. 2330, also cited by Murphy, *Fallen Is Babylon*, p. 44.

32 *The Apocalypse*

Roman Emperor	A	B	C	D	E	F	G	H
Julius Caesar (101-44 BCE)	1	1						1
Augustus (31 BCE -14 CE)	2	2	1	1				2
Tiberius (14-37 CE)	3	3	2	2				
Gaius (37-41 CE)	4	4	3	3	1			
Claudius (41-54 CE)	5	5	4	4	2			3
Nero (54-68 CE)	6	6	5	5	3	1		
Galba (June 68-Jan 69 CE)	7		6		4	2	1	
Otho (69 CE)			8		7	5	3	2
Vitellius (69 CE)			8		6	4	3	
Vespasian (69-79 CE)	7		6		7	5	4	4
Titus (79-81 CE)		8			7	8	6	5	5
Domitian (81-96 CE)					8		7(8)	6	6
[Neronic Antichrist]								7(8)
Nerva (96-98 CE)							7(8)	
Trajan (98-116 CE)								

The chart lists all the Roman Emperors from Julius Caesar to Trajan, while the letters across the top of the chart represent different ways in which the Emperors may be numbered. Does one begin with Julius Caesar (as in A, B, and H), or Augustus (as in C and D), or Gaius (as in E), or Nero (as in F) or Galba (as in G)? Are the three so-called minor emperors included (as in A, C, D, E, F, and G) or excluded (as in B, D, and H)? Does one only count those emperors deified by the Roman Senate or who claimed divinity for himself (as in H)? From an examination of the list it is apparent that a variety of attempts can be made to determine which figure is to be identified as the sixth king, with little scholarly consensus. Suffice it to say that the reference to the seven kings in Revelation 17 is not sufficient on its own to determine the date of the book's composition. Rather, one might observe that, if one can determine the date of the book on other terms, the list of kings can be manipulated to fit it.

Mention of the Temple in Revelation 11 might also be thought to help establish the date of the Apocalypse. The present tense reference to the Temple could suggest that it was still standing in Jerusalem at the time of the book's composition, thus, arguing for a pre-70 date of composition. However, this literal reading of the text does not square with the details, owing to the fact that the dimensions of the Temple described in chapter 11 reveal that this Temple is not the Herodian structure, but appears to resemble the one described in Ezekiel 40-48.[53] Neither is it altogether clear that the Temple described in Revelation 11 is actually located in Jerusalem.

The use of the term Babylon as having reference to Rome might also have some bearing on the topic of date since it appears that such references to Rome do not appear in apocalyptic documents until after 70 CE. Part of this move seems to be based upon the fact that just as Babylon had destroyed Jerusalem in 586 BCE, so now Babylon (Rome) again destroys Jerusalem.[54] While such evidence would seem to indicate that the book was written after 70 CE, it should be remembered that the reference to Rome as Babylon in early Christianity seems to have already taken place in the 60's, when Peter says, 'she who is chosen together with you in Babylon greets you' (1 Pet. 5.13).

Another tantalizing reference in the text with regard to establishing the date of the book is the reference to the Beast with the wounded head that has been healed (13.3, 12). On one level, the reference is a clear parody of the Lamb who looked as if he had been slain in chapter 5, but on another level numerous interpreters have seen a not so subtle reference to the legend that emerged sometime after Nero's death, that the dead Emperor would return alive. Obviously, this myth could not have occurred before Nero's death in 68 CE, but from the evidence it appears that the rumor did not circulate widely until near the end of the first century when various impostors turned up claiming to be Nero![55]

It is also possible that the phrase 'the twelve apostles' occurring in the description of New Jerusalem in 21.14 reveals something about the date of the Apocalypse. Here several points should be made. While reference to 'the Twelve' does appear on occasion in the FG (6.67, 70, 71; 20.24), in the Johannine literature there are no occurrences of the term ἀπόστολος ('apostle') outside of the Apocalypse, where it occurs twice, here and in 2.2 with reference to those who claimed to be apostles but were not. At the same time, while the term apostle occurs frequently in other strands of NT thought, the term 'the Twelve Apostles' is relatively rare, occurring only in Mt. 10.2 and the textually uncertain Lk. 9.1 and 22.14. The

---

[53] Beale, *The Book of Revelation*, p. 21.

[54] Beale, *The Book of Revelation*, pp. 18-19.

[55] On this whole question cf. Bauckham, *The Climax of Prophecy*, pp. 407-41.

term is also found in the title of the Didache.[56] Taken together, this evidence appears to indicate that the designation appears for the first time in the last quarter of the first century CE, perhaps implying a later date for the Apocalypse.

As noted earlier, the audience envisioned by the text of the Apocalypse is one familiar with persecution. If the specific persecution which lies behind the text were identifiable, it would, quite obviously, be possible to be more certain about the date of the document. Before looking at specific examples of persecution, it should be remembered that the extent of the persecution envisioned by the text is not altogether clear. While some persecution has been experienced and more is anticipated, in the seven prophetic messages, for the most part, the suffering of the Christians comes from the hands of the 'Jewish Community' rather than the Romans.[57] However, if Roman persecution is part of the landscape, as the book may suggest, then two primary options present themselves.

It is well known that Nero initiated a severe persecution of Christians. According to Tacitus (*Annals* 15.44), in order to divert the blame from himself for the fire that devastated Rome, Nero blamed and persecuted the Christians:

> Therefore, to scotch the rumour, Nero substituted as culprits, and punished with the utmost refinements of cruelty, a class of men, loathed for their vices, whom the crowd styled Christians. Christus, the founder of the name, had undergone the death penalty in the reign of Tiberius, by sentence of the procurator Pontius Pilate, and the pernicious superstition was checked for a moment, only to break out once more, not merely in Judea, the home of the disease, but in the capital itself, where all things horrible or shameful in the world collect and find a vogue. First, then, the confessed members of the sect were arrested; next, on their disclosures, vast numbers were convicted, not so much on account of arson as for hatred of the human race. And derision accompanied their end: they were covered by wild beasts' skins and torn apart by dogs; or they were fastened on crosses, and when daylight failed were burned to serve as lamps by night. Nero had offered his Gardens for the spectacle, and gave an exhibi-

---

[56] Aune, *Revelation 1-5*, p. lxiv.
[57] Aune, *Revelation 1-5*, p. lxvi.

tion in his Circus, mixing with the crowd in the habit of a charioteer, or mounted on his car. Hence, in spite of a guilt which had earned the most exemplary punishment, there arose a sentiment of pity, due to the impression that they were being sacrificed not for the welfare of the state but to the ferocity of a single man.[58]

Suetonius (*Nero* 16.2) simply observes:

> Punishment was inflicted on the Christians, a class of men given to a new and mischievous superstition.[59]

Clearly these texts indicate that a persecution of Christians did take place under Nero, a figure who could be called or likened to a beast in non-Christian documents[60] and about whom a legend arose of his return after his 'death'. This sort of evidence makes an early date appealing. However, evidence for a persecution that extends to Asia (Minor), leading to exile, is still not forthcoming for this period. Consequently, while appealing, such evidence does not prove conclusive with regard to the date of the Apocalypse.

There is also some evidence of a persecution of Christians under Domitian. In addition to the uncomplimentary picture of Domitian which emerges from the Roman historians, Tacitus and Suetonius, there are a few other pieces of relevant information. Melito of Sardis (quoted in Eusebius, *Ecclesiastical History* 4.26.9-10) reminds his reader, Marcus Aurelius, of the fact that Christians got on quite well with Rome for the most part, with two ominous exceptions.

> The only emperors who were ever persuaded by malicious men to slander our teaching were Nero and Domitian, and from them arose the lie, and the unreasonable custom of falsely accusing Christians. But their ignorance was corrected by your pious

---

[58] Cited according to the translation of J. Jackson, *Tacitus* IV (London: Heinemann, 1962), pp. 283-85.

[59] Cited according to the translation of J.C. Rolfe, *Suetonius* II (London: Heinemann, 1965), p. 111.

[60] Cf. Philostratus, *Life of Apollonius* 4.38 and perhaps the *Sibylline Oracles* 5.343.

fathers, who wrote many rebukes to many, whenever they dared take new measures against Christians.[61]

Tertullian (*Apology* 5.4) specifically states that Domitian was involved in the persecution of Christians but that he eventually relented:

> Domitian, too, a man of Nero's type in cruelty, tried his hand at persecution; but as he had something of the human in him, he soon put an end to what he had begun, even restoring again those whom he had banished.[62]

The closest one comes geographically to evidence of a persecution of Christians in Asia (Minor) is found in the written correspondence between Pliny, Trajan's legate in Bythinia, and the emperor (Pliny's *Letters*, 10.46, 47). These letters reveal several things about the nature of the persecution. It is clear from the correspondence (*Letters*, 10.46) that Pliny is not at all certain about how to proceed with his interrogations and decisions, indicating that there was no formal policy on the matter, a fact which Trajan confirms in response. It is also obvious that a number of Christians had been put to death as a result of the investigations. Not only were suspects interrogated, but some were also tortured in order for Pliny to get to the truth of the matter. Pliny indicates that formal worship of Trajan's statue and the images of the gods, along with cursing Christ, was treated as sufficient evidence that such ones were no longer considered Christian, a strategy with which Trajan agrees. This evidence, which may be dated somewhere around 111 CE, is almost fifteen years removed from the reign of Domitian. However, unlike the evidence regarding Nero and Domitian, this evidence of persecution is not far removed geographically from the churches mentioned in the Apocalypse.

It may be tentatively concluded that while the evidence for persecution at various periods might be of some assistance in constructing general attitudes with regard to the persecution of Chris-

---

[61] Cited according to the translation of K. Lake, *Eusebius* I (London: Heinemann, 1926), p. 391. Cf. also Melito Fragment 1 in *Melito of Sardis: On Pascha and Fragments* (ed. & trans. S.G. Hall; Oxford: Clarendon Press, 1979), p. 65.

[62] Cited according to the translation in *The Writings of Tertullian* I (eds. A. Roberts and J. Donaldson; Edinburgh: T. & T. Clark, 1869), p. 64. This passage from Tertullian is also cited by Eusebius (*Ecclesiastical History* 3.19-20).

tians in this general timeframe, it does not in and of itself settle the issue of the date of the Apocalypse.

The emphasis upon worship of the Dragon and beast, combined with the implicit identification of the beast with Rome, might be taken as evidence that at the time of the book's composition the community was faced with enforced emperor worship. Part of the problem in using this topic to gain leverage on the issue of date is the fact that solid evidence for such a practice is very late. In point of fact, Pliny offers the earliest unequivocal testimony of such a practice and even it does not seem yet to be a formal practice. This is not to suggest that such temptation was not part of the audience's horizon, but again to note that such a possibility does not settle the issue of date.

Finally, it is possible that the condition of the seven churches described in chapters 2-3 could provide clues as to the date of the document's composition.[63] Yet, such a procedure is notoriously dangerous and fraught with the challenges of getting the interpretive 'cart before the horse', creating a life setting to read the text over against. While it is possible that these descriptions can bring clarity to a variety of issues once a date has been established, such an approach cannot speak to the issue in a definitive fashion.

The ambiguity of much of the internal evidence makes a decision with regard to date difficult if not impossible. There are so many uncertainties and the attempt to reconstruct the original life setting so hypothetical that certainty on the matter is perhaps beyond the reach of the interpreter. However, if pressed, on balance the internal evidence tends to favor a later date of composition, if only slightly.

External Evidence

The external evidence is hardly more helpful than the ambiguity of the internal textual indicators with regard to date. What may be said with certainty is that the Apocalypse was known to exist by 135 CE, owing to the words of Justin Martyr in *Dialogue with Trypho* (81.4):

> And further, there was a certain man with us, whose name was John, one of the apostles of Christ, who prophesied, by a revela-

---

[63] On this cf. C.J. Hemer, *The Letters to the Seven Churches of Asia in their Local Settings* (JSNTS 11; Sheffield: JSOT Press, 1986), pp. 2-5.

tion that was made to him, that those who believed in our Christ would dwell a thousand years in Jerusalem; and that thereafter the general, and, in short, the eternal resurrection and judgment of all men would likewise take place.[64]

It is also possible that the Apocalypse was known by Papias, who is cited as bearing witness to its genuineness by Andreas of Caesarea in his *Preface to the Apocalypse*, written sometime in the sixth or seventh century.

> Regarding, however, the divine inspiration of the book [i.e., the Revelation of John] we think it superfluous to speak at length, since the blessed Gregory [I mean the Theologian] and Cyril, and men of an older generation as well, namely Papias, Irenaeus, Methodius, and Hippolytus, bear witness to its genuineness.[65]

If this testimony does indeed go back to Papias, it would indicate that the Apocalypse was known to exist perhaps as early as 115 CE. While Irenaeus (*Against Heresies* 2.22.5; 3.3.4) states that John lived into the time of Trajan, Clement of Alexandria (quoted in Eusebius' *Ecclesiastical History* 3.23.5-6; cf. also Clement's *Who Is the Rich Man that Is Saved?* 42) gives some evidence as to the timing of John's days on Patmos when he notes:

> For after the death of the tyrant he passed from the island of Patmos to Ephesus, and used also to go when he was asked, to the neighbouring districts of the heathen (ἐθνῶν), in some places to appoint bishops, in others to reconcile with whole churches, and in others to ordain some one of those pointed out by the Spirit.[66]

From the context, it appears that the tyrant in question is Domitian. Such a statement would suggest that the Apocalypse was written (or experienced) sometime during the reign of Domitian (81-96 CE). This testimony would appear to be in agreement with Irenaeus'

---

[64] Cited according to the translation found in *The Ante-Nicene Fathers I* (eds. A Roberts and J. Donaldson; Grand Rapids: Eerdmans, 1989), p. 240.
[65] Cited according to the translation of M.W. Holmes, *The Apostolic Fathers: Greek Texts and English Translations* (Grand Rapids: Baker, 1992), p. 577.
[66] Cited according to the translation of Lake, *Eusebius: The Ecclesiastical History* I, p. 243 [3.23.5-6].

statement (*Against Heresies* 5.30.3) which seems to place the appearance of the Apocalypse in the reign of Domitian:

> ... for if it were necessary that his (the Antichrist's) name should be distinctly revealed in this present time, it would have been announced by him who beheld the apocalyptic vision. For that was seen no very long time since, but almost in our day, toward the end of Domitian's reign.[67]

All in all, the external evidence is quite meager but would appear to confirm, if ever so slightly, suspicions that the Apocalypse was written down near the end of the first century CE.[68]

A Modest Proposal with regard to Date

Despite the fact that both the internal and external evidence slightly favors a late date, it appears from the text that, with perhaps one exception, John has been intentional (and successful) in disguising the date of composition from the hearers and readers. In other words, it appears that the text may intend to conceal rather than reveal the date of the document's composition. If such is indeed the case, it would seem to be more in keeping with the S/spirit of the text to respect its intentional ambiguity and look one more time for any internal indicators that might shed light on the intentions of the text.

The closest the Apocalypse comes to offering a date for its composition may be a phrase found in 1.10 where John says, 'I was in the Spirit on the Lord's Day'. It is commonly thought that this phrase, τῇ κυριακῇ ἡμέρᾳ ('on the Lord's Day'), is simply an early equivalent for 'Sunday'. Evidence offered in support of this interpretation is the fact the phrase seems to have this meaning in documents in some close temporal proximity to the Apocalypse (i.e. *Did.* 14.1; Ign., *Magn.* 9.1; and *Gos. Pet.* 35, 50). On this view, Rev. 1.10 is the first extant example of the evolution of this term. The accuracy of this explanation would be hard to disprove or deny, though the traditional Johannine designation for Sunday is τῇ δὲ μιᾷ τῶν σαββάτων ('on the first day of the week'). But at the

---

[67] Cited according to the translation found in *The Ante-Nicene Fathers I*, pp. 559-60. For the critical questions surrounding the meaning of this quote cf. Aune, *Revelation 1-5*, pp. lviii-lix.

[68] Beale, *The Book of Revelation*, p. 4.

same time, in a book known for its pregnant imagery, it is possible that the hearers and readers are being given more than a detail about the day of the week on which John experiences the revelation. This statement may also convey something else about the document's (or experience's) date. By means of the phrase, 'on the Lord's day', John may be giving his writing an eschatological date. On this reading the phrase, τῇ κυριακῇ ἡμέρᾳ ('on the Lord's Day'), might very well cause the hearer to think of the OT idea of יוֹם יהוה (*yom Yahweh*, 'The Day of the Lord/Yahweh'). But the hearer is not likely simply to see here a reference to the OT 'Day of the Lord', but that day as the Lord's day when Jesus himself will appear to resurrect the righteous dead. As ever, the intertext that is the Apocalypse is the point of convergence of various 'texts' (people, ideas, experiences, written texts). Here the convergence includes the OT idea of the 'Day of the Lord', John's experience 'in the Spirit', the person of the resurrected Jesus, and the anticipation of his return and the resurrection of the dead. This intertextual understanding of the phrase goes some way toward explaining why John does not simply utilize the OT language for יוֹם יהוה (*yom Yahweh*, 'The Day of the Lord/Yahweh'), for it is that day and more! Origen comes close to this understanding when he uses ἐν τῇ μεγάλῃ κυριακῇ ('on the great day of the Lord'), to describe the resurrection of all, which follows Jesus' resurrection 'on the third day'.[69] Not only would this reading of 'the Lord's day' be consistent with the rich symbolism of the document, but it would also dovetail nicely with the eschatological context in which Rev. 1.10 is located, between vv. 7-8 and vv. 12-20.[70] What would be the significance of this date for the book? Simply that the Lord's day relativizes all other days, indicating that the only day that matters is the Lord's day, the end of all days.[71] The convergence of this dimension

---

[69] Origen, *Commentary on John's Gospel* 10.35.

[70] On the significance of the place of 1.10 in the narrative of the Apocalypse for this understanding of 'the Day of the Lord' and other aspects of the question cf. A. Bacchiocchi, *From Sabbath to Sunday: An Historical Investigation into the Rise of Sunday Observance in Early Christianity* (Rome: Pontifical Gregoriam University Press, 1977), pp. 111-31, esp. pp. 123-30.

[71] At this point it might prove beneficial to consider this very phenomenon within the prophetic literature of the OT, for such a practice is not wholly without precedent. The typical way by which the date of an OT prophetic book is revealed is by means of the phrase, 'the word of the Lord came to (a certain

of the phrase, with the emerging understanding of this term as a designation for Sunday, would also not be without significance for the writer and his community.

Authorship

In contrast to the issue of date, determining the authorship of the Apocalypse is a bit more straightforward, for unlike the Four Gospels, Acts, Hebrews, and 1-3 John, all anonymous documents, the Apocalypse actually names its author. In point of fact, four times does this author identify himself as John, twice in the prologue (1.1, 4), once at the beginning of the inaugural vision (1.9), and once in the epilogue (22.8). However, no other appellations are given to describe this individual. No titles or additional names are used, nor does the author claim to be a physical relative of Jesus or some other authoritative figure within early Christianity. Yet, despite the scarcity of descriptive titles, much may be learned about the author from the text.

John the Prophet

Primarily, the text reveals that John is regarded as, and regards himself to be, a prophetic figure. Though he never technically calls

---

prophet) in the days of (a certain) king(s)' (cf. Jer. 1.2-3; Ezek. 2.3; Hos. 1.1; Amos 1.1; Mic. 1.1; Zeph. 1.1; Hag. 1.1; Zech. 1.1). However, on occasion, a book does not contain this phrase and, consequently, does not make reference to the reign of a certain king. With the book of Joel it appears that this lack of an internal indicator of the book's date is an intentional device to draw attention to 'the day of the Lord'. Cf. the perceptive comments of R.D. Moore ('Joel', in *The Book of the Twelve*) who notes:

> My alternative suggestion is that Joel intentionally refrains from assigning a date, not because he wants to establish a 'dehistoricized' liturgy relevant for all time, but rather because he sees the Day of the Lord eclipsing all of time and all of our days to the point of rendering them irrelevant – irrelevant enough to be left unspecified. Refusing to tell us in the first verse, as we would expect, that the word of the LORD came to Joel '*in the days of (a certain) king*', Joel seems deliberately to accentuate this omission in the second verse by prefacing the prophetic word with the question, 'Has anything like this happened *in your days or the days of your father?*' ... This day is so much bigger than the big days (viz., royal coronations) by which time has previously been calculated, that it blows away the entire dating system to become for Joel the new referent point for all future generations (cf. 1.3) (p. 6).

Given the Apocalypse's self conscious identification with the prophetic literature, perhaps a similar phenomenon may be at work here.

himself a prophet in the text, there are numerous indicators that he does indeed fulfill this function. The book begins with a description of the revelation of Jesus Christ given by God to 'his servant John' who testifies of the things he saw and heard (1.2). The next verse (v. 3) identifies the content of what John wrote as 'the words of this prophecy'. One of the primary hints as to John's prophetic identity is the fact that on at least two occasions the text describes John's prophetic commissioning(s). The first of these commissionings is described in 1.9-20, where John, 'in the Spirit on the Lord's day' hears a loud voice which twice instructs him to write what he sees and hears (vv. 11, 19). The second commissioning occurs in Revelation 10, where John is instructed to take the open scroll from the hand of the angel and to eat it (v. 8). After ingesting the scroll he is instructed, 'You must prophesy again …' (v. 11). This call narrative greatly mirrors OT call narratives, especially that of Ezekiel, virtually establishing that John is indeed a prophet.[72] John's prophetic activity is communicated to the hearer by means of the fact that his book is closely identified with 'the word of God', 'the testimony of Jesus', and the fact that he is repeatedly said to be 'in the Spirit' during the experience of the revelation.[73] Revelation 19.10 plays a significant role in this understanding where it is stated, 'The testimony of Jesus is the Spirit of prophecy'. John's prophetic identity is also made known by his instructions to engage in the prophetic activity of measuring the temple (Revelation 11), and the utilization of prophetic formulae that are also found amongst the classical prophets.[74]

Not only is there evidence of John's own identity as prophet, but as noted earlier, there are also signs of prophetic activity within the community from which the Apocalypse comes. The presence of a rival prophetess, on the concrete level (2.20), and the appearance of the false prophet, on the cosmic level (16.13; 19.20; 20.10), are negative testimony to the fact that the community was not unaccustomed to prophetic activity. But such negative evidence does not

---

[72] On this whole matter cf. Mazzaferri, *The Genre of the Book of Revelation from a Source-Critical Perspective*, pp. 264-96.

[73] Cf. Mazzaferri, *The Genre of the Book of Revelation from a Source-Critical Perspective*, pp. 296-317.

[74] Cf. Mazzaferri, *The Genre of the Book of Revelation from a Source-Critical Perspective*, pp. 317-30.

stand alone, for the community represented by the Apocalypse knows of other prophetic figures functioning within the community, such as John's brother prophets (22.6, 9). Prophetic activity seems to have been so widespread that it is possible for the Apocalypse to use 'prophets' to describe the activity of faithful members of the community: 'the prophets and the saints' in 11.18, 'saints and prophets' in 16.6, and 'the saints and the prophets' in 18.24.[75] The prophetic nature of the community would say much, not only about John's identity, but also about the way he would function as part of it. Hints in the text suggest that the brother prophets (if they need be distinguished from others in the community) might have a role in the reading (hearing and keeping) of the text at different meetings in various locations across the community. Perhaps prophetic instruction accompanied the successive multiple readings of the Apocalypse, but well within the boundaries set by the warning with which the book concludes (22.18-19). No doubt such activity would involve the kind of 'pneumatic' interpretation called for in the Apocalypse itself. The role of the other prophetic figures within the community in the composition of the book is difficult to determine. Part of the difficulty here is owing to questions about the way in which the book was composed. Was it experienced in a short period of time, and then written up shortly thereafter, as the text suggests? Or is it the product of an extended time of reflection, as the complex literary structure would suggest? On the former view, the involvement of other members of the prophetic community would perhaps be limited to discerning responses when the prophecy is read and heard by the community in times of worship. On the latter view, it might not be hard to imagine that John's own prophetic activity is joined by others as together the implications of the vision(s) and their intertextual significance are creatively constructed.[76]

The text may also reveal two other aspects of the author's identity. First, it appears that John was from a Jewish home, as his knowledge of the OT and his appreciation for the Jewish heritage

---

[75] Bauckham, *The Climax of Prophecy*, p. 84.

[76] On the extent of the activity of the prophetic community cf. Bauckham, *The Climax of Prophecy*, pp. 83-91. The idea that the Apocalypse was written down some time after it was experienced is found as early as Victorinus, *Commentary on the Apocalypse of the Blessed John* in his comments on 10.11.

would seem to make clear.[77] Second, if Rev. 1.9 speaks of banishment, then something else about John's social location is revealed. Since banishment under the Romans was reserved for royalty and members of the priesthood, the implication is that John may have come from a priestly family, as Polycrates testifies (Eusebius, *Ecclesiastical History*, 5.24.3).[78]

Writing in the Spirit

The text of the Apocalypse indicates that John experiences this revelation whilst 'in the Spirit' and that it is whilst 'in the Spirit' that he is commanded to write what he sees and hears. It is clear from this and other dimensions of the text that John regards the document as carrying a spiritual authority, one might even say that he seems to regard the words of this prophecy as an 'inspired' document. Therefore, to speak of writing 'in the Spirit' in a discussion of authorship would appear to be most appropriate. But what does it mean to write 'in the Spirit'?

Obviously, given the fact that John is 'in the Spirit' when he is given the command to write and that it is 'in the Spirit' that he experiences the revelation, there is a very tight interplay between the experiences of seeing and hearing and the experience of writing. But can anything else be said of this phenomenon? While it is possible to treat John primarily as an exegete of OT Scripture[79] or to view him as a passive instrument who simply records what is seen or heard in an automatic fashion, neither of these conceptions appear to fit the situation envisioned by the text.

---

[77] Contra R.K. MacKenzie, *The Author of the Apocalypse: A Review of the Prevailing Hypothesis of Jewish-Christian Authorship*, (MBPS 51; Lewiston, NY: Edwin Mellen Press, 1997).

[78] On this aspect of John's identity cf. Hengel, *The Johannine Question*, pp. 125-26.

[79] Note Waddell's perceptive criticism of one such approach in *The Spirit of the Book of Revelation*, p. 85.

> In conclusion, I have a few concerns with Beale's hermeneutics. Although I highly value Beale's detailed analysis of John's use of the Old Testament in the Apocalypse, at the end of the day, as a Pentecostal I find it inadequate. He leaves insufficient room for John to be recording an actual vision as opposed to solely exegeting scripture. When I read the text I assume John is interpreting and relaying an experience in the Spirit, albeit not void of Old Testament allusions. The Apocalypse ought not be reduced solely to a contextually sensitive exegesis.

The text says that John saw a vision. But what did he see and how much of what he saw made sense to him because of who he was? The concrete dimensions of his visionary experience notwithstanding, does John see the vision he does because of who he is and how he is formed? If some other early Christian experienced the revelation, would it look the same or would it take a different form? Or, does the Spirit use *John's* knowledge of the OT for the vision to take the form it does? If so, then the intertext that is John's life, his acquaintance with the OT, apocalyptic traditions, the Jesus tradition, his worshipping community, and the experience of the revelation itself is used 'in the Spirit' to produce the text of the Apocalypse. Thus the Apocalypse is that point of dynamic convergence and intersection of all that John is, including the revelation he experiences. Consequently, it is precisely because of John's knowledge of the OT, the apocalyptic tradition, the Johannine Jesus tradition, and the worshipping community of which he is a part that enables him to write 'in the Spirit'. One might go so far as to say that John's life is such that he is especially prepared for this prophetic activity, which the Spirit integrates into a profound 'inspired' text. On this view, the tension between the text's claim that this is a visionary experience, and the document's intricate design and literary complexity that suggest it is the product of a long period of time gives way to the fact that the Spirit encounters John in such a way that the convergences take place before his very eyes (and ears). Perhaps the phenomenon of glossolalia and its interpretation in contemporary Pentecostalism might function as an analogy, where the Spirit speaks through an individual believer in ways that draw upon all that he or she is, while not obliterating his or her heritage or personality.[80]

John the Prophet and the other Johannine Literature

The relationship between the Apocalypse and the FG and 1-3 John has presented a perennial challenge to NT interpreters. Though commonly identified as part of the Johannine community, there is some question as to whether or not the Apocalypse was an integral part. A brief comparison indicates some of the reasons for these attitudes.

---

[80] On this analogy cf. S. Moyise, *The Old Testament in the Book of Revelation*, p. 40.

On the one hand, there are numerous points of continuity amongst the documents. In both the FG and the Apocalypse a great deal of emphasis is placed upon the issue of witness or testimony. The anticipation of persecution owing to one's witness found in the FG (16.1-4), gives way in the Apocalypse to the reality of such persecution (2.3, 9-10, 13). The 'Word of God' is a theme common to the three major community documents (FG, 1 John, and Revelation). It has already been noted how the pneumatology shows signs of development from the FG to 1 John to the full blown prophetic pneumatology of the Apocalypse. A final example is the way in which the 'revelation of Jesus Christ', to which the Apocalypse is devoted, accomplishes this task by following the revelation of his identity by means of the imagery of the Lamb. The paschal overtones of the lamb imagery in the FG (1.29; 19.33-34), while present in the Apocalypse (5.6) are supplemented by a vision of the wrath of the Lamb (6.16, 17), who is powerful in battle.

On the other hand, there are several differences between these documents. Perhaps the most notable differences to readers of the Greek NT are those of vocabulary, phraseology, style, and syntax.[81] Some of these differences in vocabulary and style were noted as early as the third century CE. Such differences may be taken to imply that the hands of different writers are to be detected in these documents. At the same time, the grammatical style of the Apocalypse is a very curious matter and there may be more than one way to interpret the evidence. Quite clearly there are significant differences between these texts. However, one of the results emerging from additional analyses of the grammar of the book is the belief by some that the style of the Apocalypse is an intentional device by which the author seeks to confront the hearers and readers with a style that replicates that of the OT prophets. Such a device would not only have implications with regard to the prophetic genre of the book,[82] but also have affective and dispositional implications for its

---

[81] The most comprehensive study on this topic to date is Frey, 'Erwägungen zum Verhältnis der Johannesapokalypse zu den übrigen Schriften des Corpus Johanneum', pp. 326-429. Cf. also the still influential work of R.H. Charles, *The Revelation of St. John* I (ICC; Edinburgh: T. & T. Clark, 1920), pp. xxix-xxxi.

[82] F.J.A. Hort, *The Apocalypse of St. John* I (London: Macmillan, 1908), p. xxxviii; C.G. Ozanne, 'The Language of the Apocalypse', *TynB* 16 (1965), pp. 3-9; Ruiz, *Ezekiel in the Apocalypse*, pp. 224, 518, 529.

hearers as well.[83] In keeping with what has earlier been observed about John 'writing in the Spirit', it might not be going too far to ask whether it is not rather the prophetic experience itself which generates the employment of the prophetic language and style found in the Apocalypse.[84] Such an interpretation would fit nicely both with John's immersion in the OT prophetic literature and the phenomenology of his prophetic experience, while leaving open issues related to authorial intent.[85]

The differences between the documents are indeed enough to suggest that different writers produced the FG and 1-3 John, on the one side, and the Apocalypse, on the other. Yet, if the style of the Apocalypse is an intentional strategy or the result of John's prophetic experience, and there are substantial similarities between the documents, then one should not assume that the author is incapable of writing in different styles.[86] Such differences in writing style do seem to occur in Luke, where the first two chapters appear more Semitic in nature, than do the chapters that follow.[87] In addition, there is always the possibility that other hands were involved in 'assisting' the writer in the process of composition.

John in Early Christian Tradition

How does this emerging picture of the author of Apocalypse fit with the testimony about authorship found in the early church? The earliest extant witness is that of Justin Martyr (*Dialogue with Trypho*, 81.4) cited in the discussion on date above. There it was seen that Justin identifies the author as 'John, one of the apostles of Christ'. It would appear safe to assume that Justin believes that John the Son of Zebedee wrote the Apocalypse. Part of the strength of Justin's testimony is that he actually lived in Ephesus for a while in the

---

[83] A.D. Callahan, 'The Language of the Apocalypse', *HTR* 88 (1995), pp. 453-70.

[84] I am indebted to my colleague R.D. Moore for this observation. Cf. also G.R. Osborne, *Revelation* (ECNT; Grand Rapids: Baker, 2002), p. 4.

[85] In any case, the Apocalypse's grammatical style is not without theological significance. Cf. Resseguie, *The Revelation of John*, pp. 49-53.

[86] Beale, *The Book of Revelation*, p. 35.

[87] As G.B. Caird (*A Commentary on the Revelation of St. John the Divine* [London: A & C Black, 1966], p. 5) observes, '… because a man writes in Hebraic Greek, it does not inevitably follow that this is the only Greek he is capable of writing. He may have adopted this style for quite deliberate reasons of his own, as Luke appears to have …'

first half of the second century CE. Similar testimony continues to be found amongst various early Christian writers. Tertullian identifies the author as 'the Apostle John' (*Against Marcion*, 3.14.3; 3.24.4), as does Clement of Alexandria (*Who Is the Rich Man that is Saved?* 42), and Hippolytus (*De Antichristo*, 18, 36-42).

The evidence from Irenaeus is in some ways the most extensive, and at the same time, perhaps the most frustrating. For while it may be that Irenaeus believes that the Son of Zebedee wrote the Apocalypse, he never actually calls him an apostle, preferring simply to use the name John without other attribution (*Against Heresies*, 1.26.3; 4.14.2; 5.26.1), or the FG designation, 'the Lord's disciple' (*Against Heresies*, 4.20.11).

Not everyone in the early church agreed with such an assessment. Perhaps the best known of the dissenting voices is that of Dionysus who is quoted extensively on this subject by Eusebius (*Ecclesiastical History*, 7.25.1-27). In this testimony Dionysus notes that some not only reject John as the author, but even go so far as to attribute it to his arch-enemy, Cerinthus (7.25.2-3). Dionysus says:

> That, then, he was certainly named John and that this book is by one John, I will not gainsay; for I fully allow that this book is by some holy and inspired person. But I should not readily agree that he was the apostle, the son of Zebedee, the brother of James, whose are the Gospel entitled According to John and the Catholic Epistle. For I form my judgement from the character of each and from the nature of the language and from what is known as the general construction of the book, that [the John therein mentioned] is not the same (7.25.7-8a).[88]

Dionysus goes on to point out the following differences: the Apocalypse names its writer, the Gospel and Epistles do not (7.25.8b-11); the Gospel and Epistle share numerous ideas and vocabulary, while the Apocalypse is utterly different (7.25.17-24); and the style and grammar of the Gospel and Epistle are in faultless Greek, while that of the Apocalypse 'is not accurate' and employs 'barbarous idioms' that are too many to number (7.25.25-26). Lest he be misun-

---

[88] Cited according to the translation of K. Lake, *Eusebius: The Ecclesiastical History* II (London: Heinemann, 1932), p. 199.

derstood, Dionysus adds, 'For I have not said these things in mockery (let no one think it), but merely to establish the dissimilarity of these writings' (7.25.27).[89]

Given the testimony cited above, the question must be raised, is it possible that John the Son of Zebedee is to be identified with the John of the Apocalypse? While it is theoretically possible to make this identification there are at least three complications that should be noted.[90] First, there is no evidence until the latter half of the second century CE that the Son of Zebedee was ever in or near Ephesus. Ignatius, writing to the church at Ephesus ca. 110-115 CE, makes no mention of John but goes to great lengths to demonstrate his close relationship to Paul. Although others claim (Ireneaus, in particular) that both Polycarp and Papias had a personal relationship with the Son of Zebedee, neither Polycarp nor Papias make such a claim. Second, some evidence exists which suggests that John the Son of Zebedee was martyred early in the church's history. In Mk 10.39, Jesus appears to prophesy the martyrdom of both James and John, while Papias, as quoted by Philip of Side (ca. 430 CE), states that both James and John were killed by the Jews.[91] Third, if the Son of Zebedee were the author, it would indeed be odd that he never identifies himself as an apostle and is so reticent to use apostolic language. On only two occasions does the term ἀπόστολος ('apostle') appear in the Apocalypse. Once, the term is used to describe 'those who claim to be apostles but are not' (2.2). The term also once appears in the description of New Jerusalem, where the names of the twelve apostles of the Lamb are said to appear on the twelve foundations of the wall of the city. In this later text it appears that the author of the Apocalypse sees himself as distinct from this 'foundational' group (from another generation?). In the end it would appear that there is little reason to identify the author of the Apocalypse as the Son of Zebedee.

Is it possible that the author of the Apocalypse is to be identified with John the Elder, who is sometimes identified as the BD, the

---

[89] Cited according to the translation of K. Lake, *Eusebius: The Ecclesiastical History* II, p. 209.

[90] Cf. the relevant discussion in Thomas, *1 John, 2 John, 3 John*, pp. 7-8 from which this section draws.

[91] The statement of Papias is also recorded by Georgius Monachus (in the ninth century) and is supported by Syriac and African martyrologies.

author of the other Johannine documents?[92] Such an identification would explain the relationship between the name John, which appears in the text of the Apocalypse and the titles of the Gospel and Epistles. It would further explain the virtual absence of apostolic language in the Johannine literature and the treatment of the apostles as a foundational group at some distance from the author. It would perhaps also explain why the Son of Zebedee, an apostle, is not mentioned by Ignatius in his letter to the Ephesians. On this view, the Elder, not being one of the twelve, would perhaps not be on the Ignatian radar screen. This identification would also have in its favor the fact that both John the Prophet and John the Elder could independently be placed in, or around, Asia. The former is, of course, placed off the coast of Asia near the book's beginning and clearly knows a number of the churches in Asia, as the seven prophetic messages imply. The latter appears to be one of the Asiatic sources from which Papias of Hierapolis (*Ecclesiatical History*, 3.34.2) draws. Papias appears to have actually interviewed the Elder, perhaps in Asia, where he is said to have interviewed Philip (*Ecclesiatical History*, 3.39.8-17). Such an explanation is possible, but is it plausible? The answer to this question will depend in large part on how one accounts for the differences in vocabulary, phraseology, style and syntax that exist between the Johannine documents. If John the Prophet is thought to be John the Elder, such an identification would require that either John purposely adopted a style different from his normal one or that such a style was generated from his prophetic experience. Or it would require that he composed the Apocalypse himself, while relying on the assistance of others in the composition of the FG and 1-3 John, which the texts themselves may imply.[93] But in the end, it is impossible to be certain about this identification. Consequently, perhaps the best course of action is simply to hear the voice of John the Prophet alongside the other

---

[92] On the relationship between the BD, the Elder, and the authorship of the FG and 1-3 John cf. the discussion in Thomas, *1 John, 2 John, 3 John*, pp. 8-10 and Hengel's *The Johannine Question*.

[93] G.D. Fee (*Revelation* [NCCS; Eugene, OR: Cascade Books, 2011]) makes a similar argument in defense of authorship by the Son of Zebedee.

Johannine voices, content with the knowledge that they come from the same community if not the same hand.[94]

The Apocalypse and Its Streams of Influence: The History of Effects

It almost goes without saying that the Apocalypse has had an extraordinary influence upon a variety of hearers and readers throughout the centuries. Not only do the varied responses generated by the Apocalypse reveal something of the document's power, but they also suggest that attention paid to specific responses will enrich one's own grappling with this remarkable text. In this section, the book's effective history is selectively reviewed by surveying a few examples from the following categories: disastrous interpretations of the Apocalypse, other apocalyptic 'Johaninne' documents, art, music, film, and commentaries.

Disastrous Interpretations of the Apocalypse

When pondering the effective history of the Apocalypse perhaps one of the first things to cross the interpreters' minds is the disastrous interpretations that have resulted over the centuries. Of the many such interpretations only three representative interpretations and their results are here described, all of which involve the loss of life owing to the interpretations espoused.

During the sixteenth century a convergence of influences produced one of the most bizarre and tragic events in the effective history of the Apocalypse. Within a decade of the infamous Peasant Revolt of 1524-25, with which the influential reformation figure Thomas Münzter became involved, and the devastating defeat in the battle of Frankenhausen, where Münzter was captured and eventually put to death, another social uprising occurred fueled in part by the fire of the Apocalypse; the acquisition and transformation of the city of Münster. The seeds for the establishment of the Anabaptist kingdom of Münster may be found in the thought and writings of the prophetic figure Melchior Hoffmann, whose

---

[94] As for the likelihood of several leaders in the community bearing the same name, it should perhaps be observed that in the FG there were three women at the foot of the cross who share the name Mary (19.25) and two disciples named Judas.

commentary on Revelation identified the Emperor as the Dragon, the Pope as the beast, and the monks as the false prophets. Owing to various prophetic encounters and experiences, Hoffmann became convinced later in his life that he was the Elijah that was to come and that the identity of the corresponding Enoch was either Cornelius Poldermann of Middleburg or Caspar Schwenckfield; that the spiritual Jerusalem was the present Christian community, which he identified with Strassburg; that the downfall of Babylon (i.e. all priests) must take place before the coming of the Lord; that an earthly theocracy must be established in the intervening period; and that violence could be used in the annihilation of the godless.[95] Though Hoffmann's views proved too much for the authorities in Strassburg, leading to his arrest there, his teaching won many adherents from the populace in the city of Münster in Westphalia. Upon Hoffmann's arrest, a Dutch baker from Haarlem named Jan Matthys became the inspirational leader of the movement, identifying himself as Enoch who is to come and sending word that it was time to raise the 144,000 warriors of which Revelation 7 and 14 speak.[96] Seizing control of the city council, he and his followers sought to establish the New Jerusalem by, among other things, driving from the town Catholics and Protestants who refused rebaptism. As a result of the various proceedings an army from the Bishop of Münster surrounded the city. Though being victorious in previous encounters, Matthys along with several followers were killed before the city's eyes in a skirmish just outside the city walls. It appears that at this point one of his 'apostles', Jan Bockelson, became the unchallenged ruler of the kingdom, pronouncing himself king of the city, eventually instituting the practice of polygamy,[97] and seeking to export this eschatological movement to other cities throughout Europe.[98] However, the kingdom died a somewhat rapid death, falling in 1536, along with the capture, torture, and execu-

---

[95] K. Deppermann, *Melchior Hoffman: Social Unrest and Apocalyptic Visions in the Age of Reformation* (trans. M. Wren; ed. B. Drewery; Edinburgh: T. & T. Clark, 1987), pp. 254-62.

[96] Deppermann, *Melchior Hoffman*, p. 336.

[97] G.H. Williams, *The Radical Reformation* (Philadelphia: Westminster, 1962), p. 511 notes that the practice of polygamy might not be unrelated to the desire to fill out the number of 144,000 as quickly as possible.

[98] A.W. Wainwright, *Mysterious Apocalypse* (Nashville: Abingdon, 1993), pp. 90-92.

tion of its king. Thousands lost their lives as a result of these disastrous interpretations of the Apocalypse.

During the summer of 1969, Los Angeles, California was shocked by the ruthless, ritualistic murders that occurred on Saturday, 9 August 1969, of Steven Earl Parent, Voytek Frykowski, Abigail Folger, Sharon Tate Polanski, and Jay Seabring, and on the following Sunday night, 10 August 1969, the murders of Leno and Rosemary LaBianca. Though baffling to police investigators for some time to come, the bizarre clues of the murder-scene would serve to reveal the motives for these horrendous acts. As Deputy District Attorney Vincent Bugliosi would discover these terrible acts were in part the result of the disastrous interpretation of the book of Revelation by Charles Manson.[99] The illegitimate son of a teenage mother who repeatedly abandoned him, Charles Manson would spend most of his life in a variety of institutional settings, owing both to his frequent abandonment and as a result of local, state, and federal crimes that he would commit. Upon his release after the completion of a ten-year prison sentence, Manson would gather a number of followers, who became known as 'the Manson Family', over whom he exerted near absolute control. As the Deputy District Attorney who prosecuted the case discovered, the motivation for these savage murders was grounded in Manson's interpretation of the Book of Revelation. For Manson Revelation 9 held the key. He identified the four angels of Revelation 9, who would kill a third of humankind, as having reference to the four-member rock band called 'the Beatles'. The following details confirmed this interpretation for Manson: 1) the four angels would, like the locusts who arise from the abyss, have the faces of men; 2) hair as that of a woman (an obvious reference to the long haired look of the Beatles); 3) fire coming from their mouths (taken as a reference to the influence of their words); and 4) breastplates of fire (seen as a reference to their electric guitars). Manson himself was thought to be the angel who held the key to the bottomless pit from which all manner of evil would arise and would be a place of refuge for Manson and his followers. This hermeneutical key enabled Manson to interpret a number of songs from the Beatles' so-called 'White Album' (offi-

---

[99] Much of what follows draws upon Vincent Bugliosi (with Curt Gentry), *Helter Skelter: The True Story of the Manson Murders* (New York: Norton and Company, Inc, 1974 [1994]), pp. 320-28.

cially entitled simply as 'The Beatles') as prophesying an imminent racial war in which blacks would rise in revolt against white oppression. Manson hoped to initiate this cataclysmic bloodbath, which he called 'Helter Skelter', a phrase he took from the Beatles' song by that title, by directing murderous activities that would gain national, if not global, attention. In the end, his apostles of murder savagely butchered seven people in Los Angeles. When questioned by the Deputy District Attorney about his role in the murders, Manson responded, 'It's the Beatles, the music they are putting out. They're talking about war'.[100]

One of the better-known disastrous interpretations of the Apocalypse resulted in the horrendous events that took place on 19 April 1993 in Waco, Texas. Here, eighty members of a religious group known as the Branch Davidians met their death in a fiery confrontation with the Federal Bureau of Investigation following an extended siege of the community.[101] With roots deep in Seventh-day Adventist thought, and more specifically the 'Shepherd's Rod' movement, the leader of this group had come to have specific ideas about his own prophetic role, as well as the identity of the second beast of Revelation 13 and 17. The son of an unwed teenage mother, Vernon Wayne Howell would struggle in, and eventually drop out of, high school, owing in part to dyslexia. After claiming a born-again experience in a Baptist church, he would make his way to the church of his mother, the Seventh-Day Adventist Church. He would follow this trajectory to the Shepherd's Rod movement making his way to Davidian Seventh-day Adventism, a group from which the Branch Davidians would come and locate on property they called Mount Carmel. Eventually assuming leadership of the group, Howell would later change his name to David Koresh, drawing upon the biblical name David as well as the name Cyrus [כורש] whom he said came to destroy Babylon, a task in which he would share. Whilst his interpretations drew heavily from the traditions to which he was heir, Koresh seemed to sharpen the somewhat stand-

---

[100] Barry Miles, *Paul McCartney: Many Years from Now* (New York: Henry Holt and Co., 1997), pp. 488-90.
[101] Much of what follows draws heavily from K.G.C. Newport, *Apocalypse & Millennium: Studies in Biblical Eisegesis* (Cambridge: Cambridge University Press, 2000), pp. 197-236, who offers an excellent theological analysis of Koresh and the events that led to the horrible events of 19 April 1993.

ard identification of the Lamb-like beast of Revelation 13 as the United States of America. Consequently, his extended confrontation with governmental representatives such as the Bureau of Alcohol, Tobacco, Firearms, and Explosives, and later the FBI would reinforce this identification for Koresh, especially when his compound was surrounded by the Lamb-like beast, who, he was convinced, sought to persecute and kill him. At the end of an extended siege, the FBI moved on the compound and when the smoke cleared from the resulting fires, eighty members of the community, including women and children, were dead, as was Koresh, who died from a gunshot to the head.

But the effective history of the Apocalypse is far richer than a chronicling of its disastrous interpretations, as is seen in the next sections of the commentary devoted to the effective history of the Apocalypse in the categories of other apocalyptic 'Johaninne' documents, art, music, film, and commentaries.

Other Johannine Apocalyptic Documents

One of the places where the influence of the Apocalypse may be seen is its role in generating other Johannine apocalyptic literature. Although this aspect of the book's effective history is not always fully appreciated, it is not surprising that the Apocalypse has acted as a catalyst in the production of other 'Johannine' apocalyptic documents.[102]

The first document that may safely be identified as being located in the Johannine apocalyptic trajectory is a work known as 'The Second Apocalypse of John' (*2AJ*).[103] Structurally, this book (which may be dated as early as ca 400 CE or as late as the ninth century CE)[104] takes the form of a series of questions raised by 'righteous John' and answered by 'our Lord Jesus Christ'. The temporal location of this apocalypse is 'after the ascension' on Mt Tabor, the traditional site of Jesus' ascension (*2AJ* 1). The influence of the Apoc-

---

[102] On this topic cf. esp. J. Court, *The Book of Revelation and the Johannine Apocalyptic Tradition* (JSNTS 190; Sheffield: Sheffield Academic Press, 2000).

[103] Court [*The Book of Revelation and the Johannine Apocalyptic Tradition*, pp. 32-65] provides the Greek text of the *2AJ*, an English translation, as well as a useful commentary.

[104] For the evidence in favor of this later date cf. A. Whealey, 'The Apocryphal Apocalypse of John. A Byzantine Apocalypse from the Early Islamic Period', *JTS* 53 (2002), pp. 533-40.

alypse of John is evident at many places throughout the document. After praying for seven days, the heavens are opened and John sees a book sealed with seven seals (*2AJ* 2-3). Later, this book is opened by the Lamb (*2AJ* 18-19). The imagery of the Apocalypse (esp. chapter 21) is also quite apparent at the close of the *2AJ* (27) where the nature of existence in heaven is described in some detail. Many of the issues addressed in the *2AJ* are very much what one might expect to be of interest to those who know the Apocalypse and other early Christian documents dealing with various eschatological topics. For example, one of the first topics discussed in the *2AJ* concerns ὁ ἀρνητής ('the Denier'), also known as ὁ ἀντίχριστος ('the Antichrist'). Specifically, there is a description of his physical appearance (*2AJ* 7) and the length of his reign (*2AJ* 8). Other topics addressed include: the nature of the resurrection body (*2AJ* 10-11), the descent of the heavenly things to earth (*2AJ* 17), the order of divine judgement upon the Greeks, the Heretics, the Hebrews, and the baptized (*2AJ* 20), the depth of the Underworld where the unclean spirits and the Adversary are located (*2AJ* 20), and the proportionality of punishment based upon one's social location (*2AJ* 24).

Another apocalyptic text that stands within the Apocalypse's stream of influence is 'The Apocalypse of St John Chrysostom' (*AStJC*).[105] This document, the date of which appears to be somewhere between the sixth and eighth centuries CE, resembles the *2AJ* in that it too takes the form of a dialogue between Jesus and John the Theologian, also known as 'righteous John'. Unlike the *2AJ*, the fifty-one verses that comprise the *AStJC* are not as concerned with eschatological details as they are with contemporary issues of relevance. The first issue raised by John and addressed by Jesus deals with the number of different kinds of sins and the identification of those sins deemed to be unforgivable (*AStJC* 1-4). This initial discussion is followed by one devoted to how one's actions honor or dishonor Sunday (*AStJC* 5-10), which evolves into a discourse on the nature and purpose of fasting (*AStJC* 8-19). Of particular interest is the fact that the word used in the *AStJC* for Sunday, is the same word found in Revelation 1.10 when John says 'I

---

[105] Court [*The Book of Revelation and the Johannine Apocalyptic Tradition*, pp. 74-103] provides the Greek text of the *AStJC*, an English translation, as well as a useful commentary.

was in the Spirit on the Lord's (κυριακῇ) day'. The final twenty-two verses of this document are devoted to explanations about a variety of liturgical practices (*AStJC* 20-51). These issues range from an explanation of the symbols of the church, the individuals involved in worship, words and phrases used in worship, and even the length of hair for men and women involved in baptism and communion.

The Third Apocalypse of John (*3AJ*) continues to give evidence of the Apocalypse's influence upon other Johannine apocalyptic documents. Like the first two documents described in this section, this book also incorporates the dialogue format, only in this case the dialogue takes place between Saint John the Theologian and James the Lord's brother. The primary focus of *3AJ* is the fate of sinners and the righteous.[106] After an introductory question as to when the soul leaves the body (*3AJ* 1) there is as extended description of the fate of unrepentant sinners (*3AJ* 2-10). Angelic guides lead sinners to torment that lasts forever, including the river of fire and the worm that never dies. The next major section of *3AJ* (11-35) focuses upon the fate of the righteous who, full of light, pass over the torments of the unrepentant. Worthy of mention from this section is the catalog of sinners who are offered as examples of recipients of God's grace as a result of their repentance (*3AJ* 23-27). Included in this list are: Peter, who denied the Lord three times (*3AJ* 23); Mary the prostitute, who had sinned indiscriminately with 1,703 men; Manasseh, who killed his own son, 40 elders, as well as Isaiah; the thief on the cross, who had committed 99 murders (*3AJ* 24); David, who sinned with Bathsheba, one of 100 women he kept (*3AJ* 25); Andrew of Crete, who committed incest with his own mother, but later became a bishop (*3AJ* 26); and Cyprian, who was born of a race of demons and destroyed 1,300 children, before his conversion and call as a bishop (*3AJ* 27). The document concludes with a warning that there is no opportunity for repentance or forgiveness after one's death (*3AJ* 35). Clearly, the document's major emphasis is upon the importance of repentance and God's free forgiveness.

A final document, to be mentioned in this section devoted to the Apocalypse's influence upon later Johannine apocalyptic texts, is

---

[106] Court [*The Book of Revelation and the Johannine Apocalyptic Tradition*, pp. 108-31] provides the Greek text of the *3AJ*, an English translation, as well as a useful commentary.

the *Coptic Apocalypse of John* (*CAJ* 2).¹⁰⁷ This work, which appears to date from the eleventh century CE, continues the now familiar dialogue format found in the previous three books described. On the Mount of Olives, just before the ascension of Jesus, John the Apostle and Holy Virgin requests that he be taken to heaven by Jesus in order to see all the mysteries contained therein. Granting his request, Jesus entrusts John to a great Cherubim [*sic*], covered with eyes, who could answer all John's questions, for the words of the Father are hidden within the Cherubim (*CAJ* 2). John's journey includes a visit to the seven heavens. Here he discovers that water, which existed before the creation of heaven and earth (*CAJ* 3), is scarce at times owing to the sin of humanity. He finds that Michael is an unrivaled angelic being whose name is found upon the garments of all angels who come to earth, because his name keeps such ones from being lead astray by the Devil (*CAJ* 7). John discovers that Eve was hidden in Adam's rib from his creation and separated from him later (*CAJ* 13). He finds that after Solomon had the demons reveal the origins of illness and their remedies, he inscribed them on the Temple wall. Hezekiah plastered over this information and when he was found in need of healing Hezekiah prayed and was sent the prophet Isaiah with the remedy (*CAJ* 14). Finally, John is told that God determines a soul's destiny and that animals also have souls, though they always remain on earth (*CAJ* 18).

Art

The influence of the Apocalypse upon countless artists is hard to overestimate. In fact, it is not going too far to say that artists have been among the most attentive interpreters of the Apocalypse. The reason for this is not difficult to ascertain, for the book's aesthetic beauty speaks very powerfully to those with artistic sensibilities and connects with them at very deep levels. Thus, while the sometimes bizarre imagery of the Apocalypse can serve to frighten off certain textually inclined individuals, this same imagery often proves to be an irresistible invitation to the imaginations of various artists who devote their energies to artistic conceptualizations of the Apoca-

---

¹⁰⁷ Court [*The Book of Revelation and the Johannine Apocalyptic Tradition*, pp. 137-63] provides E.W. Budge's English translation of the *CAJ*, as well as Court's own useful commentary.

lypse. The influence of the Apocalypse in the realm of art is so vast, the challenges involved in attempting to describe artistic depictions without benefit of all the visual images themselves, so great, that one could almost despair of attempting to include a section in this part of the introduction devoted to history of effect. However, the significance of this voluminous evidence necessitates the inclusion of a survey of the art (including representative pieces) inspired by the Apocalypse despite the limitations of the presentation.

The effective history of the Apocalypse in art can be detected as early as the possible depictions of scenes from Revelation found within the Catacombs in Rome. Here, among the numerous representations drawn from both the OT and the NT, appear to be drawings inspired by the Apocalypse. One example of this effective history is a picture of 'Christ the Judge', surrounded by stacks of books, the basis of the judgment of the dead (cf. Rev. 20.12), and sheep, which represent the elect (Figure 1).[108]

Figure 1
Christ the Judge (Coemeterium Maius, Rome)

---

[108] J. Stevenson, *The Catacombs: Life and Death in Early Christianity* (Nashville, TN: Thomas Nelson, 1985), pp. 107-108.

60   *The Apocalypse*

Other depictions informed by the Apocalypse include the conquering Christ entering the Holy City in triumph and Christ teaching the multitude in the heavenly Jerusalem.[109]

One of the ways to gain entry into the art of the Apocalypse in general is to become aware of the variety of mediums used in creating these artistic depictions. These mediums include the following (with an example of the medium provided within parentheses): illuminated manuscripts (*The Trinity Apocalypse*, Figure 2, below), oil

Figure 2
Worship of the Beast and War with the Beast
(*Trinity Apocalypse*, Trinity College Library, Cambridge, England)

paintings (Raphael's *The Vision of Ezekiel*), stained glass (the Great East Window of York Minster), frescoes (Correggio's Painted Cuploa, Giovanni Evangelista at Parma), mosaics (the Triumphal Arch of S. Maria Maggiore in Rome), relief sculptures (*Majestas*

---

[109] Stevenson, *The Catacombs*, pp. 114-16.

Domini, Chartres [Eure-et-Loir], Notre Dame, Portail Royal), and tapestries (The Brussels Tapestries).[110]

Another avenue by which to gain some understanding of the effective history of the Apocalypse in the realm of art is to give some attention to the scenes from the Apocalypse that are most often depicted. One of the more popular scenes amongst artists is the attempt to depict John near the beginning of his visionary experience. Sometimes the focus is upon John taking the book from the angel or writing in it, though often these scenes include some aspect of the vision that awaits John. One of the best examples is the well-known fifteenth century altarpiece by Hans Memling (*Saint John the Evangelist on Patmos*), depicted on the front cover of this volume. In this oil on wood painting, John sits writing in the foreground, while in the background many of the prominent aspects of the vision are depicted. It almost goes without saying that the vision of heaven in Revelation 4-5 is an extraordinarily popular one among artists of the Apocalypse. Another prominent theme found in the artistic depictions generated by the Apocalypse are the angelic beings. As would be imagined, special attention is given to the seven angels with the seven trumpets (8.2), the sounding of which accompanies significant events on the earth, the seven angels with the seven bowls of judgment (14), as well as the angels who accompany and/or speak with John during the course of the visionary drama. Equally influential are the images of the opening of the seven seals and the four horsemen who accompany the opening of the first four of these seals. Other prominent images of the Apocalypse to be found in art include the four living beasts, the woman clothed with the Sun, the beast and the dragon, and Babylon the Harlot. As could be expected much attention is devoted to depictions of the new heaven and new earth.

Yet another way to gain some appreciation for the art inspired by the Apocalypse is to give attention to a few individual contributions of special significance. Some of the most exquisite and moving artistic depictions of scenes from the Apocalypse are to be

---

[110] All these examples may be found in the small but helpful introduction to the art of the Apocalypse N. Grubb's *Revelations: Art of the Apocalypse* (New York: Abbeville Pub., 1997) and in the more exhaustive treatment by F. van der Meer, *Apocalypse: Visions from the Book of Revelation in Western Art* (New York: Alpine Fine Arts, 1978).

found in a group of illuminated manuscripts that contain a commentary on the Book of Revelation, written sometime during the eighth century by Beatus, a resident of the Benedictine abbey of S Turribo at Liébana, Spain. The commentary Beatus produced could more properly be considered a catena, a collection of comments from a variety of earlier writers (Figure 3).[111] Several illuminated manuscripts appeared over the next few hundred years which illustrate a number of scenes from the Apocalypse. It appears that the original cycle of illustrations consisted of 108 somewhat disparate images. Of these, one illustration accompanies each chapter of text as well as an introductory image. These illustrations are among the most beautiful and emotive devoted to the Apocalypse.[112]

Figure 3
The Fifth Angel Empties His Bowl on the Throne of the Beast
(*Beatus of Liébana, Commentary on the Apocalypse (Morgan Beatus)*
The Pierpont Morgan Library, NY)

---

[111] According to Beatus' preface, these included the writings of 'Jerome, Augustine, Ambrose, Fulgentius, Gregory, Tyconius, Irenaeus, Apringius and Isidore'.

[112] On the Beatus cycle cf. van der Meer, *Apocalypse*, 108-27. Cf. also J. Williams, *The Illustrated Beatus: A Corpus of the Illustrations of the Commentary on the Apocalypse* 5 vols (London: Harvey Miller Publishers, 1994-2003).

In 1498 Albrecht Dürer produced a series of fifteen wood-cuts, based on the Apocalypse, that brought him immediate fame. These black and white depictions are staggering in terms of their vision, intricacy, and detail (cf. Figure 4). Introduced by a depiction from *The Life of John*, where John is in a cauldron of oil, they include many of the major scenes from the Apocalypse. His work, considered by many to have superseded everything that preceded it, inspired other scenes by later artists in order to compliment those offered by Dürer.

Figure 4
Albrecht Dürer, *John Devours the Scroll*
(State Art Gallery in Karlsruhe, Germany)

64 *The Apocalypse*

Perhaps the single, best-known artistic depiction generated by the Apocalypse is *The Adoration of the Lamb* by Jan van Eyck, which is part of the Ghent Altarpiece (Figure 5). While any artistic depiction of a scene from the Apocalypse involves interpretation on the part of the artist(s), the integrative vision that produces *The Adoration of the Lamb* may be without rival.

Figure 5
Jan van Eyck, *Adoration of the Lamb*
(Ghent Altar Piece, Saint Bavo, Ghent, the Netherlands)

The focal point of the scene, as the name indicates, is the Lamb standing upon an altar with his blood from an open wound flowing directly into a chalice. He is surrounded by angels, two of whom continually minister incense around him, while twelve others are given to other forms of adoration. For example, two of the twelve stand on either side of a large wooden cross which they gently embrace, a crown of thorns in the hand of one and a spear in the hand of the other. In the background is a sun-like sphere, the rays of which disperse in all directions, from which the Spirit as a dove descends. All around the Lamb are groups of saints who worship him. These include the martyrs, confessors, virgins, apostles, prophets, pilgrims, and soldiers of the cross. In the foreground is the fountain of the water of life, which the death of the Lamb makes available to all who believe (Rev. 22.1-2). The indescribable beauty of *The Adoration of the Lamb* makes it one of the most magnificent pieces of the artistic effective history of the Apocalypse.[113]

Music

When reflecting upon the Apocalypse's effective history in the realm of music, one of the first compositions to come to mind is the 'Hallelujah Chorus' in G.F. Handel's, *The Messiah*. Written over a twenty-four day period in 1741 (21 August through 14 September, 1741),[114] this ambitious oratorio in three parts covers the life of Christ beginning with the Nativity and concluding with the apocalyptic vision of the Lamb of God glorified in heaven. *The Messiah*, along with *Israel in Egypt*, consists entirely of texts taken from Scripture.[115] Coming at the end of part two, *The Messiah* climaxes in the crescendo entitled 'Hallelujah'. Relying heavily upon Rev. 19.6, from which the title 'Hallelujah' comes, the chorus incorporates the well-known phrase 'for the Lord God Omnipotent reigneth' as a repeated refrain. This refrain then gives way to additional words that come from Rev. 11.15, 'The Kingdom of this world is become the Kingdom of our Lord and of his Christ, and of His Christ and He shall reign forever and ever'. As the chorus draws to its climatic conclusion the words 'King of Kings and Lord of Lords', also from Rev. 19.16, are incorporated into the vigorous, almost overpowering integration of words from these texts; words which are brought together in an extraordinary marriage of lyrics, voices, notes, and instruments. The influence of the Apocalypse upon *The Messiah* is not limited to its effect upon the 'Hallelujah Chorus', but continues to be seen in the oratorio's very last chorus entitled, 'Worthy Is the Lamb that Was Slain', with which the composition concludes. On this occasion it is Rev. 5.12-13 that provides the lyrics:

---

[113] For an extensive discussion of van Eyck's *Adoration*, cf. van der Meer, *Apocalypse*, pp. 236-57.

[114] The Autograph Score of the Messiah bears these dates, written in German in Handel's own hand, at the beginning and the end of the manuscript, respectively. J. Tobin, *Handel at Work* (New York: St. Martin's Press, 1964), p. 2.

[115] E. Smith, 'Handel's English librettists', in *The Cambridge Companion to Handel* (ed. D. Borrows; Cambridge: Cambridge University Press, 1997), p. 103.

> Worthy is the Lamb that was slain, and hath redeemed us to God by His blood, to receive power, and riches, and wisdom, and strength, and glory, and blessing.

Followed by:

> Blessing and honor, glory and pow'r, be unto Him, be unto Him that sitteth upon the throne, and unto the Lamb.

It is even possible that the 'Amen' of Rev. 5.14 inspires its repeated use as *The Messiah* concludes. When one hears *The Messiah*, first performed in Dublin and regularly at the Foundling Hospital in London for charitable purposes,[116] the effect of the text of the Apocalypse is unmistakable. However, it is not only possible to detect the Apocalypse's effect upon *The Messiah*, it is also possible to detect something of this text's effect upon the composer himself. For it is said that upon the completion of the 'Hallelujah Chorus', Handel commented to his servant, 'I think I did see all Heaven before me and the Great God Himself'.[117]

The effective history of the Apocalypse upon music may also be observed in the hymns of Charles Wesley (1707-1788).[118] The son of an Anglican cleric (Samuel) and a mother (Susanna) fiercely devoted to religious training, Charles worked closely with his better-known brother John. On 21 May 1738, three days before John's experience of the assurance of his salvation (when his heart was 'strangely warmed'), Charles had his own religious awakening. Often referred to as the poet of the Methodist movement, Charles would pen more than 6,000 hymns. Rich in biblical content and theological reflection, a not insignificant number of these hymns clearly show the impact of the Apocalypse. For example, in the 1909 edition of *The Methodist Hymn-Book* more than 110 of Charles' hymns make explicit reference to the words and/or imagery of the Book of Revelation. Some of the hymns reflect a single idea such as the 'cleansing blood of Jesus' found in Rev. 1.5 (cf. hymns 525.1;

---

[116] A. Hicks, 'Handel and the Idea of an Oratorio', in *The Cambridge Companion to Handel*, p. 157 and D. Burrows, 'Handel's Oratorio Performances', in *The Cambridge Companion to Handel*, p. 265.

[117] Tobin, *Handel at Work*, p. 2.

[118] On the eschatological views of Charles Wesley cf. esp. Newport, *Apocalypse & Millennium: Studies in Biblical Eisegesis*, pp. 119-49. Newport confines his fine study to the prose of Charles Wesley.

708.5; 709.4), 'following the Lamb wherever he leads' in Rev. 14.4 (541.1; 787.1; 788.1; 857.2), or 'come quickly Lord Jesus' from Rev. 22.20 (66.6; 291.4; 529.5; 546.4; 554.2; 829.6). The ideas and wording of the Apocalypse are so embedded in the hymns of Wesley that such examples could be offered almost *ad infinitum*. In addition to traces of the Apocalypse's effective influence across a wide range of compositions, a number of hymns are devoted wholly to a specific text or an amalgam of texts from Revelation. The three examples selected for inclusion here each reveal something of the extent to which the Apocalypse penetrated Charles Wesley's very soul.

The first example (Hymn 200) offers Wesley's meditation upon and mediation of the prophetic word contained in Rev. 1.7:

> 1 Lo! He comes with clouds descending,
>   Once for favored sinners slain;
> Thousand thousand saints attending,
>   Swell the triumph of his train:
>   Hallelujah!
>   God appears on earth to reign.
>
> 2 Every eye shall now behold Him
>   Robed in dreadful majesty;
> Those who set at nought and sold Him,
>   Pierced and nailed him to the tree,
>   Deeply wailing,
>   Shall the true Messiah see.
>
> 3 The tokens of His passion
>   Still his dazzling body bears;
> Cause of endless exultation
>   To His ransomed worshippers:
>   With what rapture
>   Gaze we on those glorious scars!
>
> 4 Yea, Amen! let all adore thee,
>   High on Thy eternal throne;
> Saviour, take the power and glory,
>   Claim the kingdom for Thine own;

>   Jah, Jehovah,
> Everlasting God, come down!¹¹⁹

Another example (Hymn 802) is a moving reflection upon the description of those who passed through the great tribulation described in Rev. 7.13-17:

> 1 What are these arrayed in white,
>   Brighter than the noonday sun?
> Foremost of the sons of light,
>   Nearest the eternal throne?
> These are they that bore the cross,
>   Nobly for their Master stood;
> Sufferers for His righteous cause,
>   Followers of the dying God.
>
> 2 Out of great distress they came,
>   Washed their robes by faith below
> In the blood of yonder Lamb,
>   Blood that washes white as snow:
> Therefore are they next the throne,
>   Serve their Maker day and night;
> God resides among His own,
>   God doth in His saints delight.
>
> 3 More than conquerors at last,
>   Here they find their trials o'er;
> They have all their sufferings passed,
>   Hunger now and thirst no more;
> No excessive heat they feel
>   From the sun's directer ray,
> In a milder clime they dwell,
>   Region of eternal day.
>
> 4 He that on the throne doth reign,
>   Them the Lamb shall always feed,
> With the tree of life sustain,

---

[119] *The Methodist Hymn-Book* (London: Wesleyan Conference Office, 1904), p. 78.

> To the living fountains lead;
> He shall all their sorrows chase,
>   All their wants at once remove,
> Wipe the tears from every face,
>   Fill up every soul with love.[120]

A final example (Hymn 848) draws upon the concluding chapters of the Apocalypse, focusing upon the future reward and place of abode awaiting the saints:

> 1 Away with our sorrow and fear!
>   We soon shall recover our home,
> The city of the saints shall appear,
>   The day of eternity come:
> From earth we shall quickly remove,
>   And mount to our native abode,
> The house of our Father above,
>   The palace of angels and God.
>
> 2 Our mourning is all at an end,
>   When, raised by the life-giving word,
> We see the new city descend,
>   Adorned as a bride for her Lord:
> The city so holy and clean,
>   No sorrow can breathe in the air;
> No gloom or affliction of sin,
>   No shadow of evil is there.
>
> 3 By faith we already behold
>   That lovely Jerusalem here;
> Her walls are of jasper and gold,
>   As crystal her buildings are clear;
> Immovably founded in grace,
>   She stands as she ever hath stood,
> And brightly her Builder displays,
>   And flames with the glory of God.

---

[120] *The Methodist Hymn-Book*, p. 303.

70 *The Apocalypse*

> 4 No need of the sun in that day,
>   Which never is followed by night,
> Where Jesus's beauties display
>   A pure and a permanent light:
> The Lamb is their light and their sun,
>   And lo! By reflection they shine,
> With Jesus ineffably one,
>   And bright in effulgence divine.[121]

Other Wesley compositions heavily influenced by the Apocalypse include Hymns 227 and 848.

Though many other examples could here be offered,[122] the work of Handel and Charles Wesley illustrate the powerful influence of the Apocalypse in the realm of music.

Poetry

The first example here offered of the effective power of the Apocalypse in the world of English poetry comes from the so-called *Gawain*-Poet. Written near the close of the fourteenth century in the North-West Midlands of England, the *Gawain*-Poet produced four works contained in a single Medieval manuscript. The name *Gawain* comes from the first poem in the manuscript, 'Sir Gawain and the Green Knight'. The similarity of dialect and vocabulary, among other things, lead most scholars to conclude that these four works come from the same author.[123] The effect of the Apocalypse is quite pronounced in the most ambitious of the *Gawain* pieces,[124] a poem entitled 'The Pearl'. This influence is seen in the occasional direct references to 'the Apostle John' or to 'the Apocalypse', the numerous direct quotations of the book, and a variety of other more subtle appearances of the language and imagery of the Apocalypse. One extended passage illustrates something of the extent of the theological integration of the Apocalypse into the poetry of the

---

[121] *The Methodist Hymn-Book*, pp. 321-22.

[122] Though the effective history of the Apocalypse in the so-called 'main-line churches' is often hard to discern, it has recently been demonstrated that the music known in this tradition reveals that even here the Apocalypse is not without influence. Cf. the very helpful work of C.R. Koester, *Revelation and the End of All Things* (Grand Rapids: Eerdmans, 2001), esp. pp. 33-38.

[123] On this and other introductory questions cf. esp. A. Putter, *An Introduction to the* Gawain-*Poet* (London: Longman, 1996), pp. 1-37.

[124] Putter, *An Introduction to the* Gawain-*Poet*, p. 147.

Gawain-Poet. The passage is devoted to reflection upon the relationship between Christ and his bride, the Church.

64
'O spotless Lamb who doth defeat
All ills, my dearest Destiny
Chose me His mate, although unmeet
At first had seemed that unity
From the world of woe I did retreat.
He called me to His company:
'Come hither to me, my belovèd sweet;
There is no mote nor spot in thee'.
Might and beauty He gave to me.
In His blood He rinsed my robes before
He crowned me clean in virginity,
Adorning me in pearls so pure'.

65
'Why, spotless bride who flames so bright,
Possessed of royalty rich and rife,
What kind of Lamb is He who might
Wed thee and take thee to his wife?
Above all others thou climbedst the height
To lead with Him so noble a life!
So many, comely combed, did fight
For Christ and live in constant strife,
And all those dear ones thou didst drive
Out from that marriage and so assure
Thy place alone, so bold and blithe,
A peerless maid, matchless and pure'.

66
'spotless', quoth that merry queen,
Unblemished I am, without a blot,
And that I might bear with stately mien,
But 'unmatched queen', that said I not.
All wives of the Lamb in bliss we have been,
A hundred and forty thousand lot,
As in the Apocalypse it is seen.
St. John saw them gathered all in a knot,

> On the hill of Sion, that seemly spot.
> The Apostle saw them, in his vision's dream,
> Arrayed for the wedding on that hill top,
> The fair new city, Jerusalem.[125]

Another witness to the effective history of the Apocalypse comes from the work of William Blake (1757-1827). Perhaps 'the best poetry in English since Milton', Blake's work is widely known for its beauty, masterful design, and minute articulations.[126] Traces of the Apocalypse's influence can be detected throughout much of the Blake corpus. For example, in 'The Marriage of Heaven and Hell' (Plate 19) one encounters the phrase 'seven houses of brick' which has reference to the seven churches of Revelation 1-3. It is sometimes argued that if Oothoon's search for Theotormon were successful, in 'Vision of the Daughters of Albion', there would be no more sea (Rev. 21.1). Clear reference to Revelation 11 is made in a passage from 'Milton: the First Book' (Plate 24, Lines 59-61):

> The witnesses lie dead in the Street of the Great City
> No Faith is in all the Earth: the Book of God is trodden under
>   Foot:
> He sent his two Servants Whitefield & Westley: were they
>   Prophets
> Or were they Idiots or Madmen? shew us Miracles.[127]

Also being informed by the Apocalypse (21-22) are the descriptions and measurements of Jerusalem in 'Jerusalem: Chapter 1' (Plates 12-13). However, by far the composition with the greatest concentration of Apocalypse imagery is Blake's epic, 'The Four Zoas'. Not only is the title taken from the four living beasts of Rev. 4.6 (τέσσαρα ζῷα), but there are also references to a number of terms and topics also found in the Apocalypse. For example, the numerology of the Apocalypse is reflected in 'The Four Zoas: Night The First':

---

[125] *The Pearl* (trans. & ed. S. Deford, et al; New York: Appleton-Century-Croft, 1967), pp. 65-67.

[126] H. Bloom, *Blake's Apocalypse: A Study in Poetic Argument* (Garden City: Doubleday, 1963), p. 9.

[127] From *The Complete Poetry and Prose of William Blake* (ed. D.V. Erdman; New York: Doubleday, 1988), p. 118.

> Then they Elected Seven, called the Seven
> Eyes of God & the Seven lamps of the Almighty
> The Seven are one within the other the Seventh is named Jesus
> The Lamb of God blessed for ever ...[128]

In addition to the numerology, descriptive terms like 'The Synagogue of Satan' and 'the Harlot of the Kings of Earth', also known as 'Mystery the Harlot', frequently appear. Throughout the piece special standing is given to 'the Lamb of God' who, among other things, creates for Himself a bride and wife. While numerous other observations could be made about the effect of the Apocalypse upon the poetry of Blake, perhaps something of the creative integration of these powerful images in his vision might best be captured in a passage from 'The Four Zoas: Night the Eighth':

> We now behold the Ends of Beulah & we now behold
> Where Death Eternal is put off Eternally
> Assume the dark Satanic body in the Virgins womb
> O Lamb divin[e] it cannot thee annoy O pitying one
> Thy pity is from the foundation of the World & thy Redemption
> Begun Already in Eternity   Come then O Lamb of God
> Come Lord Jesus come quickly.[129]

The Apocalypse's effective history in the realm of poetry is also evidenced within the Pentecostal tradition in a composition that appeared in 1907, written by an individual identified simply as Bro. A. Beck. The poem, entitled 'The First Resurrection', was inspired by the words of Rev. 20.6, 'Blessed and holy is he that hath part in the first resurrection; On him the second death has no power'.

'The First Resurrection'

> Behold the sight most wonderful;
> From every grave beneath the skies,
> From ocean depth and mountain peak,
>   The righteous dead arise.
>
> With bodies glorified they come,
> With faces radiant and sublime;

---

[128] From *The Complete Poetry and Prose of William Blake*, pp. 312-13.
[129] From *The Complete Poetry and Prose of William Blake*, p. 377.

With shouts of victory ascend,
  All in a moment's time.

Changed in the twinkling of an eye,
Immortal bodies they put on;
Swifter than any lightning's ray
  And brighter than the sun.

Oh, what vast and joyous host,
When dead and living are called out,
From silent grave, and worldly crowd,
  At the archangel's shout.

No wicked one amongst that host,
Shall rise to life on that great day;
The flowers above their graves still bloom,
  Over their lifeless clay.

In that great resurrection morn,
Oh, grant us all a standing place;
That we with all the Bloodwashed saints
  May see Thy blessed face.[130]

Film

While the effective history of the Apocalypse in the medium of film is vast, this brief section focuses upon two distinct celluloid interpretations which find their *raison d'etre* in the Book of Revelation. Distinct in their emphases and target audiences, each film exhibits clear signs of the effect of the Apocalypse.

One motion picture that draws heavily upon Revelation is *End of Days*, a dark Arnold Schwarzenegger film. Timed for release to coincide with the turn of the millennium, the imprint of the Apocalypse is obvious throughout *End of Days*. The premise of the film is that a female baby, born 20 years before the turn of the millennium, is dedicated and prepared to bear a child fathered by Satan upon his release from the Abyss. This tale of struggle at the cosmic level draws upon the Apocalypse at a number of points as the story unfolds. Perhaps the clearest sign of the Apocalypse's effect upon the

---

[130] *Apostolic Faith* 1.8 (May, 1907), p. 2.

film is the way in which Rev. 20.7 serves as a refrain throughout the piece. The words of this verse ('And when the thousand years have ended Satan will be loosed from his prison') appear as early as the opening credits and are read by the viewer or heard from the lips of various characters in the film on several occasions. In fact, the viewer is not permitted to allow the importance of the Apocalypse to go unnoticed as part of the mystery of these words is revealed when Jericho (Schwarzenegger's character) actually reads them from the Bible. The release of Satan, accompanied by explosions and earthquake like phenomena, is depicted as a phantom-like presence, who searches New York City until the right man is found, of whom Satan takes possession. The plot develops as the powers of Satan are manifested and the diverse strategies of the church are unveiled. Satan's identity is developed in ways clearly indebted to the Apocalypse, as both serpent and hideous beast are either associated with his activity or is an image he takes on at some point. While the adulterous activities of the great πόρνη ('whore') of Revelation 17-18 find no place in the film, the sexual immorality of this female figure appears to be lived out in the figure of Satan, who is sexually immoral from his first appearance to his last one. The purpose of his release, 'to deceive the nations', is represented by the numerous individuals he co-opts or attempts to seduce in order to accomplish his goal. The witnesses of the church, who seek to oppose Satan at every point, meet fates similar to that of the witnesses found in the Apocalypse. The gematria of the Beast's number (666) is inverted (999) in this movie in order to produce the meaning that Satan's release coincides with the year 1999. The woman clothed with the Sun, whose child the beast opposes in Revelation 12, is transformed in this story into Christine York (Christ in New York!), who must be protected from the Dragon by God and his agents, so that she *not* become impregnated. Her principle defender, Jericho, though a person on the verge of suicide as the movie opens – who has had a disagreement with God when his wife and daughter are ruthlessly murdered, mirrors Christ in several ways. At one point, Satan, seeking the whereabouts of Christine, tempts Jericho with the promise of the return of his dead wife and daughter in exchange for the information. Perhaps the most explicit example of the similarities between Christ and Jericho is the moment in the movie when Jericho, whilst seeking to protect Christine, is betrayed by his

76 *The Apocalypse*

best friend, attacked and beaten by a mob, finally being crucified in a dirty alleyway. Furthermore, near the conclusion of the film, Jericho renounces violence, asks God for strength and seeks to face Satan through his faith in God/Christ. Despite Satan's attack, which includes Satan's entering him in order to accomplish his purpose for Christine, Jericho successfully fights off these internal struggles and like Christ, goes to his death in order to save others. Jericho's death not only protects Christine, but also culminates in Satan's return to the Abyss.[131] The effect of the Apocalypse upon this film, intended for a mainstream audience, is obvious.[132]

Another film that shows the clear effects of the text of the Apocalypse is *The Omega Code*, a TBN Ministries production. In keeping with a popular line of eschatological thought, this movie traces the rise of a world leader to a position of religious, political, and economic control. In addition to a plot readily recognizable to many (dispensational) students of 'Bible prophecy', *The Omega Code* utilizes in its story line The Bible Code, a recent theory that there lies deep within Scripture a secret code that emerges after painstaking numerical and linguistic analysis. The world leader of *The Omega Code*, Stone Alexander (played by Michael York), makes use of the Bible Code to gain dominance of the world. From the beginning of the film, where explicit reference is made to the books of Daniel and Revelation, the significance of the Apocalypse is clear. Throughout *The Omega Code* characters and events found in Revelation are highlighted. For example, the two witnesses described in Revelation 11 figure prominently at numerous points throughout the film. Not only do they function as prophetic figures, appearing before the world on cable TV, but they are also martyred, humiliated, and then raised from the dead. As the story unfolds, messages from the Biblical text, discovered by means of the Bible Code, appear on a computer screen. Among the messages having clear reference to the Apocalypse are the following: 'TEN HORNS UNITE

---

[131] It is perhaps not insignificant to note that in contrast to numerous other films in which the effect of the Apocalypse can be detected, the term 'antichrist' appears nowhere in *End of Days*.

[132] For a somewhat different analysis of this film cf. R. Walsh, 'On Finding a Non-American Revelation: *End of Days* and the Book of Revelation', in *Screening Scripture: Intertextual Connections Between Scripture and Film* (ed. G. Aichele and R. Walsh; Harrisburg, PA: Trinity Press International, 2002), pp. 1-23.

UNDER WORLD LEADER', 'AROMA OF END ENCHANTS ALL FOR 3 AND 1/2 YEARS', 'BLOOD POURS FROM STONE – WORLD WONDERS', 'SEVEN HORNS BOW TO WOUNDED HEAD' and the final message which reads '0000 DAWN OF A NEW MILLENIUM'. In addition to these messages, which act as a refrain throughout the film, is the rebuilding of Solomon's Temple (based upon an interpretation of Revelation 11), the worship of the beast and reference to his (false) prophet, a wound to the head of Alexander and his subsequent recovery, the reading of the text of Revelation 13 by the two witnesses, and the appearance in a vision of the Four Horsemen described in Revelation 6. It is difficult to over estimate the significance of this and other films like it,[133] for they represent the thinking and expectations about the end time of a significant number of Christians worldwide.

Commentaries

This section concludes that devoted to the Apocalypse's streams of influence as well as the introduction proper. The four commentaries surveyed at this point each represent a significant contribution and movement in the study of the Apocalypse over the centuries.

The first extant commentary on the Apocalypse is that by Victorinus, Bishop of Pettau († ca. 304), written sometime around 260 CE and preserved by Jerome. This work offers comment on a number of verses in almost every chapter, except 16 and 18. Victorinus' interpretative approach is symbolic, if not allegorical, in nature, as the following examples illustrate. Commenting on the open door John saw in Rev. 4.1, Victorinus notes, 'The new testament is announced as an open door in heaven'.[134] His comments on the open book in the hand of God continue this thought, 'This book signifies the Old Testament, which has been given into the hands of our Lord Jesus Christ, who received from the Father judgment'.[135]

---

[133] Cf. also movies based upon the *Left Behind* series of books by Tim LaHaye.

[134] Cited according to the translation of R.E. Wallis in *The Ante-Nicene Fathers* VII (Edinburgh: T. & T. Clark, 1989), p. 347.

[135] Cited according to the translation of R.E. Wallis in *The Ante-Nicene Fathers* VII, p. 349.

But perhaps the nature of Victorinus' approach is captured better by his comments on Rev. 6.12-14:

> 12. 'And I saw, when he had opened the sixth seal, there was a great earthquake'. In the sixth seal, then, was a great earthquake: this is that very last persecution.
>
> 'And the sun became black as sackcloth of hair'. The sun becomes as sackcloth; that is, the brightness of doctrine will be obscured by unbelievers.
>
> 'And the entire moon became as blood'. By the moon of blood is set forth the Church of the saints as pouring out her blood for Christ.
>
> 13. 'And the stars fell to the earth'. The falling of the stars are the faithful who are troubled for Christ's sake.
>
> 'Even as a fig-tree casteth her untimely figs'. The fig-tree, when shaken, loses its untimely figs when men are separated from the Church by persecution.
>
> 14. 'And the heaven withdrew as a scroll that is rolled up'. For the heaven to be rolled away, that is, that the Church shall be taken away.
>
> 'And every mountain and the islands were moved from their places'. Mountains and islands removed from their places intimate that in the last persecution all men departed from their places; that is, that the good will be removed, seeking to avoid the persecution.[136]

He offers an extensive explanation of how the numerical calculation of the number of the Beast, found in Rev. 13.18, works in Greek, Latin, and even Gothic. For Victorinus, there is no doubt as to the identity of the seven hills upon which the woman sits in Rev. 17.9. It is 'the city of Rome'. On the identity of the kings in 17.10-11 he writes:

> 10. 'And there are seven kings: five have fallen, and one is, and the other is not yet come; and when he is come, he will be for a

---

[136] Cited according to the translation of R.E. Wallis in *The Ante-Nicene Fathers* VII, p. 351.

short time'. The time must be understood in which the written Apocalypse was published, since then reigned Caesar Domitian; but before him had been Titus his brother, and Vespasian, Otho, Vitellius, and Galba. These are the five who have fallen. One remains, under whom the Apocalypse was written Domitian, to wit. 'The other has not yet come', speaks of Nerva; 'and when he is come, he will be for a short time', for he did not complete the period of two years.

11. 'And the beast which thou sawest is of the seven'. Since before those kings Nero reigned.[137]

In his more extensive comments on Rev. 20.1-6 Victorinus appears to argue for an earthly millennial reign of Christ at the end of which Satan will be released for a period of three and one-half years. He goes on to say:

> I do not think the reign of a thousand years is eternal; or if it is thus to be thought of, they cease to reign when the thousand years are finished. But I will put forward what my capacity enables me to judge. The tenfold number signifies the decalogue, and the hundredfold sets forth the crown of virginity: for he who shall have kept the undertaking of virginity completely, and shall have faithfully fulfilled the precepts of the decalogue, and shall have destroyed the untrained nature or impure thoughts within the retirement of the heart, that they may not rule over him, this is the true priest of Christ, and accomplishing the millenary number thoroughly, is thought to reign with Christ; and truly in his case the devil is bound. But he who is entangled in the vices and the dogmas of heretics, in his case the devil is loosed. But that it says that when the thousand years are finished he is loosed, so the number of the perfect saints being completed, in whom there is the glory of virginity in body and mind, by the approaching advent of the kingdom of the hateful one, many, seduced by that love of earthly things, shall be overthrown, and together with him shall enter the lake of fire.[138]

---

[137] Cited according to the translation of R.E. Wallis in *The Ante-Nicene Fathers* VII, p. 358.

[138] Cited according to the translation of R.E. Wallis in *The Ante-Nicene Fathers* VII, p. 359.

The second commentary to be considered comes from (the Venerable) Bede (ca. 672-735).[139] Bede's work is a running commentary on every verse in the Apocalypse and is over 40,000 words long. Several aspects of this volume merit comment.

As far as can be determined, Bede is the first interpreter to offer a seven-part structure for the Apocalypse. His view of the structure is roughly as follows:

Preface - Rev. 1.1-8
Rev. 1.9-3.22
Rev. 4.1-7.17
Rev. 8.1-11.18
Rev. 11.19-15.8
Rev. 16.1-16.21
Rev. 17.1-18.25
Rev. 19.1-22.21

However, in the commentary itself, Bede's work takes the form of three books (Book I, Revelation 1-8; Book II, Revelation 9-14; Book III, Revelation 15-22). He explains this move in a letter to Eusebius as owing to the fact that three short books relieve the mind of the readers, rather than seven. Bede is clearly indebted to interpreters before him. There are places where his interpretative decisions mirror those of Victorinus. He not only cites the interpretive rules of Tyconius in his letter to Eusebius, but he also quotes Tyconuis some ten times in the body of the commentary. Generally, Bede sees recapitulation at work in the Apocalypse, specifically mentioning that the story is recapitulated at several points (4.1; 8.1; 9.20; 11.18; 20.1). Like Victorinus before him, much of the interpretive approach could be described as spiritual or even allegorical in nature. He offers some 'philological' evidence in his exposition, as for example when he gives a definition of the meaning of the names of six of the seven churches in Revelation 2-3. The four living creatures are the Evangelists and when they preach, everyone falls down. The book in the hand of the One who sits on the throne, described in chapter 5, is the Bible: the writing on the outside is the OT, while the writing on the inside is the NT. At a num-

---

[139] Bede (The Venerable Beda): *The Explanation of the Apocalypse*, (trans. E. Marshall; Oxford and London: James Parker and Co. 1878).

ber of points Bede sees the symbols of the Apocalypse as pointing to the heretics with which the church is confronted. They are identified as the pale horse in Revelation 6 and one of the trumpets in Revelation 8. There are extensive explanations offered for the order and significance of the twelve tribes of chapter 7 and the jewels found in the description of the New Jerusalem in chapter 21. The theophanic element of lightning is identified on several occasions as having reference to the working of miracles. Those playing harps are those who have been crucified. Mention of the Sea of Glass has reference to baptism, as does mention of the first resurrection in 20.5. Apparently influenced by Tyconius and Augustine, Bede interprets the 1,000 year reign as the present time, i.e. what remains of the sixth day, at the end of which, Satan is loosed for 3 1/2 years. The liars mentioned in 21.8 are those who claim to be Jews but are not.[140]

The third commentary to be discussed is the *Expositio in Apocalypsim*[141] by the medieval abbot Joachim of Fiore (ca. 1135-1202). This commentary is considered to be the abbot's greatest work and incorporates earlier writing on Revelation entitled the *Enchiridion super Apocalypsim*. Following an introduction, the commentary is divided into eight books, each devoted to a section of the Apocalypse. The books are as follows:

Book 1 – Rev. 1.1-3.22 – Letters to the Seven churches
Book 2 – Rev. 4.1-8.1 – The Opening of the Seven Seals
Book 3 – Rev. 8.2-11.18 – The Seven Trumpet Blasts
Book 4 – Rev. 11.19-14.20 – The Two Beasts
Book 5 – Rev. 15.1-16.17 – The Seven Bowls
Book 6 – Rev. 16.18-19.21 – The Destruction of Babylon
Book 7 – Rev. 20.1-10 – The Millennium
Book 8 – Rev. 20-11-22.21 – The Heavenly Jerusalem.

These eight parts of the Apocalypse correspond to the seven special times (eras) of the church, followed by the eighth, which

---

[140] On Bede and others cf. the discussion by G. Kretschmar, *Die Offenbarung des Johannes: Die Geschichte ihrer Auslegung im 1. Jahrtausend* (CTM 9; Stuttgart: Calwer, 1985), pp. 116-22.

[141] For the text cf. Joachim of Fiore, *Expositio in Apocalypsim* (Frankfurt am Main: Minerva, 1964).

corresponds to the glorification of the heavenly Jerusalem.[142] Crucial to Joachim's interpretation is his understanding of redemptive history as being divided into three eras or statuses namely, the era of the Father, the era of the Son, and the era of the Holy Spirit. While these eras have distinct points at which they begin and end, they also overlap with one another. Joachim, who produced a number of *Liber Figurarum* by which he taught theological truths, conveyed this reality as three successive circles that overlap with one another. However, they are arranged in such a way that all three converge at the center most part, signifying the unity of the Father, Son, and Holy Spirit. The Age of the Father can be traced from Adam until Christ's first advent, the Age of the Son begins there, and the Age of the Spirit is still to come. Within these three eras the seven ages of redemptive history may be fitted. The first five (Adam, Noah, Abraham, David, and Babylonian Exile) occurring in Age of the Father, the sixth (John the Baptist) in the Age of the Son, with the seventh awaiting the beginning of the Era of the Spirit.

Part of Joachim's contribution is the employment of historical referents in the interpretation of the Apocalypse. For example, in his discussion of the Beast with seven heads found in Revelation 12 and following, Joachim offers these identifications set out in the chart that follows:

Head	Person	Persecution by	Time Period Reflected
First	Herod	Jews	Apostles
Second	Nero	Pagans	Martyrs
Third	Constantius	Heretics	Doctors
Fourth	Mohammed	Saracens	Virgins
Fifth	Mesomoth	Son of Babylon	Conventuals
Sixth	Saladin		Spiritual Men in Joachim's Time
Seventh	Gog	Second Antichrist	End of Time

As the chart indicates, these historical identifications enable the reader to make their way through redemptive history. The mention of Joachim's contemporary, Saladin (1138-1193), as the sixth head of the beast, reveals something of the eschatological expectancy of Joachim's thinking, for Saladin was the Muslim leader who recap-

---

[142] Cf. the web site of the International Center for Joachim Studies in San Giovanni in Fiore [www.centrostudigioachimiti.it/Benvenuti/benvenutieng.asp].

tured Jerusalem from the Crusaders. From Joachim's perspective, the seventh head could appear at any time, signaling the end of time and the beginning of the Age of the Spirit in earnest. Challenging the a-millennial views of interpreters like Tyconius and Augustine, Joachim's work fueled the fire for millennial expectation in numerous later interpreters.[143]

A final commentary to be mentioned in this survey is by Allan A. Boesak.[144] Writing during the time of Apartheid in South Africa, Boesak combines an analysis of the text that focuses on the message of the book for John as well as its contemporary significance. Following an extensive introductory chapter the little book is divided into seven chapters entitled:

The Blessing
The Scroll
The Seven Seals Opened
The Woman and the Dragon
The Beast from the Sea and the Beast from the Earth
The Fall of Babylon
The End and the Beginning.

Boesak sees the Apocalypse as underground protest literature written within the context of a persecuted church. Bringing considerable attention to historical issues of introduction, Boesak argues that ultimately such issues are of secondary importance for readers of the book. For example, though he will argue vigorously for a date of composition sometime during the reign of Domitian, in comparison to the context of the 'oppressed' reader this is relatively inconsequential. He observes:

> The arguments around the different hypotheses seem to lead always to an effort to establish the truth about judging the *degree* of oppression that was meted out by one or another emperor.

---

[143] In addition to the web site mentioned above, cf. also the helpful discussions of Joachim by Wainwright, *Mysterious Apocalypse*, pp. 49-53 and J. Kovacs and C. Rowland, *Revelation* (Oxford: Blackwell, 2003), pp. 17-19. For excerpts of Joichim's work in English cf. *Apocalyptic Spirituality: Treatises and Letters of Lactantius, Adso of Montier-en-Der, Joichim of Fiore, The Franciscan Spirituals, Savonarola* (New York: Paulist Press, 1979), pp. 97-148.

[144] A.A. Boesak, *Comfort and Protest: Reflections on the Apocalypse of John on Patmos* (Edinburgh: The Saint Andrew Press, 1987).

Whether it was Nero or Domitian or even Galba (as John A.T. Robinson suggests) is ultimately of secondary importance. To the suffering people of God it did not really matter who they suffered under. What mattered is that they suffered … It is the fact that the weak and the destitute remained oppressed which provides the framework for understanding and interpreting history.[145]

Describing his work as 'biblical exegesis from the underside', he writes specifically with the Black South African Church in mind. He notes:

For people who face situations like these, the Apocalypse is an exciting, inspiring, and marvellous book. It is a book which, in our sociopoltical situation, is a constant call to conversion and change. It is prophetic, historical, contemporary. But we shall have to learn to read it differently. We shall have to do away with those sterile escape mechanisms and dead-end arguments about numbers and symbols and signs by which the real message is so often paralyzed.[146]

Boesak's reading is one in which the text of the Apocalypse, its first century context, and the context of the Black South African Church interact on an almost constant basis. Examples of the power of this interaction abound as the following citations reveal. Note his comments on the meaning of the song in Rev. 5.12:

On a Sunday afternoon young black Christians pick up this ancient song and make of it a new song as they dance around a police vehicle just after a student has been arrested at our church service … In translation it goes something like this:

'It is broken, the power of Satan is broken!
We have disappointed Satan, his power is broken.
Alleluia'.

As we sing, the song is picked up by others. The police somewhat confused, somewhat bewildered, somewhat scared, release our friend. Others join us as we march, singing and dancing, back into the church. This is a new song, a freedom song, and

---
[145] Boesak, *Comfort and Protest*, p. 25.
[146] Boesak, *Comfort and Protest*, pp. 38-39.

the power of it, the sheer joy of it, the amazing truth in it captivate and inspire thousands upon thousands throughout South Africa. For although the seals of the scroll must still be opened, the scroll is not in the hands of Caesar but in the hands of the Lamb. And we will sing this new song until 'every creature in heaven and on earth and under the earth and in the sea, and all therein', will say (5.13):

'To him who sits on the throne and to the Lamb be blessing and honour and glory and might for ever and ever!'[147]

His interpretation of the 'souls under the altar' in 6.9-10 is no less insightful.

The martyrs are dead, but their witness is still alive. Their voices can still be heard; they still inspire the church. They remind the church of what it means to be faithful to Jesus the Messiah, of the price one must pay for testimony to the one true God. They remind the church also of the true character of the powers of this world. The church must not forget who and what it is facing.[148]

To interpreters who are repelled by the vengeful nature of the martyrs' prayer, Boesak responds:

People who do not know what oppression and suffering is react strangely to the language of the Bible. The truth is that God *is* the God of the poor and the oppressed ... The oppressed do not see any dichotomy between God's love and God's justice. Why is there this division between the God of the Old Testament and the God of Jesus? Why, on this point, does white Western Christianity go back to the heresy of Marcion?[149]

On the identity of the number of the Beast, Boesak says:

For the key here is not who the beast is; the church knows that. Neither is the key whether we begin counting from DF Malan, or HF Verwoerd or PW Botha, from 1910 or from 1948. The key here is the understanding of the mystery: this beast, this

---

[147] Boesak, *Comfort and Protest*, pp. 61-62.
[148] Boesak, *Comfort and Protest*, p. 68.
[149] Boesak, *Comfort and Protest*, p. 72.

powerful merciless, violent beast, was and is not and goes to perdition ... It has no life and no future. It comes from hell and goes to hell.[150]

On the prophecy about the fall of Rome and by extension the fall of the Apartheid regime, he notes:

We must remember that as John writes there is no sign whatsoever of the imminent fall of Rome. He speaks like an Old Testament prophet. The vision is so clear, God's decision so certain, that for all intents and purposes it has already happened. Rome still stands, but John already can hear and see the rumblings and ripples of the mighty earthquake that will hit the city. He knows the end of Rome is near ... Rome may still have power, but John knows that we are seeing the beast's final convulsions.[151]

A final example comes from his stinging words on the need for a new heaven and new earth:

How well should we understand this, we people of the twentieth century. We saw the heavens polluted by the foul and vile smoke from the factories, made hopelessly inhabitable for the birds of the sky in the name of progress. We know about 'missiles carving highways of death through the stratosphere' ... Can the heavens ever be clean again after Hiroshima and Nagasaki? Can the heavens ever be purified of the stench of gas ovens, burnt-out villages in Asia, or utterly destroyed Palestinian camps in Lebanon? And the vilest stench of all: those powerful and mighty men in top hats, sashes, and uniforms who threaten and maim, kill and destroy, and then go to prayer breakfast and call upon the name of God ... No, John is so right – there must be a new earth and new heaven.[152]

Though Boesak would have his own temptations and struggles with the seduction of the beast, his commentary has few rivals among those seeking to bring one's context to bear on the interpretation of the Apocalypse.

---

[150] Boesak, *Comfort and Protest*, pp. 115-16.

[151] Boesak, *Comfort and Protest*, p. 119.

[152] Boesak, *Comfort and Protest*, pp. 127-28.

THE PROLOGUE – REVELATION 1.1-8

Verse 1 – The first thing encountered by a hearer of the Apocalypse is a prologue that contains the title of the book, a formal greeting that follows epistolary convention, a doxology, and two prophetic words.[1] The very first word encountered by the hearer of the Apocalypse is the Greek word ἀποκάλυψις ('revelation'), a term which means a 'revelation' or an 'unveiling'. Modern readers are sometimes fascinated by the fact that the word that appears here is used as the name of an entire genre of writings. However, Johannine hearers would likely be impressed by the fact that in early Christian circles an ἀποκάλυψις ('revelation') is understood to be a revelatory word of the Spirit. For example, 1 Cor. 14.6 lists this kind of Spirit-inspired revelation (ἀποκάλυψις) alongside other activities of the Spirit such as tongues speech, knowledge, prophecy, and teaching. Such a beginning suggests to the hearers that all that follows is closely connected to the work of the Spirit.

The next words quickly identify this work as an 'apocalypse of Jesus Christ'. Grammatically, the phrase ἀποκάλυψις᾽ Ἰησοῦ Χριστοῦ ('revelation of Jesus Christ'), can mean a revelation given by Jesus (a subjective genitive) or a revelation about Jesus (an objective genitive). While arguments can be set forth in favor of each possibility, it appears that to insist on choosing between these interpretive options is to advocate a false choice.[2] For the book's content reveals that the apocalypse is both a revelation from Jesus and is, at the same time, a revelation about Jesus.[3] Johannine hearers are not surprised to learn that this revelation 'was given to him (Jesus Christ) by God', for in the FG the Son only speaks those things

---

[1] G.R. Beasley-Murray, *Revelation* (Grand Rapids: Eerdmans, 1981), p. 50.

[2] Resseguie, *The Revelation of John*, p. 62.

[3] As E.-B. Allo [*Saint Jean L'Apocalypse* (Paris: J. Gabalda, 1921), p. 3] observes, 'C'est une Révélation de Jésus-Christ sur Jésus-Christ'.

which the Father gives him to speak (cf. Jn 1.18; 8.28; 12.49-50; 14.10; 15.15; 17.8, 14). This Apocalypse is given '... to show (δεῖξ-αι) his servants what is necessary to take place quickly'. This purpose is borne out by the fact that on seven subsequent occasions this verb is used 'to designate an unveiling of the future' (Rev. 4.1; 17.1; 21.9, 10; 22.1, 6, 8).[4] The intended recipients of this Apocalypse are 'his servants', which could be a reference to believers in general. However, given the OT usage of this term to designate prophets it is likely that its occurrence here anticipates the numerous mentions of prophets in this book and may even be evidence that the community of the Apocalypse is a prophetic community.[5] The content of the revelation is further identified as 'that which is necessary to take place quickly'. Something about the necessity of God's gift of this revelation is conveyed by the appearance of the word δεῖ ('it is necessary'), a term which appears in the Apocalypse a total of eight times (4.1; 17.1; 21.9, 10; 22.1, 6, 8). The fact that the contents of the book must take place quickly indicates something of the urgency of this message.[6]

The revelatory chain of transmission, which includes God and Jesus Christ in the first part of the verse, continues in its conclusion to include Jesus' angel and 'John his servant'. While it is not uncommon for angelic guides to play a leading role in various apocalyptic documents, the introduction of the angel in Rev. 1.1 is a bit odd in that the angel does not really function in this capacity until Revelation 17. The order of the revelation's transmission makes clear that Jesus Christ is not in a subordinate position to the angel but, as learned later, is so far superior that he is worthy of receiving worship alongside God. The verb ἐσήμανεν ('he showed') is yet another word utilized to indicate the manner of the revelation here described. On this occasion, the term carries with it the idea of indicating the meaning of prophetic (Acts 11.28) and/or metaphorical (Jn 12.33; 18.32; 21.19) language. It is not without significance that this verb comes from the same word family as σημεῖον ('sign'), the preferred Johannine word for sign. As such, the hearer is put on

---

[4] G. Schneider, 'δείκνυμι, δεικνύω', *EDNT*, I, p. 280.
[5] Cf. esp. Hill, *New Testament Prophecy*, pp. 87-93 and Smalley, *The Revelation to John*, p. 27. Beale (*The Book of Revelation*, p. 183) argues that this points to the community's 'general prophetic vocation'.
[6] Osborne, *Revelation*, p. 55.

notice that the meaning of that which is revealed has a significance that transcends a literal or surface meaning.[7]

Verse 2 – The identity of the individual to whom this apocalypse is entrusted is 'his servant John'. As noted in the introduction, this John is a well-known prophetic figure in the Johannine community, possibly to be identified with John the Elder, likely author of other Johannine documents. It is this John 'who has borne witness … to whatsoever he saw'. The fact that John bore witness is significant for several reasons. First, the idea of witness or testimony is a dominant one in the FG. Second, this idea is a very prominent one in the Apocalypse, where one's witness is intimately connected to one's identity as a believer. Third, the idea of John's bearing witness is very closely connected to the witness or testimony of Jesus Christ, the content of those things which John saw. The content of this revelation is described as 'the word of God and the witness of Jesus'. This combination of phrases conveys several ideas to the hearers at once. The phrase 'the word of God' occurs at a number of places in the Apocalypse (1.2, 9; 6.9; 19.13; 20.4; cf. also 17.17 and 19.9 where the plural 'words' occurs). It is reminiscent of numerous OT texts where a prophetic call is being recounted (Hos. 1.1; Joel 1.1; Jer. 1.2, 4, 11) and, consequently, prepares the way for v. 3, where the book is referred to as 'the words of this prophecy'. But for the Johannine hearers, the phrase may also point to Jesus, who is known as the Word of God in the FG (1.1-18) and appears to be the one named 'the Word of God' in Rev. 19.13. Thus, while an emphasis upon the prophetic aspect of the phrase is primary, it carries with it a Christological dimension from the beginning. The Christological inference of the first phrase is made explicit in the second, 'the witness of Jesus'. As such, it becomes clear that the content of the Revelation is not twofold ('the word of God and the witness of Jesus'), but that these two phrases have reference to the same reality, the second phrase clarifying the first.[8] It is difficult not to see in this phrase, which occurs six times in the Apocalypse (1.2, 9; 12.17; 19.10 a, b; 20.4), reference both to Jesus' life and witness as evidenced in the FG and that which follows in the Apocalypse.

---

[7] Smalley, *The Revelation to John*, p. 27.
[8] Resseguie, *The Revelation of John*, p. 64.

Therefore, the hearers are assured of the continuity between this revelation and what is already known of Jesus.

Verse 3 – The first of seven beatitudes found in the Apocalypse (1.3; 14.13; 16.15; 19.9; 20.6; 22.7, 14) occurs in v. 3. In content, this beatitude most resembles that found in 22.7. This blessing is pronounced upon all those involved in the prophetic interpretive task. Specifically, this process includes a reader (designated by the singular ὁ ἀναγινώσκων ['the one who reads']), who reads aloud, and those who '*hear* the words of this prophecy and *keep* the things written in it'. The construction of the verse reveals that 'those who hear' are identical with 'those who keep', indicated in part by the fact that both participles, ἀκούοντες ('hearing') and τηροῦντες ('keeping') are governed by the same article, οἱ ('the').[9] The verse makes clear that not only are all individuals in the community invited to participate in this process, but also that this book is considered to be a prophetic document. As such, this apocalypse claims to stand in the tradition of the OT prophetic literature. In the Johannine literature the idea of hearing is closely associated with belief. Those who hear Jesus believe in him (Jn 1.37, 40; 4.42; 14.28), belong to God (8.47), have eternal life (5.24), show that they are Jesus' sheep (10.3, 8, 16, 27), and will rise from their graves (5.25, 28). Thus, in Rev. 1.3 hearing the words of this prophecy entails the appropriate response to them.[10] This emphasis upon appropriate response to the prophetic word is continued by the fact that the blessing pronounced includes those who keep the things written in this book. For in the Johannine literature, keeping the words or commands of Jesus entails more than simple conformity to a set of principles, but includes an identification with and incorporation of the words and commands of Jesus. Such a response to his words results in eternal life (Jn 8.51-55) and a sharing in the kind of love characteristic of the Father and the Son (Jn 14.15-24; 15.10, 20; 17.6, 11-15). Therefore, hearing and keeping are no passive responses on the part of the prophetic community but entail active and sustained responses. The urgency of such responses is made clear by the concluding statement in v. 3, 'for the time is near'. Not

---

[9] On the relationship of hearing and doing (obeying) in the OT and in a Pentecostal Hermeneutic, cf. L.R. Martin, *The Unheard Voice of God: A Pentecostal Hearing of the Book of Judges* (JPTSup 32; Blandford Forum: Deo, 2008), pp. 61-79.

[10] Smalley, *The Revelation to John*, p. 31.

only is this a second reference in these first three verses to the fact that the things described in this book are soon to take place, but it also anticipates an identical statement in 22.10, where emphasis is placed upon the nearness of Jesus' return.

Verses 4-5a – The next part of the prologue is devoted to the formal opening of this circular letter in vv. 4-5a. Here one finds the standard A (author) to B (recipients) greeting found in a variety of letters in Graeco-Roman antiquity. For a second time the author, names himself. First introduced as the servant who testified, John is now the author. The addressees are the seven churches in Asia. As noted in the introduction, the number seven is not exclusive but inclusive, as it is a number of completion in the Apocalypse.[11] On this reading, John is addressing all the (Johannine) churches in Asia.[12] In Johannine thought the blessing of grace and peace is no perfunctory formula, for these terms are of special significance for the community. The pronouncement of grace comes with the knowledge that the Logos is the one full of grace and that out of his fullness we have all received one grace after another (Jn 1.14, 16). Consequently, the hearers understand that the grace conveyed in this greeting ultimately comes from Jesus Christ (Jn 1.17). In the same way the other element of the blessing is also Johanninely charged owing to Jesus' use of the term. On three occasions in the FG, Jesus himself speaks peace to his disciples. First, in Jn 14.27 Jesus promises to give the disciples peace when they face the prospect of his departure. Later, after the resurrection, he speaks peace both to the disciples (20.19) and later to Thomas (20.26). This same peace is now spoken to the seven churches who may also share with the disciples in the FG a 'troubled' context.

The gifts of grace and peace have a threefold origin. They come from 'the One who is, who was, and is coming', the Seven Spirits, and Jesus Christ. The second mention of God in the Apocalypse takes the form of a statement which underscores the fact that there is no time (or place?) at which God does not exist. He is, and was, and is coming. Present, past, and future converge in his presence and being. Consequently, the grace and peace that come from him have no limits in time and space. These gifts are also said to come

---

[11] Beale, *The Book of Revelation*, pp. 186-87.
[12] Simoens, *Apocalypse de Jean*, p. 16.

from 'the Seven Spirits before his throne'. As with the seven churches, so reference to the Seven Spirits implies completion, the fullness of the Spirit in the presence of the One who sits on the throne.[13] It is sometimes argued that the hearers would be reminded of seven angelic beings.[14] However, the Seven Spirits are no angelic beings, but the Spirit himself, who will take different forms as the words of this prophecy unfold. More probably the intertext which converges with John's experience here is Zech. 4.2, where the seven branched lampstand stands in the holy place in the Temple.[15] Mention of the Spirits' location before the throne conveys two things to the hearers. First, it is perhaps not without significance that God, who is named at the beginning of the book, is here described as 'the One who sits on the throne'. For, the sovereignty of God over all creation is affirmed often in the Apocalypse and his throne is viewed in great contrast to the thrones of others. He is quite simply without rival. Second, the close proximity of the Seven Spirits to the One who sits on the throne implies their nearness to God and the fact that when they act, it is God himself who acts. Therefore, this grace and peace comes from the throne of God by means of the Seven Spirits before the throne. As is no surprise to the Johannine hearers, these gifts also come from Jesus Christ. Three things are said about him in this verse. First, he is 'the faithful witness'. This phrase not only underscores the fact that John's own witness is faithful owing to the fact that he has witnessed to (testified of) the witness of Jesus (v. 2), but it also anticipates the connection between witness and death which the second description conveys. Second, Jesus is called 'the firstborn of the dead'. Clearly, there is a connection between his faithful witness and death, but at the same time there is an emphasis upon the fact that, while he experienced death, he is no longer dead. Neither would it be lost on the hearers that if he is the 'firstborn of the dead', others are also to follow. Third, Jesus is called 'the ruler of the kings of the earth'. With this description, the hearers are again put on notice that the revelation of Jesus Christ they are hearing will reveal things about him not yet fully appreciated. In the FG, Jesus is known to be the King of Israel

---

[13] Resseguie, *The Revelation of John*, p. 66.

[14] Aune, *Revelation 1-5*, pp. 34-35.

[15] Cf. the helpful discussion in Bauckham, *The Climax of Prophecy*, pp. 162-66.

(Jn 1.49), for a true Israelite declares him so (1.47). In the Apocalypse, this reign is now understood to extend over all kings of the earth! As with mention of God's throne, so mention of Jesus as ruler over all the kings of the earth serves to prepare the readers for the further explication of this dimension of Jesus' identity that follows in the Apocalypse. It also conveys to the hearers a sense of assurance in the face of the kings of the earth, who are often experienced in opposition to God and his kingdom. In addition it is a subtle signal of the later positive role of the kings of the earth in the New Jerusalem (21.24). That such a king as this speaks grace and peace to the hearers would communicate at a very deep and emotive level as it does with John.

Verses 5b-6 – Reflection upon the extraordinary nature of Jesus Christ explodes into a spontaneous doxology of praise focusing upon his redemptive work (vv. 5b-6).[16] The doxology is constructed in such a way that the object of the praise is described first. Three things are said about Jesus. He is 'the One who loves us'. The nature of this love for the community is reflected in the FG. There it is clear that this love is complete and ultimate, for Jesus 'loved his own εἰς τέλος ('until the end')' (Jn 13.1). It is like the love of the Father (17.23), which resulted in the sending of his Son (3.16). The definition of Jesus' love is also made known in 1 Jn 3.16, which says, 'in this we have known love, because that one laid down his life on our behalf'. Thus, mention of 'the One who loves us' continues the thought of Jesus' death from v. 5 and anticipates the next description of him as he 'who loosed[17] us from our sins by his blood'. The fact that Jesus is the one who sets free from sin is also well known within the community, for he is the 'Lamb of God who takes away the sin of the world' (Jn 1.29). This implicit paschal imagery points in the direction of the efficacious power of Jesus' blood noted later in the FG (6.53-56; 19.34), and made explicit in 1 Jn 1.7-2.2 and 5.6-7. The power of Jesus' blood to destroy sin and

---

[16] Beale, *The Book of Revelation*, p. 191.

[17] There is some question as to the original reading at this point in the manuscript tradition. The bulk of the best manuscripts support λύσαντι ('who loosed' or 'who destroyed'). The other option, λούσαντι ('who washed'), would fit well with the idea of the washing away uncleanness (sin) found in Jn 13.10, while the former would fit well with the fact that in the Apocalypse a variety of things are loosed (Rev. 5.2; 9.14, 15; 20.3, 7).

make clean is a recurrent theme found throughout the Apocalypse. The statement that Jesus loves us and destroyed our sins also prepares the hearers for the paschal imagery in Rev. 5.6. The idea that Jesus destroyed sin is in a great deal of continuity with 1 Jn 3.8 which states, 'the Son of God was manifested in order to destroy the works of the Devil', which in this context are identified as sin (cf. 1 Jn 3.4-10). In addition to these two dimensions, the object of the doxology is also said to have 'made us a kingdom, priests to God and his Father'. This kingdom is that into which the hearers have been made. It is, like the later imagery of the New Jerusalem, something that believers share in or of which they are a part (Rev. 1.9). Very similar language ('kingdom and priests') reappears in 5.10, where reference is again made to the powerful effects of the blood of Jesus (5.9). The relationship between the blood of Jesus and the kingdom is also underscored in 12.10. This kingdom is identified as 'priests to God', indicating that they are set apart for service unto him. As the book unfolds there is a clear connection between their service to God, the effects of the blood of Jesus, and reigning with God (cf. esp. 5.9-10 and 20.6). By placing the object of the doxology first in the Greek sentence, emphasis is placed upon the worthiness of this one to receive praise, before praise is given. It is to the one who has accomplished all these spectacular things that glory and honor are given eternally. In this first occasion of worship in the Apocalypse, John leads the way in giving glory and honor to Jesus. By this he anticipates and joins in with all those who will lift their voices in praise as the book unfolds. This two-fold praise, which reappears in 4.9, gives way to additional three-fold and four-fold formulae later in the volume. The unlimited praise 'for ever and ever' matches the unlimited worthiness of Jesus. The prayer, 'amen', 'so let it be', concludes the doxology.

Verses 7-8 – Within this context of worship the prologue reaches its crescendo as two prophetic words explode into the hearers' ears. It should come as no surprise that in a community known for its prophetic orientation, prophetic utterances explode upon the scene.[18] The hearers learn that these words are most appropriate for

---

[18] It should perhaps be noted that the placement of these prophetic words within a context of worship in the prologue may indicate something of the way in which prophecy functioned within community gatherings. From these verses it

this context in that they continue the worship of God and they contribute toward the development of at least two themes revealed in the first six verses. Appropriately enough, the first prophetic utterance consists of words about the resurrected Jesus, while the second prophetic utterance consists of the words of God.

As the hearers encounter the words spoken about Jesus in v. 7, sacred texts, sacred teaching, and the experience of the Spirit converge. It is the 'faithful witness', 'the firstborn of the dead', 'the ruler of all the kings of the earth' who will 'come with the clouds'. Such a word indicates continuity with Daniel's Son of Man imagery (Dan. 7.13) and Jesus' eschatological teaching as reflected in the Synoptic tradition (Mk 13.26) and the teaching of Paul (1 Thess. 4.17). But within the Johannine trajectory something else is being revealed about Jesus and by Jesus. For while the promise of his return is part of the Johannine tradition, 'coming with the clouds' is not. From very early on in this book, the hearers are left with no doubts about the promise that Jesus himself will appear, an emphasis still in tact as the book concludes (22.7, 12, 20). At his appearing 'every eye will behold him' – 'even those who have pierced him'. For Johannine hearers, such language indicates that even those responsible for Jesus' death will look upon him (Jn 19.37). But in this prophetic word, the fulfillment of Scripture in the FG is extended beyond the cross to a different kind of beholding. If the cross is the moment of Jesus' glorification in the FG, this appearance is the moment of his vindication in the Apocalypse. For 'all the tribes of the earth will mourn because of him'. As with the oracle from Zech. 12.10-12, so in this prophetic utterance, every tribe will mourn who sees him. It is the mourning of lost opportunity, of opposing this returning one. Such mourning will be encountered at various points as the book unfolds. The conclusion of this first prophetic word is indicated by the addition of John's own 'yes' and 'amen'.

The second prophetic utterance begins with words familiar to Johannine hearers, for ἐγώ εἰμι ('I Am') are words often on the lips of Jesus in the FG. There they convey the idea of identification

---

would appear likely that prophetic utterances came forth in moments when the community was engaged in times of spontaneous praise.

with Yahweh.[19] In Rev. 1.8, the predicate to the 'I Am' statement is 'Alpha and Omega'. But as the hearers quickly discover, this 'I Am' statement is not in reference to Jesus at this point but to the Lord God. Here, in a move reminiscent of those in 1 John, a statement normally associated with Jesus (in the FG), is reappropriated with reference to God. This identification conveys the idea that God is the beginning and the ending, the first and the last, he is the all in all. Nothing exists outside of him. But before the hearers can catch their collective breath after this unexpected identification, the eternality of God is underscored once again by his identification as 'the One who is, and was, and is coming'. The last words of this prophetic utterance, and the prologue as a whole, further identify God as ὁ παντοκράτωρ ('the All Powerful One'), an identification that will act as a refrain throughout the rest of the Apocalypse (4.8; 11.17; 15.3; 16.7, 14; 19.6, 15; 21.22). Along with the other ways by which God has been identified, his claim to be the All Powerful One places an exclamation point as to his sovereignty, power, and unrivaled status.[20]

---

[19] Cf. the very helpful piece by D. Ball, *'I Am' in John's Gospel: Literary Function, Background and Theological Implications* (JSNTS 124; Sheffield: JSOT Press, 1996).

[20] Osborne, *Revelation*, p. 72.

'IN THE SPIRIT ON THE LORD'S DAY' – REVELATION 1.9-3.22

As noted in the introduction, the first major section of the Apocalypse is comprised of 1.9-3.22, the onset of which is indicated by the first 'in the Spirit' phrase found in 1.10. This section, which is divided into two major parts, is devoted to the inaugural vision of Jesus (1.9-20) and the seven prophetic messages he speaks to the seven churches of Asia (2.1-3.22). This section is held together, not only by the fact that it is the resurrected Jesus seen by John who speaks prophetically to the seven churches, but also by the fact that an element from the inaugural vision of Jesus is incorporated into each of the seven prophetic messages. As the hearers may have come to suspect from the prologue there is much about Jesus that remains to be revealed. This first major section will go some way toward informing the hearers about him.

The Inaugural Vision of Jesus (1.9-20)

In this inaugural vision of Jesus, the hearers learn of John's geographical location, his spiritual location, his initial commissioning for his prophetic task, the stunning description of the resurrected Jesus, and something about the hermeneutics of the Spirit.

Verse 9 – For a third time in nine verses the author identifies himself as John. On this occasion his name is made emphatic by the appearance of the personal pronoun ἐγώ ('I'). In the three verses that follow, the hearers learn several things about John. First, he reminds them that he is their 'brother'. While the preponderance of occurrences of this term in the FG has reference to a physical relationship, by the time of Jn 21.23 the term appears to have taken on a spiritual connotation, which is its dominant meaning in 1 John and 3 John. While the term 'brother' certainly retains this spiritually intimate meaning in the Apocalypse, it shows signs of taking on the added meaning of prophet (cf. esp. Rev. 22.9 and its close proximity to 'fellow servants' in 6.11 and 19.10).

Second, the hearers are told that John is their συγκοινωνὸς ('participant' or 'sharer'). Clearly, the idea of fellowship is not far from the thought expressed,[1] a theme especially significant within the Johannine community (1 Jn 1.3, 6-7; 2 Jn 11). In what is John a participant with the community? Three things are singled out. He is a participant in tribulation. For the Johannine community, tribulation is a bittersweet reality for although it entails suffering, it is not suffering without reward. In the FG Jesus reminds the disciples that though they suffer tribulation in this world, they will rejoice as surely as a woman who rejoices at the sight of her child after suffering the tribulation of childbirth (Jn 16.21). In the midst of such tribulation Johannine hearers are comforted by the fact that Jesus has overcome the world (Jn 16.33). No doubt the hearers of the Apocalypse understand John to share with them in this bittersweet experience. As the book will reveal, such tribulation is known all too well by the hearers (Rev. 2.9-10; 7.14). Not only does John share with them in tribulation, but he also is a participant in the kingdom, the kingdom into which Jesus has made the believers (1.6). Additionally, he is a participant with them in ὑπομονῇ ('faithful endurance'). Such steadfastness is an absolutely essential quality for those who seek to be faithful witnesses to Jesus in the Apocalypse (2.2-3, 19; 3.10; and esp. 13.10; 14.12). Each of the things in which John is a participant with the community are said to be 'in Jesus' and each of them are connected to Jesus in a special way.[2] For he has overcome the world, made them into a kingdom, and has himself been a faithful witness.

Third, the hearers learn of John's geographical location on the island called Patmos and they learn of the reason for his location. As is well known, Patmos is a ten mile by six mile island located about thirty-six miles off the coast of Asia (Minor) in the Aegean Sea. It was near a group of islands where, according to Tacitus (*An-*

---

[1] Smalley, *The Revelation to John*, p. 49.
[2] Smalley, *The Revelation to John*, p. 50.

nals 4.30), political prisoners were regularly exiled. As noted earlier, if John were indeed on Patmos owing to political banishment it might reveal something of his social location, as only nobility and priests were afforded the luxury of exile. The hearers learn that John's location on Patmos was owing to 'the word of God and the testimony of Jesus'. There are several ways to understand this phrase. It could be taken to mean that John had gone to Patmos to engage in missionary activity there, or that John had been exiled owing to his 'Christian' identity, which fits with the theme of suffering and persecution in the book. It is also possible to take the phrase διὰ τὸν λόγον τοῦ θεοῦ καὶ τὴν μαρτυρίαν Ἰησοῦ ('on account of the word of God and the testimony of Jesus') as indicating that it was for the purpose of witnessing to all he would see ('the word of God and the testimony of Jesus') that John was on Patmos.[3] At any rate, his location there is clearly tied to his activity as witness.

Figure 6
Hieronymus Bosch, *John on Patmos*

---

[3] Smalley, *The Revelation to John*, p. 51.

Verses 10-11 – If the hearers believe that the Apocalypse now takes a turn in the direction of the mundane, after the high octane prologue, this impression is only temporary, for as v. 10 unfolds, extraordinary events take place. The fourth thing learned about John by the hearers appears to be paired and contrasted with the third. Previously, the hearers are told ἐγενόμην ἐν τῇ νήσῳ τῇ καλουμένῃ Πάτμῳ ('I was on an island called Patmos'). In v. 10 they hear ἐγενόμην ἐν πνεύματι ἐν τῇ κυριακῇ ἡμέρᾳ ('I was in the Spirit on the Lord's Day'). While the identical construction with which these statements open clearly connects John's geographical location with his spiritual location, it also serves to contrast these two locations. Although John may be on an island, he is at the same time 'in the Spirit'.

The connection between the Seven Spirits before the throne and the fact that John is 'in the Spirit' would not be lost on the hearers. As noted, the fact that the Seven Spirits are in such close proximity to the throne reveals that when they act, it is God himself who acts. Given the fact that this revelation of Jesus Christ is given by God, it should come as no surprise that the Spirit is involved in such a crucial way. It also reveals the ways in which the work attributed to the Spirit in the Apocalypse is at the same time the work of God. As noted in the introduction the phrase 'in the Spirit' is an important one for it occurs four times in very significant locations. In point of fact, it is by means of this phrase that the book is given its structure. By its strategic occurrences the hearers come to know that the Spirit is the means by which the revelation of Jesus Christ takes place. Furthermore, it is in this state that John sees things, hears things, tastes things, touches things, and interprets things. 'In the Spirit' there are moments of convergence where all that John is, is drawn upon as new and constructive dimensions of present and future reality are experienced. It would appear to be a given that the community would understand being 'in the Spirit' as intimately connected to prophetic activity (i.e. the way in which one receives and makes known prophetic visions, messages, and words). It would not appear to be going too far to say that the community would likely see their own participation in the discerning process as being 'in the Spirit' as well. The only indication of when John is initially 'in the Spirit' is conveyed by the phrase 'on the Lord's day'. As noted in the introduction, in a book known for its pregnant imagery, it is possible that the hearers are being given more than a detail about the day of the week on which John experiences the revelation. By means of this phrase, John may be giving his writing an eschatological date.[4] On this view the phrase, τῃ κυριακῇ ἡμέρᾳ ('on the Lord's Day'), might very well cause the hearers to think of the OT idea of יום יהוה (*yom Yahweh*, 'The Day of the Lord/Yahweh'). However, the hearer is not likely to take this simply as a reference to the OT 'Day of the Lord', but that day as the Lord's day when Jesus himself will appear to resurrect the righteous dead. This intertextual understanding of the phrase may also explain why John does not simply utilize the OT language for יום יהוה (*yom Yahweh*, 'The Day of the Lord/Yahweh'), for it is that day and more! Not only is this reading of 'the Lord's day' consistent with the rich symbolism of the document, but it also dovetails nicely with the eschatological context in which Rev. 1.10 is located, between the prophetic word by Jesus about his return (v. 7) and the vision of the resurrected Jesus (vv. 12-20). As noted in the introduction, the Lord's day relativizes all other days. Thus, the hearers stand with John on the verge of the day to which all of history points, the Lord's day.

It is while in the Spirit on this day that John hears 'behind him a great voice as a trumpet'. If there is a blessing upon those who hear and keep the words of this prophecy (1.3), in this verse John, who hears a great many things in the Apocalypse, hears the words of this prophecy for the first time himself. Mention of a great voice introduces an idea that follows often in the book. The likening of this voice to a trumpet is significant for a couple of reasons. First, whenever mention is made in the Apocalypse of a trumpet (4.1; 8.2, 6, 13; 9.14) or the sounding of a trumpet (8.6, 8, 10, 12-13; 9.1, 13; 10.7; 11.15), the sound comes from God either directly or indirectly. Second, many of the sounds John describes to his hearers in the book are the loudest human-made or natural sounds possible in the first century CE. The effect of such intensity of sound upon the hearer(s) should not be ignored nor minimized.[5] In these, the initial words of Jesus in the Apocalypse, John receives a commissioning

---

[4] Bacchiocchi, *Sabbath to Sunday*, pp. 111-31.

[5] On the trumpet, cf. R. Skaggs and P. Benham, *Revelation* (PCS: Blandford Forum: Deo Publishing, 2009), p. 27.

for his prophetic task. His commission is two-fold: to write and to send. The hearing of this command for John to write what he sees in a book is doubly comforting for the hearers who are reaping the fruit of John's faithful witness as they hear this book read. The hearers also understand that 'the words of the book of this prophecy' is a book written at divine direction. What John sees he writes, something he claims as early as Rev. 1.2. Near the end of the account of this inaugural vision of Jesus, John will again be instructed to write (v. 19). In addition to writing, John is commissioned to send the book to the seven churches. Although not identified as the seven churches of Asia, as in v. 4, the seven churches are here individually named. They are the churches in Ephesus, in Smyrna, in Pergamum, in Thyatira, in Sardis, in Philadelphia, and in Laodicea. Conveniently, these cities are mentioned in a clockwise fashion, beginning in the southwest with Ephesus and ending in the southeast with Laodicea,[6] perhaps conforming to a circular ancient postal route.[7] Clearly, all the Johannine churches are the intended audience of this book.

Verse 12 – With the onset of v. 12 the hearers are introduced to what will be a recurring phenomenon within the book, where John hears something, but what he sees has changed (before his eyes), not unlike psychedelic imagery where one form morphs into another before one's eyes (and ears!). On this occasion John, who has just been told to write what he sees, turns to 'see' the voice that was speaking with him, a reference that may very well underscore the significance of the commission that comes from this voice in 1.10-11.[8] Perhaps the hearers would be reminded of the way in which Mary Magdalene turns to see the resurrected Jesus in Jn 20.14, as the same Greek verb occurs in both contexts.[9] Underscoring his activity designed to facilitate his 'seeing', John says, 'And I turned to see ... And turning I saw'. However, what he sees is not a voice but 'seven golden lampstands'. Though the hearers may suspect a connection between the Seven Spirits, seven churches, and seven lampstands, they are not allowed the luxury of contemplating these

---

[6] Smalley, *The Revelation to John*, p. 52.
[7] Osborne, *Revelation*, p. 85.
[8] Osborne, *Revelation*, p. 86.
[9] Smalley, *The Revelation to John*, p. 52.

connections for John's focus goes immediately to the midst of the lampstands.

Verse 13-16 – In the stunning vision of Jesus that follows, elements from a variety of OT texts converge in new and creative ways, giving John a glimpse of one who combines numerous characteristics of God, the Son of Man, and his servants. There are from Zechariah lampstands (4.2); from Daniel characteristics of 'one like the son of man' (7.13), 'the Ancient of Days' (7.9), the fiery furnace (3.6), the man dressed in linen with a gold belt around his waist (10.4-6); from Ezekiel elements from the wheel within a wheel (1.24) and the man in linen (9.11); from Isaiah a mouth like a sharpened sword (49.2); and from Judges words about the face of the Lord (5.31). Yet none of these details on their own, nor simply an accounting for them from their OT texts, does justice to the vision.[10] Such a convergence of elements and details indicate that the revelation of Jesus Christ continues in astounding fashion as he is seen and experienced in ways as never before. The fact that he is identified with enigmatic figures as well as God himself, indicates that in Jesus there is a culmination of God's purposes and activities. As Son of Man, the promise of Jesus' return rings in the ears of the hearers from v. 7. As one attired in the robe and sash, with eyes that are ablaze, feet like glowing brass, and a voice of many waters, he is securely in control of the future. With head and hair white like wool he is intimately identified with the Ancient of Days. With the stars in his hands and a mouth sharp as a double-edged sword, he too speaks and acts prophetically. And the brilliance of his face ... is like the sun, shining with all its power ... like that of God's face. Such brightness, such radiance is almost blinding, impossible to comprehend. Yet John's hearers take in every word as the vision is recounted.

Verses 17-18 – John's response when he saw him, the third time in this section John makes reference to seeing, was to fall 'at his feet as though dead'. This response is not an unexpected one, given John's encounter with the resurrected Jesus, revealed in all his glory, but it also sets a precedent of sorts for an element often found in contexts of worship in the Apocalypse (4.10; 5.8, 14; 7.11; 11.16;

---

[10] Cf. Osborne, *Revelation*, p. 89.

19.4; and 22.8). Such prostration would appear to be an involuntary reflex by John, who is clearly overwhelmed by the glory of Jesus.

John's response is met by Jesus' own response, a combination of touching and speaking. The fact that Jesus places his right hand, which has the seven stars in it, upon John suggests that this touch is not a mere sign of comfort. But as the hearers are to learn, such a description suggests that this act has something to do with prophetic communication. As might be expected, this action is accompanied by the words of the One who has a sharp two-edged sword in his mouth and conveys the sound of many waters when he speaks. He utters words that are both recognizable and, at the same time, continue to reveal aspects of Jesus' identity not yet known. His words, 'fear not, I Am', remind the hearers of Jesus' words in the FG to the fearful disciples who had just seen Jesus walk to them on the water (Jn 6.19-20). On that occasion Jesus says, 'I Am, fear not'. On this occasion, the command, 'fear not', is followed by the predicate use of 'I Am'. In words reminiscent of the prophetic words of God about being the Alpha and Omega in 1.8, Jesus says 'I Am the first and the last …' in 1.17. His appropriation of language clearly synonymous in meaning to the words of God, confirms what the vision has implied; a deep and intimate identification between God and Jesus. As with God, Jesus himself embraces beginning and end. There is nothing that lies outside him and his influence or power. This penetrating speech continues in v. 18, where Jesus identifies himself as 'the living one'. For Johannine hearers, such a statement is not surprising for 'in him was life' (Jn 1.4) and he is 'the Way, the Truth, and the Life' (14.6). In this passage (Rev. 1.18), Jesus' emphasis appears to be upon the fact that he is continually alive, as the present participle ὁ ζῶν ('the living one') implies. This suspicion is confirmed by the next words of Jesus, who says, 'I was dead and behold I am living forever and ever'. The grammar makes clear the primary point. Jesus had been dead at one point, but he is now alive forever. Such a statement expands the previous description of Jesus as the firstborn of the dead, which also implies that he *was* dead, but dead no longer. Attention to his present state is underscored by the word 'behold'. Just as God is the one 'who is, who was, and who is coming', so Jesus is 'the first and the last' and 'is living forever more'. His past experience with death and continuous experience with life have made him a captor of and victor over death and his companion Hades (cf. Rev. 6.8; 20.13, 14). This mastery is conveyed by the imagery of Jesus having 'the keys of death and Hades'.[11] The one who holds the keys controls the door, determining who goes in and who goes out. The not so subtle message to John and his hearers; there is no need to fear death and Hades because Jesus holds the keys! His death and continual life have given him possession of these keys.[12] Jesus' words function to fill out the picture that emerges from vv. 12-16. The one who is seen in all his glory is first and last, was dead and lives forever, has dominion over death and Hades.[13] What an extraordinary figure he is!

Verse 19 – At the beginning of this inaugural vision John is commanded to write what he sees (v. 11) and again near the end of this vision John is commanded to write what he has seen. These commands serve to function as borders or boundaries (an inclusio) around this vision of Jesus. By this means, there is a close connection drawn between the authority of John's commission and the authority of the one who commissions. Therefore, in the light of all this, John is again commanded to write. The use of the term 'therefore' serves to underscore the fact that John is commanded to write owing to his experience of the resurrected Jesus. On this occasion he is specifically instructed to write 'what he has seen, and what is, and what is about to happen after these things'. Thus, the urgency with which the book begins, with regard to things that must take place quickly or soon (vv. 1-3), reappears in v. 19. There are present and future realities that John will see ('after these things') about which he must write. As the book unfolds the relationship between these two will be the interpretive challenge of the discerning community.

Verse 20 – In this vein, John and his hearers receive their first overt instruction about pneumatic interpretation as Jesus himself, on this occasion, offers an explanation of 'the mystery of the seven stars ... and the seven golden lampstands'. Several observations should be offered on v. 20. Mention of the word 'mystery', a term that also occurs in 10.7 and 17.5, 7, alerts the hearers to the fact that at least these details in the vision of Jesus call for interpretation

---

[11] Beale, *The Book of Revelation*, pp. 214-15.

[12] Osborne, *Revelation*, p. 96.

[13] Smalley, *The Revelation to John*, p. 56.

106 *The Apocalypse*

Figure 7
Albrecht Dürer, *Christ Among the Lampstands*
(State Art Gallery in Karlsruhe, Germany)

that is only available by means of divine (Jesus' own) explanation. Such an occurrence conveys both to John and his hearers the reality that writing (and reading, hearing, and keeping!) 'in the Spirit' is facilitated by the intervention of God himself. Two aspects of the vision are here explained by Jesus. The seven stars in his right hand, which has been placed upon John, are the seven ἄγγελοι ('angels' or 'messengers') of the seven churches. On this understanding, the seven stars in his hand are the means by which he communicates with the churches. Such an understanding, in some ways, minimizes the importance of the debate which seeks to determine whether these ἄγγελοι ('angels' or 'messengers') are human messengers or angelic beings. While either interpretation can do justice to the text, given the prominent role of angels in the rest of the Apocalypse and the lack of a human referent for this term within the book, it would appear that 'angels' is the best translation/interpretation here.[14] In addition to this identification, Jesus makes known to John the meaning of the seven lampstands in the midst of which Jesus stands. They are the seven churches, already mentioned twice before. Jesus' presence in the middle of these lampstands and the fact that all churches are represented by these seven underscores the vital relationship that exists between Jesus and the churches. As will become clear, it is his presence that determines whether or not the church is a church, as he can remove the lampstand if necessary (2.5). The relationship between the seven Spirits and the seven stars and seven lampstands will be revealed as the text unfolds.

---

[14] Osborne, *Revelation*, p. 99.

The Seven Prophetic Messages to the Seven Churches of Asia (2.1-3.22)

Though many translations and commentators treat chapters two and three as distinct from chapter one, it should perhaps be observed that there is no break in thought or sequence in the Greek text of the Apocalypse. As far as the hearers are aware, the things described in the next two chapters are experienced by John in a position of prostration with the right hand of Jesus upon him the entire time. It is the same right hand in which he holds the seven stars, stars that have just been identified as the seven messengers of the seven churches. And it is he who holds them who stands in the midst of the seven lampstands, which are identified as the seven churches. As the hearers encounter the things that John 'sees', this circle of lampstands in which Jesus stands is not far from their minds.

Though each of the prophetic messages is distinct in terms of content and detail, they share a similar structure and for the most part each is comprised of the same elements.[1] First, underscoring the previous instructions to John 'to write', each of the messages begins with the command, 'To the Angel of the church in … write'. Second, the connection between the inaugural vision of Jesus in chapter 1 and the seven prophetic messages in chapters 2-3 is also borne out by the fact that each of the prophetic messages contains a description of Jesus taken from the inaugural vision. As noted in the introduction, several of these elements reappear near the book's conclusion in a description of the 'King of Kings and Lord of Lords' (19.11-16). Third, each prophetic message contains words of Jesus that reveal his intimate knowledge of the church being addressed, often with the phrase, 'I know your works', appearing. Fourth, five of the prophetic messages contain a call for repentance. Fifth, each of the prophetic messages contains a promise to those who overcome or are victorious. Sixth, each of the prophetic messages includes the refrain, 'The one who has an ear, let him or her hear what the Spirit says to the churches'. In the first three prophetic messages this refrain stands next to last, while in the last four the phrase stands last.

---

[1] Simoens, *Apocalypse de Jean*, pp. 28-30.

A final observation might be in order before examining the seven prophetic messages in detail. The fact that Jesus stands in the midst of the seven lampstands, that he has identified these lampstands with the seven churches being addressed, and that the churches are addressed in a particular order (that appears to follow an ancient trade route), may suggest that the hearers would not experience the individual messages in some indiscriminate and disconnected fashion, but rather would be drawn into the visual imagery, mentally making their way around Jesus as the individual messages unfold. More specifically, perhaps the hearers would see some convergence between the circle of lampstands and the 'circle' of Asian churches. In other words, perhaps the convergence of the circle of lampstands with the circle of churches serves to facilitate the transportation of the hearers into the very presence of Jesus' prophetic messages to the churches of which they themselves are a part.

To the Angel of the Church in Ephesus (2.1-7)
Verse 1 – Without a break in the Greek text, Jesus' explanation of the mystery of the stars and the lampstands is followed by seven additional commands to write. The first of these occurs in 2.1 where the angel of (and in turn) the church in Ephesus is addressed. While it is likely that the appearance of ἀγγέλῳ ('angel' or 'messenger') at this point has reference to an angelic messenger, owing to the fact that an individual 'human' messenger would no doubt deliver the Apocalypse to the individual congregations, perhaps the hearers would not be overly preoccupied with the meaning of the term. The fact that the angel of the church at Ephesus is addressed first is no surprise to the hearers, for they have earlier learned of the somewhat circular order of the churches to be addressed (1.11). Nor would the close proximity of Ephesus to Patmos be lost on the hearers, as Ephesus was known as the place of first landing in Asia.[2] It may even be thought that the address of Ephesus first would reflect its standing amongst the other churches in the community.[3]

It is not altogether clear how important knowledge of the ancient city of Ephesus is for the hearers in the proper interpretation

---

[2] Ramsay, *The Seven Letters to the Seven Churches of Asia and their Place in the Plan of the Apocalypse*, pp. 227-28.

[3] Smalley, *The Revelation to John*, p. 59.

of the prophetic messages. While much has been done to provide a historical backdrop against which to read chapters 2 and 3,[4] in the end there is relatively little in terms of interpretive value that has resulted from such historical investigation. Precious little is known about the churches themselves and the most reliable information available to interpreters of the Apocalypse seems to come directly from the text itself.[5] It does not appear that the interpretation of the text is dependent upon a knowledge of the individual cities addressed. For while it may not be unlikely that residents of a particular location would pick up on subtleties in the text about the city in which they live, it is clear that all the hearers are the intended audience, many of whom would not be in the same interpretive position.

What would the hearers think of when encountering the name Ephesus? Perhaps they would think of one of the great cities of the Roman world with a population of around 250,000 inhabitants. Perhaps they would think of a leading religious center in which was located one of the seven wonders of the ancient world, the Temple of Artemis, 'the Mistress of Wild Animals', whose image was comprised of various fertility symbols, i.e. her chest was covered with breasts.[6] Perhaps they would think of a center of commerce, despite the progressive silting up of its harbor, or think of the leading city in the province, though Pergamum was the official provincial capital.[7]

Whatever the hearers may think when encountering the name Ephesus, they soon discover what Jesus thinks. In this first prophetic message, Jesus is identified as 'the One who holds the seven stars in his right hand, the One who stands in the midst of the seven lampstands'. With this description the hearers are introduced to a phenomenon whereby one or two characteristics used to describe Jesus in the inaugural vision reappear in the seven prophetic mes-

---

[4] Cf. esp. the work of Ramsay, *The Seven Letters to the Seven Churches of Asia and their Place in the Plan of the Apocalypse* and Hemer, *The Letters to the Seven Churches of Asia in their Local Settings*.

[5] On this cf. the work of Moyise *The Old Testament in the Book of Revelation*, pp. 24-44 and Koester, *Revelation and the End of All Things*, pp. 41-72.

[6] For an image of the Ephesian Artemis cf. *National Archaeological Museum of Naples* (ed. S. DeCaro; Naples: Electa Napoli, 1999), p. 30.

[7] C.J. Hemer, 'Seven Cities of Asia Minor', in *Major Cities of the Biblical World* (ed. R.K. Harrison; Nashville, TN: Nelson, 1985), p. 236.

sages. In addition to providing a link to the vision of Jesus in chapter one, these descriptions convey other subtle details to the hearers. For example, in 1.16 Jesus is described as 'having in his right hand seven stars', while in 2.1 he is described as 'the One who holds seven stars in his right hand'. Though subtle, the shift in vocabulary from 'having … seven stars' to 'holding seven stars' is not insignificant. For in the Apocalypse the term 'holding' implies something firmly in one's grasp (2.1; 7.1; 20.2) or a strong attachment to a teaching or person (2.13-15, 25; 3.11). Thus, the shift in vocabulary conveys to the hearers a sense that the seven stars, identified in 1.20 as the seven messengers to the seven churches, are firmly in the hand of Jesus and, consequently, at his full disposal. Therefore, the relationship between John's instruction to write to the messenger of the church in Ephesus and the direct connection with Jesus is underscored. The second phrase contains an additional detail that also further informs the hearers. In 1.13 Jesus is described as 'in the midst of the lampstands', while in 2.1 he is described as 'the One who walks in the midst of the seven golden lampstands'. The fact that he is now said to be 'walking' in the midst of the lampstands conveys both the notion of intimate relationship between Jesus and the churches (3.4; 21.24) and the idea of activity on Jesus' part. The one who is in the midst of the churches is the one who knows the churches and is active within them. The hearers are implicitly invited to walk with Jesus in the midst of the lampstands.

Verse 2 – In v. 2, as in each of the prophetic messages, the word οἶδα ('I know') stands immediately after Jesus' self-description. In this verse, as in 2.19, 3.1, 8, 15, the phrase the hearers encounter is οἶδα τὰ ἔργα σου ('I know your works'). By this phrase the hearers are introduced to a term, 'works', which is a most significant one in the Apocalypse. In this book the word can be used of good (2.2, 5, 19, 26; 3.1, 8, 15), bad (2.6), or incomplete (3.2) works. There are works for which repentance should be, but is not always, offered (2.22; 9.20; 16.11). Some works are an extension of one's witness beyond death (14.13). Other works are the direct actions of God (15.3). On several occasions, works are the basis of one's (future) judgment (18.6; 20.12, 13) and/or one's reward (2.23; 22.12). Clearly, the idea of works is an integrative one which includes one's activity or actions, that carries with them a sign-like quality which reveals something about one's relationship with God and/or Jesus.[8] In the Apocalypse, the term 'works' is not a vulgar word to be avoided, as is sometimes the case in various English translations of or commentaries upon the text of Revelation, but is a term that must be embraced in order to appreciate fully this dimension of the Apocalypse's meaning.

In the prophetic message to Ephesus, the phrase 'I know your works' introduces the hearers to the content of the bulk of this communiqué, to which vv. 2-6 are devoted. For in this section several dimensions of Jesus' knowledge of this particular church are revealed. Specifically, the church is commended for her 'works', 'labor', and 'patient endurance'. It appears that this description not only introduces the content of the message but also reveals something of the content of the message, for the theme of 'works' figures prominently in it (2.5, 6), as does labor (2.3) and patient endurance (2.3). Apparently, each of these qualities is to be understood as related to the church's resistance of 'evil ones', manifested in the form of false apostles and teachers. This emphasis would be made clear to the hearers in part by the fact that the content of this prophetic message begins and ends with reference to such individuals, in the form of the 'evil ones'/'false apostles' (2.2), on the one hand, and the Nicolaitians (2.6), on the other. One important dimension of the church's commendation is that they οὐ δύνῃ βαστάσαι κακούς ('are not able to bear/support evil ones'). This congregation is known for what it is able and is not able to support. While they are not able to support evil ones, they do 'support/bear on account of my name' (2.3).[9] As will become apparent later in the narrative, in this they stand in great contrast to the beast who supports the Great Whore (17.7).

Their lack of support for such 'evil ones' is illustrated initially by their ἐπείρασας τοὺς λέγοντας ἑαυτοὺς ἀποστόλους ('testing those who say of themselves that they are apostles'). While it is possible that the hearers might take the mention of apostles in this verse as a reference to the twelve apostles, the evidence of the broader Johannine tradition would seem to subvert such an under-

---

[8] Though nuanced differently cf. the definition offered by Osborne, *Revelation*, p. 113.
[9] Aune, *Revelation 1-5*, p. 143.

standing, for the term apostle never appears in the FG or 1-3 John with that meaning. In point of fact, the lone appearance of the term ἀπόστολος ('apostle' or 'sent one') in these documents is found in Jn 13.16, where the term is part of a proverbial saying used alongside the verbal form πέμψαντος ('sent one'), not as a reference to the Twelve. In that context, it appears that the proverbial use of ἀπόστολος ('apostle' or 'sent one') prepares the reader of the FG for 13.20, which has clear reference to the mission of the disciples, where again one finds forms of the verb πέμπω ('send').[10] Discerning Johannine hearers would, of course, also be aware of the fact that often in the FG John the Baptist (Jn 1.6; 3.28), the Son (3.17, 34; 5.36, 38; 6.29, 57; 7.29; 8.42; 10.36; 11.42; 17.3, 8, 18, 21, 23, 25; 20.21; cf. also 1 Jn 4.9, 10, 14), and the disciples of Jesus (Jn 4.38; 17.18) are spoken of as being or having been sent by God, with a form of the verb ἀποστέλλω ('send') occurring. Similarly, a form of the verb πέμπω ('send') has reference to John the Baptist (Jn 1.33; 13.20), the Son (4.34; 5.23, 24, 30, 37; 6.38, 39, 44; 7.16, 18, 28, 33; 8.16, 18, 26, 29; 9.4; 12.44, 45, 49; 13.20; 14.24; 15.21; 16.5), the Paraclete (14.26; 15.26; 16.7), and Jesus' disciples (20.21). Such usage suggests that for the Johannine community 'sending' language has become theologically conditioned with special reference to divine mission, but has stopped short of becoming technical language for the Twelve. Thus, on the surface the occurrence of apostle in Jn 13.16 might appear simply to be proverbial language, the theologically freighted 'sending' language elsewhere in the FG might well point to a divine sending for the practice of footwashing, as Jesus himself sends them with this commission. With such an extensive theological background, it is likely that when the hearers of the Apocalypse learn of those who claim to be apostles in Rev. 2.2, they would understand such language as having reference to individuals who claim a special status has having been sent by God to the community. This interpretation would appear to be consistent with the egalitarian nature of the Johannine community, where the only 'ecclesiastical' title to be found is in 2 and 3 John where the author refers to himself as *the* Elder. However, as is widely recognized, no evidence exists to suggest that there were other elders within this

---

[10] On this cf. J.C. Thomas, *Footwashing in John 13 and the Johannine Community* (JSNTS 61; Sheffield: JSOT Press), p. 111.

community. While there is somewhat frequent mention of prophets within the Apocalypse, as has been seen there is some reason to believe that the community would understand itself to be a prophetic community, a move which appears to underscore further the egalitarian nature of the Johannine community. Thus, it appears that there were those in Ephesus making claims to having been sent by God to the community! Yet, while these individuals claim to be apostles, Jesus declares that they are not. This verdict is in agreement with the discernment of the Ephesian church whose testing of these would-be-apostles results in finding that they are not apostles at all, but liars. Such a description would perhaps remind the hearers of the way Jesus speaks of the Devil in Jn 8.44, as a liar and the father of lies. The implication about the relationship between these lying apostles and the devil would not be lost on the hearers. Although nothing is said about how the church tested these claimants, two clues may reveal something about the nature of this activity. First, the use of the term πειράζω ('test') in its other occurrences in the Apocalypse (2.10; 3.10) suggests that this testing be understood as a quite intense process. Second, it would be surprising indeed if the admonitions with regard to the testing of the S/spirit(s) found in 1 Jn 4.1-6 did not play some role in the community's actions.[11] If the instruction found in 1 Jn 4.1-6 informs this process, then perhaps the following may be assumed about the testing of the would-be apostles.[12] First, as the discernment called for in that passage is directed to the entire community, not simply a special group of leaders, it might be assumed that the testing of these would-be 'sent ones' involved a discernment process that included the entire Ephesian church community. Second, since prophetic activity attributed to the Spirit must be in conformity to the Spirit confession, 'Jesus Christ coming in the flesh', which focuses upon the significance of Jesus' Incarnation, his pre-existence, and the believers' experience of Jesus in a personal way, it might be inferred that these would-be 'sent ones' were found lacking in this regard. Third, since prophetic activity attributed to the Spirit was expected to exhibit continuity with the community's experience of and belief in Jesus, it appears there was a lack of the necessary dynamic interaction be-

---

[11] Osborne, *Revelation*, p. 113.
[12] On this cf. Thomas, *1 John, 2 John, 3 John*, pp. 197-214.

tween these individuals and the church in Ephesus to which they speak. Apparently, the words and actions of these would-be apostles were found to be the result of the spirit of deception rather than the Spirit of Truth. It should, of course, be obvious that the process of testing would-be 'sent ones', and finding that these particular ones are liars, would imply that other 'sent ones' are indeed sent by God to the community and would be judged accordingly.

Verse 3 – In the face of such liars, the church at Ephesus exhibits patient endurance, a spiritual characteristic that John himself shares with them (1.9). While such patient endurance is exhibited in the church's not being able to 'bear'/support such evil ones, they do 'bear' certain unnamed burdens 'on account of my name'. These words not only commend the church's patient endurance but also introduce the hearers to a very significant term in the Apocalypse, Jesus' name. A great many things are attributed to Jesus' name in the Johannine literature. The hearers would know that belief in his name leads to: the authority to become children of God (Jn 1.12), eternal life (Jn 20.31; 1 Jn 5.13), and the forgiveness of sins (1 Jn 2.12). Furthermore, the hearers know that anything they can ask for in his name will be received (Jn 14.13, 14, 26; 15.16; 16.23, 24, 26). They also know that solidarity with the name brings persecution (Jn 15.21) and that belief in his name is closely associated with loving one another (1 Jn 3.23). As a result of this rich understanding of Jesus' name, its appearance in the Apocalypse carries with it a deep sense of solidarity and personal identification with Jesus. This understanding is conveyed by the fact that the hearers bear adversity on account of his name (2.3), they hold onto his name (2.13) as he holds the seven stars in his right hand, and they do not deny his name (3.8). As a result of such identification with his name, those who overcome are assured that his new name will be written upon them (3.12; 14.1); the name of the One who is 'the Word of God' (19.13), 'King of Kings' and 'Lord of Lords' (19.16). In what they bear on account of the name they have not grown weary. To those of whom Jesus says in v. 2, 'I know your ... labor' (κόπον), he now says 'you have not labored out' (οὐ κεκοπίακες). The church in Ephesus is clearly commended for its tenacious loyalty in difficult circumstances.

Verse 4 – Owing to such stellar praise, the hearers are hardly prepared for the direction Jesus' address takes in v. 4. For at this point, the hearers encounter a phrase that reappears on two other occasions in the seven prophetic messages to the churches of Asia (2.14, 20); ἀλλὰ ἔχω κατὰ σοῦ ὅτι ('but I have against you that'). Not only are the hearers alerted to this change in tone and direction by the introduction of the strong word of contrast ἀλλά ('but'), but they also learn that Jesus holds a grievance against the church in Ephesus. In these first words of rebuke by Jesus in the Apocalypse, the church in Ephesus is told, 'you have left your first love'. While a certain amount of ambiguity surrounds this charge, a number of clues in the text reveal something of its significance for the hearers. The first clue is the phrase's structural location. For it stands at the center both of the content of the message (vv. 2-6), as well as the entire message to the church at Ephesus (vv. 1-7), and it is bounded on either side by Jesus' words of commendation in vv. 2-3 and v. 6. Thus, the central significance of the rebuke is made clear. Closer examination reveals that the rebuke itself has a very interesting structure with the words 'first' and 'repent' playing important roles. The rebuke begins with 'first love', moves to a call to 'repent' and to do 'first works' and closes with words of 'repentance'. Among other things, such a structure implies a connection between the 'first love' and 'first works' as well as a connection between repentance and 'first works'.

Standing first in the rebuke (in the Greek text) are the words 'first love', indicating something of their importance in the sentence and thought. Clearly the idea is important, but what would it mean to Johannine hearers? It is sometimes thought that the words 'first love' would have reference to the zeal of a new believer, and in this context the waning of such zeal. However, the role and function of love within the Johannine literature suggest that the phrase would have a more concrete meaning for hearers of the Apocalypse. In point of fact, the concept of love is so important in the Johannine literature that it would not be going too far to say that it is the central theological theme for the community. Love is understood as shared by God, Jesus, and his disciples and/or members of the community. Love is dynamic, active, and relational. It begins with God (1 Jn 4.7, 16b), who loved the world so much that he sent his unique Son (Jn 3.16; 1 Jn 4.9-10). Jesus' love for his own is understood to be complete and ultimate (Jn 13.1), leading to the laying down of his life for others (1 Jn 3.16). This love, identified with

God and Jesus, can even be spoken of as 'perfected' or 'completed' in believers (1 Jn 2.5; 4.12, 17-18). Such love is no abstract concept but is understood as manifest in work and truth, i.e. the concrete actions of emotive, sacrificial giving to the point of giving one's life (1 Jn 3.16-18). It may not be insignificant that the command for believers to love one another is rooted and grounded in the fact that αὐτος πρῶτος ἠγάπησεν ἡμᾶς ('he first loved us') – 1 Jn 4.19. It would appear, then, that the words, 'first love', stand for an amalgam of ideas fused together throughout the Johannine literature.

Given the earlier mention of Jesus' love for the hearers (1.5) and the fact that he later speaks of his love for the church in Philadelphia (3.9), it may be that the 'first love' in 2.4 has primary reference to Jesus. If so, Jesus' rebuke that they have left their first love is especially stinging, owing to the fact that the church in Ephesus has earlier been praised for bearing opposition on account of his name. The existence of this rebuke on the heels of such stellar praise introduces the hearers for the first time to a phenomenon that occurs frequently throughout the Apocalypse. That is, the dialectic created by the tension of the call to faithful witness in the face of temptation to compromise that witness in some way. Here as later in the Apocalypse, the dialectic focuses upon one's relationship with Jesus – they hold to his name but have left their 'first love'.

Verse 5 – However, before the hearers have time to contemplate this dialectic, Jesus issues a command that grows out of this rebuke, as the presence of the postpositive οὖν ('therefore') indicates. The command to remember may suggest that this rebuke takes the church in Ephesus by surprise. That is to say, these hearers may not be aware until this moment that they have left their 'first love'. At the least, it implies that they have forgotten this fact. The call to remembrance challenges the hearers to recall all that their 'first love' entitled and how far they have fallen from that place. Perhaps the appearance of the word πέπτωκας ('fallen') would remind the hearer that while John fell at the feet of Jesus as though dead, they have fallen away from him. At the same time, the imagery of falling is quite significant in the Apocalypse. Often it is used in positive ways to describe the posture of worship (4.10; 5.8, 14; 7.11; 11.16; 19.4) or protection of the saints (7.16). More often, it appears in negative contexts conveying the idea of judgment

(6.13; 8.10; 9.1; 11.13; 14.8; 16.19; 17.10 18.2, 3), the desire for death (6.16), or false worship (19.10; 22.8). Clearly, the hearers are told that they have fallen from the 'first love'. The exact meaning of their 'fallen' situation is quickly revealed in the double command to 'repent and do your first works'. Such an instruction would be a bit of a surprise to Johannine hearers, as the word 'repent' does not occur in the FG or 1-3 John. Yet, it is a very important theological concept in the Apocalypse. On the one hand, the majority of the term's occurrences appear with reference to the seven churches in the seven prophetic messages (2.5, 5, 16, 21, 22; 3.3, 19). On the other hand, four times the word appears with reference to those who refuse to repent of the 'works of their hands' (9.20, 21; 16.9, 11) despite the gracious judgments of God. From its other occurrences in the Apocalypse it becomes obvious that here the command to repent calls for a turning away from the action which Jesus judges, leaving their 'first love'. The hearers discover that there is an explicit connection between repenting and doing 'first works'. Such a connection implies that if there is a need to repent for leaving one's first love, the doing of 'first works' must also involve love.

Within the Johannine community, there could hardly be any misunderstanding about that of which first works consists: love for one another. This is, after all, the new command which Jesus gives to his disciples (Jn 13.34), the criteria by which all will know that 'you are my disciples' (Jn 13.35), and the way in which we know that we love God and Jesus (1 Jn 4.7-5.5). It appears then that whilst the hearers in Ephesus have been extraordinarily resilient in opposing 'evil ones', they have left their 'first love', Jesus, by their lack of love for one another.[13] On this view, repentance for leaving the first love necessarily entails the first works of loving one another, whilst loving one another is the fruit that they have truly repented.

The absolute necessity of repentance is underscored in the following sentence by a veiled threat contained in Jesus' next words 'If not, I will come to you'. The hearers learn much from this first of seven places in the Apocalypse where Jesus announces his imminent 'coming' (2.5, 16; 3.11; 16.15; 22.7, 12, 20). First, the hearers already know from the prophetic word found in 1.7 that the ap-

---

[13] Fee, *Revelation*, p. 27.

pearance of Jesus is connected with judgment in that it will generate mourning on the part of all the peoples of the earth. Therefore, the hearers would hardly be surprised that Jesus' own first words about his coming, prophetically spoken to the church at Ephesus, have an ominous tone. Second, the hearers are introduced to the fact that Jesus' words about his 'coming' in the Apocalypse often function both to spur them on to proper action/works and encourage them in their activity as faithful witnesses. Third, while there is continuity between the prophetic word about Jesus' eschatological return in 1.7 and the threat of his 'coming' in 2.5, there is also discontinuity between these words. On the one hand, the prophetic words of 1.7 rather clearly speak of Jesus' eschatological return. On the other hand, Jesus' words in 2.5 appear, at the least, to carry with them the idea that this coming of Jesus to the church at Ephesus has reference to his ongoing activity, not necessarily to his eschatological return mentioned in 1.7. However, rather than taking these ideas as having reference to wholly distinct activities of Jesus, there are hints in the text that the hearers would likely see a great deal of continuity between them, while holding them in some tension.[14] One of the clues pointing to this interpretation is the fact that references both to the ongoing activity of Jesus and to his eschatological return are to be found in the seven 'I come' promises of Jesus in the Apocalypse. Given Jesus' close proximity to the lampstands, as the One who walks among them, words about his coming to a particular church would not necessarily be unexpected. At the same time, seeing the eschatological coming of Jesus in too great a tension with his ongoing activity ignores the fact that there appears to be a certain merging of these ideas in the Apocalypse. Specifically, it would not be lost on the hearers that it is the Jesus who is coming in eschatological glory (1.7) who comes even now to the seven churches (2.5). Consequently, Jesus' ongoing activity would be seen as eschatological activity, an understanding not far removed from the eschatological emphases of the FG.

Jesus' specific threat to the church at Ephesus, should she refuse to repent, is 'I will remove your lampstand from its place'. The implications of this devastating prospect are all the clearer in the light of Jesus' earlier words (1.20) that 'the seven lampstands are the sev-

---

[14] Osborne, *Revelation*, p. 118.

en churches'. That is to say, the lampstand will be extinguished; the church at Ephesus will cease to exist.[15] Something of the portentous nature of this threat is revealed by the fact that the only other place where the term 'remove' occurs in the Apocalypse has reference to the results of the opening of the sixth seal where every mountain and island is removed from its place (6.14). The lampstand will be removed from its place, by the One who walks among the lampstands, as surely as every mountain and island will be removed from theirs unless repentance occurs. If leaving their first love has reference to Jesus, it is not surprising that such action will ultimately result in the destruction of the church by the one abandoned, Jesus.

To underscore the seriousness of the situation facing the church at Ephesus, a call for repentance concludes v. 5, balancing the call that appears at the beginning and middle of the verse. This explicit emphasis not only alerts the hearers to the need for repentance on behalf of the church at Ephesus, but also puts the hearers on notice that the issue of repentance will turn out to be a major one in the Apocalypse.

Verse 6 – The prophetic words of Jesus in v. 6 reveal that the content of the message (about Jesus' knowledge of the works of the church at Ephesus) is coming to a close, for this verse connects with what precedes it in at least two ways. Most immediately, the words of v. 6, 'But you have ...', stand in contrast to the words of v. 4, 'But I have ...' While the words of v. 4 were words of rebuke, the words found in v. 6 are words of encouragement. As such, they indicate to the hearers that all is not lost. In addition, these words also mark a return to the theme of the evil ones that the Ephesian believers cannot bear/support. Earlier such evil ones were identified as 'those who claim to be apostles but are not' (v. 2). Here they are identified as the Nicolaitans. The chiastic balance of these examples in vv. 2 and 6 does not necessarily imply that 'those who claim to be apostles' are understood to be synonymous with 'the Nicolaitans', but it does suggest that both are to be identified as 'evil ones'. What might be somewhat surprising to the hearers is the positive use of the word 'hate' on this occasion, for in the Johannine literature the term rarely has a positive meaning. It often appears in describing the world's hatred of the Father (Jn 15.23-24),

---

[15] Aune, *Revelation 1-5*, p. 147.

Jesus (Jn 3.20; 7.7; 15.18, 23-25), and his followers (Jn 15.18-19; 17.14; 1 Jn 3.13). Its primary use in 1 John is in association with John's rebuke directed to the one who hates one's brother (2.9, 11; 3.15; 4.20). In point of fact, the lone positive use of the term in the FG is found in 12.25 where Jesus says, 'The one who loves his life will lose it, and the one who hates his life in this world will guard it unto eternal life'. In Rev. 2.6, the Ephesian believers are praised for hating the 'works of the Nicolaitans'. What is more, they learn that Jesus himself 'hates' such works as well! Perhaps in such shocking language the hearers would discern a distinction between their own works, which Jesus knows (and praises), and the works of the Nicolaitans, which Jesus (apparently knows and) hates. While little is known about the Nicolaitans outside the Apocalypse, a few additional details are revealed in 3.14-15.[16] At this point it is enough to know that they are the adversaries of Jesus and his church. In this, the church in Ephesus stands in solidarity with Jesus.

Verse 7 – Jesus' prophetic message to the church in Ephesus reaches its conclusion in v. 7 where two distinct components of the seven prophetic messages occur for the first time in the Apocalypse. The first component is a refrain found in each of the messages. It is a call to discerning obedience, 'The One who has an ear let that one hear what the Spirit is saying to the churches'. While this phrase will appear seven times in chapters 2-3, it is anything but perfunctory, for a number of ideas converge in it, making it a very rich theological refrain indeed. Owing to its importance several observations are here offered. First, this invitation to hear what the Spirit says is in keeping with the earlier divine guidance offered by Jesus regarding the mystery of the seven stars and seven lampstands in 1.20. As such it suggests to the hearers that the interpretive, discerning process to which they are called is not only a Christological endeavor but is also a Pneumatological one as well. This motif will continue to develop as the Apocalypse unfolds. Second, while the refrain places emphasis upon what the Spirit is saying, it is clear that these words are the prophetically spoken words of Jesus. As noted earlier, Jesus begins speaking in 1.17 and continues uninterrupted

---

[16] One of the only other occurrences of the word 'hate' in the Apocalypse is in 17.16, where it describes the eventual hatred of the Great Whore by the Beast and the Ten Horns. Such a linguistic connection might imply a religio-theological between the Great Whore and the Nicolaitans.

until 3.22, so it is clear that the words the Spirit is saying are coterminous with the words prophetically spoken by Jesus. In point of fact, Jesus himself makes this identification between his words and that which the Spirit is saying. Such a declaration reminds the hearers of the relationship between Jesus and the Spirit of Truth in the FG. He will say what he hears and make known the things of Jesus (Jn 16.13-15). It also puts the hearers on notice that the relationship between Jesus and the Spirit is an especially close one in the Apocalypse. At this point it is sufficient to note that Jesus and the Spirit speak with one voice.[17] Third, the hearers cannot help but remember that the Spirit who is speaking now in the prophetically spoken words of Jesus, is the same Spirit who is before the One who sits on the throne (1.4) and is the same Spirit who makes possible John's revelatory experience (1.10). The former idea may even suggest to the hearers that these words of Jesus are not only coterminous with the Spirit's words, but are also directly connected with the One who sits on the throne. Finally, for a third time in the Apocalypse the term 'hear' appears. It has occurred in the beatitude near the book's beginning (1.3) and is used to describe John's initial revelatory encounter (1.10). The former occurrence is closely connected to the idea of 'keeping' (i.e. 'obeying') the words of this prophecy. As the book unfolds it becomes obvious that the call to 'hear' is a call to obedience (cf. esp. 3.3). The hearing called for here is a specifically pneumatic activity. Owing to the fact that John is 'in the Spirit' when he sees (and writes!), the fact that these words are the prophetically spoken words of Jesus, and the fact that John and his hearers have already received divine interpretive assistance from Jesus himself, it stands to reason that the entire process from first encounter to discerning obedience is a pneumatic experience. In this activity, the hearers stand in solidarity with John, Jesus, and the Spirit. If John's role is to 'write in the Spirit', the role of others in this prophetic community is to 'hear in the Spirit'. If part of the discerning obedience called for in the Apocalypse is one of the ways in which the hearers 'keep the words of this prophecy', then the first

---

[17] It might be worth noting that the phrase, 'The one who has an ear to hear, let that one hear', occurs often in the sayings of Jesus in several synoptic texts (cf. Mt. 11.15; 13.9, 43; Mk 4.9, 23; Lk. 8.8; 14.35). Such evidence, if known by the hearers, would underscore the fact that these are indeed Jesus' words. On this cf. Aune, *Revelation 1-5*, p. 155.

concrete call for such obedience involves continued 'hard labor', 'patient endurance', and 'bearing the name of Jesus'. It also involves repentance for any abandonment of one's first love (Jesus) and a doing of 'first works' (loving one another). The hearers learn that there is more to keeping the words of this prophecy than having knowledge of inside information on the unfolding of history. It involves discerning obedience.

The conclusion of this first prophetic message is marked by another component characteristic of each of the seven prophetic messages, a promise for the one who overcomes. Before examining the promise made to those who overcome, perhaps a few observations should be made about the term itself. Structurally, the hearers may pick up on the word play between τῶν Νικολαϊτῶν ('the Nicolaitans') and τῷ νικῶντι ('those who overcome'). However, the similarity between these groups extends only to the sound of the terms, for the works of the former, Jesus hates, while the works of the latter, Jesus rewards. This idea of overcoming would, no doubt, be informed by the fact that in the FG Jesus himself states, 'I have overcome (νενίκηκα) the world', a victory over both the world that hates him (15.18-16.4) and its ruler who is already being judged (16.11). Through Jesus (1 Jn 5.5) believers also overcome the evil one (1 Jn 2.13-14) and the world (1 Jn 4.4; 5.4). The hearers would likely identify immediately with this term and the realities it conveys. In the Apocalypse, the term takes on additional shape and color. In keeping with the FG, the word can be used to describe the activity of Jesus as Lion (5.5) and Lamb (17.14), as well as the rider on the white horse Jesus unleashes with the opening of the first seal (6.2). The term is even used of the activity of the beast against the saints (11.7; 13.7). But the vast preponderance of its occurrences is in contexts used to describe believers in the Apocalypse. Early in the book the term appears in the context of promises to those who overcome (2.7, 11, 17, 26; 3.5, 12, 21). But as the Apocalypse unfolds this overcoming on the part of the saints is spoken of in the past tense, as an accomplished reality (12.11; 15.2). This combination of promise and fulfillment culminates in the term's final occurrence in the eschatological promise of 21.7. Thus the idea of overcoming is a most powerfully rich theological concept in the book.

The first of the seven promises made to those who overcome in Revelation 2-3 reveals that the promises are eschatological in nature. It also indicates that Jesus is the one who will make good on these promises with his words 'I will give …' Perhaps the hearers would not be surprised to learn that Jesus on this occasion will give those who overcome something to eat, for such an idea is common in the FG, where Jesus gives a variety of things to be eaten including himself (cf. esp. John 6)![18] Here the promised gift is 'to eat of the tree of life, which is in the Paradise of God'. This promise, pregnant with meaning, immediately takes the hearers to the beginning of the biblical canon where there is in the paradise of God, a tree of life (Gen. 2.9). This tree, which God provides, produces fruit which, when eaten, enables one to live forever (Gen. 3.22). However, as a result of the disobedience of Adam and Eve, God denies access to the tree by barring entry into his garden (Gen. 3.23-24). Jesus' promise to give those who overcome to eat of this tree is not some vague eschatological promise, but carries with it concrete evidence of the reversal of the curse found in Genesis, for access to the Tree of Life is no longer denied but is granted. Clearly, one implication of this OT text is that access to the Tree of Life, means access to eternal life. It, of course, comes as no surprise that those who overcome are promised by Jesus to eat of the Tree of Life, for in the stunning vision with which the Apocalypse opens Jesus identifies himself as 'the One who lives', 'who was dead and is living forevermore' (1.18). It is only natural that the One who is alive forevermore, the one identified as Life (Jn 1.4; 14.6), even Eternal Life (1 Jn 1.2) is the one able to promise and give access to the Tree of Life. It may not be without significance that whilst God originally barred access to the Tree of Life owing to disobedience, access is granted by Jesus owing to the overcomers' obedience. As with all the promises to those who overcome, the full force of this eschatological promise will not be fully appreciated until the description of the New Jerusalem at the book's end, where these elements figure prominently. Consequently, whatever the hearers' perception of this extraordinary promise might be in 2.7, they have no way of knowing just how extraordinary it truly is. Mention of the location of the Tree of Life as in the Paradise (or Garden) of God reminds the hearers of the idyllic environment of creation described

---

[18] On this theme cf. esp. J.S. Webster, *Ingesting Jesus: Eating and Drinking in the Gospel of John* (Atlanta: SBL, 2003), pp. 149-50.

in Genesis, the standard by which other locales are judged (13.10), while drawing upon the eschatological associations Paradise comes to have in the Hebrew Bible (Isa. 51.3; Ezek. 28.13; 31.8-9).[19] Together they anticipate the idea of paradise fulfilled in the city of the New Jerusalem. With these words, the first prophetic message of Jesus to the seven churches comes to a close.

To the Angel of the Church in Smyrna (2.8-11)

Verse 8 – Without any delay, Jesus next instructs John to write to the angel of the church at Smyrna, using the identical construction used in 2.1 with reference to Ephesus. As the hearers encounter the name Smyrna, they are led to the next lampstand some forty miles north of Ephesus. Perhaps they think of the city's remarkable history that involved destruction (ca. 600 BCE) and rebuilding (ca. 300 BCE). Or perhaps they would think of its acropolis, located on a hill more than 500 feet high, often likened to a crown, depicted on its coins and monuments. Or perhaps they thought of the fact that it rivaled Ephesus as the 'first city' of Asia.[20]

Whatever, the hearers think of with regard to Smyrna, they soon find out what Jesus thinks. As in the first prophetic message Jesus identifies himself by means of elements familiar to the hearers from John's description of his inaugural vision of Jesus. Thus, the hearers could hardly experience this description without being reminded of that stunning event. For a second time he calls himself 'the first and the last' (1.18), reminding the hearers of his deep and intimate identification with God – the fact that there is nothing that lies outside his influence.[21] This phrase also is the first of several contrasts found in this prophetic message.[22] As in chapter one so here the identification of Jesus as 'first and last' is followed by reference to his death and life. As in 1.18 his death is described as a past event. However, in contrast to 1.18, where emphasis is placed upon the reality of his continuing life, the aorist tense ἔζησεν ('became alive')

---

[19] Aune, *Revelation 1-5*, p. 152.

[20] Cf. Hemer, 'Seven Cities of Asia Minor', pp. 239-40 and Murphy, *Fallen Is Babylon*, pp. 118-19.

[21] Resseguie, *The Revelation of John*, p. 88.

[22] Note the contrasts between 'first and last', 'was dead became alive', 'poverty and rich', 'claim to be Jews but are not', 'those faithful to death receive a crown of life'. Murphy, *Fallen Is Babylon*, p. 120.

is used, focusing attention on the point at which he became alive, his resurrection from the dead.

Verse 9 – Owing to the duplication of the specific elements with which these first two prophetic messages begin, the hearers would hardly be surprised that the formula Οἶδα σου ('I know your') next occurs. The one outside of whose influence nothing lies knows the Smyrnean believers well. Specifically, he knows of their 'tribulation, poverty ... and the blasphemy of those who claim to be Jews but are not'. Several things would be conveyed to the hearers by Jesus' mention of the word 'tribulation'. First, they would likely remember the transitory nature of tribulation, for Jesus himself has assured that though his disciples are certain to experience tribulation in this world (Jn 16.33), joy is sure to follow (Jn 16.21). Thus, in the midst of their tribulation, the certainty of its arrival brings the reminder that it is temporary. Second, knowledge that John the prophet is himself their brother in tribulation would encourage the hearers that tribulation is shared by the servant chosen to testify of this extraordinary revelation (Rev. 1.9). Third, evidence awaits the hearers later in the Apocalypse of the faithfulness possible despite great tribulation (7.14). Fourth, they will also learn that Jesus himself can bring tribulation upon those who do not repent (2.22). Not only does Jesus know of their tribulation, he also knows of their poverty. Though Smyrna itself was a prosperous city, the members of the church are poor. It is not altogether clear whether their poverty is owing to their faithful witness, but given the extent of the persecution of which Jesus speaks such is a distinct possibility.

The next word spoken, ἀλλά ('but'), might lead the hearers to expect a rebuke of the Symrneans, owing to the pattern of 2.4 where a rebuke follows ἀλλά ('but'). However, instead of a rebuke at this point Jesus offers a prophetic insight into their situation. Despite their poverty, Jesus declares that they are rich. Normally, mention of riches or being rich will have a negative connotation in the Apocalypse (cf. 3.17-18; 6.15; 13.16; 18.3, 15, 19), but here it is clearly positive. One implication of such juxtaposition is that Jesus uses this word to describe 'spiritual', rather than material riches.[23] The only hints as to the identity of these riches are that there is no rebuke of the church at Smyrna and the fact that they have endured

---

[23] Osborne, *Revelation*, p. 130.

great hardship for their faith. Perhaps such riches enable their faithful obedience.

After the prophetic insight about their riches, the hearers learn of a third aspect of Jesus' knowledge of the church at Smyrna, 'the blasphemy of those who say of themselves to be Jews and are not but are a synagogue of Satan'. The charge of blasphemy may strike the hearers as a bit unexpected for the term does not appear in the FG or 1-3 John. However, its appearance serves to introduce the hearers to an ideal that reappears on numerous occasion later, describing the appearance and activity of the beast (13.1, 5, 6; 17.3) and human beings who suffer from the seven bowls of plagues (16.9, 11, 21). Its meaning in other places in the Apocalypse suggests that it here carries the ideas of accusation and contempt for the church at Smyrna. Though the specifics of such blasphemy are not described, something may be deduced about them from the remainder of the verse. This blasphemy comes from 'those who say of themselves to be Jews but are not ...' The phrase would remind the hearers of a similar construction in 2.2, where reference is made to 'those who claim to be apostles and are not'. Those individuals were tested and found to be liars by the church at Ephesus. On this occasion, there is no evidence to suggest that those who claimed to be Jews were tested and found not to be Jews by the church at Smyrna. Rather, it appears that this declaration by Jesus is akin to his previous prophetic insight about the church being rich, revealing a reality not previously understood. How would the hearers understand these words? Despite arguments to the contrary,[24] it appears that the hearers would most likely understand these individuals to be identified with part or all of the Jewish community in Smyrna.[25] On this reading, the same prophetic dynamic is present here as in the previous portion of this verse where despite the church's outward experience of tribulation and poverty, they are in reality rich. So in the latter portion of the verse, despite these individuals' outward appearance as Jews, in reality they are not. The point of both contrasts is the importance of the spiritual reality. The implication here is that although these individuals may be eth-

---

[24] However, cf. the comments in the introduction, p. 29.
[25] Cf. esp. P.L. Mayo, *'Those Who Call Themselves Jews': The Church and Judaism in the Apocalypse of John* (PTMS; Eugene, OR: Pickwick Pub., 2006), pp. 51-76.

nic Jews, they are not Jews spiritually; they are not the legitimate heirs of Israel. These stinging words, which are not out of keeping with the thought revealed in other NT documents and theologies,[26] give way to even more stinging words from Jesus when he calls them 'a synagogue of Satan'. Just as those who claimed to be apostles where found to be liars in 2.2, so these who claim to be Jews are found to be 'a synagogue of Satan'. This first mention of Satan in the Apocalypse would convey several things to the hearers. First, such a harsh judgment may very well remind the hearers of Jesus' words about his Jewish opponents in the FG (8.44), whom he calls children of their Father the devil, owing to their behavior. Second, these words carry with them the scathing indictment that their synagogue, meant to be a gathering place for the people of God, has been turned into a place of the adversary of God's people, Satan.[27] Third, mention of the blasphemy of this synagogue of Satan indicates that the accusations being brought against the church in Smyrna actually have a satanic origin. Fourth, the phrase 'synagogue of Satan' serves to introduce the hearers to the primary adversary of God and his people in the Apocalypse (cf. esp. 2.13, 24; 3.9; 12.9).[28] It is not surprising that his first mention comes in the context of accusations being brought against the church. Before leaving this phrase a final observation should perhaps be offered. Although these scathing words are spoken about the Jewish community in Smyrna, it should be remembered that, as noted in the introduction, the implied audience of the Apocalypse appears to be one with a clear appreciation for its Jewish heritage. Not only does its presumed familiarity with the OT point in this direction, but also the way in which certain 'Christian' details are grounded in Jewish roots. At the same time, the words of 2.9 make clear that there is tension between some of the churches of the Apocalypse and the broader Jewish community. Rather clearly, this tension appears to revolve around the issue of identity, specifically, the identity of God's people.

---

[26] Indeed, it appears that many NT documents share the idea that Christians are the legitimate heirs to Israel, not the non-Christian Jewish community.

[27] R.H. Gause, *Revelation: God's Stamp of Sovereignty on History* (Cleveland, TN: Pathway Press, 1983), p. 53 and Mayo, *'Those Who Call Themselves Jews'*, pp. 71-73.

[28] As the name implies. Cf. Osborne, *Revelation*, p. 132.

Verse 10 – Instead of the rebuke of 'I have something against you' in v. 9, the church at Smyrna received a positive assessment as to their being rich. Instead of a call for repentance in v. 10, they receive words of warning bounded on either side by words of instruction. Such words indicate that not only does Jesus know the current situation of the church at Smyrna, but he also knows its future. The verse opens with the words of instruction, 'Do not fear what you are about to suffer'. The words, 'do not fear', would remind the hearers of Jesus' words in the FG to the fearful disciples who had just seen Jesus walk on the water (Jn 6.19-20), as well as the words of the resurrected Jesus to John in Rev. 1.17. On both those occasions the words imply that despite the circumstances faced, the individuals in question should take courage from the fact that Jesus is with them. By implication, so these words convey the same assurance to the church at Smyrna. However, on this occasion, the words 'do not fear' are given in advance of the circumstance that might otherwise produce fear, specifically, that which they are about to suffer. The appearance of the word μέλλεις ('about to') underscores the immediacy of the suffering, while the word πάσχειν ('to suffer') conveys something of its severity. Perhaps this term would also remind the hearers of Jesus' own suffering, explicitly identified with the πάσχα ('Passover') in the FG and alluded to in the reference to 'the lamb that looked as if it had been slaughtered' in Rev. 5.6. The hearers are hardly able to begin to reflect upon the implications of these ominous words before they hear a warning that makes explicit the kind of suffering they are about to experience.

This warning begins with a formula of revelation, found often in the FG (Jn 1.19-34; 1.35-39; 1.47-51; 5.14; 19.24b-27). There, an individual sent by God sees a person, says ' Ἴδε ' ('Behold'), and then describes the person in such a way so as to reveal something about his or her situation, mission, or destiny.[29] This formula very appropriately introduces the warning found in Rev. 2.10. The fact that μέλλει ('about to') reappears so quickly after its mention in v. 9 and is the first word to follow 'Behold', demonstrates the connection between the warning that follows and the words found in

---

[29] Cf. the discussion of M. de Goedt, 'Un Scheme de Revelation dans le quatrieme Evangile', *NTS* 8 (1961-62), pp. 142-50.

the previous sentence.[30] Specifically, the church is warned, 'The Devil is about to cast some of you into prison in order that you might be tested and have tribulation for ten days'. This first mention of the Devil in the Apocalypse is quite appropriate in this context which has just mentioned the slander of blasphemy, as the Devil is described by Jesus in the FG as the 'Father of Lies' (Jn 8.44). It is also appropriate owing to the fact that the Devil put [βεβληκότος ('placed')] into Judas' heart that he should betray Jesus (13.2). The fact that the Devil is about to cast some of them into prison may also remind the hearers of the fact that John (the Baptist) had been cast into prison before them (3.24). In any event, thoughts of prison would no doubt convey to the church an inhospitable place where individuals might be held indefinitely at the whim of those in power. The fact that they are imprisoned for the purpose of being tested and having tribulation for ten days would also be of significance to the hearers for several reasons. In the number ten, they encounter for the first time a number that will always have negative connotations in the Apocalypse, having reference to the ten hours of the dragon (Rev. 12.3) and the ten horns of the beast (13.1; 17.3, 7, 12, 16), which are identified as the ten kings (17.12). Yet, despite the ominous foreboding such a number might bring, it is likely that even though the church at Smyrna knows tribulation, here they are encouraged by several facts. First, if John is indeed on Patmos owing to exile, his role as their 'brother in tribulation' (1.9) would take on even greater significance and encourage them all the more. Second, the fact that this tribulation is described as lasting ten days indicates that it is of a limited, not an unlimited, duration. Third, a great sense of encouragement might also be conveyed by the fact that Daniel provides a most important intertext. Such a source is not surprising, as Danielic influence can be detected as early as the inaugural vision of Jesus in chapter one. On this occasion, mention of the church being tested for ten days may well remind the hearers of the LXX version of Dan. 1.12, 14, where the three young Israelite men, refuse the food of the Babylonians and

---

[30] Perhaps the hearers would also see a connection between what the church at Smyrna is about to suffer and the things that are about to take place spoken of in 1.19.

propose that they be tested for ten days.[31] Such an intertext from Daniel might encourage the church at Smyrna to turn what, on the surface, could be interpreted as a passively experienced persecution into active witness, with the anticipation of God's intervention on their behalf. Finally, mention that the Devil will cast some of them into prison, anticipates the fact that the Devil will himself be cast into the Abyss where he will be kept, not for ten days but for 1000 years (20.3). After release from 'his prison' (20.7), he will then be cast into the lake of fire and sulfur with the beast and the false prophet, where they will be tormented forever and ever (20.10).

This warning is followed by the second admonition found in this verse and serves to balance the first. The words 'Continue to be faithful unto death' would connect with the hearers in several ways. This command is reminiscent of Jesus' words to Thomas μὴ γίνου ἄπιστος ἀλλὰ πιστός ('do not continue to be unfaithful but faithful') in Jn 20.27 in the face of his struggle to believe in Jesus' resurrection. Such similar language would not be lost on the hearers. Primarily, the hearers would be reminded that already in the Apocalypse Jesus has been identified as 'the faithful witness' (Rev. 1.5), a title clearly connected with his witness unto death and one which will reappear on other occasions to describe Jesus (3.14; 19.11). The phrase will also be used with reference to Antipas (2.13), while the word πιστός ('faithful') will describe those with the conquering Lamb (17.14), as well as words that are 'faithful and true' (21.5; 22.6). The faithfulness called for, like the faithfulness of Jesus and Antipas, is a 'faithfulness unto death'. While the term ἄχρι ('until' or 'unto') is used often in the Apocalypse to convey the completion of a given task (2.25, 26; 15.8; 17.17; 20.3, 5), the clearest parallel will occur in 12.11 where it is said of the martyrs who overcome, 'they did not love their lives unto death' (ἄχρι θανάτου). Clearly, the faithfulness called for could very well entail a witness that results in the death of some of those in the church at Smyrna. But the hearers would not be unaware that such a call comes from 'the One who was dead and came to life' (2.8), 'the One who holds the keys to death and hades' (1.18). Consequently, it is this one who promises to give those who exhibit such faithfulness τὸν στέφανον τῆς

---

[31] Note especially Dan. 1.14 which reads, 'ἐπείρασεν αὐτοὺς ἡμέρας δέκα' ('he tested them ten days'). Prigent, *L'Apocalypse de Saint Jean*, pp. 128-29.

ζωῆς ('the crown of life'). While this image could be an intentional reference to Smyrna's acropolis, often likened to a crown, crown imagery is used often in the Apocalypse (3.11; 4.4, 10; 6.2; 9.7; 12.1; 14.14). In yet another contrast, the one faithful to death is given a crown of life. The crown imagery clearly indicates a reward for the successful completion of a difficult challenge. The image also anticipates the overcoming language to follow in v. 11. It is not surprising that the One who is alive can give such a crown, for the gift and the giver are coterminous.

Verse 11 – The refrain with which the hearers are familiar from the message to the church at Ephesus occurs here for the second time in the book, 'The one who has an ear to hear let that one hear'. How would the hearers respond to this pneumatic call for discerning obedience? How would they be challenged to 'keep the words of this prophecy' in the light of the prophetic message to the church at Smyrna? Specifically, this second concrete call for discerning obedience would involve a conscious reflection upon a) the fact that despite their physical poverty, they are deemed 'rich' by the resurrected Jesus, b) a refusal to fear in the face of suffering, and c) a faithfulness even unto death. Once again, keeping the words of this prophecy is more than having knowledge of future events in advance, it necessitates complete and utter faith in and faithfulness to 'the One who is the first and the last, who was dead and came to life'.

As with the prophetic message to the church at Ephesus, the message to the church at Smyrna also concludes with a promise to those who overcome. In keeping with the first promise this one too is eschatological in nature. As might be expected from the description of Jesus in v. 8 and the promise of 'the crown of life' by Jesus in v. 10, those who overcome are assured that they will not be harmed at all by the 'second death'. This eschatological idea will await further definition for the hearers (20.6; 20.14; 21.8), but at this point is an appropriate gift from the One who was dead and came to life.

To the Angel of the Church in Pergamum (2.12-17)

Verse 12 – Again, without any delay, Jesus next instructs John to write to the angel of the church at Pergamum, using the identical construction used in 2.1 and 2.8 with reference to Ephesus and Smyrna, respectively. As the hearers encounter the name Pergamum, they are led to the next lampstand some 45 miles north of Smyrna. Perhaps they think of the imposing sight of the city built upon a thousand-foot high cone shaped mountain; a city whose very name means citadel. Or, perhaps they think of the fact that it is to Pergamum that people came to receive administrative Roman justice, signified by the sword. Perhaps they think of the city's fame as a religious center with its enormous sculptured altar dedicated to Zeus. Or, perhaps they think of the other religious sites built for Athena, Dionysus, or their most characteristic god Askelpios, whose image was a snake. Perhaps they think of the numerous religious pilgrims who come to the Askelpios shrine in search of healing. Or perhaps their thoughts are dominated by the fact that in Pergamum was the first officially sanctioned temple dedicated (in 29 CE) to 'divine Augustus and the goddess Roma' (Tacitus, *Annals* 3.37).[32]

Whatever the hearers think of with regard to Pergamum, they soon find out what Jesus thinks. As in the first two prophetic messages Jesus identifies himself by means of elements familiar to the hearers from John's description of his inaugural vision of Jesus. Thus, the hearers could hardly experience this description without being reminded of that stunning event. On this occasion, he calls himself 'the One who has a double-edged sword'. Earlier in the vision, a double-edged sword came out of his mouth (1.16). This detail served to highlight the fact that Jesus speaks prophetically. While reference to his mouth is omitted in 2.12, it is hardly likely that the hearers would have forgotten that detail. Perhaps its absence here might cause more of the hearers' attention to be focused upon the dangerous nature of this instrument.

Verse 13 – For a third time in the Apocalypse, a prophetic message from Jesus begins with the word Οἶδα ('I know'). As before, this word introduces the hearers to the bulk of the content of this communiqué, here found in vv. 13-17. The first part of the content is marked out by the verb κατοικέω ('I live') which stands at both the beginning and end of v. 13. While the first two appearances of the word are followed by attributes (2.2) or experiences (2.9), here attention is focused upon the church's location. Specifically, Jesus

---

[32] Cf. Hemer, 'Seven Cities of Asia Minor', pp. 241-42 and R.H. Mounce, *The Book of Revelation* (Grand Rapids, MI: Eerdmans, 1977), pp. 95-96.

knows where the church lives, 'where the throne of Satan is'. Normally in the Apocalypse, this verb appears in describing 'those who live upon the earth' (3.10; 6.10; 8.13; 11.10; 13.8, 12 2x, 14 2x; 17.2, 8). Only in 2.13 does it occur to denote a specific location.

Clearly, this statement would assure the hearers that Jesus knows the church in Pergamum lives in the same place where Satan's throne is located. Perhaps it would not surprise the hearers to find that not only is Satan active in afflicting the church in Smyrna, but that he is also present in Pergamum. The fact that his throne is located in Pergamum, described by the articular construction 'where the throne of Satan is',[33] may indicate that his presence may be felt more intensely there owing to the fact that it is the center of his activity. Why would Pergamum merit such a description? Perhaps it is owing to a variety of associations found within the city; the massive altar dedicated to Zeus, the temple of Augustus and Roma, and the Asklepios cult, whose sign of the snake can still be found among the archeological remains. This combination of ideas may uniquely qualify Pergamum for such a description over against the other cities addressed in these opening chapters. Yet, the message conveyed to the hearers is more than this, for mention of Satan's throne also indicates that Satan is in direct contrast and conflict with the One who sits on the throne. In this, it also anticipates mention of the Dragon's rival throne, which is given to the beast later in the book (13.2; cf. also 16.10). However, owing to the fact that the designation, 'the One who sits on the throne' is used on numerous occasions in the Apocalypse with reference to God, it leaves no doubt as to his sovereignty.

Despite living in the city where Satan's throne is located, the church at Pergamum is commended by the resurrected Jesus for two specific things. First, 'you are holding to my name'. Such an expression indicates a firm grasp or strong attachment, owing in part to the fact that the same verb is used to describe Jesus holding the seven stars in his hand (2.1), with which the prophetic messages commenced. The fact that this strong attachment is directed to Jesus' name reminds the hearers of the patient endurance of the church at Ephesus, who bore a number of things on account of Jesus' name (2.3). Given the rich Johannine understanding of Jesus'

---

[33] Aune, *Revelation 1-5*, p. 182.

name and the fact that the church at Pergamum firmly holds on to it, suggests that they have a deep sense of solidarity and personal identification with Jesus. It may also prepare the hearers for the mention of the 'new name' in v. 17. The second commendation is closely related to the first, as the church is told 'you did not deny my faith'. The first part of this statement is fraught with Johannine meaning. Positively, the one who does not deny is in company with John (the Baptist) who did not deny but confessed 'I am not the Christ' (Jn 1.20). Negatively, the primary use of the term occurs in describing the prediction (13.38) and occurrence of Peter's denial of Jesus (18.25) and the activity of the antichrists in 1 John (2.22-23). The significance of the fact that the church at Pergamum exhibits the kind of witness characteristic of John, rather than succumbing to the temptation of denying Jesus would not be lost on the hearers. While the words τὴν πίστιν μου ('my faith') might be taken to mean 'faith in me',[34] it appears likely that this phrase would convey a different meaning to the hearers. The meaning of the preceding construction κρατεῖς τὸ ὄνομά μου ('you are holding to my name') suggests that this similar construction τὴν πίστιν μου ('my faith') would have a similar meaning. This similarity is shared by the following construction with reference to Antipas, ὁ μάρτυς μου ὁ πιστός μου ('my faithful witness'). The lone occurrence of 'faith' in the FG and 1-3 John might also shed some light on its first appearance in the Apocalypse. 1 John 5.4-5 reads, 'Because each one who has been born of God overcomes the world. And this is the overcomer who has overcome the world, our faith. Who is the one who overcomes the world except the one who believes that Jesus is the Son of God?' In this passage 'our faith' is closely connected to overcoming the world and belief in rather than a denial of Jesus. In addition, the broader context of Rev. 2.13 argues for this meaning, as it focuses upon faithfulness. Therefore, it would seem that the phrase 'my faith' would suggest something of the church's solidarity with the faithfulness of Jesus, i.e. they did not deny the faithfulness of Jesus by their own faithful actions.

Such an interpretation fits well with the phrase that follows – 'even in the days of Antipas, my faithful witness, who was killed

---

[34] So Prigent, *L'Apocalypse de Saint Jean*, p. 132 and G.R. Beasley-Murray, *Revelation* (Grand Rapids, MI: Eerdmans, 1981), p. 84.

among you, where Satan lives'. Several things are significant about this statement. First, while it is sometimes argued that since Antipas is the only person named as a martyr to this point, it is likely that no one else had been put to death in the community. But such an interpretation misses the point of the text. This individual named Antipas is cited as an example of one who held on the Jesus' name and did not deny his faith. Second, by mention of Antipas, the hearers learn that the possibility of being put to death owing to one's faithfulness described in the previous message to the church in Smyrna, has become a reality in the message to the church in Pergamum. Consequently, the warning of the previous passage takes on an even more solemn tone. Third, the only thing known about Antipas from this verse is that he stands in extremely close solidarity with Jesus. For Antipas, like Jesus, is described by the words ὁ μάρτυς μου ὁ πιστός μου ('my faithful witness'), words that echo the first description of Jesus in 1.5, ὁ μάρτυς ὁ πιστός ('the faithful witness'). Such similarity of language would not be lost on the hearers. Fourth, as with the description of Jesus in 1.5 as 'the faithful witness', so here these words about Antipas are followed up by reference to the death of the faithful witness. Fifth, Antipas' death is situated in two locations. On the one hand, it is placed among the community ('among you'), underscoring the intimate relationship between Antipas and the church in Pergamum, perhaps suggesting that others may be called upon to die as well. On the other hand, Antipas' death is located in the place 'where Satan lives'. This latter phrase indicates the close connection between where Satan lives and the deadly persecution of the church. Earlier in v. 13, mention of Satan's throne underscored his power in Pergamum. Now, the hearers learn that they live where he lives. The end of the first portion of the message's content is revealed by the reappearance of the word κατοικεῖ ('lives'), which forms an inclusio with its appearance at the beginning of this verse.

Verse 14 – As in the message to the church in Ephesus, the onset of the second portion of the message's content is marked by the words, 'But I have against you', indicating a change in the tone of the message and the introduction of words of rebuke. Unlike its previous appearance (2.4), here the phrase contains the word ὀλίγα ('a little'), at least initially suggesting that the rebuke to follow will not be as severe as the one to the church in Ephesus. Jesus' words of rebuke focus on two related activities. In each case the church at Pergamum have some among them who are holding to the teaching of Balaam and the teaching of the Nicolaitans. Significantly, in each of these condemnations the same verb is used to describe the relationship to the false teaching as is earlier used to describe their holding to Jesus' name. Such a phenomenon creates a tension which the hearers must hold together, similar to the tension found in the message to the church at Ephesus, where they have an intimate relationship with Jesus, and yet have left their first love, Jesus. Here, the contrast is between those who 'hold to my name' in 2.13, and those who 'are holding to the teaching of Balaam … and the Nicolaitans'.

Although the teaching of the Nicolaitans will continue to be cloaked in ambiguity, the teaching of Balaam is identified further in this message by connecting the teaching to actions described in the OT. In this message, the name Balaam is apparently assigned by Jesus to a teacher within the community. Perhaps the choice of this name is an acknowledgement that the teacher in question is regarded to be a prophetic figure. Mention of this name would no doubt remind the hearers of the story of Balaam in Numbers 22-24. This prophetic figure is called upon by Balak, the king of Moab, to curse the Israelites who are making their way to Canaan. But Balaam's encounter with God, God's angel (who bears a sword), and even Balaam's donkey, results in him blessing Israel three times instead of cursing them. However, immediately following his faithful prophesying, the Israelites enter into sexual immorality and apparently eating food sacrificed to idols (Num. 25.1-2). Despite his earlier prophetic words, Balaam's counsel is blamed for these activities (Num. 31.16). Jesus' words in Rev. 2.14 focus upon Balaam's culpability by his teaching Balak 'to place a σκάνδαλον ('stumbling block') before the sons of Israel to eat food sacrificed to idols and πορνεῦσαι ('to commit sexual immorality')'. σκάνδαλον ('stumbling block') language would no doubt remind the hearers that in the FG this terminology occurs in contexts that describe the refusal of disciples to remain with Jesus (Jn 6.61-66) or as a warning not to leave (16.1). Here it serves to register the level of threat such teaching poses to the church. It may even be possible that mention of Balak is a subtle allusion to Rome, with mention of Israel an allusion to the believing community in Pergamum. At any rate, the specifics of the stumbling block placed before Israel, 'eating food sacrificed to idols' and 'committing sexual immorality', both provides continuity with the OT story with regard to Balaam, and introduces for the first time major themes in the Apocalypse.

The issue of eating food sacrificed to idols, inferred in Num. 25.2, is of significance for a couple of reasons. On the level of the narrative, this mention introduces the theme of idolatry, one that is very prominent in the Apocalypse. Not only will there be an additional mention of eating food sacrificed to idols (2.20), but also idols (9.20) and idolaters (21.8; 22.15). But what exactly would the idea of eating food sacrificed to idols mean to the hearers? The Numbers text indicates that such activity occurred in the context of offering sacrifices to idols. Given the attention this theme receives in the Apocalypse, such a context is certainly a possibility. However, the case might not be so clearcut, as food sacrificed to idols was widely available in a variety of other contexts in first century Asia. This would be particularly true of Pergamum, owing to the prominence of its many religious centers. Among these other possible contexts would be public feasts, where food earlier sacrificed to idols would be distributed to the populace. Civic and religious banquets of various sorts would often include the symbolic presence of a particular deity and, consequently, an offering to him or her. In addition, food available in the local market often came from surplus meat earlier sacrificed to a particular deity. The temptation to participate in one or more of these activities would be strong for believers seeking to make their way within the social and commercial life of Pergamum. It is not altogether clear if the language of the Apocalypse would allow for a position with regard to such food as one finds in the Pauline admonition of 1 Cor. 10.25-30, though it appears most likely from the language that the Apocalypse adheres to a more rigid approach.

The other primary activity associated with the teaching of Balaam is sexual immorality, an enormously important theme in the Apocalypse. From the Numbers text the hearers would be prone to take the reference to 'sexual immorality' literally, as this seems to be its primary meaning there. However, it is also clear that this imagery functions metaphorically at a number of places in the Apocalypse to denote religious infidelity, a not uncommon image in the OT. As with any number of terms and images within the Johannine literature, it is possible that reference to sexual immorality may convey both ideas; a lax attitude toward issues of sexual purity and an unfaithfulness with regard to commitment to Jesus. At any rate, the occurrence of this term anticipates the theme's later development (2.20, 21; 9.21; 14.8; 17.2, 4; 18.3; 19.2; 21.8; 22.15), culminating in the appearance of the Great Πόρνη ('whore') (17.1, 5, 15, 16; 19.2).

Before leaving a discussion of Balaam, one final observation should be offered. Perhaps the intertext that results in v. 14, where despite Balaam's faithful prophesying he is only remembered for his leading the children of Israel astray, would convey to the hearers a warning that despite any prophetic activity that comes from their own Balaam, in the end all that will be remembered is his own involvement in leading 'Israel' astray. Such a parallel would not likely be lost on the hearers.

Verse 15 – The second activity against which Jesus speaks is closely related to the first, 'so, you also have some who are holding to the teaching of the Nicolaitans as well'. For a second time the Nicolaitans are mentioned by Jesus. Earlier, he told the church at Ephesus that he hated their works (2.6). Here they are grouped alongside the teaching of Balaam. From their previous mention and their association here with Balaam, they are clearly viewed in an antagonistic position to Jesus and his followers. At the same time, it is not altogether clear that the hearers know anything more about the Nicolaitans than they did before their second mention. For, unless they are to be identified with the teaching and practices of Balaam, which is grammatically possible, they continue to be cloaked in ambiguity.[35] If the Nicolaitans are to be identified with the teaching of Balaam, there would be an emphasis upon their 'prophetic' claims, as well as advocating an accommodating view toward the surrounding pagan society.

Verse 16 – In keeping with the order established in the message to the church in Ephesus, these words of rebuke are followed by a call to repentance on the part of the church. On this occasion, such repentance would no doubt involve a repudiation of the teaching of Balaam and the Nicolaitans, which Jesus himself repudiates. As before (2.5b), failure to repent will be met by an eschatological fate, with the words, 'I will come to you quickly', conveying such a

---

[35] On this cf. Mounce, *The Book of Revelation*, p. 98.

meaning. Whereas the warning received by the church at Ephesus was directed to the entire church, here the warning seems to be directed to those who continue to hold to the teaching of Balaam and the Nicolaitans. For Jesus here uses the words, 'I will make war with them', not you. The occurrence of war language at this point introduces the hearers to a major theme within the Apocalypse, where the verb form (12.7; 13.4; 17.4; 19.11) and noun form (9.7, 9; 11.7; 12.7, 17; 13.7; 16.14; 19.19; 20.8) appear often. While an immediate visit by Jesus in judgment is not ruled out altogether, such significant occurrences of this terminology in eschatological contexts further supports the eschatological nature of the judgment spoken of to the church at Pergamum. The instrument of war on this occasion is the same instrument described at the beginning of this prophetic message, 'the sword of my mouth'. Several ideas converge at this point. First, there is an obvious reference to the prophetic mouth of Jesus, which is able to speak and to bring judgment. Significantly, it is with this sword that Jesus will destroy the nations who oppose him (19.15, 21). Second, the convergence of this sword and that of the angel of the Lord in the Balaam story would underscore the fact that such a fate awaits any prophetic figures who mislead God's people as had Balaam. Third, perhaps the hearers would also pick up on the contrast between the sword which comes from Jesus' mouth to make war and the one possessed by the Roman ruler of Pergamum, who can judge but for a while. Perhaps it should be noted that unlike the prophetic message to the church in Ephesus (2.6), this call for repentance is not softened in any way. It stands without final words of commendation.

Verse 17 – For a third time in the book, Jesus' prophetic message concludes with a call to discerning obedience. What is the Spirit saying to (all) the churches through this prophetic message to the church in Pergamum? Clearly, the churches are to keep the words of this prophecy by holding on to Jesus' name even in the face of Satan's rule, even in the face of death. They may also be kept by repenting of any identification with the teaching of Balaam or the Nicolaitans, which would encourage accommodation to the surrounding world. The lines of demarcation between the church and the world must be clear; otherwise one faces imminent judgment.

The eschatological promise made to those who overcome on this occasion includes two items. Initially, Jesus promises to give such a one 'the hidden manna'. This promise would connect with the hearers at several levels. First, mention of manna would remind the hearers of the gracious gift of God to Israel in the wilderness. This provision was ongoing until Israel left the wilderness and entered into the land of promise (Exodus 16; Josh. 5.12). That Jesus promises those who overcome such a provision underscores the eschatological nature of the gift. Second, the description of the manna as 'hidden' would also be of significance. As was well known, the manna given by God would not last until the next day, except on the Sabbath. Yet, God instructs Moses to take some of the manna for future generations as a testimony of God's gracious provisions. This manna was preserved, despite the fact that it would normally spoil if kept longer than commanded. That Jesus promises manna he describes as hidden would both remind the hearers of the miraculous nature of the divinely preserved manna and also point forward to the eschatological nature of his manna. Third, the Johannine hearers would also be aware of the close connection between the manna in the wilderness that God gave (Jn 6.31, 49) and the bread from heaven which is given by and is Jesus (6.29, 33, 35, 50-51). If one eats his flesh and drinks his blood, such a one has eternal life (6.53-58). If there is a subtle hint that Jesus gives of himself in giving the overcomer to eat of the tree of life in Rev. 2.7, the hint is less subtle in 2.17. Fourth, neither would it be lost on the hearers that in contrast to those who eat food sacrificed to idols, those who overcome are promised supernatural provision of an eschatological nature. Finally, the promise of the hidden manna may also point forward to the marriage supper of the Lamb (19.9).

In addition to the hidden manna, Jesus promises to give the overcomer 'a white stone and upon the stone a new name written which no one knows but the one who receives it'. It would not surprise the hearers to learn that Jesus promises to give a 'white' stone as this color would indicate a high degree of solidarity with Jesus, whose head and hair are earlier described as white as wool and snow, and with any number of other white objects.[36] Though the

---

[36] Murphy (*Fallen Is Babylon*, p. 133) notes, 'The whiteness of the stone fits well with the use of white in the rest of Revelation. White appears twenty-one times in Revelation, symbolizing purity, that is, fitness for entering the heavenly world where God is enthroned, and readiness for being part of the new Jerusalem. It represents victory over evil and the joy of communion with God and

meaning of the stone is somewhat debatable, its significance is clearly connected to that which is written upon it, 'a new name'. While it is possible that the new name mentioned is a new name for the overcomer, as when Jesus renames Peter in the FG (Jn 1.42), for several reasons it is more likely that these ambiguous words would be taken as having reference to Jesus' new name.[37] First, this initial occurrence of the word 'new' in the book, introduces the hearers to a universe of 'new' things they will encounter in the Apocalypse.[38] These include the New Jerusalem (Rev. 3.12; 21.2), Jesus' new name (3.12), new songs sung in heaven (5.9; 14.3), a new heaven and a new earth (21.1), and the fact that all things are made new (21.5). Second, Jesus will again make reference to his new name in a later prophetic message, where he promises to write his new name on the one who overcomes (3.12). Third, it would be most significant that those who have been described as holding to Jesus' name at the beginning of this message (2.12) are promised his name as an eschatological reality as the message ends (2.17). Fourth, the fact that the name is only known to those who receive it anticipates the new song sung, that no one else could learn except the 144,000 who had been redeemed from the earth (14.14). The sense of experiential and/or existential knowledge appears to be the same in each case. In any event, the recipient of such a stone stands in continuity with Jesus and his future.

To the Angel of the Church in Thyatira (2.18-29)
Verse 18 – Continuing without delay, Jesus instructs John next to write to the angel of the church in Thyatira, using the identical construction used in 2.1, 2.8, and 2.12 with reference to Ephesus, Smyrna, and Pergamum, respectively. As the hearers encounter the name Thyatira, they are led to the next lampstand, though this time they turn south, as Thyatira is located some 40 miles southeast of Pergamum. Perhaps they think of a former military outpost located in the broad and fertile Lycus valley. Or perhaps they think of the image found on its coins of a warrior with an axe ready to smash

---

Christ. The color white figures in the vision of Christ (1.14 [three times]), the white garments of the saved (3.4, 5, 18; 6.11; 7.9, 13, 14), Christ's white horse for the final battle (19.11), the garb of the heavenly army (19.14 [twice]), and the great white throne on which God sits at the end of time (20.11)'.

[37] Beale, *The Book of Revelation*, pp. 254-56.
[38] Wall, *Revelation*, p. 76.

his enemies. Perhaps they think of the numerous industries and professional trade guilds located there, well known in Asia. Or perhaps the hearers are conscious that since there are seven churches to be addressed, the message to the church in Thyatira is the central one, and conceivably the most important.[39] The fact that this prophetic message turns out to be the longest of the seven would be corroborating evidence of its importance.

Whatever the hearers think of, with regard to Thyatira, they soon find out what Jesus thinks. Before Jesus identifies himself by means of elements familiar to the hearers from John's description of his inaugural vision of Jesus, as in the first three prophetic messages, he introduces himself by means of a different phrase, the Son of God. While such a departure from his established convention might take the hearers by some surprise, they would certainly be familiar with this title from other places in the Johannine tradition (Jn 1.18, 34, 49; 3.16-18, 35; 5.25; 10.36; 11.4, 27; 19.7; 20.31), 1 Jn (1.3, 7; 2.22-24; 3.8, 23; 4.9-10, 14-15; 5.1, 9-13, 20), and 2 Jn (3, 9). By use of this title, Jesus underscores yet again his intimate relationship to 'the One who sits on the throne'. Included in the stunning inaugural vision of Jesus are elements that point to a connection between this Son of Man and Daniel's Ancient of Days. By use of the title Son of God, this relationship is made even more explicit, if such were possible! Although this is the only occurrence of this title in the Apocalypse, it also fits nicely with other statements about the relationship between the Father and the Son in the book (1.6; 2.28; 3.5, 21; 14.1). The appearance of this title, along with the words 'my Father', form an inclusio of sorts for the message to this church.

Picking back up on the previously established pattern, Jesus again describes himself with elements taken from the inaugural vision. Here he is described as 'the One who has his eyes as flaming fire and his feet as glowing brass'. Mention of his flaming eyes, a direct quote from the earlier vision, remind the hearers of his penetrating prophetic vision. Likewise, the mention of his feet, again a direct quote though one which omits the phrase 'as in a refining furnace', point to Jesus' strength and stability. Thus, the hearers could hardly experience this description without being reminded of

---

[39] Charles, *The Revelation of St. John* I, pp. 67-68 and Murphy, *Fallen Is Babylon*, p. 133.

the earlier stunning vision of Jesus. Consequently, the impact of his prophetic words that follow would be all the more powerful.

Verse 19 – For a second time, Jesus' 'I know' statement makes reference to 'your works' (2.2), the first of six occurrences of the term in this message. In fact, the first portion of this prophetic message (v. 19) begins and ends with reference to their works. Jesus' knowledge of their works reveals the most comprehensive list of works to be found in any of the seven prophetic messages in these two chapters. Specifically, the church at Thyatira is commended for their love, faith, service, and patient endurance. The mention of the church's love connects with the hearers at various levels. They have already been introduced to this language in the letter's greetings, where reference is made to Jesus' love for the Johannine believers. Such love is foundational for the community. The hearers have also encountered this terminology in Jesus' rebuke of the church in Ephesus (2.4), a church that left its first love. The commendation of the church at Thyatira for its love indicates that it is in solidarity with Jesus who loved them. It reveals that they exemplify the characteristic identified by Jesus as most essential in Johannine discipleship, 'By this all will know that you are my disciples, if you have love for one another' (Jn 13.35). It is difficult to imagine a higher commendation in the Johannine community. At the same time, such a commendation appears to place the church in Thyatira in contrast with the church at Ephesus, who had forsaken their first love. The intentionality of this contrast becomes even more apparent as the message continues. The church at Thyatira is also commended for its τὴν πίστιν ('faith'). As the hearers know, in the Johannine literature generally and the Apocalypse in particular, this term is very closely associated with the idea of faithfulness[40] and the idea of faithful witness. Generally speaking, it appears that 'faith' in the Apocalypse is intimately connected with patient endurance and overcoming. Thus, not only does the church in Thyatira identify with Jesus, who is love, but with the kind of faith(fulness) which he too possesses (2.13) and has demonstrated as a faithful witness.

Jesus also commends the church for its τὴν διακονίαν ('service'). While it is not altogether clear what this term would convey

---

[40] Prigent, *L'Apocalypse de Saint Jean*, p. 139.

to the hearers, it is likely that its meaning would be distinctively Johannine. Attempts to define the term in the light of its occurrences in other NT literature, though well intended, may not necessarily be as helpful as seeking for hints in the Johannine literature. Two clues may indicate something of the term's meaning for the hearers. In the FG, the verbal form of the term occurs in passages fraught with allusions as well as explicit references to Jesus' death (Jn 12.2, 26). In point of fact, the disciples are instructed that whoever would serve Jesus, such a one must follow him. The immediate context makes clear that following Jesus entails following him in death, giving his life. For 'the one who loves his life will lose it, and the one who hates his life in this world will keep it unto eternal life' (Jn 12.25).[41] The term's appearance in Rev. 2.19, alongside 'love' and 'patient endurance', would be in keeping with this emphasis found in the FG. At the same time, it is just possible that this term may convey a bit more to the hearers. For διακονίαν ('service') is one of several Greek terms used to denote service of one kind or another. Thus, it is related to the term δοῦλος ('servant') that regularly appears in the Apocalypse, sometimes with the meaning of 'prophet'. It may very well be that the term 'service' would on this occasion convey to the hearers both the idea of loving service[42] manifested in one's faithfulness unto death as well as the service of prophetic vocation, which is intricately connected to the former. The church at Thyatira is also commended for its 'faithful endurance', a term which draws the experience of John (1.9), the church at Ephesus (2.2, 3), the church of Thyatira, and Jesus (3.10) together. This work is a defining one for the saints in the Apocalypse (13.10; 14.12) and reveals something of the steadfastness of the church's life and witness for Jesus. Along with the other works delineated, this commendation reveals the extraordinary nature of this church.

The commendation of the church at Thyatira concludes with an affirmation of the progressive nature of the church's works, 'and your last works are more than your first ones'. These words would again remind the hearers of the contrast between this church and the church in Ephesus, who left its first love. In fact, Jesus calls the Ephesian church back to its first works, owing to the place from

---

[41] A. Weiser, 'διακονέω', *EDNT*, I, p. 304

[42] For this dimension of the term cf. H. Beyer, 'διακονία', *TDNT*, II, p. 87.

which it has fallen (2.4-5). By contrast, the works of the church in Thyatira is ever increasing. Perhaps the hearers would even take such praise as an indication that the church brought forth more fruit as a result of their remaining in Jesus (Jn 15.2). As noted earlier, this section of the message both begins and ends with a reference to 'works'.

Verse 20 – Given such stellar praise the hearers might be a bit surprised to encounter for a third time in these four prophetic messages the phrase, 'But I have against you', indicating that words of rebuke are to follow. By this phrase, they are reminded once more of the dialectic created by the tension of the call to faithful witness in the face of temptation to compromise that witness in some way. The specifics of the dialectic on this occasion are revealed as this message unfolds. Jesus' words of rebuke focus upon a particular 'prophetic' figure, her teaching and practices, and those who align themselves with her and her activity. The church at Thyatira 'tolerates the woman Jezebel, who says of herself that she is a prophetess'. Jesus' choice of the word ἀφεῖς ('tolerate') to describe the action of the church is quite an interesting one. It does not necessarily convey the idea of active participation, but rather of permitting, or allowing something or someone to continue, as with the words of the chief priests and Pharisees about Jesus: 'If we leave him alone (tolerate him), all will believe in him' (Jn 11.48). This term is the first hint to the hearers that toleration of the false prophetess may be the extent of their inappropriate activity. However, as will be seen, such toleration has eternal consequences. The construction, which follows, indicates that the harm is not in tolerating a woman or women in general, but of the particular woman 'Jezebel'. The name 'Jezebel' appears to have been assigned to this woman by Jesus himself, as the One whose eyes of fire has penetrating prophetic insight. The significance of this name for the hearers would in itself indicate why toleration of such a person is inappropriate, for the name reminds them of one of the arch enemies of Israel, the wife of Ahab, the opponent of the prophet Elijah. Ahab's marriage to Jezebel, daughter of Ethbaal the king of the Sidonians, resulted in his adopting Baal worship, going so far as to erect an altar and temple for Baal in Samaria (1 Kgs 16.31-32). Jezebel's impact is not confined to offering sacrifices to foreign gods (which implies eating meat sacrificed to them), she is remembered years later in the LXX

(2 Kgs 9.22) as promoting πορνεῖαι ('sexual immoralities') and φάρμακα ('sorceries'). For Jesus to name this woman 'Jezebel' is enough to alert the hearers as to her true identity and perhaps to suggest that their discernment with regard to this figure was lacking.

After learning of Jesus' assessment of 'Jezebel', the hearers learn of the claims she makes for herself. The language used is reminiscent of that found in 2.2 of those who say of themselves to be apostles, but after testing by the church have been found to be liars instead. It is also reminiscent of that found in 2.9 of those who claim to be Jews and are not, but are a synagogue of Satan. As such, it reminds the hearers that one's claims with regard to one's spirituality are not always in keeping with Jesus' own penetrating insight and knowledge. On this occasion, the problem is not that the claims come from a woman, for given the nature and role of women within the community it is altogether likely that women were numbered among the prophets in this prophetic community. Rather, the problem is with her activity and lifestyle. 'Jezebel' 'teaches and deceives my servants to commit sexual immorality and to eat food sacrificed to idols'. Perhaps the first thing to strike Johannine hearers would be the fact that 'Jezebel' teaches. For within the Johannine tradition, 'teaching' is the exclusive domain of Jesus (Jn 1.38, 49; 3.2; 4.31; 6.25, 59; 7.14, 28, 35; 8.20; 9.2; 11.8, 28; 13.13-14; 18.20; 20.16; 2 Jn 9), the Father (Jn 6.45; 8.28), and the Paraclete/Chrisma (Jn 14.26; 1 Jn 2.27). In point of fact, outside of one reference to John (the Baptist) as 'Rabbi', there are no positive examples of human teachers to be found in the Johannine literature.[43] Rather, she stands in line with the antichrists and deceivers (1 Jn 2.27), Balaam (Rev. 2.14), and the Nicolaitans (2.15) in her attempts to teach. Not only does she 'teach' but also she 'deceives'. Again, Johannine hearers encounter a term familiar to their ears, owing to its prominent place in 1-2 John, here deception is the exclusive domain of the community's opponents (1 Jn 1.8; 2.26; 3.7; 4.6; 2 Jn 7). There the deception had to do with the fact that they were not able to confess 'Jesus coming in the flesh'. While there is no indication that such deceptive Christological teaching was part of the teaching of 'Jezebel', mention of her deceiving my servants does stand in

---

[43] Cf. the negative attribution of the title 'teacher of Israel' to Nicodemus in Jn 3.10.

solidarity with others who deceive in the Apocalypse; namely, Satan (12.9; 20.3, 8, 10), the second beast/false prophet (13.14; 19.20), and the Great Whore (18.23). The deception of which Jesus speaks is so dangerous, that even his servants, the prophets, are susceptible to the teaching of 'Jezebel'. Perhaps such imagery would shake the hearers to their core, to think that servants/prophets of God could be deceived to take the side of Jezebel instead of Elijah. No doubt, the prospect of the Mt. Carmel events is part of this mental picture, functioning as an implicit warning with regard to such an association. Specifically, she advocates sexual immorality and eating food sacrificed to idols, the very activities promoted by 'Balaam'. Given Thyatira's dependence upon professional trade guilds and industries, where commercial activities inevitably led to participation in banquets honoring the gods, such temptations to accommodate were very real indeed. No doubt, the positions of 'Jezebel' were quite appealing indeed. Neither can it be ruled out that such accommodation led to immoral sexual activities.

Perhaps it would strike the hearers that the church in Thyatira continues to stand in contrast to the church in Ephesus. Earlier, Thyatira compared favorably, owing to its persistence in love and its last works which are more than the first. Now, however, the comparison is unfavorable, owing to the fact that the church in Ephesus was able to discern that those who claimed to be apostles were in reality liars, while Thyatira could not discern that the woman who claimed to be a prophetess was in actuality 'Jezebel'.

Verse 21 – If the church's relationship with 'Jezebel' has been one of toleration, Jesus' relationship can be described as giving her time. While these relationships might seem similar, they are different in at least one significant fashion. Jesus does not give her space to operate, but he gives her time 'in order that she might repent'. It is not altogether clear how or when time was given to 'Jezebel' to repent. Owing to the dynamics of the Johannine community, perhaps this came forth from Jesus in a prophetic utterance in the context of community worship. Or, perhaps a prophetic figure within the community had confronted the woman with these words of Jesus.[44] Or, perhaps John himself was involved in conveying Jesus' words to 'Jezebel'. In any event, the hearers would be left in no

---

[44] Osborne, *Revelation*, p. 158.

doubt that Jesus had given 'Jezebel' sufficient time to repent. Initially, the hearers might take this statement as a call to repentance consistent with other calls for repentance found in the messages to Ephesus (2.5) and Pergamum (2.16). But if this is the hearers' initial take on these words, they quickly find that this call for repentance will have more in common with later occurrences of this word, where a variety of individuals refuse to repent (8.3, 19; 9.20, 21; 16.9, 11). For Jesus reveals that despite the time and opportunity given for her to repent, 'she does not desire to repent of τῆς πορνείας αὐτῆς ('her sexual immorality'). Not only do the hearers learn that 'Jezebel' has no intention or willingness to repent,[45] they also learn that her teaching 'my servants' (to commit sexual immorality) grows out of her own identity (and practice of sexual immorality). From this identity and activity she has no intention of repenting. Such a description of 'Jezebel' and her activities prepares the hearers for their encounter with the Great Whore later in the book. Thus, the hearers encounter their first example of obstinate disobedience.

Verse 22 – The next portion of this prophetic message (vv. 22-25), which is clearly defined by a couple of literary markers, conveys Jesus' intentions for the woman, her lovers, her children, and the rest of those in Thyatira. The hearers would pick up on the fact that these verses stand together, as near the beginning and the end of this section are Jesus' words, βάλλω ('I cast') and οὐ βάλλω ('I will not cast/place'). One result of this construction is that Jesus' promised actions to and upon a variety of individuals are held together in both solidarity and contrast.

As for the obstinate sexually immoral 'Jezebel', Jesus says, 'I will cast her upon a bed'. Such graphic language is suggestive at two levels. The phrase could be taken to mean, 'I will place her upon a bed', which would be a usual place for a sexually immoral person. For a bed is the place where such activity would normally take place, as the following statement makes clear. However, the phrase βάλλω αὐτὴν εἰς κλίνην ('I will cast her upon a bed') can also be taken as an idiom which means 'I will cast her upon a sick bed'.[46]

---

[45] Perhaps she saw no need to repent as Murphy (*Fallen Is Babylon*, p. 137) notes.

[46] Cf. F.G. Untergassmair, 'κλίνη', *EDNT*, II, p. 300.

The idea that Jesus would bring punishment for sin upon an individual is consistent with Johannine thought, where at least one infirmity is the result of sin (Jn 5.14).[47] 'Jezebel' will suffer physically for her obstinate disobedience.

Not only will 'Jezebel' be cast onto a sick bed, but 'those who commit adultery with her (will be cast) into great tribulation if they do not repent of her works'. The language of sexual immorality gives way to the related language of adultery. By speaking of those who commit adultery with 'Jezebel', Jesus conveys at least two things to the hearers. First, adultery language carries with it the idea of participation in illicit sexual activities, here represented by 'Jezebel' and her teaching. Second, adultery language implies more than inappropriate sexual activity, for it also conveys the idea of unfaithfulness on the part of the ones who commit adultery. Specifically, this imagery suggests that such ones were at one time part of the community but have been unfaithful to their legitimate partner, committing adultery with 'Jezebel' instead. Just as 'Jezebel' is to be punished, so those who commit adultery with her will be cast into great tribulation. To this point in the Apocalypse, those who share in tribulation have been those who have sought to be faithful witnesses to Jesus like John (1.9) and the church at Smyrna (2.9, 10). On those occasions it appears certain that the suffering experienced comes at the hands of Satan and those who stand with him. However, the suffering that awaits those who commit adultery with 'Jezebel' comes from the hand of Jesus. Such an ominous statement, not only underscores the need for repentance by such individuals, but also anticipates the wrath of the Lamb described later in the book (6.16). At the same time, the language of 'great tribulation' may also indicate something of the eschatological nature of such a judgment, a judgment that is imminent. Yet, just as 'Jezebel' was given time to repent, so those who commit adultery are given an opportunity to repent. They need not share her fate provided they repent of her works. Reference to the 'works' of 'Jezebel', for which

---

[47] On this whole question cf. J.C. Thomas, *The Devil, Disease, and Deliverance: Origins of Illness in New Testament Thought* (Cleveland: CPT Press, 2011), pp. 81-113. It may also not be without significance that the condition of the man born blind is said to have occurred 'in order that the works of God might be manifest in him' (9.3) and Lazarus' condition is 'in order that the Son of God might be glorified through him' (11.4).

repentance is called, stand in strong contrast to the works commended by Jesus in v. 19, which should be emulated. The choice between these 'works' is stark and makes all the difference. The repentance here called for would doubtless involve a repudiation of those activities that would compromise their faithful witness. Despite any social and/or commercial repercussions, absolute faithfulness to Jesus, the faithful witness, is required.

Verse 23 – As for her children Jesus says ἀποκτενῶ ἐν θανάτῳ ('I will kill in death/with a plague'). This phrase could have one of two meanings.[48] It can be taken as an idiom meaning, 'I will surely kill', indicating the certainty of the promised death. Or, it can be translated as 'I will kill with a plague' as appears to be the phrase's meaning in Rev. 6.8. How would the hearers take the phrase? Perhaps it might not be going too far to suggest that both meanings would register with the hearers. On the one hand, none of them would doubt the certainty of the fulfillment of such words. On the other hand, the idea that the children of 'Jezebel' might suffer death owing to a plague, would not be out of keeping with the sickness with which their mother is to be struck. In point of fact, both ideas seem to be present in this phrase. Who are the children of 'Jezebel'? Although it is possible to take this phrase as having reference to her physical children, given the metaphorical nature of the passage, it is likely that 'children' also function metaphorically. But who are they metaphorically? If those who commit adultery with 'Jezebel' are unfaithful members of the Johannine community, then it would appear that her children are likely those born of her sexual immorality.[49] Such ones would undoubtedly bear the characteristics of their mother with regard to sexual immorality and eating food sacrificed to idols, and would likely be the heirs who would continue her works. If such ones were ever a part of the Johannine community, there are no hints of that in the text. Given their fate, they seem to be wholly identified with their mother. The severity of the punishment described would be yet another point at which the experience of the church in Thyatira would intersect with the story of 'Jezebel' in the OT. Not only would it be difficult for the hearers not to be reminded of the slaughter of Ahab's children (his seventy sons – 2

---

[48] Aune, *Revelation 1-5*, p. 198.
[49] Smalley, *The Revelation to John*, p. 75.

Kgs 10.1-11), but it would also be a powerful reminder of the certainty of the fate prophesied.[50] As Elijah's words had come to pass, how much more the words of Jesus!

The significance of these words of warning and judgment should not be lost on any of the hearers, for the resurrected Jesus next addresses all the churches at once. 'And all the churches will know that I Am the one who searches minds and hearts, and I will give to you each according to your works'. This sentence is significant for several reasons. First, it indicates that what happens in Thyatira has significance for all the churches everywhere and that his actions at Thyatira have a testamentary nature for all.[51] Second, it reinforces the idea that the Apocalypse is in reality one circular letter, the contents of which is important to all its hearers. Third, Jesus uses the ἐγώ εἰμι ('I Am') formula, well-known from the FG, which here lays claim to his intimate identity with the Father, who also uses the words with reference to himself in the Apocalypse (1.8). Fourth, this emphasis is reinforced by the way in which Jesus further identifies himself as 'the one who searches minds and hearts', as very similar constructions are used to describe the activity of God at various places in the OT (Ps. 7.10 [9]; Jer. 11.20; 17.10; 20.12). Such an association makes his activity in this regard all the more powerful. Fifth, the fact that Jesus introduces himself in Rev. 2.18 as the One whose eyes are as fire coincides with, and may be the basis of his ability to search the inner recesses of individuals and churches. At any rate, the hearers would hardly be surprised that he is able to search minds and hearts. Perhaps it should also be noted that Jesus will see/know what is in the heart of the Great Whore in 18.7. Sixth, Jesus' promise to 'give to you each according to your works' heightens the level of his hearers' awareness with regard to whether they will align themselves with the works he commends or the works he will judge in Thyatira. The use of emphatic second person plural language also serves to underscore the fact that such words occur in direct address. At the same time, this phrase aptly describes in summary fashion, the criterion that is the basis of Jesus' discerning judgment in all the churches. Finally, the structural location of these words is not without significance. Located midway

---

[50] Beale, *The Book of Revelation*, pp. 263-64.
[51] Smalley, *The Revelation to John*, p. 75.

through this prophetic message that is located midway through the seven prophetic messages, these words of Jesus take on an even more universal quality. For they are not only directed to the church at Thyatira, but are also explicitly directed to all the churches of the Apocalypse. In point of fact, these words serve as a summary of Jesus' activity among the lampstands; searching minds and hearts, giving according to one's works. The statement may indeed be the theological zenith of the seven prophetic messages.

Verse 24 – With these centrally located words ringing in their ears, this section of the message (vv. 22-25) continues with attention now focused upon 'the rest of you in Thyatira'. For a third time in the last seven words, the term 'you' again appears, underscoring the connection between the rewards 'you' receive according to 'your' works, and the admonition to 'you' which follows. These words also make clear that not all in the church in Thyatira have committed adultery with 'Jezebel'. 'The rest' are quickly identified by Jesus as 'those who do not have this teaching'. Unlike those who hold to the teaching of Balaam and those who hold to the teaching of the Nicolaitans, the rest in Thyatira do not have the teaching of 'Jezebel'. This statement reinforces the idea that the fault of the church at Thyatira is the toleration of 'Jezebel', not active participation with her. 'Not having this teaching' means that they do not 'know the deep things of Satan'. Clearly, in this verse, 'the deep things of Satan' are viewed as synonymous with 'this teaching' of 'Jezebel'. However, it is not at all clear what the 'deep things of Satan' are or how the hearers would understand this reference. It is possible that these words of the resurrected Jesus reflect his prophetic insight whereby he assigns names that reflect the true identity of those he encounters (2.9, 14, 20). On this view, Jesus' words imply that though they may make claims to know the 'deep things of God', in reality they know the 'deep things of Satan'. While such a meaning would be in keeping with the broader phenomenon in the Apocalypse, there is one aspect of the verse that tends to subvert this meaning, the phrase, 'as they say', which follows. Normally, when certain false claims are being made by those deemed to be opponents in the Apocalypse, one encounters the phrase, 'who say of themselves to be', or something very much like it. Owing to this pattern, what one might expect here something like 'who say of themselves to know the deep things of God, but they do not. Rather, they know the deep things of Satan'. The absence of such a formulation and the presence of the phrase, 'as they say', combine to suggest that 'Jezebel' and her associates indeed claimed to know the 'deep things of Satan'. What such a claim entails is difficult to determine. It may be inferred from the terminology that these 'deep things' were not known by everyone, but only by those who identified with 'Jezebel'. It is likely that they would have something to do with attitude and teaching of 'Jezebel' toward eating food sacrificed to idols and sexual immorality, perhaps being the basis of such belief and practices. Perhaps knowledge of Satan's deep things was believed to enable believers to participate in commercial and social activities with immunity. Perhaps it was thought that such knowledge would nullify his powers or at the least allow believers to avoid areas and actions where they would be most vulnerable. In the end, while it is impossible to know exactly what such knowledge entails, it would not be lost on the hearers that just as the churches in Smyrna and Pergamum have to contend with Satan, so the church in Thyatira. As such, 'Jezebel' and those who stand with her are seen by Jesus as in association with Satan's work elsewhere; his synagogue and his throne.

The hearers are alerted to the fact that this section of the message, vv. 22-25, is drawing to a close by Jesus' next words οὐ βάλλω ('I will not cast/place'). Just as the section begins with reference to the fact that Jesus would cast 'Jezebel' upon a bed of suffering and those who commit adultery with her into great tribulation, it concludes with his words that he will not cast another burden upon the rest of those in Thyatira. There would be at least two significant things about this statement for the hearers. First, there appears to be a certain word play in the Greek text at this point between βαθέα ('deep things'), βάλλω ('I will cast'), and βάρος ('burden'). This word play suggests a direct connection between the activity of the hearers in Thyatira and Jesus' subsequent action; since the rest of the Thyatirans do not know the deep things of Satan, Jesus will not cast another burden upon them. Second, the hearers would likely be struck by the convergence of language about sexual immorality and eating food sacrificed to idols and Jesus' refusal to place another burden upon them. Such a convergence of ideas and words occur elsewhere in the NT. In Acts 15.28-29, a decision was reached with regard to appropriate Gentile Christian behavior in order to promote table fellowship with Jewish Christians. The agreement was to abstain from 'food sacrificed to idols, blood, strangled food, and sexual immorality'. The convergence of the words βάρος ('burden'), εἰδωλοθύτων ('food sacrificed to idols'), πορνείας ('sexual immorality') in both passages is striking at the least. It may even indicate something of the direction the resurrected Jesus desired for the Johannine believers to take in attempting to discern their relationship with their culture, especially with regard to these two issues. Such would confirm the non-accommodating approach advocated in the Apocalypse.

Verse 25 – The final words of this section of the message call for specific action on the church's part. 'In any case, that which you have, hold until I come'. While they do not have the teaching of 'Jezebel', they do have certain things, identified earlier (2.19) as love, faith(fulness), service, and patient endurance. Owing to the fact that their last works have been more than their first, these words call for the church at Thyatira to continue with such works until Jesus comes. Perhaps the command κρατήσατε ('hold') would convey the promise of divine assistance as this word is found as part of the divine title παντοκράτωρ ('all powerful one').[52] Such language would perhaps remind the hearers of Jesus' earlier call for faithfulness unto death (2.10) and his promises to come to two of the churches in judgment (2.5, 16). The same kind of faithfulness is here implied, whilst the reference to his coming is obviously comforting and points to his eschatological advent more clearly than in the other messages.

Verses 26-28 – For the first time in the prophetic messages, the promise to the overcomers precedes the call for discerning obedience, indicating a change in order that will be followed in the next three messages as well. It is difficult to determine the precise significance of this subtle change within the messages for the hearers, though they would no doubt be a bit surprised by this new order. Perhaps such an inversion would underscore the significance of discerning obedience by focusing attention a bit more on this dimension than the promise of rewards.[53] This inversion may also have some structural significance, owing to the way in which this

---

[52] Simoens, *Apocalypse de Jean*, p. 33.
[53] Murphy, *Fallen Is Babylon*, p. 142.

seven is divided into the sub-groups of three and four, as opposed to the subsequent divisions of the sevens into groups of four and three.[54] Such a subtle move indicates that this first series of sevens is distinct from the following series of sevens. This point is reinforced by the fact that the other series of sevens all appear in the section governed by the 'in the Spirit' phrase found in 4.2.

In the identification of the one who overcomes in Thyatira several elements converge, for the one who overcomes is 'the one who keeps my works until the end'. The language of keeping is familiar to the hearers from its earlier occurrence in the admonition to keep the words of this prophecy (1.3). By means of such an active and sustained response the hearers share in the beatitude spoken by Jesus on that occasion. Here, the idea of keeping is combined with the theme of works, the sixth and final occurrence of this term in the message to the church in Thyatira. Earlier, the church is commended by Jesus for both the quantity and quality of their works (2.19). In the center of the passage (2.23), Jesus makes clear that works are the basis of the future judgment of the hearers. Now, the earlier works are identified as Jesus' own works. No doubt, the hearers would understand their works to stand in some continuity with his works. A third Johannine element to appear in this phrase are found in the words ἄχρι τέλους ('until the end'). In this, perhaps the hearers would be reminded of the way Jesus' love is described in the FG 'he loved his own εἰς τέλος'('until the end'). This phrase, which can be translated as 'until the end' or 'completely', likely means both in Jn 13.1.[55] Perhaps the phrase used by Jesus here in the Apocalypse would also emphasize both qualitative and quantitative dimensions, in keeping with the emphasis of 2.19. On this view, the church is both praised for past and present faithfulness, while being encouraged to continue such faithful activity until completion.

To such a one, Jesus says, 'I will give to him authority over the nations'. It would come as no surprise that Jesus would be the one in a position to give authority over the nations as he is 'the ruler of all the kings of the earth' (1.5). In these words is the promise that those who overcome will participate in this activity of Jesus. As the

---

[54] Bauckham, *The Climax of Prophecy*, p. 10.
[55] Thomas, *Footwashing in John 13 and the Johannine Community*, pp. 81-82.

hearers of the Apocalypse will learn, authority is transferred from one figure to another on a great many occasions. However, despite any rivals that may arise, these words will continue to ring in their ears – Jesus will give the one who overcomes authority over the nations. The fact that the overcomers will share in Jesus' rule becomes even clearer as his words of promise continue, for the hearers begin to understand that his words echo those found in Ps. 2.8-9, a psalm widely regarded as a messianic psalm. Not only does the messianic nature of the psalm point in this direction, but on two occasions these very words are also used with reference to Jesus, who 'rules with a rod of iron' (12.5; 19.5). Thus, the connection between Jesus' rule and that of those who overcome is clear. But as the details of this authority are revealed, the hearers understand that this authority is one to be exerted with power, for 'he will rule (shepherd) them with a rod of iron, as he breaks the clay vessels'. At first, the appearance of the word ποιμανεῖ ('rule' or 'shepherd') in the same context as the breaking of vessels to bits might strike the hearers as a bit unexpected if not inappropriate. For the activity of smashing pottery to pieces does not seem to fit the meaning often attributed to 'shepherd'. However, amongst the shepherd's duty was the protection of the sheep, which might involve the use of the rod as a weapon. Just as Jesus' rule will be spoken of as firm, so that shared by those who overcome; it will be firm but sure.[56] Though the church in Thyatira may face the possibility of suffering for Jesus in the present, one day the roles will be reversed and they will rule over the nations with him. In an expression that would remind the hearers of the thought contained in the other Johannine literature, Jesus makes clear that his giving of authority is based upon what he has received from the Father. The same preposition ὡς ('as') that connects the second phrase in v. 27 with the first, now connects the first portion of v. 28 with that which precedes. This construction results in a meaning something like, 'I give … as even I received'. After all, Jesus' Father is the one who gave him authority over all flesh (Jn 17.2) and is the One who sits on *the* throne (Rev. 1.4), a throne he will share with his son (3.21). In addition to authority to rule, Jesus will give to the one who overcomes τὸν ἀστέρα τὸν πρωϊνόν ('the morning star'). Although, reference to Jesus' authori-

---

[56] Skaggs and Benham, *Revelation*, p. 44.

ty over the stars and, therefore, astrology cannot be dismissed, there appears to be more to this promise than that Jesus will give them Venus. For the one who makes this promise is the one who holds the seven stars in his right hand (even as he speaks these words!). But more than this, Jesus will identify himself later in the Apocalypse as 'the morning star' in Rev. 22.16,[57] where this description appears alongside his words 'I am the root and offspring of David', a clear messianic claim. Earlier promises have implied a giving of Jesus himself to those who overcome (2.7, 17).[58] Here, the promise is more explicit, as the identity of overcomer with Jesus appears more extensive.[59]

Verse 29 – For a fourth time in the book, Jesus' prophetic message concludes with a call to discerning obedience. On this occasion, the call to discerning obedience is heightened by the fact that the call follows, rather than precedes the promise to the one who overcomes, and by the fact that previously in this message (v. 23) Jesus makes clear that his message is indeed to all the churches. What is the Spirit saying to all the churches through this prophetic message to the church in Thyatira? Quite obviously, keeping the words of this prophecy are intimately connected to holding to what they have and keeping Jesus' works until completion. Their love, faith(fulness), (prophetic) service, and patient endurance must continue, even as 'Jezebel', her lovers, and her children meet their appointed judgments. The line of demarcation between the church and the surrounding (commercial and social) world is clearly drawn by Jesus. There is to be no toleration of even 'prophetic' figures who advocate a theology of accommodation by means of the deep things of Satan.

To the Angel of the Church in Sardis (3.1-6)

Verse 1 – Continuing without delay, Jesus instructs John next to write to the angel of the church in Sardis, using the identical construction employed in 2.1, 2.8, 2.12, and 2.18 with reference to Ephesus, Smyrna, Pergamum, and Thyatria, respectively. As the

---

[57] Resseguie, *The Revelation of John*, p. 94.

[58] Aune, *Revelation 1-5*, p. 212 and Fee, *Revelation*, p. 44.

[59] If the message to the church in Pergamum is still in the ears of the hearers, perhaps they would see both the star and the scepter as issuing out of Balaam's prophecy in Num. 24.17. Cf. Murphy, *Fallen Is Babylon*, p. 141.

hearers encounter the name Sardis, they are led to the next lampstand, moving southeast, as Sardis is located some thirty miles southeast of Thyatira. What would the hearers think of when they hear the name Sardis? Perhaps they would think of the prosperous city located on the western end of the famous highway that ran all the way from ancient Susa, the former capital of Elam, through Asia (Minor). Or, perhaps they thought of the way the city dominated the rich Hermus valley from its location on the spur of Mt Tmolus. Perhaps they thought of the natural citadel where Sardis was originally located, with rocks that go up some 1,500 feet, forming an almost impregnable defense. Or, perhaps they thought of Roman life reflected in its theatre and stadium. Perhaps they thought about its exceptionally large temple dedicated to Artemis, which was never completed. Or, perhaps they thought about the image of the deified empress Livia, found on coins struck in Sardis, who is viewed as the new mother of prosperity, with a sheaf of grain in her hand. Or, perhaps they thought of the fact that, though impregnable to hostile attack, the city fell twice, once to Cyrus and once to Antiochus the Great, owing to a lack of vigilance on the part of its inhabitants.[60]

Whatever the hearers think of when encountering the name Sardis, they soon find out what Jesus thinks of the church there. For a second consecutive time, the resurrected Jesus first identifies himself by words that are not contained in his description in the inaugural vision. Previously (2.18), he identified himself as the Son of God, a title well known to those familiar with the Johannine tradition. On this occasion, he identifies himself as 'the one who has the Seven Spirits of God and the seven stars'. While not part of the inaugural vision 'the Seven Spirits of God' have been encountered by the hearers in the document's prologue, where they are located 'before his (God's) throne' (1.4) indicating something of the Spirit's very close association with God. This same Spirit is the means by which John receives the revelation, as he is 'in the Spirit on the Lord's Day' (1.10). The words of this same Spirit are coterminous with the words of the resurrected Jesus, as is made clear by the refrain, 'the one who has an ear to hear let that one hear what the

---

[60] Caird, *The Revelation of St. John*, pp. 47-48 and Mounce, *The Book of Revelation*, p. 109.

Spirit is saying to the churches'. Now the intimate connection between Jesus and the Spirit is made even clearer with the phrase, 'the one who has the Seven Spirits of God'. Such a statement not only makes clear the close association between God and the Spirit, but may also be a hint that Jesus now shares the throne with God,[61] a fact explicitly stated later in the seven messages (3.21), and as a result 'has' the Seven Spirits of God. The intimate connection between Jesus and the Spirit becomes even clearer as the Apocalypse unfolds, where the Lamb's seven eyes are described as the Seven Spirits of God sent out into all the earth (5.6). Such an association further underscores his ability to 'search hearts and minds' and see into the inner recesses of men and women. The results of such an ability will become known to the hearers before this first verse is finished.

Not only is he 'the one who has the Seven Spirits of God', but 'the seven stars' as well. This description, modified from its previous occurrences in the vision (1.16) and in the message to the church at Ephesus (2.1), is important in at least two ways. First, Jesus' words about 'having the seven stars' remind the hearers of the location of these stars, his right hand, which is still upon John as Jesus prophetically speaks. This imagery conveys the idea that these messengers are firmly under his control, and consequently, speak truthfully. The one who 'has the seven stars' in his control, is the one who has earlier threatened to remove the lampstand from the church in Ephesus, if the church does not repent. Second, it may not be without significance that the message to the church at Sardis begins and ends with reference to angels, as the seven stars (3.1) have earlier been identified as the seven ἄγγελοι ('angels' or 'messengers') by Jesus (1.20), and the resurrected Jesus mentions angels again in 3.5. Such a structure would not be lost on the hearers. In both occurrences, there appears to be an emphasis upon the truthfulness of Jesus' words to the church at Sardis and in turn to all the churches of the Apocalypse.

It comes as no surprise to the hearers that Jesus' next words are the familiar, 'I know your works'. Not only is this formula known from its earlier occurrences (2.2, 19), but it is also no surprise that

---

[61] A. Yarbro Collins, *The Apocalypse* (NTM 22; Collegeville, MN: Michael Glazier Press, 1979), p. 24.

'the one who has the Sevens Spirits of God and the seven angels' would know the works of this church. These words form an inclusio around the first part of the message (vv. 1-2). What is somewhat surprising to the hearers is the stark nature of Jesus' words that follow. For there are no words of affirmation as there are in the other messages; simply words of rebuke, making this message the most severe judgment amongst the seven messages.[62] 'You have a name that you are alive, and you are dead'. These words would be pregnant with meaning for the hearers. First, the emphasis placed upon the word ὄνομα ('name'), which stands first in the Greek sentence, introduces the hearers to one of the major terms and themes in the passage. Second, perhaps the hearers would pick up on the implicit contrast between Jesus' name, as it has appeared in the messages to the churches in Ephesus and Pergamum, and the name of the church in Sardis. The church in Ephesus bore many things on account of his name (2.3), while the church in Pergamum held firmly to his name, even to the point of death (2.13), and are promised Jesus' name if they overcome (2.17). Here, it is the church that has a name. Third, there also appears to be a contrast between Jesus, who 'has' the Seven Spirits of God and the seven stars, and the church in Sardis that 'has' a name. Fourth, there is a further contrast between Jesus, who was dead and is alive (1.18), and the church in Sardis who has a name that they are alive, but they are in fact dead (3.1). Fifth, it would not be lost on the hearers that Jesus is uniquely qualified to judge those who are alive and those who are dead owing to the fact that he was dead but is now alive (2.8). He is alive; they are not. Sixth, the hearers would likely pick up on the contrast between the name of the church, and the reality of its true identity. Such prophetic insight on Jesus' part would no doubt remind the reader of other situations in the seven prophetic messages where the claims do not match the reality (2.3, 9, 20).[63] What would the statement that the church in Sardis is dead convey to the hearers? It would appear to be clear that the 'death' here spoken of has reference to some sort of 'spiritual' death. Such an idea, though in different terminology, is found elsewhere in the Johannine literature. 1

---

[62] As Prigent (*L'Apocalypse de Saint Jean*, p. 147) notes, 'C'est sans doute le jugement le plus sévère des sept Lettres'.

[63] Resseguie, *The Revelation of John*, p. 95.

John 3.14 reads, 'We know that we have passed out of death into life, because we love the brothers; the one who does not love remains in death'. A similar contrast between life and death also occurs in 1 Jn 5.16, which may echo Jesus' words to his Jewish opponents in the FG that it is possible 'to die in your sins' (Jn 8.24). The fact that the hearers know that there is a 'sin unto death' (1 Jn 5.16) and a 'second death' (Rev. 2.11; cf. also 20.6, 14; 21.8) would perhaps make Jesus' statement here all the more ominous.

Verse 2 – Jesus' next words seem to stand in some contrast to what he has just stated, for he now indicates that even though dead, they are to 'Wake up and strengthen that which remains, which is about to die'. Jesus' use of the term γρηγορῶν ('awake' or 'watchful') conveys both the idea of wakefulness and watchfulness, combining the idea of vigilance with eschatological expectation. Thus, his address to those in Sardis is an appropriate follow-up to his previous words of stern rebuke. This word is paired with another, στήρισον ('strengthen'), that combines the idea of 'strengthening' in the light of the return of Jesus (cf. Jas 5.8). The idea of resoluteness is not far removed here. Such strong language is called for, owing to the fact that the rest of the things that remain amongst the church at Sardis are on the verge of death. Thus, the hyperbolic language of v. 1, gives way to the more precise language of v. 2. The tension created by such contrast is not something that would take the hearers by surprise, as the church in Ephesus has learned, in that they have bore many things on account of Jesus' name but have left their first love. The more precise language of v. 2 reveals that the situation is very desperate indeed for the church in Sardis. The little that they have is near death. 'For I have not found your works fulfilled before my God'. The one who knows their works has not found them to be complete. Rather, as the temple of Artemis has not been completed, neither have the works of the church. The term Jesus here uses πεπληρωμένα ('fulfilled') often occurs in the Johannine literature to designate the fulfillment of Scripture (Jn 12.38; 13.18; 15.25; 17.12; 19.24, 36), Jesus' word (18.9, 32), or joy that has been made complete (Jn 3.29; 15.11; 16.24; 17.13; 1 Jn 1.4; 2 Jn 12). Thus the hearers are likely to understand Jesus' words here as indicating that the works of those in Sardis have stopped short of their completion. In this they stand in contrast to the church in Thyatira, whose last works were more than the first (Rev. 2.19), and who were recipients of the promise to those who 'keep my works until the end' (2.26). Their works, which are incomplete before my God, stand in contrast to the Seven Spirits, which are complete (Seven) before the One who sits on the throne. The resurrected Jesus, who has the Seven Spirits of God, now makes reference to God as 'my God', further developing the tight association between them, a theme to which he returns near the end of the message (v. 5).

Verse 3 – In the light of such a dreadful situation, indicated by the word οὖν ('therefore'), the resurrected Jesus calls for specific action from the church at Sardis. Like the church at Ephesus, they are called upon to 'remember'. On this occasion two specific things are to be remembered. First, they are to remember what they received. Among the many things about which the hearers might think, perhaps two things would stand out. Jesus' words to 'receive the Holy Spirit' (Jn 20.22), which are reinforced by the Elder's words 'you have an anointing which you received from him' (1 Jn 2.27), and 'the command received from the Father' to love one another (2 Jn 4). Thus, the call, to remember things received, is of fundamental importance within the Johannine community, as both the emphasis upon the Spirit and the love command are central in Johannine theology. Second, they are to remember what they have heard. Owing to the extremely close connection between hearing and belief in the FG, this admonition is equally important for it, in essence, is a call back to belief, another fundamental element in Johannine thought. The impact of the refrain 'to the one who has an ear to ear, let that one hear' would not be missed by the hearers, who would understand the things heard earlier by the church in Sardis are to be heard once again. As Jesus' words unfold, he instructs those in Sardis to 'keep' those things they received and heard, and to repent for their incomplete works before God. As seen in 1.3, there is a close connection between hearing and keeping. As noted earlier, in the FG keeping the words or commands of Jesus entails more than simple conformity to a set of principles, but includes an identification with and incorporation of those words and commands. Such a response to his words results in eternal life (Jn 8.51-55) and a sharing in the kind of love characteristic of the Father and the Son (Jn 14.15-24; 15.10, 20; 17.6, 11-15). Therefore, the command to keep underscores two of the basic components of

Johannine thought, eternal life and love. The fact that these words are spoken to those who are dead or who are about to die would make this emphasis all the more significant. Not only are they to keep such things, they are also to repent. The call for repentance, which is by now a familiar element of the prophetic messages to the hearers, is the culmination of a series of five imperative verbs beginning in v. 2. The expectations of this direct call for repentance would appear to involve the activity of being awakened, the strengthening of what remains, remembering things received and heard, as well as keeping those things. Thus, concrete action is envisioned in this call.

For a second time in this message the word οὖν ('therefore') occurs, revealing the interconnection of the message and the relationship of what follows to that which precedes. 'Therefore, if you do not wake up, I will come as a thief, and you will not know the hour when I come upon you'. Directing the hearers' attention back to the first imperative in the passage (v. 2), which no doubt underscores the connection between repentance and waking up, Jesus makes clear the consequence of failing to comply with his commands. As with several of the other prophetic messages, failure to repent is met with a threat, the threat 'I will come as a thief'. Again the tension between Jesus' ongoing juridical activity in the life of the churches and his eschatological advent is felt in such words. However, on this occasion it appears clear that reference is being made to Jesus' eschatological return. One reason the hearers would likely take these words as having reference to Jesus' eschatological return is owing to the fact that 'thief' imagery is frequently found in early Christian eschatological discourse (Mt. 24.43; Lk. 12.39; 1 Thess. 5.2; 2 Pet. 3.10). The appearance of this phrase here anticipates its later occurrence in the Apocalypse (16.15) with precisely this eschatological meaning. Although it might strike the hearers as odd that Jesus would identify himself as a thief given its meanings in the FG (Jn 10.1, 8, 10; 12.6), such language conveys the suddenness of an event, for a thief, as opposed to a robber, takes the victim by surprise.[64] It is precisely this suddenness that is brought out in Jesus' next words, 'and you will not know what hour I will come upon you'. While he knows their works, they will not know the hour of

---

[64] Yabro Collins, *The Apocalypse*, p. 24.

his coming, owing to the fact that without repentance they will not know him. Thus, the threat/promise of Jesus' return to the church in Sardis is not conditional, predicated by whether or not they repent. Rather, the emphasis here is upon the suddenness and certainty of his coming to them in judgment, and the fact that they are unprepared for it, and consequently unaware of its timing. The only conditional aspect of his words is whether or not they will be prepared for and aware of his coming. Perhaps these words would cause the hearers to think of the way in which Cyrus and Antiochus the Great came upon Sardis unawares.[65] The 'hour' of which the resurrected Jesus speaks would no doubt remind the hearers of its soteriological significance in the FG (Jn 2.4; 7.30; 8.20; 12.23, 31-32; 13.1; 17.1). Yet, while this theological significance would not be lost in its use here, its occurrences in the Apocalypse carry with them eschatological significance.[66]

Verse 4 – In v. 4, the hearers encounter the word ἀλλά ('but'), which on several previous occasions in the prophetic messages (Rev. 2.4, 14, 20) introduces the words of rebuke, 'but I have this against you'. However, instead of the words, 'But I have', the hearers encounter the words, 'But you have'. Such an inversion of personal pronouns prepares the hearers for the inversion of content. For normally, the churches hear words of rebuke at this point, after having heard words of commendation. Earlier in 2.14, Jesus told the church at Pergamum 'But I have against you ὀλίγα' ('a little' or 'a few'). Now he tells the church in Sardis, 'But you have ὀλίγα ('a little' or 'a few') names'. The contrast would be apparent. Whilst there was much to praise about the church at Pergamum, and little to criticize, there is little to praise and much to criticize in Sardis. Earlier (3.2), Jesus had said to the church in Sardis, 'You have a name that you are alive, but you are dead', indicating that the church's name did not match its spiritual reality. In the words he speaks here in v. 4, the name is the reality, so much so that the names of individual believers are not given; reference is made simply to them as 'a few names in Sardis'. These names are described by means of their clothing. Two specific things about these names are noted. Jesus observes that they have not 'stained their clothes and

---

[65] Sweet, *Revelation*, p. 99.
[66] Cf. H. Giesen, 'ὥρα', *EDNT*, III, pp. 507-508.

they walk with me in white'. Mention of stained or defiled garment imagery would likely remind the hearers of similar imagery found in Zech. 3.3-5, where Joshua the high priest stands in filthy garments before the face of the angel of the Lord. The symbolic nature of these garments is revealed when, after they are removed and replaced by clean garments, the Lord says, 'Behold I have taken away your iniquities' (Zech. 3.4).[67] While it is not altogether clear how the hearers would take this imagery, as the Apocalypse unfolds it appears that the imagery of having stained or defiled garments carries with it the idea of moral impurity, perhaps involving sin, idolatry, and/or sexual immorality (Rev. 14.4). Such defilement indicates one's estrangement from God and Jesus. Apparently, stained garments of this nature can only be made clean by washing them and making them white in the blood of the Lamb (7.14). From the context in 3.1-6, perhaps spiritual slumber, weakness, and incomplete works are part of such defilement. There are a few names in Sardis who have avoided such contamination. However, the description of such names is not limited to a negative assessment, indicating what they have not done, for Jesus also describes them actively as those 'who walk with me in white, because they are worthy'. Walking is a familiar metaphor in the Johannine literature. Walking with Jesus (Jn 6.66), walking in the Truth (2 Jn 4; 3 Jn 3, 4), and walking in the Light (1 Jn 1.6-7) all seem to have reference to the same spiritual reality that conveys the idea of fellowship with and/or being with Jesus.[68] Jesus' words that 'they will walk with me in white' further underscores the idea of their identity with Jesus, for as is already known, white is a color intimately connected with Jesus (Rev. 1.14). As they will learn, white garments become even more closely identified with him and those who follow him. The fact that they appear in white, here anticipates the eschatological reality that awaits those who overcome (2.5), just as their walk anticipates the eschatological promise of being with Christ during the thousand year reign (20.4) and the nations walking in the light of the Lamb (21.24). The phrase that follows, 'because they are worthy', is typically Johannine in that it is capable of a double meaning. On the one hand, the phrase could be taken to mean, they will walk with Jesus in white

---

[67] Smalley, *The Revelation to John*, p. 84.
[68] Cf. the discussion in Thomas, *1 John, 2 John, 3 John*, pp. 23-24, 75-76.

because they have proven themselves worthy of such a close association. On the other hand, the phrase could imply that the rest of those in Sardis are worthy because of their close association with Jesus. Such Johannine ambiguity may invite the hearers to reflect upon the integral connection between the two ideas, seeing a symbiotic relationship between them rather than a purely causal one. At the least, it makes explicit the connection between being in white and being worthy. Something of the meaning of being worthy will be revealed later in the prophecy, when it is seen that the only other individuals described as worthy are God (4.11) and the Lamb (5.2, 4, 9, 12).[69]

Verse 5 – For a fifth time the hearers encounter eschatological promises made to the one who overcomes. On this occasion, three promises are made; one with reference to the overcomer's clothing, two with reference to the overcomer's name. The first promise is stated by Jesus as follows, 'Thus the one who overcomes will be clothed in white garments'. The appearance of the term οὕτως ('thus' or 'so') indicates that this first promise is closely connected to the description of the rest in Sardis that precedes this statement.[70] The hearers would likely understand such an explicit connection as overt evidence that those in Sardis who presently walk with Jesus in white anticipate this eschatological reward and in good Johannine fashion, already experience it to a certain degree. White clothing is a theological reality in the Apocalypse, which, as noted in the previous verse, indicates that the wearer has an intimate association with Jesus by proving to be a faithful witness and thus experiencing this eschatological reward. Not only is this association underscored by the number of individuals described as wearing white garments and/or robes (cf. 3.18; 4.4; 6.11; 7.9, 13), but also the mention of many other white objects with clear associations to God and/or Jesus (1.14; 2.17; 6.2; 14.14; 19.11, 14; 20.11). On this occasion, the hearers are no doubt encouraged by the fact that their appearance will be like unto that of the resurrected Jesus.

The second and third promises to the one who overcomes hearken back to the theme of one's name, introduced at the begin-

---

[69] Smalley, *The Revelation to John*, p. 85. The only other occurrence of the word ἄξιος ('worthy') is found in 16.6, where it appears to have the meaning of 'fitting', 'appropriate', or 'proper'.
[70] Aune, *Revelation 1-5*, p. 223.

ning of the message. Whilst this church's name does not match its spiritual reality (3.1), there are those in Sardis whose names *are* the spiritual reality (3.4). To such ones as these the second and third promises are directed, one negatively stated and one positively stated. The second eschatological promise, 'I will never erase his name out of the book of life', introduces the hearers to book imagery, which is important in the Apocalypse. For the hearers such language is no doubt grounded in the language of Exod. 32.31-33,[71] which reads:

> So Moses went back to the Lord and said, 'Oh, what a great sin these people have committed! They have made themselves gods of gold. But now, please forgive their sin – but if not, then blot me out [ἐξάλειψον ('blot out me')] of the book you have written'. The Lord replied to Moses, 'Whoever has sinned against me I will blot out [ἐξαλείψω ('I will blot out')] of my book'. (NIV)

From this text the hearers would know that there is a book in which God has written names and that God can expunge names from this book, owing to sinful activity on the part of those whose names appear in the book. In Rev. 3.5, it is the resurrected Jesus who has the authority to take such an action. The fact that the name of the one who overcomes will never be erased suggests that they have not defiled their garments and that they have continued to walk with Jesus in white. Absence of sin is also implied. Appropriately enough, the book in which these names appear is the Book of Life. It would follow that only the names of those who are alive would appear in a Book of Life. Clearly, the names of those who are dead would not be written there or would be erased.[72] It would not surprise the hearers to find that the one who is alive, who is Life, is the one who has authority to expunge names from the Book of Life. For this book appears to belong to him, a point that will be confirmed later (21.27). This first mention of the Book of Life prepares the hearers for additional references to it in the Apocalypse, where the lines of demarcation become clearer and clearer between

---

[71] Smalley, *The Revelation to John*, p. 86.

[72] As M. Kiddle (*The Revelation of St. John*, [London: Hodder and Stoughton, 1940], p. 47) astutely notes, 'This promise ... is made with a backward glance at the atrophied members of the church at Sardis'.

those whose names are and are not written in this book (13.8; 17.8; 20.12, 15; 21.27). The possibility that names can be erased from the Book of Life by Jesus will create the context for understanding the later statement that such names are written in the book before the creation of the world (17.8). The tension created by these two ideas is typically Johannine.[73]

The third eschatological promise found in this message also involves the name of the one who overcomes. Jesus says, 'And I will confess his name before my Father and before his angels'. Jesus' language at this point would at the same time be both familiar and startling, as 'confession' language is found at various places in the Johannine literature (Jn 1.20; 9.22; 12.42; 1 Jn 1.9; 2.23; 4.2, 3, 15; 2 Jn 7). With one exception, where the term is used to describe the confession of sin (1 Jn 1.9), every other occurrence of the word is related to the confession of Jesus. Thus, this language would be familiar enough to the hearers. However, an inversion takes place on this occasion, for it is Jesus who confesses and it is the name of the one who overcomes that is confessed! The power of this promise, that the confessed one will do the confessing, indicates something of the faithfulness Jesus feels towards those who have been faithful to him. They have been faithful to confess in the face of excommunication, persecution, even death. His faithfulness to confess such ones would not likely be less than theirs. Such an inversion in this lone appearance of the word 'confess' in the book would be enough to leave the hearers somewhat breathless, but there is more. For his confession of them takes place before the ultimate authority; the One who sits on the throne, the Alpha and Omega, the one who is and was and is coming, the All Powerful One. If it is a name that is important to the church in Sardis, with these words Jesus reminds them that what is of ultimate importance is the one before whom this name is confessed. As this message closes, Jesus' reference to 'my Father' balances his claim to be 'the one who has the Seven Spirits of my God' with which this message began. Likewise, his reference to confession of the name 'before his angels' in v. 5, balances his claim to have 'the seven stars' in v. 1. Mention of 'his angels' at this point reminds the hearers both of the location of this confession, heaven, and its veracity, as the angels are witnesses to it.

---

[73] Cf. the discussion by H. Balz, 'βιβλίον', *EDNT*, I, pp. 217-18.

Verse 6 – This message closes with the now familiar call for discerning obedience, as do all the messages. What is the Spirit saying to those who have ears to hear? How can the hearers keep the words of this prophecy? Perhaps part of the answer to this question is to be found in the many imperatives that come from Jesus in this message. Thus, the churches should wake up, strengthen what is about to die, and bring their works to completion before God. They are to remember what they have received and heard, faithfully keeping all those things, while repenting for their spiritual death. They must give urgent attention to keeping their garments pure, maintaining their uninterrupted fellowship with Jesus. Perhaps what the Spirit is saying to the churches is that it is all about a name.

To the Angel of the Church in Philadelphia (3.7-13)

Verse 7 – Continuing without delay, Jesus instructs John next to write to the angel of the church in Philadelphia, using the identical construction employed in 2.1, 2.8, 2.12, 2.18, and 3.1 with reference to Ephesus, Smyrna, Pergamum, Thyatria, and Sardis, respectively. As the hearers encounter the name Philadelphia, they are led to the next lampstand, moving south-southeast, toward Philadelphia located some thirty miles away from Sardis. What would the hearers' think of when they encounter the name Philadelphia? Perhaps they would think of the founder of Philadelphia, Attalus II, whose love for and devotion to his brother, Eumenes II, gave rise to the city's name. Or, perhaps they would think of its strategic location at the junction of routes leading to Mysia, Lydia, and Phrygia, making it the gateway to the east. Perhaps they would think of its intended function as a 'missionary city' from which the Greek language and culture could be spread to the east. Or, perhaps they would think of its location on rich, fertile, volcanic soil, and the fact that it frequently experienced earthquakes. Perhaps they would think of the fact that on at least two occasions the city changed its name. Once the name was changed to Neocaesarea as a sign of gratitude to Tiberius for the aid received in rebuilding after a devastating earthquake in 17 CE. Later, it adopted the family name of Emperor Vespasian, changing its name to Philadelphia Flavia. Or, perhaps they would think of the city's economic prosperity and its many religious temples and festivals.[74]

Whatever the hearers think of when encountering the name Philadelphia, they soon find out what Jesus thinks of the church there. For a third consecutive time, the resurrected Jesus first identifies himself by words that are not contained in his description in the inaugural vision. Previously, in the message to Thyatira (2.18), he identified himself as the Son of God, a title well known to those familiar with the Johannine tradition. In the message to Sardis (3.1), he identified himself as the one who has the Seven Spirits of God. On this occasion, he first identifies himself as 'the holy one, the true one'. The first term used by Jesus, 'the holy one', would be a familiar one to Johannine hearers. In the FG, Jesus is called 'the holy one of God' by Peter (Jn 6.69; cf. also 1 Jn 2.20), refers to himself as the one whom the Father has sanctified (Jn 10.36), and says that he sanctifies himself (17.19). Since such holiness and/or sanctification rather clearly come from God, it is no surprise that God is himself also called 'Holy Father' by Jesus in prayer (Jn 17.11). That such holiness and/or sanctification is to extend to the followers of Jesus is revealed in his prayer that they be sanctified in the Truth (Jn 17.17, 19) and in the admonition in 1 John for believers to purify themselves just as Jesus is pure (1 Jn 3.3).[75] Such an understanding of Jesus as 'the holy one' converges nicely at this point with the picture of Jesus that continues to emerge as the Apocalypse unfolds. As noted, Jesus also identifies himself as 'the true one'. For Johannine hearers such a designation taps into an extremely rich and deep theological reality. Not only is Jesus 'full of truth' (Jn 1.14), but he is also identified as 'the Truth' (Jn 14.6). Thus, in Johannine thought truth is Christologically conditioned and defined. Consequently, in any number of Johannine expressions that mention the Truth, a Christological understanding cannot be ruled out, but is likely present. Examples include, but are not limited to, references to 'the Spirit of Truth' (Jn 14.17; 15.26; 16.13), 'walking in the Truth' (2 Jn 4; 3 Jn 3, 4), worshipping 'in

---

[74] On this cf. Mounce, *The Book of Revelation*, pp. 114-15, Hemer, 'Seven Cities of Asia Minor', p. 245, and Koester, *Revelation and the End of All Things*, p. 65.

[75] J.C. Thomas, *He Loved Them until the End: The Farewell Materials in the Gospel according to John* (Pune, India: Fountain Press, 2003), pp. 59-61 and Thomas, *1 John, 2 John, 3 John*, pp. 152-53.

Spirit and in Truth' (Jn 4.23). Such a rich theological concept would, no doubt, color the way that the phrase, 'the true one' would be understood by the hearers. But in addition to this, the term ἀληθινός ('true' or 'genuine') takes on the distinct nuance of true as opposed to false, genuine or real as opposed to fake or unreal, authentic as opposed to inauthentic. In the FG Jesus is the true light (Jn 1.9; cf. also 1 Jn 2.8), the true bread from heaven (6.32), the true vine (15.1), the one whose judgment is true (8.16). As with 'the holy one', this term is also shared by God (Jn 17.3; cf. also 1 Jn 5.20). Again, such an understanding of Jesus as 'the true one' converges nicely at this point with the picture of Jesus that continues to emerge as the Apocalypse unfolds. Specifically, it reinforces for the hearers the reality that Jesus has no rivals on this earth, for he is 'the ruler of the kings of the earth'. It also places Jesus and his words in contrast to a variety of others who have proven to be liars, or not what they have claimed to be, encountered in the preceding messages. In addition, this title prepares the hearers for the liars and deceivers who will be encountered in this message and in the later unfolding of the Apocalypse. Significantly, the terms 'holy' and 'true' are combined to describe God later in the Apocalypse (6.10), where he is called 'the holy and true δεσπότης ('despot' or 'master')'.

In the previous messages, titles used in Jesus' self-designation that have not appeared in the inaugural vision give way to those familiar to the hearers from that vision. This emerging pattern appears to be replicated in the message to the church in Philadelphia, though in this verse the hearers are presented with an additional modification. For on this occasion, Jesus identifies himself as 'the one who has the key of David, the one who opens and no one can close, who closes and no one can open'. The intertext which results in this passage for the hearers is a combination of images which emerges from Isa. 22.22, the inaugural vision of the resurrected Jesus (Rev. 1.18), and the FG (Jn 10.7). This intertext communicates at several levels. First, 'the key of David' clearly reflects imagery found in Isa. 22.22, where the glory and authority of David's throne are transferred to Eliakim. The text reads, 'I will place on his shoulder the key to the house of David; what he opens no one can shut, and what he shuts no one can open'. The use of such imagery makes clear to the hearers that Jesus is making certain messianic claims for himself and claims about who is part of his messianic kingdom and who is not. For the one who possesses David's key is the one who can determine who enters and who is denied entry. This imagery contributes to the theology of the book at the levels of both the meta-narrative and the micro-narrative. With regard to the former, Jesus' relationship to David continues to be of interest at strategic points in the Apocalypse (Rev. 5.5; 22.16).[76] With regard to the latter, Jesus' words are of particular relevance to the church in Philadelphia, which must contend with 'the synagogue of Satan' (3.9). Second, 'the key of David' imagery also reminds the hearers of a detail found within the inaugural vision of Jesus, where he says, 'I have the keys of death and Hades' (1.18). There, Jesus is depicted as having complete mastery over death and Hades, indicating that there is no need for the believer to fear these foes for Jesus holds the keys, determining who goes in and who goes out. In other words, he opens and closes death's door, he provides the way to life! Third, the hearers are likely to be reminded of the fact that in the FG Jesus identifies himself as 'the Door of the sheep', the door through whom anyone who enters will be saved, who will have life and have it in superabundance (Jn 10.7-10).[77] Before the message to the church in Philadelphia concludes, Jesus' vital role in determining who enters the New Jerusalem will become clear to the hearers (Rev. 3.12).

Verse 8 – The content of the message begins with 'I know your works', a familiar phrase to the hearers by this point. However, before an enumeration of these works is given, a parenthetical statement breaks into the message, a statement that stands in great continuity with the last description of Jesus. 'Behold I have placed before you an opened door, which no one is able to shut it'. Given the previous words of Jesus, this statement comes as no surprise for he is the one who has the key of David and can open, and no one can shut. Owing to those previous words, it appears these words would be understood by the hearers in relationship with Jesus' messianic claims including his ability to make alive, open the door to life, for he is the Door. The perfect tense forms of the verbs δέδωκα ('I have placed' or 'I have given') and ἠνεῳγμένην ('opened') implies

---

[76] Smalley, *The Revelation to John*, p. 88.
[77] Yarbro Collins, *The Apocalypse*, p. 27.

that this opened door was placed before them at some point in the past and remains open before them even now. If, as seems likely, this door has reference to their invitation to be 'saved' and experience eternal life, as implied in Jn 10.7-10, then this moment in the past likely has reference to the point at which they heard the witness of Jesus Christ and responded in faith to him.[78] Perhaps in the mention of the open door before the church there is also conveyed a very subtle hint that this church, as all the churches, is to play a role in the conversion of those around them, culminating in the conversion of the nations later described in Rev. 21.24. At any rate, the interruption which this parenthetical statement brings to the continuity of the 'I know your works' statement and the enumeration of those works would serve to encourage the hearers in advance of Jesus' words with regard to the hardships facing this church. Following the parenthetical statement, Jesus now enumerates the church's works, 'you have little power and you have kept my word and have not denied my name'. It is not altogether clear how the hearers would understand the statement 'you have little power'. Although it is possible that this phrase conveys the idea of poverty and/or lack of social standing, such is not its normal Johannine meaning. Often this language is associated with the ability or inability to do or accomplish something, as the frequent appearance of the verbal form of the word demonstrates. In this context, it is interesting that despite the church's little δύναμιν ('power'), the door which Jesus has placed before them no one δύναται ('is able' or 'has the power') to shut. Thus, their little power does not make them vulnerable to those who would wish to counteract Jesus' salvific activity on their behalf. Though they have little power, still they have demonstrated an extraordinary commitment to Jesus, having kept his word, having not denied his name. In the phrase 'having kept my word' several ideas converge for the hearers. In Johannine thought there is an extremely tight interplay between keeping Jesus' word or commands, eternal life (8.51), loving Jesus and being loved by the Father (Jn 14.15, 23-24; 15.10; 1 Jn 2.3-4; 5.3), mutual indwelling (1 Jn 3.22-24), as well as walking as Jesus walks (1 Jn 2.5). The hearers would also be aware of the beatitude with which the Apocalypse begins with regard to keeping the things

---

[78] Smalley, *The Revelation to John*, p. 89.

written in this book (1.3). Such a matrix of thoughts indicate that Jesus' words in Rev. 3.8 reveal something about the intimate relationship shared by the church in Philadelphia and Jesus. Yet, these words of affirmation are followed by others, 'they have not denied my name'. As with those in the church at Pergamum (2.13), the church at Philadelphia exhibits the kind of witness characteristic of John (the Baptist), rather than succumbing to the temptation of denying Jesus. The fact that they did not deny Jesus' name reminds the hearers of the patient endurance of the church at Ephesus, who bore a number of things on account of Jesus' name (2.3). It also reminds them of the fact that the church at Pergamum firmly holds on to it as well (2.13) and are even promised his new name (2.17). These earlier associations, and the rich Johannine understanding of Jesus' name, suggest that the church in Philadelphia has a deep sense of solidarity and personal identification with Jesus even at the risk of personal vulnerability. This mention of not having denied his name also prepares the hearers for the emphasis given to names in the eschatological promises with which this message concludes. It may not be without significance that both the verbs in the phrases 'having kept my word' and 'having not denied' appear in the aorist tense, indicating that a particular point in the past is in mind, where they kept his word and did not deny his name.

Verse 9 – The next verse is composed of two sentences, each of which begins with the word ἰδοὺ ('behold') indicating that they stand together. In fact, it appears that the second occurrence of this term actually picks up on the previous one, owing to the way the sentence becomes focused upon the identity of this 'synagogue of Satan'. This phenomenon is quite like the interruption found in the previous verse with regard to Jesus' words about the opened door. It may well be that v. 9 offers an implicit commentary on the previous one, providing the context for understanding the phrases 'having kept my word' and 'not having denied my name'. On this view, the hearers would see a connection between the adversities experienced by the church in Philadelphia and the 'synagogue of Satan' mentioned in v. 9. Such a connection would not come as a complete surprise to the hearers, owing to their knowledge of this same connection in the message to the church in Smyrna.

The contrast between the church in Philadelphia and the 'synagogue of Satan' to which v. 9 is devoted is initially indicated by the fact that in each case a construction occurs which begins with 'behold', followed by a form of δίδωμι ('I give'). In v. 8 this construction alerts the hearers to the fact that an opened door has been 'given' or 'placed' before them.[79] In v. 9 the construction indicates that some of the 'synagogue' of Satan would be 'given' or 'made' to 'come and worship'. This is reminiscent of Jesus' use of βάλλω ('I cast') in 2.22 and 25. In 3.9 Jesus' mention of the 'synagogue of Satan' gives way to a description reminiscent of its description in the message to the church in Smyrna (2.9), for the phrase, 'they say of themselves to be Jews' reappears here. On that occasion it was seen that in all likelihood, this 'synagogue of Satan' has reference to some or all of the Jewish community in Smyrna. On this occasion, it appears that at least some of the Jewish community in Philadelphia is in view. As before, the prophetic insight of Jesus reveals that although these individuals may be ethnic Jews, they are not Jews spiritually, they are not the legitimate heirs of Israel.[80] In keeping with his earlier words to Smyrna, Jesus says that despite their claims, 'they are not' Jews. However, on this occasion his language escalates as he charges, 'but they are lying'. Such language would remind the hearers of the description of the would-be apostles who were found to be liars by the church in Ephesus (2.2). It also provides part of the rationale for why this 'synagogue' is called a 'synagogue of Satan', for through its 'lying' activity this 'synagogue' exhibits one of the characteristics of the Devil, who is a liar and the father of lies (Jn 8.44).

As the resurrected Jesus picks back up the earlier train of thought by the second use of ἰδοὺ ('behold') in v. 9, a most remarkable statement is made: 'Behold I will make them, in order that they might come and worship before your feet and know that I have loved you'. Once again, Jesus' words to this church echo the words of Isaiah, with several passages converging in such a way that they produce an intertext of astounding significance. More than one of the Isaianic prophecies envisions a time when the kings of the nations and the wealth of land and sea will come to Jerusalem (Isa.

---

[79] The term that appears in v. 9 διδῶ ('I will make') is related to δίδωμι ('I give'), but appears to be on its way to a transition to a ω form rather than a μι verbal form. On this cf. Charles, *Revelation*, I, p. 88.

[80] Murphy (*Fallen Is Babylon*, p. 154) notes, 'For the author, who is himself Jewish, the definition of "Jew" has changed'.

60.1-22). It will be a time when those from afar will come to worship and serve Israel because God is with them (Isa. 45.14). A time when the Holy One of Israel will declare, 'I have loved you' (Isa. 43.3-4). This matrix of passages clearly anticipates a time of vindication for Israel, when the Gentiles will acknowledge that they have truly been chosen by God. Yet, no sooner than these promises of Israel's future vindication begin to swirl in the minds of the hearers, does the irony of reality settle in upon them. In a stark reversal of fortunes, this 'synagogue of Satan, who claim to be Jews but are not' will not receive the long awaited vindication before the Gentiles, but will themselves be required by Jesus to take the role of the Gentiles in the vindication of the church in Philadelphia.[81] These ethnic Jews, who are not Jews spiritually, have forfeited their inheritance, while the church in Philadelphia receives the heritage of Israel.[82] Specifically, Jesus' words to the church reveal that they will inherit these eschatological promises and vindication before the very ones who have caused them such distress.[83] Perhaps the hearers would see some connection here to the kind of vindication Jesus himself receives when he comes with the clouds; when every eye will see him, even those who have pierced him (Rev. 1.7). With the words προσκυνήσουσιν ἐνώπιον τῶν ποδῶν ('and they will bow down or worship before your feet'), Jesus introduces the hearers to a most significant theme in the Apocalypse. In some ways it could be said that it is around the issue of worship that the lines of demarcation are drawn in the book. The Apocalypse will prove to be consistently ruthless in its insistence that only God and the Lamb are worthy of worship. The hearers are instructed time and again that neither the dragon (13.4), the beast (13.4, 8, 12; 14.9, 11; 20.4), the image of the beast (13.15; 14.9, 11; 16.2; 19.20), demons or idols (9.20) – nor even God's servants and/or angels (19.10; 22.8) – are to be worshipped. Only God (4.10; 5.14; 7.11; 11.1, 16; 14.7; 15.4; 19.4, 10; 22.9) and the Lamb (5.14) are to be worshipped. It is possible to take this term in 3.9 to mean 'to bow down', as it appears to mean in Isa. 45.14 (LXX). However, owing

---

[81] Smalley, *The Revelation to John*, pp. 90-91 and Mayo, '*Those Who Call Themselves Jews*', p. 70.

[82] Prigent, *L'Apocalypse de Saint Jean*, p. 156.

[83] Cf. Beale, *The Book of Revelation*, p. 288.

to its meaning in its occurrences elsewhere in the Apocalypse (and the FG for that matter, Jn 4.20-24; 9.38; 12.20), it seems likely that the hearers would take the term as at least pointing in the direction of its fuller meaning in Rev. 3.9. What would this phrase mean to the hearers in that case? While it is likely that they would take the word to mean vindication in some sense, perhaps the word points in the direction of the worship of Jesus, in that Jesus stands behind this church.[84] On this view, perhaps this language anticipates the eschatological conversion of the nations (21.24).

It is not without significance that the words, 'and they will know that I have loved you', not only echoes the words of the Holy One of Israel, but also comes from 'the holy one', a title by which Jesus earlier identified himself to the church in Philadelphia. At the same time, this phrase calls the hearers back to the prologue of the Apocalypse, where John described Jesus as 'the one who loved us and loosed us from our sins and made us a kingdom, priests to God and his Father'. For the 'synagogue of Satan' to know that Jesus has loved the church would, by implication, entail an acknowledgement that the church is indeed the kingdom of the Father and priests dedicated to his service. Such an acknowledgement would further underscore the inversion motif found in this verse, where the promises made to Israel are fulfilled in the church.

Verse 10 – Jesus' message continues in v. 10, developing earlier themes while introducing new dimensions to the hearers. The main idea of the verse is conveyed to the hearers by means of its structure around two primary and interrelated parts: 'Because you have kept my word … even I will keep you'. One of the church's works was identified by Jesus previously in the statement, 'you have kept my word' (v. 8). Something of the quality of the believers' commitment to Jesus and his word by the church in Philadelphia is indicated by the fact that there has been no rebuke of the church to this point, nor will there be. But apparently, this particular work is so significant that Jesus specifically returns to it in v. 10. On this occasion, the phrase Jesus uses is modified slightly, 'you have kept my word of patient endurance'. From this modification the hearers learn that there is a deep connection between 'keeping my word', which is part of Johannine spirituality, and 'patient endurance',

---

[84] J.M. Nützel, 'προσκυνέω', *EDNT*, III, p. 175.

which is exhibited already by John (1.9) and the churches in Ephesus (2.2, 3) and Thyatira (2.19). This combination of ideas would no doubt remind the hearers of the faithful witness which has been modeled by Jesus (1.5), followed by Antipas (2.13), and implicitly called for in Smyrna (2.10). Such an expression indicates that the faithfulness of the church in Philadelphia is beyond doubt. Their lives of faithful witness are in keeping with that of the resurrected Jesus who speaks.[85] Owing to their having kept his word, Jesus says, 'even I will keep you from [ἐκ, 'from' or 'out of')] the hour of testing that is about to come upon the whole inhabited world to test the inhabitants of the earth'. These eschatological words of promise would communicate with the hearers at several levels. Perhaps one of the first things to jump out to them is the familiarity of this language to Johannine hearers. In the FG, Jesus says:

> I have given them your word and the world has hated them, because they are not of the world just as I am not of the world. I do not ask in order that you take them out of the world, but in order that you keep them from [ἐκ ('from' or 'out of')] the evil one (Jn 17.14-15).

The parallels between these sayings are even more obvious when it is noted that before uttering these words in the FG, Jesus describes the disciples as having kept God's word (17.6). Thus, the prospect of those who have kept the word being kept from some ominous future event(s) would not be a wholly new concept for the hearers.

One of the significant aspects of this verse is the fact that the hearers are here introduced to the idea of the hour of testing that is to come upon the whole earth. The ominous combination of the words, 'hour' and 'testing', would indicate to the hearers something of the extraordinary importance of this impending event. Perhaps the relationship between 'hour' and suddenness would still be in the hearers' minds from the warning of Jesus in 3.3 that he comes as a thief and no one knows the hour that he comes. They will also learn that in the Apocalypse, 'hour' often carries with it the idea of an appointed time (9.15; 11.13; 14.7, 15; 18.10, 16, 19). This particular

---

[85] Sweet (*Revelation*, p. 104) is close to this idea when he observes that the word of my patient endurance has reference to 'not merely Jesus' sayings, but his whole self-revelation, characterized as *endurance*'.

hour is one of testing. The idea of testing can carry with it both positive and negative connotations in Johannine thought. For it can be the activity of Jesus (Jn 6.6) and his church (Rev. 2.2), on the one hand, or that of the Devil (Rev. 2.10), on the other hand. While the identity of the one who brings this hour of testing might not be altogether clear to the hearers, it is clear that Jesus has the power to keep them from it. As will be seen, since God will be closely associated with the preponderance of the appointed hours in the Apocalypse, it is likely that this hour of testing is closely associated with him as well. The scope of the testing might also indicate something of its origin. The hour of testing is about to come upon the οἰκουμένης ὅλης ('whole inhabited world'). With these words the hearers are introduced to a phrase that appears three times in the Apocalypse. In its other two occurrences (12.9; 16.14), it clearly has reference to God's opponents and/or those who do not believe.[86] This phrase indicates that, with the exception of those whom Jesus will keep from it, this hour of testing will be experienced by all of the world's inhabitants. The scope of this hour of testing is made clearer by the following words, 'to test those who live upon the earth'. Not only does this phrase reinforce the universal scope of this testing, but it also offers implicit corroborating evidence that this testing comes from God and is directed to those who are his opponents and/or fail to believe. For in many other occurrences in the Apocalypse the phrase has reference to those who: have caused the death of the saints (6.10); will experience the final three trumpet blasts (8.13); rejoice over the death of the two witnesses (11.10); worship the beast (13.8, 12) and are deceived by him (13.14); have drunk the wine of sexual immorality with the Great Whore (17.2), and marvel at the beast (17.8). The hearers are not yet in a position to understand that 'those who live upon the earth' will be defined in these ways. However, they are in a position to understand that this hour of testing will come upon these inhabitants, not upon those who, like the church in Philadelphia, have kept Jesus' word of patient endurance. Reference to this ominous hour of testing, the arrival of which is imminent, could not help but heighten the dramatic tension for the hearers. For while its content and nature are

---

[86] H. Balz, 'οἰκουμένη', *EDNT*, II, p. 504.

not yet known, the certainty of its arrival is! The intent of this testing will only become apparent as the Apocalypse unfolds.

Verse 11 – With Jesus' words in v. 11, 'I come quickly; hold on to what you have, in order that no one may take away your crown', the content of the message comes to a close. If some of Jesus' previous words about his coming (2.5, 16; 3.3) left a degree of ambiguity as to whether or not they had primary reference to his eschatological return, these words do not. It is the clearest of Jesus' promises to return to this point, following up nicely on 3.3 and anticipating those that follow (16.15; 22.7, 12, 20). These bold words, coming on the heels of those found in v. 10 about the hour of testing, may suggest to the hearers a somewhat close connection between this hour of testing and Jesus' return. If so, the relationship between the hour of testing, the church's being kept from it, and Jesus' return would be all the clearer and the expectancy level of the hearers all the higher. Previously, mention of Jesus' return has come as part of a warning to some of the churches in need of repentance (2.5, 16; 3.3). On this occasion, Jesus' words are not part of a call to repentance but do constitute a warning of sorts. For they precede the admonition to 'hold on to what you have'. The occurrence of the word κράτει ('hold on' or 'grasp') calls to mind its earlier appearances in the Apocalypse. It is used to describe Jesus' grasping the seven stars in his hand (2.1), the church in Pergamum who holds on to Jesus' name (3.13), even though there are those there who hold to the teaching of Balaam (3.14) and the Nicolaitans (3.15). But its nearest parallel to its occurrence in 3.11 is found in Jesus' admonition to the church in Thyatira to 'hold what you have until I come' (2.25). Although the church in Philadelphia has little power, they do have certain works. They have kept Jesus' word of patient endurance and they have not denied his name, despite apparent opposition from a 'synagogue of Satan'. Neither have they been rebuked by Jesus for any sin or shortcoming for which repentance must be offered. The reason for this call for continued vigilance on their part is 'in order that no one take away your crown'. The hearers would know that this crown is likely to be identified with 'the crown of life' which Jesus promises to those in the church in Smyrna who are faithful unto death (2.10). As in that context, Jesus' mention of στέφανόν σου ('your crown') implies that it is a reward for the successful completion of a very difficult task. Such a statement here implies that already the church in Philadelphia has received their crown, they have already completed their task and been rewarded for their faithfulness. Such a situation is similar to that of the few names in Sardis who already wear white because they had not soiled their garments. They were worthy to wear white already but are promised white garments to wear as part of their eschatological reward (3.4-5). The thrust of Jesus' words 'in order that no one takes away your crown' reveal that despite the fact that they have already been rewarded for completing their task, it is still possible for them to have their crown (of life) taken away from them.[87] Thus, the eschatological tension felt at various places in the Apocalypse is quite discernible here as well. Such language also suggests that despite the fact that they will be kept from the hour of testing, the church will still face opposition and persecution capable of causing them to forfeit their crown. Vigilance is called for in even the best of circumstances.

Verse 12 – The eschatological promises to the one who overcomes consist of two primary actions on Jesus' part: making and writing. While these actions are primary, it is significant that the phrase 'of God' occurs four times in this verse alone, indicating the close relationship that exists between Jesus, God, and those who overcome. The first of Jesus' promises is, 'I will make him a pillar in the temple of my God and I will never cast him out'. This first promise would be an especially powerful one to the church in Philadelphia, owing in part to its context of conflict with a 'synagogue of Satan'. In the face of the claims to Jewish identity on the part of those who claim to be Jews and are not but are lying, such a statement makes abundantly clear that it is the church and not the 'synagogue of Satan' who are the true Jews. It also underscores the promise of vindication Jesus makes earlier to this church in 3.9. The imagery of being a pillar in the temple also conveys the idea of stability and permanency to the hearers.[88] This imagery, combined with the promise 'I will never cast him out', would be especially significant to those who live in an area so often destabilized by earthquakes. Since a temple is inextricably linked to the presence of a deity (in antiquity as well as the Apocalypse), the primary meaning

---

[87] Mounce, *The Book of Revelation*, p. 155.
[88] Resseguie, *The Revelation of John*, p. 99.

of the imagery, 'a pillar in the temple of my God', has to do with the overcomer's permanent location in God's presence. The promise that the overcomer will never be cast out underscores this point. The one who overcomes is promised a permanent place in God's presence with no fear of being removed from his presence.

The second set of promises is closely connected to his second primary activity: writing. Jesus says, 'And I will write upon him the name of my God and the name of the city of my God, the New Jerusalem coming down out of heaven from my God, and my new name'. The writing of these names rather clearly indicates the idea of solidarity with, even possession by, those whose names are written upon the item or person. In this case, the overcomer is promised absolute identity and solidarity with God, his city, and Jesus, his Son. This inscription anticipates the act of placing the seal of God upon the foreheads of the servants of God in 7.3, as well as the fact that the 144,000 (14.1) and those in the New Jerusalem (22.4) have the name of God inscribed upon them. This overt identity marker will stand in sharp contrast to another identity marker (i.e. the mark of the beast) encountered later in the book, revealing it to be the counterfeit that it is. The inscription of God's name upon the overcomer might also remind the hearers that in the Torah the priest of God was instructed to wear a gold plate inscribed with the words 'Holy to the Lord' attached to the turban. This name was to be worn upon the forehead in order that the people might be accepted before the Lord (Exod. 28.36-38). The fact that Jesus has made these Johannine believers priests unto God (Rev. 1.6), would not be lost on the hearers who have just learned that the one who overcomes will be a pillar in God's temple.

Not only is the name of God written upon the overcomer, but Jesus also promises to write the name of God's city upon the overcomer. The phrase used by Jesus to describe this city would be fraught with meaning for the hearers. The imagery of writing the name of the city upon an individual would without question identify such an individual as a member or citizen of that city. Just as the name of God would mark out these individuals as belonging to God, so the name of the city would identify them as belonging to this city. The fact that this city belongs to God would further underscore the identity of the overcomer with God. The hearers are introduced for the first time to the 'New Jerusalem', a city which will be mentioned two more times in the book (21.2, 10). On each occasion it is described as 'coming down out of heaven from God'. The repetition of this phrase, and the fact that a present participle is used on each occasion in it, implies that this 'coming down out of heaven from God' is a permanent characteristic of this city.[89] It is always coming down out of heaven from God! It is an eschatological promise of immediate and direct access to God; a promise fulfilled later in the Apocalypse (21.2, 10). Owing to the implied continuity between the New Jerusalem and the city of Jerusalem, perhaps the hearers would not be surprised that its mention comes so closely on the heels of the promise that the overcomer will be made a pillar in the temple of God. For Jerusalem was God's chosen site for his temple.[90] At the same time, the name New Jerusalem conveys a certain degree of discontinuity as well, for this Jerusalem, unlike its predecessor, is characterized both by its newness and its permanent coming down from heaven of God quality. Thus, its mention here also creates a certain anticipation and expectancy amongst the hearers. It should perhaps be observed that mention of the New Jerusalem may also remind the hearers of how this message began with reference to Jesus' possession of the key of David, as David's relationship to Jerusalem is well known. It would only be fitting that the one who holds that key has authority to write its name upon the one who overcomes. At any rate, Jesus' promise to write this name upon the one who overcomes indicates that the future of this city and the future of the one who overcomes are coterminous.

Finally, Jesus promises to write 'my new name' on the one who overcomes. Perhaps reference to 'my new name' would remind the hearers of the promise for vindication, made to Israel, that involves a new name that will come from the mouth of the Lord (Isa. 62.2). Certainly, this promise would be reminiscent of the promise made to the church in Pergamum of a white stone with a new name writ-

---

[89] Caird (*The Revelation of St. John*, p. 55) describes this construction as an 'iterative present, denoting a permanent attribute of the new Jerusalem'.

[90] The temple imagery found within the Apocalypse is quite complex, eventually giving way to the reality that there is no need for a temple in that city, for God and the Lamb is its temple. Yet, there will be many mentions of God's (heavenly) temple following this initial one, before that culmination. Once again, the psychedelic quality of the Apocalypse's imagery is evident.

ten upon it (2.17). The inscription of Jesus' new name upon the one who overcomes anticipates the fact that the 144,000 (14.1) and those in New Jerusalem (22.4) have the name of the Lamb inscribed upon them. Furthermore, it is indeed fitting that those in Philadelphia who 'have not denied my name' (3.8) are those who will receive 'my new name' (3.12)! The writing of Jesus' new name upon the one who overcomes makes the intimate connection between the resurrected Jesus and the one who overcomes complete. They belong to Jesus; they stand in solidarity with him.

Verse 13 – This message closes with the familiar call for discerning obedience, as do all the messages. What is the Spirit saying to those who have ears to hear? How can those who hear keep the words of this prophecy? Primarily, the hearers are to continue holding on to what they have: keeping Jesus' word of patient endurance and not denying his name even in the face of persecution. Continued vigilance is important lest the crown (of life) that they already possess be taken away by someone or something. By continuing to keep these things, those in the church in Philadelphia will be kept from the hour of testing. They will receive the promises of a permanent location in the presence of God and of full identification with him by bearing the names of God, his city, and his Son.

To the Angel of the Church in Laodicea (3.14-22)

Verse 14 – Continuing without delay, Jesus instructs John next to write to the angel of the church in Laodicea, using the identical construction employed in 2.1, 2.8, 2.12, 2.18, 3.1, and 3.7 with reference to Ephesus, Smyrna, Pergamum, Thyatria, Sardis, and Philadelphia, respectively. As the hearers encounter the name Laodicea, they are led to the final lampstand, moving southeast toward Laodicea, located some 40 miles away from Philadelphia. What would the hearers think of when they encounter the name Laodicea? Perhaps they think of a major commercial center located at the intersection of the road that runs through Pergamum, Thyatira, and Philadelphia and another road that leads west all the way to Ephesus. Or, perhaps they think of its bank and medical school. Perhaps they think of the black wool for which Laodicea was famous. Or, perhaps they think of the city's rebuilding after a deadly earthquake in 60 CE, without imperial aid, on which occasion a stadium and other large civic buildings were donated by Laodicean benefactors. Perhaps they think of the aqueduct system by which means the city received much of its water supply. Or, perhaps the hearers understand that this is the seventh and final church to be addressed by the resurrected Jesus and anticipate its climactic significance.

Whatever the hearers think of when encountering the name Laodicea, they soon find out what Jesus thinks of the church there. On this occasion, Jesus identifies himself by three titles, at least two of which are familiar to the hearers from the prologue. The first title the hearers encounter is ὁ ἀμήν ('the Amen'). The use of 'Amen' as a title or proper name is most unusual and is the only time this word is used in such a way in the whole of the NT.[91] It is possible that the hearers would be reminded of the fact that God himself is once referred to as 'God, the Amen' in Isa. 65.16, which is often translated as 'the true God', by whom one may swear both blessings and curses. As such, he is the highest and ultimate authority or truth. Part of the significance in Jesus' use of the title, then, is his appropriation of yet another title and/or name for himself that otherwise is reserved for God.[92] But such a connection would not exhaust the meaning of this identification for the hearers, owing to the term's well-known liturgical significance. Johannine hearers would be quite familiar with the way the double 'amen' is used by Jesus in the FG to introduce a variety of important utterances. On these occasions, the term serves as part of an oath formula 'amen, amen, I say to you', indicating the reliability and trustworthiness of the words that follow. This formula occurs so often in the FG that it is very difficult to believe that Johannine hearers would not be aware of this connection. On this view, Johannine hearers would understand that the one who uses this 'amen, amen' formula does so because he is *the* 'Amen'. Neither should it be ignored that the previous liturgical uses of the term in the Apocalypse (Rev. 1.6, 7) have clear Christological connections, for on each occasion it appears on the heels of words said about Jesus. The resurrected Jesus next identifies himself as 'the faithful and true witness'. These words would be quite significant for the hearers for they both hearken back to his identification in 1.5 as 'the faithful witness' and the way he has introduced himself to the church in Philadelphia as

---

[91] Smalley, *The Revelation to John*, p. 96.
[92] Aune, *Revelation 1-5*, p. 255.

'the true one'. The convergence of these ideas in 3.14 once more draws the hearers' attention to the place of faithful witness in their lives. For in this identification as 'the faithful and true witness', Jesus again serves as the model after which the believers are to pattern themselves. His faithful and true witness entails suffering and death, as well as being raised from the dead. He, along with Antipas, and others who face death, has shown the way for believers to follow. Perhaps the mere appearance of this title already raises the question of the faithful witness, or lack thereof, of the church in Laodicea.[93] Coming on the heels of his identification as 'the Amen' and his earlier claim to be 'the True One', the fact of his trustworthiness and identification with and as the Truth underscores the authenticity of his words to the church in Laodicea (as well as all the churches). As the 'faithful and true witness' his words are amplified in this last of the seven prophetic messages. Finally, he identifies himself as 'the origin (ἡ ἀρχὴ) of the creation of God'. Hearers would have reason to see in this title a variety of nuances of meaning. Perhaps their first associations would be with Jesus' identity in the FG as λόγος ('Word'), whose role in creation is central. For 'all things came to be through him, and without him not one thing came to be' (Jn 1.3). The fact that in Jn 1.1 the Word was ἐν ἀρχῇ ('in beginning'), before creation, might go some way toward contributing to this identification as 'the Origin of God's creation' here in Rev. 3.14. Thus, for Jesus to call himself 'the Origin of God's creation' would not surprise the hearers of the Apocalypse.[94] Neither is it without significance that Jesus will twice more identify himself as ἡ ἀρχὴ ('the origin' or 'the beginning') in the Apocalypse, where he is 'the origin/the beginning and the completion' (21.6; 22.13). At the same time, it is also possible that the hearers would discern in this phrase an echo of Rev. 1.5, where Jesus is identified by John with a related term 'the ruler (ὁ ἄρχων) of the kings of the earth'.[95] At any rate, Jesus' self-designation as 'the

---

[93] Yabro Collins, *The Apocalypse*, p. 30.

[94] Although it is possible to translate this phrase 'the beginning of God's creation' implying that Jesus was the first thing created, such an idea is at odds with the rest of Johannine thought, which seems to go to great lengths to demonstrate that Jesus was not 'created' by God.

[95] On this possibility cf. Murphy, *Fallen Is Babylon*, p. 160.

Origin of God's creation' alerts the hearers to the fact that God's creation will figure prominently in the remainder of the book.

Verses 15-16 – The content of the message is marked by the familiar phrase 'I know your works'. On this occasion the phrase not only introduces the content of the message but also prepares the hearers for the contrast between Jesus' knowledge and the Laodicean church's lack of knowledge.[96] Jesus' statement reveals that, unlike other churches, there are no words of praise or commendation offered to the church in Laodicea. Their works consist of nothing that merits his affirmation, making this church the object of his severest judgment found amongst the seven prophetic messages.[97] The first thing the hearers learn is that the church's works are identified in the negative. 'You are neither hot nor cold. Would that you were either hot or cold. So because you are lukewarm and neither cold nor hot, I am about to spit you out of my mouth'. As the hearers encounter these words they quickly learn that whatever the characteristics conveyed by the terms 'hot' and 'cold', they are deemed positively by Jesus, for they are placed in contrast, not to one another, but to the state of being 'lukewarm'. It is clear that both 'hot' and 'cold' states are acceptable to Jesus. In point of fact, he declares them to be such. The primary hint as to the meaning of these three terms comes from the fact that they are placed in a dining context by Jesus' reference to spitting out the 'lukewarm' substance. Such a context makes clear that the church's problem is its uselessness. Its works are completely worthless. The dining context would likely remind the hearers of the common practice of using both 'hot' and 'cold' drinks with a meal and on other occasions, with both 'hot' and 'cold' water often being available to be added to wine and other beverages.[98] Jesus' graphic description of spitting out the 'lukewarm' substance would also be familiar to hearers in that this action was repeated at any number of banquets in antiquity when a diner was not pleased with the taste of something served. 'Lukewarm' water or beverages were less distinctive than their 'hot'

---

[96] Murphy, *Fallen is Babylon*, p. 162.

[97] Prigent, *L'Apocalypse de Saint Jean*, p. 164.

[98] On this whole matter cf. the extremely insightful work of Craig R. Koester, 'The Message to Laodicea and the Problem of its Local Context: A Study of the Imagery in Rev. 3.14-22', *NTS* 49 (2003), pp. 407-24. These comments are heavily indebted to his fine analysis.

and 'cold' counterparts. In point of fact, it could even be used to induce vomiting! In this message, the 'lukewarm' imagery would likely convey the idea of reflecting the temperature of the environment, rather than the very distinctive imagery of something being 'hot' or 'cold'. While some degree of work is involved in keeping a substance 'hot' or 'cold', nothing is required for a substance to be 'lukewarm'. This condition develops simply by the accommodation of the substance to its surroundings. Jesus' message to the church in Laodicea could well be that its works reflect accommodation to its environment and the loss of its distinctive 'Christian' temperature. Its own 'faithful witness' is now indistinguishable from its surroundings. As such, these works will be spit out of Jesus' mouth because they are so unpalatable. In fact, the word ἐμέσαι ('spit out') may even indicate that such works cause Jesus to become sick to his stomach and to vomit out these works![99] Given the earlier prophetic associations with regard to the sword of Jesus' mouth, such a startling description is indeed an ominous sign to the hearers. It may not be without significance that Jesus returns to dining imagery near the end of this message (v. 20).[100]

Verse 17 – It is not altogether clear to the hearers at this point, exactly what these sickening works are, aside from the fact that they are 'lukewarm' and may result from accommodation to their surroundings. But Jesus' words in v. 17 offer some clarification as the statement begins with the term ὅτι ('because' or 'for'), which appears to indicate that the words which follow in v. 17 are directly connected to those which precede them in vv. 15-16. Their sickening works are directly connected to their claims, 'I am rich and I

---

[99] Aune, *Revelation 1-5*, p. 258.

[100] The oft-repeated line of interpretation which posits that the 'hot', 'cold', and 'lukewarm' language draws upon the fact that Heiropolis was known for its 'hot' water, Colossae for its the 'cold' water, and Laodicea for its 'lukewarm' water (brought via an aqueduct) does not quite fit the evidence. Such an interpretation does not take the dining context into sufficient account. Nor does it take into account the fact that Strabo (*Geography*, 13.4.14) declared the water in Laodicea to be fine for drinking. Nor does it pay sufficient attention to the fact that several of these seven cities had at least a portion of their water needs supplied by aqueducts. There were three aqueducts in Ephesus, two in Smyrna, and one each in Pergamum and Sardis. Unfortunately, such a line of interpretation has concealed, rather than revealed the meaning of the text. On all this cf. the excellent work by Koester, 'The Message to Laodicea and the Problem of its Local Context', pp. 407-24.

have become rich and I have need of nothing'. The hearers might discern an echo in Ephraim's similar claim to be rich in Hosea (12.8), a claim which God himself subverts. The triple emphasis of Rev. 3.17 underscores the confident self-assessment of the church with regard to its riches and independence. Owing to the previous inversion of poverty and riches in the message to the church at Smyrna, a church which was financially poor but declared to be spiritually rich by Jesus, it is likely that the emphasis of 3.17 would be understood to mean that the church in Laodicea was rich financially and materially. It might also indicate that in such claims the church understood itself to be rich spiritually as well, having need of nothing. On this view, it is significant that the accommodating attitude to their environment, which apparently led to their 'lukewarm' status, may also have led to their financial stability, as well as their prosperous spiritual self-assessment. Whatever may have led the church to this self-assessment, nothing could be farther from the truth. For Jesus knows ('I know your works', v. 15) what they do not know ('and you do not know', v. 17), 'that you are miserable and pitiable and poor and blind and naked'. This construction, where each of these terms appears in the nominative case and is connected by καὶ ('and'), underscores for the hearers the deplorable condition of the church.[101] As the resurrected Jesus relentlessly piles term upon term, the weight of the desperate situation of the church becomes heavier and heavier. Rather than being wealthy and having no need for anything, the church is in reality a miserable entity, something to be pitied owing to its dreadful condition. While the first two terms in this list of five are general descriptions of the appalling state of the church, the last three terms in this list describe concrete characteristics of the church in Laodicea, and serve as the basis of Jesus' words which follow in v. 18. In contrast to their claims to be rich, they are actually poor. Jesus' statement here is the reverse of his words to the church in Smyrna, which is poor but Jesus describes as rich (2.9). The irony of this comparison would hardly be lost on the hearers, making the contrast all the more powerful. Clearly their poverty is a spiritual poverty that must in some way be connected to their 'lukewarm' nature resulting from accommodation to their surroundings. They are also spiritually

---

[101] Aune, *Revelation 1-5*, p. 259.

'blind', a condition that in Johannine thought is the result of one's location in spiritual darkness and is a sign that one remains in sin (Jn 9.1-41). The one blinded by the darkness, walks in darkness and does not know where he or she is going (1 Jn 2.11). Owing to these associations, a more damning Johannine indictment of a church is difficult to imagine. The church is also described as spiritually 'naked'. Once again the irony of Jesus' words would be immediately recognizable to the hearers, as wealth in antiquity was often measured in part by one's wardrobe. Thus, for a church that considers itself wealthy, to be declared naked is quite unexpected. Peter's action in the FG, where he clothes himself before jumping into the water to swim to Jesus because he was naked (Jn 21.7), suggests that there is something inappropriate about the naked condition. The appearance of this term elsewhere in the Apocalypse conveys the idea of exposure and humiliation (Rev. 16.15; 17.10). Here Jesus' charge clearly indicates that the church in Laodicea is in an exposed and humiliating position.

Verse 18 – These final three descriptions of the church's deplorable condition in v. 17 become the basis of Jesus' admonition to those in Laodicea in v. 18, as each of these conditions is singled out as a need to be remedied. Thus, Jesus says, 'I advise you to buy from me …' Perhaps Jesus' words would remind the hearers of this term's earlier appearance in the Johannine literature, where Caiaphas' advice that it is better for one man to die for the people (Jn 18.14) proves discerning.[102] The occurrence of the emphatic personal pronouns, 'you' and 'me', may heighten the contrast between the need of the Laodiceans and the resources of Jesus. There is also the interesting phenomenon of Jesus advising those who are spiritually poor to 'buy' certain needed things from him. Clearly, his counsel assumes that the Laodiceans must learn to purchase, not out of their material wealth, but in keeping with the admonition found in Isa. 55.1-3, where those without money are invited to 'come and buy' in order that their souls may live. In this Isaianic text, such purchases are synonymous with listening to the Lord and following his ways. No doubt the purchases of which Jesus speaks are to be made in a similar fashion. The church is advised to buy gold, white garments, and eye salve from Jesus. The interrelation

---

[102] Osborne, *Revelation*, p. 208.

between these three items is indicated by the fact that the one verb 'buy' governs all three. The first thing to be purchased from Jesus is 'gold refined in fire'. The mention of gold would no doubt cause the hearers to pause owing to the fact that if the church in Laodicea is rich materially in any sense, then they would possess some gold already. But just as the imagery of riches has more than one meaning, so does the imagery of gold. Gold can have negative associations. There are locusts that wear crowns of gold (9.7) and there are idols of gold (9.20). The Great Whore is bedecked with gold while in her hand is a golden cup full of her abominations and the uncleanness of her sexual immorality (17.4). The merchants, who have gold among their cargo (18.12), bring gold into the evil city (18.16). Conversely, the hearers are aware that gold has numerous positive associations as well, for Jesus has already been seen in a golden girdle (1.13) while the seven golden lampstands have appeared several times (1.12, 20; 2.1). Gold will also be associated with the twenty-four elders, who wear crowns of gold (4.4), the golden bowls of incense which are the prayers of the saints (5.8), the angel with a golden censer (8.3), the golden altar before the throne of God (8.3; 9.13), the Son of Man who wears a golden crown (14.14), the angels with golden girdles (15.6), and golden bowls full of the wrath of God (15.7). Gold will also be intimately identified with the New Jerusalem for it is to be measured with a golden rod (21.15), while the city (21.18) and its streets (21.21) are made of pure gold. That Jesus has gold is clear from the golden girdle, which he wears, and the seven golden lampstands, in the midst of which he walks. But he reveals more about this gold when he describes it further to the church in Laodicea as πεπυρωμένον ἐκ πυρός ('refined by fire'). This phrase literally means 'fired by fire', as both the noun and the verb come from the same root word. Normally such language would convey the idea of the removal of impurities from a substance by refining it in fire, so that it comes out pure. In this context it is difficult not to see here a reference to the fire of suffering which opposition and/or persecution brings to the community. Perhaps the hearers would discern in these words of Jesus a call to reject their accommodating disposition to their surroundings that has resulted in their 'lukewarm' condition, identifying more fully with Jesus the faithful and true witness. The purchase of such gold will result in their being spiritually 'rich'. The relationship between suffering for one's faithful witness and riches declared to the church in Smyrna would not be lost on the hearers at this point, making clearer the point that obtaining gold fired by the fire of suffering owing to one's faithful witness results in true riches.[103] Ironically, the acquisition of this 'gold' might very well involve the relinquishment of the gold they currently possess.

Jesus also advises the church to purchase 'white garments'. Again the irony of those who think they are rich being instructed to buy white garments would not be lost on the hearers as one of the ways wealth was gauged in antiquity was in terms of one's wardrobe, or changes of clothes. The instruction to purchase 'white garments' would also be appropriate coming from Jesus for white is intimately connected with him (1.14) and those who walk with him (3.4). As has been seen, white clothing is a theological reality in the Apocalypse, which indicates that the wearer has an intimate association with Jesus by proving to be a faithful witness and thus experiencing the promised eschatological reward of being dressed in white (3.6). Jesus' admonition is an implicit call to those in Laodicea to be dressed like their resurrected Lord. The fact that there are already some names who walk in white with Jesus underscores the fact that 'white garments' are not simply an eschatological promise to be experienced at the return of Jesus, but is a present possibility, even necessity, for those who are part of the church. The purchase of these garments would no doubt be made in precisely the same way as the purchase of gold from Jesus; hearing his word and following his commands. The purpose of such garments is 'in order that you might be clothed and the shame of your nakedness might not be manifested'. In addition to the way the imagery of white garments points to the church's identification, in this context it is clearly connected to the reversal of their spiritual 'lukewarm' state of nakedness. The shame of their nakedness is no doubt in reference to the fact that their 'works' leave much to be desired. In point of fact, their works are revolting. Reference to the shame of nakedness might well remind Johannine hearers of the possibility of being ashamed at Jesus' parousia (1 Jn 2.28), where both the idea of 'being ashamed' and 'being put to shame' are present.[104] The occur-

---

[103] Beale, *The Book of Revelation*, p. 305.
[104] Thomas, *1 John, 2 John, 3 John*, pp. 144-45.

rence of the word 'manifest' in both 1 Jn 2.28 and here in Rev. 3.18 suggests that such an eschatological nuance would not be missed by the hearers. Thus, in this verse, the shame or disgrace of their nakedness has reference to the 'lukewarm' and sickening state of their works, which need to be reversed by the buying of white garments. Such a purchase will ensure that they do not have to face Jesus at this coming in disgrace, but rather can be clothed like unto him and resemble him in appearance.

The third thing Jesus advises the church to buy is 'salve to anoint your eyes'. While commentators debate whether or not the powder used for eye salve produced in nearby Phyrgia is in mind, Johannine hearers are likely to discern a deeper meaning for a couple of reasons. First, there is a remarkable similarity between the word used here ἐγχρῖσαι ('to anoint'), to describe the anointing of the eyes, and the word used in Jn 9.6, ἐπέχρισεν ('to anoint'), to describe Jesus' anointing the eyes of the man born blind in John 9. The relationship of the blind man receiving his physical sight to his receiving spiritual sight is made clear as the pericope unfolds. The result in both the FG and the Apocalypse is the receiving of sight.[105] Such similarities would hardly go unnoticed by the hearers. Second, neither would the similarity between this anointing and the anointing that all believers have received from the Holy One be ignored (1 Jn 2.20). The former allows one to receive spiritual sight, the latter enables one to know all things (1 Jn 2.27). The purpose of the anointing described by Jesus in Rev. 3.18 is in order that 'you might see'. This anointing would result in a move from darkness to the light, a receiving of sight that would enable them to know where they are going. The fact that the remedy for blindness occurs last in the series of remedies, while occurring next to last in the list of v. 17 may suggest that spiritual blindness is the church's major problem. In any event, Jesus makes clear to the church in Laodicea that he has the remedy for their deficiencies and he can transform their works from those that are sickening to those that are worthy of their Lord.

The hearers understand that they are listening to the last of the seven prophetic messages. This realization would likely heighten the

---

[105] The fact that a form of βλέπω ('I see') occurs in both passages makes this connection all the stronger.

dramatic effect of Jesus' words for them. It might also cause them to hear these final words not simply as the conclusion of this message, but as in some ways the conclusion of all the messages. If so, perhaps this blurring of the lines begins to be seen with the end of v. 18 and the beginning of v. 19.

Verse 19 – The hearers might catch an echo of Prov. 3.12 when Jesus says, 'Those whom I love, I rebuke/convict and discipline'. The emphatic personal pronoun 'I' reminds the hearers of all that Jesus has spoken to this point and that he is in a position to rebuke and discipline. It also continues the practice in the Apocalypse where titles and actions normally attributed to God are attributed to or self-ascribed by Jesus. Mention of Jesus' love not only reminds the churches of Jesus' love for them declared earlier (1.5; 3.9), but also of its rich theological meaning within Johannine thought. Its occurrence in this context comes as a welcome sign of encouragement in a message that has contained no affirmation for the church in Laodicea. It suggests that despite the sickening condition of this church Jesus still loves them and, consequently, speaks these words to it. At the same time, these words serve to remind the hearers that all his prophetic words spoken to the seven churches are spoken in love. Those he loves he 'rebukes' and 'disciplines'. Both these words communicate to the hearers at a couple of levels. For while the word ἐλέγχω ('rebuke') can be translated as 'rebuke' in this verse, in the FG it also carries with it the idea of 'convict' or 'prove wrong' (Jn 16.8-11). And while the word παιδεύω ('discipline') can be translated as 'discipline', Johannine hearers would not likely be able to forget that the noun form of the word, παιδία ('children'), often appears in 1 John as a term of endearment for the believers, 'children'. Thus, even these words that convey rebuke and discipline also carry a hopeful expectation that such conviction and discipline will be met with an appropriate response. In this case, the appropriate response is made clear. 'Therefore, be zealous and repent!' The call for being zealous might at first strike the hearers as odd, until Jesus' words from the FG are remembered, 'Zeal for your house will destroy me'. In this quotation of Ps. 69.9 (LXX), Jesus indicates that his zeal for God's house will ultimately lead to his own death, a scripture which the disciples later believe, after the resurrection. Perhaps the not so subtle message to the church in Laodicea is that there is no substitute for a zealous commitment to

Jesus; even if that commitment leads to the loss of one's life! At the same time, this word of challenge to the church in Laodicea would function as a word of encouragement to those churches that have and continue to demonstrate such a zealous commitment in their faithful witness. Such a zealous commitment would lead quite naturally to repentance. That Jesus calls the church in Laodicea to repentance is not surprising in the least, given the church's deplorable condition. Given the context, the concrete elements of this repentance would no doubt include the buying of gold, white garments, and eye salve and a rejection of the environment that leads to a 'lukewarm' nature. No longer are they to be complacent, allowing their surroundings to dictate their condition, but they are to be zealous so that they might move from a state of being 'lukewarm' to being 'hot' or 'cold'. The intensity of this call to repentance is heightened in importance in that it is the final call for repentance to be found in the seven prophetic messages.

Verse 20 – The content of this message comes to a close in v. 20 with words that are, appropriately enough, a fitting conclusion to the seven prophetic messages as a whole, for it draws on various ideas that have appeared in Jesus' earlier words to the seven churches. The complexity of this verse is witnessed with Jesus' first words: 'Behold, I stand at the door and I knock'. His words reveal that despite the sickening condition of the church in Laodicea, Jesus is still present and active. The perfect tense verb ἕστηκα ('I stand') indicates that Jesus has taken up a position outside the door of the church where he continues to be located. Not only is he located outside the door of the church, but as the present tense verb κρούω ('I knock') reveals, he is continuously knocking, seeking entry.[106] Part of the irony of this statement for the hearers is that Jesus, who is the door, stands before the door of the church. This image would suggest that the church is not in fellowship with Jesus, despite his continued entreaties toward it. Such words might well remind the hearers of those found in Song 5.2, where the lover knocks on the door of the beloved, perhaps introducing for the hearers the imagery of marriage between Jesus and his church.[107] If this image leads the hearers to believe that the church is not in fel-

---

[106] Smalley, *The Revelation to John*, p. 101.
[107] Beale, *The Book of Revelation*, p. 308.

lowship with Jesus, Jesus' next works confirm this understanding: 'if anyone hears my voice and opens the door, I will enter in to it and I will dine with him and he with me'. The idea of 'hearing my voice' is a familiar one in Johannine circles as it echoes numerous words of Jesus in the FG. In point of fact, the imagery is so rich and complex that for the hearers it may be a comprehensive cipher indicating one's total solidarity and complete identification with Jesus and his mission. The idea of hearing the voice of Jesus includes an eschatological dimension in the FG, for the dead who hear the voice of the Son of Man will be made alive (Jn 5.24-28). It is also closely associated with identity and discernment, for Jesus' own sheep hear his voice and will not follow another (Jn 10.3-5, 16, 27). Finally, in his last, climatic response to Pilate, Jesus says, 'Each one who is of the Truth hears my voice' (Jn 18.37). For the hearers of the Apocalypse such a rich image would surely indicate that the activity of hearing Jesus' voice reveals whether or not they know him and are identified as his sheep, who have eternal life and will come to life in the last day. Thus, this image of hearing his voice pushes the hearers toward discerning their own status before and relationship with the resurrected Jesus. The fact that it is the one who hears his voice 'and opens the door' is significant. The hearers know, from Rev. 3.7, that Jesus has the power to open this door, for he is the one who can 'open and no one can close' and 'close and no one can open'. Yet, this door will not be opened by Jesus.[108] Rather, it must be opened by the church(es).[109] Such a reality suggests that unless the church is active in its response to Jesus' entreaty, it will not share a meal with him, for it is not in fellowship with him.[110] Its 'lukewarm' condition must give way to an active response to Jesus. The result of a positive response, the opening of the closed door, is the fellowship of a meal between Jesus and his church. The idea of sharing a meal together is clear enough. But perhaps it should also be pointed out that Jesus has already hinted about an eschatological fellowship meal in his promise to give the church in Ephesus to eat of the tree of life (2.7) and the church in Pergamum some hidden

---

[108] Mounce (*The Book of Revelation*, p. 129) insightfully observes, 'In an act of unbelievable condescension he requests permission to enter and re-establish fellowship'.

[109] Osborne, *Revelation*, p. 213.

[110] Resseguie, *The Revelation of John*, p. 102.

manna (2.17). The appearance of the verb δειπνήσω ('I will eat') might well remind the hearers of the fact that a δεῖπνον ('dinner') takes place on three occasions in the FG (Jn 12.2; 13.2, 4; 21.20). Owing to the fact that each of these meals has sacramental overtones, perhaps Jesus' words in Rev. 3.20 would be taken as a subtle reference to the Eucharist, as a sign of the fellowship to be enjoyed by Jesus and the church.[111] It is also possible that this dining anticipates the eschatological marriage δεῖπνον ('dinner') of the Lamb mentioned in Rev. 19.9,[112] that appears to include a gruesome dimension as well (cf. 19.17). Whatever its full meaning, the intimacy of this meal is made clear by the phrase 'I with him and he with me'.

Verse 21 – For a seventh time in the seven prophetic messages, an eschatological promise is made to the one who overcomes. On this occasion Jesus promises, 'I will give to him to sit with me on my throne, even as I have overcome and I have sat with my Father on his throne'. It is difficult to overestimate the significance of this statement for the hearers. To be promised access to a throne would be stupendous enough. But to be promised to sit with Jesus, the ruler of the kings of the earth (1.5), on his throne is almost beyond comprehension! To this point in the Apocalypse, mention has been made of the throne of the One who is and was and is coming, before which are the Seven Spirits of God (1.4), and Satan's throne (2.13). Owing to the fact that Jesus is proclaimed to be 'the ruler of the kings of the earth', the hearers would not be completely surprised that he here reveals that he has a throne. The throne is Jesus' to give owing to the fact that he himself is one who has overcome. Thus, the explicit connection between Jesus' throne and his experience of overcoming would be difficult for the hearers to miss. No doubt, the mention of Jesus' overcoming would remind the hearers of his words to the disciples in the FG: 'in this world you have tribulation; but be courageous, I have overcome the world' (Jn 16.33). Tribulation as the context of Jesus' overcoming in the FG would be an obvious parallel with the broader context of the Apocalypse. In addition, Jesus overcoming activity is developed further in 1 Jn 5.4-5, where there is an extremely tight connection between Jesus'

---

[111] Smalley, *The Revelation to John*, p. 102.
[112] Sweet, *Revelation*, p. 109.

overcoming and the believer's overcoming. In Rev. 3.21, this connection becomes even clearer, for Jesus' overcoming work is the explicit model for the believer's overcoming work.[113] 'The one who overcomes will sit ... even as I have overcome and sat'. The word ἐνίκσα ('I have overcome'), an aorist tense verb, indicates that Jesus has a specific past event in mind. To this point one phrase stands out in the Apocalypse as the most likely candidate for this past event. Most recently, this title appears at the beginning of the message to the church in Laodicea. Jesus is 'the Faithful and True Witness', the kind of witness all believers are called to be. While the hearers would doubtless look upon Jesus' entire life as comprising his overcoming work, this victory is intimately connected to his death and resurrection in this book. Thus, the overcoming work of Jesus as Faithful and True Witness is inextricably bound to his place on the throne and his ability to give to others the right to sit on his throne. Jesus' faithful witness would stand in stark contrast to the 'lukewarm' witness of the church in Laodicea. The eschatological tension found in the Apocalypse is reflected by the fact that although Jesus makes this statement, there will be another place in the Apocalypse where he is described as overcoming his foes (17.14). The conclusion of v. 21, with its reference to Jesus sitting on the Father's throne, informs the hearers in several ways. First, it continues to develop the close identification between Jesus and God. The one who sits on the throne is God, Jesus' Father. The fact that the overcomers would share the throne not only reinforces the idea that they share a variety of attributes, but also suggests that their identities are mysteriously interconnected. Second, if the one who overcomes is promised to sit on Jesus' throne with him, and Jesus sits on the throne of his Father, then by implication the one who overcomes will participate in the activity of God and at some level share in his identity. Such an implication, though stupendous, is not out of keeping with the promises that the one who overcomes will be a pillar in God's temple, will have authority over the nations, and have God's name, the name of God's city, and Jesus' name written upon him or her. In some ways this promise, though given to the church in Laodicea, is a fitting conclusion to the seven messages, for it appears to be the comprehensive promise to the one who

---

[113] Prigent, *L'Apocalypse de Saint Jean*, p. 168.

overcomes. Third, the emphasis placed upon the throne(s) continues to develop a theme that becomes dominant in the rest of the book,[114] and provides the perfect transition to the next major section of the Apocalypse.

Verse 22 – The seven prophetic messages of this first section of the vision end with the familiar call to discerning obedience. At one level, this call is specific to the church in Laodicea. But owing to its strategic location as the final church addressed and the fact that the horizons of this message and all the messages begin to merge from about v. 19 onwards, the hearers would have reason to pause and reflect upon the words of Jesus in this entire section of the book. So, what response should be given to the words of the resurrected Jesus, which are spoken by the Spirit? How can the hearers keep the words of this prophecy? With regard to the message to the church at Laodicea it is clear. The faithful witness of the church must remain active and not become diluted through accommodation to its environment. Whatever the costs it must be 'hot' or 'cold', not 'lukewarm'. Jesus, the true and faithful witness, has all the provisions to enable believers to see spiritually with eyes that he has healed, to appear as him in white garments, and to possess the gold that has been tried by the fire of persecution. Jesus' entreaties are to be met with an active response. It involves a demonstration of zeal for him and his cause as well as repentance. For one's response will determine one's fate. While numerous ideas would perhaps be swirling in the hearers' minds as a result of their reflection upon all the messages, one theme stands out above all others; the theme of faithful witness. Jesus and the Spirit continually and consistently call for faithful witness from the churches. Such faithful witness is to be given in the face of persecution that could result in death, the teaching and presence of false prophets and apostles, and the temptation to accommodate their witness to the surrounding religious and commercial environment. Faithful and true witness is the appropriate response to the faithful and true witness, Jesus Christ. It is this witness offered by means of discerning obedience that will be the focus as the Apocalypse continues to unfold.

---

[114] D. Sanger ('θρόνος', *EDNT*, II, p. 156) notes that of the some sixty occurrences of the word θρόνος ('throne') in the NT, three-fourths of them appear in the Apocalypse.

'IN THE SPIRIT' IN HEAVEN – REVELATION 4.1-16.21

With the conclusion of the seven prophetic messages to the seven churches, the first major section of the Apocalypse (1.9-3.22) comes to a close. The second and largest section of the Apocalypse (4.1-16.21) includes the inaugural vision of heaven (4.1-5.14), the opening of the scroll sealed with seven seals (6.1-8.5), the seven angels with the seven trumpets (8.2-11.19), the struggle of God's people in cosmic perspective (12.1-15.4), and the seven angels with the seven bowls of plagues (15.1-16.21). In this largest major section of the book, the hearers encounter the second occurrence of the phrase ἐν πνεύματι ('in the Spirit'), indicating the beginning of a new section of the Apocalypse. Immediately after the seventh bowl of plagues is poured out, the phrase ἐν πνεύματι ('in the Spirit') occurs for a third time, indicating the onset of the third major section in the Apocalypse. As noted in the introduction, this section of the Apocalypse is not only connected to what precedes and follows it, but it also stands together as a distinct section by means of a variety of literary markers.

The Inaugural Vision of Heaven, the One Who Sits on the Throne, the Lamb, and the Scroll Sealed with Seven Seals (4.1-5.14)

Verse 1 – The hearers of the Apocalypse are alerted to the transition from the first major section of the book to the second major section in two ways. For the first time since Jesus began speaking in 1.17, the hearers again encounter John's voice. This change of speaker would prepare the hearers for a shift of focus. The transition is also indicated by means of the phrase 'After these things I saw', signaling the conclusion of the seven prophetic messages to the seven churches spoken by the resurrected Jesus to John. Earlier John saw the risen Jesus (1.12-20). In 4.1 John saw 'a door which had been opened in heaven'. Mention of the opened door would convey several things to the hearers. First, it reminds them of another open door that Jesus himself had placed before the church in Philadelphia (3.8). In that passage there is an extremely tight interplay between Jesus who opens the door and Jesus as the door of the sheep, through whom those who enter are 'saved' and experience 'eternal life'. As on that occasion, this door too represents access to God.[1] Second, the passive form of the verb ἠνεῳγμένη ('which had been opened') grammatically is a divine passive, indicating that the door had been opened by God, or in this case, Jesus.[2] It may not be going too far to suggest that the hearers would understand this door being opened by Jesus as somehow the result of his possession of the 'key of David'. Third, the perfect tense of this verb suggests that the door had been opened and remains open for John and perhaps others (in the prophetic community) as well. For not only does John make his way through this opened door, but the hearers also accompany him on his journey and are called upon to discern what they experience as they engage in pneumatic interpretation. Fourth, the contrast between Jesus standing at and knocking on the door of the church in Laodicea, asking the church to open the door, and the door which Jesus has opened in heaven would be difficult to miss for the hearers.[3]

But before the hearers are able to ponder this mysterious scene, their attention is directed elsewhere. For John says, 'And the first voice which I heard as a trumpet was speaking with me saying, "Come up here, and I will show you that which is necessary to take place after these things".' Such language reveals that the one who was speaking, Jesus,[4] continues to speak to John at this point. The phrase, 'the first voice which I heard as a trumpet', takes the hearers

---

[1] Yarbro Collins, *Apocalypse*, p. 34.
[2] Smalley, *The Revelation to John*, p. 113.
[3] Koester, *Revelation and the End of All Things*, p. 71.
[4] Osborne, *Revelation*, p. 224.

back to John's initial prophetic encounter with Jesus described in the Apocalypse (1.10). It was this voice that commissions John to write what he sees. It was this voice that gives way to the incredible vision of the resurrected Jesus, which follows. The fact that the first voice speaking with John now speaks to him again underscores the continuity that exists between Jesus' words in Revelation 1-3 and his words to follow in 4.1. The words 'Come up here' are an invitation to enter into heaven through the opened door. Such an incredible invitation would likely fill the hearers with anticipation, reminding them of certain OT prophetic figures who were also given visions of heaven. While there will be differences between the visions of heaven which Isaiah and Ezekiel received and the one John receives, it will become clear that they and John see the same God.[5] The invitation to come up to heaven accompanies Jesus' promise to show John that which is necessary to take place. This promise reminds the hearers of similar language that occurs at the beginning of the book (1.1) and just before the seven prophetic messages (1.19), indicating that what is to follow is not disconnected from that which precedes. This language carries with it the idea of divine sovereignty, as 'it is necessary' for these things to take place. The introductory nature of 4.1 is indicated by the fact that this verse begins and ends with the words μετὰ ταῦτα ('after these things'). The latter occurrence of these words carries with them a certain sense of ambiguity, as the identity of these things is not at all clear at this point. All the hearers know is that such things are likely to take place soon (cf. 1.1, 3, 19).

Verses 2-3 – The effects of Jesus' words are immediate and suggest something of John's willingness to 'come up here'. For John exclaims, 'Immediately I was in the Spirit'. Several things are significant about the appearance of this phrase. First, since there is no hint in the text that John was no longer 'in the Spirit' as chapter 4 begins, the phrase's appearance here would convey a sense of continuity between John's experience in chapters 1-3 and his experience in chapter 4 and following.[6] Second, owing to what the hearers learn after last encountering this phrase, they are likely to expect additional prophetic words from or about Jesus in what follows. As

---

[5] Kiddle, *The Revelation of St. John*, p. 67.

[6] Smalley, *The Revelation to John*, p. 114.

the Apocalypse unfolds they learn that this phrase is central to the book's structure and that the means by which the revelation is given is 'in the Spirit'. Third, on this occasion, the 'in the Spirit' phrase follows the words of Jesus, while in 1.9-10 the words of Jesus follow this phrase. In the former it appears that being 'in the Spirit' leads to the revelation of Jesus' words, whilst in the latter it appears that the words of Jesus leads to John's being 'in the Spirit'. Such an inversion reinforces once again the emerging picture of the relationship between Jesus and the Spirit in the Apocalypse, whose words and activities seem to be coterminous. Finally, there appears to be a connection between certain geographical locations and being 'in the Spirit'. In chapter one there was a connection between John being on the island of Patmos when 'in the Spirit' (1.9-10), while in Rev. 4.2, there appears to be a connection between John being 'in the Spirit' and being in heaven. This trend continues in the last two passages that contain the 'in the Spirit' phrase. In Rev. 17.3 John is taken to the wilderness while 'in the Spirit', whilst in Rev. 21.10 John is 'in the Spirit' on a great mountain.

As the narrative continues it is clear that John's vantage point is now heaven for he says, 'And behold, a throne stood in heaven and upon the throne one was seated'. Not only does this statement indicate a change in John's geographical location, but it also continues the throne emphasis that has been building in the book. The hearers were introduced very early in the book to the throne of the One who is and was and is coming, before which are the Seven Spirits of God (1.4), and later learn that Satan too has a throne (2.13). But what is still ringing in the hearers' ears at this point is the promise to the one who overcomes with which Jesus concludes the seven prophetic messages to the seven churches to 'sit on my throne even as I ... have sat on my Father's throne'. Thus, as John describes his vision of heaven, the hearers would have not been completely surprised that there is a throne in heaven, nor that there is one who sits on this throne! Later, the vocabulary of one sitting on the throne often appears in the Apocalypse as a title for God in the phrase, 'the One who sits on the throne' (4.9-10; 5.1, 7, 13; 6.16; 7.10, 15; 11.16; 19.4; 21.5). Perhaps in this text these words would cause the hearers to expect a description of 'the One who sits on the throne', along the lines of the earlier description of Jesus in 1.12-20. However, unlike the descriptions of God in Isaiah and

Ezekiel, John is reticent about describing 'the One who sits on the throne' in concrete terms. Rather, John's description of what he sees takes the form of beautiful translucent objects and colors that convey theological truths to the hearers.[7] For 'the One who sits on the throne' was in appearance as the stones jasper and sardius, while a rainbow encircled the throne in appearance as emerald. The hearers may well be taken back by the fact that God is described by such objects and colors. But they might also be impressed by the fact that these particular colors appear here in connection with the description of God. For these colors are also found together on the sacred breast piece worn by the High Priest as described in Exod. 28.17-21. In that text, twelve different stones are sewn on this garment, with the name of one of the twelve tribes being engraved on each one. Significantly, jasper is the final stone of the twelve, while the first row of three stones begins with sardius. With these two colors, representing the whole of Israel in inverse order, the hearers would learn of the close connection that exists between the One who sits on the throne and his people. This detail of the vision perhaps reveals to the hearers why these particular colors are present on the High Priest's breast piece, for they are tied to the identity of God. The relationship between these twelve stones and God's identity becomes even clearer when the foundations of the New Jerusalem are described in Rev. 21.19-21, where all but one of these stones appear.[8] The first foundation is jasper and the sixth foundation is sardius. It may not be insignificant that jasper stands first in both these texts. Thus, the presence of God is first conveyed to John and his hearers by means of these theologically significant stones. In addition, the hearers learn that there is a rainbow, in appearance as emerald, encircling the throne. Several things are conveyed to the hearers by this statement. First, it would be very difficult for the hearers not to see here a reference to the sign of God's covenant with Noah not to destroy the earth by a flood again (Gen. 9.8-17).[9] Standing as it does in this inaugural vision of God in heaven, this sign would serve as a constant reminder throughout the

---

[7] Smalley, *The Revelation to John*, p. 115; Osborne, *Revelation*, p. 226.

[8] Ten of the stones described in the Hebrew Scriptures appear here, combined with another of the stones (χρυσόλιθος ['chrysolite']) from the LXX version of Exodus 28.

[9] Smalley, *The Revelation to John*, p. 115.

Apocalypse, that despite the divine judgment poured out upon the world, God's mercy is not forgotten.[10] This detail about the rainbow would underscore God's faithfulness to his creation.[11] Second, the rainbow that here appears is the first in a series of things described as encircling the throne in Revelation 4-5, anticipating the circle that encompasses the whole universe. Third, the rainbow's emerald color reminds the hearers of God's identity as this color too is found on the High Priest's breast piece, appearing as the first stone in the second line of twelve stones. Emerald also appears as the fourth foundation in the New Jerusalem (21.19). With these theologically significant objects and translucent colors, the hearers receive their first glimpse of the One who sits on the throne.

Verse 4 – 'And encircling the throne were twenty-four thrones, and upon the thrones were sitting twenty-four elders clothed in white garments and upon their heads were golden crowns'. As the hearers learn of the twenty-four thrones that encircle the throne, they can hardly but think of the promise just spoken to the one who overcomes in 3.21. Such a one will be given authority to sit on the throne with Jesus, just as he sits on the throne with his Father. Thus, the unbelievable promise of the resurrected Jesus is fulfilled before John's eyes (and the hearers' ears). Not only would this imagery convey something about the promise of authority given to the one who overcomes to rule the nations, but the hearers would no doubt also be struck by the close proximity such overcomers have to God and his throne! Those who sit on these thrones are described in some detail, indicating at most every point the connection between the twenty-four who sit on the thrones and the promises to those who overcome.[12] Significantly, those who sit on these thrones are not described in language typical for heavenly beings, such as angels, but are described as elders. The appearance of groups of elders in the NT is remarkably widespread. They are mentioned in connection with the Jerusalem church (Acts 11.30;

---

[10] As Caird (*The Revelation of St. John*, p. 63) observes, 'The rainbow … tells us that there is no triumph for God's sovereignty at the expense of his mercy, and it warns us not to interpret the visions of disaster that follow as though God had forgotten his promise to Noah'.

[11] Bauckham, *Climax of Prophecy*, p. 254 and Wall, *Revelation*, p. 92.

[12] On the identity of the elders cf. the helpful piece by L.W. Hurtado, 'Revelation 4-5 in the Light of Jewish Apocalyptic Analogies', *JSNT* 25 (1985), pp. 105-24 (esp. pp. 111-16). Cf. also Fee, *Revelation*, p. 69.

15.2, 4, 6, 22-23; 16.4; 21.18), the Pauline mission (Acts 14.23; 20.17-38), the Pauline circle (1 Tim. 4.14; 5.17-19; Tit. 1.5), and the Petrine churches (1 Pet. 5.1). Within the Johannine community, the author of 2 and 3 John refers to himself as *the* elder. Clearly, these uses suggest that within these early Christian communities, elders, or *the* elder, are leaders who in some ways represent the entire community or church. Owing to the unique position of *the* elder in 2 and 3 John, the exemplary and representative nature of the term would be all the more striking for Johannine hearers. The fact that there are twenty-four thrones and elders is pregnant with meaning, as a number of ideas converge at this point. The number itself invites reflection on its biblical significance. Owing to the prominence of the number twelve in the OT, perhaps the first thing the hearers would discern here is a doubling of that number. Such a doubling would result in the discovery that this number (12), which is full of theological significance, is ultimately part of a fuller number still. Like so many other things in this book, its significance can only be fully appreciated in relationship to its larger theological meaning. It is very difficult to imagine that the hearers would not see in this number some kind of combination of the theological significance of the number twelve in both the OT and the Johannine tradition. Specifically, the hearers will learn that both the twelve tribes of Israel and the twelve apostles have a significant place in heaven (Rev. 7.4-8) and the New Jerusalem (21.12-14). At this point, one of the things the number twenty-four would suggest to the hearers is that there is a profound relationship between these twenty-four elders and those represented by the twelve tribes and the twelve apostles. In this instance, the whole is certainly greater than the sum of its parts. The hearers might also discern in this comprehensive number reference to the role of believers as priests to God (1.6). On the one hand, the division of the priesthood into twenty-four courses would be common knowledge (1 Chron. 24.4-6).[13] On the other hand, the hearers will discover that the elders exhibit various priestly functions as the book unfolds. The identity of the twenty-four elders is further confirmed by the description of their white garments and golden crowns. The appearance of the elders in white garments fulfills the eschatological promise given by

---

[13] Simoens, *Apocalypse de Jean*, p. 43.

Jesus in 3.5 that the one who overcomes will wear white garments. These garments indicate that one has an intimate association with Jesus. Their appearance in white mirrors his appearance, just as their faithful witness is patterned on his faithful witness. The golden crowns on the heads of the elders also appear to indicate fulfillment of the resurrected Jesus' promise that the one who is faithful unto death will be given a crown of life (2.10). The fact that the crown is now described as 'golden crowns' indicates something about the way in which the fulfillment of eschatological promises is even greater than anticipated. The 'white garments' and 'golden crowns' the elders possess demonstrate that the promises to the one who overcomes are based upon heavenly realties.[14] The fact that 'crowns' have already been received by the church in Philadelphia (3.11) indicates something of the eschatological interplay between present and future realities, reassuring the hearers of the reality of these promises. Owing to the convergence in 4.4 of ideas found in 2.10, 3.5, and 3.21, it is clear that these standing nearest the throne are those who have been faithful witnesses, like their Lord. If a rainbow of mercy encircles the throne, those who have experienced God's mercy themselves next encircle it.

Verses 5-6a – The hearers are told three additional things about the throne in vv. 5-6a, the grammar indicating that these three details are to be understood together. First of all, it is learned that out of this throne come 'lightnings, sounds, and thunders'. For the hearers, there would be no mistaking the significance of such language, for it is standard theophany vocabulary indicating the presence and activity of God (cf. Exod. 19.16; Ezek. 1.13; Ps. 77.18; Dan. 7.9). In Rev. 4.5, these theophanic elements reveal the awesome presence and power of God as they proceed directly from his throne and are some of the loudest and most impressive phenomena with which first century individuals would be familiar. The present tense verb ἐκπορεύονται ('coming out/from') indicates that these are on-going phenomenon.[15] At the same time, this language conveys the idea that God is not some distant passive deity, but is a God who is active in creation and human history. For, as noted in

---

[14] Hurtado, 'Revelation 4-5 in the Light of Jewish Apocalyptic Analogies', p. 114.
[15] Aune, *Revelation 1-5*, pp. 294-95.

the introduction, the theophanic elements, that appear here for the first time in the Apocalypse, will reappear with growing intensity on three subsequent occasions in this section of the book (8.5; 11.19; 16.18). Significantly, these theophanic elements appear at the conclusion of the opening of the seventh seal, the blasting of the seventh trumpet, and the pouring out of the seventh bowl of plagues. The relationship between the rumblings of God's presence in 4.5 and the theophanic elements at the completion of each of these sevens underscores the fact that these activities come from the same God who is depicted here.[16] Their growing intensity conveys a sense of progression and completion of the divine judgments.

Next, the hearers are told that 'seven torches of fire are burning before the throne, which are the Seven Spirits of God'. Mention of these seven torches before the throne would no doubt call the hearers' minds to the seven lamps that were to stand in the holy place in the temple (Exod. 25.31-40; 40.4, 24-25) and the seven lamps that stand on Zechariah's golden lampstand (Zech. 4.1-14).[17] Such a convergence of ideas would contribute to the heavenly 'temple' scene, indicating that what John sees is the heavenly reality to which other texts and visions point. This somewhat familiar imagery would propel the hearers forward in their understanding of the Spirit in several ways. First, this statement makes clear that 'the Seven Spirits before the throne' described by John in the prologue (1.4) are indeed to be understood as 'the Seven Spirits of God', as Jesus' statement in 3.1 has implied. Second, the close proximity of the Seven Spirits to God underscores the fact that, when they act, He acts. Third, the reappearance of the 'Seven Spirits' language at this point, after the numerous references to the Spirit in chapters 2-3, underscores the fact that the Seven Spirits of God and the Spirit are indeed identical.[18] Fourth, the picture of the Spirit that continues to emerge in the Apocalypse is a complex one. The Spirit's close proximity and relationship to God is strategically noted in 1.4, 3.1, and now again in 4.5. The Spirit's role as the means by which this revelation is experienced is also clear from its strategic location in 1.10 and 4.2. The intimate relationship between the Spirit and

---

[16] Beale, *The Book of Revelation*, p. 326; Osborne, *Revelation*, p. 232.
[17] Bauckham, *Climax of Prophecy*, pp. 162-63.
[18] Simoens, *Apocalypse de Jean*, p. 44.

Jesus, who speak with one voice, is emphasized throughout chapters 2-3 in the refrain that calls for discerning obedience. The fact that Jesus claims to have 'the Seven Spirits of God' (3.1) indicates something of the extent of their relationship. After this emphasis upon Jesus' relationship with the Spirit, the mention of 'the Seven Spirits of God' before the throne reminds the hearers that the Spirit's identity cannot be understood apart from his intimate relationship with God. This is to say, 'the Seven Spirits of God' which Jesus 'has' are indeed 'the Seven Spirits *of God*'.

In addition to encountering the theophanic elements and the Seven Spirits of God before the throne, the hearers learn that 'before the throne is as a glass sea like crystal'. The appearance of this sea presents the hearers with an enigma, for in the biblical tradition and in the Apocalypse itself, the sea often has negative associations.[19] It is the place from which the beast arises (13.1) and in the new heaven and new earth it has no place for 'there is no more sea' (21.1), a point John emphasizes by mentioning it before anything else is offered in describing these new entities. And yet, here in John's vision of heaven there is a glass sea as crystal. Rather clearly the glassy crystal appearance of this sea is designed for reflection. In this context the sea would reflect the lightning and other visual theophanic qualities of the throne.[20] In other words, this glassy crystal sea is designed to reflect the glory of God. This characteristic of the sea may also go some way toward explaining its presence here in heaven, despite its negative connotations. Perhaps the hearers discern in this somewhat 'mixed' image the theological truth that even those objects that have negative associations somehow reflect the glory of God![21]

Verses 6b-8b – With the reflection of God's theophanic presence still in their minds, John next describes another group of beings located around the throne. 'And in the midst of the throne and around the throne were four living beings full of eyes in front and in back'. Like the twenty-four elders sitting on the twenty-four thrones, these too are described as being around or encircling the

---

[19] Caird, *The Revelation of St. John*, p. 65.

[20] Schüssler Fiorenza, *Revelation: Vision of a Just World*, p. 59. It should also be noted that the grammatical construction of vv. 5-6a makes clear that these sentences stand together.

[21] I am indebted to my colleague L.R. Martin for this insight.

throne. Yet, before being described in this way, they are said to be located in the very middle of the throne. This combination of ideas conveys the sense of extraordinarily close proximity to and dynamic movement in and around the throne.[22] As with other elements in this vision of heaven, neither John nor his hearers are allowed to think in static terms but dynamic ones. The imagery used in describing these four beings invites the hearers to reflect upon their unique identity, as they are called ζῷα ('living beings'). While this term is sometimes rendered as 'beasts', such a translation is misleading for it is not at all connected to the word θηρίον ('beast') which appears later in the book. Though the translation 'living beings' is technically accurate, given the fuller description of these beings that follows it becomes clear that perhaps a better contextual translation would be 'living creatures', as a comprehensive term for representatives of the created order, including humankind.[23] Thus, these 'living creatures' are connected to creation, yet they appear in heaven, in and around the throne. Mention of these four 'living creatures' would remind the hearers of similar creatures described by Ezekiel in one of his visions of heaven (Ezek. 1.4-28), reinforcing the celestial nature of what is being described by John. But unlike those creatures, the four that John sees are 'full of eyes in front and in back'. This somewhat startling image conveys the theological truth that these 'living creatures' possess complete and comprehensive vision with which to see completely all the magnificence, omnipotence, and holiness of the One who sits on the throne.[24] Nothing escapes their sight. The comprehensive nature of their vision will serve to underscore their qualification to praise God as ὁ παντοκράτωρ ('the All Powerful One'). The initial description of the 'four living creatures' in v. 6b gives way to a more detailed one, in which each of the living creatures is enumerated and given a more extensive physical description. For the first time in the book, John

---

[22] The attempt to understand the phrase 'in the midst and around the throne' as having reference to the design of the throne, fails to convince owing in part to the dynamism of the passage. On this view the four living creatures are an integral part of the throne, its back and legs, just as the cherubim are part of the mercy seat on the ark of the covenant owing to their location on or in it. For this proposal cf. R.G. Hall, 'Living Creatures in the Midst of the Throne: Another Look at Revelation 4.6', *NTS* 36 (1990), pp. 609-13.

[23] Simoens, *Apocalypse de Jean*, p. 45.

[24] Resseguie, *The Revelation of John*, p. 111.

and his hearers encounter an enumerated series whereby the things in the series are numbered in order, a practice that appears frequently in the remainder of the book. Sometimes such enumeration carries with it the idea of progression leading to a specific culmination. On other occasions the enumeration appears simply to draw specific attention to the individual objects in the series, which appears to be the case here. The first living creature is in appearance as a lion, the second as an ox, the third has the face of a man, and the fourth as a flying eagle.[25] Both the number four[26] and the individual physical forms of the living creatures indicate that they are connected in some way to the created order. Owing to their extraordinarily close proximity to the throne and their strategic role as worship leaders here and elsewhere in the book, their significance is difficult to overestimate. On the one hand, the physical descriptions of the four living creatures appear to be representatives of the different realms of creation.[27] There is the ferocious and terrifying lion (9.8, 17; 10.3; 13.2), the domesticated ox, the human being, and the eagle whose domain is the heavens (8.13; 12.14).[28] Thus, these four creatures seem to have a representative function for all of creation. On the other hand, it is significant that things do not revolve around humankind, but rather in this context it is clear that humanity is simply a part of this heavenly vision. God is central.[29] As the description of the four living creatures continues in v. 8, the hearers have cause to think of the vision which Isaiah describes, as the four living creatures are said, like the seraphim that appear in Isa. 6.2, to have six wings. Such imagery reinforces the sense of awe and holiness of this scene in the Apocalypse, as the hearers recall the activi-

---

[25] Irenaeus (*AH*, 3.11.11) appears to be the first to equate the four living creatures with the four evangelists (Matthew/Lion, Mark/Ox, Humanity/Luke, and John/Eagle), an identification that has proven to be very popular in the history of the church.

[26] As Bauckham (*Climax of Prophecy*, pp. 30-32) points out, the number four is the number of the created world in the Apocalypse. For example, the earth has four corners (7.1; 20.8), four winds (7.1), and can be divided into four divisions (5.13; 8.7-12; 14.7; 16.2-9).

[27] Fee, *Revelation*, pp. 72-73.

[28] B.M. Metzger (*Breaking the Code* [Nashville: Abingdon, 1993], p. 50) describes the four living creatures as follows: 'These symbolize, respectively, what is the noblest, strongest, wisest, and swiftest in creation'.

[29] Koester, *Revelation and the End of All Things*, p. 72.

ty of the seraphim in Isaiah. For a second time, reference is made to the fact that the four living creatures are full of eyes. Earlier, the description was that they are 'full of eyes in front and in back', while in v. 8 they are 'full of eyes all around and within'. In addition to reminding the hearers of the creatures' comprehensive vision yet again, perhaps this change in description suggests some connection between them being 'full of eyes all around and within' and their location 'in the midst of and all around the throne'. Of these four living creatures it is said, 'and they do not cease day and night saying'. Very literally, the Greek text says 'and they have no rest from saying'. Such a statement indicates that their praise offered to the One who sits on the throne is an on-going, never ending activity. They are creatures designed to praise God, and when they do this unceasingly, the reason for their existence is fulfilled. At this point, the description of the four living creatures gives way to their words of praise contained in the first of numerous hymns the hearers encounter in the Apocalypse.[30] These hymns not only serve to underscore the theological importance of worship in the book, but also convey numerous theological truths.[31] As the hearers encounter this portion of the Revelation they cannot help but be impressed by the role of the hymns as they will encounter five such hymns before this section devoted to the inaugural vision of heaven (Revelation 4-5) comes to a close.

Verse 8c – The opening words of the hymn that comes from the four living creatures are 'Holy, holy, holy'. This triple declaration of the holiness of the One who sits on the throne echoes the words of the seraphim in Isa. 6.3, focusing attention upon the absolute holiness of the One who sits on the throne. For the hearers, such words of praise are consistent with those of Jesus, who himself has called God 'Holy Father' (Jn 17.11). This triple declaration may also remind them of the fact that Jesus has earlier identified himself as 'the Holy One' in the Apocalypse (3.7), suggesting that even when the focus of attention is upon the One who sits on the throne, thoughts of Jesus are never far away. While the opening

---

[30] Hymns appear in the Apocalypse in 4.8, 11; 5.9b-14; 7.10-12; 11.15-18; 12.10-12; 13.4; 14.1-2; 15.3-4; 16.5-7; 18.20; 19.1-8.

[31] Cf. R. Morton, 'Glory to God and the Lamb: John's Use of Jewish and Hellenistic/Roman Themes in Formatting his Theology in Revelation 4-5', *JSNT* 83 (2001), pp. 89-109.

words of the hymn echo those of the seraphim in Isaiah, the words that follow echo those of God himself, spoken in the prophetic utterance with which the prologue concludes (1.8), as well as some of John's own words in 1.4. The combination of the close proximity of the four living creatures to the throne and their being full of eyes ensures that their knowledge of God is accurate. And since true knowledge of who God is inevitably leads to true worship of God,[32] their worship is indeed true worship (Jn 4.23). He is 'Lord, God, the All Powerful One, the one who was, the one who is, and the one who is coming'. Consistent with this heavenly setting is the fact that God is praised by the four living creatures because he is the All Powerful One, the one who has no rivals. He is praised because in him the past, present, and future converge; because there is no place or time in which he does not exist. This opening volley of praise sets the stage for that which follows. The four living creatures praise him for who he is; Holy, Lord, God, All Powerful, Eternal – Never Ending.

Verse 9 – John and his hearers soon discover that the four living creatures are not alone in their worship of God for 'whenever the living creatures give glory and honor and thanks to the One who sits on the throne, the One who lives forever and ever, the twenty-four elders fall before the One who sits upon the throne and they worship the One who lives forever and ever and they cast their crowns before the throne ...' The occurrence of the word 'whenever' is a most fascinating introduction to this verse, for on its own it implies particular times at which a certain action takes place. But on this occasion the 'whenever' is governed by the previous verse which says that the four living creatures never stop offering praise to God. Thus, the 'whenever' means all the time, always, continuously. The verse also reveals that the rendering of 'glory and honor and thanks' is somehow related to their words of praise recorded in the previous verse. That is to say, whenever they sing this hymn, they are giving 'glory and honor and thanks'. In the FG, glory is associated with God and his Son, Jesus. Clearly, such glory belongs to the realm of God as it precedes the creation of the world (Jn 17.5). It is especially reflected in the incarnation of Jesus (1.14) and is manifested at numerous points in his ministry (2.11; 11.4, 40).

---

[32] Bauckham, *The Theology of the Book of Revelation*, p. 32.

Jesus makes clear that above all one should seek the glory of God (7.18; 8.50-54). This stands in contrast to those who love the glory of men more than the glory of God (Jn 12.43). Such a rich theological understanding is extended in the Apocalypse where glory is intricately connected with God (Rev. 4.11; 5.13; 7.12; 11.13; 14.7; 15.8; 16.9; 19.1, 7; 21.11, 23). That glory is the first element in this trilogy of praise would not surprise John or his hearers. Honor, the second element, is also intricately connected to God in the Apocalypse (4.9, 11; 5.13; 7.12). Perhaps John and his hearers would be struck by the contrast with Jesus' words in the FG that a prophet is not without honor except in his own country (Jn 4.44), with the fact that in God's own 'house' he is always being given honor. Thanks is also closely associated with God in the Apocalypse (Rev. 7.12; 11.17), though it is not mentioned as often as the other elements of the trilogy of praise. The clear object of this glory and honor and thanks is the One who sits on the throne. To this point John and his hearers have learned a number of things about this one, most recently through the hymn of the four living creatures. Here the emphasis is upon the fact that he is the One who lives forever and ever. This emphasis is made clear by the fact that the One who sits upon the throne is described this way twice in vv. 9-10, almost in stereotypical fashion. Such emphatic language follows up nicely on the fact that he has on three previous occasions in the book been described as 'the one who was and the one who is and the one who is coming'. Together these descriptions underscore for John and his hearers the fact that the One who sits on the throne is eternal,[33] his existence never comes to an end.[34] One of the implications of all this is that if his existence never comes to an end, neither does his reign.[35] The significance of this aspect of God's nature, existence, and reign will perhaps only be fully appreciated by the hearers when they later encounter others who sit on thrones, but whose reigns are of a limited duration.

Verse 10 – Whenever the four living creatures worship the One who sits on the throne in this manner, which is continually, the twenty-four elders follow their lead by doing three things. The ac-

---

[33] Smalley, *The Revelation to John*, p. 123.
[34] Beale, *The Book of Revelation*, p. 333.
[35] Osborne, *Revelation*, p. 239.

tions of these individuals, who look as though they have received the promises to those who overcome, are described in such a way that each action is specifically linked to a particular aspect of the One who sits on the throne. First, John and his hearers learn that the twenty-four elders who sit upon twenty-four thrones leave their thrones and 'fall before the One who sits on the throne'. Like John, who falls as though he were dead at the feet of Jesus (1.17), so the twenty-four elders fall before the One who sits on the throne. Since John's prostration before Jesus appears to be an involuntary response by John, who is overwhelmed by the glory of Jesus, the hearers may assume a similar response on the elders' part. Such a response would not be wholly unexpected given the extraordinarily awesome description of the One who sits on the throne that has precedeed. The similarity of the responses of John and the elders may also encourage the connection between those who overcome and the elders. At any rate, the habitual leaving of their thrones and falling down before the throne will be seen as a characteristic of the twenty-four elders, who are always falling down to worship. Second, the elders 'worship the One who lives forever and ever'. In this first clear reference to the worship of God, the hearers encounter a term that they will often hear as the book unfolds. In this statement, they are reminded that the worship of God is absolutely fundamental and necessary. Owing to the fact that this worship is rendered to one who lives forever and ever, it becomes clear that such worship is to be restricted to such a one. The effects of this magnificent scene will continue to be felt when this basic theological and existential affirmation is challenged later in the book, as the hearers encounter those who worship the beast (13.4, 8, 12, 15; 14.9, 11; 16.2; 19.20). On the two occasions when John is tempted to worship one of God's servants he is instructed to 'Worship God!' (19.10; 22.8). Third, the twenty-four elders 'cast their crowns before the throne'. This imagery conveys a very powerful message to the hearers, for it indicates that despite the rewards which they have received owing to their overcoming faithful witness, they do not celebrate their own accomplishments or reign, but that of the One who sits on the throne.[36] This activity makes clear that these rewards are gifts of God, who has made all possible. Such powerful

---

[36] Koester, *Revelation and the End of All Things*, pp. 74-75.

imagery reveals that despite their wearing golden crowns and the authority they represent, they recognize that there is only one authority, the throne of God.[37]

Verse 11 – As had the four living creatures, so too the twenty-four elders worship with a hymn.

> You are worthy, our Lord and God,
> to receive the glory and the honor and the power,
> because you created all things
> and on account of your will they are
> and they have been created.

The first word to appear in this hymn in the Greek text is ἄξιος ('worthy'), a word that has already appeared in 3.4 to describe those in Sardis who have not defiled their garments and, consequently, are worthy to walk with Jesus. The word itself is a commercial term often used in the context of weights and balances to determine if something was equal or adequate.[38] In the Apocalypse, someone is deemed worthy to receive something or to do something owing to who they are or what they have done. Often these latter two ideas are integrally connected. Thus, to be worthy becomes a theologically freighted word. The one addressed in this hymn is 'our Lord and God', echoing the words of the living creatures but with the addition of the pronoun 'our', indicating something of the personal nature of the relationship between the elders and God.[39] This addition may also remind the hearers that despite others who may claim to be lord and god, the One who sits on the throne is 'our' Lord and God.[40] In this context, what 'our Lord and God' is worthy of is 'to receive the glory and the honor and the power'. Like the activity of the living creatures in v. 9, the hymn of the elders in v. 11 makes reference to a trilogy of praise, though there are a couple of differences. While they, too, join in ascribing glory and honor to our Lord God, in their hymn of praise the definite article is used along with each element of praise. Such articular constructions may be a way of underscoring the fact that God is worthy of 'the' glory and

---

[37] Smalley, *The Revelation to John*, p. 124,

[38] P. Trummer, 'ἄξιος', *EDNT*, I, p. 113.

[39] Resseguie, *The Revelation of John*, p. 113

[40] Cf. Aune, *Revelation 1-5*, pp. 310-12 for a discussion of the possible Roman background against which such claims are made.

'the' honor and 'the' power in a way like no other. Instead of thanks, the elders' trilogy contains reference to power. The hearers would not likely see in this change an indication that the elders are not thankful, but rather that power is closely associated with God's creative activity. As John and his hearers will discover, power too is closely associated with God in the Apocalypse (7.12; 11.17; 12.10; 15.8; 19.1). All other power(s) described in this book pale in comparison with 'the' power of God (13.2; 17.13; 18.3). 'Our Lord and God' is deemed worthy of such worship owing to his role as creator. As befitting the hymn, these statements take on a chiastic structure where the first part of the statement is mirrored by the final portion.[41] It could be set out as follows:

'You created all things'
　'and on account of your will they are'
'and they have been created'.

Set out in this fashion it is clear that the statements begin and end with reference to God's creative activity. These similarities are even clearer in the Greek text where a form of the word κτίζω ('create') appears at the beginning and the end. The middle statement then in some ways becomes the focal point, as God's creative will is emphasized. This emphasis upon God as creator is not only foundational in terms of God's identity, but is also important as it will leave no doubt as to who is responsible for the creation of the new heaven and new earth later in the book. Despite this strong affirmation of God as creator, thoughts of Jesus are never far from the hearers' minds, as a very similar statement is made about the Logos in Jn 1.2-3. Here 'our Lord and God' has created all things – even those things, as it turns out, that will rebel against him and refuse to repent. His work as creator is connected to the core of his being for it is on account of his will that they are. For Johannine hearers God's creative activity and will cannot properly be understood without the understanding that God does not will that any be lost (Jn 6.38-40). The divine passive rendered 'they have been created' conveys something of his active agency in creation, balancing the active voice statement with which this chiastic section begins. Thus,

---

[41] Osborne, *Revelation*, p. 242.

despite any marring of his creation that may have taken place, God is still praised for his creative activity by the twenty-four elders.

Chapter 5, Verse 1 – As the vision continues in chapter five, the hearers' attention is directed to a new development within the vision by the phrase καὶ εἶδον ('and I saw').[42] With all the activity in and around the throne described in chapter four, John now sees something new, for 'in the right hand of the One who sits on the throne is a book with writing on the inside and outside sealed with seven seals'. Numerous aspects of this detail would prove intriguing to John and his hearers. First, the fact that this scroll is in the 'right' hand of the One who sits on the throne continues to place emphasis upon the power of this one who created all things, as the right hand would be regarded as the hand of power.[43] Second, John and his hearers would no doubt be intrigued by this book and its contents, for any book that is in the right hand of God would be a most significant one indeed. While the identity of the scroll is much debated, its significance for the hearers at this point is conveyed by its location and physical description. Third, this scroll, like the one given to Ezekiel by God, has writing on the inside and outside. Normally a scroll would have writing on the inside only, protecting what is written from becoming worn by frequent handling. That the scroll John sees is two sided suggests its contents can barely be contained by it. Perhaps John knows it is a two-sided scroll by the fact that he could see writing on the outside and assumes there is writing on the inside as well. Fourth, it is also discovered that this scroll is sealed with seven seals. Such a detail indicates two things to John and his hearers. Seals upon a legal document often were placed there by witnesses, who would stand ready to testify to the authenticity and trustworthiness of its contents. The fact that seven seals are affixed to this scroll suggests that the One who sits upon the throne himself, and/or the Seven Spirits located before his throne, is the one who validates the scroll's contents. At the same time, the fact that seven seals are affixed to this scroll indicates that its contents have been made completely inaccessible to anyone whom God does not authorize to open it.

---

[42] Smalley, *The Revelation to John*, pp. 126-27.
[43] Resseguie, *The Revelation of John*, p. 115.

Verse 2 – For a second time in as many verses John says 'and I saw', again directing the hearers' attention to a new development in this vision. What John sees on this occasion is 'a mighty angel preaching with a great voice'. The appearance of this angel in such dramatic fashion focuses attention upon the significance of the unfolding events. Another angel will appear in equally dramatic fashion later in the Apocalypse (10.1). This mighty angel's great voice is apparently strong enough to be heard by all creation[44] and its intensity is in keeping with the other extraordinarily loud sounds described to this point. It may strike John and his hearers as significant that the angel's activity is described by the word κηρύσσοντα ('preaching')[45] which normally has the meaning of 'preaching'. Such a detail could well convey the idea that this angel's activity is not simply an invitation to anyone who might be worthy to open the scroll, but, owing to the theological significance of the term, carries with it implicit proclamation; a proclamation suggesting that there is indeed one who is worthy to open the scroll. Such a meaning is made more likely by the fact that this is the only appearance of this term in the whole of the Johannine literature.[46] The mighty angel's proclamation is, 'Who is worthy to open the book and to loose its seals?' The words 'who is worthy' would remind John and his hearers of the One who sits on the throne, who himself has been praised as 'worthy' in the hymn with which chapter four comes to a close. Here as there, the term 'worthy' conveys the idea of one who is adequate or equal to the task. In other words, they would hear in this question a call for one who is qualified for such a task, and would perhaps be wondering what would qualify one for such an act. Owing to the fact that the One who sits on the throne is deemed worthy (4.11), that the book is in his right hand, and that the book has been sealed by him or his Seven Spirits, the hearers may well conclude that the one who is worthy to open the book is no less worthy than the one who holds the book. Only such a one would be worthy (and authorized!) to open the scroll that God has closed and loose the seals with which he has sealed and authorized

---

[44] Mounce, *The Book of Revelation*, p. 143.

[45] Smalley, *The Revelation to John*, p. 129.

[46] E. Lohse [*Die Offenbarung des Johannes* (NTD; Göttingen: Vandenhoeck und Ruprecht, 1960), p. 38] goes so far as to call κηρύσσω ('preach'), 'The decisive key word of the entire vision'.

its contents. The mighty angel's preaching is concerned with a uniquely qualified one indeed![47]

Verse 3 – But alas, no one in all of creation, 'in the heaven or upon the earth or under the earth', was able, very literally 'had the power', 'to open the book nor to see it'. This three-tiered description of those unable to open the book adds to the heightened drama experienced by John and his hearers, further underscoring the unique qualifications of the one who *is* worthy. Given the fact that the One who sits on the throne is ascribed 'power' owing to his creative activity (4.11), it would not surprise the hearers that the one deemed worthy to open the book and see it would also require power (5.3). The shift from the phrase 'loosing the seals' in v. 2, to the phrase 'nor to see it' in vv. 3-4, would perhaps link in the hearers' minds the one worthy 'to see' this book with those things which John himself is commissioned to 'see' (1.11).

Verse 4 – This disappointing turn of events proves to be quite traumatic for John who says, καὶ ἔκλαιον πολύ ('and I wept much'). As the Greek imperfect tense often conveys the idea of continuous past action, this phrase might better be translated, 'I wept and wept much' or 'I was weeping much'. The appearance of this verb, often used to describe strong emotions with regard to something or someone lost,[48] would remind the hearers of the weeping that takes place in the FG. For there, such weeping accompanies the death of Lazarus (Jn 11.31, 33) and the death of Jesus (20.11, 13, 15), as Mary's weeping is the occasion of her encounter with the resurrected Jesus. Thus, John's continuous weeping in Rev. 5.4 indicates that John is clearly distraught owing to the fact that 'no one was found worthy to open the book nor see it'. Perhaps the occurrence of the divine passive εὑρέθη ('was found') adds to the desperation of the situation, implying that God himself could find no one worthy for this essential task. There appear to be at least two reasons for John's tears. First, there is the incredible dramatic tension of the scene where everything seems to be moving to this point, only to be frustrated by the fact that no one in all of creation is found worthy to open the book. If the divine will can be frustrated in the very throne room of God, what are the implica-

---

[47] Kiddle, *The Revelation of St. John*, p. 97 and Aune, *Revelation 1-5*, pp. 347-48.
[48] H. Balz, 'κλαίω', *EDNT*, II, p. 293.

tions for those on earth who are called to fight the fight of faithful witness in the face of powerful opponents including Satan himself? Second, owing to his commission to write what he sees in a book, John may very well understand that his prophetic task is being abraded owing to the lack of one worthy to open the book. Such a devastating disappointment is more than personal regret that *he* will not see the things promised,[49] but is evidence that the frustration of the prophetic call and vocation is much more significant than any personal disappointment.

Verse 5 – At this point, one of the elders speaks to John instructing him μὴ κλαῖε ('stop weeping'). This construction, a present tense prohibition, is used in order to stop an action already in progress. The translation 'stop weeping' is not only an adequate rendering of this construction but also sits well with the preceding imperfect tense verb in v. 4, where John says 'I was weeping much'.[50] The elder's next words indicate that more than comfort is being offering to John. They reveal that John has no reason to weep for all is not lost. The divine will is not frustrated after all. John's prophetic mission is to be completed. 'Behold, the Lion of the Tribe of Judah has overcome, the Root of David, to open the book and loose its seals'. The emphasis of this statement in the Greek text is placed upon the word ἐνίκησεν ('has overcome'),[51] as it stands second in this sentence after the word 'Behold', a term used to direct John's attention to this new development. This 'overcoming' terminology is, of course, familiar to the hearers owing in part to its prominence in chapters 2-3, where those who overcome are promised eschatological rewards on seven separate occasions. Neither would it be lost on John and his hearers that the elder who speaks with John is representative of those who have themselves overcome, which may also suggest why it is one of the elders who speaks with him at this point.[52] But perhaps the most important association this terminology would evoke is found in the last pro-

---

[49] Smalley, *The Revelation to John*, p. 130.
[50] Aune, *Revelation 1-5*, p. 322.
[51] Osborne, *Revelation*, p. 253.
[52] Allo notes (*L'Apocalypse*, p. 62) that the intervention of one of the elders with John shows very well the special rapport between these personages and humanity, though, interestingly enough, he does not identify the twenty-four elders with the saints.

phetic message spoken by the resurrected Jesus to the church in Laodicea, where he identifies himself as one who has overcome (3.21) and, consequently, sits on the throne with his Father.[53] Jesus' Johannine identity, as one who has overcome (Jn 16.33; 1 Jn 5.4-5), would create within the hearers an expectancy that he is the one to whom the elder has reference in Rev. 5.5. The elder identifies the one who has overcome as 'the Lion of the Tribe of Judah' and 'the Root of David'. These two titles would be most significant for John and his hearers for in them a number of OT messianic ideas converge. The first message is, at one and the same time, connected to the patriarchal blessing spoken by Jacob to Judah in Gen. 49.8-12, and the image of the lion as ferocious, destructive, and irresistibly strong figure.[54] From the Torah the hearers would know that Judah is 'a lion's whelp', who stoops and crouches as a lion (Gen. 49.8). Not only this but it is also said of Judah that the scepter in his hand and the ruler's staff between his feet will not depart from this tribe until Shiloh comes, to whom all people will be obedient (Gen. 49.10). This pregnant image is joined by another which is no less potent, for he is also identified as the Root of David. This title would not likely come as a surprise to John and his hearers for they already know that the resurrected Jesus is 'the one who has the key of David' (Rev. 3.7), who, as David's descendant, determines who enters his kingdom and who is excluded from it. This title would also draw upon the hearers' knowledge of Isa. 11.1-10, which speaks of the shoot that will come from the root of Jesse. Significantly, in describing this individual as one upon whom the Spirit will rest, there appears to be a seven-fold emphasis:

> And the Spirit of the Lord will rest upon him, the spirit of wisdom and understanding, the spirit of counsel and might, the spirit of knowledge and the fear of the Lord.

Such a detail would not likely be lost upon John or his hearers as the connection between Jesus and the Seven Spirits of God has already been seen to be an intimate one (Rev. 3.1) and reappears in this very verse. In addition, this root of Jesse will smite the earth

---

[53] L.L. Johns, *The Lamb Christology of the Apocalypse of John* (WUNT 2 Reihe 167; Tübingen: Mohr Siebeck, 2002), pp. 178-79.
[54] Bauckham, *The Climax of Prophecy*, p. 182.

with the word (LXX) of his mouth (Isa. 11.4), usher in eschatological peace (Isa. 11.6-8), and be an ensign to the nations who will seek him (Isa. 11.10). It is difficult to overestimate the impact of the convergence of these two titles on John and his hearers at this point, for they go a long way toward summing up the messianic hope found within the OT.[55] Given the many messianic associations of these titles,[56] it would not come as a surprise that the Lion of the Tribe of Judah, the Root of David, 'has overcome ... to open the book and its seven seals'.

Verse 6 – For a third time in six verses the phrase 'and I saw' occurs, indicating the introduction of yet another new detail in the vision. The object John sees is 'in the midst of the throne and the four living creatures and in the midst of the elders'. While the description is somewhat surrealistic, the impression left upon the hearers is that the object John now describes is closer to the throne than any of those previously mentioned. Such a description serves to heighten the dramatic tension of this heavenly scene. At precisely this point, a phenomenon occurs which has happened once before in the book and will occur again. The thing, which John hears, is not exactly what he sees. In the augural vision of Jesus that John describes, he heard a voice like a trumpet, but when he turned to see the 'voice' he saw seven golden lampstands and one like a Son of Man in their midst (Rev. 1.12). On this occasion, John hears about the Lion of the Tribe of Judah, the Root of David, but what he sees is 'a Lamb standing, as if slaughtered'. This psychedelic-like morphing of one form into another is both as unexpected as it is meaningful. While it is possible that John and his hearers would, in the light of this vision, be tempted simply to replace all OT lion imagery with slaughtered Lamb imagery,[57] it is much more likely that each of these images would interpret and clarify the other.[58] For in truth, the Lamb is, at one and the same time, the Lion.[59] He does not stop being the Lion owing to the appearance of Lamb im-

---

[55] Ladd, *A Commentary on the Revelation of John*, p. 83.
[56] Cf. G. Schimanowski, *Die himmlische Liturgie in der Apokalypse des Johannes: Die frühjüdischen Traditionen in Offenbarung 4-5 unter Einschluß der Hekhalotliteratur* (WUNT 2 Reihe 154; Tübingen: Mohr Siebeck, 2002), pp. 197-204.
[57] So Caird, *The Revelation of St. John*, p. 74.
[58] Michaels, *Revelation*, p. 95.
[59] Murphy, *Fallen Is Babylon*, p. 193.

agery. But just as the 'voice' heard in 1.10 could not be understood fully without the vision of the one like a Son of Man, so the Lion in 5.5 cannot be fully understood without the vision of the Slaughtered Lamb. Such dialectical imagery means that the voice cannot be thought of any longer without thinking of the one like the Son of Man, nor the Lion without the Slaughtered Lamb.

The image of the slaughtered Lamb in itself would be pregnant with meaning for John and his hearers, for a number of associations converge here.[60] There is, of course, knowledge of the Passover lamb of the Exodus story, whose death brought life to those Israelites who participated in the Passover feast, which involved the requisite placing of blood upon the door posts. The verb σφάζω ('slaughter') would also remind the hearers of Isa. 53.7 (LXX) where the same root word appears in describing the suffering servant 'as a lamb led to the slaughter'. The place and significance of Jesus as the paschal lamb in the FG would also be well known, beginning with John's (the Baptist) identification of Jesus in the revelatory formula, 'Behold the Lamb of God who takes away the sin of the world' (Jn 1.29).[61] The narrative of the FG soon makes clear its preoccupation with Passover imagery at many places, including the fact that Jesus dies at the time the Passover lambs are slain (Jn 19.31). Consequently, there would be no mistaking the identity of this Slaughtered Lamb for Johannine hearers. The occurrence of the perfect passive participle ἐσφαγμένον ('slaughtered') would also point in the direction of Jesus' death as a one-time event, the effects of which are still felt.[62] The fact that John describes the Slaughtered Lamb as standing may even be an oblique reference to the resurrection of this Slaughtered Lamb,[63] for he is no longer dead. Such an image would contribute additional depth and richness to Jesus' earlier claims about his death and resurrection (Rev. 1.18; 2.8).[64]

---

[60] Cf. N. Hillyer, '"The Lamb" in the Apocalypse', *EQ* 39 (1967), pp. 228-36.

[61] Though the FG and the Apocalypse use different words for lamb, ἀμνός ('lamb') and ἀρνίον ('lamb' or 'sheep') respectively, the words appear to be theological equivalents. Cf. Prigent, *L'Apocalypse de Saint Jean*, p. 191.

[62] Smalley, *The Revelation to John*, p. 132.

[63] Aune, *Revelation 1-5*, p. 352.

[64] Prigent (*L'Apocalypse de Saint Jean*, p. 192) notes that in these images we have the equivalent of Christological propositions.

This Lamb becomes one of the dominant figures in the Apocalypse, as the term occurs twenty-eight times with reference to Jesus. But the lamb is not to be understood simply as one that has been slaughtered, for he is described as having seven horns. Not only is he the first animal in the Apocalypse described as having horns,[65] clearly a reference to his power, but he is also described as having *seven* horns, an indication that his power is complete. While this detail is not what one might expect to be said of a Slaughtered Lamb, it does provide a point of real continuity between the image of the Lion and that of the Lamb. At the same time, this detail prepares John and his hearers for the fact that when other animals with horns appear in the book, they will be understood as the imitators and rivals that they are. However, it will become equally clear that their power does not compare with the complete power of the Slaughtered Lamb. In addition to the seven horns, John sees that the Lamb has seven eyes. Taken on its own this image would convey the idea that the Slaughtered Lamb has perfect vision and, consequently, perfect knowledge, for he sees all. This image would sit well with Jesus' numerous 'I know' statements found in the seven prophetic messages in Revelation 2-3.[66] But, as John and his hearers discover, there is even more to this particular detail in this vision, for the seven eyes are identified as 'the Seven Spirits of God sent out into all the earth'. Obviously, such an image would imply that the Lamb possesses the fullness or completeness of the Spirit.[67] But this image would convey much more than this simple statement, for by it the intimate relationship between Jesus and the Spirit continues to develop. To this point in the Apocalypse John and his hearers have learned that the words of Jesus and those of the Spirit are coterminous and that Jesus boldly claims to have the Seven Spirits of God. They know of the tight interplay between John's visionary encounters with Jesus and being 'in the Spirit'. Now, they learn that the Seven Spirits of God are identified as the Lamb's seven eyes. In the Apocalypse, the eyes of Yahweh, as depicted in Zech. 4.10, are also depicted as the eyes of the Lamb.[68] Such intriguing imagery

---

[65] Prigent, *L'Apocalypse de Saint Jean*, p. 193.
[66] Metzger, *Breaking the Code*, p. 53.
[67] Prigent, *L'Apocalypse de Saint Jean*, p. 193.
[68] Bauckham, *The Climax of Prophecy*, p. 164.

continues to underscore the intimate nature of the relationship between the One who sits on the throne and Jesus, the Lamb. But there is more, for these Seven Spirits of God, these seven eyes of the Lamb, go out into all the earth.[69] While this statement would convey the idea that the Lamb has perfect knowledge and vision, such an understanding would not appear to exhaust its meaning in this verse. For John and his hearers two additional ideas would appear to be present in these words. First, these words are likely to remind them of Jesus' own words with regard to the Paraclete who will convict the world concerning sin and righteousness and judgment (Jn 16.8-11). Thus, there is a very active dimension to the activity of the Seven Spirits of God. Second, as the Apocalypse will make clear, there is a very tight connection between the activity of the Seven Spirits of God and the prophetic witness of the church. It might not be going too far to say that Spirit is that which inspires the faithful witness of all those who are part of this prophetic community.[70] Such witness is in keeping with the faithful witness of Jesus (1.5), Antipas (2.13), the two witnesses (11.3-13), and the statement in 19.10 that 'the witness of Jesus is the Spirit of prophecy'.

When John and his hearers discover that 'the Lion of Tribe of Judah, the Root of David' is the Slaughtered Lamb, it becomes clear that the victory of the Lion has been won through the sacrificial death of the Lamb. Israel's hopes of messianic liberation and conquest are accomplished through the sacrificial death of Jesus. The juxtaposing of the contrasting images of 'the Lion of the Tribe of Judah, the Root of David' and the Slaughtered Lamb reveals that the symbol of conquest is the symbol of sacrificial death.[71] This juxtaposition of images makes clear to John and his hearers that their own 'faithful witness' and 'overcoming' is intimately connected to the sacrificial death of Jesus, and may even necessitate their own death.[72] Such a realization would make Jesus' words to the church in Smyrna (2.10) 'to be faithful unto death' all the clearer.

---

[69] Resseguie, *The Revelation of John*, p. 120.
[70] Bauckham, *The Climax of Prophecy*, pp. 165-66.
[71] Bauckham, *The Climax of Prophecy*, pp. 179-85.
[72] Johns, *The Lamb Christology of the Apocalypse of John*, pp. 175-80.

Verse 7 – The words of v. 7 are anything but inconsequential for they describe one of the most significant events in the book, an event so important that it triggers the most incredible acts of worship contained within the Apocalypse. For it is here that John describes the long awaited activity of the one who is worthy to open the book and loose its seals. The Lamb, who is the Lion and the Root, 'went and took out of the right hand of the One who sits upon the throne'. Several aspects of this statement would strike the hearers as significant. First, the occurrence of the perfect tense verb εἴληφεν ('took') at this point indicates that the results of this past action continue to be felt into the present. The book has been taken by the Lamb and even now is in his possession. Second, this act indicates the unique worthiness of the Lamb, as no one in all creation is qualified to take the book but he. Third, in many ways this act could be seen as the central moment in salvation history,[73] for the one who takes the book from the One who sits on the throne is the one who has been slain but is now alive. Owing to its strategic location and its theologically freighted associations, it would be exceedingly difficult for John and his hearers not to see in this image of taking the book a symbol of the obedient death of the Lamb.[74] Fourth, immediately after the Lamb takes the book instantaneous worship results, indicating the significance of the Lamb's actions.[75] When the Lamb takes the book, John and his hearers find themselves at a remarkable turning point within the plot of the Apocalypse, for the following narrative is very much dependent on this act.

Verse 8 – In order that the significance of this event not be missed, the very next verse begins with the phrase, 'and when he took the book'. When the Lamb took the book attention is again focused upon the four living creatures and the twenty-four elders who encircle the throne and constantly worship the One who sits on the throne. Almost unbelievably, John and his hearers discover that as soon as the Lamb takes the book, he too becomes an object of worship![76] The connection between the Lamb's taking the book

---

[73] Prigent, *L'Apocalypse de Saint Jean*, p. 194.
[74] Kiddle, *The Revelation of St. John*, p. 102.
[75] Aune, *Revelation 1-5*, p. 355.
[76] Michaels, *Revelation*, p. 95.

and the subsequent worship of the Lamb also makes clear the extraordinary importance and significance of his action. It is truly remarkable that in a book which underscores the importance of true worship given to God alone, worship which is not to be shared with any other figure whether beastly or angelic, that in this verse another figure would receive the worship that God himself receives.[77] Such a description indicates rather certainly that the Lamb shares in divine worship; that his identity and relationship with God is an extremely close one. The fact that they would share worship at this point, though a remarkable development in the story, is not unanticipated given the earlier emphases of the prophecy. For not only does Jesus 'have' the Seven Spirits of God (3.1; 5.6), but he also shares his Father's throne (3.21). Thus, the intricate nature of their identity and relationship continues to unfold before the 'eyes' of John and the ears of his hearers. The nature of the worship rendered to the Lamb consists of four activities. First, as John had earlier done before Jesus (1.17) and the elders constantly do before the One who sits on the throne (4.10), the four living creatures and the twenty-four elders fall down before the Lamb. Second, each of them had κιθάραν ('harps' or 'lyres'). While at first glance it might appear that both groups of living creatures and elders had harps, the hearers would understand that only the elders are likely to possess such instruments. The masculine phrase ἔχοντες ἕκαστος ('each one having') clearly goes with the elders, which appears in the masculine gender in the Greek text as well, and would not include the four living creatures, which appears in the neuter gender in Greek.[78] John and his hearers would be familiar with the harps, as such stringed instruments often appear in worship contexts in the OT (Pss. 33.2; 98.5; 147.7). In the Apocalypse the harps are found exclusively in heaven and are always connected with singing (Rev. 5.8-9; 14.2; 15.2). Third, each of the twenty-four elders also has 'golden bowls full of incense'. Again, these priestly functions would not be lost on John and his hearers and would be further evidence of the connection between the twenty-four elders and their counterparts on earth.[79] This description envisions the burning

---

[77] Bauckham, *The Climax of Prophecy*, pp. 133-38.

[78] Beale, *The Book of Revelation*, p. 357.

[79] J.D. Charles, 'The Apocalyptic Tribute to the Lamb (Rev. 5.1-14)', *JETS* 34 (1991), p. 470.

incense that goes up before God in his temple and is a sweet smell to him. Just as the hearers are earlier told of the meaning of the Seven Eyes of the Lamb, so here they are told the meaning of the 'bowls full of incense' – they 'are the prayers of the saints'. Among other things, this image indicates that the relationship between the twenty-four elders and the 'saints' is an especially close one. It would also serve to comfort John and his hearers with the knowledge that rather than being a burden to God, the prayers of the saints are an aroma that is pleasing to him. In addition, this image makes clear that there is a connection between the worship of those on earth and those in heaven![80] The prayers of the saints are not simply a ritual to be rendered in a perfunctory way, but are reflected in the activity around the throne of God himself. If the prayers of the saints on earth enable them to participate in heavenly worship, surely the same would be true of other forms of worship. Would they too not find a place in the worship found in heaven? Here for the first time in the book the term ἁγίων ('saints') appears. The term would suggest their special relationship to Jesus and God, owing to the fact that both have earlier been called ἅγιος ('holy') (3.7; 4.8). The term also takes on growing importance as the book unfolds, becoming the term of choice for believers in the Apocalypse.[81]

Verses 9-10 – Fourth, 'and they sang a new song'. Given the fact that in the OT new songs are frequently the response of God's people to new acts of salvation (Pss. 33.3; 40.4; 96.1; 98.1; 144.9; 149.1; Isa. 42.10), the singing of a new song on this occasion is not at all surprising. Although other hymns precede it in the Apocalypse (Rev. 4.8, 11), this is the first time in the book that specific lyrics are identified as a 'song'. The importance of this point is made all the clearer by the cognate accusative construction, ᾄδουσιν ᾠδὴν ('they sang a song'), where the same root word is found in both the verb and the noun in the direct object. The appropriateness of their singing a new song on this occasion would be apparent to John and his hearers, for no other action in all of history parallels those things described in Revelation 5. This becomes clear in the song itself, which can be set out as follows:

---

[80] Metzger, *Breaking the Code*, p. 53.
[81] Murphy, *Fallen Is Babylon*, p. 196.

You are worthy to take the book
and to open its seals,
because
you were slaughtered
and you have purchased for God in your blood
out of every tribe and tongue and people and nation
and you made them for our God a kingdom and priests,
and they will reign upon the earth.

This song begins with the identical words that did the previous hymn to God in 4.11, a detail that underscores the fact that the Lamb is worshipped in the same way as the One who sits on the throne is worshipped![82] The fact that the Greek sentence begins with Ἄξιος ('worthy') makes this parallel all the more obvious. As God before him, the Lamb is now declared to be qualified for a specific task. Here the task is 'to take the book and open its seals'. The unique worthiness of the Lamb made known previously in 5.2-8, now becomes the basis of this new song sung to him. For he is not only worthy to take the book, but also to open its seals!

The qualifications for this worthiness are set out in the next three stanzas; because 'he was slaughtered', 'and he purchased', 'and he made'. The reappearance of 'slaughter' language calls to mind the numerous associations the Slaughtered Lamb imagery first triggers when mentioned in v. 6, for example Exodus' Passover lamb, Isaiah's Suffering Servant, and the FG's Lamb who takes away the sin of the world. The fact that this stanza consists of only one word in the Greek text [ἐσφάγη ('you were slaughtered'], dramatically underscores the crucial significance of the sacrificial death of the Lamb. In many ways this reality stands alone. The next stanza focuses upon the second qualification lifted up in this new song, 'and you purchased for God in your blood out of every tribe and tongue and people and nation'. The term ἀγοράζω ('purchase'), though carrying a commercial meaning in its occurrences in the FG (Jn 4.8; 6.5; 13.29), takes on a decidedly theological meaning in the Apocalypse. Its only other appearance to this point in the Apocalypse is found in Jesus' words to the church in Laodicea to purchase gold, white garments, and salve from him (Rev. 3.18). Later the term appears with reference to those who receive the mark of the Beast

---

[82] Sweet, *Revelation*, p. 130.

(13.17), and to describe the mourning of those who committed adultery with the Great Whore (18.11). In 5.9, as later in 14.3, 4, the term is used to describe the purchase of individuals for God. The language itself implies ownership of those purchased. It also places a great deal of emphasis upon the price of the purchase, 'your blood'. As seen in 1.5, the blood of Jesus is efficacious for the loosing or destroying of sins. Its mention here rather obviously is connected to the discussion of the Slaughtered Lamb in the previous verses, indicating that the sacrificial death of the Lamb makes possible such a purchase. The other aspect of this purchase is its universal quality, for individuals are purchased for God from 'every tribe and tongue and people and nation'. Four-fold designations which have reference to all of humanity occur seven times in the Apocalypse, five times using these specific elements (5.9; 7.9; 11.9; 13.7; 14.6), and two other times where 'tribe' is replaced by 'kings' (10.11) and 'crowds' (17.15). Interestingly enough, in none of the lists is the same order given, nor does any of the lists begin with 'tongues', suggesting that the lists are anything but haphazard. Rather the order and specific elements that appear reflect their immediate contexts.[83] Here the occurrence of this listing underscores the universality of those purchased in the Lamb's blood for God. Those whom he purchased are not restricted to any particular ethnic, national, or linguistic group; the redemptive work of the Lamb knows no such limits. The song's final stanza is devoted to the third qualification of the Lamb to take the book and open its seals, 'and he made them to our God a kingdom and priests and they will reign upon the earth'. These lyrics reiterate John's words about Jesus in the prologue that 'he made us a kingdom, priests to our God and Father'. There, too, this activity is closely associated with his blood. Here, it becomes clear that such a kingdom and such priests come from all groupings of humankind. John and his hearers also learn from this song that those in this kingdom 'will reign upon the earth'. The earlier promises from the resurrected Jesus to those who overcome with regard to the wearing of crowns and the sitting upon thrones, and the presence of the twenty-four elders who wear crowns and sit upon thrones anticipate the words of this song. Given the song's emphasis upon reigning on the earth, the hearers

---

[83] Cf. Bauckham, *The Climax of Prophecy*, pp. 326-37.

might also be reminded of the earlier promise to the one who overcomes in the church in Thyatira that Jesus will give him/her authority over the nations and he/she will rule with a rod of iron (2.25-27). Though the promise that such lyrics carry is a staggering one, its full potential cannot be appreciated until its fulfillment becomes clear later in the book.

Verses 11-12 – No sooner do the words of this new song conclude than the attention of John and his hearers is directed to another dimension of the vision as yet unseen. For a fourth time in this chapter the words 'and I saw' occur, yet what John describes actually focuses upon what he hears. Unlike earlier episodes where John hears something and looks to see it, here what he sees leads him to what he hears. The impression left is that what John encounters, he encounters both visually and audibly. What he hears is 'the voice of many angels'. These angels are encircled around the throne as well as around the living creatures and the twenty-four elders. Until this point, the focus upon the throne has moved from the outside in; from the twenty-four elders who encircle the throne, to the four living creatures who seem to dart in and around the throne, to the Lamb who is in the midst of, even on, the throne. But with the introduction of the angels, the focus moves further out, to a larger circle. These angels speak with one voice, though their number is exceedingly great. Although the living creatures have been enumerated, these angels are the first objects to be described by the word ἀριθμὸς ('number'). The description of their number is given in an almost poetic fashion in the Greek text. For their number was μυριάδες μυριάδων καὶ χιλιάδες χιλιάδων ('tens of thousands of tens of thousands and thousands of thousands'). Such staggering numbers of angels indicates that for John and his hearers the heavens are literally filled with angelic beings around the throne and the living creatures and the twenty-four elders, leaving the impression that there is no creature in heaven that is not preoccupied with worship of the Lamb. When such a group as this speaks with one voice it is a very great voice indeed, the intensity of sound being hardly possible to imagine. The words that come from this great voice raised by the angels echo those of the twenty-four elders in 4.11. Just as their first words in the worship of God declare that he is 'worthy', so the first words of the angels declare, 'Worthy is the Lamb that was slaughtered'. The angels' words also build upon and reiterate the words of the new song (5.9-10), underscoring the fact that the Lamb is worthy precisely because he was slaughtered. In 5.9 he is declared worthy 'to take the book and open its seals', while in 5.12 he is declared worthy to receive worship in a seven-fold way. Just as God was deemed worthy to receive a trilogy of praise (4.11), consisting of 'the glory and the honor and the power', so the Lamb is deemed worthy to receive seven-fold praise, which includes the trilogy of praise rendered to God in inverse order.[84] The fact that the praise rendered to the Lamb is seven-fold would be appropriate given the number's association with completeness and the fact that the heavens appear to be completely full of angels rendering such praise. It also sits nicely with the three-fold praise rendered to God as each number has 'divine' associations. It may not be without significance that this seven-fold doxology begins with the element with which the trilogy of praise of God concludes, 'the power'. Not only does this occurrence provide a point of continuity between God and the Lamb, but it also underscores 'the power' of the one who has overcome by his own blood to be worthy to take the book and open its seals. The attribution of 'wealth' to the Lamb would no doubt remind the hearers of the wealth of the church in Smyrna, despite their poverty and tribulation (2.9), and of the poverty and wretchedness of the church in Laodicea, despite their claims to be rich (3.17). Later, when 'the rich' as a social class (6.15; 13.16) and those 'rich' through association with the Great Whore (18.3, 15, 17, 19) are encountered, their wealth will be evaluated by means of the 'wealth' that belongs to the Lamb. The attribution of 'wisdom' to the Lamb will later be understood by the hearers as a quality shared by God (7.12) and essential for pneumatic interpretation on the part of the hearers (13.18; 17.9). The fourth element in this seven-fold doxology, 'strength', is also one that will be intimately associated with God (7.12; 18.8), as well as his angels (5.2; 10.1; 18.2, 21) and worshippers (19.6). When this idea is later used of a social class (6.15; 19.18) and Babylon the Great City (18.10), the contrast between their 'strength' and the Lamb's 'strength' will again be striking to the hearers. The fifth element of praise is the theologically rich, 'glory', part of the trilogy of praise rendered to God by the four living creatures (4.9). Its intri-

---

[84] Resseguie, *The Revelation of John*, p. 122.

cate connection with God in the Apocalypse (4.11; 5.13; 7.12; 11.13; 14.7; 15.8; 16.9; 19.1, 7; 21.11, 23), as well as its deep association with Jesus in the FG, make its occurrence here all the more significant. For not only does the close relationship between God and the Lamb continue to develop, but there is also the implicit answer to Jesus' prayer for the Father to glorify him consistent with the glory he shared before the world began (Jn 17.5). The sixth element of this seven-fold formula, 'honor', appears as the second element in the trilogy of praise rendered to God in Rev. 4.9. Again, the Lamb receives that which is intricately connected to God in the Apocalypse (4.9, 11; 5.13; 7.12). The seventh and final element in this angelic chorus of praise rendered to the Lamb is 'blessing', which is also intimately connected with God in the Apocalypse (5.13; 7.12). For John and his hearers, the implication of this deafening chorus is clear. The Lamb is worthy to receive praise that is worthy of God himself. It is impossible to imagine a more complete heavenly song of praise than this. And yet …

Verse 13 – Unbelievably, as the vision continues, the throng of worshippers expands beyond the boundaries of heaven to include the entire universe. The hearers could hardly miss the universalistic emphasis of this verse as it begins with the words καὶ πᾶν κτίσμα ('and every creature'). Not only does it serve this function, but the occurrence of this phrase also takes the hearers back to the song of the twenty-four elders in 4.11 which underscores God's creative activity and will, where both ἔκτισας ('you created') and ἐκτίσθησαν ('they were created') occur. Lest the hearers miss the inclusive nature of this group, there appears to be a comprehensive listing of the created order to underscore this point: 'And every creature which is in heaven and upon the earth and under the earth and upon the sea and all the things in them'. With this the hearers are introduced to the phenomenon of four-fold divisions to refer to the created order in the Apocalypse.[85] In addition to mention of the four-fold division of the created order, the universal aspect of this praise is again emphasized by the words 'and all the things in them', which in some ways serves as an inclusio with 'every creature', which surrounds the four-fold division of creation. The clear implication is that all the things God created (4.11) are included in this

---

[85] Bauckham, *The Climax of Prophecy*, p. 31.

236   *The Apocalypse*

grouping. What John hears them saying is truly astounding for these words of praise are directed to the One who sits on the throne *and* to the Lamb.

> To the One who sits on the throne and to the Lamb
> be the blessing and the honor and the glory and the might
> for ever and ever.

The Lamb, who earlier has received praise in his own right, now joins the One who sits on the throne as the object of praise. The

Figure 8
The Adoration of the Lamb
(Golden Codex of St Emmeran, Ratisbon, Munich, Bayrische Staatsbibliotek)

Lamb does not replace the One who sits on the throne,[86] but is inextricably joined to him as the object of universal worship.[87] Given the four-fold division of the created order it is not surprising that the praise rendered by them comes in the form of a four-fold doxology. But the significance of this doxology is not limited to its four-fold structure, for its four individual components are themselves a provocative integration of doxological elements that have been used to describe God and/or the Lamb. By this means, the intimate nature of their identity and relationship is again highlighted. This four-fold doxology begins with 'the blessing', the last element listed in the seven-fold angelic doxology directed to the Lamb in 5.12 and one that has not yet been rendered to God. The ascription of this element of praise to both God and the Lamb, after its previous ascription to the Lamb, makes clear that the Lamb is not in a superior position to the One who sits on the throne, but is worshipped along with him. The ascription of 'honor and glory' to the One who sits on the throne and to the Lamb has previously been rendered to the Lamb by the angelic chorus in 5.12 and to God by the four living creatures as 'glory and honor' in 4.9. These attributions continue to emphasize their shared worship. The final doxological element κράτος ('might' or 'power') has earlier appeared with reference to the Lamb (1.6). It is also found on the lips of the four living creatures in the title ὁ παντοκράτωρ ('the Almighty One' or 'the All Powerful One') with reference to the One who sits on the throne in 4.8. Fittingly, the praise rendered by every creature in the universe is intended to last for every moment of existence, 'for ever and ever'.

Verse 14 – The last word of praise spoken in this inaugural vision of heaven comes from the four living creatures, who also spoke the first words of praise in it (4.8). At the end of scenes of praise that have included songs from the four living creatures, the twenty-four elders, myriads of angels, and every creature in the universe, the four living creatures add their 'Amen'. Not only does the utterance of the 'Amen' have good liturgical precedence in the Apocalypse (1.6, 7), but it is also closely associated with Jesus in

---

[86] Koester, *Revelation and the End of All Things*, p. 80.

[87] Michaels, *Revelation*, p. 97. Kiddle (*The Revelation of Saint John*, p. 105) notes, 'Nowhere else in the New Testament is Christ adored on such absolutely equal terms with the Godhead'.

each of those contexts and even becomes a title by which Jesus identifies himself (3.14). John and his hearers are likely to pick up on both emphases here. Upon hearing the 'Amen', the twenty-four elders fall down yet again. It is altogether fitting that the words with which this section concludes are καὶ προσεκύνησαν ('and they worshipped')!

The Opening of the Book Sealed with Seven Seals (6.1-8.5)

The extraordinary scene of worship gives way to the continuation of the major section devoted to John in the Spirit in Heaven that comprises 4.1-16.21. The second section of this largest portion of the book witnesses several significant events. Primarily, this subsection is devoted to a description of the opening of the seven seals by the Lamb. Three things will strike John and his hearers as especially significant about this portion of the text. First, the opening of each enumerated seal is accompanied by eschatologically and theologically significant events. Second, the first of several interludes found throughout the book occurs here, separating the opening of the sixth seal from the seventh seal (7.1-17). Third, the opening of the seventh seal (8.1-5) is intimately connected to the seven angels with seven trumpets, which immediately follows (8.2-11.19).

The Opening of the First Six Seals (6.1-17)

With the extraordinary praise of every creature in the universe still ringing in their ears, John and his hearers now have their attention focused upon the opening of the seven seals by the Lamb. The opening of the seven seals fall into a four-three pattern, where the first four stand together, while the fifth, sixth, and seventh seals stand on their own to a certain extent. There is clearly a tight connection between the actions of the Lamb in chapter five and his actions here in chapter six. For the one who is worthy to take the scroll and open its seals, the one who is worshipped by every creature in the universe, is the one who now actually opens the seals one by one. Sometimes this connection is not fully appreciated owing to the fact that the opening of the seals is accompanied by suffering and death inflicted upon the world. Contemporary readers are sometimes tempted to believe that such activity is not appropriate for the Slaughtered Lamb who has just received such universal worship. However, John and his hearers are likely to see a very tight connection between the events of chapters five and six, for the eschatological events that accompany the opening of the seals are under the control of God and the Lamb is the one worthy to open them.

Verse 1 – The scene opens with the familiar 'I saw', indicating that a new detail or development is now within John's field of vision. Following fast on the heels of chapter five, there is a climactic nature to the actions described. 'When the Lamb opened one of the seven seals' indicates to the hearers that the long awaited action of the Lamb is now underway. The seals of the book, which was in the hand of the One who sits on the throne, are now being opened. Somewhat unexpectedly, when the Lamb opens one of the seven seals, John does not immediately describe what he sees but what he hears. For one of the four living creatures was speaking with a voice like thunder. The appearance of one of the four living creatures at this point reminds the hearers of the creatures' strategic location in and around the throne. The creature's voice as 'thunder' also suggests a close association between this living creature and the throne of God, for in Rev. 4.5 thunder was one of the theophanic elements to come from the throne. Such an indicator suggests that when the living creature speaks, he speaks for the One who sits on the throne.[1] The fact that the living creatures are those with whom worship of God and the Lamb begins and ends in Revelation 4-5 points to the continuity that exists between those who act in those chapters and those who act in chapter six.[2] The utterance of this thunderous voice is the command Ἔρχου ('come' or 'go'). This command will be heard as each of the first four seals is opened. Near the book's conclusion this word is also found as an invitation from the Spirit and the Bride (22.17), an admonition to be spoken by the one who hears (22.17), and a cry for the return of Jesus (22.20). This enigmatic command from the throne of God will not leave the hearers puzzled for long, for after hearing this command John immediately sees something.

---

[1] Beale, *The Book of Revelation*, p. 374.
[2] Wall, *Revelation*, p. 109.

Verse 2 – Once again the words 'I saw' appear, followed by 'and behold', indicating the sight which John next encounters is an especially significant one. What John sees is described as 'a white horse, and the one sitting upon him having a bow and there was given to him a crown and he went out overcoming even in order that he might overcome'. For John and his hearers, the appearance of this horse and its riders would evoke a number of associations. The horse is in itself a powerful figure, often being used to dominate those on foot. This particular horse is reminiscent of the white horse and white horses mentioned in Zech. 1.8 and 6.2-6, respectively, which appear with horses of other colors. In Zechariah, these horses and teams of horses are sent by the Lord to patrol the earth. Given these associations and the fact that this horse and rider come as a result of the opening of the first seal by the Slaughtered Lamb, the appearance of this horse and rider, here, would create a sense of extraordinary expectancy on the part of the hearers. This expectancy is heightened all the more by the fact that this horse and rider resemble to an astonishing degree the emerging picture of Jesus and his followers in the Apocalypse. This striking resemblance is owing to three specific details revealed in v. 2. First, the color of the horse, white, is one that has been intimately associated with Jesus and his followers to this point in the book (1.13; 2.17; 3.4, 5, 18; 4.4). Thus, the appearance of the white horse would at least give the hearers pause as to whether or not this rider is somehow connected with Jesus. Second, not only is Jesus involved in the giving of crowns (2.10), implying that he has crowns to give, but the retaining (3.11), wearing (4.4), and casting down (4.10) of crowns all are characteristic of his followers. Such associations would perhaps be taken as a further clue that this rider is associated with Jesus. The connection between the giving of the crown to the rider and his overcoming activity is reminiscent of the connection between Jesus having overcome and being given the right to sit on the throne with God (3.21). Third, throughout the book to this point, there has been an emphasis placed upon the need for Jesus' followers to overcome (2.7, 11, 17, 26; 3.5, 12, 21) and the fact that Jesus has himself overcome (3.21; 5.5). The emphatic statement that this rider goes out 'overcoming in order that he might overcome' would not be lost on the hearers, as Jesus is the one who has overcome! The fact that Jesus, who has already been portrayed as one like a son of man, the

Lion of the Tribe of Judah, and the Slaughtered Lamb, could now be portrayed as the rider on a white horse would not be all that surprising. This is especially true owing to the fact that Jesus will appear in just this fashion in Rev. 19.11-16. At the very least, this imagery of v. 2 would convey to the hearers the idea that wherever this horse and rider go Jesus himself goes.[3] The bow, which this rider has, indicates that he is not unarmed, but rather is an offensive force. The bow as an offensive weapon is not only known from the OT (Isa. 21.17; Jer. 50.29; 51.3), but would also be an especially powerful image given the close association of the bow with the Parthians, dreaded enemies of Rome. As the narrative unfolds, it may not be insignificant that the calamities of famine, plague, wild beasts, and sword are the very arrows of God mentioned in Deut. 32.23-25 and Ezek. 5.16-17. The last words of this verse indicate that this white horse and its rider actually go out to accomplish the assigned task.

Verses 3-4 – No sooner have this horse and rider gone out to overcome than the Slaughtered Lamb opens the second seal. The enumeration of this 'second' seal is a new development in the Apocalypse and will be followed consistently throughout the book with regard to the seals, trumpets, and bowls in this section (4.1-16.21). Its mention here also indicates that the seals will be opened quickly and in order. Just as with the opening of the previous seal, so the opening of the second seal is accompanied by a sound, for John says, 'I heard the second living creature saying'. Although it is not clear to the hearers to which of the four living creatures reference is being made, it is enough to know that one of those intimately connected with the throne is active here. As with the first living creature mentioned, the hearers would detect in the voice of this living creature the voice of the One who sits on the throne. This one too gives the identical command Ἔρχου ('come' or 'go'). 'And another red horse went out'. Whereas the first horse and rider's activity of going out is described at the conclusion of the verses devoted to their description, in v. 4 the activity of going out precedes the rest of their description. It is possible that the occurrence of the word ἄλλος ('another') would be an indication to the hearers that

---

[3] The identification of Jesus with the white horse and its rider has a long and rich history in early Christian interpretation of the Apocalypse beginning with Victorinus. Cf. Kovacs and Rowland, *Revelation*, pp. 78-80.

the first horse is separate from those that follow, implying that they form a distinct group, perhaps of a different kind than the first.[4] Such a hint would be in keeping with the interpretation that the white horse and rider are closely associated with Jesus. Yet, while such an interpretation is possible, there appears to be little need to drive too deep a wedge between any of these four horses and riders for all four are sent from heaven,[5] from those very near the throne, one might say from God himself. If the color of the first horse indicates something of its association with Jesus, the color of the second horse also reveals something of its mission and identity. As becomes clear shortly, red is the appropriate color for this horse and rider for he takes peace from the earth, encourages slaughter, and bears a great sword. The fact that red is the color of the great dragon of chapter 12 may be an indication that its color would alert the hearers to the fact that it too will bring bloodshed. Thus, rather than being a signal that this horse and rider are directly connected to the great red dragon, the color of the former may illuminate the color of the latter. The activity and function of the rider is given in a chiastically structured statement focusing upon what is divinely given to this rider and his primary task.

> There was given to him to take peace from the earth
>   in order that they might even slaughter one another
> and there was given to him a great sword (Rev. 6.4).

It is significant that the divine passive ἐδόθη ('there was given') stands at the beginning and end of the statement, revealing that the ability to take peace from the world is accomplished by means of the great sword with which the rider is entrusted. How ironic that the one who earlier gives peace to Johannine believers (1.4) is now the one who commissions the taking of peace from the earth. The purpose of these gifts is made clear in the purpose clause that stands in the middle of this chiastic statement; 'in order that they might slaughter one another'. Upon hearing these words, the color of the horse makes perfect sense for wherever he goes, blood will be spilt. The occurrence of the word σφάξουσιν ('they might slaughter') at this point might come as a bit of a surprise to John

---

[4] Aune (*Revelation 6-16*, p. 395) mentions this possibility.
[5] J.C. Poirier, 'The First Rider: A Response to Michael Bachmann', *NTS* 45 (1999), p. 257.

and his hearers, as the term has earlier been exclusively associated with the Slaughtered Lamb. It may not be without significance that it is this Slaughtered Lamb who opens the seal that occasions the emergence of this horse and its rider. Would such a linguistic connection suggest to John and his hearers that there may be some relationship between the slaughter of the Lamb and the slaughter of one another by those upon the earth? In other words, have the slaughterers now become the slaughtered?

Verses 5-6 – While the hearers ponder these possibilities their attention is directed to yet another development with the words, 'and when he opened the third seal'. Rather than simply being taken as a formulaic statement, these words convey to John and his hearers the ongoing activity of the Lamb who is worthy to take the book and open its seals. Thus, as the third seal is opened the hearers are mindful that the work of the Lamb continues. As with the opening of the first two seals, so the opening of the third is accompanied by the voice of one of the four living creatures. The word of this third living creature is identical to that of the first two: Ἔρχου ('come' or 'go'). John's next words are identical to those in v. 2, 'And I saw, and behold', which serve to direct the hearers' attention to a new detail and at the same time underscores its significance. What John sees is 'a black horse, and the one who sits upon him having a scale in his hand'. If the color of the first two horses is significant, it stands to reason that the color of this horse will be as well. Not only is the black horse's color an ominous sign for John and his hearers owing to its general association with darkness, but also owing to the fact that within the Johannine community darkness takes on spiritual overtones. In all likelihood, the first mention of the black horse would convey a sense of foreboding to John and his hearers. The fact that this rider has a scale in his hand indicates that the domain of his mission is commercial, as the scale is an instrument of commerce. For the first time, the emergence of one of these horses and riders is accompanied by another voice. In keeping with the other voices heard to this point in chapter six this one too is associated with the four living creatures. However, on this occasion there is one crucial difference. This voice is heard coming from the midst of the four living creatures! While it is possible that the location of the voice would suggest that it comes from one of the creatures or from them all corporately, the precise location as 'in the midst of the four living creatures' suggests otherwise. For to this point in the book, there are only two entities located in the midst of the four living creatures; the throne of God and the Slaughtered Lamb. If the four living creatures earlier speak for God, owing to their close geographical proximity around the throne, this voice makes clear that God[6] and/or the Lamb is speaking more directly,[7] giving the horse and its rider a specific directive. The directive takes the form of a description followed by a prohibition. First, the voice from the midst of the four living creatures describes famine like conditions with the words, 'A quart of wheat for a denarius and three quarts of barley for a denarius'. Since one quart of wheat and three quarts of barley were a meager ration for a cavalryman and his horse or barely enough for an individual and a domestic animal, it is clear that basic necessities are in view.[8] Owing to the fact that a denarius was the usual daily wage, the implications of the situation are easy to see. These prices, which appear to be ten to twelve times higher than normal,[9] reveal a siege like economy.[10] Second, the description of these famine-like conditions is followed by the prohibition, 'and do not harm the oil or wine'. It is possible to take this prohibition as a sign that despite the famine the rich are not denied their accustomed luxuries, in this case oil and wine. While it is true that landowners could make more money from olive groves and wine vineyards than wheat, and were sometimes tempted to develop the former as opposed to growing the latter,[11] such evidence hardly demonstrates that oil and wine are luxuries enjoyed by the wealthy. For while oil and wine are not as important as wheat and barley, they are not luxuries limited to the rich but commodities utilized by all.[12] In point of fact, their mention here seems to have more to do with the fact that neither the olive tree nor the vine is as susceptible to drought owing to the fact that their roots

---

[6] Sweet, *Revelation*, p. 140.

[7] Smalley, *The Revelation to John*, p. 153.

[8] Aune, *Revelation 6-16*, p. 397.

[9] This observation is based upon remarks about normal prices by Cicero, *Verr.* 3.81.

[10] Wall, *Revelation*, p. 110.

[11] Yarbro Collins, *The Apocalypse*, p. 46.

[12] Aune, *Revelation 6-16*, p. 398.

go deeper than wheat and barley.[13] On this view, the divine command connotes a limitation to the famine. Though severe, it is not severe enough to affect olive trees or grape vineyards.[14]

Verse 7 – But before the hearers can ponder fully the implications of the message of the voice from the midst of the four living creatures, they encounter the words, 'And when he opened the fourth seal', reminding them of the Slaughtered Lamb's ongoing activity as the one worthy to open the seals. Mention of the fourth seal would lead the hearers to expect to encounter the voice of the fourth living creature, owing to the pattern established with the opening of the first three seals. This expectation is immediately fulfilled with John's words, 'I heard a voice of the fourth living creature saying'. In one sense the mention of the fourth living creature conveys a sense of anticipation owing to the fact that there are only four living creatures, but seven seals to be opened. Consequently, despite the fact that three other seals remain to be opened, at one level there is a kind of finality with the reference made to the voice of the fourth living creature. As with the first three living creatures, the fourth one also says Ἔρχου ('come' or 'go').

Verse 8 – For a third time the hearers encounter the identical words, 'And I saw, and behold a horse', again indicating a new element in the vision as well as underscoring its significance. The color of the fourth horse is χλωρός ('pale' or 'yellowish green'). It would not be lost on John or his hearers that χλωρός ('pale' or 'yellowish green') is the color of sickness and death.[15] It is the color of a corpse! Following fast on the heels of the words from the midst of the four living creatures about famine conditions, this color alone indicates that the arrival of the fourth horse is even more ominous than the one that preceded it. But the color of the horse is not the only ominous feature of this scene for the one who sits on this horse, unlike the other riders, is given a name[16] and has a companion! 'His name is Death and Hades follows along with him.' Their appearance here may send mixed signals to John and his hearers. For, on the one hand, while these two figures would normally strike

---

[13] Mounce, *The Book of Revelation*, p. 155.
[14] Resseguie, *The Revelation of John*, p. 128.
[15] Smalley, *The Revelation to John*, p. 155,
[16] Beale, *The Book of Revelation*, p. 382.

terror in the hearts of humankind, on the other hand, the resurrected Jesus has already made the claim to have the keys of Death and Hades (1.19). His control of their domain translates into his admonitions to the seven churches with regard to how they should face death (2.10, 11, 23). For a second time Death is personified, as it will be two more times in the Apocalypse (20.13, 14) and on each occasion that Death is personified it is linked to Hades.[17] The imagery of Death as the rider being followed along with Hades produces a gruesome picture indeed. For it generates a scene where all the victims of Death are quickly captured by Hades.[18] To this rider and his companion, as with two of the previous riders, something is divinely given. On this occasion Death and Hades are given 'authority over one-fourth of the earth to kill with sword and with famine and with death and by means of the beasts of the earth'. The fact that authority is given over one-fourth of the earth indicates that as with the famine described in v. 6, even the devastation described with the opening of the fourth seal is not without its limits, for only one-fourth of the earth is affected.

The connection between the opening of the fourth seal, the voice of the fourth living creature, and the fate of one-fourth of the earth would not be lost on John and his hearers. Such a linguistic emphasis would indicate that the while the first four seals have been opened, in tandem with the activity of the four living creatures and the consequences for one-fourth of the earth, other seals remain to be opened. This first set of four seals within the seven is now completed. The revelation that one-fourth of the earth would be killed, reminds the hearers of Jesus' warning to the 'children' of 'Jezebel', that they too would be killed if repentance was not forthcoming (2.13). The fact that this devastation is to be accomplished by elements that bear a remarkable similarity to those envisioned in Jer. 15.2 suggests that this activity is the direct result of the fact that

---

[17] Aune, *Revelation 6-16*, p. 401.

[18] This scene is captured well in Albrecht Dürer's *The Four Horsemen of the Apocalypse*, where Hades' gaping mouth quickly swallows Death's victims. Cf. van der Meer, *Apocalypse*, p. 289. The image generated by Rev. 6.8 leads Kiddle (*The Revelation of St. John*, p. 118) to observe, 'The sufferer does not find peace as his tortured heart stops beating; he must wait the final judgment in the cheerless underworld of the dead, full of unknown terrors'.

God's patience has run out with those in question.¹⁹ It appears that these four elements are a culmination of the effects that accompany the opening of the first four seals. The mention of the sword may even call to mind the fact that Jesus has a double-edged sword coming from his mouth (1.16). Is it possible that such a detail might suggest to John and his hearers that the Lamb who opened this seal is present in its effects as well?

Figure 9
Facundus, *The Four Horsemen, Rev. 6*
(Madrid, Biblioteca Nacional)

Verse 9 – Though the first four seals hold together in a unique way, the description of the opening of the fifth seal is quite similar to the previous four, with the words, 'And when he opened the

---

¹⁹ Poirier ('The First Rider: A Response to M. Bachmann', p. 260) goes so far as to say of this verse, 'Rev 6.1-8 seems to be Jer 15.2 in apocalyptic dress'.

fifth seal'. While in English this phrase sounds identical to the previous four, there is one modification in the Greek text, for here, unlike its other appearances in this chapter, the number precedes the word 'seal'. To the discerning hearer, such a slight modification might very well indicate that the opening of this seal stands in some distinction to the previous four. Such suspicions are quickly confirmed by the fact that on this occasion John does not hear one of the four living creatures say Ἔρχου ('come' or 'go') nor does he see a horse and its rider. Rather, he sees something else, 'I saw under the altar the souls of those who had been slaughtered on account of the word of God and the witness which they had'. The hearers' initial encounter with the altar in the Apocalypse would unleash a variety of associations for them, for the altar is a most important article in God's house, coming to represent his very presence! It is here that sacrifices are offered, with the blood of the sacrifices running down from the top and sides of the altar, collecting under it. The location of these 'souls' under the altar would indicate to John and his hearers that they are sacrifices that have been offered to God.[20] The fact that they are under the altar reveals their extraordinary close proximity to him. The idea that these dead believers are already to be found in heaven would not be a complete surprise to Johannine hearers, for such an expectation is to be found in the words spoken by Jesus in the FG (Jn 14.2-3; 17.24). Such a detail would prove to be theologically significant for those within the community confronted by death in this world owing to their identification with Jesus.[21] For Johannine hearers the word ψυχὰς ('souls') conveys more than the idea of disembodied spirits, for in the Johannine literature the word often has the meaning of 'life' that may be laid down on behalf of another individual (Jn 10.11, 15, 17; 13.37, 38; 15.13; 1 Jn 3.16). Such a meaning would fit well with its use in Rev. 6.9, for these 'souls' or 'lives' have indeed been laid down on behalf of another for they have been slaughtered. The appearance here of the word slaughtered to describe these 'souls' points to the intimate connection that exists between these 'souls' and Jesus. For they, like the Lamb, have been slaughtered. They

---

[20] Yarbro Collins, *The Apocalypse*, p. 47.
[21] Aune, *Revelation 6-16*, pp. 403-404.

have suffered the same fate as Jesus[22] and, no doubt, bear the same marks as he. The implication being that they too look as though they have been slaughtered and they have! John and his hearers know very well the connection that exists between the Slaughtered Lamb's blood and those purchased from every tribe and tongue and people and nation people (5.9). Now the connection between those slaughtered 'souls' who are under the altar and their identification with Jesus is revealed. For these 'souls' have been slaughtered on account of the Word of God and the witness which they have. Such language brings to mind John, who 'has witnessed the word of God and the witness of Jesus Christ' in the writing down the words of this prophecy (1.2), who is on the Island of Patmos 'on account of the Word of God and the witness of Jesus' (1.9). It reminds them of Jesus, 'the faithful witness' (1.5; 3.14), whose faithful witness was manifested in his death. It also reminds them of Antipas, 'my faithful witness', who followed Jesus in his faithful witness, giving his life in Pergamum (2.13). Clearly, these 'souls' under the altar have been slaughtered owing to their identification with Jesus, his witness, and his message.[23] Just as the hearers would have likely seen a connection between the slaughtering of one another in 6.4 and the slaughter of the Lamb, so they would likely see this connection extended to include those 'souls' under the altar who have themselves been slaughtered in 6.9. Reference to 'the witness which they have' underscores the fact that their deaths are not viewed simply as random acts of violence, but as sacrifices actively offered to God through their intentional participation in the witness of Jesus. Their complete solidarity with Jesus could not be more explicit.[24]

Verse 10 – These slaughtered souls under the altar 'cried out with a great voice, "How long, O Master, the Holy and True One,

---

[22] Smalley, *The Revelation to John*, p. 157.

[23] S. Pattemore, *The People of God in the Apocalypse: Discourse, Structure and Exegesis* (SNTSMS 128; Cambridge: Cambridge University Press, 2004), p. 79.

[24] Two details in this verse might lead Johannine hearers to conclude that OT believers might very well be included amongst the souls under the altar. First, in 1 Jn 3.12 reference is made to Cain who slaughtered his brother. Second, in the Apocalypse one would normally expect 'on account of the witness of Jesus' in Rev. 6.9 instead of 'on account of the witness which they had'. Perhaps this less overtly Christological reference would give John and his hearers pause at this point. Cf. A. Feuillet, 'Les Martyrs de l'humanité et l'Agneau égorgé: Une interprétation nouvelle de la prière des Égorgé en *Ap* 6.9-11', *NRT* 99 (1977), pp. 189-207 and Pattemore, *The People of God in the Apocalypse*, pp. 78-79.

will you not judge and avenge our blood on those who dwell upon the earth"?' This fourth loud voice found in the Apocalypse (1.10; 5.2, 12), comes from the souls crying out in unison. The first words voiced by the slaughtered souls stand in clear continuity with a number of the voices in the Psalms, where the Psalmists ask the same question, 'How long, O Lord' (Pss. 13.1, 2; 74.10; 79.5; 82.2; 89.46; 90.13; 94.3). Thus, the first words that come from the slaughtered souls reveal that they speak with the authority of Scripture; their question is a biblical one, conditioned by the numerous questions put to God for justice, vengeance, and vindication. Their cry most parallels that found in Psalm 79 (LXX 78), where similar terminology is found. It is not altogether clear whether this prayer is directed to God or to Jesus. On the one hand, the term δεσπότης ('Master' or 'Lord') is used some seventeen times for God in the LXX[25] and would appear to fit the context well here, as in the Apocalypse God is normally the one who judges. On the other hand, the adjectives ὁ ἅγιος καὶ ἀληθινός ('the Holy and True') have previously been used by the resurrected Jesus with reference to himself in the prophetic message to the church in Philadelphia (3.7). The fact that the Lamb is the one who opens the seals, is in some way identified with the first rider, and will be identified with wrath later in this passage, all suggest that the term δεσπότης ('Master' or 'Lord') may on this occasion have reference to Jesus. In addition, it appears that the term is used with reference to Jesus in two other NT books (2 Pet. 2.1; Jude 4). The fact that on this occasion it is not altogether clear to whom this title has reference would not be lost on John and his hearers, as the intricate nature of the relationship between and identity of God and Jesus is becoming more and more apparent. Perhaps John and his hearers would be thinking primarily of God in this verse and secondarily of Jesus.[26] The cry of the slaughtered souls, 'How long ... will you not judge and avenge our blood on the inhabitants upon the earth', focuses upon the divine delay in the dispensing of justice and vindication. As the Apocalypse unfolds both God (Rev. 11.18; 14.7; 16.5, 7; 18.8, 10, 20; 19.2; 20.12, 13) and the Lamb (19.11) will be involved

---

[25] Aune, *Revelation 6-16*, p. 407.

[26] Pattemore (*The People of God in the Apocalypse*, p. 83) notes, 'It may well be that John is deliberately creating an overlap of reference as part of his narrative christology'.

in the dispensing of judgment. Owing to the souls' close proximity to God, and consequent knowledge of him, the certainty of God's judgment in the OT as well as later in the Apocalypse, the delay in its arrival is all the more difficult to understand. The cry for judgment is a cry for justice from one who has the power to execute judgment, for he is the all-powerful One. Accompanying this cry, indeed part of it, is the cry for God to avenge their blood. The term ἐκδικεῖς ('avenge'), which comes from the root word for 'justice',[27] conveys the idea of vindication. True to its OT heritage, such vindication is not simply a matter of the reputation of God's people but of God himself.[28] It will become clear later in the book (19.2) that the judgments of God are intimately connected to avenging the blood of his servants, i.e. vindicating them in the face of their enemies, fulfilling the proleptic promise made in 1.7. The introduction of the words 'our blood' makes a number of things clear. First, it reveals that the slaughtering of these 'souls' is no less real than the slaughtering of the Lamb (5.6, 12). Second, it further underscores the identification that exists between the Slaughtered Lamb and his slaughtered followers. It now becomes even clearer than before that the faithful witness to which they are called is patterned on Jesus' own faithful witness, being faithful unto death. The cry of these slaughtered 'souls' also makes clear the identity of those deserving of such judgment by God, they are 'the inhabitants upon the earth'. This phrase, which comes to represent those opposed to God and his work in the Apocalypse, conveys at least two things to the hearers. First, it reveals a basic division in the ranks of humanity between those who follow the Lamb and those who oppose him, a division anticipated in 3.10.[29] Second, this phrase implies that the events that have accompanied the opening of the first four seals are not deemed sufficient to vindicate the blood of these 'souls'. This is true despite the fact that authority was given to the fourth rider to kill one-fourth of humanity. Such a visceral prayer reveals something of the depth of the pain and anguish of these 'souls'. While such strong language has often struck a variety of commentators as being 'unchristian' and/or unworthy of the love ethic found in the

---

[27] Murphy, *Fallen is Babylon*, p. 210.
[28] Cf. the remarks of Beale, *The Book of Revelation*, p. 392.
[29] Pattemore, *The People of God in the Apocalypse*, p. 85.

NT, such reactions may well have more to do with the context of contemporary readers than the content of the text. Perhaps the testimony of readers of the Apocalypse from outside the context of comfort and affluence would go some way toward enabling a more authentic and robust hearing of this verse.[30]

Verse 11 – The divine response to their cry is two-fold. First, 'and there was given to each of them a white robe'. The divine passive ἐδόθη ('there was given') indicates that this gift has a divine origin. Apparently, 'the holy and true Master' himself responds to their prayer. The fact that each of these 'souls' is given 'a white robe' reveals that their identification with Jesus is an intimate one indeed. For not only is white the color closely associated with Jesus in the Apocalypse (1.14), but also those who follow him have been promised white garments in which they will walk with him (3.4, 5, cf. also 3.18). In fact, such white garments are already worn by the twenty-four elders who are seated around the throne (4.4). Thus, the gift of a white robe conveys the idea that the promises made to those who overcome are being fulfilled before their very eyes or ears. These elders come to represent all those who have been faithful even unto death. They have not soiled their garments, they are faithful witnesses like their Lord. Second, 'and it was said to them that they should wait a little time more, until they might be full, both their fellow servants and their brothers who are about to be killed even as they'. Again a divine passive, ἐρρέθη ('it was said'), reveals that this response comes from the one addressed by the 'souls'. The word ἀναπαύσονται ('they should wait') introduces a theme that will reappear at strategic locations throughout the Apocalypse, the theme of delay. Despite the desires of the 'souls under that altar', their cry for judgement and vindication that is long overdue is met with the instruction to wait a little while longer. It is just

---

[30] As Boesak (*Comfort and Protest*, p. 72) notes, 'People who do not know what oppression and suffering is react strangely to the language of the Bible ... The oppressed do not see any dichotomy between God's love and God's justice'.

To this might be added the observations of Schüssler Fiorenza (*Revelation*, p. 64), 'Exegetes, who generally do not suffer unbearable oppression and are not tormented by God's apparent toleration of injustice, tend to label this outcry for justice as unchristian and contrary to the preaching of the Gospel. One can adjudicate the central quest of Revelation in theological terms, however, only if one comprehends the anguish that fuels this outcry for justice and vindication, for divine revenge and restitution for so many lives taken, and for so much blood unnecessarily shed.'

possible that this instruction might carry with it the more positive idea of 'resting', as the term can also be translated in this way. On this hearing, the 'souls under the altar' are being informed that their vindication is no longer tied to their own 'works' but is now exclusively in the hands of God. Consequently, they are invited to 'rest' for a little while longer.[31] While such an idea might possibly be present, the rest of the verse seems to argue against this as the primary meaning. The 'souls' are to wait ἕως πληρωθῶσιν ('until they are full' or 'complete'), indicating that to this point justice and vindication would be premature owing to the fact that there are others who must first join these 'under the altar'. John and his hearers do not need the sentence to be completed for them to understand its implications. These 'souls' will only be 'full' or 'complete' when others who have also been slaughtered join them. But the sentence *is* finished, making clear who these individuals are and how they will join these 'souls under the altar'. The ones whom the 'souls' await are 'their fellow servants and their brothers who are about to be killed even as they'. Such language would not be lost on John and his hearers. For not only are these terms closely associated with prophetic vocation in the Apocalypse, but they have also been used previously by John to describe himself as a servant of God (1.1) and a brother of the hearers (1.9). The stark truth is that these 'souls under the altar' will be full or complete only when John and his hearers join them. This warning is made explicit in that those who will join the 'souls under the altar' are those 'who are about to be killed even as they'. The same fate awaits these fellow servants and brothers that met these 'souls'. They will be slaughtered even as these 'souls' had been, even as the Lamb whom they follow. Thus, as these 'souls' wait, their earlier cry would be understood to expand to include the prayer for justice and vindication both for them and those who will complete them. And John and his hearers wait too …

Verses 12-14 – The description of the opening of the fifth seal is so extensive that the hearers might have momentarily forgotten that they are in the midst of the opening of the seven seals, as their minds ponder the implications of the 'souls under the altar'. But if such is the case, John and his hearers are jolted back into their

---

[31] A suggestion made by Pattemore, *The People of God in the Apocalypse*, p. 88.

broader context with a description of the opening of the sixth seal that parallels the opening of the first seal, 'and I saw when he opened the sixth seal'. Such a parallel may serve as an inclusio, indicating that these first six seals stand together. The interlude that is chapter seven will confirm such a suspicion, as the opening of the seventh seal, which must await the conclusion of this interlude, will not be described until chapter eight. The way in which the sixth seal rounds out the first six will also be impressed upon the hearers by the fact that the description devoted to it is nearly twice as long as that devoted to the opening of the fifth seal. In addition, there is a sense of finality conveyed in the opening of this sixth seal for within it two non-enumerated sets of sevens are found. The first set of sevens describes the cosmic upheavals that accompany the opening of the sixth seal, while the second set describes the human reactions to these cosmic events.[32] What John sees when the sixth seal is opened by the Lamb is the eruption of seven cosmic events which suggest a cosmic collapse. These elements include those that appear in a variety of OT texts. Their convergence at this point would not be lost on John or his hearers. The cosmic upheaval revealed in vv. 12-14 begins with reference to a great earthquake. This mention would no doubt remind John and his hearers of the many references to earthquakes found in OT eschatological contexts (Isa. 13.13; Joel 2.10; Hag. 2.6) and also serve to introduce a detail in the Apocalypse that will figure prominently at various points. This great earthquake would serve as a sign of the beginning of the end. Next, the sun becomes black as sackcloth (Isa. 50.3), a cloth especially suitable for mourning, while the whole moon becomes as blood (Joel 2.31). Not only does the sun cease to shine and the moon take on an ominous color, but 'the stars of heaven fell upon the earth as a fig tree casts its fruit when shaken by a great wind' (Isa. 34.4). No sooner do the stars of heaven fall to earth than the heaven itself vanishes as a scroll vanishes when it is rolled up (Isa. 34.4). Finally, 'every mountain and island was removed from their places' (Jer. 4.24). Several aspects of these verses would be of significance to John and his hearers. First, the fact that there are seven elements included in these cosmic upheavals would convey a sense of finality. At this point in the narrative, it is impossible to imagine that all of

---

[32] Aune, *Revelation 6-16*, p. 391.

creation itself is not being destroyed.[33] Second, the fact that so many of these elements are associated with the promised eschatological activity of God in the OT, many of which signal the 'Day of the Lord', would leave no doubt that in these events God himself is present. Third, the theme of shaking, removing, even vanishing is clearly at the heart of the activities that accompany the opening of this seal. The earth, the stars, heaven, mountains and islands all feel the effects of such movement. Fourth, a number of the details mentioned in these verses, might very well remind the hearers of other details occurring earlier. Mention of the sun turning black as sackcloth would remind the hearers of the third horse and his mission. The moon appearing as blood would remind them of the blood of the Lamb and the souls under the altar. The falling of the stars 'to the earth' might be seen in connection with the cry for vindication of the souls under the altar that their blood be avenged upon 'the inhabitants upon the earth'. The vanishing of the book appears ironically in the midst of the opening of the seven seals in order that this book might be opened, not rolled up! And perhaps the mention of the removal of every mountain and island from their places is a tacit reminder that even the island of Patmos, where John is located, will at some point be removed from its place. Suffice it to say that the content of vv. 12-14 and their connections with what has come before would be swirling in the minds of John and his hearers.

Verses 15-17 – The human reaction to these cosmic events, which accompany the opening of the sixth seal, follows immediately. This reaction is united and complete, for the seven distinct classes of human society speak in unison in response to the cosmic upheaval. Not only does the number seven indicate that humanity in its entirety is here represented, but the groups themselves span the range of humankind from kings to slaves and free persons. Five of these groups will reappear together in Rev. 19.18, when the birds of the air are called together for a great feast. The first group, 'the kings of the earth', are those over whom Jesus has already been said to be ruler (1.5), but who function as the adversaries of God throughout the Apocalypse (17.2, 18; 18.1, 9; 19.1). Apparently their opposition will come to an end when the kings of the earth

---

[33] Resseguie, *The Revelation of John*, p. 131.

bring their glory into the New Jerusalem (21.24). However, at this point they first appear in their adversarial role. Joining them are the great men, later identified with Babylon the Great City (18.23), and the Generals (19.18). The rich (13.16) and the strong (16.15, 18.2, 8, 10, 21; 19.6, 18) are also part of this vast society of individuals, as are every slave (13.16; 19.18) and every free person (13.16; 19.18). These last two groups stand in special relationship to one another owing to the word πᾶς ('each' or 'every') which governs them both in the Greek text, similar to the way in which mountain and island stand together in 6.14. These seven classes of humanity join together as they hide themselves 'in the caves and in the rocks of the mountains', an eschatological activity anticipated in Isaiah (2.10, 19, 21) where the enemies of God are said to hide themselves in order to escape his terror. Not only do they hide themselves, but they also call upon the mountains and the rocks in which they are hiding saying:

> Fall upon us and hide us from the face of the One who sits on the throne and from the wrath of the Lamb, because the great day of their wrath has come, and who is able to stand?

These words reveal a number of things to John and his hearers. First, they indicate that despite the staggering activities that accompany the opening of the seals, especially the first four seals, a portion of humankind survives. Perhaps they would assume this number to be three-fourths based upon 6.8. Second, it becomes clear that these individuals consider themselves helpless in the face of their adversaries, as they call out to inanimate objects for protection and lament the fact that none can stand against them. Third, the events that accompany the opening of the seals are, no doubt, viewed as the reason that they hide themselves and call out to the rocks and mountains to hide them. However, it is very clear that they consider God and the Lamb to be responsible for these calamities and, consequently, those from whom they desire to be hidden. Fourth, humanity's description of both God and the Lamb might strike the hearers as a bit odd for a couple of reasons. For while the whole of chapter four is devoted, for the most part, to a description of the heavenly court focusing upon the One who sits on the throne, there is no description of his face! Such a statement may reflect the well-known OT understanding that no one can see the face of God and live (Exod. 33.20). If such an idea is here present it indicates that in the events that accompany the opening of the seals the presence of God is manifest in such a way his face is being revealed. John and his hearers would not have forgotten that the book being unsealed has its origin in the right hand of the One who sits on the throne. Thus, his face is being revealed. It is the Day of the Lord! Closely associated with the face of the One who sits on the throne is 'the wrath of the Lamb', from which humankind also desires to be hidden. If there was any question with regard to the Lamb's involvement with the events that accompany the opening of the seals, these words remove all doubt. While such a description might not seem quite appropriate for one earlier identified as the Slaughtered Lamb, it does fit well with the Lamb's activity in chapter six and continues the idea contained in the title of the Apocalypse, it is a revelation of Jesus Christ. The fact that the first mention in the book of the word 'wrath' comes in association with the Lamb[34] is even more significant owing to the fact that in all its other occurrences it is used in association with God (6.17; 11.18; 14.10; 16.19; 19.15). Such an attribution continues the practice in the Johannine literature where a characteristic of God is attributed to Jesus. In addition, this attribution might also bring some clarity to the identity of the rider on the white horse. For, if that rider is identified as the Lamb, reference to the wrath of the Lamb in v. 16 would form an inclusio with the reference in v. 2. In other words, not only is the on-going activity of the Lamb chronicled with the opening of each seal, but his overall involvement is also underscored by his presence at the beginning and end of this section devoted to the opening of the first six seals. Given the close association and identity between God and the Lamb, it comes as no surprise that this eschatological moment is identified as 'the great day of their wrath', revealing further the intimate nature of their relationship.[35] Perhaps the discerning Johannine reader would remember that instead of receiving eternal life, the one who does not obey the Son incurs the wrath of God (Jn 3.36). The theme of the Day of the Lord continues with humanity's last question, a question that calls to mind the prophecies of Nahum (1.6) and Malachi (3.2), 'and

---

[34] Osborne, *Revelation*, p. 296.
[35] Smalley, *The Revelation to John*, p. 170.

who is able to stand?' The intensity of their situation and the despair in which they find themselves makes the emphasis of this question all the more striking. It is the Day of the Lord, who is able to stand?

The 144,000 and the Great Multitude (7.1-17)

Verse 1 – With the final words of chapter six still in their minds and hearts, John and his hearers anxiously anticipate the opening of the seventh and final seal by the Lamb. However, the next words encountered are not 'And I saw when he opened the seventh seal' but rather, 'And after this I saw', indicating that the seventh seal is not to be opened quite yet. In other words, John's hearers must await the end of the seal sequence, which must to them signal the end of all things.[36] But before this end, John describes 'four angels standing upon the four corners of the earth, grasping the four winds of the earth in order that the wind might not blow upon the earth nor upon the sea nor upon any tree'. The appearance of the four angels indicates that despite the break in recounting the opening of the seventh seal God continues to be active, for these angels as some others mentioned in the book (9.11; 14.18; 16.5) have control over various portions of nature. The fact that there are four angels standing at the four corners of the earth also suggests that there are indeed certain heavenly beings who are able to stand before the One who sits on the throne and the Lamb, partially answering the question with which chapter six concludes. At the same time, this emphasis upon the number four might also point to God's complete control over the earth, as the four corners of the earth suggest the world in its entirety.[37] Owing to the fact that these four angels are prepared to unleash the four winds might suggest to the hearers that 'the four living creatures' have morphed into these four angels, but this is uncertain. The four winds, a traditional sign of God's destructive power in the OT (Jer. 49.36; cf. also 4.11-12; 51.1-2; Ezek. 5.12),[38] might also remind the hearers of the four riders described previously in the opening of the first four seals, who bring various degrees of destruction upon the earth. Such an association is all the more likely owing to the fact that there is a close

---

[36] Resseguie, *The Revelation of John*, p. 135.

[37] Pattemore, *The People of God in the Apocalypse*, p. 125.

[38] Smalley, *The Revelation to John*, p. 181.

connection between the four chariots of horses and the four winds of heaven described in Zech. 6.5.[39] As noted earlier in the reading of Rev. 6.2, the images from this passage may well be in the minds of the hearers as this vision unfolds. Clearly, the purpose of the angels' restraining activity is to keep these winds from prematurely bringing destruction upon the earth, sea, and trees. The scope of the winds' potential activity is not only conveyed by 'the earth' and 'the sea', which denote the major components of the world, but also by 'any tree', which represents those things most vulnerable to the destructive force of the wind.[40] Such a surrealistic scene leaves the hearers contemplating at least two questions. First, owing to the numerous implicit connections between this verse and the previous chapter, what is the temporal relationship between the things described in each? In other words, does what is described in 7.1 follow on from 6.17 chronologically, or does mention of the four winds which are being restrained take the hearers back to before the opening of the first seal? Second, if these four winds are at present being held back by the four angels, can the unleashing of their destructive powers be far away?

Verse 2 – But before much reflection can be given to these questions John recounts seeing yet another event. 'And I saw another angel coming up from the rising of the sun having a seal of the living God. And he cried with a great voice to the four angels to those to whom had been given to harm the earth and sea saying …' The appearance of this other angel is most significant, for it is clear that he is closely associated with God. This angel is identified as coming from the realm of God, ἀπὸ ἀνατολῆς ἡλίου ('from the rising of the sun' or 'from the east of the sun'), indicating something of his close proximity to God. In addition, this angel is said to possess a 'seal of the living God'. The term σφραγῖδα ('seal') would likely be taken to have reference to a signet ring, commonly used in antiquity by kings and their designees to 'seal' or 'mark' those things which they regarded to be their personal property.[41] The fact that this seal is identified as belonging to 'the living God' could not help but remind the hearers of the book, sealed with seven seals, that

---

[39] Caird, *The Revelation of St. John*, p. 94 and Allo, *L'Apocalypse*, p. 91.
[40] Sweet, *Revelation*, p. 147.
[41] Metzger, *Breaking the Code*, p. 60.

was in the hand of the One who sits on the throne in 5.1. What was inferred there becomes clearer here. The seven seals are indeed the seals of God. The significance of this seal is underscored by the fact that God is here referred to as 'the living God', which might call to mind the fact that Yahweh is referred to by this title twice in the LXX in contexts where he has been reproached (2 Kgs 19.4, 16). This title serves to contrast the true and living God with the idolatry of the false gods.[42] At the same time, the hearers would be mindful of the fact that earlier in the book God has already been called 'the One who lives forever and ever' (Rev. 4.9, 10). The angel's possession of 'the seal of the living God' makes clear that this angel is God's authorized agent, acting on his behalf. It is this authorized angel, with the seal of the living God, who now cries out with a great voice, speaking for God. The subjects of his words are the four angels mentioned previously. Earlier in v. 1 it was implied that these angels held back the four winds from harming the earth, sea, and trees. Now it becomes clear that they themselves have been given the authority to harm the earth and sea, the divine passive ἐδόθη ('was given') indicating that their authority comes from God.

Verse 3 – Following this dramatic description of this other angel, authorized by God, he addresses the other four saying, 'Do not harm the earth nor the sea nor the trees, until we seal the servants of our God upon their foreheads'. The prohibition against harming the earth and sea and trees follows naturally upon the revelation that these angels have the authority to do such harm, and apparently have been commissioned to do so. But the prohibition is of a temporary nature, postponing the work of harming, rather than prohibiting it altogether. The destructive work of the four angels is to be delayed until which time 'we can seal the servants of our God upon their foreheads'. It appears from the first person plural verb σφραγίσωμεν ('we seal') that this other angel is to be joined in his work of sealing by the four angels who at present are at the four corners of the earth grasping the four winds. Thus, it seems that this other angel has some degree of authority over the four angels who hold back the wind. Clearly, 'the servants of God' are to be sealed with the seal of the living God, but of what does this sealing consist? For the Johannine hearers such language would evoke a

---

[42] Mounce, *The Book of Revelation*, p. 167.

host of images. In point of fact, it is likely that its mention would generate a convergence of ideas drawn from the biblical tradition where God marks an individual or individuals to protect them from harm or death. Such stories are plenteous beginning with that recorded in Gen. 4.15, where God places a mark upon Cain in order that no one would take his life. Owing to the numerous paschal allusions, perhaps the Passover story itself would be prominent in their minds (Exodus 12), where the blood of the Passover lamb is placed upon the door-posts of the Israelites insuring that the Destroyer angel would pass over that house sparing the lives of its firstborn. The similarities between the words of the angel and the actions described in Ezek. 9.1-11 where a mark is placed upon the foreheads of those who 'sigh and groan' over the sin of the city, and as a result their lives are spared, would perhaps also stand out.[43] But such biblical associations would not exhaust the meaning of this image for there are other connections that would be generated by it. As noted earlier, mention of the seal of the living God would no doubt be taken as having reference to God's signet ring. In appearance a signet ring would have on its top side raised letters or a symbol that when pressed upon a soft surface would leave its impression on that object. God's signet ring would likely be thought of as bearing his name, an idea that will be made obvious later in the book (14.1), leaving its imprint upon any so sealed. Such an idea is not far removed from the way in which this verb is used in the FG to indicate authentication of the witness of Jesus, by the one who believes (Jn 3.33), and the person of Jesus, by God the Father (6.27). Nor is it likely that the hearers would miss the way in which this seal and sealing stands in the context of and in contrast to the seven seals and their unsealing by the Slaughtered Lamb. Not only would John and his hearers be struck by the fact that this sealing takes place just before the seventh seal is unsealed, but also by the fact that it is the same God who does both! The fact that this verb will occur five times and the noun form once in a span of seven verses highlights the importance of this activity.[44] Those to be sealed are identified as 'the servants of our God', a designation that

---

[43] Already with Origen the similarities between these passages have been noted, cf. Allo, *L'Apocalpse*, p. 91.

[44] Resseguie, *The Revelation of John*, p. 136.

appears to have prophetic associations in the Apocalypse (cf. the discussion of 1.1; 2.20).[45] These servants of God are to be sealed upon their μετώπων ('foreheads'). Significantly, this term appears only in the Apocalypse in the whole of the NT and always designates a place where a seal (7.3; 9.4), mark (13.16; 14.9; 20.4), or name (14.1; 17.5; 22.4) is placed.[46] It would appear that the seal is placed upon the forehead owing to the fact that this is the most visible place on the face, immediately indicating that these individuals belong to God. In addition to identifying the sealed as belonging to God, the purpose of this sealing appears to be for protection, the implication being that these servants of God would be protected from the harm about to be unleashed by the four angels.

Verse 4 – With the conclusion of these words the angel speaks to the other four angels, the hearers might expect John next to observe the sealing of the servants of God. But this is not to be, for at this point John does not see but hears. 'And I heard the number of those sealed, 144,000, sealed out of every tribe of the sons of Israel'. The hearers are not told how John hears this number (are they counted individually aloud? is their number called out? does he hear the sound of their sealing and add the numbers himself?), but it is clear that the number sealed is the result of the activity of these angels commissioned for this task. The significance of what John heard is not how he hears the number of those sealed, but the number itself. As the following verses make clear this number is a perfect square number being the sum of 12,000 from each of the twelve tribes of Israel.[47] Perhaps the hearers are reminded of Numbers 31, where Moses takes 12,000 men, one thousand from each of the twelve tribes of Israel, into battle with Midian. If so, the fact that such a force is here squared would suggest not only that it is a perfect force in number, but also that the whole is represented by each of its parts. This number suggests perfection and completion, not one member is excluded.

Who are these described as being from 'each tribe of the sons of Israel'? Who are the 144,000? The first hint as to their identity is found already in v. 3, where those to be sealed are called 'the serv-

---

[45] Kiddle, *The Revelation of St. John*, p. 134 and Caird, *The Revelation of St. John*, p. 95.

[46] P. Lampe, 'μέτωπον', *EDNT*, III, pp. 421-22.

[47] Bauckham, *The Climax of Prophecy*, p. 218.

ants of our God'. In its earlier (and later occurrences) in the Apocalypse, this phrase is used with reference to John and other Johannine Christians, underscoring their prophetic identity. Thus, the hearers' first inclination would be to see some connection between these 'servants of God' and these 'sons of Israel'. Related to this, the earlier words of the resurrected Jesus indicate that there are those in the cities where the churches are located who claim to be 'Jews', but they are not (2.9; 3.9). The clear implication of such revelations is that those who identify with and believe in Jesus are those who may lay claim to being God's people. While the Johannine believers are not ever directly called 'Jews' in the book it appears that they would have a close affinity with the name Israel, for in the FG Israel is closely identified with Jesus and his followers. There, John comes baptizing in order that the 'Lamb of God that takes away the sin of the world' might be revealed to Israel (Jn 1.31). It is by means of his witness that the earliest disciples encounter Jesus, resulting in the declaration by 'the true Israelite', Nathaniel (1.47), that Jesus is 'the King of Israel' (1.49). Though the 'Teacher of Israel', Nicodemus, does not understand Jesus' teaching about 'birth from above' (3.10), Jesus is declared to be 'the King of Israel' by those who receive him in Jerusalem (12.13). The clear implication of such passages is that Jesus and those who believe in him are identified with Israel. The initial occurrence of the phrase 'sons of Israel' in the Apocalypse also implies some identification between this title and the Johannine believers (Rev. 3.14). Later 'the names of the twelve tribes of the sons of Israel' will reappear, being inscribed upon the twelve gates in the New Jerusalem. Thus, it appears likely that John and his hearers would understand mention of 'the tribes of the sons of Israel' as having reference to Johannine believers. Clearly, such language continues to make explicit the connection between Jesus, 'the Lion of the Tribe of Judah', the one who has the 'Key of David', his redemptive work, and the heritage of Israel. On this occasion, the heritage of Israel is most important, but as will be seen it is Israel in its transformed state. Something more of this 'transformed' role of the heritage of Israel is revealed as the hearers' encounter the list of the twelve tribes in vv. 5-8.[48] The delineation of these tribes is almost inexplicable if not to in-

---

[48] Smalley, *The Revelation to John*, p. 187.

form John and his hearers as to the nature of this 'Israel'. Otherwise, the main point regarding the identity of the 144,000 could have been made without their specific mention in vv. 5-8.

Verses 5-8 – It would seem likely that John and his hearers would be familiar with various listings of the twelve tribes of Israel, as some twenty different such lists appear in the OT. While it might be possible to derive something of the significance of the list encountered in 7.5-8 by its formal comparison to other lists, this approach does not seem to be the best way forward. Rather, in keeping with the approach of the reading offered in this commentary, it would seem advantageous to ask how the hearers would be affected by what they encounter in this list as it unfolds. The list found in 7.5-8 begins with reference to the fact that 12,000 are sealed from the tribe of Judah. For the hearers, the appearance of Judah as the first tribe listed would make perfect sense, though Judah is not normally the first tribe in most lists. Judah is, after-all, the tribe from which the messiah is prophesied to come, the tribe of David from which come all but one of the kings of Israel and Judah.[49] It is the tribe with which Jesus, the Slaughtered Lamb, is identified. And Jesus is the one who has 'the key of David'. He is 'the Lion of the Tribe of Judah'. Thus, as the hearers first encounter this list of 'the tribes of the sons of Israel', they perhaps discern that they are encountering a unique listing of the twelve tribes. The appearance of the participle ἐσφραγισμένοι ('who were sealed') reaffirms the purpose of this activity. The fourth appearance of this verb in three verses keeps before the hearers the fact that these are identified as belonging to God and being protected by him. The hearers next encounter 12,000 from the tribe of Reuben. Often Reuben appears first in listings of the twelve tribes, owing to the fact that he was Jacob's first-born. His appearance at this point might convey two things to the hearers. First, that he stands in a subordinate position to the tribe from which the messiah comes. Second, despite any demotion or displacement in order, the tribe of the first-born son is still important in this transformed Israel. Perhaps his mention underscores the importance of the heritage of Israel in a way hard to parallel. If the hearers assume from the mention of Reuben after Judah that this list will now follow convention,

---

[49] Smalley, *The Revelation to John*, p. 187.

they quickly discover that this is not the case, for the next 12,000 sealed is not from the tribe of Simeon, Jacob's second-born, but the son of a handmaid, Gad. In fact, the next three groups of 12,000 come from tribes whose heads were born not by Leah or Rachel, but by Zilpah and Bilhah, their respective handmaids. The tribes of Gad and Asher trace their origin to Jacob by means of Zilpah, Leah's handmaid who bore children from Jacob for her mistress. The same phenomenon is true of the next tribe, Naphtali, from which 12,000 are sealed, whose origin is traced to Jacob by means of Bilhah, Rachel's handmaid who bore children from Jacob for her mistress.[50] The unusual placement of these three tribes might convey to the hearers the sense of inversion, where less important tribes find themselves elevated in this group. Often the tribes that come from the handmaids are listed last, or near last, and their treatment and status sometimes even borders on second-class stature. The hearers could not help but be impressed by the fact that those sealed from these 'tribes of the sons of Israel' come from an Israel that has been transformed, not only in its messianic quality, but its egalitarian nature. Owing to the placement of these three tribes from the handmaids, the hearers might next expect to encounter the tribe of Dan, as Dan is the other head to come from the handmaid Bilhah. However, the next group of 12,000 sealed comes not from Dan but from the tribe of Manassah. Not only does this appearance come as a bit of a surprise, given the fact that Dan is expected at this point, but also because this grandson of Jacob appears before a number of other prominent tribes. Manassah's displacement of Dan would perhaps register with the hearers in at least three ways. First, it might imply that Dan's propensity toward idolatry has resulted in a forfeiture of his place among the tribes (Judg. 18.30-31; 1 Kgs 12.25-33). Second, the fact that Manassah is a grandson of Jacob may say something about the extent of this new and transformed Israel. Third, the mention of Manassah at this point could not help but remind the hearers of Joseph, his father, whose prophetic nature was well known from the OT. Owing to the mention of Manassah, the hearers might next expect the mention of his brother, Ephraim. But again, they find their expectations

---

[50] C.R. Smith, 'The Portrayal of the Church as the New Israel in the Names and Order of the Tribes in Revelation 7.5-8', *JSNT* 39 (1990), p. 113.

to be unfulfilled. For instead of Ephraim, the next 12,000 sealed come from the tribe of Simeon. For the hearers at least part of this diversion might not be completely unexpected, for the omission of Ephraim in some ways fits well with the omission of Dan, as Ephraim was also given to idolatrous activity. Thus, oddly enough, the mention of Manassah where Dan is expected and its implicit reference to Ephraim, which is also omitted, places Manassah in a most strategic position. As with Reuben, mention of 12,000 sealed from Simeon reminds the hearers of the importance of the heritage of Israel, as does the fact that the next three groups of 12,000 sealed come from tribes traditionally given places of importance, Levi, Issachar, and Zebulon. While often omitted from lists of tribes in contexts devoted to discussion of the distribution of the land, the mention of Levi is most fitting in Rev. 7.7, as Levi's presence would underscore for the hearers, in a most significant way, the priestly theme that has been developing as the book unfolds. Specifically, the presence of this tribe at this point reinforces the identification of the Johannine believers as priests to God (1.6; 5.10),[51] providing yet another point of contact between these 'sons of Israel' and the Johannine 'servants of God'. The eleventh group of 12,000 sealed comes from the tribe of Joseph. The mention of this tribe is again something of a surprise, owing to the fact that normally when Manassah appears in a list, Joseph does not appear, rather his other son Ephraim appears. Joseph's mention would not only highlight Ephraim's omission, again raising the issue of the implications of idolatry for the hearers, but also again would remind the hearers of Joseph's prophetic activities and in turn their own prophetic vocation. Significantly, Joseph's appearance at this point stands in chiastic parallel to Reuben, who was the one brother who did not wish to kill Joseph, thereby preserving his life. The final group of 12,000 sealed comes from the tribe of Benjamin, the last son of Jacob. Four things stand out about the mention of this tribe at this point. First, Benjamin is listed alongside his brother Joseph, the only other son borne by Rachel. As such, the hearers' may be reminded of Jacob's special love for both Rachel and her sons. Second, the mention of Benjamin last forms an inclusio of sorts with Judah, as these two tribes are the only tribes from which the kings

---

[51] Smalley, *The Revelation to John*, p. 189.

of Israel and Judah arose, thus, emphasizing the messianic nature of the list yet again. Third, this inclusio might also be an implicit acknowledgement of the place of the nation of Judah, which was comprised of Judah and Benjamin, in this transformed Israel. Fourth, the participle ἐσφραγισμένοι ('who were sealed'), which last appeared with the mention of the tribe of Judah reappears here, again forming an inclusio around the tribes and reinforcing the purpose of this sealing.[52] These 144,000 belong to God, bearing his seal, being protected by him.

What would the hearers gather about the identity of this 144,000 who are sealed from 'the tribes of the sons of Israel'? Perhaps a brief summary would be helpful at this point. First, in all likelihood they would see a strong connection between their own community and the 144,000. While the extent of this continuity is not certain, there is no evidence to suggest that this number is disconnected from Johannine believers, the churches described in Revelation 2-3. Second, it is obvious that the 144,000 would be thought of as a messianic group. Third, clearly this group would be seen as the heirs to what God has done through Israel, owing in part to the presence of the historically important tribes. Fourth, like the Johannine believers, this group is marked in part by its priestly identity. Fifth, the prophetic characteristics of this group would not be lost on the hearers, as they too share in this prophetic identity. Finally, this group is clearly one marked out as belonging to God and protected by him. The extent and scope of this protection will become clearer as the book itself unfolds.

Verses 9-10 – As the hearers ponder the significance of this 144,000, they are immediately confronted by the description of yet another scene signified by the phrase 'after these things I saw', indicating a new direction in the vision but one that is not discontinuous with what precedes. For by this time the hearers know full well that it is not unusual for a description of that which John 'hears' to be followed by a description of that which he 'sees'. It is further the case that what John earlier 'hears' is directly connected to and transformed into what he 'sees'. The greatest example of this phenomenon to this point is found in Revelation 5. There John hears the

---

[52] Smalley, *The Revelation to John*, p. 189 and Resseguie, *The Revelation of John*, p. 137.

description of the Lion of the Tribe of Judah, but what he sees is a Lamb that looks as if it had been slaughtered. Despite the clear differences in these images and their descriptions, they refer to the same person and the differing images interpret and clarify one another, so much so that the Lion cannot be fully understood without the vision of the Lamb. Owing to the way in which things heard sometimes morph into things seen in the Apocalypse, John's words 'I saw' alert the hearers to the possibility that the description which follows may indeed be related at a profound theological level to that which precedes. The extent of this relationship becomes clear as the chapter unfolds.

With the word 'Behold' John directs the hearers' attention to 'a great crowd', the first 'crowd' to be mentioned in the book. The description of this crowd stands in contrast to the group previously described, for while that group had a 'number', this crowd no one is able to 'number'. The contrast conveyed by the noun ἀριθμὸν ('number') and the verb ἀριθμῆσαι ('to number') would not be lost on the hearers. The fact that this crowd is innumerable would be all the more astounding for John and his hearers, owing to the fact that the number of Christians within the Johannine community would not likely be very large.[53] The sheer magnitude of this innumerable crowd could not help but be an extraordinary encouragement to them as they face what at that point must seem to be insurmountable odds. While the previous group was composed 'out of each tribe of the sons of Israel', this crowd is composed 'out of all nations and tribes and peoples and tongues'. Though in a different order, these four components earlier appeared in 5.9, describing those purchased by the blood of the one who was slaughtered. Here, as there, these four components point to the universal nature of this crowd. The contrast between those who comprise the previous group and this crowd is clear, as is the move from a somewhat nationalistic group focused upon Israel to a more inclusive and universalistic crowd. Of extraordinary significance is the fact that this innumerable, universal crowd is said to be 'standing before the throne and before the Lamb'. For the hearers, this description directly answers the question with which chapter six closes, 'Who is able to stand' before the One who sits on the throne and the

---

[53] Aune, *Revelation 6-16*, p. 467.

Lamb? It is this innumerable crowd drawn from every nation, tribe, people, and tongue![54] In contrast to those who fear the revelation of the face of the One who sits upon the throne and the wrath of the Lamb, this crowd shares intimate fellowship with God and the Lamb and stand in very close proximity to them. Rather than hiding from the divine presence, these participate in it in a three-fold fashion. First, they are clothed in 'white robes', attire that suggests this crowd has proven faithful in its witness to Jesus. In this it reminds the hearers of the 'white robes' given to the souls under the altar that had been slaughtered 'on account of the Word of God and the witness which they had'. The white robes point to a direct connection between the souls mentioned in 6.9-11 and the crowd mentioned here in 7.9. Second, this crowd is described as having 'palm branches in their hands'. Johannine hearers would no doubt be reminded of the only other occasion where this word is found in the Johannine literature (in fact, in the whole of the NT!). Upon Jesus' triumphal entry into Jerusalem the crowd that greets him with the words, 'Hosanna; Blessed is the one who comes in the name of the Lord, and the King of Israel' is described as having palm branches in their hands (Jn 12.13).[55] In Rev. 7.9, the appearance of palm branches would be a sign of the victory of the Lamb and the identification of this innumerable crowd with their King. Such details are appropriate for those who follow the one who is characterized as being the one who has overcome. As their attire and activity reveal, they too have overcome. Third, the crowd also participates in the divine presence by crying out with a great voice, 'Salvation to our God who sits upon the throne and to the Lamb'. This hymn-like confession conveys a sense of finality, as it appears to focus upon salvation in its most comprehensive, eschatological sense as belonging to 'our God Who Sits on the throne and the Lamb'.[56] Such attributions of salvation occur three times in the Apocalypse, each time emphasizing this eschatological salvation (7.10; 12.10; 19.1). While the salvific nature of 'overcoming' or being 'victorious' is clearly a part of the salvation mentioned here, for Johannine hearers

---

[54] Resseguie, *The Revelation of John*, p. 138.
[55] Fee, *Revelation*, p. 111.
[56] Schüssler Fiorenza, *Revelation*, p. 68.

this 'salvation' is likely to have a more comprehensive meaning.[57] For its meaning here would, no doubt, be informed by Jesus' words in the FG that 'salvation is of the Jews' (4.22) and the Samaritan believers' declaration that Jesus is 'truly the savior of the world' (4.42). The trajectory present in these words of Jesus in John 4 is, interestingly enough, present in the movement of Revelation 7. Just as the statement that 'salvation is of the Jews' precedes the affirmation that Jesus is 'the savior of the world', so the sealing of the 144,000 precedes the innumerable crowd. The implicit implication of this order is that a necessary connection exists between the mission of the 144,000 from the transformed Israel and the universal, eschatological people of God present in 7.9. This parallel helps to define these two groups and their relationship to one another. In both John 4 and Revelation 7 it appears that universal salvation grows out of Israel and its strategic salvific role.

Verses 11-12 – The hymn-like confession of the innumerable crowd, drawn from every group on earth, generates a resounding heavenly response. 'All the angels standing around the throne and the elders and the four living creatures both fell before the throne upon their faces and worshipped God'. When hearing that all the angels were involved, John's hearers are likely to think of the thousands of thousands and ten thousands of ten thousands of angels mentioned in 5.11-12. The word 'all' implies that no fewer than this number is in view. Like their earlier appearance, these angels are standing around the throne, the elders, and the four living creatures, the latter two standing in inverse order from their earlier appearance. The act of prostration before the throne reminds the hearers of John's response to the resurrected Jesus (1.17) and the constant reaction of the twenty-four elders, who are always falling down before the One who sits on the throne (4.10; 5.8, 14). The fact that the angels are said to fall upon their faces underscores the extent of their obeisance. In addition to their prostration, the angels 'worshipped God', again paralleling the activity of the twenty-four elders. Among other things this worship consists of the praise that the angels render to God saying, 'Amen, the blessing and the glory and the wisdom and the thanksgiving and the honor and the power and the strength to our God forever and forever; Amen'. Several

---

[57] Pattemore, *The People of God in the Apocalypse*, p. 146.

things stand out about this seven-fold doxology. First, the doxology begins and ends with 'Amen'. In one sense the first 'amen' is the angelic response to the hymn-like confession of the innumerable crowd found in 7.10. At the same time, the fact that the 'amen' surrounds this angelic doxology underscores its liturgical character, calling to mind the earlier appearances of the term and its Christological associations (1.6, 7; 3.14; 5.14). Second, the doxology takes a seven-fold form, indicating the completeness of this act of worship. In fact, except for the substitution of 'the thanksgiving' for 'riches', the individual elements of this doxology are the same as the one offered by the angels to the Lamb (5.12).[58] Appropriately enough, 'thanksgiving' has earlier been rendered to the One who sits on the throne by the four living creatures (4.9). The repetition of these elements again underscores the way in which both God and the Lamb share in the worship rendered by various groups in the Apocalypse, continuing to reveal something of the unique nature of their identity. Third, each of the elements in the doxology are articular in form, paralleling the four-fold doxology rendered to the One who sits upon the throne and the Lamb by every creature in all of creation (5.13). This construction would further heighten the meaning of each element in the doxology for John and his hearers.[59] The angelic doxology ends as it begins with an 'amen'.

Verses 13-14 – The appearance of the innumerable multitude and their activities not only generate the response of the all the angels, but also a response on the part of one of the elders. Normally, mention of the twenty-four elders is accompanied by reference to the fact that they fall down and worship, so John and his hearers might be a bit surprised to find that on this occasion one of the elders speaks. Both the description and content of his speech indicate that they are offered in response to the appearance and activity of the innumerable crowd. For John says 'one of the elders answered saying to me, "These who are clothed in white robes, who are they and from whence did they come?"' Although the earlier reference to the white robes generates a variety of associations with regard to the identity of the innumerable crowd, the question of the elder suggests to the hearers that there is even more to be revealed about

---

[58] Prigent, *L'Apocalypse de Saint Jean*, p. 224.
[59] Mounce, *The Book of Revelation*, p. 172.

the identity of this crowd. For John and his hearers have come to know that they are sometimes assisted in their pneumatic interpretation by direct divine intervention (e.g. 1.20). While John and his hearers might at first be startled by the fact that the elder asks John about the crowd's identity, this gives way to the understanding that sometimes in prophetic encounters the prophet or seer is asked certain questions by God and/or his agent. Thus, the opportunity for this exchange underscores once again John's prophetic identity. The question is also helpful in establishing the scope and limit of John's prophetic ability and/or knowledge, implying that his prophetic ability and function is absolutely dependant upon that which is made known to him. John's reply to the elder's question is 'Sir, you know'. These simple words reveal the similarity of John's response to that of other prophetic figures (Ezek. 37.3),[60] an acknowledgement of the limits of his knowledge, and may be understood as an indication that John expects additional revelation to come from this elder. If so, John is not disappointed, for the identity of those dressed in white is made clear by the elder's words, 'These are the ones coming out of the great tribulation and they have washed their robes and made them white in the blood of the Lamb'. The first thing John and his hearers learn from the words of this elder is the origin of this innumerable crowd. They are described as 'coming out of the great tribulation'. Though the present tense participle ἐρχόμενοι ('coming') will be governed by two aorist verbs which follow, and thus translated as a past tense, its initial impact upon the hearers is likely to suggest that this crowd is coming out of the great tribulation before John's eyes. Mention of 'the great tribulation' as the place of the innumerable crowd's origin would connect with the hearers in several ways. First, it is clear from the Apocalypse that tribulation is regarded as a necessary part of the believer's life. Not only does Jesus speak of such tribulation in the FG (Jn 16.21, 33), but John himself also speaks of his own tribulation (Rev. 1.9). At the same time, the resurrected Jesus speaks of the tribulation awaiting the church at Smyrna (2.9-10) and warns of 'great tribulation' that awaits those who do not repent of their adultery with 'Jezebel' (3.22). Thus, it would appear that the hearers would see some continuity between tribulation already experienced by be-

---

[60] Murphy, *Fallen Is Babylon*, p. 226.

lievers and 'the great tribulation' out of which this innumerable crowd comes. Second, the construction of the phrase τῆς θλίψεως τῆς μεγάλης ('the great tribulation'), in which the words 'tribulation' and 'great' are both accompanied by the definite article, indicates that a particular ordeal is here in mind.[61] Not only this, but the phrase indicates that this ordeal is unlike other times of tribulation in terms of intensity and duration. Third, such language would likely remind John and his hearers of the tribulation unlike all other tribulations of which Daniel speaks (12.1-2).[62] If so, it is significant that this tribulation also speaks of the complete deliverance of the people of God. Fourth, it is just possible that Jesus' words with regard to the 'tribulation unlike any since the creation of the world' (Mk 13.19) would further inform the hearers' understanding of 'the great tribulation' mentioned in Rev. 7.14. However, there is little other evidence to suggest the hearers' knowledge of the Synoptic apocalyptic tradition. Whatever else might be in the hearers' minds at this point, the innumerable crowd's experience in 'the great tribulation' is defined in the rest of v. 14 in terms of the activity of the crowd, 'and they washed their robes and made them white in the blood of the Lamb'. Whatever they experienced in 'the great tribulation' this innumerable crowd did not experience it passively but were active in it. To this point, John and his hearers may have been under the impression that those who are clothed in white robes are simply given them to wear (3.4, 5; 4.4; 6.11). But here it becomes clear that this crowd actively participates in the receiving of them by washing them and making them white. How would these ideas fit together for the hearers? Perhaps they would think of the ways in which the resurrected Jesus continually speaks to the seven churches about their works and the implicit relationship between them and the believers' ability to overcome. Perhaps it would remind them of the way in which believers are called upon to offer an active, faithful witness to Jesus. The fact that their robes are made white in the blood of the Lamb makes clear the connection between their own faithful witness and the faithful witness of the Lamb, whose blood stands at the center of redemptive history. The hearers know full well that confession of sin is met with cleansing and forgiveness

---

[61] Murphy, *Fallen is Babylon*, p. 226.
[62] Beale, *The Book of Revelation*, p. 433.

from that sin, accomplished by the blood of Jesus (1 Jn 1.7, 9). They know that his blood looses from sin (Rev. 1.5) and purchases for God out of 'every tribe and tongue and people and nation' (5.9). The fact that this crowd, comprised of those from all nations and tribes and peoples and tongues, has washed its robes and made them white in the blood of the Lamb, among other things, indicates that they have confessed their sin and stand in solidarity with Jesus. Given the fact that the 'souls under the altar' were slaughtered and their blood shed 'on account of the Word of God and the witness which they have' (6.9-11), perhaps the hearers would suspect that this crowd's solidarity with Jesus' blood might entail their own slaughter and shed blood.

Verse 15 – The words of the elder about the innumerable crowd continue taking the form of eschatological promises that both reveal continuity with the promises to those who overcome in the seven prophetic messages and, like them, point to their final fulfillment that will be witnessed near the book's end. The connection between the crowd's activity in coming through 'the great tribulation' and these promises is made clear by the phrase διὰ τοῦτο ('on account of this'). The statement 'they are before the throne of God' picks up on the earlier similar statement in v. 9. Now John and his hearers understand why they are before God's throne, because they have come out of 'the great tribulation'. The word εἰσιν ('are') is a present tense verb reemphasizing their intimate relationship with God exemplified by their close proximity to him. At this point, the promises shift from present tense to future tense verbs. For the hearers such a shift would suggest a focus upon the final realization of these eschatological promises, though they are already experienced in part. Given their close proximity to the throne it is not surprising to find that 'they will serve him day and night in his temple'. This statement calls to mind the eschatological promise made to those who overcome in the church in Philadelphia (3.12) that they will be 'pillars in the temple of my God', never departing from the divine presence. Here in 7.15 the promise of being in the permanent presence of God again focuses upon the temple as the place of the divine presence. In addition, it moves from the somewhat passive image of 'pillar', which conveys stability in 3.12, to the more active image of 'serving'. The appearance here of the term λατρεύουσιν ('they will serve') would not be surprising to John or his hearers, for they are already well aware of their own priestly identity (1.6; 5.10). At the same time, this democratic word, rarely used for the ministry of priests in the LXX, would fit well with the idea that those who 'serve' God in this verse come from 'all nations and tribes and peoples and tongues'.[63] In serving God 'day and night' this innumerable crowd stands with the four living creatures who 'day and night' never cease to sing to the One who sits on the throne. Those who serve God in this way will find that 'the One who sits on the throne will tabernacle over them'. For Johannine hearers the appearance of the verb σκηνώσει ('tabernacles') would unleash a variety of significant theological ideas. For such language calls to mind the OT Tabernacle as the place of God's dwelling among his people.[64] This visible sign of God's presence gives way to the Incarnation, which in Johannine thought is forever remembered by the words, 'And the Word became flesh and tabernacled among us, and we beheld his glory, glory as the unique Son of the Father, full of grace and truth' (Jn 1.14).[65] The fact that the One who sits on the throne will tabernacle over this crowd indicates that he will offer protection by the shelter of his divine presence.

Verses 16-17 – In language reminiscent of the promises to those who return from exile in Babylon (Isa. 49.10), the elder informs John of the provisions promised this innumerable crowd, 'They will not hunger anymore nor will they thirst anymore nor will the sun beat upon them nor any scorching heat'. This promise of food, drink, and shelter are here more than simply the basic concerns of humankind but take on eschatological and salvific import. Not only do such words echo those of Isaiah, but also those of Jesus. Johannine hearers remember that as the Bread of Life Jesus says, 'the one who comes to me will never hunger, and the one who believes in me will never thirst' (Jn 6.35). In addition, they would be familiar with the frequency with which Jesus speaks of quenching the thirst of those who come to him (4.13-15; 6.35), for out of his belly flows rivers of living water (7.37-39). The eschatological nature of this promise will become even clearer near the close of the Apocalypse

---

[63] Pattemore, *The People of God in the Apocalypse*, p. 155.

[64] J.A. Draper ['The Heavenly Feast of Tabernacles: Revelation 7.1-17', *JSNT* 19 (1983), pp. 133-47] goes so far as to suggest that the feast of Tabernacles underlies and informs this entire section.

[65] Osborne, *Revelation*, p. 329.

(21.6). Joined to these promises is the promise of shelter, which might be expected from the fact that the One who sits on the throne tabernacles upon them. Specifically, protection from the destructive effects of the sun and scorching heat are singled out, elements about which the majority of the world's population are still concerned. These promises spoken by the elder about the innumerable crowd guarantee that all their 'physical' needs are to be met, even as they are already met in part for the hearers. But such promises are not simply the result of the fact that the One who sits on the throne tabernacles over them, but as the Johannine language of v. 16 suggests are also closely connected to the Lamb. In point of fact, this connection is made explicit by the words of v. 17, 'for the Lamb in the midst of the throne will shepherd them and guide them unto wells of living water'. The identity of the Lamb as 'in the midst of the throne' makes clear that his own activity is not discontinuous from that of the One who sits on the throne. For the Lamb is at the very center of God's throne and activity, having been given authority to sit upon his Father's throne (3.21) and being located in its midst (5.6). Reference to 'the Lamb ... who will shepherd them' generates a variety of diverse images that converge at this point for John and his hearers. Among them is the fact that this Slaughtered Lamb is the Lion of the Tribe of Judah, who has the key of David. He is the one who gives those who overcome the authority to rule over the nations with an iron rod (2.27), as he himself will rule (12.5; 19.15). But perhaps most significant is the fact that he is the Good Shepherd who loves his sheep so much that he lays down his life for them (Jn 10.1-21). It is this same Slaughtered Lamb who will shepherd the innumerable crowd. Chief amongst his activity will be to 'guide them unto wells of living water' (lit. living wells of water), further emphasizing the theme of life.[66] Such a description would be particularly potent for Johannine hearers for it calls to mind both the guiding activity of the Spirit of Truth (Jn 16.13) and the emphasis placed upon wells of living water found in the FG (4.14; 7.38). Both of these emphases would once again remind the hearers of the intimate relationship that exists between Jesus and the Spirit in the Apocalypse. This detail also goes some way toward explaining why this innumerable multitude will never be thirsty again, ow-

---

[66] Smalley, *The Revelation to John*, p. 201.

ing to the fact that the Lamb who shepherds them leads them to 'wells of living water'! Apparently, Jesus' promise to the Samaritan woman (4.14) continues to ring eternally in the ears of Johannine hearers. The final promise spoken by the elder about the innumerable crowd once again echoes the words of Isaiah (25.8), 'and God will wipe away each tear from their eyes'. Such a comforting act on God's part appears to be in response to tears of death. Not only does the text in Isaiah make this connection, but also in the FG Jesus weeps at the tomb of Lazarus (Jn 11.35). In response to whatever the innumerable crowd has endured in the great tribulation, including death, God will wipe away each tear. As with other promises, this one too reappears near the book's conclusion (Rev. 21.4) again pointing to eschatological fulfillment. Such comfort, offered in this context of death, is a fitting conclusion to the interlude that is chapter seven.

How would the extraordinary images contained in this chapter impact John and his hearers? Taken together these two images appear to be two distinct but related representations of God's people. Further, it seems that these images appear before and after 'the great tribulation'. Both images offer encouragement in their own ways for the messianic 'tribes of the sons of Israel' are sealed by God before the four angels unleash the four winds of the earth, while the innumerable crowd comes forth from the great tribulation clothed in white robes, standing before the throne. John and his hearers would also likely be struck by the fact that these two images are related to one another, for that which is heard gives way to that which is seen. While numerous questions remain, there is little doubt for the hearers that the 144,000 from the tribes of the sons of Israel are transformed before their very 'eyes' into a universal innumerable crowd that stand before the throne having come out of the great tribulation. Owing to the fact that many of the promises mentioned with regard to this crowd will reappear near the book's conclusion, John and his hearers may come to regard this particular image as a prolepsis of the end.[67] At any rate, it is likely that both these images give the hearers a great deal of encouragement that despite the horrific effects of the opening of the seven

---

[67] Murphy, *Fallen Is Babylon*, p. 228.

seals, they as God's people are not forgotten, in fact, they stand before his very presence!

The Opening of the Seventh Seal and the Golden Altar (8.1-5)

Verse 1 – John's hearers could be forgiven if they have momentarily forgotten that they are in the midst of the opening of the seven seals, owing to the incredible images they have just encountered. However, they are abruptly reminded of this fact with the words found in 8.1, 'And when he opened the seventh seal …' Suddenly, John and his hearers are jolted back into the reality of the seven seals and the Slaughtered Lamb who is worthy to open them. Their last memory of the opening of the sixth seal would lead them to expect that, with the opening of the seventh seal, the end of all things has been reached, for, the beatific image with which chapter seven closes strongly implies that the end is very near indeed. And yet, when the seventh seal is opened rather than encountering the end, John and his hearers encounter silence; 'there was silence in heaven as a half hour'. John and his hearers are likely to be impacted by such silence in several ways. First, this surprising silence would perhaps evoke reflection and contemplation about the fact that at the very moment the final activity of God is expected, silence comes instead. Such silence would be striking owing to the fact that the heavens have literally been teeming with the sounds of praise that have come from all creation! That such thunderous sounds of praise are here replaced by silence could not help but to have a stunning effect upon the hearers.[68] Second, such silence is likely to remind the hearers of the prophetic call for silence before the presence of God (Hab. 2.20), especially as he is roused to action (Zech. 2.13).[69] Owing to the hearers' expectation of the end at this point in the Apocalypse, perhaps this silence would call to mind the words of Zephaniah (1.7), 'Be silent before the Lord God, for the Day of the Lord is near'. Third, John and his hearers are well aware of the fact that at various places in the Apocalypse things heard are paired with things seen generating dialectical images that are theologically potent. Could it be that this silence will give way to some-

---

[68] Gause (*Revelation*, p. 127) notes, 'When God holds in suspension the chief function of all his creatures, the glorifying of his name, it can only mean one thing. God is about to do something awesome'.

[69] Murphy, *Fallen is Babylon*, p. 231.

thing seen in ways similar to earlier occurrences of this phenomenon in the Apocalypse? The significance of the silence's duration, 'as a half hour', is not altogether clear. In part this is true owing to the fact that ἡμιώριον ('half an hour') is the first such temporal indicator to appear in the book. While it is possible that this has reference to a specific period of time that is not obvious to modern readers,[70] its significance for John and his hearers may not be so very different from that for modern hearers. Perhaps the impact of this short, impressive break can best be gauged in real time. For although it is the shortest of the temporal indicators to appear in the book, if the reader of the Apocalypse (1.3) stopped reading for about half an hour at this point, the extent of the delay and the significance of the silence would become all the more real.

Verse 2 – The half-hour of silence recounted gives way to a description of something John saw, 'I saw the seven angels who were standing before God, and seven trumpets were given to them'. Perhaps the first thing these words would convey to the hearers is the possibility that these seven angels stand in juxtaposition to the silence, in ways not unlike the Lamb to the Lion, and the innumerable crowd to the 144,000 from the tribes of the sons of Israel. As with the previous images, the silence and the seven angels with seven trumpets seem to stand in opposition to one another, with silence being the absence of sound while the seven trumpets represent one of the loudest human made sounds. The silence might seem to imply a certain passivity, while the seven angels with the seven trumpets are clearly at the ready to act. On this view the silence morphs into the seven angels and indicates rather explicitly that when the seventh seal is opened by the Lamb, the half hour silence and the seven angels with the seven trumpets are the result. In other words, the content of the seventh seal is the silence which morphs into the seven angels with the seven trumpets. As such, the hearers' expectation of the imminence of the end is frustrated as its description is to be delayed by both the silence and the seven angels. In point of fact, knowledge of the opening of the seven seals would suggest that the activity of each of the seven angels will be recounted before the description of the end is offered. Though the

---

[70] For example, Bauckham (*The Climax of Prophecy*, p. 83) argues that this is the amount of time it would take to offer incense at the morning ritual in the temple in Jerusalem.

hearers are well acquainted with the significance of the number seven, they might be somewhat surprised with the emergence of these seven angels instead of the four angels who hold back the four winds, whose activity had appeared to be imminent in 7.1-3.[71] And yet, instead of four angels there are seven. Four things are revealed about these seven angels in 8.2. First, their number implies perfection, implying that what they do is complete and full. Second, the appearance of the definite article τοὺς ('the') in describing 'the seven angels' indicates that they are introduced here for the first time to the hearers but are at the same time known to them.[72] The reappearance of the seven angels later in the book (15.1; 16.1-21) would seem to confirm this hint. Third, the angels are in very close proximity to God as they stand before him, indicating not only their willingness to serve him but also, as a result of their intimate location, their direct access to him. Fourth, these seven angels are given seven trumpets. The fact that the passive voice verb ἐδόθησαν ('were given') is used to describe the gift of the seven trumpets to these seven angels reveals the origin of this gift. They are divine gifts, coming from God himself. As such, the hearers understand that whatever use is made of the trumpets by the angels is in accordance with God's own will and desires.[73] Perhaps the first thing the hearers would think of at the mention of the trumpets would be the fact that twice to this point in the book the word trumpet has been used with reference to the voice of Jesus (1.10; 4.1). Such a Christological and prophetic association would make reference to the trumpets in 8.2 all the more significant, indicating that these trumpets are indeed to be closely identified with God. More of a signal instrument than a musical one, as it is capable of only a few notes,[74] its various OT uses reveal the trumpet to be the instrument *par excellence* that signals the grand moments of Israelite history and life.[75] The mention of the seven trumpets in the hands of the seven angels at this point in the Apocalypse would indicate to John and his hearers that they are on the verge of witnessing additional signif-

---

[71] Ladd, *Revelation*, p. 124.
[72] Aune, *Revelation 6-16*, p. 509 and Smalley, *The Revelation to John*, p. 213.
[73] Resseguie, *The Revelation of John*, p. 142.
[74] H. Lichtenberger, 'σάλπιγξ', *EDNT*, III, pp. 225-26.
[75] Prigent, *L'Apocalypse de Saint Jean*, p. 230.

icant acts of God. Owing to the way in which these seven angels continue God's activities described in the opening of the first six seals, the hearers are prepared for the additional forthcoming judgments.

Verse 3 – However, before the activities of these seven angels are described, the attention of John and his hearers is directed to another angel. This angel, distinct from the seven just mentioned, 'came and stood at (or over) the altar having a golden censer, and there was given to him much incense, in order that he might place with the prayers of all the saints upon the golden altar before the throne'. These words could not help but remind the hearers of two scenes previously encountered in the Apocalypse. The first is the only other place where incense and prayers have been mentioned together in the book, around the throne in chapter five. There, the incense is identified as 'the prayers of the saints' (5.8). Such a recollection could very well lead to the realization that the offering of incense and the prayers of the saints frame the recounting of the opening of the seven seals, suggesting a very tight connection between the prayers offered and the activity of God in the seals.[76] The second scene that would, no doubt, spring to the hearers' minds is that recounted in 6.9-11 where 'the souls under the altar' cry out to God for justice and vindication. Owing to the fact that the response described in 6.11 makes clear their cries were heard by God, the hearers in 8.3 would be encouraged to expect a divine response on this occasion as well. Thus, the activity described in this verse has close associations with previous scenes that inform the hearing of this passage.[77] Based upon this verse and the information contained in v. 5, this censer appears to be a ladle shaped object, its composition of gold indicating that it is worthy of its purpose.[78] The fact that θυμιάματα πολλά ('much incense') was given to this angel prepares the hearers for the fact that it is to be offered with the prayers of *all* the saints.[79] In 6.10 it is the cries of those who had been slaughtered that are heard, here it is the prayers of *all* the

---

[76] Murphy, *Fallen Is Babylon*, p. 234.

[77] Beale, *The Book of Revelation*, pp. 454-55.

[78] On the previous use of gold in the Apocalypse cf. 1.12, 13, 20; 2.1; 4.4; and 5.8.

[79] Smalley (*The Revelation to John*, p. 215) notes that the vast amount of incense is for the vast amount of prayers.

saints. The broadening of the scope of the prayers offered has increased to include not only those who have been martyred but those who are alive as well.[80] Such a move would serve to inform and encourage the hearers that their prayers are not perfunctory, but actually make their way to the very presence of God and are even now before him. As in 5.8, the term ἁγίων ('holy') suggests their special relationship to Jesus and God, owing to the fact that both have earlier (3.7; 4.8) been called ἅγιος ('holy'). While in 5.8 the incense is identified as being the prayers of the saints, here in 8.3 the incense appears to be offered along with the prayers of the saints. The fact that they are offered together underscores the pleasing, fragrant nature of the prayers that can be seen to rise visibly before the Lord. Being placed upon the golden altar before the throne, not only reveals that these prayers will be heard by God, owing to their close proximity to him, but also suggests that there is something sacrificial about them.[81] This imagery further suggests that the incense and prayers kindle and sustain the fire of the altar.[82] The importance of the altar's location receives additional emphasis in that it is mentioned at the conclusion of this verse as well as the next (v. 4).

Verse 4 – With the words of the next verse the hearers learn that the angel accomplishes his task: 'And the smoke of the incense with the prayers of the saints arose out of the hand of the angel before God'. The agency of the angel underscores the fact that these prayers do indeed reach the ear of God, the smoke being a visible sign of the prayers' ascent. At this point, the content of the prayers is not revealed, but the hearers would likely understand them to stand in some continuity with those offered in 5.8 and perhaps with the cries of 'the souls under the altar'. The fact that the smoke arises 'before God' not only stands in parallel with 'before the altar' of the previous verse, but also encourages the hearers of the certainty that their prayers are indeed received by God himself.

Verse 5 – As John's narration continues the hearers learn of the unique relationship that exists between the prayers of the saints and the activity of God. For of the same angel who places the incense

---

[80] Michaels, *Revelation*, p. 118.

[81] Mounce, *The Book of Revelation*, p. 182.

[82] Schüssler Fiorenza, *Revelation*, p. 71.

with the prayers upon the altar John next says 'and the angel took the censer and filled it with (out of) the fire of the altar and cast it upon the earth'. The significance of such extraordinary imagery would hardly be lost on the hearers. It is the same angel who performs the remarkable double action of placing the incense and prayers of the saints upon the golden altar and casting fire from the altar upon the earth.[83] It is the same censer used to place the incense and prayers upon the altar that is used to scoop out of the fire and cast it upon the earth.[84] It is the same altar upon which the incense and prayers are placed out of which the fire comes which is cast upon the earth. The point could not be clearer. There is an intimate relationship between the prayers of the saints and the latter activity of the angel who casts down fire upon the earth. In point of fact, it appears that the fire that is cast down from the altar is fueled by the prayers of the saints.[85] The idea that the censer is 'filled' or 'full' of fire from the altar coincides with the fact that 'much' incense is used and the prayers of 'all' the saints are in view. The interesting construction ἐκ τοῦ πυρὸς τοῦ θυσιαστηρίου ('out of the fire of the altar') makes explicit the connection between the prayers and the fire.[86] As at many other points in the Apocalypse such imagery would call to the minds of the hearers a number of OT stories. It almost goes without saying that fire falling from heaven would be an especially familiar OT image of judgment (Gen. 19.24; 2 Kgs 1.10, 12, 14; Job 1.16; Ps. 11.6). Perhaps the story of Elijah's encounter with the prophets of Ba'al, who prays for God to send a consuming fire in order to turn the hearts of the people back to him (1 Kgs 18.36-40), is of special relevance.[87] It is quite likely that John and his hearers would also be mindful of the parallel between this description in Rev. 8.5 and that of the man dressed in linen found in Ezek. 10.2-8. This one is instructed to fill his hands with burning coals from between the cherubim and scatter them over the city in judgment of the guilt of the house of Israel and Judah. Such a visual parallel would be all the more striking

---

[83] Allo, *Saint Jean L'Apocalypse*, p. 104.

[84] Murphy, *Fallen Is Babylon*, pp. 234-35.

[85] Resseguie, *The Revelation of John*, p. 143.

[86] On the nature of this relationship Michaels (*Revelation*, p. 118) states, 'Prayer is the engine driving the plan of God toward completion'.

[87] Wall, *Revelation*, p. 123.

when it is recalled that the man dressed in linen is commissioned to scatter the coals of fire only after he has placed a mark upon the foreheads of those who sigh and groan over all the abominations that have been committed (9.4).[88] The hearers would likely understand the mention of the angel casting fire from the altar 'upon the earth' as an indication that the prohibition against harming the earth given to the four angels in Rev. 7.3 is no longer in effect. In point of fact, it may even suggest that the four winds held back by the four angels in 7.1 are somehow to be identified with the action of the angel here in 8.5. In any event, the expectant silence with which this section begins (8.1), gives way to the unleashing of additional judgments of God portended in the pregnant imagery of fire being cast down from heaven. The fact that the initiation of this judgment comes from God is further emphasized by the reappearance of the theophanic elements the hearers first encountered in the heavenly throne room scene in 4.5. Their reappearance here would convey several things to the hearers. First, the reappearance of the theophanic elements would convey a real sense of continuity between the God who is active in creation and human history in 4.4 and the God who is active in judgment in 8.5. Second, the inverted order of the original list, which only occurs here out of the four lists of theophanic elements in the book moves from thunder to sounds (voices) to lightning, perhaps suggesting that on this occasion the idea of lightning is being underscored. On this view, it may not be without significance that lightning comes forth from the coals of fire located in the midst of the four living creatures described in Ezek. 1.13, providing yet another point of continuity between this passage and that prophetic writing.[89] Third, the introduction of an additional theophanic element, earthquake, in this list indicates an intensification of God's presence and introduces the idea of judgment. Such intensification will increase with each appearance of the theophanic elements. The addition of σεισμός ('earthquake') would be especially significant as it was perhaps the most feared natural disaster with which the hearers would be familiar and the occurrence of which was not infrequent in Asia Minor. The theophanic elements occur at a strategic location at this point in the Apoca-

---

[88] Bauckham, *The Climax of Prophecy*, p. 82.
[89] Bauckham, *The Climax of Prophecy*, p. 82.

lypse, at the conclusion of the opening of the seven seals and the beginning of the sounding of the seven trumpets. Such a location reveals something of its structural significance, a characteristic that will continue with later appearances of the theophanic elements.

Seven Angels with Seven Trumpets (8.6-11.19)

Verse 6 – The relationship of the activity of this other angel to that of the seven angels with the seven trumpets is revealed in part by the fact that reference to the seven angels reappears at the conclusion of the passage devoted to the activity of this other angel (vv. 2-5). 'And the seven angels who have the seven trumpets prepared them in order that they might trumpet'. Such a reference reveals that the activity of this other angel is framed by reference to the seven angels with seven trumpets, suggesting a tight interplay between their activities. Specifically, it suggests that the activity of the seven angels stands in continuity with and is grounded in the activity of this other angel. The casting of fire from the altar upon the earth will be seen as coterminous with the sounding of the seven trumpets, especially given the fact that the first four trumpets will themselves contain fire imagery. Owing to this sense of continuity, the hearers would be ever mindful of the fact that this activity is directly related to the prayers of the saints. Seen in this light, reference to the seven angels preparing the trumpets is more than a dramatic pause, drawing out the action still further, for it envelops and links the previous section with what follows.[1] At the same time, this mention does alert the hearers to the fact that the opening of the seventh seal is now to be discussed more fully. Before leaving this verse, it should perhaps be observed that the noun σάλπιγγας ('trumpets') and the verb σαλπίσωσιν ('sound' or 'play') are very similar. In fact, rather than translating the verb as 'to sound' or 'to play', it might more appropriately be translated as 'to trumpet', in order to bring out the word play going on in the Greek text. Thus, on this occasion, the sentence could be translated, 'And the seven angels who have the seven trumpets prepared them in order that they might trumpet'.

---

[1] Murphy, *Fallen Is Babylon*, p. 235.

The Sounding of the First Six Trumpets (8.7-9.21)

Verse 7 – At long last, the activity of the seven angels commences with the words, 'And the first one trumpeted'. The blasting of this signal instrument calls attention to that which follows. When the first trumpet sounds 'there was hail and fire mixed with blood and it was cast upon the earth'. The imagery of hail and fire mixed with blood would be pregnant with meaning for the hearers. For not only do each of these elements appear in the plagues God sent upon Egypt in the deliverance of his people during the Exodus (Exod. 9.22-26; 7.20-21), but they are also significant in the Apocalypse as well. Such connections with the Exodus tradition perhaps suggests to the hearers that just as God sent plagues upon the enemies of his people, while preserving them from their tormenting effects, so he is about to act in the present. If these elements raise the Exodus motif for the hearers, then it is likely that they understand the purpose of such divine intervention as to bring their enemies to repentance, a purpose made clear later (Rev. 9.20-21). This first reference to 'hail' in Revelation points to its later appearances and its emerging significance, as it is always closely associated with the activity of God himself (11.19; 16.21). As powerful as these associations would likely be, they do not exhaust their potency for the hearers, for the significance of the other elements would also be informed by their previous placement within the narrative of the Apocalypse. When reference is made to fire, they could hardly forget the relationship between the fire from the altar that was cast upon the earth by the other angel. In fact, just as that fire was cast upon the earth (8.5), so too this fire (with the other elements) is also explicitly said to be 'cast upon the earth', the passive voice further underscoring that this activity comes from God himself. The fact that the 'hail and fire was mixed with blood' would also be informed by the previous meaning of 'blood' within the Apocalypse. Specifically, the tight connection between the cry of the souls under the altar for God to 'avenge (or vindicate) their blood' (6.10) and the moon turning to blood, with the opening of the next seal (6.12), would remind the hearers of the relationship between this judgment of God and the witness of the saints. The consequence of the casting of these elements upon the earth is that 'a third of the earth was burnt up, and a third of the trees were burnt up and all the green grass was burnt up'. Such a consequence would register immediately with the hearers, for this judgment is quite devastating and at the same time is not final, nor complete. The fact that it is more intensive than the judgments that accompany the opening of the seals, in which one-fourth of the earth's population is killed (6.8), would not be lost on the hearers.[2] Such a detail would indicate that the judgments that seemed so final with the seals were not final but a first step in God's judgment. As such, the increase in the severity of the judgments would suggest these judgment cycles are not merely repetitious but that they are moving along in a somewhat linear fashion. At the same time, the fact that a third of the earth is affected, rather than the whole of the earth, would clearly convey the idea that while judgment is certain, there may yet be room for repentance. If Zech. 13.8-9 is at all in the hearers' minds then the fact, that only one-third survived there, while two-thirds survive here, might be taken as a hopeful inversion.[3] Such an inversion would reveal that while the judgments that await the inhabitants of the earth are indeed terrifying, they could, almost inconceivably, be worse. The devouring of pastures and trees by the flame would also perhaps call to mind Joel's prophecy (1.19-20), indicating the arrival of the Day of the Lord.

Verses 8-9 – 'And the second angel trumpeted; and something like a great mountain burning with fire was cast into the sea'. With the sounding of the second trumpet the fire that was cast upon the earth from the altar continues to burn. This time the fire imagery takes the form of a burning mountain.[4] Such an overwhelming image continues the continuity with the fire from the altar, as the passive voice verb ἐβλήθη ('was cast') underscores the fact that this action too has a divine origin. As with the consequences of the events that accompany the sounding of the first trumpet, the consequences of the fiery mountain being cast to the sea is equally as devastating. For when the mountain of fire falls upon the sea 'a third of the sea became blood and a third of the creatures having life in the sea died and a third of the ships were destroyed'. For a second time the consequence of this judgment is reminiscent of the plagues that befell Egypt. Here, the image of the first plague, where

---

[2] Metzger, *Breaking the Code*, p. 64.

[3] Resseguie, *The Revelation of John*, p. 145.

[4] Michaels (*Revelation*, p. 122) suggests that it is as if the whole of Mt. Sinai were on fire.

the water of the Nile turns to blood causing the death of all the fish (Exod. 7.20-21), immediately comes to mind. As with the first judgment, the appearance of blood would again point to the connection between these judgments and the witness of the saints. Again, as with the first judgment, the extent of the destruction, though severe, is limited to a third. Whilst the first judgment points to the death of a third of the inhabitants of the earth, the second points to the death of a third of the creatures that have life in the sea. Not only is the loss of life of the living creatures in the sea described, but there is considerable economic loss as well, for a third of the ships that sail the sea are destroyed. Something of the nature of the destruction that ensues is conveyed by the fact that the compound verb διεφθάρησαν ('were destroyed') occurs here.[5] In the Apocalypse, God is uniquely the one who brings such destruction (11.18). The role of such ships in commerce, known on a small scale from the FG (Jn 6.17, 19, 21-23; 21.3, 6), is made clear later in the Apocalypse (18.19).

Verses 10-11 – As with the opening of the seals, so with the angels trumpeting their trumpets, the remaining ones follow in rapid-fire succession, 'And the third angel trumpeted; and a great star burning like a torch fell out of heaven'. As with the first two trumpets, that which accompanies the blasting of the third trumpet demonstrates that it too is in continuity with the casting upon the earth the fire from the altar. On this occasion, the fire is seen in the great star that is burning like a torch. The falling of a great star is a remarkable enough occurrence, owing to the rarity of such an event and the enormity of the ensuing destruction caused by its impact. The impression that such a cosmic sign would have on the hearers is difficult to overestimate. On its own it would no doubt be taken as a sign from God, but the words 'out of heaven' make this conclusion all the clearer. This star, as the other activities described with the blasting of the trumpets, is the work of God. The fact that the previous occurrence of the word λαμπὰς ('torch') comes in reference to the seven torches before the throne in 4.5 further underscores the connection of this star to God. This star 'fell upon a third of the rivers and upon the fountains of water'. In contrast to the object of the second trumpet, the object of this star appears to

---

[5] A. Sand, 'διαφθείρω', *EDNT*, I, pp. 315-16.

be sources of drinking water. In the Apocalypse rivers will be the object of God's judgment (12.15, 16; 16.4, 12), until the emergence of the river of the water of life in the New Jerusalem (22.1, 2). Although the fountains of water are on occasion the object of God's judgment (8.10; 16.4), they are said to be the creation of God (14.7) and fountains of living water are promised to those faithful to God (7.17; 21.6; cf. also Jn 4.6, 14). Before proceeding to describe the consequences of this star's falling upon the rivers and fountains of water the star is identified by name, 'And the name of the star is called Apsinth'. John and his hearers are familiar with the fact that from time to time their pneumatic interpretation is aided by direct divine instruction. The revelation of the name of this star may be a case in point, as there is no evidence of a star being called by this name in antiquity.[6] The word Ἀψινθος ('Apsinth', 'Wormwood', or 'Bitter') appears to come from the plant by this name, which is quite bitter to the taste and from which an oil can be abstracted that can be used medicinally to kill intestinal worms. This etymology explains why the term is often translated 'Wormwood'.[7] Its potency is revealed by the fact that it can still be tasted when one ounce has been diluted in 524 gallons of water![8] The potency of a star named 'Apsinth' would not be difficult to imagine. 'And a third of the waters became wormwood (or bitter) and many men died from the water because they had been made bitter'. Such a result indicates that the bitterness of this star far exceeds the bitterness of the Aspinth plant, for the bitterness of this star is lethal, while that of the plant was not considered so.[9] Such a fate is grave enough, but John and his hearers may understand that such word play does not exhaust the meaning of this verse on two counts. First, the divine insight with regard to the star's name may also encourage them to discern the way in which these events intersect with Jeremiah's prophecy regarding his idolatrous people and their adulterous shepherds, the prophets. So upset is God that he vows to feed his people (Jer. 9.15) and their prophets (Jer. 23.15) with wormwood and give poisonous water for them to drink. Second, John and his

---

[6] Aune, *Revelation 6-16*, p. 521.
[7] Smalley, *The Revelation to John*, p. 222.
[8] Aune, *Revelation 6-16*, p. 522.
[9] Contra Beale, *The Book of Revelation*, p. 479.

hearers would also likely pick up on the irony and inversion pervasive in this verse. On the one hand, the poisoning of the rivers and fountains of water is in some ways an inversion of the events at Marah, where God makes the bitter water sweet (Exod. 15.25). Such an inversion would not be lost on the hearers. On the other hand, Johannine hearers would likely pick up on the fact that 'star', 'rivers', and 'fountains' are all terms that have a special relationship to Jesus. Previously, the resurrected Jesus promised to give to the one who overcomes 'the Morning Star' (Rev. 2.28), while in the FG he spoke of a 'fountain' or 'well' of water springing up unto eternal life (Jn 4.14) and a river of living water flowing from his belly (Jn 7.38). The contrast between the use of these objects in association with Jesus and here in this passage is striking. Thus, as with a number of places in the Apocalypse, the interpretive possibilities for the hearers are enormous.

Verse 12 – When the fourth angel trumpeted 'a third of the sun and a third of the moon and a third of the stars were struck'. As with the previous three trumpets, the judgment that accompanies this sounding affects one third of the objects, a refrain that would leave a significant auditory impression upon the hearers.[10] The sun, which had earlier become as sackcloth, the moon, which had earlier become as blood, and the stars, which earlier fell from heaven (6.12-13), are now struck. The term ἐπλήγη ('were struck') not only carries with it the idea of being struck with force,[11] but also introduces the hearers to a term whose cognate πληγή ('plague') will figure prominently in the remainder of the book. The force of this blow, which comes from God owing to the passive voice of the verb, is so strong, 'that a third of them were made dark and the day was not allowed to shine for a third of it and the night as well'. Once again the imagery of the Exodus looms large in the events that accompany the blasting of the trumpets, as the events of 8.12 are reminiscent of the plague of darkness that fell upon Egypt in Exod. 10.21-23. Such similarity reminds the hearers that the same God active in the Exodus is once again active in the face of stubborn unbelief. At the same time, it is likely that the relationship between darkness and the Day of the Lord would not be lost on John

---

[10] Sweet, *Revelation*, p. 164.
[11] Smalley, *The Revelation to John*, p. 223.

and his hearers (Amos 5.18). With the blasting of this fourth trumpet, all four spheres of God's creation (earth, sea, fresh water, and heavens) have been affected.[12]

Verse 13 – When the fourth seal was unsealed, the hearers were met by a break in continuity as the opening of the fifth seal departed from the horse and rider motif, shifting attention to the souls under the altar. A similar break greets the hearers after the fourth angel sounds his trumpet. On this occasion, the break is marked by language now long familiar to the hearers as John says, 'And I saw, and I heard …' However, unlike previous occurrences there is an inversion of the normal order of hearing and then seeing. The order of these words in v. 13 would convey to the hearers that John's visionary experience continues and at the same time would underscore the importance of that which John hears. John heard, 'an eagle flying in the middle of the sky (or heavens) saying with a great voice'. Several things about these words would be of interest to the hearers. First, the words ἑνὸς ἀετοῦ ('an eagle') very literally means 'one eagle'. While ἑνὸς ('an') could function as an indefinite article in this verse,[13] it might very well remind the hearers of any number of things for which 'one' is used to designate between similar beings, such as 'one of the living creatures', or 'one of the elders'. While it is not likely that the hearers would think of a group of eagles, this designation might indeed remind them of 'one of the living creatures' that was 'flying like an eagle' encountered earlier (Rev. 4.7). While it would be unwise to push this identification too far, it should not be forgotten that this living creature is, after all, described as 'flying like an eagle' and has been involved in some of the events that accompany the opening of one of the seals in Revelation 6. It would seem that his appearance at this point would surprise neither John nor his hearers. Second, the location of this eagle, ἐν μεσουρανήματι ('in the middle of the sky' or 'heaven'), is at the highest point reached by the sun in the sky, its zenith,[14] indicating the prominence of his position. Owing to this location, the flying activity of the eagle could hardly be missed, nor his words unheard, for they are spoken with a great voice, a description which

---

[12] Michaels, *Revelation*, p. 121.
[13] Smalley, *The Revelation to John*, pp. 224-25.
[14] W. Radl, 'μεσουρανήμα', *EDNT*, II, p. 412.

has greeted the hearers on numerous occasions (1.10; 5.2, 12; 6.10; 7.2, 10). His proclamation, which figures prominently in the narrative that follows, is introduced by a triple woe followed by an urgent warning, 'Woe, woe, woe to the inhabitants upon the earth at the rest of the sounds of the trumpets of the three angels that are about to trumpet'. The woe, well known from the OT prophetic literature as a divine warning and/or threat (Hos. 7.13; Isa. 1.4; 10.5; Jer. 23.1; Ezek. 24.6; and the six-fold woe in Isa. 5.8-22),[15] appears here in a three-fold form, indicating something of the magnitude of the warning therein contained. Not only this, but as the hearers will learn the triple woe is tied to the three remaining trumpets and angels. The fact that these woes are directed to 'the inhabitants of the earth', would remind the hearers of the cry of the souls under the altar that their blood be avenged upon 'the inhabitants of the earth' (6.10). Given the fact that these woes are clearly directed to those who stand in opposition to God and his people, perhaps John and his hearers would recall that the 144,000 have been sealed for protection by God's angels. Such knowledge would provide some reassurance to the believers that despite the woes awaiting 'the inhabitants of the earth' those of 'the tribes of the sons of Israel' will be protected. The three woes are explicitly tied to the remaining trumpets and the three angels about to trumpet them. Such an explicit warning suggests that the blasting of these three trumpets will be accompanied by events even worse than the first four, if such is possible to imagine! The relationship between these woes and trumpets will be made explicit as the Apocalypse unfolds (9.12; 11.14), while three two-fold woes will greet the destruction of Babylon (18.10, 16, 19). Something of the imminence of these blasts is conveyed by the words τῶν μελλόντων ('which are about'), a term that has appeared frequently throughout the Apocalypse to designate those things on the verge of taking place (Rev. 1.19; 2.20; 3.2, 10, 16; 6.11). The appearance of this language to describe the last three trumpets would convey to the hearers an even greater sense of urgency with regard to this warning.

Chapter 9, Verse 1 – At last then, the fifth angel trumpets. When he does John says, 'And I saw a star fallen out of heaven unto the earth, and a key of the shaft of the Abyss was given to him'.

---

[15] H. Balz, 'οὐαί', *EDNT*, II, p. 540.

Apparently, John does not actually see the star falling to earth, but that it had fallen. Mention of a star falling to earth would be reminiscent of the activity that accompanies the blasting of the third trumpet where a great star, burning as a torch, fell upon a third of the rivers and fountains of water (8.10-11). Here, as there, the fact that the star is described as having fallen does not suggest anything negative about the star with regard to its 'fallenness'. Rather, the star that accompanies the blasting of the fifth trumpet, like that of the third has its origin in heaven. Owing to the warning given with regard to the inhabitants upon the earth in 8.13, the hearers might well imagine that the falling of this star unto the earth has repercussions for the earth's inhabitants. Unlike the star described in 8.10, this star bears personal characteristics for there was given to him 'the key of the shaft of the Abyss'. The divine passive ἐδόθη ('was given') once again indicates the activity of God, making clear this star's divine commission.[16] The articular phrase 'the shaft of the Abyss' suggests that John and his hearers are likely familiar with this place. The shaft, mentioned four times in the first two verses of chapter nine, is the place of access to the Abyss. In the Apocalypse the Abyss will be seen as a place of imprisonment from which the beast emerges (11.7) and into which Satan is cast for 1,000 years (20.1, 3). Earlier in the book the resurrected Jesus claims to have the key of Death and Hades (1.18), as well as the key of David (3.7), indicating his mastery over the former and authority to act on behalf of the latter. Owing to the widespread perception that the Abyss is the realm of the dead (Hades) and the place of punishment (Gehenna),[17] the hearers would perhaps see a connection between the authority of this star and that of the resurrected Jesus. While the divine passive certainly implies that the key is given to the star by God,[18] the activity of the resurrected Jesus in this gift would not be far from the hearers' minds. At any rate, this star has the authority to open (and shut) the shaft of the Abyss.

Verses 2-3 – When he opened it, 'smoke arose out of the shaft as smoke from a great furnace, and the sun and the air were darkened by the smoke of the shaft'. The image conveyed by smoke

---

[16] Osborne, *Revelation*, p. 362.

[17] O. Böcher, 'ἄβυσσος', *EDNT*, I, p. 4.

[18] Resseguie, *The Revelation of John*, p. 146.

pouring forth from a great furnace heightens the ominous sense of expectancy on the part of the hearers, for it results in the darkening of so great an object as the sun, as well as the air, which stands between the earth and the heavens. It is probably worth noting that the hearers might well associate the darkness here mentioned with the ninth plague of darkness inflicted upon the Egyptians during the period of the Exodus. 'And out of the smoke came locusts upon the earth, and authority was given to them as the scorpions of the earth have authority'. As smoke comes out of the shaft of the Abyss, so locusts come out of the smoke. Given the psychedelic fashion with which one image can morph into another in the Apocalypse, it is not clear whether the hearers would conceive of the locusts coming out of the smoke or would take the smoke as resolving itself into locusts. In any event, the emergence of locusts upon the earth would be a terrifying sight indeed for their destructive power was well known. Not only could locusts 'travel in columns several feet deep, and up to four miles in length, stripping the earth of all its vegetation',[19] but they were also widely regarded in the OT as a sign of God's judgment (Deut. 28.42; 1 Kgs 8.37; Ps. 78.46). Of special significance to the hearers would be the fact that an infestation of locusts was the eighth plague God sent upon Egypt during the period of the Exodus (Exod. 10.4-20). Like the star that was divinely commissioned for its task, so the locusts receive divine authority, revealed in the reoccurrence of the divine passive ἐδόθη ('was given'). Such a statement is reminiscent of Rev. 6.8 where Death and Hades are given authority over a fourth of the earth to kill those who reside therein. In 9.3, the image of divinely ordained locusts coming out of the shaft of the Abyss to carry out their mission is frightening enough. But what the hearers next learn about the locusts' authority serves to heighten their anxiety level considerably. For the locusts' authority is like the authority that the scorpions of the earth have. Scorpions were well known for the fact that they could dominate their opponents in the insect and animal world by using their poisonous stingers. While non-lethal in humans, the sting of a scorpion was an extraordinarily painful torment. In this light, it would appear that the authority of the scorpions, which the locusts are given, is their ability to terrorize humankind owing to

---

[19] Smalley, *The Revelation to John*, p. 228.

fear of being stung. Thus, the tyranny of these locusts is greater than the tyranny of this insect in general.

Verse 4 – In words reminiscent of those spoken to the four angels holding back the four winds at the four corners of the earth (7.1-3), these locusts are given specific instructions. 'It was said to them in order that they not harm the grass of the earth nor any green thing nor any tree, except those men who did not have the seal of God upon their foreheads'. The hearers discover several things in the words of this command. First, the divine passive ἐρρέθη ('it was said') makes clear that this command comes from God. Second, the prohibition with which this verse begins reveals a most unusual characteristic about these locusts, for the devastation which locusts bring is very much tied to green vegetation. In point of fact, locusts were feared precisely because they could strip bare all manner of green vegetation that happens to lie in their path. Locusts prohibited from devouring green vegetation are very peculiar locusts indeed. Third, not only would the prohibition against harming any green vegetation remind the hearers of the similar prohibition in chapter seven, but the identity of those whom the locusts may harm would also point them back to this passage. For the prohibition against harming anything except for humans who do not have the seal of God upon their foreheads would explain to the hearers the purpose of the sealing of the 144,000 by the other angel and the four angels located at the four corners of the earth (7.3-8). These individuals bear the seal of the living God in order that they might be protected from the judgments that accompany the opening of the seventh seal, which are the judgments that accompany the blasting of the seven trumpets by the seven angels. The implication of these words is very clear. Just as God had protected Israel from the plagues directed against Egypt, so God will protect those who have the seal of God upon their foreheads, the transformed Israel, from this judgment.

Verses 5-6 – A third divine passive in as many verses, ἐδόθη ('was given'), reveals the nature of the harm that these locusts are authorized to bring to those humans who do not have the seal of God upon their foreheads. Authority was given to them, 'that they might not kill them, but that they might be tormented five months, and their torment will be as torment of a scorpion when it has stung a man'. Like Death and Hades the locusts are given authority.

Unlike them, the locusts are not given authority to kill. Rather, the locusts' authority is to torment those who do not have the seal of God upon their foreheads. The nature and extent of this torment is conveyed to the hearers in several ways. First, the verb βασανισθήσονται ('might be tormented') together with its cognate βασανισμὸς ('torment') appear a total of three times in this verse alone. This concentration of language would hardly be lost on the hearers. Second, these Greek words for torment convey the idea of intense bodily pain, so intense, in fact, that this language is often used to describe eschatological torment.[20] Third, the torment which these locusts are to inflict is limited in nature, for the humans in question are to be tormented for a period of 'five months'.[21] It is possible that the significance of 'five months' for the hearers would be connected to the fact that 'five' can serve as a round number meaning 'a few', as it does on occasion in both the OT (Lev. 26.8) and the NT (1 Cor. 14.19).[22] However, given the fact that five months is the locust's normal life cycle, it is perhaps more likely that the hearers would see the significance of this time period in relation to this specific detail. If so, it would reveal yet another unexpected characteristic of these locusts. These locusts would afflict those without God's seal for the entire period of their existence. The implication is that unlike the insect which does not normally afflict a particular place for more than a few days, before moving on, the torment of these locusts is prolonged while at the same time being just as concentrated. Fourth, the nature of the torment is likened to the torment brought to human beings when they have been stung by a scorpion. The intense pain is an agonizing ordeal for the sufferer. Not only does this detail reveal something of the intensity of the torment, but it also explains why the locusts' authority had earlier been likened to that of the scorpions of the earth. The locusts are authorized to terrorize humankind owing to the fear of being stung. In fact, the agony caused by these stings is so great that

> in those days men will seek death and they will not find it, and they will desire to die and death flees from them.

---

[20] W. Stenger, 'βασανίζω', *EDNT*, I, pp. 200-201.

[21] Resseguie, *The Revelation of John*, p. 147.

[22] Aune, *Revelation 6-16*, p. 530.

This poetic couplet[23] stands in parallel to a certain degree with the content of 6.16. There, the seven classes of humankind cry out to the mountains and the rocks to fall upon them in order that they might be hidden from the face of the One who sits upon the throne and the wrath of the Lamb. Such a parallel reinforces the fact that those described in 9.6 stand in solidarity with those who fear close contact with God and the Lamb, rather than those who stand before them (7.9). Among other things, the hearers are likely to be struck by the irony contained in this couplet. For in contrast to the way in which Death pursues and kills one-third of humanity when the fourth seal is unsealed (6.8), here Death cannot be found. In point of fact, Death flees (keeps on fleeing)[24] from those who desire it! Owing to the control which the resurrected Jesus has over Death in the Apocalypse (1.18; 2.11; 6.8), it would seem that Death cannot be found by those who seek it during the torment of the locusts because the one who controls Death will not allow Death to be found. Thus, the torment of the locusts is made all the more painful as not even Death can save those afflicted from it. At the same time, one of the implications of the fact that no lives are lost during this judgment might be that humanity is being given a specific period of time in which to repent, just as had the false prophetess 'Jezebel' (2.21).

Verses 7-11 – The hearers could be forgiven if they assume the description of the activities that accompany the blasting of the fifth trumpet was now complete, for the amount of space devoted to the description of this trumpet is about the same as that devoted to the first four combined! Yet surprising as it may be, there is much more that awaits the hearers with regard to the description of that which accompanies the blasting of the fifth trumpet. For, after the initial and rather extensive description of the locusts and their mission, the hearers encounter another description that focuses upon the locusts' dreadful and terrifying appearance. The shift of emphasis to the appearance of these creatures is signaled by the word play with which this verse begins, τὰ ὁμοιώματα ('the appearances' or 'likenesses') of these locusts ὅμοια ('was like' or 'as'). The hearers learn nine things about the appearance and characteristics of these lo-

---

[23] Wall, *Revelation*, p. 129.
[24] So Osborne, *Revelation*, p. 369.

custs. First, they are said to look like 'horses prepared for battle'. Such a description would not only convey something of the size and power of these creatures but would also remind the hearers of a similar description of locusts found in the book of Joel, where such creatures have a special association with the Day of the Lord (Joel 1.4-7; 2.1-11). Second, upon their heads these locusts have crowns as of gold. Owing to the exclusively positive connotations that the word στέφανος ('crown') has elsewhere in the book (Rev. 2.10; 3.11; 4.4, 10; 6.2; 12.1; 14.14) it is likely that the hearers would take its appearance here in a positive rather than negative fashion. Therefore, rather than being a parody of the Lamb,[25] these golden crowns appear to indicate that these locusts have the power and authority to accomplish their (divinely authorized) task. Third, the locusts are said to have 'faces as the faces of men'. While this detail might well indicate that these locusts have intelligence,[26] such a statement could not help but remind the hearers of the description of the third living creature around the throne of God in Rev. 4.7, perhaps underscoring the idea that even these hideous locusts are divinely commissioned. Fourth, the hair of these locusts is 'like the hair of women'. Although effeminate associations cannot be ruled out with regard to the imagery of the (long) hair of women, it is more likely that this image would convey a sense of vitality, as it does with Samson (Judg. 16.13-22) and Absalom (2 Sam. 14.25-26).[27] Fifth, the teeth of these locusts are like the teeth of lions. With this detail the ferocious nature of these locusts comes into sharper focus. For not only would this imagery convey a sense of dread and fear amongst the hearers, owing to the incredible destruction of which a lion's teeth is capable, but it would also remind the hearers of the first living creature described in Rev. 4.7. As with the description of their faces, so this association with the four living creatures again underscores the divine nature of these locusts' commission. Sixth, the phrase, 'and they have breastplates as iron breastplates', suggests that the scales normally found on the chests of locusts are very strong indeed, being like iron breastplates. The mention of such armor continues to emphasize the abilities of these

---

[25] So Sweet, *Revelation*, p. 169.

[26] Prigent, *L'Apocalypse de Saint Jean*, p. 243.

[27] Smalley, *The Revelation to John*, p. 232.

locusts to accomplish their task; they are virtually indestructible.[28] Seventh, 'and the voice of their wings is as the voice of many chariots of horses running into war'. This thunderous voice carries with it the familiar sounds of war, a war that these locusts are well equipped to carry out. Eighth, 'and they have tails as scorpions, and stingers, and in their tails their authority to harm men for five months'. These words serve to clarify the earlier statements made with regard to the scorpion like torment of these locusts (9.5), the length of their activity, and the nature of their authority. The things implied there are made explicit here. Ninth, the hearers learn that unlike the locusts described in Prov. 30.27, these locusts have a king over them, revealing something of the intentional nature of their task. If locusts that have no king manage to maintain rank as they march, these insidious locusts are even more organized! The king of the locusts is identified as 'the angel of the Abyss', perhaps a reference to the angel, who had been given the key to the Abyss who clearly has a certain authority over them, or another angel associated with these locusts. At any rate, this angel is named in a rather striking way, for his name is given in both Hebrew and Greek, a move reminiscent of the FG (Jn 5.2; 19.13, 17, 20). The Hebrew name is given (in Greek translation) as Ἀβαδδών ('Destruction'), a term that would be familiar to the hearers from its somewhat frequent appearance in the Writings where it often is closely associated with Death (Job 26.6; 28.22; 31.12; Prov. 15.11; Ps. 88.11). For the most part it is the name of a place, never the name of an angel. However, its appearance in Rev. 9.11 as a proper name for the Angel of the Abyss would fit well with the context and would serve to personify Destruction for the hearers. When the Greek name is given there is a small surprise for the hearers as they might very well expect the word, Ἀπώλεια ('Destroyer') rather than Ἀπολλύων ('Destroyer'), as the former is normally used in the LXX to translate the Hebrew equivalent not the latter. This shift would suggest to the hearers that this 'Greek' name is more than a mere translation but is one that carries with it a deeper significance. One possible association would likely stand out above the others. As has been observed, Exodus motifs are abundant in this section of the Apocalypse. Owing to a number of indicators it is clear that God himself

---

[28] Mounce, *The Book of Revelation*, p. 197.

is responsible for the Angel who unlocks the Abyss and in turn the emergence of these locusts, as he had been in Joel. Given such associations, it may very well be the case that mention of this 'Destroyer' would remind the hearers of the Destroyer found in the Exodus story,[29] who is also under divine commission and leaves those with God's mark unharmed. The fact that a different word is used here than the one that appears in Exod. 12.23 may be in accord with the fact that at this point in the Apocalypse the Destroyer does not bring death, but organizes excruciating suffering. At the same time, the association of death with the Destroyer in the Exodus story might very well anticipate the events that will accompany the next trumpeting. In any case, the emphasis conveyed by the fact that this name is given in both Hebrew and Greek would hardly be lost on the hearers and further underscores the dreadful nature of these locusts.

Verse 12 – The conclusion of the description of the events that accompany the blasting of the fifth trumpet is signaled in v. 12, where the fifth trumpet is identified with the first of the three remaining woes of which the eagle speaks in 8.13. Specifically, the hearers are told, 'The first woe has departed; behold two woes are still coming after these things'. By this explicit connection between the fifth trumpet and the first of the three woes, the ominous nature of the final two trumpets is made all the clearer to the hearers. For the events associated with the blasting of the fifth trumpet are by far the worst in this series and are the most extensively described. Clearly, the warning that two woes are still to come prepares the hearers for the blasting of the next two trumpets.

Verses 13-14 – When the sixth angel trumpeted John says, 'And I heard one voice out of the four horns of the altar of gold before God'. These words remind the hearers of other references to the altar, all of which are closely associated with the prayers of the saints (6.9; 8.3), suggesting that the directives of this voice are in some way related to the prayers that have previously been mentioned. The close proximity of the altar to God suggests that this is the voice of God, either directly or indirectly. It is the voice of divine authorization,[30] the four horns conveying the image of divine

---

[29] Beale, *The Book of Revelation*, p. 504.
[30] Smalley, *The Revelation to John*, p. 235.

strength.³¹ The redundancy of the words with which v. 14 begins, 'saying to the sixth angel, the one who has the trumpet', makes the identity of this angel very clear. Such emphasis would perhaps heighten the sense of dramatic tension experienced by the hearers, for after the first five trumpets have blasted, the expectation of that which follows could hardly be higher. This sixth angel is directed to 'Loose the four angels who have been bound at the great Euphrates River'. Mention of these four angels would no doubt remind the hearers of the four angels located at the four corners of the earth holding back the four winds of the earth (7.1). The fact that the phrase 'the four angels' is an articular construction suggests that the hearers are familiar with these four, perhaps implying that these two groups would be identified as the same.³² Or, perhaps reference to 'the four angels' would put the hearers on notice that yet another group of four angels also stands ready to fulfil God's commission. The perfect passive participle τοὺς δεδεμένους ('who have been bound') is used to describe these angels, implying that they have been bound by God at some point in the past and remain bound even now. While it is possible that their 'being bound' implies something negative about these angels, given the fact that Satan will be bound for 1,000 years later in the book (20.2), such a conclusion might be a bit premature. For in the Johannine literature, this verb is used to describe the binding of Lazarus (Jn 11.44) and Jesus (19.24) as part of their respective burials, as well as to describe the binding of Jesus during his arrest (18.12, 24). On several occasions, the appearance of binding is used in conjunction with loosing (Jn 11.44; Rev. 9.14; 20.2), indicating that the binding in question is for a specific purpose. Given the term's use in the FG, the hearers would not necessarily view these angels in a negative light upon learning that they 'have been bound' (by God).³³ The location of these four angels at the great Euphrates River would strike an ominous note for not only is this one of the historical boundaries for Israel (Gen. 15.18; Josh. 1.4), but it also is the location of some of Rome's most feared enemies, the Parthians.

---

³¹ Kiddle, *The Revelation of St. John*, p. 161.

³² Murphy, *Fallen Is Babylon*, p. 146.

³³ Wall, *Revelation*, p. 132.

Verse 15 – The next words in the Greek text indicate that these angels were indeed released, the divine passive ἐλύθησαν ('were loosed') standing in the place of emphasis, underscoring God's continued activity in these events. John and his hearers learn that these four angels are those 'who had been prepared for the hour and day and month and year'. Just as the seven angels prepared to trumpet their trumpets (8.6), and the locusts looked like horses prepared for battle (9.7), so these four angels had been prepared (by God) for this very moment. Throughout the Apocalypse the verb, ἑτοιμάζω ('prepare'), is used to designate something or someone prepared by God (9.15; 12.6;) and/or prepared to accomplish his purpose (8.6; 9.7; 16.12; 19.7; 21.2). The extent of the preparation of these four angels goes all the way to the very moment they are to carry out their mission. It points to the exact hour, day, month, and year. While such a formulation is unique in Scripture, it is paralleled to a certain extent in Num. 1.1 and Zech. 1.7 (cf. also Hag. 1.15), where day, month, and year are cited with reference to the coming of the word of the Lord. Perhaps the unique formulation found in Rev. 9.15 would propel the hearers forward into this prophetic encounter. At any rate, the passive participle, οἱ ἡτοιμασμένοι ('those prepared'), and this peculiar means of temporal calculation combine to convey the extent of God's involvement in and orchestration of the activity of these angels. The reason for the angels' divine commission is revealed by a purpose clause, 'in order that they might kill a third of men'. In continuity with the first four trumpets, a third of the objects concerned are affected. In discontinuity with the previous five trumpets, for the first time human beings are killed. The escalation in the numbers of those who are killed from when the fourth seal is opened (one-fourth) to the blasting of the sixth trumpet (one-third) would hardly be lost on the hearers. Such an increase would fit well with the intensification of judgment expected in the second and third woes (8.13) and at the same time contribute to the sense of an accelerated movement toward the end for the hearers.

Verse 16 – Yet, the hearers do not next encounter a description of these four angels personally killing one-third of humankind but rather encounter a description of a massive army. It appears that these four angels, loosed to kill a third of humankind, have morphed into an unbelievably large force! The first thing revealed about this force is 'the number of the soldiers of horses (cavalry)'. The astronomical number is δισμυριάδες μυριάδων ('twice ten thousand times ten thousand'), a number reminiscent of the angels described in 5.11. The hearers might also be reminded of Ps. 68.17, where this very number appears with reference to the chariots that accompany the Lord as he comes to his Holy Place from Sinai. Perhaps such similarity would reinforce the fact that the army of which Rev. 9.16 speaks does indeed come from the Lord, just as had the chariots in Psalm 68. The enormity of this number indicates its supernatural nature.[34] This force, 200,000,000 strong, cannot conceivably be resisted.[35] It will accomplish God's purpose. John next informs his hearers, 'I heard their number'. These words, reminiscent of those in 7.4, not only indicate the source of his knowledge, but also create within the hearers an expectancy of what follows, for when John heard the 144,000 numbered, he then saw an innumerable crowd.

Verse 17-19 – True to form, what John heard in v. 16 gives way to what he saw in v. 17, 'And I saw horses in the vision and those sitting upon them as …' In recounting what he saw on this occasion, John makes explicit reference to 'the vision' for the only time in the whole of the Apocalypse. By this means of expression, the significance of what is seen is emphasized and the visionary nature of his experience underscored. Whereas in v. 16 reference to soldiers precedes that of the horses, in v. 17 mention of the horses precedes that of those who sit upon them. However, when John actually describes their appearance it is as though horse and rider converge into one entity,[36] for the ascription of breastplates that appear fiery, hyacinth-like, and sulfurous does not distinguish between horses and riders in any way. Rather, it appears that these breastplates make horses and riders indistinguishable with regard to this detail. Significantly, the constituent parts of the breastplates are described by adjectives that convey a less than clear picture of the breastplates. The focus is not so much on a variety of colors, though colors may be implied, as upon breastplates that appear somewhat hazy while reflecting elements capable of destruction.

---

[34] Prigent, *L'Apocalypse de Saint Jean*, p. 246.
[35] Gause, *Revelation*, p. 142.
[36] Beasley-Murray, *Revelation*, p. 165.

Such is clearly the case with the elements 'fiery' and 'sulfurous', and may also be the case with ὑακινθίνους ('hyacinth-like'), which appears to have reference to a gem that generates a dark-blue, or dark-red bordering on a black luster,[37] perhaps resembling the appearance of smoke. As John's words continue, the hearers learn that the true objects of focus are the horses, as their riders receive no more attention, and that this army is not only well protected by their breastplates, but they are also well armed. Something of the offensive nature of this army is revealed by the words 'and the heads of the horses were as the heads of lions, and out of their mouths came fire and smoke and sulfur'. The description of their heads as those of lions would remind the hearers of the description of the locusts' teeth as lions' teeth in 9.8, as well as the physical appearance of the first living creature in 4.7. By this image, both the ferocious nature of this army and its divine commission are conveyed. Out of the mouth of these lion-like heads come ominously destructive elements, which bear a striking resemblance to the appearance of this army's breastplates; fire, smoke, and sulfur. Something of the cumulative nature of this army's activities is revealed by the way in which these three particular elements function within the trumpet sequence, for some form of fire appears with the sounding of the first four trumpets, smoke with the fifth, and sulfur with the sixth. Owing to the fact that these three elements go on to become basic elements in the divine punishment that emerges in the book (14.10-11; cf. also 18.9, 18; 19.3, 20; 20.10, 14; 21.8), their appearance in 9.17 appears to anticipate that which is to come![38] In order that the hearers not misunderstand what they have heard, they are told, 'From these three plagues a third of men were killed, out of the fire and the smoke and the sulfur that were coming out of their mouths'. Adding to their ominous identity and function, these destructive elements are called πληγῶν ('plagues'), the first attribution of this word to a judgment in the Apocalypse. Such an attribution would again underscore the divine nature of these events as this language would immediately call to mind the ten plagues directed toward Egypt during the period of the Exodus, continuing this em-

---

[37] J.H. Thayer, *Greek-English Lexicon of the New Testament* (Grand Rapids: Zondervan, 1975), p. 633.
[38] Michaels, *Revelation*, p. 131.

phasis in the Apocalypse, as this term appears on numerous subsequent occasions in the book. These three plagues, coming out of the horses' mouths, are explicitly identified as those elements responsible for the killing of a third of humankind. The impression left is that these plagues represent eschatological judgments inflicted in advance of the end. It comes as no surprise, then, when the hearers are informed, 'For the authority of the horses is in their mouths ...' Such destructive abilities are horrendous enough, but there is more. For just as the authority of the locusts was in their tails (9.10) so the hearers learn that the authority of the horses is not confined to their heads. Their authority is also 'in their tails, for their tails are like serpents, having heads and with which they harm'. Serpent imagery used for the tail of an animal may not be so unusual, as various animals have tails that might appear to be similar in form to serpents, but these 'serpents' have heads with which to harm its victims. Though the hearers are not told, they may very well assume that the heads of these serpents also take the form of lions' heads, with the three plagues coming from them as well. Thus, in addition to their breastplates that make them virtually indestructible, their ability to inflict harm is doubly impressive, as they possess heads on either part of the torsos. While such fearful images would strike terror in the hearts and minds of most, perhaps the hearers would recall from Ps. 91.13 that the lion and serpent pose no danger to those who dwell in the shelter of the Most High.[39]

Verse 20 – Despite these judgments, 'the rest of the men, those who were not killed by these plagues, did not repent of the works of their hands, in order that they not worship the demons and the idols of gold and silver and bronze and stone and wood, which are not able to see nor hear nor walk'. It now becomes clear that these plagues were designed to give humankind an opportunity for repentance.[40] In this light, the death of a third of humanity, following on the death of a fourth of humanity (6.8), is now seen as gracious restraint that affords an opportunity for those who survive to repent! Such a call and opportunity for repentance would not surprise the hearers in a book that has called for repentance from the churches on numerous occasions (2.5, 16, 21, 22; 3.3, 19). The fact

---

[39] Sweet, *Revelation*, p. 173.
[40] Osborne, *Revelation*, p. 385 and Resseguie, *The Revelation of John*, p. 149.

that this is the first mention of repentance since near the end of the seven prophetic messages by the resurrected Jesus would not be lost on the hearers. For in this refusal to repent the Johannine hearers would be confronted with the prospect of those who have seen the arm of God himself revealed and yet choose not to repent! Such an encounter could hardly help but pose the question in the form of a warning, are we too failing to repent despite God's own direct intervention in our lives? At the same time, this failure to repent could not help but remind the hearers of Pharaoh's repeated failure to repent at the conclusion of each and every plague which the Lord sent upon Egypt. Specifically, the rest of humanity is said not to repent of 'the works of their hands'. As has been seen, in the Apocalypse the idea of works is an integrative one which includes one's activity or actions, that carries with them a sign-like quality which reveals something about one's relationship with God and/or Jesus. On this occasion there is a close connection between 'the works of their hands' and the worship of demons and idols. The mention of demons at this point in the Apocalypse might come as a bit of a surprise to the hearers, as there appears to be little to no interest in demons or the demonic in the Johannine literature. For example, there are no exorcisms described in the FG and the only person accused of being demon possessed there is Jesus (Jn 7.20; 8.48, 49, 52; 10.20, 21)! Neither are demons, as such, mentioned in 1-3 John. Later in the Apocalypse the hearers learn that demonic spirits in the form of frogs come from the mouth of the Dragon and the beast and the false prophet to perform signs and gather the kings of the world together for battle on the great day of the Lord (Rev. 16.13-14). They also later learn that fallen Babylon has become the haunt of demons and unclean spirits (18.2). The appearance of demons here in 9.20, apparently in connection with idolatry, suggests some relationship between their worship and idolatry. While it is possible that the hearers would take this mention to indicate that the worship of demons is to be equated with the worship of idols, the rest of the verse, which makes clear that idols are impotent, suggests otherwise. Rather it seems to indicate that the relationship between demons and idols is that the former inspires the worship of the latter. Even more significant than the issue of demons is the fact that for the first time in the Apocalypse the hearers encounter the word worship in connection with one other than

God and/or his people (3.9; 4.10; 5.14; 7.11). In this way, the theme of false worship is introduced into the book, a theme that will function prominently and gain significance as the book unfolds. On this occasion, it makes the choice between the worship of God and the worship of demons and idols all the clearer for the hearers. The description of the idols, which sits nicely with the phrase 'the works of their hands', could not help but evoke for the hearers the biting words of numerous OT writers with regard to the foolishness and futility of idolatry (Isa. 40.18-20; 41.6-7; 44.9-20; Jeremiah 10; Ps. 115.3-8).[41] Despite their composition, whether of gold, silver, bronze, stone, or wood, they are unable to act, to see or hear or walk. And yet, these impotent idols and the demons that inspire their worship are tenaciously grasped by those who, ironically enough, have seen firsthand the activity of 'the living God' in the form of the plagues and judgments wrought upon the earth and its inhabitants!

Verse 21 – Not only this but 'neither did they repent of their murders, nor their sorcery, nor their sexual immorality, nor their thefts'. These 'works of their hands' also go without repentance. It is significant that each of these activities is specifically condemned in the Torah (Exod. 20.13; 22.18; 20.14, 15, respectively), and that three of the four appear in texts which describe those whose eschatological fate is the lake of fire (21.8) and those excluded from the New Jerusalem (22.15). In addition to these major associations, each of these activities may also have other specific associations within the Apocalypse and/or the other Johannine literature. In addition to its other references in the Apocalypse (21.8; 22.15), Johannine hearers would likely regard those who commit murder as children of the Devil, who, according to Jesus, 'was a man killer from the beginning' (Jn 8.44). One wonders if they would not also see those who would not repent of their murders as including those responsible for the death of Antipas (2.13). Sorcery,[42] which appears here in 9.21 as well as the eschatological contexts of 21.8 and 22.15, will become closely associated with the activity of Babylon, who deceived the nations by her sorcery (18.23). Sexual immorality

---

[41] Murphy, *Fallen Is Babylon*, p. 249.

[42] Here the term for 'potions' instead of the normal word for 'magic' appears, perhaps indicating that even the paraphernalia used with sorcery is condemned, so Osborne, *Revelation*, p. 387.

would call to mind the teaching of Balaam (2.14) as well as the activity and teaching of 'Jezebel' and her followers (2.21). Such sexual immorality will come to be intimately connected to Babylon the Great Whore (17.1, 2, 4, 5, 15, 16; 18.3, 9; 19.2). Despite the fact that Jesus elsewhere in the Apocalypse says, 'I come as a thief!' (3.3; 16.15), it is clear that those who have committed theft in 9.21 are viewed, not like Jesus, but as those who enter the sheep fold illegally (Jn 10.1), to kill, steal, and destroy (10.10). Perhaps even more ominously for Johannine hearers, such language would be reminiscent of Judas (Jn 12.6), the archetype of one who refuses to repent. Thus, the refusal of the rest of humankind to repent of such activities reveals something of the level of their obstinate refusal to respond to the hand of God. Such a response could not help but leave the hearers with a sense of hopefulness, that God will avenge his faithful witnesses, and a sense of bewilderment, that the people of the world could be so adamant in their refusal of God and his work. Or perhaps it is that they are so blind that they cannot see the hand of God in the activities associated with the sixth trumpet.[43]

Prophetic Witness (10.1-11.14)

Verse 1 – As chapter ten begins John and his hearers are, no doubt, awaiting the news that the second woe has come and the blasting of the seventh trumpet. Yet, as with the delay between the opening of the sixth and seventh seals in the seals sequence, so there is a delay between the blasting of the sixth and seventh trumpets. However, the latter delay is more pronounced than the former in that, unlike the sixth seal, which is completely opened before the delay begins, the events associated with the sixth trumpet are not completed, for the second woe has not yet been described as having departed. Thus, John and his hearers experience something new in this emerging pattern of delay. Instead of hearing the seventh angel blast his trumpet, John says, 'And I saw another mighty angel coming down out of heaven'. Here, the language, 'And I saw', alerts the hearers to the fact that a new dimension of the vision is being introduced, directing their attention to a different object than the ex-

---

[43] Yarbro Collins (*Revelation*, p. 63) concludes, 'Verses 20-21 express the prophet's conviction that the people of his day were so alienated from the creator that no crisis could move them to repentance. Events in which the faithful would see divine providence and justice are simply acts of blind fate to others'.

pected conclusion of the second woe and blasting of the seventh trumpet. Mention of 'another mighty angel' not only indicates this but directs their attention back to the only other mighty angel to appear in the book to this point; the mighty angel in 5.2. Such a reference would remind them of a mighty angel in heaven who preaches, 'Who is worthy to open the book and loose its seals?' Like that mighty angel, this one is also originally located in heaven. But as he descends, the attention of the hearers is directed back to earth. This mighty angel is described in terms unlike any other angel in the book and indicates something of his unique importance and function.[44] Like Jesus, who 'comes with the clouds' (1.7), this mighty angel is 'clothed with the cloud'. Like God, whose throne is surrounded by a rainbow (4.3), this mighty angel has 'the rainbow around his head'. The fact that ἡ ἶρις ('the rainbow') is articular in 10.1 almost certainly points back to the rainbow mentioned in 4.3. Like Jesus, whose 'countenance is as the sun shining in its power' (1.16), the mighty angel's 'face is as the sun'. Like Jesus, whose 'feet are like bronze glowing in a furnace' (1.15), the feet of this mighty angel are 'as pillars of fire'. Like the One who sits on the throne (5.1) and the Lamb (5.7), this mighty angel too has a book in his hand. While other similarities occur in the verses that follow, these remarkable characteristics are enough to make clear the extraordinary identification of this mighty angel with both Jesus and God. What response would the revelation of such characteristics generate within John and his hearers? Perhaps they would be tempted to see in this angel a manifestation of the risen Christ, who now appears to John in angelic form. Or, realizing that Jesus has not been described as an angel yet in the Apocalypse (nor will he at any subsequent point), perhaps they are tempted to see in this angel a Christophany on the order of the appearance of 'the angel of the Lord' found in the OT.[45] Or, perhaps, owing to the remarkable convergence of the divine characteristics of both God and Jesus, and the intimate connection that exists between Jesus and the Spirit in Johannine thought, the hearers would be tempted to see in this angel

---

[44] Bauckham, *The Climax of Prophecy*, p. 253.

[45] For example, Gen. 16.10; 22.11-18; 24.7; 31.11-13; Exod. 3.2-12; 14.19; Judg. 2.1; 6.22; 13.20-22. For an extensive argument favoring this interpretation cf. Beale, *The Book of Revelation*, pp. 522-26.

the Spirit herself.[46] While any or all of these identifications might theoretically be entertained by the hearers, it is quite likely that they would not long hold to any one of them. For it is clear that this mighty angel is identified as 'another mighty angel' underscoring the fact that this angel is similar in some respects to the previous 'mighty angel'. In addition, some of the details that follow are difficult to reconcile with any of these identifications, such as when the mighty angel swears an oath by heaven. But, perhaps most importantly, the hearers could not help but be struck by the remarkable consistency with which the Apocalypse keeps the lines of demarcation between Jesus and the angels clear.[47] If such identifications are unlikely, what would these (divine) characteristics convey? It would seem very clear that at this point, John and his hearers would see in this mighty angel a being intimately associated with God and Jesus, one authorized to act on behalf of and in accordance with the divine will, representing the divine presence and glory.[48] The angel's unique description would perhaps also prepare them for his unique function and underscore the importance of the events described here.

Verse 2 – One of the most intriguing aspects of this mighty angel's description is that he has 'in his hand an opened book'. The appearance of the perfect passive participle ἠνεῳγμένον ('opened') to describe this book indicates that it had been opened at some point in the past and remains open even now. Mention of an opened book could not help but to suggest to John's hearers the possibility that it is the same book that was taken from the hand of God by the Lamb, who subsequently opened its seals. If so, the book sealed with seven seals has been opened, having made its way from God to the Lamb to the mighty angel to John, an order of transmission remarkably consistent with the order set forth in 1.1. On this view, the events described in chapters 6-9 are those that accompany the opening of the seals and are not necessarily the revelation of the book's contents. For only when the book has been opened are its contents accessible to John and, in turn, his hearers. While the fact that the word βιβλαρίδιον ('little book') occurs here

---

[46] For this fascinating interpretation cf. Waddell, *The Spirit in the Book of Revelation*, pp. 159-63.
[47] Bauckham, *The Climax of Prophecy*, pp. 118-49.
[48] Gause, *Revelation*, p. 145

Figure 10
William Blake, *The Angel of Revelation*
(Metropolitan Museum of Art, NY)

rather than βιβλίον ('book') found in chapter five might be taken to suggest that the little book of 10.2 is different from the book of 5.1, such a conclusion would be premature. On closer examination one finds that both these terms are diminutives, indicating that the force of 'little' is relative. At the same time, the angel's instruction to John later in 10.8 indicates that these two terms function as synonyms in the Apocalypse, for βιβλίον ('book') appears there with reference to the angel's book.[49] One can only imagine the excitement felt by John and his hearers given the prospect that they are finally encountering the opened book! Neither, in this book, is the posture of the angel without significance as the hearers learn that 'he placed his right foot upon the sea and the left upon the earth'. The location of these feet, like 'pillars of fire', indicates something of the scope and the authority of this mighty angel's universal mission and message, as he stands upon the two major components of earthly creation (Gen. 1.10).[50] The fact that the activity of his feet is described first encourages the hearers to take earth as their vantage-point for viewing this enormous figure.

Verse 3 – Whilst contemplating his incredible posture, the hearers learn more about this mighty angel, for 'he cried out with a great voice as a lion roaring'. In a book filled with loud sounds and great voices, the revelation that this enormous mighty angel cries out with a great voice is no surprise. Even so, the hearers would surely imagine that, owing to his enormous stature, the sound of his voice must be deafening! The intensity of the voice is likened to 'a lion roaring'. The association of the angel's voice with that of a lion would remind the hearers of OT descriptions of God's voice (Hos. 11.10; and esp. Amos 3.8), and be yet another way in which this mighty angel reminds of Jesus, the Lion of the tribe of Judah (5.5). Interestingly enough, the words of this angel are not recorded, rather the hearers learn 'And when he spoke, the seven thunders spoke their own voices'. Several things are significant about these words. First, this is the first (and only) time in the Apocalypse when the words of an angel are not recorded.[51] Second, it appears that there is some connection between the crying out by the mighty an-

---

[49] Cf. the very helpful discussion of the book's identity by Bauckham, *The Climax of Prophecy*, pp. 243-57.

[50] Resseguie, *The Revelation of John*, p. 153.

[51] Aune, *Revelation 6-16*, p. 559.

gel and the seven thunders that follow. While it is possible that the voice of the angel morphs into the seven thunders, the fact that the seven thunders are explicitly said to speak with their own voices makes such an interpretation unlikely. Rather, it appears that the seven thunders are the result of the angelic crying out and/or sound in response to the cry of the mighty angel. Third, the sounding of the voices of thunder clearly conveys to the hearers extraordinarily loud sounds, as thunder was one of the strongest natural sounds encountered in antiquity. Fourth, it is exceedingly difficult to imagine that mention of the seven thunders would not be taken by the hearers as the introduction of yet another series of sevens, along the lines of the seven seals and seven trumpets. After all, this seven is introduced near the end of the sequence of the seven trumpets, and like the others would appear to be of heavenly origin. Fifth, the fact that this construction is articular, '*the* seven thunders', suggests that the hearers would be familiar with this group. If so, it is likely that they would be reminded of the voice of God as reflected in Psalm 29, where the voice of the Lord is mentioned seven times, with its initial description likening it to thunder.[52] The equation of thunder with God's voice would also be familiar to Johannine hearers from the tradition found in the FG (Jn 12.29). Neither would the significance of the role of thunder in the strategically located theophanic displays in the Apocalypse be lost on the hearers (Rev. 4.5; 8.5; 11.19; 16.18), two of which they have already encountered. Thus, as the hearers encounter the seven thunders, they may very well be preparing themselves for yet another series of sevens of even greater intensity than those that have precedeed.

Verse 4 – In contrast to the words from the voice of the angel, which John does not appear to understand, it seems that he does understand the words of the thunders for the hearers learn, 'And when the seven trumpets spoke I was about to write'. In keeping with Jesus' command to 'write what you see' (1.11, 19), John prepares to continue in his faithful obedience to write down those things which he witnesses. The hearers could hardly be surprised by John's intentions and, no doubt, anticipate an immediate recounting of the thunders' words. However, whilst preparing to record what he heard, John says, 'I heard a voice out of heaven saying, "Seal up

---

[52] Sweet, *Revelation*, p. 178.

the words of the seven thunders, and do not write them'". While the hearers may not have been surprised by John's intention to write what he heard, they must be astounded by this heavenly prohibition, for it appears to stand at odds with Jesus' previous commands (1.11, 19).[53] While not identified, the heavenly origin of this voice would indicate that it could hardly be other than that of Jesus or God, making the contrast all the greater. In any event, whether directly or indirectly, the voice gives a divine prohibition. Significantly, this prohibition takes a two-fold form, perhaps balancing the two-fold command to write found earlier in the book (1.11, 19). Positively, John is commanded to 'seal' the words of the seven thunders. Such language is exceedingly provocative, for much of what John writes in this book is the direct result of the unsealing of the book sealed with seven seals. In addition, this command seems to stand in sharp contrast to the presence of the unsealed book in the mighty angel's hand! And yet, John is commanded to seal these words. To this point in the Apocalypse, the idea of sealing is found in conjunction with words that have been written, and individuals who have been marked out for God's protection. Is there any way in which the words of the thunders may be understood as having a special significance, as those individuals sealed appear to have? While such an interpretation is possible, the second part of the prohibition indicates that John is to conceal these words by not writing them down. This aorist subjunctive prohibition conveys that John is forbidden to take a course of action he has not yet commenced,[54] an idea that dovetails nicely with John's earlier words that he 'was about to write'. It should be noted that while the words of the seven thunders do not become part of John's book, they are part of John's experience and do not seem to be invalidated or suspended. Rather, they remain sealed because they are not written down. What then is the significance of the seven thunders for John and his hearers? If, as seems likely, the seven thunders are deemed to be yet another series of God's judgments, in line with the seven seals and seven trumpets,[55] it is probable that this series would bring with it an increase in intensity of the judgments to be experienced. Thus,

---

[53] Mounce, *The Book of Revelation*, p. 209.
[54] Aune, *Revelation 6-16*, p. 549.
[55] Skaggs and Benham, *Revelation*, p. 108.

whereas the opening of the seven seals saw the death of a fourth of humankind and the blasting of the seven trumpets saw the death of a third, would the words spoken by the seven thunders not involve the death of a half of humankind?[56] If so, the command to omit these words from the book John is writing would serve to hasten the pace by which the hearers move toward the end, shortening any delay.[57] It moves them toward an acknowledgement that the second woe has passed and toward the blasting of the seventh (and final) trumpet.

Verses 5-6 – But before the hearers can contemplate further the implications of the sealing of the words of the seven thunders, attention is directed back to the mighty angel. As if to make certain that the hearers would not confuse him with the voice from heaven or the seven thunders, he is described by John as 'the angel, the one whom I saw standing upon the sea and upon the earth'. Not only does this distinguish this angel from the voice out of heaven and the seven thunders, but it also draws specific attention to the posture of the mighty angel. For this gigantic figure now raises 'his right hand into the heavens and swears' an oath. The picture of this mighty angel standing on the sea and the land with his hand extending all the way up into the heavens is one of the most incredible images to appear to this point in the Apocalypse. The only concrete analogy that John and his hearers might have for such an incredible sight would be the Colossos of Rhodes, one of the Seven Wonders of the ancient world, which stood about 105 feet tall on the promontory overlooking the harbor of Rhodes. Destroyed by an earthquake in 224 BCE the ruins of the Colossos were well known, inspiring awe at such a spectacular structure.[58] And yet, even this incredible analogy is dwarfed by the stature of this mighty angel, whose cosmic posture connects the heavens with land and sea![59] By means of this dramatic posture, the mighty angel makes clear the basis of the oath he swears, a power above all others. For this mighty angel 'swore by the One who lives forever and ever, who created the heaven and the things in them and the earth and the

---

[56] A.M. Farrer, *The Revelation of St. John the Divine* (Oxford: Clarendon, 1964), p. 125.

[57] Resseguie, *The Revelation of John*, p. 154.

[58] Aune, *Revelation 6-16*, pp. 556-57.

[59] Bauckham, *The Climax of Prophecy*, p. 253.

things in it and the sea and the things in it'. For Johannine hearers, no more solemn oath could be undertaken than the one sworn here. The mention of 'the One who lives forever and ever' along with 'the one who created' carries the hearers back to the throne-room scene of chapter 4, where the former is twice used with reference to the One who sits on the throne. The designation 'the living God' also appears in 7.2 with reference to his seal. Likewise, the reference to God as creator occurs twice in 4.11, where in a chiastic song of praise God receives the worship of the four living creatures for his strategic role in the creation of all things. On this occasion, the comprehensive nature of God's creative activity is further underscored, not only by the three-fold mention of heaven, earth, and sea, but also by the explicit mention of 'the things that are in it' which follows each of these major divisions of creation. Thus, the hearers would well imagine that the oath of the mighty angel, which is to come, is of extraordinary importance. John and his hearers are not to be disappointed, for the mighty angel of cosmic stature utters an incredible statement, χρόνος οὐκέτι ἔσται ('there is no more time'). This utterance would, no doubt, have a startling effect upon John and his hearers for they are filled with anticipation that the end of all things is near. After all, the words of the seven thunders had just been sealed in order to avoid further delay, while the pronouncement of the passing of the second woe and the blasting of the seventh trumpet must surely be at hand. Thus, at one level, these words would carry with them the idea that the end itself is soon to be experienced and may be taken as a response of sorts to the cries of the souls under the altar in 6.9-11. But, as they will learn, this statement does not apparently mean that time itself has already come to an end, as the rest of the angel's words will reveal, for the days of the seventh trumpet are yet to come. At any rate, it is difficult to imagine that these words would not create within John and his hearers the expectancy that the end of all things is imminent.

Verse 7 – However, despite this statement with regard to time, the hearers are alerted to the fact that a bit more time remains. For the mighty angel continues his message saying, 'but in the days of the voice of the seventh angel, when he is about to trumpet, and the mystery of God will have been fulfilled, as he preached to his servants the prophets'. The first word encountered by the hearers is the strong word of contrast ἀλλ᾽ ('but'), leading to a translation something like, 'there is no more time, but ...' The contrast means that despite the fact that there is no more time, 'the days of the voice of the seventh angel' do remain, and of course mention of the seventh angel reminds the hearers that they have not yet encountered the seventh trumpet or an acknowledgement that the second woe has passed! Not only is there reference to the seventh angel, but explicit mention of the fact that he 'is about to trumpet'! Thus, it appears that the blasting of the seventh trumpet is here closely associated with the fact that there is no more time. There is no more delay for the seventh trumpet is about to sound. Further, it appears that in the days when the seventh trumpet sounds, 'the mystery of God will have been completed'. From the previous occurrence of the word μυστήριον ('mystery'), the hearers would understand this word as having reference to something in need of interpretation. In Rev. 1.20 it is the mystery of the seven stars and the seven lampstands that is explained by the resurrected Christ, an example of the pneumatic interpretation needed for understanding this Revelation. The occurrence of 'the mystery of God' in 10.7 would alert the hearers to the fact that something else is in need of (divine) explanation. While the meaning of this mystery is left uninterpreted for the moment, owing to the eschatological context of the mighty angel's words John and his hearers would likely understand this mystery as having reference to God's eschatological plan. The hearers would perhaps be struck by the fact that the aorist passive ἐτελέσθη ('has been completed') appears here with reference to the future, conveying an additional sense of certainty with regard to the completion of the mystery of God.[60] It is also likely that the occurrence of this term would remind Johannine hearers of Jesus' desire to complete the work of his Father in the FG (Jn 4.34; 5.36; 17.4) and of Jesus' last words on the cross, 'It is completed' (19.30). The implications with regard to the relationship between Jesus' death and the completion of the mystery of God in the Apocalypse are not difficult to see, for the one is coterminous with and makes possible the other. Neither would Johannine hearers be unaware of the fact that the love of God can be completed in the lives of believers (1 Jn 2.5; 4.12, 17, 18). Perhaps the convergence of these

---

[60] Smalley, *The Revelation to John*, p. 265.

ideas indicate to the hearers the way in which the mystery of God will be completed and prepare them for what follows in Revelation 11. One of the other things John and his hearers learn about this mystery is that God preached it to his servants the prophets. The occurrence of the word εὐηγγέλισεν ('preached') to describe God's revelation of this mystery to his servants further underscores the connection between this mystery and the life and death of Jesus for its association with the Gospel and Gospel proclamation was well known in early Christianity. Though not the word of choice in the Johannine literature, it does reappear later in the Apocalypse (14.6). It is striking that the term κηρύσσοντα ('proclaiming') is used of mighty angel's proclamation in 5.2, while the mighty angel of chapter 10 uses the word εὐηγγέλισεν ('preached') to describe God's making known this mystery. Thus, both mighty angels are connected in one way or another with terms associated with Gospel proclamation and are connected to one another in still another way! Who are these servants, these prophets? Rather clearly this statement would have reference to OT prophets, as the words of Amos 3.7 would almost certainly come to the hearers' minds. But, it is also quite likely that Christian prophets would be included as the recipients of this preaching. Three reasons may be offered for this conclusion. First, many of the occurrences of servants (1.1; 2.20; 7.3; 11.18; 22.6) and prophets (10.11; 11.2, 10, 18; 16.6; 18.20, 24; 22.6, 9) in the Apocalypse appear to have reference to Christian prophets. Second, a very similar phrase will appear in 11.18 where servants and prophets are again connected and this phrase appears at least to include Christian prophets. Third, it should not be forgotten that John is himself engaged in just such an experience in writing down the words of this prophecy and finds himself among certain other 'brothers the prophets' (22.9). Thus, the 'mystery of God' has been revealed, at least in part, to God's servants the prophets, a revelatory process that includes John and his community.

Verse 8 – Before the hearers have time to take in the full implications of the angel's words, the voice from heaven again speaks to John saying, 'Go, take the opened book in the hand of the angel who was standing upon the sea and upon the earth'. As in v. 4, it is likely that the hearers would understand this voice as either the voice of God or Jesus. Earlier, this divine voice prohibits writing down the words of the seven thunders. Now this divine voice commands John to take the opened book in the hand of the mighty angel. Given the enormous stature of the mighty angel, noted for a third time here in the span of eight verses, such a command is almost unbelievable if not for the fact that it comes from God himself. The episode takes on the form of a prophetic commissioning as John is directed to come and take the open scroll, perhaps reminding the hearers of Ezekiel's prophetic commission (cf. esp. Ezek. 2.8-3.2). The command Ὕπαγε ('go') may carry with it additional theological weight for Johannine hearers, as the term often appears in the FG in close association with the mission of Jesus, while the command λάβε ('take') is defined in large part by its appearance in describing the activities of the Lamb in taking the book in Revelation 5. Such a two-fold command suggests that John is no passive instrument in prophetic communication, but is called to active participation in this prophetic call. The fact that the opened book is the object John is to take indicates that John himself will now have access to the book that had been sealed with seven seals, that had been in the hand of the One who sits on the throne, that had been in the hand of the Lamb, and now is in the hand of the mighty angel! Since so much of what the hearers have recently encountered points them to the fact that they and John are very near the end of all things, such a commission seems a bit oddly placed, for normally the call of a prophet comes early, rather than near the end of a prophetic book.

Verse 9 – Despite the formidable stature of the mighty angel John is obedient to the heavenly command, doing precisely as he was instructed. In fact, the hearers might smile at the fact that John does not take the book from the gigantic figure but rather says, 'And I went to the angel asking him to give to me the little book'. No sooner does John obey the heavenly voice than he receives a command from the mighty angel, 'Take and eat it, and your stomach will be bitter, but in your mouth it will be sweet as honey'. If the words from the heavenly voice reminded the hearers of Ezekiel's commission, the words of the mighty angel show remarkable similarities to those words, indicating that indeed John is receiving a(nother) prophetic commission. Not only is John told to take the book, but now he is also instructed to eat it. While the word κατάφαγε ('eat') can be translated as 'eat', in this context, as in the Johannine literature as a whole (Jn 2.17; Rev. 11.5; 12.4; 20.9), the term has the stronger connotation of 'devour' or 'consume'.⁶¹ Clearly, the image conveys the idea that John is to devour the book by ingesting it and in so doing the content of the book will become a part of him. There can be little doubt that there is a direct relationship between the contents of this book and John's prophetic ministry. The warning that the book would be bitter to the stomach of John but sweet as honey in his mouth would rather obviously be of special significance with regard to the book's contents. While such imagery might remind John and his hearers that the word of the Lord is sweet as honey to the taste (Ps. 119.103) and that the prophetic message can sometimes be a bitter one, as with the case of Ezekiel,⁶² it appears that this imagery points to specific dimensions of the little book's content. Generally speaking, the hearers would be aware of the fact that the activity of God and his agents could sometimes involve bitterness for many people were described as having died in 8.13 owing to the fact that a third of the rivers and fountains of water had been made bitter by the star that had fallen upon them. Though the hearers could not likely discern the full meaning of this bitter and sweet imagery at this point, the meaning will become clear by the conclusion of this section of the book. By way of preview, it appears that the reason the book is bitter to John's stomach while sweet as honey to his mouth is very much related to the implications of the book's contents for John and his hearers. Specifically, as has been hinted to this point, it will be made clear to John and his hearers that their prophetic witness will result in death, though they will receive divine protection until their witness is complete (cf. esp. 11.7). The fact that the mighty angel mentions bitterness before sweetness might well alert the hearers to the dangerous nature of their activities as faithful witnesses. When John devours the book, it will devour him; it will indeed be both bitter and sweet.

Verse 10 – John is faithful to this prophetic call as he actively takes the little book out of the hand of the angel and devours it. The results of his ingesting this book are just as the mighty angel had said they would be. In John's description of his experience he inverts the words of the angel noting first that the book was as

---

⁶¹ Mounce, *The Book of Revelation*, p. 214 n. 37.
⁶² Wall, *Revelation*, pp. 139-40.

sweet as honey in his mouth and then noting that his stomach was made bitter when it had been consumed. Not only does John's description follow the normal digestive order, but it also alerts the hearers to the fact that in the prophetic words to follow, they will first encounter their sweetness, the promise of divine protection, and then their bitterness, the call to martyrdom.[63] It is probably not lost on the hearers that Daniel's own prophetic encounter left him physically ill (Dan. 10.8-17). Nor would the repetition of these verses with regard to John taking and devouring the book (Rev. 10.8-10) be lost on the hearers, as it would serve to emphasize the importance of this event for John and his hearers. Perhaps it should also be noted that nowhere in the Apocalypse does John more fully enter into this visionary drama than here, which says something about the extent of his active participation in the prophetic task. It is also significant that his actions here are similar to those of the Lamb in chapter 5, who also takes the book. At the very least, such similarities convey a sense of John's identification with the Lamb and his own participation in the salvific activity of the Lamb. It may even imply that John, too, will follow in the way of martyrdom.[64]

Verse 11 – Following this prophetic action, John again receives divine instruction, which on this occasion contains an explicit prophetic call, 'And they say to me, "It is necessary for you to prophesy again unto many people and nations and tongues and kings"'. The hearers might be a bit surprised by the fact that in describing this experience John says, 'they say to me'. While it is theoretically possible that 'they' would be understood to mean both the voice from heaven and that of the mighty angel, such would be unusual in a prophetic call narrative, especially in the light of the fact that John has earlier been commissioned by the resurrected Jesus himself (1.11, 19). It is more likely that the indefinite plural λέγουσίν ('they say') would be understood as an idiomatic substitute for the passive, which is found in both Hebrew and Aramaic, resulting in a translation something like, 'I was told'.[65] Such a meaning would fit well both with the context of the prophetic call and the frequent occurrence of divine passives in the book. Thus, the words of

---

[63] Koester, *Revelation and the End of All Things*, p. 104.

[64] Smalley, *The Revelation to John*, pp. 266-67.

[65] Aune, *Revelation 6-16*, p. 573.

commission to follow have a divine origin. The first word spoken to John in the Greek text is Δεῖ ('it is necessary'), a word which conveys the idea of divine compulsion or necessity, making clear that John has no option – he must prophesy![66] Neither should it be ignored that this word has twice appeared previously in the Apocalypse with reference to those things that must take place (1.1; 4.1). The reappearance of the term here would imply that John is to be a very real part of those things that are to take place. It is necessary for John to prophesy again. Such a statement reveals that John has already been prophesying as he has faithfully recorded the things that he has seen and heard up to this point, especially the seven prophetic messages found in chapters 2-3. It is difficult to ignore the implication that John's previous prophesying is at or is coming to an end and is to give way to another round of prophesying.[67] This commission to prophesy again, as well as the fact that John has recently devoured the open book, suggests that John's future prophetic activity will take on a more intense and personal dimension, if such is possible! The focal point of John's prophetic task to this point has been the church, and this emphasis will continue to the book's conclusion. But this verse indicates that John is now to prophesy ἐπὶ ('to', or 'about') 'many peoples and nations and tongues and kings'. While it is possible to translate ἐπὶ ('to', or 'about') as 'against', reminiscent of Ezekiel's prophesying against the nations,[68] as the following verses will make clear John's prophetic mandate, and that of the church with him, is to prophesy to all nations by bearing faithful witness to the Lamb. Thus, the translation 'to' is the likely meaning of ἐπὶ ('to', or 'about') in this context.[69] The four-fold phrase 'many peoples and nations and tongues and kings' is reminiscent of the four-fold formulae that have previously occurred in 5.9 and 7.9. However, the list found in 10.11 differs in two ways. First, the word 'kings' appears here in the place of tribes, perhaps preparing the hearers for the emphasis upon kings that follows in chapters 16-21. Second, while the first two lists occur in contexts where they testify to the universality of the people

---

[66] Smalley, *The Revelation to John*, p. 249.

[67] Yarbro Collins, *The Apocalypse*, p. 65.

[68] Beale, *The Book of Revelation*, pp. 554-55.

[69] D.E. Holwerda, 'The Church and the Little Scroll (Revelation 10,11)', *CTJ* 34 (1999), p. 154.

of God, here the list describes the nations, as it will from this point on in the Apocalypse.[70] Such philological links suggest that individuals from these groups have not simply experienced salvation in order that the people of God might be universal in its composition, but also in order that members of these very groups might become witnesses to the groups from which they come.[71] Thus, John (and his hearers with him?) is commissioned to prophesy yet again, this time on the world stage.

Chapter 11, Verse 1 – No sooner are these words of prophetic commission spoken than John is given a prophetic task to accomplish for he writes, 'And there was given to me a reed as a rod, saying, "Rise and measure the temple of God and the altar and the worshippers in it"'. Such a close connection between John's prophetic commission and the prophetic task given suggests that at least a portion of the activity described in the following chapter in some way functions as the accomplishment of that commission.[72] The divine origin of this commission is made clear by the divine passive ἐδόθη ('there was given'). The instrument John is given, with which he is to accomplish this act, is a κάλαμος ('reed'), a term that appears later in the Apocalypse in the context of measuring the New Jerusalem (21.15-16). However, at this point it might strike Johannine hearers as significant that this instrument is the same as the instrument the Elder uses to write the epistle of 3 John, perhaps implying that John's activity of measuring is not far removed from his activity of writing. Symbolic prophetic acts are, of course, well known in the OT and even the act of measuring is not an unusual one (2 Sam. 8.2; 2 Kgs 21.13; Isa. 28.16-17; 34.11; Jer. 31.38-40; Ezekiel 40-48; Lam. 2.8; Amos 7.7-9; Mic. 2.5; Zech. 1.6; 2.1-2). Thus, in one sense the command to measure would be a prophetic act with which the hearers would be familiar. However, while the significance of measuring in many of the OT texts indicates impending destruction or points to the promise of reconstruction, the hearers of the Apocalypse would come to learn that the significance of John's measuring is different from any of its predecessors. In these first two verses of chapter 11 the hearers learn that John is

---

[70] Bauckham, *The Climax of Prophecy*, p. 265.
[71] Koester, *Revelation and the End of All Things*, p. 103.
[72] Prigent, *L'Apocalypse de Saint Jean*, p. 260.

instructed to measure certain things but not to measure others. What would the command for John to 'measure the temple of God and the altar and those who worship in it' mean to the hearers? It is clear that this action is to mark out the temple, the altar, and the worshippers for some purpose. But what purpose is conveyed by this act of measuring and how would these three items be understood? While it is possible that mention of the temple, altar, and worshippers would be taken by the hearers as having reference to a current or future temple complex, upon closer inspection such an interpretive option does not appear to be likely. One of the first things the hearers would likely pick up on is the fact that when the term ναός ('temple' or 'sanctuary') appears in the Johannine literature, it does not normally have reference to the literal temple complex. Rather, ἱερόν ('temple') appears to be the term of choice for the temple complex in the FG (Jn 2.14, 15; 5.14; 7.14, 28; 8.20, 59; 10.23; 11.56; 18.20). In point of fact, the term ναός ('temple' or 'sanctuary') appears only three times in the FG, each time with reference to the temple of Jesus' body (2.19-21). Such a theologically significant understanding of the term ναός ('temple' or 'sanctuary') would no doubt open the hearers up to the possibility that the temple here in view is not a literal temple complex, but one that is filled with theological significance. Such an understanding would also be confirmed by the appearance of ναός ('temple' or 'sanctuary') earlier in the Apocalypse, where Jesus promises the one who overcomes that he will make him 'a pillar in the temple of my God' (Rev. 3.12), clearly implying that such a one has a permanent place in God's presence. The other occurrence of ναός ('temple' or 'sanctuary') to this point in the book has reference to God's heavenly temple, where those who have come out of the great tribulation serve him day and night (7.14). In fact, this use of ναός ('temple' or 'sanctuary') is consistent with what follows throughout the Apocalypse as temple is clearly identified as the heavenly temple (11.19; 14.15, 17; 15.5, 6, 8; 16.1, 17). This understanding of temple will only give way to the fact that in the New Jerusalem there will be no temple, for, in imagery hearkening back to the FG, the Lord God Almighty and the Lamb 'is' the temple (21.22). Given all these indicators, it appears likely that mention of the temple in 11.1 has reference to God's temple in heaven with which believers are intimately connected. Significantly, mention of the second component to be measured τὸ θυσιαστήριον ('the altar') points in this same direction, for the hearers' previous acquaintance with 'the altar' in the Apocalypse has reference to the heavenly altar (6.9; 8.3; 9.13) and will throughout the rest of the book (14.18; 16.7). As with the temple imagery, so the altar imagery is intimately connected to believers to this point in the book. Previously, the hearers have encountered the 'souls under the altar' (6.9) and the relationship between altar and 'the prayers of the saints' (8.3), which appear to be related to the judgments of God released from the altar (9.11). The fact that the heavenly altar is in the very presence of God confirms the same message that the temple imagery conveys. The third component to be measured also points in the direction of this interpretive option. Johannine hearers would be well aware that true worshippers are those who worship the Father in Spirit and in Truth (Jn 4.23). Such worship is not tied to a particular geographical location (4.20-24). In the Apocalypse, the twenty-four Elders, who bear a striking resemblance to those who overcome, are always falling down and worshipping in heaven (Rev. 4.10; 5.14; 7.11; 11.16). In addition, hearers of the Apocalypse would be well aware of the fact that Jesus has made those who believe in him into priests to our God (1.6; 5.10), at least part of which is understood to take place in heaven (5.10) and/or in the 1,000 year reign (20.6). Thus, when the hearers encounter these three components that are to be measured, or marked out, it is very likely that they would understand them as having reference to the believing community in the very presence of God.

Verse 2 – This command to measure is followed by words that include both a command and a prohibition. John is told, 'And the court outside the temple leave out (cast outside) and do not measure it, because it has been given to the nations, and they will trample the Holy City for forty-two months'. What would the hearers make of such an enigmatic statement? First, it is likely that given the previous associations between the temple and the believing community that the shift in focus to the 'outer court of the temple' would carry with it at least some of its previous associations. For 'the outer court of the temple' is still part of the temple, and if the temple is closely associated with the believing community in the very presence of God so the outer court of the temple would carry some of those positive connotations. In point of fact, for Johannine hearers the term αὐλή ('courtyard') would likely be informed by its use in the FG, where it is identified both with the safety of the sheepfold (10.1, 16) and as a place of vulnerability as Peter discovers in the court of the High Priest (18.15). Second, the graphic language encountered describing that John is to leave out and not measure the outer court would not be lost on the hearers for the phrase ἔκβαλε ἔξωθεν ('cast outside') underscores the idea of vulnerability if not outright abandonment! And yet, Johannine hearers would know full well that being cast out into a world of vulnerability would not leave them without hope. For, as the formerly blind man in the FG discovers, Jesus himself is waiting there for those who believe in and worship him (Jn 9.34-38)! Third, the reason why the outer court is not to be measured becomes clear in the next phrase, for 'it has been given to the nations'. Significantly, the same divine passive that appeared in 11.1 to make clear the divine origin of John's prophetic task reappears here to make clear the divine origin of the outer court of the temple being given to the nations. Such a divine act will result in the trampling of the Holy City for forty-two months. Thus, the vulnerability of being left out or cast outside, of not being measured, becomes clear. Perhaps the hearers would even see in this image of trampling a convergence of ideas found in Zech. 12.3 (LXX) and Dan. 8.11-14,[73] adding to the ominous nature of what is being described. Fourth, it would also be obvious to the hearers that 'the outer court of the temple' and 'the Holy City' are identical in this verse. The linkage between the people of God as temple, altar, worshippers, outer court of the temple, and Holy City not only reveals the meaning of these images in these first two verses of chapter eleven but also prepare the hearers for the way in which certain cities to be encountered later are defined more as people than as buildings or geographical locales. Specifically, they will learn of the way in which the holy city and the New Jerusalem stand in continuity with one another and will be coterminous (Rev. 21.10). Fifth, the hearers learn that the time of the holy city's vulnerability is of limited duration, forty-two months. This reference to a limited period of time would likely remind the hearers of Daniel's 'time, times, and half a time' (Dan. 7.25; 12.7), which designates a period of unprecedented trauma and persecution for

---

[73] Waddell, *The Spirit in the Book of Revelation*, pp. 169-70.

the people of God. This specific temporal designation will appear once more in Rev. 13.5.

What would the hearers make of this prophetic task entrusted to John? What would be its significance? From the foregoing it appears likely that they would see here reference to the people of God marked out as being in his very presence. As such, there is the implicit promise of protection.[74] At the same time, it is clear that the people of God, who are in his very presence, are still subject to vulnerability, owing to the response of the nations to them. Thus, the protection and vulnerability of the people of God sit side by side in a way remarkably reminiscent of the picture of God's people in chapter seven, where the 144,000 are sealed by God for protection against the impending divine judgments, while the universal, innumerable crowd is identified as coming out of the great tribulation! This combination of protection and vulnerability for the people of God in 11.1-2 results in a certain merging of the people of God in their heavenly and earthly manifestations. Therefore, the hearers are now very near the theological heart of the Apocalypse, for the images of 11.1-2 appear to reveal something of the content of the opened book that John has devoured and makes more explicit the nature of Christian prophetic witness, a theme which immediately takes center stage in the next section the hearers encounter.

Verse 3 – It is interesting that John is nowhere described as carrying out this prophetic task, a wholly unprecedented event in the Apocalypse for John appears to be very faithful in carrying out all the commands he is given. Such an unresolved tension may leave the hearers wondering if the description to follow is in some way connected to or a fulfillment of John's prophetic task. For without any break the divine voice continues to speak, 'And I will give to my two witnesses and they will prophesy 1,260 days being clothed in sackcloth'. These words convey a number of things to the hearers. First, the divine voice speaks in the first person, 'I will give to my two witnesses', indicating the close connection that exists between the prophetic activity to follow and the divine speaker. God, and or Jesus, is the initiator of prophetic witness.[75] Second, it is sig-

---

[74] Even though measuring in and of itself never means protection in the OT texts where measuring is described. On this cf. M. Jauhiainen, 'The Measuring of the Sanctuary Reconsidered (Rev. 11.1-2)', *Biblica* 83 (2002), pp. 507-26.

[75] Gause, *Revelation*, p. 151.

nificant that there are two witnesses who are described as the recipients of the divine gift. While interpretive history is full of attempts to identify these two witnesses,[76] the hearers might be struck by the fact that their number is in accord with the Torah stipulations with regard to the minimal number of witnesses needed to validate a truth claim (Num. 35.30; Deut. 17.6; 19.15).[77] Third, the fact that they are identified as witnesses could not help but remind the hearers of the other witnesses encountered to this point in the book which include: John, who has witnessed to the witness of Jesus (Rev. 1.2); Jesus, who is the faithful witness (1.5);[78] and Antipas, whom the resurrected Jesus describes as 'my faithful witness' who was put to death on account of his faith (2.13). Thus, these two witnesses stand in continuity with the witness of the community and her Lord. Neither should it be ignored that these two witnesses are called 'my' witnesses, underscoring further that they and their prophetic activity belong to God. Fourth, the activity of these witnesses is described as prophesying, a detail that emphasizes further the connection between witness and prophetic activity in the Apocalypse. Here it appears that the activity of witnessing and prophesying are synonymous. It is prophetic witness. The hearers would also be aware of the fact that to this point in the book, prophetic language has been used previously with reference to 'the words of this prophecy' to which John gives careful witness (1.3) and the commission John receives to 'prophesy again' (10.11). Clearly, John would not be far from the minds of the hearers when mention is made of the prophetic work of these witnesses. Fifth, the duration of their prophetic activity is the exact length of the period of time during which 'the outer court of the temple', 'the Holy City', will be trampled by the nations (11.2). However, instead of hearing this temporal period described as forty-two months, it now appears as 1,260 days. While it is possible that such a designation is no more than literary variation,[79] such a conclusion might be a bit premature. For while both designations, forty-two months and 1,260 days, are used but twice each in the book, it is significant that the former is

---

[76] On this cf. the discussion by Kovacs and Rowland, *Revelation*, pp. 126-30.
[77] Resseguie, *The Revelation of John*, p. 162.
[78] Osborne, *Revelation*, pp. 419-20.
[79] Smalley, *The Revelation to John*, p. 276.

found in contexts describing opposition to God (13.5) or his people (11.2), while the latter is found in contexts describing the activity of God's people (11.2) or their divine protection (12.6).[80] Perhaps these designations suggest that the same period of time looks different depending upon one's perspective, whether the perspective of God or his opponents. At any rate, it would hardly be lost on the hearers that the trampling of God's people by the nations will not be experienced passively, but will be met during the entire period with active prophesying.[81] Sixth, the attire of these two witnesses, sackcloth, might well remind the hearers of the fact that in the OT sackcloth was a sign of mourning (Isa. 22.12; Jer. 4.8; Jon. 3.6-8). Here, it may suggest something of the nature of the two witnesses' prophesying. Specifically, the wearing of sackcloth may indicate that their message is closely related to the mourning that results from divine judgment, while at the same time holding out the hope that those who hear their prophetic message might respond with repentance.[82]

Verse 4 – As the description of these two prophetic witnesses continues to unfold, the parallels between the stunning vision of the resurrected Jesus with which John's vision begins (1.9-20) and the description of these two prophetic witnesses would be apparent to the hearers. For just as in the inaugural vision of Jesus, where the hearers encounter an incredible convergence of intertexts from a variety of OT locations, so they immediately detect in the description of these two prophetic witnesses a similar intertextual convergence.[83] There are olive trees and lampstands from Zechariah, the ability to bring forth fire and close the heavens like Elijah, the ability to turn water into blood and bring other plagues like Moses, and incredibly a death, resurrection, and ascension like that of Jesus. As the description unfolds, the remarkable convergence that emerges would make the role and function of these two prophetic witnesses all the more significant and meaningful to the hearers. After learning of their mission in v. 3, the hearers discover more about their

---

[80] Bauckham, who makes a similar point, refers to the 42 months as 'the Beast's time' and the 1,260 days as 'the church's time' (*The Climax of Prophecy*, p. 402).

[81] Resseguie, *The Revelation of John*, p. 162.

[82] Cf. esp. Waddell, *The Spirit in the Book of Revelation*, p. 173.

[83] Koester, *Revelation and the End of All Things*, p. 108.

identity in John's next words, 'These are the two olive trees and the two lampstands which are before the Lord of the earth'. As with the revelation of the mystery of the seven stars and the seven lampstands in 1.20, so now the hearers are assisted in their interpretation by divine guidance as the divine voice makes this identification. Significantly, both αἱ δύο ἐλαῖαι ('the two olive trees') and αἱ δύο λυξνίαι ('the two lampstands') are articular constructions suggesting that they are well known entities to the hearers.[84] There should be little doubt as to why these items would be known to the hearers for their mention could not help but remind them of Zechariah 4, where two olive trees stand on either side of the central lampstand with seven lamps on it. In the elaborate description that follows, Zechariah learns that two branches of the two olive trees are connected to the golden pipes through which the oil is poured out. Both the word of the Lord spoken to Zerubbabel, 'Not by might, nor by power, but by my Spirit says the Lord of Hosts' (Zech. 4.6), and the identification of these two olive branches as 'the two anointed who stand before the face of the whole earth' in 4.14 would invariably assist the hearers in discerning that in these two prophetic witnesses of which the Apocalypse speaks they are encountering Spirit anointed prophets. This identity is further underscored when the hearers learn that these witnesses are described as the two lampstands (Rev. 11.4). Clearly, the lampstand imagery from Zechariah 4 would inform the hearers' understanding of the two lampstands in Rev. 11.4 as closely associated with the activity of the Holy Spirit. However, the hearers would also be aware of other dimensions of the meaning of the lampstands. For earlier, the resurrected Jesus identifies the seven golden lampstands in the midst of which he stands as the seven churches whom he will prophetically address (1.20). In the inaugural vision of heaven, the hearers learn that the seven lampstands of fire located before the throne are the Seven Spirits of God (4.5). Such previous associations indicate that in the description of the two prophetic witnesses in 11.4 there is a convergence of the churches, the Spirit, and these witnesses. Thus, there would appear to be in these two prophetic witnesses a convergence of the activity of Jesus, the prophetic ministry of the Holy Spirit, and the ongoing witness of the churches.

---

[84] Allo, *L'Apocalypse*, p. 132.

Given these associations and the way in which the temple, the altar, the worshippers, the outer court of the temple, and the Holy City have reference to the believing community in 11.1-2, perhaps it would not be going too far to suggest that the hearers would likely see in these two figures reference to the prophetic, Spirit inspired ministry of the church itself.[85] The mention of the witnesses' location as 'standing before the Lord of the earth' underscores their close proximity to God, being in the same location as the Spirit herself, indicating that the actions and words of these witnesses are to be identified with the actions and words of God himself. It may also occur to the hearers that just as the words of the resurrected Jesus are coterminous with those of the Spirit, so the words and deeds of these witnesses are as well.[86]

Verse 5 – As the description of the two witnesses continues the hearers learn of their divine protection for 'if anyone desires to harm them, fire comes out of their mouth and consumes their enemies'. The grammatical form, which the construction 'if anyone desires to harm' takes, is known in Greek grammar as a first class conditional clause, which places emphasis upon the reality of this condition.[87] Thus, this grammatical construction underscores the certainty that there will be those who desire to harm these two witnesses. However, the certainty of this potential opposition will be met with the certainty of the witnesses' divine protection. These words could not help but remind the hearers of Yahweh's words to Jeremiah, 'I will make my words in your mouth a fire and these people the wood, and it will consume them' (LXX Jer. 5.14). Likewise, they would remind them of Elijah, who called down fire from heaven against the messengers of Ahaziah (2 Kgs 1.10).[88] This imagery would also call to the hearers' memory the fire that plays such a major role in some of the judgments that accompany the trumpet blasts described earlier in the Apocalypse (Rev. 8.6-11). It might even remind them of the power ascribed to the mouth of the resur-

---

[85] Beale, *The Book of Revelation*, p. 573.

[86] On all this cf. the helpful discussion by Waddell, *The Spirit in the Book of Revelation*, pp. 174-77, who aptly concludes, 'As a priesthood of all believers, the church offers worship to God, but as a prophethood of all believers, the church bears the witness of God to the world' (pp. 176-77).

[87] Aune, *Revelation 6-16*, p. 613.

[88] Beasley-Murray, *Revelation*, p. 184.

rected Jesus, which has coming out of it a double-edged sword (1.16) with which he makes war (2.16).[89] The fact that the fire in 11.5 is described as coming from the mouth, not mouths, of these two witnesses underscores the fact that they work in unison and cannot be identified separately from one another. In point of fact, the emerging description of these two prophetic witnesses suggests that they be understood almost as prophetic identical twins.[90] The essential nature of the witnesses' mission and the extent of their protection are further underscored by the next words which the hearers encounter, 'And if any desire to harm them, in this manner it is necessary for them to die'. The idea of divine necessity, conveyed by the word δεῖ ('it is necessary'), reiterates the fact that their protection is of divine origin. Together with the previous words in v. 5a, this statement about the necessity of the death of the witnesses' opponents would add to the hearers' expectations that any opposition would meet with a fiery end.

Verse 6 – In addition to divine protection offered against the malicious desires of their opponents, the two prophetic witnesses have prophetic authority. The authority is spoken of in ways fraught with meaning owing to the numerous ways it intersects with OT thought and events. For any hearer would immediately recognize the authority of these witnesses as being in keeping with the authority exercised by some of Israel's most famous prophetic figures. Like Elijah, who caused a drought (1 Kgs 17.1) and Jesus who shuts and no one can open (Rev. 3.7), 'these have the authority to shut the heaven in order that no rain would fall during the days of their prophecy'. It may not be lost on the hearers that the period of the witnesses' prophesying, 1,260 days, is in early Christian tradition, equivalent to the length of the drought (three and a half years) associated with Elijah (Jas 5.17). This extraordinary authority is present during the entire period of their ministry of prophetic witness. Thus, their witness appears to take place during the entire time the nations trample the Holy Place (Rev. 11.2). Like Moses, who struck the water in Egypt causing it to turn into blood (Exod. 7.17) and caused all kinds of plagues to fall upon Egypt (1 Sam. 4.8), these

---

[89] Sweet, *Revelation*, p. 185.
[90] C.H. Giblin, 'Revelation 11.1-13: Its Form, Function, and Textual Integration', *NTS* 30 (1984), p. 442.

prophetic witnesses 'have authority over the waters to turn them into blood and to strike the earth with every plague as often as they desire'. It would perhaps not go unnoticed that while the desire [θέλει ('desires')] of the witnesses' enemies would be frustrated, the accomplishment of the desire [θελήσωσιν ('they desire')] of the witnesses would know no limits, an idea present in the teaching of Jesus in the FG (Jn 15.7).

Perhaps by this point it is beginning to dawn on the hearers that these two prophetic witnesses, who stand in continuity with the prophetic witness of the churches, are endowed with prophetic powers that appear to be the accumulation of all the prophets who have preceded them. In them, the prophetic anointing by the Spirit seems to be complete. Their prophetic message of repentance is demonstrated at every point by the power of the Spirit.

Verse 7 – The hearers now learn that the two witnesses' impenetrable invincibility has its limits after all, 'and when they completed their witness, the beast the one who comes up out of the Abyss will make war against them and will overcome them and will kill them'. These words are filled with significance for the hearers. The temporal indicator 'when' is a subtle hint that the activity of the two witnesses is about to change, a change made clear by the fuller statement, 'and when they completed their witness'. The word τελέσωσιν ('completed') conveys a number of things to the hearers. The fact their witness can be spoken of as completed suggests that while their prophetic activity comes to an end it does not come to an end until their witness has been fully offered. In this regard, the witness and activity of the two witnesses mirrors that of Jesus, for Johannine hearers would be well aware that when Jesus completes the work of his Father on the cross he himself says τετέλεσται ('It is completed').[91] This similarity would be all the more significant given the fact that Jesus' faithful witness is tied so closely to his own death in the Apocalypse. Thus, the end of the prophetic witness offered by these two witnesses does not come prematurely, but only when it has been completed. It is at this moment that a significant figure is introduced into the book, 'the beast'. While this is the first mention of the beast in the Apocalypse, the articular construction indicates that the hearers are already familiar with

---

[91] Wall, *Revelation*, p. 145.

him.[92] Perhaps this familiarity is based upon the resemblance this figure bears to the fourth beast of Dan. 7.7-23, when this terrible, dreadful, exceedingly strong beast made war with the saints and overcame them (7.21).[93] The origin of the beast mentioned in Rev. 11.7 is revealed by the modifying phrase 'the one coming up out of the Abyss', indicating the place from which he comes not the moment of his ascent from the Abyss.[94] The beast's activity is described in three-fold form, with each verb appearing in the future tense, perhaps pointing to the beast's opposition to the one who stands behind their witness, as the beast 'makes war against them and overcomes them and kills them'. Upon first encountering the imagery of war in this verse, the hearers could hardly avoid thinking of the way in which the fourth beast of Daniel 7 made war against the saints, thus indicating something of the beast's evil nature. Significantly, when war imagery has previously appeared in the Apocalypse it has been in connection with other figures that also come up out of the Abyss (Rev. 9.7, 9) and increasingly will be associated with the activity of the beast and those identified with him (12.7, 17; 13.7; 16.14; 17.14; 19.19; 20.8). In fact, the beast will come to be thought of by the inhabitants of the earth as invincible in war (13.4). At the same time, the hearers also know of one capable of making war with the sword of his mouth (2.16); one who will ultimately judge and make war in righteousness (19.11). In 11.7 the making of war against the two witnesses by the beast is clarified by the second phrase in this triology, 'and he will overcome them'. Such a statement might be a startling one to the hearers owing to the fact that nowhere to this point in the Apocalypse have the opponents of God's people ever been spoken of as overcoming. In point of fact, only Jesus (3.21; 5.5) and those faithful to him (2.7, 11, 17, 26; 3.5, 12, 21) have been spoken of as overcoming.[95] Thus, to learn that the beast overcomes these two witnesses threatens to subvert the hearers' understanding of what it means to overcome. The third part of the triology makes even clearer the nature of the warring in which the beast engages, 'and he will kill them'. This

---

[92] Resseguie, *The Revelation of John*, p. 163.

[93] Prigent, *L'Apocalypse*, p. 273.

[94] Smalley, *The Revelation to John*, p. 280.

[95] The lone exception is the rider on the white horse in 6.2, who as noted earlier bears a striking resemblance to Jesus.

statement would remind the hearers yet again of 'my faithful witness Antipas' who was killed in Pergamum owing to his allegiance to Jesus. Although their witness is complete before their death, the hearers might well suspect that their death is intimately connected to their witness, being an essential part of it.

Verse 8 – The beast's opposition to these two witnesses is not limited to making war upon them during their lifetimes but extends to the humiliation of denying them burial. For the hearers learn 'and their body upon the streets of the Great City lies'. Since proper burial was a near universally recognized right in antiquity, its denial was associated with absolute disregard for decency and would convey utter disrespect and hatred for those so affected.[96] In this case, it is an indication of the beast's hatred for and opposition to Jesus and his witnesses. Perhaps Johannine hearers would think of the contrast between these actions and Pilate's desire to have the bodies of Jesus and those crucified with him buried before the Sabbath began in the FG (Jn 19.31-37).[97] The fact that their corpses are spoken of in the singular as πτῶμα αὐτῶν ('their body') reinforces the singularity of their witness.[98] The location where these dreadful events take place is conveyed to the hearers in almost kaleidoscopic[99] or psychedelic fashion, for the description of this Great City changes before the eyes and ears of the hearers with each new detail. The way in which a number of details converge at this point is reminiscent of the intertextual convergence already encountered in the description of the two witnesses here in this chapter and that of the resurrected Jesus (Rev. 1.12-20). While the Great City could be thought of as any great city of antiquity, in the Apocalypse this designation will come to be identified more and more with Babylon (16.19; 17.18; 18.10, 16, 18, 19, 21). If the hearers are initially puzzled by mention of the Great City, they find immediate divine assistance offered for its interpretation when they are told, 'which is called pneumatically Sodom and Egypt, where also their Lord was crucified'. Just as Jesus offered the hearers assistance in their pneumatic interpretation earlier, so here they find similar divine assis-

---

[96] Beasley-Murray, *Revelation*, p. 186.
[97] Aune, *Revelation 6-16*, pp. 617-18.
[98] Osborne, *Revelation*, p. 426 n. 9.
[99] Koester, *Revelation and the End of All Things*, p. 110.

tance. The Greek text makes explicit the nature of this interpretative assistance for this city is called Sodom and Egypt πνευματικῶς ('pneumatically'). While this term is often translated as 'figuratively', 'metaphorically', 'symbolically', or even 'spiritually', none of these translations are adequate for they fail to bring out the fact that this identification comes by means of the Spirit.[100] Just as Jesus has earlier revealed the identity of the seven lampstands and the seven stars (1.20), so now the Spirit reveals the identity of this Great City. The hearers learn that this city is called Sodom, in that it is a place of moral degradation,[101] one so filled with vice that normal standards of hospitality and decency are turned upside down, as the refusal of burial for the two witnesses indicates. It is also called Egypt in that it too is a place of tyranny,[102] associated with slavery and oppression, as the making of war by the Beast upon the two witnesses indicates. This Great City is also 'the place where their Lord was crucified'. While this phrase is sometimes taken as an indicator that reference is here made to the literal Jerusalem, such an interpretive conclusion appears to be a bit premature.[103] On the one hand, this reference is a clear indication that the two witnesses experienced the same fate as Jesus, perhaps suggesting that any city in which his faithful witnesses die is the same city in which he was crucified. The fact that Jesus is here called Lord for the first time in the Apocalypse underscores this identification.[104] On the other hand, the hearers will learn that just as this Great City is the place where their Lord was crucified, the Great City will also be identified as the place in which 'the blood of the prophets and the saints is found and of all those who have been slain upon the earth' (18.24).[105]

Verse 9 – Apparently this city morphs into a globally diverse cosmopolitan center for 'some out of the peoples and tribes and

---

[100] Waddell (*The Spirit in the Book of Revelation*, p. 183) notes, 'In the center of the Apocalypse, John places the story of the two witnesses, and in the center of this brief narrative, John describes the spiritual insight of the church discerning the reality of the great city ... Like John, who was in the Spirit when he saw his visions, the church must also see Spiritually'.

[101] Metzger, *Breaking the Code*, p. 70.

[102] Caird, *The Revelation of St. John*, p. 138.

[103] Resseguie, *The Revelation of John*, p. 164.

[104] Pattemore, *The People of God in the Apocalypse*, p. 164.

[105] Kiddle, *The Revelation of St. John*, pp. 185-86.

tongues and nations see their body for three and one-half days'. Three aspects of this description are worthy of note. First, the composition of those who see the body of the two witnesses reveal that this city has representatives of those from all cities, suggesting that the Great City which is called Sodom and Egypt and is identified as the place where their Lord was crucified, is now viewed as having inhabitants from all over the world in its constituency. It is the global city. Second, the hearers would likely be struck by the similarity between the constituency of this city and 'the peoples and nations and tongues and kings' to which John is earlier commissioned to prophesy (10.11), providing yet another link between the prophetic witness of these two witnesses and that of John. Third, the fact that individuals from all over the world see their body in the streets indicates something of the extent of the humiliation inflicted upon these two witnesses, for it is complete and absolute. They are humiliated before the entire world! But even as their humiliation is seen to be complete, the hearers learn that their humiliation has its limits for their body will be exposed for three and one-half days. This temporal designation would alert the hearers to the fact that this humiliation is of limited duration, especially when compared to the duration of their prophetic witness, 1,260 days. But perhaps more importantly, this period of time could not help but remind the hearers of the length of time of Jesus' own death.[106] As such, this designation would make clear to the hearers the fact that this time of humiliation is drawing to a close. Before v. 9 concludes, the hearers learn of the reason for the location of the witnesses' body in the streets of the Great City; for those who see them 'would not allow their bodies to be placed into a tomb'.

Verse 10 – Not only this, but 'the ones who dwell upon the earth will rejoice over them and will celebrate and will send gifts to one another, because of these two prophets who tormented the ones who dwell upon the earth'. The words of this verse reveal a chiastic structure that places a certain emphasis upon 'the ones who dwell upon the earth', as reference to these individuals stands both at the beginning and the end of this sentence. These individuals are known to the hearers as those upon whom the great time of testing will come (3.10), as those responsible for the slaughter of the souls

---

[106] Bauckham, *The Climax of Prophecy*, p. 280.

under the altar (6.10), and those to whom the three woes have been spoken (8.13). As such, they are perceived as the opponents of God and his people. As had the actions of the beast, so the activities of these individuals are described in triple form. It is first said that these individuals 'will rejoice over them'. Johannine hearers might see in this rejoicing over the two slain witnesses a fulfillment of Jesus' words in the FG that upon his departure, whilst his disciples mourn 'the world will rejoice' (Jn 16.20). The phrase ἐπ' αὐτοῖς ('over them'), makes clear that this rejoicing, like the denial of burial, will be at the expense of these witnesses. The second activity described, 'and they will celebrate', underscores the disgraceful nature of their response and will be set in contrast to proper celebration mentioned later in the book (cf. Rev. 12.12; 18.20). The third component in this triology of disgrace is the fact that those who dwell upon the earth will be so overjoyed at the death of these two witnesses that they will actually mark this event as a festival complete with the exchanging of gifts![107] All this rejoicing is owing to the death of 'these two prophets who tormented those who dwell upon the earth'. This phrase, which describes the cause for their activity, is not simply a superfluous restatement of the obvious but conveys new information to the hearers. Though the prophetic nature of their witness has been inferred, here for the first time these two witnesses are clearly called 'prophets', confirming for the hearers that their activity is Spirit inspired prophetic witness. It is also revealed that their prophetic activity, like that of certain judgments before them (9.5), involved tormenting those to whom they prophesied, underscoring yet again their status as servants of God. The hearers would likely understand such a statement as having reference to the whole of their prophetic activity.

Verse 11 – Already alerted to the fact that this humiliation has its limits (v. 9), the hearers now learn that this period has come to an end as they encounter the phrase 'and after three and a half days'. The fact that this temporal designation would remind the hearers of the period of time during which Jesus was dead, no doubt, increases their level of anticipation and expectancy. They are not to be disappointed, for immediately following these words the hearers learn that 'a Spirit of Life out of God entered in them, and

---

[107] Wall, *Revelation*, p. 147.

they stood upon their feet, and great fear fell upon those beholding them'. Significantly, the Spirit who now enters the two prophets is the same Spirit who has inspired their prophetic activity. If the opposition of the beast lasts beyond their life so does the activity of the Spirit, in and through them. Thus, there is continuity with what has preceded in that this same Spirit, who stands before the throne, who speaks the words that Jesus speaks, in whom John experiences the visions of this book, who inspires prophetic witness, now enters into these two prophets. There is also progression of development in that the Spirit's relationship to God is now expressed in still another way, she is the Spirit ἐκ ('out of') God. The Spirit, who earlier is located in close proximity to God, is now said to have her origin in God, an idea familiar to the hearers from the FG (Jn 14.17). Such language about the 'Spirit of Life' could hardly help but remind the hearers of Ezek. 37.5 (LXX), where the identical phrase, πνεῦμα ζωῆς ('spirit' or 'breath of life'), also occurs. Consequently, this Spirit, who has her origin in God, is now intimately connected with the activity of the resurrection of these two prophets. The certainty of the witnesses' resurrection is also underscored by the next words the hearers encounter, ἔστησαν ἐπὶ τοὺς πόδας αὐτῶν ('they stood upon their feet'), for they are identical to those that occur in Ezekiel (37.10) as well. Perhaps there is in these words a subtle anticipation of the first resurrection, which will be introduced later in the Apocalypse (20.5-6).[108] At any rate, this extraordinary sight, the divine vindication and resurrection of the two prophets who experienced total and absolute humiliation at the hands of those who dwell upon the earth, results in great fear falling upon those who behold this. While it is possible to take this fear simply as the fear that results from a frightening experience, for several reasons such an interpretation does not here seem likely. First, Johannine hearers would know that a similar fear was experienced by those who behold Jesus walking on the water in the FG (Jn 6.19). Second, the participle τοὺς θεωροῦντας ('those beholding') comes from a verb that in the FG is often associated with divine signs or activity (John 2.23; 4.19; 6.2, 19, 40; 12.45; 14.19; 17.24; 20.14). Often, such usage reveals a deeper understanding that leads to initial or deeper faith in Jesus. That such a verbal form appears at this point in the Apoca-

---

[108] Beasley-Murray, *Revelation*, p. 187.

lypse (Rev. 11.11), suggests that the hearers would understand the fear experienced in a more positive sense. Third, later in this chapter there will be a clear equation drawn between those who fear God's name and those who worship him (11.18). In point of fact, this very equation comes to be stated more clearly as the book unfolds (14.7; 15.4; 19.5). It might not be going too far to say that the resurrection of these two prophets results in a reverential fear on the part of those who behold them. Thus, it would appear that the resurrection of these prophets would not be seen in isolation from the rest of their Spirit inspired prophetic ministry, but as a further vindication of it and its completion.

Verse 12 – However, before being allowed to take in the full implications of this amazing turn of events, the hearers' attention is directed to heaven with the words, 'And they heard a great voice saying to them, "Come up here". And they went up to heaven in a cloud, and their enemies beheld them'. Reminiscent of the voice John hears at the beginning of this section of the Apocalypse (4.1), these two witnesses are themselves invited up to heaven. Perhaps this identical invitation[109] serves as an inclusio with that in 4.1, suggesting that in one sense this section is coming to a close, or at least a pause. At the same time, the similarity between the invitation of 4.1 and that of 11.12 would once again point to the connection between John's own prophetic work and that of the two prophets. While the 'great voice' that speaks here is not identified, as was the one in 4.1, it clearly is a heavenly voice, being understood as the divine voice. The invitation to 'come up here' indicates that the mission of the two prophets is over and all that awaits them is to be in the heavenly presence of God, joining the souls under the altar and the innumerable crowd coming out of the Great Tribulation. No sooner was the invitation voiced than they went up to heaven in a cloud. The hearers would no doubt be struck by the parallel between the words of the resurrected Jesus that he will come with the clouds (1.7) and the fact that the witnesses go up in the cloud. Furthermore, just as every eye will see Jesus, even those who have pierced him, so their enemies behold the two prophets being taken up into heaven! The parallel between Jesus' own experience of death, resurrection, and ascension and that of these two prophets

---

[109] Aune, *Revelation 6-16*, p. 624.

would hardly be lost on the hearers, indicating that the prophetic ministry of the church stands in direct solidarity with that of their Lord. Just as he will be vindicated, so also those faithful prophetic witnesses will be as well.

Verse 13 – Hardly allowed to catch their collective breath the hearers are next told, 'And at that hour there was a great earthquake'. These words would convey several things to the hearers. First, the fact that the great earthquake takes place at the very hour the two prophets ascend to heaven indicates that there is a concrete connection between these two events, suggesting that the earthquake is part of their vindication and their witness. Second, since this is the second great earthquake encountered by the hearers, it is likely that this great earthquake would be understood in part in the light of the first one described. The hearers know that when the sixth seal was loosed, there was a great earthquake that was part of a cosmic cataclysm apparently designed to bring people to the worship of God (6.12). However, instead of drawing human beings to God, all stratum of humankind cried for the mountains and the rocks to fall upon them in order that they might hide from the face of the One who sits on the throne and the wrath of the Lamb (6.16). On this occasion, the hearers may anticipate a different outcome as the effects of the prophets' resurrection has already resulted in fear falling upon those that dwell upon the earth. Third, the hearers might well be struck by the fact that whereas time has been measured in terms of 42 months, 1,260 days, and 3½ days, it is now measured in terms of one hour, an indication that time itself is speeding ahead toward the end. The occurrence of this great earthquake has the result that 'a tenth of the city fell and 7,000 men died in the earthquake'. These two figures would immediately suggest to the hearers the limited nature of this judgment, for in OT imagery one-tenth was equated with the remnant that survives God's judgment (Isa. 6.13; Amos 5.3). Likewise, the number 7,000 is associated with the minority who are faithful to Yahweh (1 Kgs 19.18), which also signifies the remnant. However, in Rev. 11.13 these numbers have been reversed with the remnant being identified with the majority, the ninety per-cent, the 63,000 who survive, with only the minority perishing![110] Unlike the results of the previous great

---

[110] Koester, *Revelation and the End of All Things*, pp. 110-11.

earthquake, on this occasion 'the rest were fearful and gave glory to the God of heaven'. Clearly underscoring the idea of the remnant, those who survive the judgment of the great earthquake are described as 'the rest' (cf. esp. 9.20). The level of the fear experienced by these survivors is conveyed by the emphatic term ἔμφοβοι ('terrified'), continuing the theme of fear introduced in v. 11, though showing some progression and development. Here, fear is joined with giving glory, perhaps suggesting that the words fear, worship, giving glory, and repent function as synonyms in the Apocalypse.[111] Such connections will become increasingly obvious as the book unfolds (cf. esp. 14.7; 15.4; 16.9). In this act, the rest join with the four living creatures (4.9; 7.12), the twenty-four elders (4.11; 7.12), the myriads of angels (5.12), and every creature in the universe (5.13) in giving glory to God. The fact that this remnant comes from the pagan world is made clear by the phrase, 'the God of heaven', which was a well known Jewish expression used in communication with pagans.[112] Thus, the witness and vindication of the two prophetic witnesses results in the majority of those to whom they bore witness converting to the worship of the God of Israel. Perhaps this event parallels the connection between the 144,000 and the universal innumerable crowd encountered earlier in Revelation 7. Such an extraordinary story is an incredibly optimistic one and could not help but encourage the hearers that despite their circumstances the conversion of the nations awaits them.[113]

Verse 14 – Since the end of chapter nine the hearers have found themselves in a sort of limbo. For although they have been led to believe that the three woes earlier announced by the flying eagle are identified with the last three trumpet blasts (8.13), a fact confirmed at the conclusion of the fifth trumpet blast which is identified as the first woe (9.12), the long interlude devoted to prophetic witness in 10.1-11.13 has postponed the identification of the second woe. Thus, the words of 11.14, 'the second woe has departed; behold the third woe comes quickly', serves to jolt the hearers out of their preoccupation with the prophetic witness described most recently and direct their attention back to the events that accompany the blasting

---

[111] Caird, *The Revelation of St. John*, p. 140.
[112] Aune, *Revelation 6-16*, p. 629.
[113] Bauckham, *The Climax of Prophecy*, p. 283.

of the sixth trumpet, where one-third of humankind is killed by the three plagues of fire, smoke, and sulfur which issue forth from the mouths of the horses (9.13-21). At the same time, reflection upon the events that accompany the sixth trumpet would encourage the hearers to be mindful of the fact that such judgments did not result in the conversion of those who survive, for 'the rest of the men did not repent of the works of their hands' (9.20-21). The conversion of 'the rest' awaits the completion of the witness of the two prophets, which includes their humiliating death, resurrection, and ascension. Thus, by the time the sixth trumpet is identified as the second woe for the hearers, the memory of it has been softened by the turn of events that has lead to the conversion of the majority of those to whom the two prophets bore witness. Consequently, there is evidence that the woes themselves may be in the process of transformation. As noted earlier, such a move might already be present in the command John received not to write down what he heard when the seven thunders sounded (10.4). For if the increasing intensity of judgments held true from the seals (one-fourth) and trumpets (one-third) to that of the seven thunders, then the hearers might well have understood that the thunders would affect one-half of creation and humankind. Given all these associations, the announcement 'behold, the third woe comes quickly' would fill the hearers with even greater expectancy. At least three things are worthy of note. First, it is clear that the hearers would be anticipating the third and final woe, which at this point might be taken as a sign of the end itself. Second, the hints as to the transformation of the second woe would create an expectancy that the third and final woe might be transformed in even a greater way than the second. Third, the words ἔρχεται ταχύ ('comes quickly') would no doubt remind the hearers of the resurrected Jesus' own words ἔρχομαι ταχύ ('I come quickly') found on two earlier occasions both as threat (2.16) and promise (3.11). These same words will serve as a three-fold refrain near the book's conclusion (22.7, 12, 20) indicting something of their theological and eschatological significance. Perhaps the hearers would perceive some connection between the soon coming of the third woe and the soon coming of Jesus himself!

The Sounding of the Seventh Trumpet (11.15-19)
Verse 15 – At long last the seventh angel trumpeted. For the hearers, the blasting of this trumpet signals the advent of the third terri-

ble woe and the end of all things. And yet, rather than being accompanied by still more terrifying judgments the hearers discover that 'there were great voices in heaven saying, "The Kingdom of the World has become the Kingdom of our Lord and his Christ, and he will reign forever and ever"'. This radical divergence from the previous trumpet blast pattern indicates that the woes themselves are indeed being transformed. On this occasion, it appears that the third woe is transformed into the end itself, with the praise of God and the Lamb forming the scene's center. Though mention of a great voice speaking from heaven is not unusual in the Apocalypse, for the first and only time in the book mention is here made of great voices in heaven speaking.[114] Such a grammatical shift could not help but remind the hearers of the many great voices in heaven they have encountered previously in the book. Specifically, they are likely to think of the great voice of the extraordinary number of angels who worship the Lamb (5.11-12), the great voice of the innumerable crowd coming out of the Great Tribulation who praise God and the Lamb (7.11), and perhaps even the great voice that invites the two prophets to come up to heaven (11.12), though the latter appears to be a divine voice. At any rate, the hearers are likely made to think of these many voices that have previously been heard in the praise of God and the Lamb. If so, they are probably not surprised that what comes from these great voices is yet another hymn of praise. The primary focus of this hymn is revealed by the fact that both the subject of the first phrase and the verb of the second are forms of the same Greek word, βασιλεία ('kingdom') and βασιλεύσει ('reign'), respectively. This emphasis might best be conveyed by the translation, 'the kingdom/reign of this world has become the kingdom/reign of our Lord and his Christ, and he will reign forever and ever'. Mention of 'the kingdom of this world' would likely remind Johannine hearers of the words of Jesus in the FG, which make clear that his kingdom is not of this world (Jn 18.36), a world that has its own ruler (14.30), who has already been judged (16.11). As such, the fact that 'the kingdom of this world', which has stood in such opposition to God and the Lamb throughout the Apocalypse, 'has become the Kingdom of our Lord and his Christ' conveys a sense of finality. These words imply a fundamen-

---

[114] Smalley, *The Revelation to John*, p. 289.

tal transformation of 'the kingdom of this world'. Specifically, those who formerly owed their allegiance to the world now identify with 'our Lord and his Christ'. What has caused this remarkable transformation? The hearers may well suspect that this transformation is in some way connected to the witness of the two prophets, whose life, death, resurrection, and ascension result in the conversion of the majority that survives the great earthquake.[115] Thus, through their Spirit anointed witness, 'the kingdom of this world has become the Kingdom of our Lord and his Christ'. Something of the nature of this transformation is conveyed by the fact that, in contrast to 'the kingdom of this world', which would find itself temporally restricted to a certain period of time, 'the Kingdom of our Lord and his Christ' is one which knows no temporal limitations for 'he will reign forever and ever'! It may not be without significance that the verb βασιλεύσει ('reign') is a third person singular. While such a construction might cause the hearers to wonder whether this verb has reference to the activity of God or Christ, what they will soon discover is that in the Apocalypse the singularity of God and Jesus is emphasized. This becomes apparent in a couple of different ways. They are never the subjects of a plural verb, nor are plural pronouns used with reference to them. In point of fact, the hearers discover that a singular verb can be used where God and the Lamb serve as the subjects (21.22).[116] Thus, the hearers may be encountering this phenomenon for one of the first times with reference to the phrase, 'and he will reign forever and ever'. As such it appears that the Greek grammar is not sufficient to convey the theological reality of the identity of God and Jesus. Consequently, the breaking apart of the grammar conveys something of the depth of the theological reality here described.

Verse 16 – Before the hearers can take in the full implications of the hymn coming from the great voices in heaven, their attention is directed to figures with which they are by now quite familiar, the twenty-four elders seated upon their thrones before God. In keeping with their previous activity (4.10; 5.8, 14; 7.11) these elders once again 'fell upon their faces and worshipped God'. Their appearance

---

[115] M.L. Archer, '"And the Seventh Angel Trumpeted": A Literary Analysis of Revelation 11.15-19', ThM Thesis, Columbia Theological Seminary (2006), ch. 4.

[116] Bauckham, *The Climax of Prophecy*, pp. 139-40.

and activity here, which is reminiscent of their presence and activity around the throne in chapters four and five, where similarities between their hymn found in 11.16-18 and those found in Revelation 4-5 abound, may suggest that their mention serves as an inclusio of sorts,[117] perhaps being another indication that the end of the vision draws near. In addition, their appearance in 11.16 also reminds the hearers of the elders' heavenly appearance in 7.11, where they join with the angels and four living creatures in offering hymnic praise to God (7.12). Owing to the striking resemblance they bear to those who overcome and their previous consistent activity of praise, the elders' presence here would alert the hearers to the fact that additional songs of praise await. Their expectations are not disappointed for from the elders comes yet another hymn of praise which, along with its predecessor in 11.15, focuses almost exclusively upon the finality of God's accomplishments. This is apparent to the hearers by the way in which vocabulary familiar from earlier in the book is re-appropriated and joined with new elements that underscore the finality of the scene all the more.

Verse 17 – The hymn, which the hearers encounter from the twenty-four elders, reveals a three-part structure. It begins with thanksgiving, making it the only hymn of thanksgiving in the Apocalypse,[118] as the twenty-four elders say, 'We thank you, Lord, God, the All-Powerful One, the one who is and the one who was, because you have taken your great power and reigned'. The words of the twenty-four elders, like some of those which precede, take the hearers back to the throne room scene in 4.8, where the four living creatures address the One who sits on the throne as, 'Lord, God, the All-Powerful One, the one who is and the one who was and the one who comes'. Again the hearers may be tempted to take such similarities as an inclusio, serving as still another clue that this section (4.1-11.19) is coming to a close. Such similarities also provide a sense of continuity, as the hearers are reassured that the same God who is addressed in chapter four is the same God who is now addressed as the one who rules. However, on this occasion the threefold phrase 'the one who is and the one who was and the one who comes', which by now is familiar to the hearers (1.4, 8; 4.8) as a ref-

---

[117] Michaels, *Revelation*, p. 144.
[118] Archer, '"And the Seventh Angel Trumpeted"', ch. 4.

erence to God, stands as a two-fold phrase. For God is now referred to as 'the one who is and the one who was', with no reference made to 'the one who comes'. There can be little doubt that such a modification would underscore for the hearers the fact that God is no longer described as 'the one who comes' owing to the fact that he has already come![119] Thus, the words of the hymn found in v. 15 about God's reign are treated as a present reality. The reason for the elders' thanksgiving is made clear in the following phrase in v. 17, 'because you have taken your great power and have reigned'. The hearers are familiar with the way power is earlier ascribed to God by the twenty-four elders in the throne room scene (4.11), and by the angels around the throne, the four living creatures, and the twenty-four elders with the appearance of the innumerable crowd (7.12). Now they learn that God's 'great power' has been taken up by him and manifested in his rule. Such narrative movement implies that through his great power God has begun to reign in a way not yet seen.

Verse 18 – The second stanza of this hymn indicates something about the way in which God has taken up this great power with the words, 'and the nations were enraged and your rage has come'. By means of a clever play on words the hearers learn that the wrath of the nations is met by the wrath of God. For when the nations ὠργίσθησαν ('were enraged'), God's ὀργή ('rage' or 'wrath') came. Significantly, in the Apocalypse the verb is used only with reference to the nations (11.18) and the dragon (12.17), while the noun is reserved for the Lamb (6.16) and/or God (6.17; 14.10; 16.19; 19.15). Given the overall context of the Apocalypse, the enragement of the nations has reference to their (sometimes violent) opposition to God, most recently exemplified in the martyrdom of the two witnesses, while the rage or wrath of God has reference to the judgments inflicted upon those who oppose him, most recently exemplified in the earthquake that results in the conversion of those who survive.

In some ways the next words of the hymn both continue the thought of this second stanza while providing the transition to the third and final stanza, 'and the time to judge the dead (has come)'. On the one hand, the connection between the second stanza and

---

[119] Murphy, *Fallen is Babylon*, p. 271.

this phrase is revealed in part by the fact that they both seem to share the same verb, ἦλθεν ('has come'), which is present in the previous phrase while implied in this one. On the other hand, the hearers learn that 'the time to judge the dead' is a comprehensive phrase encompassing both the giving of rewards to God's servants and the destroying of those who destroy the earth. For this is a time 'to give the reward to your servants the prophets and to the saints and to those who fear your name'. Clearly, the giving of 'the reward' is a positive activity owing in part to the identity of those who are to receive it. Though this is the first mention of τὸν μισθὸν ('the reward') in the Apocalypse, Johannine hearers would be familiar with it owing to its meaning in the FG and in 2 John. In the former Jesus speaks of the reward that awaits those who enter into the missionary harvest (Jn 4.36), while in the latter the Elder can warn his readers not to lose that for which they have been working, but receive a full reward (2 Jn 8). The relationship between 'work' and 'reward' would likely suggest a close connection between the two ideas to the hearers of the Apocalypse. This connection between works and reward, would likely indicate that their understanding of 'reward' in 11.18 would be informed by the many places where reference has been made to works earlier in the book, especially Rev. 2.23 where the resurrected Jesus promises 'I will give to each of you according to your works'. As such, works and that which is given are closely associated with the one who overcomes (2.25), suggesting that in 11.18 'the reward' is a comprehensive term having reference to all those things promised to those who overcome.[120] The intimate nature of the connection between works and reward will be made clear later in the book (22.12). Thus again, it becomes clear that the troubling nature of rewards for some contemporary readers is not in keeping with the way in which works and rewards function in this book.[121] It is possible to take the identity of those to whom this reward is to be given as being comprised of two or three distinct groups, 'your servants the prophets and the saints and those who fear your name'. One of the implications of such an interpretation is that a distinction is being made between a

---

[120] Aune, *Revelation 6-16*, pp. 644-45.

[121] Apocalypse studies still await the kind of careful treatment on this topic that Matthean studies has received. Cf. B.B. Charette, *The Theme of Recompense in Matthew's Gospel* (JSNTS 79; Sheffield: JSOT Press, 1992).

special group of Johannine believers, designated as 'prophets', and the rest of the community, designated as 'saints' and 'those who fear your name'. It is even possible to take these words as evidence of a further subdivision of the community, with 'saints' having reference to Jewish believers, and 'those who fear your name' having reference to Gentile believers. However, such an interpretation fails to do full justice to the way in which the book itself seems to define these terms. The connection between servant and prophet is not only revealed in the construction of the Greek phrase τοῖς δούλοις σου τοῖς προφήταις ('to my servants the prophets'), but also in John's own person as he is both servant (1.1) and one who prophesies (10.11). The hearers also are familiar with this equation from a similar construction found in 10.7. 'Servants' will also be closely associated with, even identical to, 'those who fear him' in 19.5, while 'saints' will be intimately connected with 'prophets' in 16.6 and 18.24. In point of fact, it appears that these terms serve very much as synonyms in the Apocalypse suggesting that on this occasion they would strike the hearers as a comprehensive reference to the believing, witnessing, prophetic community to whom this book is addressed.[122] The comprehensive nature of these terms is underscored by the words the hearers next encounter, for though they appear to stand in continuity with what precedes they also appear to stand in a certain discontinuity. While the phrase τοὺς μικροὺς καὶ τοὺς μεγάλους ('the small and the great') makes reference to those on either end of the social scale from the insignificant to the mighty,[123] and will reappear in the Apocalypse with precisely this meaning (13.16; 19.5, 8; 20.12), these words would give the hearers pause given the fact that unlike the words which precede them these words appear in the accusative case rather than the dative case. This change of case serves to inform the hearers that the 'judging of the dead' will not be exhausted by the giving of the reward to 'your servants', as it introduces yet another group of individuals to be judged. Specifically, it is time 'to destroy those who destroy the earth'. Significantly, τοὺς διαφθείροντας ('those who destroy') stands in the accusative case, suggesting that just as the giving of the reward encompasses the insignificant to the mighty, so

---

[122] Smalley, *The Revelation to John*, p. 292.
[123] Smalley, *The Revelation to John*, p. 293.

the destroying of those who destroy the earth will as well. The nature of this destruction is revealed in part by the play on words between the compound verb διαφθεῖραι ('to destroy') and the object τοὺς διαφθείροντας ('those who destroy'), indicating that the judgment rendered would be appropriate to the crime. Such a phrase would perhaps remind the hearers of the numerous OT texts (Exod. 21.24; Lev. 24.20; Deut. 19.21; Judg. 1.7; 15.11; Ps. 7.14-16) where the *lex talionas* appears to be referenced.[124] Through a clever change of cases the hearers learn that the judging of the dead (genitive) includes both those who are worthy of the reward (dative) and those who will be destroyed (accusative).[125]

Verse 19 – With the words of the establishment of the reign of God and the judging of the dead ringing in their ears, the hearers now encounter the long awaited and long promised end of all things. And the words that they next encounter do not disappoint, for 'the temple of God in heaven was opened and his ark of the covenant was seen in the temple, and there came lightings and voices and thunders and an earthquake and great hail'. The reference to God's temple reminds the hearers of its occurrence in 11.1-2 revealing that these verses form an inclusio, indicating that the narrative of the two prophetic witnesses is enveloped by references to the temple and consequently stand together in some way.[126] The significant place of the temple in this phrase is indicated in part by the fact that its mention stands at both the beginning and the end of the phrase, underscoring the locations of his Ark of the Covenant. It is also significant that all the activity described in this verse either comes from God or is made possible by him, as the divine passives ἠνοίγη ('was opened') and ὤφθη ('was seen') reveal. The activity of God is further underscored by the way in which emphasis is placed upon the fact that this temple belongs to God, noted twice, as does the Ark of the Covenant. Both images convey the idea of the presence of God in ways that take the hearers back to the throne room scene of chapter four. The fact that God's temple is placed in heaven highlights these connections all the more. The eschatological significance of the opening of God's temple and the

---

[124] Murphy, *Fallen is Babylon*, p. 271.
[125] I am indebted to my colleague L.R. Martin for this insight.
[126] Archer, "'And the Seventh Angel Trumpeted'", ch. 4.

revelation of his Ark of the Covenant would hardly be lost on the hearers, for it would be quite difficult to imagine how God's presence could be more directly described. Grammatically, the phrase ἡ κιβωτὸς τῆς διαθήκης αὐτοῦ ('his Ark of the Covenant') can be rendered either as placing emphasis upon the fact that it is 'his' Ark, or emphasizing that it is 'his' covenant. However, it is not likely that the hearers would be tempted to choose between these distinct meanings. For while in this context a great deal of emphasis is placed upon the fact that both the temple and the Ark are God's, neither would it be ignored that this broader section (4.1-11.19) begins and ends with reference to God and his covenant faithfulness. The ark is clearly a sign of such faithfulness in 11.19, just as the rainbow around the throne is a sign of his covenant in 4.3. Thus, there can be little mistaking the significance of the words found in this verse, for at this point the hearers encounter the presence of the God who reigns, rewards, and destroys in all his covenant faithfulness. It is little wonder that the theophanic elements, first observed in the throne room scene (4.5) and again at the end of the opening of the seven seals in an intensified form (8.5), reappear in 11.19 with ever-increasing intensity. Their appearance here not only conveys something of God's very presence, but also signals the end of the seven trumpet blasts. The fact that the theophanic elements are described in the same order as in 4.5 is yet another indication of the way in which chapters four and eleven form an inclusio. The addition of 'great hail' to the theophanic elements is consistent with the relationship between the blasting of the trumpets and falling of hail upon the earth (8.7), and along with reference to the Ark would tie these signs to those associated with Sinai. The increasing intensity represented by the presence of great hail is yet another sign of progression throughout the book and the nearness of the end. Thus, the hearers find themselves in the very presence of God as the end of all things has come. And yet …

Redemptive History in Cosmic Perspective (12.1-14.20)

… the book continues! In point of fact, what the first-time hearers do not yet know is that they are only now at the book's halfway point! The words of this prophecy continue to unfold in new and ever more creative ways. What the hearers soon discover is that the next major section forms an interlude of sorts telling the story of God's people in cosmic perspective. As such, characters and themes introduced earlier, at times almost in passing, reappear in this section in much greater detail. The passage, which begins with a 'great sign in heaven' (12.1) and concludes with a 'great sign in heaven' (15.1), is followed by the last cycle of seven to appear in the book, when the angel having seven bowls of plagues appears and then pours out their contents in turn (15.1-16.21). Interestingly enough, the story line that leaves off in 11.19 converges in 15.1 with that found in 12.1-14.20. Thus, in this section the hearers experience even more of the Apocalypse in new dimensions.

Signs in Heaven: The Woman Clothed with the Sun and the Red Dragon (12.1-18)

Verse 1 – Despite apparently having come to the end of the vision, the hearers, amazingly enough, begin to encounter even more fantastic images in the next unexpected words that come from John's pen, 'and a great sign was seen in heaven'. Of course, any Johannine hearer would be aware of the significance of signs from their place of prominence in the FG, where they occur in order that its readers might (continue to) believe that 'Jesus is the Christ the Son of God and that in order that believing you might have eternal life in his name' (Jn 20.31). These signs, which function to lead people to initial or deeper belief, point beyond themselves to a more profound understanding of their significance, and come only from the hand of Jesus himself. Thus, the appearance of a 'great sign in heaven' would, at one and the same time, remind the hearers of the pregnant nature of signs in the FG and perhaps cause them to expect that this sign too is somehow connected to Jesus. Despite the discontinuity these words would represent to the hearers from the words that have preceded them, at least two aspects of the first phrase found in chapter 12 provide points of continuity with that which immediately precedes these words for the hearers. First, the term ὤφθη ('was seen') would remind the hearers of the first appearance of this specific form just one verse previous, where 'the Ark of his covenant in his temple' was seen (11.19). Second, the fact that this great sign is seen in heaven would remind the hearers of this previous verse as well, for heaven is apparently the location of God's Ark. Consequently, despite the fact that the initial words found in chapter 12 introduce the hearers to a mode of expression not yet encountered, signaling that the hearers are now entering a new phase in the Apocalypse, they also reassure the hearers that there is some continuity with that which precedes. The appearance of the word σημεῖον ('sign') would also perhaps remind the hearers of the fact that the transmission of the divine revelation experienced by John is described at the beginning of the book with the word ἐσήμανεν ('he showed'), which carries with it the idea of indicating the meaning of prophetic (Acts 11.28) and/or metaphorical (Jn 12.33; 18.32; 21.19) language. Thus, when the hearers finally encounter a 'great sign', they are prepared for the fact that its meaning will have a significance that transcends a literal or surface meaning.

The great sign that John sees in the heaven is 'a woman clothed with the sun, and the moon is under her feet and upon her head a crown of 12 stars, and having in the womb, and she cried being in travail and torment to give birth'. Even as the hearers are introduced to this great sign they are likely comparing this woman to the only other woman and the only other gigantic figure to appear to this point in the book. In comparison to 'Jezebel', the false prophetess who encourages sexual immorality and the eating of food sacrificed to idols, whose judgment awaits not only her but her children as well (Rev. 2.20-23), this woman is a picture of cosmic royalty, power, and promise. In comparison to the angel who stands with one foot on the sea and one foot on the earth, whose face is as the sun and feet are as pillars of fire (10.1-2), the woman clothed with the sun dwarfs him both in size and significance. Whereas the great angel of chapter 10 was clothed with the clouds and had a face that shone like the sun, the cosmic brilliance of this woman is indicated in part by the fact that she is clothed with the sun, which conveys a sense of magnificent radiance. This description and her location in heaven underscore her close proximity to God himself. The moon, which earlier in the Apocalypse was described as turning to blood (6.12) and being struck by an angel so that a third of it was darkened (8.12), is now said to be under the feet of this woman, conveying a sense of majesty and dominion. Perhaps it would not be lost on the hearers that the moon, an apparent object of idolatrous worship for many in the OT (Deut. 4.19; 17.3; 2 Kgs 23.5; Job 31.26; Jer. 8.2), is firmly under the feet of this spectacular woman. The στέφανος ('crown') upon her head serves to underscore her extraordinary faithfulness, as it does for many others mentioned to this point in the book (Rev. 2.10; 3.11; 4.4, 10). On this occasion the crown also reveals something else about her identity, for her crown is comprised of twelve stars. While it is possible that the hearers might take the twelve stars as representing the signs of the Zodiac, especially given the woman's location in the heaven,[1] such an interpretation does not prove convincing owing to several considerations. First, it is clear from Rev. 7.4-8 that the tribes of the sons of the reconstituted Israel, numbering twelve, are extraordinarily important, as 12,000 out of each tribe are sealed at God's command. Second, the hearers will later learn that the twelve tribes are so theologically important that the names of the twelve tribes of the sons of Israel will be inscribed on the twelve gates of the New Jerusalem (21.12-13). Third, it is quite likely that the hearers would not be unaware of the fact that equation between twelve stars and the twelve tribes is made already in Gen. 37.9, where in Joseph's dream the twelve stars clearly have reference to the sons of Jacob, from whom the twelve tribes come.[2] Thus, the emerging picture of this resplendent woman is one that ties her very closely to Israel and/or Zion.[3]

Verse 2 – But there is more, for she is pregnant, being very close to delivery, crying out in pain, laboring to give birth. The fact that this woman is pregnant conveys a sense of life and hope to the hearers; a promise that more is to come. That a woman such as this is described as pregnant could not help but generate a great expectancy as to the nature of the child to be born. For although the child is not identified at this point the hearers have little choice but to think that such a child has a special connection to heaven, the location of this woman, perhaps having a special connection with God himself! The agony of the childbirth would call to mind the words spoken to Eve regarding the pain of childbearing in Gen. 3.16. As such, there would at least be the hint that the child here described in Rev. 12.1 may be the fulfillment of the words spoken to Eve about her child of promise in Gen. 3.15, an idea made clearer later in Revelation 12. At the same time, the hearers would per-

---

[1] So Murphy, *Fallen is Babylon*, p. 278 and Aune, *Revelation 6-16*, p. 681 among others.
[2] Prigent, *L'Apocalypse de Saint Jean*, p. 287.
[3] Beale, *The Book of Revelation*, p. 626.

haps be reminded of the words of promise spoken to Israel and/or Zion in Isaiah (26.16-17; 54.1; 66.7-9) or in Micah (4.9-10). These associations aside, the hearers would be struck by the fact that in crying out [κράζει ('crying out')] this woman joins a number of other positive figures encountered in the book to this point, who also 'cry out' (Rev. 6.10; 7.2, 10; 10.3). The fact that she cries out with birth pangs indicates the origin of her cries. Combined with this is the fact that she is laboring greatly to give birth. In point of fact, her ordeal bears the marks of torment as she agonizes to give birth to this child, as the word used here to describe her agony, βασανίζω ('to torment'), has already been encountered by the hearers where it has reference to intense physical (9.5) and emotional (11.10) torment. Thus, the hearers are left with a sense of awe as they witness this cosmic event filled with such pathos and agony.

Verse 3 – Still pondering this incredible sight, the hearers encounter the term ὤφθη ('there was seen') for a third time in four verses. Alongside the great sign of the woman clothed with the sun is 'another sign in heaven'. With similar expectations that this sign, as its predecessor, is filled with deeper meaning, it would not be lost on the hearers that unlike the first sign, this sign is not referred to as a 'great' sign, perhaps suggesting its inferiority to the first 'great' sign. And yet, whilst this sign is not called 'great' it does describe a 'great' figure for the hearers learn, 'and behold a great red dragon having seven heads and ten horns and upon his heads seven diadems and his tail swept the third of the stars of heaven and cast them upon the earth'. If the first sign conveys a sense of awe owing to its majestic imagery, the second sign conveys a sense of dread owing to its ominous nature! The appearance of this great red dragon at this point would likely convey a number of things to the hearers. First, it introduces them to a figure who is remarkably prominent in the narrative that follows, the term δράκον ('dragon' or 'serpent') appearing some thirteen times (12.3, 4, 7 [2x], 9, 13, 16, 17; 13.2, 4, 11; 16.13; 20.2). Second, it would hardly be lost on the hearers that in the OT this term has reference to many of the opponents of God and his people. These include Nebuchadrezzar (Jer. 51.34), Pharaoh (Ezek. 29.3; 32.3-16), Egypt (Ps. 74.14), Assyria and Babylon (Isa. 27.1). Thus, the hearers would likely take the mention of the great red dragon in Rev. 12.3 as having reference to the archetypal enemy of God. Third, something of the ominous nature of this dragon is conveyed to the hearers by means of its color. For while it is possible that there is no particular significance to the fact that the dragon is red,[4] it is more likely that this color would remind the hearers of the rider upon the red horse who was given authority to take peace from the earth in order that individuals might slaughter one another. Ominously, this rider is given a great sword (6.4). Owing to this association, the hearers would no doubt discern in this dragon, a sinister figure[5] capable of murderous activity[6] and more. Fourth, something of the magnitude of the dragon's importance is conveyed by the word μέγας ('great'), a term often encountered in the Apocalypse to distinguish the importance of one thing or event from others of the same kind. In addition to the great voices noted earlier, reference is made to a great sword (6.4), earthquake (6.12, 13; 11.13), day of wrath (6.17), tribulation (7.14), mountain of fire (8.8), star (8.10), furnace (9.2), the Euphrates (9.14), the city (11.8), fear (11.11), and hail (11.19). Thus, the description 'great red dragon' underscores the enormity of this dragon over against all others. Its great nature is made even clearer by the fact that he has 'seven heads and ten horns and upon his heads seven diadems'. Both the physical attributes of the great red dragon and their corresponding numbers are of immense significance. His seven heads indicate that the dragon's rule is perceived as complete and universal.[7] His ten horns, reminiscent of those of the fourth beast in Dan. 7.7, would convey something of the dragon's extraordinary strength and power. Not only this, but upon his seven heads were seven διαδήματα ('diadems'). In contrast to the woman clothed with the sun, whose crown was comprised of twelve stars, the dragon has seven diadems. In their first encounter with this term in the Apocalypse, the hearers would immediately understand its significance, for the diadem was widely recognized as the sign of royalty especially amongst the Persian kings. Thus, the wearing of the seven diadems corresponds to the number of the

---

[4] So Ladd, *Revelation*, p. 168.

[5] C. Hauret, 'Éve transfigurée: de la Genèse à l'Apocalypse', *Revue d'histoire et de philosophie religieuses*, 59 (1979), p. 330.

[6] Allo, *L'Apocalypse*, p. 159.

[7] Gause (*Revelation*, p. 164) makes the intriguing suggestion that, at the same time that it designates completion, this number may hint that his kingdoms have run their course.

dragon's heads, seven, suggesting once again the complete and universal nature of the dragon's rule. Whilst there may be a temptation on the hearers' part to identify the dragon's kingdoms based upon the number of his heads and horns,[8] at this point perhaps these details' immediate impact would be to focus the hearers' attention upon the brief pageantry of human history which these details embody.[9]

Verse 4 – But the description of the powerful reign of the dragon is not limited to reference to his heads, horns, and diadems, for the hearers are also given an accounting of his power in action as 'his tail swept the third of the stars of heaven and cast them upon the earth'. With these words the hearers are reminded of the cosmic nature of this dragon, who, like the woman clothed with the sun, is located in heaven. The power of his tail is reminiscent of the power of the tails of the creatures that come forth during the blasting of the fifth and sixth trumpets, who are capable of inflicting great pain and suffering (Rev. 9.10, 19). In 12.4 the tail is clearly a sign of the dragon's great and terrible power. Reminiscent of 'the little horn' of Dan. 8.10, this dragon too demonstrates his contemptuous power by casting down some of the stars of the heavenly host. But going beyond the little horn of Daniel 8, the dragon's tail of Revelation sweeps a third of the stars of heaven and casts them unto the earth. The sheer magnitude of such an action is unbelievably difficult to fathom! Yet, the enormity of this power is tempered for the hearers. For they know that just as the extent of the damage resulting from the first four trumpet blasts was limited to one-third of the objects afflicted, so the power of the great red dragon is limited in nature, for he does not sweep away all the stars, just a third of them! The hearers next learn that this ominous figure 'stood before the woman who was about to give birth, in order that when she gave birth he might devour her child'. This act makes clear the sinister and murderous intentions of the dragon, who prepares himself, even before the birth of the woman's child, to devour the child immediately upon delivery. Perhaps this depiction of the dragon would remind the hearers of Jesus' words about the devil in the FG,

---

[8] As, for example, did Joachim and countless others after him, cf. esp. Kovacs and Rowland, *Revelation*, pp. 140-42.

[9] Gause, *Revelation*, p. 164.

who is described as a murderer from the beginning (Jn 8.44). The imagery of the dragon would, no doubt, also remind the hearers of the prophetic words of Gen. 3.15-16 spoken to Eve with regard to the enmity she and her seed will experience with the serpent. Having already been made aware of the woman's travail in childbirth, they now learn of the enmity between the dragon and the child, imagery reminiscent of the words, 'he will bruise your head, you will bruise his heel'. The fact that the term δράκον ('dragon' or 'serpent') often appears in the LXX to translate serpent would not be lost on the hearers, further underscoring the connection with Gen. 3.15-16. The intention of the great red dragon that he might καταφάγῃ ('consume' or 'devour') the child is amazingly similar to the actions of King Nebuchadrezzar, who κατέφαγέν ('devoured') Zion, swallowing her like a δράκον ('dragon' or 'serpent') (Jer. 51.34 – LXX 28.34).[10] Thus, the connection between Judah and this child, on the one hand, and Nebuchadrezzar and the dragon, on the other hand, could hardly be clearer. As this cosmic standoff comes into full focus, the hearers could not help but wonder as to its outcome. Will the dragon be successful in his intentions to devour the 'heavenly' child? Or, will the woman clothed with the sun prevail?

Verse 5 – But the hearers are not left long to wonder about the outcome of this confrontation for they immediately learn that the woman clothed with the sun 'bore a son, a male child, who is about to shepherd all the nations with a rod of iron'. Not only would the hearers be taken by the rapidity with which the birth of the child is described, but also be struck by the fact that the child is called both 'son' and 'male child'. This unique reference to the child would convey several ideas to the hearers. First, the description of the child as 'son' would have a special significance to Johannine hearers owing to the fact that to this point in the Johannine literature the term υἱος ('son') is used exclusively for Jesus, while believers are called 'children'. Thus, reference to this child as son suggests to the hearers that this child is none other than Jesus, the unique Son of God. Such an identification fits nicely with the heavenly origin of this child, born of the woman clothed with the sun. Second, while the occurrence of the term ἄρσεν ('male child') could be taken as unnecessary redundancy, owing to the etymological meaning of the

---

[10] Prigent, *L'Apocalypse de Saint Jean*, p. 296.

term as something like 'that which discharges sperm',[11] it is possible that the hearers would see in its appearance here an additional reference to the discussion of the enmity between the seed of the serpent and the seed of Eve in Gen. 3.15 and in particular that this male child is the very seed who will bruise the head of the serpent. Third, the term ἄρσεν ('male child') may also remind the hearers of Isa. 66.7 where this very term is used with reference to the unrealistically quick delivery there described. After the tension filled standoff between the woman and the dragon, this detail would not likely go unnoticed by the hearers. Fourth, this double reference to the child would quite naturally underscore the importance of this child, placing unusual emphasis upon his birth. The child is further identified as the one 'who is about to shepherd all nations with a rod of iron'. This description is reminiscent of the resurrected Jesus' promise to those who overcome that 'I will give to him authority over the nations and he will shepherd them with a rod of iron' (Rev. 2.27). That this authority is his to give is made clear later in 7.17 where it is said, 'and the lamb in the midst of the throne will shepherd them'. In the words of 12.5 the hearers are introduced to a phrase, 'all nations', which will appear later in the book both as the objects of the fornication and sorcery of Babylon the Great (14.8; 18.3, 23), on the one hand, and those destined to worship the Lord God Almighty (15.4), on the other hand. The fact that this male child is described as 'about to shepherd all nations' may be an implicit continuation of the idea that this seed will bruise the head of the serpent. In addition to what the hearers learn about this son, they also learn more about the woman who gives birth, for despite the fact that she experiences the vulnerability of pregnancy combined with the menacing presence of the great red dragon, she courageously gives birth to this son, in the very face of the dragon[12] and his hostile intents. As the identity of the child becomes clearer and clearer to the hearers it slowly begins to dawn on them that this woman who bore such a striking resemblance to Eve and Israel/Zion, the mother of the messiah, has clearly morphed into the mother of Jesus. Such a discovery would be of special significance

---

[11] J.B. Bauer, 'ἄρσεν', *EDNT*, I, p. 158.

[12] J.A. Schroder, 'Revelation 12: Female Figures and Figures of Evil', *Word and Witness* 15 (1995), p. 181.

for Johannine hearers owing to the strategic role the mother of Jesus plays in the FG. Though she is never named there, referred to simply as the mother of Jesus, she is present near the beginning of Jesus' ministry being a catalyst in the performance of his first sign (Jn 2.1-12) and found near the Gospel's end at the foot of the cross (19.25-27). It is as though in the emerging image of the woman clothed with the sun that the promises regarding the messianic seed given to Eve, Israel, and Mary converge in this one image.

With thoughts of the mother of Jesus still in their minds, the hearers encounter more astonishing words, 'and her child was snatched up to God and to his throne'. Several things would strike the hearers as significant about this statement. First, the hearers might be a bit surprised to learn that at some point the location of the events described have shifted from heaven to earth, as the child is now described as being snatched up to God and his throne. Such an unexpected shift may well serve to inform the hearers that the cosmic events described in heaven in the first few verses of chapter 12 are not without significance upon earth. Rather there appears to be a symbiotic connection between the events described in the heavens and those that take place on earth. Second, the hearers would also likely be struck by the role attributed to God in this sentence. On the one hand, God and his throne technically are the objects to which the child is snatched. On the other hand, the passive voice verb ἡρπάσθη ('was snatched up') indicates that God himself is the one who snatches up the child. Thus, in this significant verse God is the one who snatches up the child and the one to whom the child is snatched. The appearance of this word would likely remind Johannine hearers of its many negative occurrences in the FG where it is used to describe the attempts of the crowd to make Jesus king (Jn 6.15), the wolf's attempt to attack the flock (10.12), and any hostile attempt to remove believers from the hand of Jesus (10.28) and/or the Father (10.29). The certain activity of God stands in stark contrast to other attempts to snatch Jesus and or his followers. Third, the depiction of the snatching up of 'her child' immediately after his birth might be taken to suggest Jesus is seen here simply as a passive infant Messiah. However, such an interpretation ultimately fails to convince. For, outside of this chapter there is no interest in the infancy of Jesus in the whole of the Johannine literature. To insist that the image here described must focus exclusively on the infancy of Jesus, to the exclusion of the rest of his life and ministry, would appear to be overly restrictive. Neither is the depiction of Jesus' life and ministry as a single moment out of keeping with the FG, for as is well known Jn 1.14 describes Jesus' life and ministry in precisely this way. Given the way in which the mother of Jesus frames his entire ministry in the FG, from the first sign to the cross, the reference to 'her child' in Rev. 12.5 might well signal for the hearers Jesus' entire life and ministry in the single moment here described. The depiction of the child being snatched up to God and his throne would also remind the hearers of the resurrected Jesus' promise to those who overcome to sit with him on his throne just as he has overcome and sits with the Father on his throne (3.21)! Clearly, the way to the throne is to be a faithful witness who overcomes. For the hearers, the child being snatched up to God's throne could not possibly exclude his faithful witness, his atoning life and death. Thus, the description of the snatching up of the child for the hearers would likely be understood to encompass the entire life, ministry, death, and resurrection of Jesus.[13] With this, it is now clear that whereas John was successful in devouring the book (10.9, 10) and the fire from the mouths of the two witnesses was successful in devouring those who oppose them (11.5), the great red dragon is unsuccessful in his attempt to devour the child. For the woman clothed with the sun did indeed give birth to him in the very face of the dragon, and God himself has protected the child from the dragon.

Verse 6 – Incredible as it is, the activity of the woman clothed with the sun is not confined to giving birth to the male child. For after giving birth to her child, and apparently witnessing his being snatched up to God and his throne, the hearers learn, 'and the woman fled into the wilderness, where she has there a place having been prepared from God, in order that there they might nourish her 1,260 days'. A number of ideas converge in these remarkable words. The description of her activity of fleeing into the wilderness indicates once again the close connection that exists between this woman and Israel, whose own time in the wilderness and her divine provisions would be well known to the hearers. Yet, these connections are now informed by the fact that reference is made to this

---

[13] Beale, *The Book of Revelation*, p. 639.

Israel after the birth and snatching up of her son is complete. Such a chronology suggests that the woman clothed with the sun, who has shown remarkable similarities to Eve, Israel, and the mother of Jesus, now shows remarkable similarities to the reconstituted Israel, the church to which John writes. It is not as though the woman simply morphs in psychedelic fashion into the church with no connection to her previous depictions. Rather, the woman who now resembles the church is informed by all her previous depictions. In brief, the divine activity present in the lives of Eve, Israel, and the mother of Jesus finds its fulfillment or culmination in the church. The depiction of the woman as fleeing into the wilderness not only reveals that she is an active participant in the events described, not a passive observer, but also reminds the hearers that the events depicted on the cosmic stage in Revelation 12 are related symbiotically to those that take place on earth. Mention of the woman's flight into the wilderness immediately conveys to the hearers that her time there will be one of provision and protection, owing in part to the fact that the wilderness often functioned in precisely this fashion in the OT (Exod. 15.22-17.7; 1 Kgs 19.1-18; and Hos. 2.14-15). Such suspicions on the hearer's part are confirmed by the very next words, 'where she has there a place having been prepared from God'. Throughout the FG, the wilderness functions as a place of witness (Jn 1.23), salvific healing (3.14), provision (6.31, 49), and protection (11.54).[14] Consequently, for Johannine hearers to discover that God has prepared a place for the woman in the wilderness would not be all that surprising but rather would be in keeping with Johannine attitudes toward the wilderness. The perfect participle ἡτοιμασμένον ('having been prepared') suggests that the place had been prepared by God at some point in the past for this very time, an idea found earlier in the Apocalypse where both locusts (Rev. 9.7) and angels (9.15) have been prepared for specific tasks at specific times. The hearers might also find in this word an anticipation of the fulfillment of Jesus' eschatological words to the disciples in the FG, 'I go to prepare a place for you and if I go I will also prepare a place for you' (Jn 14.2-3). While the place prepared for the woman is not the room in the Father's house, it does anticipate the

---

[14] In Jn 11.54 Jesus no longer walks openly among the Jews but departs for the country near the wilderness.

fulfillment of such a promise. In the divine preparation of this place, it becomes clear that God is active, not only in the snatching up of the male child, but also in the life of the woman. The purpose of the woman's fleeing is made clear in the ἵνα ('in order that') clause with which v. 6 concludes, 'in order that there they might nourish her for 1,260 days'. As Israel before her, this woman is to receive nourishment whilst she is in the wilderness. As such, the hearers might expect this nourishment to have a divine origin, especially since God has prepared this place for her. While the verb τρέφωσιν ('they might nourish') might conceivably be translated as 'he might nourish' owing to the indefinite character of the construction,[15] in any case, the divine origin of the nourishment is made clear by the way in which a variety of creatures and creation itself (agents of God) are involved in ministering to this woman in Rev. 12.13-17. The third person plural form of the verb in 12.6 might anticipate that which is to follow. Interestingly enough, this same word appears in the LXX version of 1 Kgs 18.13 to describe the divine provisions of bread and water made for Elijah.[16] Significantly, the hearers learn that the woman will be nourished in the wilderness for 1,260 days, the exact length of time the two witnesses will prophesy before a hostile world (11.3). If there is reason for the hearers to think that the woman clothed with the sun has morphed into the church at this point, this chronological detail confirms their pneumatic discernment. As such, their expectations with regard to the woman's time in the wilderness will not only include nourishment, but protection from hostility as she renders her own faithful witness.

Verses 7-8 – At this point the hearers might well expect a narration of the dragon pursuing the woman into the wilderness, as it would appear that she fled there owing to the presence of the great red dragon in the first place. However, their attention is suddenly directed not to the wilderness but back to heaven with the words, 'And there was war in heaven, Michael and his angels made war against the dragon'. While the hearers' expectation of conflict is not disappointed, the conflict is played out in heaven rather than on earth! Perhaps this discovery would cause the hearers to realize that

---

[15] Aune, *Revelation 6-16*, p. 653; BDF §130.
[16] Smalley, *The Revelation to John*, p. 321.

to this point the great red dragon has not been described as actually being located upon the earth. Rather, at last mention he was an ominous sign in the heavens, awaiting the birth of the child! Thus, to learn of the great red dragon's presence in heaven may suggest to the hearers that the story line of 12.1-6 is being temporarily suspended, a not uncommon occurrence in the Apocalypse. Normally when this happens the hearers find that they have access to more information when the story line continues. On this occasion what they learn about is a war in heaven. Such a discovery is, no doubt, startling owing to the fact that God's sovereignty in heaven to this point in the book has been absolutely certain. For this reason war in heaven would be as disconcerting as it is unexpected. What would account for such a war? Perhaps the hearers would think it the result of the male child having been snatched up to God, with the great red dragon having gone up to heaven to make war against him there owing to the fact that the dragon's intentions to consume the child have been frustrated by God himself. Yet, there is no cosmic showdown between the male child, who is about to shepherd the nations with a rod of iron, and the great red dragon. If the hearers expect a war between the one who is prepared to make war on the church in Pergamum with the double-edged sword in his mouth (2.16) and the dragon they are disappointed. In point of fact, in this war, the initiation of which does not necessarily seem to be attributed to the dragon, Michael and his angels figure prominently. In other words, if this war is deemed to be an attack of the dragon on the male child, the dragon, despite his cosmic strength, does not even merit the attention of the male child, but that of Michael and his angels. The mention of Michael at this point would both draw attention to his close relationship with God, as one who stands with him and fights (Dan. 10.21), and point attention toward the people of God, as Michael was widely regarded as the protector of Israel, God's people (Dan. 10.13; 12.1).[17] Though Michael is not called an angel in Rev. 12.7, the fact that angels are attributed to him underscores the fact that he is an authoritative figure, who would likely be understood by the hearers as warring on behalf of God (and the male child) and on behalf of God's people. But what is the nature of this war and how is it to be understood? Its results, described in

---

[17] Koester, *Revelation and the End of All Things*, p. 120.

12.8-12, suggest that it encompasses the whole of redemptive history as one moment. For, as will be discovered, this war is intimately related to the dragon being cast out of heaven, the coming of the

Figure 11
The Woman Clothed with the Sun
(*Hortus Deliciarum of Herrad*)

salvation, power, and kingdom of God, the coming of the authority of his Christ, and the overcoming of the dragon by the brothers through the blood of the Lamb and the word of their testimony. However, at this point, the focus of attention is upon the war itself.

For the hearers learn both that Michael and his angels wage war upon the dragon and that 'the dragon and his angels warred' as well. Yet, despite the troubling prospect of a war in heaven, its outcome is never in doubt for Michael and his angels are introduced first to the hearers, perhaps indicating their superior position, and when the dragon and his angels are introduced as making war it is immediately observed that 'he was not strong (enough) nor was their place found any longer in heaven'. When the hearers learn that the dragon was not ἴσχυσεν ('strong' or 'mighty'), perhaps they would see here the contrast between the dragon who was not strong, on the one hand, and the Lamb (5.12) and God (7.12) to whom ἰσχὺν ('strength' or 'might') is ascribed, on the other hand. Not only this, but the hearers might also be aware of the contrast between the dragon, who is not strong (enough), and the two ἰσχυρὸν ('strong' or 'mighty') angels whom they have encountered earlier (5.2; 10.1). Not only does the war with Michael reveal that the dragon is not strong enough to contend with him but also that the place he and his angels formerly had in heaven has been lost. In fact, the phrase 'nor was their place found any longer in heaven' suggests that their place has all but been forgotten owing to the war fought and lost with Michael. If the great red dragon was 'another sign in heaven' (v. 3), his locale is no longer heaven for he has no place there any longer.

Verse 9 – If the hearers wonder where the dragon has gone they learn very quickly, 'And he was cast down, the great dragon, the ancient serpent, the one called Devil and Satan, the one who deceives the whole inhabited world, he was cast down to the earth, and his angels were cast down with him'. Two major ideas are conveyed to the hearers in this verse. First, there is an emphatic description of the casting down of the dragon and those with him. The word translated 'cast down', the only verb occurring in this verse, appears not one but three times. In the Greek text the term ἐβλήθη ('was cast down') is the first word (after 'and') that the hearers encounter in the verse, occurring just before 'the great dragon', and is encountered again after 'the one who deceives the whole inhabited world'. Thus, this word stands as an inclusio around the names given to the dragon, indicating that he is the very one who had been cast down! Perhaps the description of the dragon being cast down would be informed for Johannine hearers by the words of Jesus who, when speaking of his own glorification (upon the cross) says in Jn 12.31, 'Now is judgment of this world, now the ruler of this world has been cast out' and those found in 16.11 where Jesus says, 'for the ruler of this world has been judged'. These words, along with those of Rev. 12.5, which narrate the snatching up of the child to God's throne, signify that in the events here described reference is being made to the implications of the salvific work of the Lamb,[18] an idea that will become even clearer in the following hymn (12.10-11). The fact that each occurrence of the verb 'was cast down' appears in the passive voice indicates that the casting down of the dragon is from start to finish divine action.[19] Second, in this context of the dragon's humiliating defeat the hearers discover his full identity. Having knowledge of his ominous power, murderous intentions, location in heaven, participation in war in heaven, and his subsequent being cast down, the hearers are now exposed to a somewhat comprehensive listing of his names and titles. From this list they discover that some of their earlier suspicions with regard to the great red dragon's identity were sound. Mention of the great dragon at the beginning of the list provides continuity that the figure earlier described is identical to the one now mentioned. As the hearers encounter the next title, 'the ancient serpent', it would be next to impossible for them not to think of the Genesis story (Gen. 3.1-7), where the serpent tempts Adam and Eve with eating from the fruit of the Tree of Life, fruit which was forbidden to them by God. It would not appear to be going too far to suggest that the serpent of which the hearers would think when hearing the words 'the ancient serpent' would be the serpent of Genesis 3. Nor would the correlation between the dragon's intention to devour the woman's child at birth and the enmity between the serpent and Eve's seed be lost on the hearers. He is the ancient serpent, the liar, and murderer from of old. Not only is he the ancient serpent, but he is also 'called Devil and Satan, the one who deceives the whole inhabited world'. When the hearers encounter the phrase 'the one called' perhaps they think of the last recent occurrence of the word 'called' (Rev. 11.8), where the great city 'is called pneumatically Sodom and Egypt'. If so, then there may be an

---

[18] Bauckham, *The Climax of Prophecy*, p. 186.
[19] Aune, *Revelation 6-16*, p. 695.

expectancy that these titles are pneumatically discerned as well. Johannine hearers would be aware that Jesus has identified the Devil as a murderer from the beginning and as one of whom it is said lying is his native tongue (Jn 8.44). In addition, they know that 'the one who commits sin is of the Devil, for the Devil sins from the beginning' (1 Jn 3.8). The antipathy between the Son of God and the Devil is made clear in that the former was manifested in order that he might destroy the works of the latter (1 Jn 3.9). In the Apocalypse, the hearers earlier encountered mention of the Devil in Rev. 2.10, where the resurrected Jesus tells the church in Smyrna, 'Behold, the Devil is about to cast some of you into prison in order that he might test you. Be faithful unto death and I will give you the crown of life'. Thus, the words of 12.9 make clear that the Devil, who poses such a threat to the church, and the great red dragon are identical. Consequently, when the church is 'faithful unto death' it too is understood to be withstanding the onslaught of the dragon. Joined to the name Devil in 12.9 is Satan. For Johannine hearers the term Satan is well known from the fact that in the FG Satan entered Judas just before this disciple goes out into the night (Jn 13.27). It probably does not surprise the hearers that in the Apocalypse this sinister figure is especially associated with Jewish opposition to the church, the synagogue of Satan (Rev. 2.9; 3.9), the powerful presence of Satan (2.13), and the ominous nature of his 'deep things' (2.24). For the great dragon to be identified as identical to Satan concretizes further for the hearers the nature of the dragon's activity and power. Nor is the final title in this series, 'the one who deceives the whole inhabited world', without significance. For Johannine hearers the phrase ὁ πλανῶν ('the one who deceives') is informed by its use especially with regard to those who would deceive themselves (Jn 7.47; 1 Jn 1.8) or others (Jn 7.12; 1 Jn 2.26; 3.7). The lone appearance of this term in the Apocalypse to this point occurs in Rev. 2.20 with reference to the false prophetess (called 'Jezebel' by Jesus), who 'teaches and deceives my servants to commit sexual immorality and to eat food sacrificed to idols'. Remarkably, in this survey of Johannine usage this verb is used exclusively to describe human agents who deceive themselves or others, as is the noun πλάνος ('deceiver') in 2 Jn 7. While 1 Jn 4.6 reveals the connection between 'the spirit of deception' and those who do not confess Jesus, here, for the first time, it becomes clear to Johannine hearers that the agent of deception *par excellence* is the great dragon. He is the one who stands behind all the human agents of deception. And when the churches oppose deception, they oppose the great dragon himself. This impressive cacophony of titles and names could well overwhelm the hearers as they reflect upon this remarkable convergence. Yet, it is this very creature, this very opponent who has been described as being cast down, and is now described as being 'cast down to the earth'. With this, the hearers are reminded of the woman's location in the wilderness and the fact that for the first time the dragon is described as being present, not in the heaven but on the earth. At the same time, they are reminded of the fact that despite the dragon's strength he is not strong enough! For he will forever be thought of as 'cast down' whenever his names or titles appear from this point forward! In addition to the dragon being cast down to the earth, those over whom he exercises authority, his angels, are also cast down to earth. The implications are clear; to stand with the dragon is to be cast down oneself. The hearers are assured that there is no future for them with the dragon.

Verse 10 – Immediately following the revelation of the dragon's full identity the hearers are greeted with another hymn of praise. This hymn is prefaced by and attributed to an anonymous voice in heaven as John says, 'And I heard a great voice in heaven saying'. By this point the hearers have encountered many 'great voices' in the book and have learned that anonymous voices from heaven, whether singular or plural, are authoritative with the mode of delivery being perfectly suited to the message attributed to the voice(s). In point of fact, the hearers' most recent encounter with 'great voices' in heaven, which introduce a hymn of praise and celebration found in 11.15, is remarkably similar to what is found in 12.10. For in the words to follow the hearers learn that in some ways the hymn of 12.10-12 expands upon that found in 11.15! Such a realization dawns upon them as they hear the first words of this hymn, 'Now has come the salvation and the power and the Kingdom of our God and the authority of his Christ'. In these words is a convergence of significant terms, themes, and emphases found at various places to this point throughout the book, as well as an expansion of that which has precedeed in 11.15. Like its first occurrence (7.10), the attribution of salvation to God in praise conveys a sense of finality, focusing upon salvation in its most comprehensive, eschatological sense. The fact that the entire hymn begins in 12.10 with the word Ἄρτι ('now') further underscores this sense of finality. Neither is the attribution of power in praise without precedent in the Apocalypse, for both God (4.11; 7.12; 11.17) and the Lamb (5.12) receive such. Its occurrence here would perhaps remind the hearers of the way this term has earlier highlighted God's creative and redemptive power. The third element in this trilogy of praise, 'the Kingdom of our God', would convey at least two things to the hearers. First, it would provide a direct link back to 11.15 where 'the kingdom of the world has become the Kingdom of our Lord', and, as other dimensions of chapter 12, would underscore for the hearers that what they are encountering in this and the following two chapters is a more expansive and detailed revelation of that disclosed in the more concise and compact chapter 11. Second, the hearers would be reminded of the close connection that exists between 'the Kingdom of God' and the Johannine believers, for they are themselves 'a kingdom of priests' to God' (1.6; 5.10), indicating that the coming of the salvation, power, and Kingdom of God is not unrelated to the believers as his priestly kingdom. Just as in 11.15 where the words 'and of his Christ' closely follow 'the kingdom of the world has become the Kingdom of our Lord', so here the words 'the salvation and the power and the Kingdom of our God' are closely followed by 'and the authority of his Christ'. Such a statement underscores the intimate relationship between God and his Christ, not only by placing them in close proximity to one another, but also by making clear that the authority of his Christ is authority derived from God, for he is again described as 'his Christ' and is attributed authority in relationship to salvation, power, and the Kingdom. Reference to the authority of Christ has already been made in 2.26, where the resurrected Jesus promised those who overcome in Thyatira, 'and I will give to him authority over the nations'. No doubt the hearers would take the words of 12.10 as evidence that Jesus does indeed have such authority.

The reason that these words of praise can be spoken with such absolute certainty is 'because the accuser of our brothers has been cast down, the one who accuses them before our God day and night'. This language reveals several things to the hearers. First, there appears to be a close connection between the coming of salvation, power, and the Kingdom of our God and the casting down of the great red dragon owing in part to the fact that these words are introduced by the word ὅτι ('because').[20] Second, it is clear that in this phrase the great red dragon and the accuser of the brothers is one and the same. Third, Johannine hearers would perhaps be aware of the fact that while Jesus does not bring an accusation before the Father against those who hoped in Moses instead of believing in him, Moses himself brings the accusation, owing to their unbelief (Jn 5.45). Fourth, the hearers might take comfort in the fact that Jesus himself faced the false accusation of the Jews before Pilate (18.29). Fifth, in contrast to the four living creatures who praise God day and night with the hymn recorded in Rev. 4.8 ('Holy, holy, holy ...') and those coming out of the great tribulation who serve God day and night (7.15), this individual is before our God accusing the brothers day and night (12.10). Yet, the continual work of the accuser of the brothers before our God has come to an end; he has been cast down from heaven! Such is indeed cause for rejoicing and is clearly connected to the coming of 'the salvation and the power and the Kingdom of our God and the authority of his Christ'. Though the accuser will no doubt continue to bring accusations against the brothers on earth, as 12.10 will reveal, his days of accusations in heaven are over!

Verse 11 – As this hymn of praise continues the connection between the coming of the Kingdom of our God, the casting down of the accuser of the brothers, and the active witness of those who overcome is made clear in the words: 'And they overcame him on account of the blood of the Lamb and on account of the word of their witness and they did not love their life unto death'. The antecedent of αὐτοί ('they') is τῶν ἀδελφῶν ('the brothers') making clear that those who have overcome are the very ones whom the accuser has constantly accused before God. But whereas the accuser of the brothers has been cast down to earth, these individuals have overcome him. For the hearers there could be little doubt that the individuals described in 12.11 are heirs to the promises given by the resurrected Jesus to those who overcome in the seven prophetic messages to the seven churches in Revelation 2-3 (2.7, 11, 17, 26; 3.5, 12, 21). As these words are heard, it becomes even clearer to

---

[20] Smalley, *The Revelation to John*, p. 326.

the hearers that the one with whom the seven churches contend in chapters 2 and 3 is none other than 'the accuser of our brothers, the great dragon, the ancient serpent, the one called Devil and Satan, the deceiver of the whole inhabited world'. Yet, this formidable foe has been overcome! The hymn attributes their having overcome to two sources, indicated by the appearance of the double διά ('on account of'), which precedes both 'the blood of the Lamb' and 'the word of their testimony'. First, the hearers are reminded that the victory of their brothers is made possible by the 'blood of the Lamb', an idea that has appeared on three earlier occasions in the book. In 1.5 they learned that the blood of the Lamb loosened them from their sins and made them a kingdom of priests to God; in 5.9 that the Lamb by means of his slaughter has purchased in his blood for God out of every tribe and tongue and people and nation a kingdom of priests who will reign upon the earth; and in 7.14 that those coming out of the great tribulation have washed their robes making them white in the blood of the Lamb and are now before the throne of God serving him day and night in his temple. The relationship between the blood of the Lamb and the Kingdom of priests is clear, as is the fact that the blood of the Lamb makes the overcoming possible. His blood looses sin, his blood purchases men and women, his blood makes white! There could be no overcoming without the blood of the one who himself overcame (3.21). Second, the hymn also attributes their overcoming the accuser to 'the word of their testimony'. For hearers of the Apocalypse such a statement would evoke a matrix of imagery for they have previously learned of the close relationship that exists between faithful witness and Jesus (1.5; 3.14), faithful witness and death (1.5; 2.13; 3.14; 6.9; 11.9), and John's witness, the word of God and the witness of Jesus (1.2, 9). Thus, to learn that these conquerors have overcome by the word of their testimony likely conveys the idea that these individuals, like their Lord, have given the ultimate faithful witness by following him in death. That their witness is rooted and grounded in his own, that it stands in direct continuity with the word of God and John's own witness would not be lost on any of them. It is, therefore, made exceedingly clear that their witness is inextricably bound up with him.[21] The last line of this stanza, 'and they loved

---

[21] As Caird (*The Revelation of St. John*, p. 157) aptly notes, 'in his story theirs

not their life unto death', makes explicit these many connections and pushes this imagery even further, for the connection between loving one's life and the laying down of life is a rich one for Johannine hearers. Johannine hearers know Jesus as the model of love for he is the Good Shepherd who lays down his life for his sheep (Jn 10.11-17), a reality acknowledged in 1 Jn 3.16. They know of Jesus' warning that the one who loves his life in this world will lose it whereas the one who hates it will guard it unto eternal life (Jn 12.25). Despite Peter's professed willingness to lay down his life for Jesus (13.37), they know how hard such a desire is to live out (13.38). Other words, no doubt, ringing in the hearers' ears are those of Jesus that there is no greater love than this that one would lay down his life for his friend (15.13). In point of fact, love itself is identified with Jesus' act of laying down his life for believers, who, as a result, are obligated to lay down their lives for the brothers (1 Jn 3.16). Thus, for the hearers there would be a convergence of thoughts and ideas in the words of Rev. 12.11, 'and they loved not their life unto death'. Structurally, these words confirm those that precede them in v. 11. Their overcoming is modeled in and made possible by Jesus, to whose faithful witness unto death they themselves have witnessed in their own life and death (Rev. 2.10; 11.3-13). Their overcoming is indeed on account of the blood of the Lamb and on account of the word of their testimony. It may not be insignificant that the term ψυχὴν ('life') is found in the singular, reminiscent of the reference to the 'body' of the two witnesses in 11.8, perhaps underscoring the communal nature of their witness and overcoming.

Verse 12 – The implications of that described in the first two stanzas are made clear in the final stanza of this hymn:

> On account of this,
> Rejoice, heavens and those who dwell in them.
> Woe to the earth and the sea
> because the Devil has come down to you
> having great anger
> knowing that he has little time.

---

was already written'.

The first two words of this stanza, διὰ τοῦτο ('on account of this'), would call the hearers' attention to all that has precedeed in the first two stanzas. Owing to the coming of salvation, power, the Kingdom of our God, the authority of his Christ, the casting down of the accuser of the brothers, and the testimony with regard to the overcoming of 'the brothers', the call goes out both to heaven and to the earth and sea. To the heavens and those who dwell in them there is the command to rejoice, conveyed by the imperative εὐφραίνεσθε ('rejoice'). The objects to whom this command is directed, 'the heavens and those who dwell in them', indicates to the hearers a most comprehensive audience. For not only is this the only place in the Apocalypse where the plural form 'heavens' occurs, but the phrase, 'those who dwell in them', would also remind the hearers of the many groups they have earlier encountered in the book numbering in the tens of thousands and beyond! Such a command reminds especially of the throne room scenes in chapters 4 and 5 colored by the specificity of those who follow, for example the souls under the altar, various angelic figures, and the two witnesses among others. Most recently, 'the heavens and those who dwell in them' would include those who witnessed the casting down of the red dragon (12.7-9) and those who have overcome him (12.11). Perhaps the hearers would also see in this command to rejoice a clear divine response to those who rejoiced over the death of the two prophetic witnesses in 11.10. Significantly, the verb σκηνόω ('dwell') is reserved in the FG for the Word (Jn 1.14) and in the Apocalypse for God and those who dwell with him in heaven (Rev. 7.15; 12.12; 13.6; 21.3). While the heavens and those who dwell in them are commanded to rejoice, the earth and the sea receive a warning that comes in the form of a woe. While at first it might appear to the hearers that this is the long awaited third woe, promised initially as part of the warning about the three woes in 8.13 (cf. also 9.12 and 11.14), it soon becomes clear that those woes signified events directed to an unbelieving world that come directly or indirectly from God himself. This woe appears to be directed to the believing community and is the result of the Devil being cast down. While mention of the earth and the sea nicely balances the earlier mention of the heavens and those who dwell in them, their appearance here may also anticipate the fact that as the story continues to unfold, two beasts will emerge from both the sea (13.1) and the earth (13.11). The warning of the woe is clearly tied to the fact that 'the Devil has come down to you having great anger, knowing that he has little time'. Just as the command to rejoice grows out of that which precedes in vv. 10-11, so the warning of the woe does as well. It is owing to the fact that he has lost his place in heaven, being cast down to the earth, that the Devil has come down with great anger. The hearers would hardly miss the emphasis of these words for in the Greek text they begin and end with a form of the verb 'has'. Translated very literally, 'having great anger, knowing that little time he has'. While the preceding verses suggest that his anger is the result of having lost his place and being cast down from heaven, the last words in the hymn indicate that his anger is because 'he knows that he has little time'. Perhaps it is not without significance that the word καιρός ('time') occurs five times in the Apocalypse with this reference standing in the middle, while the first and last references stand in inclusio fashion in the words, 'for the time is near' (1.3; 22.10). Clearly, the phrase, 'he has little time', would be understood as eschatologically conditioned, indicating that the loss of his place in heaven is the beginning of the end. The great red dragon has great anger, but he has little time.

Verse 13 – The hearers next discover that the two story lines found in 12.1-6 and 12.7-12 converge nicely in v. 13 in the words, 'And when the dragon saw that he had been cast down to the earth, he persecuted the woman who had given birth to the male child'. These words provide a sense of continuity and progression for the hearers in several ways. First, not only do these words fulfill the hearers' expectation created in vv. 1-6 that the red dragon would pursue the woman clothed with the sun, but it also builds on the knowledge of the story of his having been cast down to earth out of heaven. Second, the dragon's realization of his loss of place is clearly identified as part of the rationale for his actions, again suggesting a symbiotic connection between his war in heaven and persecution of the woman on earth. Third, though not explicitly present in vv. 7-12, the woman clothed with the sun reappears in the story in connection with the great red dragon. Fourth, upon learning that the dragon 'persecuted the woman who had given birth to the male child', Johannine hearers would no doubt be struck by the fact that not only was Jesus himself persecuted by the Jews in the FG (Jn 5.16; 15.20), but also his prediction that if the world 'persecuted me, they will persecute you as well' (15.20). Fifth, such associations, along with the reappearance of the woman who gave birth to the male child, would be added confirmation for the hearers that this woman now looks remarkably like the church,[22] the transformed Israel. As such, her persecution by the dragon would be very much at home with how Johannine believers understood the implications of following their Lord. The mention of 'the male child' at the end of 12.13 makes all the more explicit the central role he plays in the conflict between the dragon and the woman.

Verse 14 – But before the hearers can focus upon the nature of the dragon's persecution of the woman they learn, 'two wings of a great eagle were given to the woman, in order that she might fly into the wilderness into her place, where she is nourished in that place a time and times and half a time from the face of the serpent'. These words pick up directly on those heard earlier in 12.6. Common to the verses is the idea that the woman goes into the wilderness, that the wilderness is a place prepared for her, and that it is a place of nourishment for a specific period of time. In 12.14, the hearers learn that the woman's flight is actually accomplished by divine means. The divine passive ἐδόθησαν ('were given') stands first in the Greek sentence followed by 'to the woman', underscoring the fact that her means of flight is divinely provided. The significant role of the eagle to this point in the book, as closely identified with God and his work (4.7; 8.13), heightens the idea of divine activity. Neither would it be lost on the hearers that in the OT, Israel's experience of deliverance from Egypt by the hand of God is described in similar manner (Exod. 19.4; Deut. 32.11-12), as is the promise of future deliverance (Isa. 40.31). Thus, the hearers could hardly escape the conclusion that in this woman the experience of Israel is recapitulated, even as she looks increasingly like the Church. The fact that her wings are described as those of 'a great eagle' contrasts nicely the power of this divine provision with the power of the 'great red dragon', a power that is not inconsiderable. The purpose of such divinely given wings is made clear by the ἵνα ('in order that') clause which follows; these wings enable her to fly to a specific place. The significance of this place is conveyed to the hearers in part by a dual redundancy that occurs in the description

---

[22] Gause, *Revelation*, p. 172.

of this place. For the hearers to learn that she flies 'into the wilderness' would confirm for them that the description of her flight into the wilderness in v. 6 is being continued here in v. 14. Such language would likely remind them that this place in the wilderness is one prepared for her by God himself. Yet, the hearers learn more, for immediately following the phrase 'into the wilderness' are the words 'into her place'. The connection between these phrases in the Greek text is quite clear, given their identical construction. Owing to the extent of this similarity they might appear to be superfluously redundant. But, the repetitious nature of the construction would hardly be lost on the hearers who would likely take it as a point of emphasis, underscoring the fact that the wilderness to which she flies is indeed 'her place' for it had been prepared for her by God. Such emphasis via redundancy continues with the next three words encountered by the hearers, ὅπου τρέφεται ἐκεῖ ('where she is nourished in that place'). While it is possible simply to regard the combination of ὅπου ('where') and ἐκεῖ ('in that place') as pleonastic[23] and perhaps unnecessary, following on the heels of the combination 'into the wilderness into her place', such repetition would hardly be taken as anything other than continued emphasis upon the place to which she flies. The fact that the word 'nourish' stands between 'where' and 'in that place' also tends to support this understanding. Given the context of conflict with the dragon and the events that follow, it is likely that the word τρέφεται ('she is nourished') would convey not only the idea of nourishment but protection as well, as it had in 12.6. Earlier, the hearers learned that the period of divine protection offered to the woman was 1,260 days, the exact length of time the two witnesses prophesy before a hostile world (11.3). Here, they discover that this period of divine protection is coterminous with Daniel's 'a time and times and half a time' (Dan. 7.25). Yet, whilst this temporal designation is in Daniel one used to describe the time given to the fourth beast to afflict the saints, in Rev. 12.14 it is a temporal designation for the period of nourishment and protection offered to the woman! Thus, there is a subtle inversion present in the words the hearers encounter, where a time of persecution is described as a time of protection. The nature of the nourishment and protection begins to take shape when

---

[23] BAGD, p. 238.

the hearers encounter the words 'from the face of the serpent'. Harkening back to the full description of the dragon in 12.9, the hearers find that the dragon is again described as the serpent. At least two things are conveyed to the hearers by this phrase. First, mention of the serpent fast on the heels of the description of the dragon persecuting the woman would remind the hearers that when they encounter the attacks of the serpent they are encountering the dragon himself. Second, the fact that the nourishment of the woman is said to be 'from the face of the serpent' underscores the extent of the protection, for just as the woman successfully gave birth to the male child before the dragon who wished to devour him, so the woman and her witness will be protected despite the serpent's close proximity and evil intents.

Verse 15 – The hearers do not have to wait long to learn of the serpent's intentions for they next hear, 'and the serpent cast out of his mouth after the woman water as a river, in order that he might sweep her away with the river'. These words continue the cosmic imagery of the chapter underscoring the power of the serpent while making allusions to the Exodus tradition. The dragon, who was powerful enough to sweep a third of the stars out of heaven and cast them to the earth, is now described as a serpent capable of spewing an entire river out of his mouth. The mention of 'water as a river' might remind the hearers of Pharaoh's order that every male Hebrew child must be cast into the river (Exod. 1.22). At the same time, the hearers might be struck by the similarities between the woman who finds herself in the wilderness owing to divine intervention who now faces the obstacle of water designed to destroy her and the experience of Israel when confronted with the Red Sea (Exodus 14-15). Just as Pharaoh pursued Israel, so the serpent pursues the woman.[24] The intention of the serpent is made especially clear to the hearers by means of a word play in the Greek text of Rev. 12.15. Here one discovers that the serpent cast out of his mouth a ποταμόν ('river') so that he might make the woman a ποταμοφόρητον ('one swept away by a river'). Such action clearly conveys the serpent's lethal intent and reveals to the hearers some detail about the way in which the dragon persecuted the woman.

---

[24] Kiddle, *Revelation*, p. 236.

Verse 16 – As the hearers begin to ponder the implications of the serpent's actions they discover that the woman's divine protection has not yet reached its limits, for 'the earth rendered help to the woman and the earth opened her mouth and swallowed the river that the dragon cast out of his mouth'. The hearers could hardly miss the emphasis placed upon the role of the earth in these actions, for they are clearly told that 'the earth rendered help to the woman', indicating that the following actions are to be understood as the earth's intervention on her behalf in the light of the hostile actions of the serpent. The presence of the opening words of this verse is hardly explicable otherwise. This activity of the earth on the woman's behalf would likely call to mind the continued emphasis in the Apocalypse on the connection between the Creator and his creation, so much so that at this point the creation appears to be doing the bidding of the Creator himself. Given the numerous allusions to the Exodus tradition, if the hearers earlier made a connection between the water as a river and the experience of Israel at the Nile, it is possible that they might see in the earth opening her mouth a faint allusion to the earth's actions in the rebellion of Korah (Num. 16.31-33). Owing to the fact that the mouth of the earth and the dragon are mentioned in this verse, it is difficult to resist the temptation of seeing an explicit contrast between the strength of the mouth of the serpent, from which the river of water comes, and the strength of the mouth of the earth, which is able to open and drink up the entire river. Finally in this verse, the identity of the serpent as the dragon is made clear yet again for the hearers, making the contrast between the power of the mouth of the serpent/dragon and the mouth of the earth all the clearer.

Verse 17 – Just as the dragon's earlier frustration at being cast down to earth from heaven lead to his persecution of the woman, so now his frustration at the thwarting of his attempt to sweep her away with a river leads to additional anger, 'and the dragon was enraged at the woman and departed to make war with the rest of her seed who keep the commands of God and have the witness of Jesus'. These words would alert the hearers to the fact that despite his frustrated attempts the dragon's hostility toward the woman is anything but over. Yet, at the same time, they might also remember that the last time the word enraged appeared (Rev. 11.18) it had reference to the rage of the nations that proved fruitless in the face of the rage of God himself! But before they can reflect on this connection the hearers' attention is quickly diverted to a somewhat unexpected development. For instead of the dragon's rage resulting in another direct attack on the woman, on the order of seeking to sweep her away by the river that comes from his mouth, he departs 'to make war on the rest of her seed'. Reference to the dragon preparing to make war would inform the hearers in a couple of different ways. On the one hand, this language could not help but remind them of the dragon's last making of war, which proved to be extraordinarily unsuccessful as he was not strong enough and lost his place in heaven (12.7)! On the other hand, this language could not help but remind the hearers of the fact that after the two witnesses' prophetic witness was complete the beast made war against them and overcame them (11.7). The point could not be clearer. Just as the temple is protected for 1,260 days and the two witnesses are protected until their witness is complete, so the woman is protected from the attacks of the dragon for 1,260 days, a time and times and half a time.[25] But just as the two witnesses are overcome and killed by the beast when their witness is completed, so war will be made upon those loyal to the commands of God and have the witness of Jesus! The language 'the rest of her seed' conveys at least two things to the hearers. First, the term seed would perhaps remind them of the male child, borne by the woman, snatched up to heaven, the fulfillment of Gen. 3.15.[26] Second, the fuller phrase itself indicates that there is a concrete connection between the male child and the rest of her seed, suggesting that the mother of the male child is also in some sense the mother of all believers. One wonders if for Johannine hearers such language would be understood to extend the thought of the FG where 'the mother of Jesus' becomes the 'mother of the Beloved Disciple' (Jn 19.25-27). Is it possible that the words of Rev. 12.17 suggest that 'the mother of Jesus' is 'the mother of all true disciples' as well? At any rate, the transformation of the woman clothed with the sun from Eve, to Israel, to Mary, to the Church would now appear to be complete. The qualification of 'the rest of her seed' as those 'who keep the commands of God and have the witness of Jesus' expands the hearers knowledge of their

---

[25] Resseguie, *The Revelation of John*, pp. 175-76.
[26] Murphy, *Fallen Is Babylon*, p. 289.

identity considerably. For Johannine hearers know that keeping the command(s) of the Father is intimately connected to the command to love one another (Jn 13.34; 14.15, 21, 31; 15.10, 12; 1 Jn 2.3-4, 7-8; 3.22-24; 4.21; 5.2-3; 2 Jn 4-6) to the point of laying down one's life as Jesus did (Jn 10.14-18). Lest anyone be confused about its importance, the keeping of God's command is no mere exercise in conformity for, as Jesus says, 'I know that his command is eternal life' (12.50). No doubt this keeping of God's commands would also be informed by the numerous times the word 'keep' appears in the seven prophetic messages the resurrected Jesus speaks to the seven churches earlier in the Apocalypse. Specifically, such language is used with reference to keeping Jesus' works (Rev. 2.26) and words (3.8, 10), as well as keeping the things they have received (3.3). Thus, 'the rest of her seed, who keep the commands of God' is understood to be those who are faithful in living out a sacrificial love for God and others, even to the point of death. Closely related to this designation is the rest of the phrase, 'and have the witness of Jesus'. It may not be without significance that for the first time in chapter 12 the male child is identified by name as Jesus,[27] a dramatic technique with which the hearers would be familiar from the prologue of the FG (Jn 1.17) and 1 John (1.3). Coming as it does in such close proximity to the words of the hymn in Rev. 12.11, 'and they overcame him through the blood of the Lamb and the word of their testimony and they did not love their lives unto death', the meaning of the phrase could hardly be clearer. It makes explicit that the individuals against whom the dragon is preparing to make war are themselves prepared to give the ultimate faithful witness by following Jesus in death. Thus, both qualifying statements 'those who keep the commands of God' and 'who have the witness of Jesus' convey the same reality, a point confirmed by the fact that in the Greek text the same article governs both phrases.

Verse 18 – Poised to learn of the dragon's preparations for war against the rest of the woman's seed, the hearers encounter the words, 'And he stood upon the sand of the sea'. Apparently, the preparation and means of this war will emerge from the sea. This description, taken with the words of woe spoken to the earth and

---

[27] Hauret, 'Éve transfigurée: de la Genèse à l'Apocalypse', p. 335.

sea in 12.12, prepares the hearers for the ensuing war and those who wage it with and for the Dragon.

The Two Beasts (13.1-18)

Verse 1 – With attention focused upon the dragon standing on the sand of the sea, the hearers next encounter John's words describing the ensuing events, 'And I saw a beast coming up out of the sea, having ten horns and seven heads and upon his horns ten diadems and upon his heads a blasphemous name'. The first two words in the Greek text καὶ εἶδον ('and I saw') are reminiscent of a number of places earlier in the Apocalypse where John uses these exact words to describe the things he was seeing. Thus, after the absence of this mode of description for more than two chapters, the last occurrence being found in 10.5, the hearers find themselves in familiar linguistic territory even while they encounter a new visionary description. Unbeknownst to the hearers, the occurrence of this expression at this point marks the beginning of a series of things seen that begins with the sea (13.1) and climaxes with something like 'a sea of glass' in heaven (15.2). Despite the fact that reference to the beast in 13.1 is anarthrous, it is likely that his mention would remind the hearers of the reference to the beast who comes up from the Abyss who made war against, overcame, and killed the two prophetic witnesses earlier in 11.7. If, as the hearers may suspect from what has been encountered previously (Revelation 12), this section (Revelation 12-14) expands upon 11.3-13, then it would seem likely that mention of the beast in 13.1 would alert them to the fact that they are now to learn much more about this enigmatic figure than they knew previously. As the beast that emerges from the sea is described, the hearers come to realize that he bears a striking resemblance to the great red dragon, who at last mention was standing on the sand of the seashore apparently awaiting the arrival of the beast who will aid the dragon in his war on the rest of the offspring of the woman clothed with the sun. For like the dragon, the beast has ten horns and seven heads, indicating that he too is the picture of extraordinary strength and power (ten horns) as well as complete and absolute rule (seven heads).[28] Yet, the hearers are not likely to take the beast as simply identical to the dragon, for not only is the description of the beast's horns and heads in inverse

---

[28] Resseguie, *The Revelation of John*, p. 180.

order of the dragon's, but also because while the dragon has seven diadems, the beast is described as having ten. The explicit connection between the ten horns and the ten diadems underscores the power and strength of the beast all the more, suggesting to the hearers that the beast who comes up out of the sea is even more powerful than the dragon, if such a thing were possible! Not only is the beast described as having more diadems than the dragon but he is also described as bearing a blasphemous name upon his head! While the nature of the blasphemous name is not explicitly revealed at this point, from the blasphemy language it would seem likely that the hearers would suspect that the blasphemous name impinges in some way upon the identity and glory of God and his name.[29] Perhaps the hearers would be reminded of the fact that the church in Smyrna suffered 'the blasphemy of those who say of themselves to be Jews and are not but are a synagogue of Satan'. If so, it is likely that they now understand that the blasphemy they endured was a manifestation of the power of the dragon and his servant the beast. If they learned in 2.9 that such blasphemy was very much connected to the identity of God and his people,[30] it is likely that the beast's blasphemous name would be understood as closely connected to God's identity and name,[31] perhaps even having reference to a variety of divine names, which numerous contemporary rulers were so fond of appropriating for themselves.[32]

Verse 2 – As John's narration continues the hearers learn even more about the beast, 'And the beast which I saw was as a leopard and his feet as a bear and his mouth as the mouth of a lion'. On their own, these words suggest a beast that is swift, powerful, and terrifying, for the speed of the leopard, the power of the bear, and the ferociousness of the lion were well known, the latter point being especially emphasized by the double reference to the mouth of the lion in 13.2. At the same time, it is difficult to imagine that this particular combination of animals would not remind the hearers of the description of the four beasts found in Daniel 7. There, the four beasts (the lion, the bear, the leopard, and the terrible fourth beast

---

[29] H.W. Beyer, 'βλασφημία', *TDNT*, I, pp. 621-24.
[30] Cf. the discussion of Rev. 2.9 above.
[31] Resseguie, *The Revelation of John*, p. 182.
[32] Mounce, *The Book of Revelation*, p. 250.

with ten horns) represent four consecutive kingdoms, which culminate in the fourth kingdom that makes war against the saints (Dan. 7.21) and excels all the other kingdoms, as it devours the whole earth (7.23).[33] That the visions of Daniel and John are distinctive would not be lost on the hearers, for not only is Daniel's order of the beasts (lion, bear, and leopard) inverted in the Apocalypse (leopard, bear, and lion), but unlike Daniel, John does not see four separate beasts (kingdoms) but one composite terrible beast, that appears to combine dreadful characteristics of them all![34] If Daniel's vision implies chronological progression, the vision John sees suggests the culmination of all the kingdoms in one hideous beast.[35] In John's first words about the beast, the hearers learned of the striking physical resemblance between the dragon and the beast. At this point they learn that the connection between the dragon and the beast extends beyond mere appearances, for they discover, 'And the dragon gave to him his power and his throne and great authority'. Though the hearers may have assumed that the dragon is a powerful figure, owing to his ability to cast one-third of the stars of the sky from heaven with his tail, to this point in the Apocalypse the word δύναμις ('power') has only been used in association with God (4.11; 7.12; 11.17; 12.10), Jesus (1.16; 5.12), and believers (3.8). For the hearers to learn that the dragon gives his power to the beast not only indicates that the power standing behind the beast is that of the dragon, but, owing to its previous associations with God and/or Christ, also suggests that the dragon's giving of power to the beast may parody the activity of God and his Christ.[36] Likewise, reference to the dragon giving his throne to the beast is conditioned for the hearers by the numerous previous references to the word 'throne' in the Apocalypse, where with only one exception they are always mentioned in association with reference to God, the Lamb, or his followers. Thus, while the hearers would know that Satan has a throne, localized on earth in Pergamum, according to the words of the resurrected Jesus (2.13), they would likely see reference to the

---

[33] Andrew of Caesarea (*Commentary on the Apocalypse*, 13.2 [ACCS 12, p. 199] identifies the leopard as the Greeks, the bear as the Persians, the lion as the Babylonians, and the antichrist as the king of the Romans.

[34] Osborne, *Revelation*, p. 492.

[35] Gause, *Revelation*, p. 178.

[36] Resseguie, *The Revelation of John*, p. 183.

dragon giving his throne to the beast as a continuation of the parody of the relationship between God and the Lamb,[37] especially owing to the fact that Jesus promises the one who overcomes to sit on his throne just as he has overcome and sits on the Father's throne (3.22). Similarly, the dragon's giving the beast great authority is again conditioned for the hearers owing to the fact that the occurrence of authority elsewhere in the Apocalypse is always an authority that appears to have come from God or Jesus, either directly or indirectly (2.26; 6.8; 9.3, 10, 19; 11.6; 12.10). Thus, the beast's great authority derived from the dragon would likely be seen as part of the parody of divine activity as well.

Verse 3 – If the hearers suspect from v. 2 that the dragon and the beast parody the relationship between God and the Lamb, such suspicions are confirmed in the next words they encounter, 'And one of his heads was as slaughtered unto death, and the plague of his death was healed'. What perhaps first catches the attention of the hearers is the fact that the phrase ὡς ἐσφαγμένην ('as slaughtered') here used to describe one of the beast's heads is the identical phrase the hearers earlier encountered in the description of the Lamb who looked as though it had been slaughtered! Owing to the salvific implications of the slaughter of the Lamb, made clear to the hearers at numerous points throughout the book, it would seem safe to assume that mention of the beast's slaughtered head would represent to the hearers salvific claims on the part of the beast, so much so that at the very least they would likely see in the beast one who makes competing salvific claims! While it is possible that the wounding of the beast's head is not described within the Apocalypse, perhaps the hearers would suspect that such an event is alluded to in 11.7, which recounts the beast's previous though brief appearance in the book. There, in response to the prophetic activities of the two witnesses, the beast rises, makes war, overcomes, and kills them. Thus, perhaps it is the prophetic ministry of the two witnesses that results in the slaughter of one of the beast's heads,[38] a slaughter so severe that the death of the beast is imminent. Owing to the continuity of the witness borne by Jesus and his witnesses,

---

[37] Allo, *L'Apocalypse*, p. 185.

[38] Kiddle (*Revelation*, p. 245) observes, 'John believed that the death of the martyrs was of cosmic importance', while Sweet (*Revelation*, p. 210) notes, '… the *obedience* and *testimony* of Jesus and his saints wound the beast's *head*'.

the hearers might also find in this statement an echo of the Gen. 3.16 prediction that the seed of the woman would bruise the head of the serpent.[39] However, before being able to ponder the many questions that these words raise, the hearers learn, 'and the plague of his death was healed'. Three things stand out about this statement. First, the occurrence of the word plague to describe the wound to the beast's head would confirm the hearers' earlier suspicions with regard to the occasion of the wounding, for this very word, πληγή ('plague'), is used to describe some of the prophetic activities attributed to the two witnesses in 11.6 just before the introduction of the beast into the story line.[40] Second, the pronoun αὐτοῦ ('his') in the phrase 'the plague of his death' appears to have reference to the beast, not just his wounded head. In other words, it appears the wound to one of the beast's heads was a mortal wound to the beast himself. Third, the verb that describes the healing of the beast's mortal wound appears in the passive voice. To this point, verbs appearing in the passive voice have almost uniformly been forms of the divine passive, having reference to the activity of God, and such may be the case here as well. However, owing to the number of ways in which the description of the dragon and the beast are a parody of God and the Lamb, one wonders if the hearers would not see in the term ἐθεραπεύθη ('was healed') a continuation of this theme and take this 'divine passive' as having reference to the activity of the dragon. The appearance of the beast from the sea, with his similarity in appearance to and his investiture by the dragon, and the healing of the mortal wound to one of his heads have a significant result on the world, 'and the whole earth was astonished after the beast'. Johannine hearers might well detect in the presence of the term ἐθαυμάσθη ('was amazed') a continuation of the parody of the previous sentences as this very term occurs in the FG to describe the response of the disciples (Jn 4.27) and the Jews (5.20, 28; 7.15, 21) to the activity of Jesus. The earth's astonishment at all that the beast is results in a reaction to him similar to that which Jesus receives in the FG. Thus, the way in which the beast rivals Jesus is underscored once again. As the hearers learn of the beast's initial effect upon the whole earth, perhaps they remem-

---

[39] Michaels, *Revelation*, p. 156.
[40] Sweet, *Revelation*, p. 210.

ber the ominous woe directed to the earth and sea with regard to Satan's expulsion from heaven, his great anger, and his little time (Rev. 12.12).

Verse 4 – The result of the whole earth's astonishment after the beast is revealed in the next words the hearers encounter, 'And they worshipped the dragon, because he gave the authority to the beast, and they worshipped the beast saying, "Who is like the beast and who is able to war with him?"' If the earlier verses have suggested that the dragon and beast serve to mimic God and the Lamb, these words make this clear. Aside from the rest of those who would not repent and not worship demons or idols (9.20), to this point only God and the Lamb are the objects of worship in the Apocalypse (4.10; 5.14; 7.11; 11.1, 16).[41] For those steeped in the OT and the heritage of Israel, as are the hearers of the Apocalypse, the worship of other beings in the place of God and the Lamb would be especially heinous and would reveal the extreme threat posed to believers by the dragon and the beast. For the ultimate motivation for the war, which the dragon and the beast wage against the rest of the woman's offspring, is the desire to receive the worship rightly reserved for God and the Lamb alone. The hearers discover that the worship rendered to the dragon is owing to the fact that he gave the authority to the beast. Given the context, it would appear that the term authority has reference to all the things given to the beast by the dragon, 'his power and his throne and great authority'. No doubt the beast's similarity in appearance to the dragon and the healing of the beast's wounded head are part of such 'authority'. Along with the dragon, the beast is also worshipped. Although nothing is said about the form of the worship offered to the dragon, the hearers learn that the worship of the beast includes a song of praise for they are described as singing a psalm to him, 'Who is like the beast and who is able to war with him?' Such a psalm would connect with the hearers in several ways. First, this hymn's obvious mimicry of the hymns offered to God (4.8, 11; 7.10, 12; 11.15, 17-18; 12.10-12) and the Lamb (5.9-10, 12, 13) earlier in the book would hardly be lost on them.[42] For the unrivalled position and

---

[41] Even the term's appearance in Rev. 3.9 seems to have ultimate reference to the worship of Jesus.

[42] Gause, *Revelation*, p. 179.

power of God and the Lamb is rather clearly a recurring refrain to this point. Second, while the hearers are painfully aware that the beast is able to make war, overcome, and kill the two prophetic witnesses, and consequently is able to make war on them, they are likely to be struck by the absurdity of the claims to invincibility in war made on behalf of the beast owing to the fact that the dragon, who gives him authority and power, is himself not strong enough to win the war he makes in heaven but loses his place there. While the 'whole earth' might be foolish enough to engage in such empty praise, the discerning hearers are not! Third, it would be difficult for the hearers to miss the way in which this psalm is reminiscent of a variety of OT songs that acclaim God's incomparable nature (Exod. 15.11-12; Deut. 3.24; Pss. 18.31; 86.8; 89.8; 113.5; Isa. 40.25-26; 44.7; Mic. 7.18), a fact that suggests the song sung to the beast is a parody of Judaic praise as well.[43] Thus, when they hear these words of praise, the lines of demarcation are drawn all the more clearly for the hearers. The dragon and the beast are diametrically opposed to God and the Lamb, and those who side with the dragon and the beast engage in false worship and give them a place that belongs only to God.[44]

Verse 5 – But before having sufficient time to ponder the grave implications of such false worship, the hearers learn even more about this beast, 'And there was given to him a mouth speaking great and blasphemous things and there was given to him authority to act forty-two months'. Whereas the previous description of the beast had no doubt called to mind the first three beasts of Daniel 7, these words could hardly help but remind the hearers of the fourth beast with ten horns, three of which are displaced by the emergence of yet another horn with a mouth speaking great things who makes war against the saints and prevails against them (Dan. 7.20). The double appearance of the word ἐδόθη ('there was given') in Rev. 13.5 underscores the fact that the beast's authority and power is a derived authority and power. But to whom do these passives have reference as subject? At this point the hearers might be a bit confused owing to the fact that the most immediate referent to one who gave something to the beast is the dragon, who is worshipped

---

[43] Smalley, *The Revelation to John*, p. 339.
[44] Prigent, *L'Apocalypse de Saint Jean*, p. 314.

because he gave authority to the beast (13.4). Yet to this point in the Apocalypse every occurrence of ἐδόθη ('there was given') has had reference to God or the Lamb. Perhaps the hearers would discern in these passives reference to both the dragon, and to God. On the one hand, such an understanding would fit nicely with the dragon who continues to mimic the activity of God with even the 'divine passive' now having reference to him, as with ἐθεραπεύθη ('was healed') in 13.3. On the other hand, a reference to God would make sense as he is ultimately in control and without rival in the book, and clearly is the one who would place the limits of forty-two months upon the beast, a limitation that is hard to imagine as coming from the dragon who has 'little time' himself![45] The mouth given to the beast, earlier described as a mouth of a lion, is one that utters great and blasphemous things. As noted, such a mouth is reminiscent of the horn's mouth of Dan. 7.20 that speaks great things. But the hearers of the Apocalypse would no doubt see a connection between the blasphemous name upon the heads of the beast (Rev. 13.1) and the blasphemous things spoken by the mouth of this beast. If so, the nature of the names are, no doubt, related to the kind of great and blasphemous things said in 13.5. Thus, it is likely that the hearers would understand the great and blasphemous things uttered by the mouth of the beast as closely connected to God's identity and name. In addition to the mouth speaking great and blasphemous things, the beast was given authority to act for forty-two months. The words 'there was given to him authority' would take the hearers back to vv. 2 and 4 where the dragon is twice described as giving authority to the beast. Such repetition here would make it impossible to ignore the fact that the dragon himself stands behind the activity of the beast. On this occasion, however, there is a temporal limitation for the period during which the beast may act, forty-two months, a limitation that appears to have a divine origin. The first occurrence of this temporal indicator was with reference to the trampling of the holy city described in 11.2. The reappearance of this temporal indicator at this point suggests that the period of the beast's activity is coterminous with the trampling of the holy city.

---

[45] Beasley-Murray, *Revelation*, p. 213 and Smalley, *The Revelation to John*, p. 340.

Verse 6 – Having been given a mouth with which to speak great and blasphemous things, the beast, as the hearers discover, now begins to use his mouth for this precise purpose, 'And he opened his mouth unto blasphemy to God to blaspheme his name and his dwelling, those who dwell in heaven'. The fact that the beast is described as opening his mouth would suggest at least two things to the hearers. First, it would, no doubt, once again call to mind the actions of the horn in Dan. 7.25, who speaks great words against God. Second, the phrase 'he opened his mouth' would underscore the significance of the words that are to follow, perhaps indicating that the beast speaks in an official capacity.[46] The hearers could hardly miss the emphasis placed upon the blasphemous activity of the beast, as both the noun and verb forms of the word occur in this verse. While the nature of the beast's blasphemous name and blasphemous speech is not altogether clear in the previous verses, it is made explicit in the words of v. 6, for this verse clearly identifies the objects of his blasphemous acts. Specifically, the hearers learn their previous suspicions, that the beast's blasphemous activity is directed toward God, are confirmed in this verse. Though the blasphemous name of the beast is not revealed nor the content of his blasphemous words, it would appear safe to assume that the beast's blasphemous activity challenges the identity and nature of God, perhaps going so far as to appropriate divine names and attributes for himself. It is even possible that the hearers would understand that the beast's blasphemous activity would not be limited to such hubristic claims but might even involve more direct attacks upon God and his identity. The beast's blasphemous activity toward God includes his name, his dwelling, and those who dwell in heaven. Thus, the beast's blasphemous activity is a comprehensive challenge to God's identity, person, dwelling, and people. Owing to the fact that in antiquity one's name was thought to be identical with one's person blasphemy of God's name was considered to be blasphemy of God himself.[47] Such an attitude is reflected in the numerous ad-

---

[46] Aune, *Revelation 6-16*, p. 744. Gause (*Revelation*, p. 180) goes so far as to propose that this expression might very well remind the hearers of prophetic, oracular speech enabled by Yahweh. If so, such associations would suggest that the mimicry by the dragon and the beast of God and the Lamb continues to develop.

[47] L. Hartman, 'ὄνομα', *EDNT*, II, p. 519.

monitions and commands to protect and sanctify God's name in the OT. Similarly, the beast's blasphemous activity of God's σκηνήν ('dwelling') would be understood by Johannine hearers as a direct attack upon God's person for, as they learned in Rev. 7.15, God promises the eschatological provision, 'the One who sits on the throne' σκηνώσει ('will dwell') upon those coming out of the great tribulation. This eschatological reality appears later in the description of the new heaven and new earth, 'Behold the dwelling of God is with men, and he will dwell with them' (21.3). Add to this evidence the FG's testimony that the Word 'tabernacled among us' (Jn 1.14). Thus, for Johannine hearers, blasphemy of God's dwelling would not only include his person but also those who witness and are enveloped by his dwelling. This latter understanding is made explicit in the final words conveyed to the hearers in Rev. 13.6 where the phrase 'those who dwell in heaven' appears to modify 'his dwelling'. Perhaps at this point the hearers would remember the instruction to 'the heavens and those who dwell in them' to rejoice at the casting down of the dragon (12.12). There is, after all, clearly a great deal of continuity between these who dwell in heaven and the believing community in heaven and, by extension, the believing community upon the earth.[48] Consequently, the hearers learn that the blasphemous activity of the beast includes the believing community both past and present, an experience already known from the prophetic message to the church in Smyrna (2.9-10). This dimension of the beast's blasphemous activity would hardly be surprising to the hearers owing to the fact that the object of the dragon's wrath is the rest of the woman's seed. The words they encounter in the last phrase of 13.6 would indicate that the beast's blasphemous activity includes the rest of her seed in a comprehensive sense. The beast blasphemes God and all that is associated with him.

Verse 7 – The hearers learn that the beast's activities are not confined to blasphemy for they are told, 'And there was given to him to make war against the saints and to overcome them, and there was given to him authority over every tribe and people and tongue and nation'. For a second time in the span of three verses the hearers encounter the double occurrence of the term ἐδόθη

---

[48] Pattemore, *The People of God in the Apocalypse*, p. 168.

('there was given') with reference to the beast. As with its earlier occurrences in v. 5, the hearers may be a bit unclear as to the unnamed subject of these passives. Clearly, the giving of the ability to make war against the saints is something that forwards the agenda of the dragon, who himself is described as making war with the rest of the seed of the woman (11.17) and who appears to be worshipped, along with the beast, by the whole earth (13.4). Thus, it appears that these 'divine passives' yet again might have reference to the dragon, who continues to mimic God. At the same time, it is clear that nothing happens upon the earth and/or to God's people without God's expressed permission. Consequently, the hearers are likely to discern in these passives the activity of both the dragon and God. The ascription to the beast of the ability 'to make war against the saints and to overcome them' could not help but remind the hearers of the actions of the beast against the two prophetic witnesses in 11.7, where, upon the completion of their witness, 'the beast from the Abyss made war against them and overcame them and killed them'. Such near identical wording suggests that the experience of the two witnesses and the saints at the hands of the beast is coterminous and once again confirms that the description of the beast in chapter 13 is an expansion of his brief enigmatic mention in 11.7. The occurrence of the word 'saints' would not only reinforce the connection between this text and Dan. 7.25, but would also indicate that the woman's seed is indeed identical with the saints. It also serves as an ominous warning that the saints can expect similar treatment at the hands of the beast as did the two prophetic witnesses. In addition to the ability to make war against the saints, the beast receives 'authority over every tribe and people and tongue and nation'. Given the various points at which the beast is said to have received authority from the dragon, it would seem probable that the hearers would take such language here as underscoring the ultimate source of the beast's authority as the dragon. Reference to 'every tribe and people and tongue and nation' would perhaps generate two responses in the hearers. On the one hand, it is difficult to imagine that these words would not cause them to see here yet another point at which the activity of the beast parodies that of God and the Lamb, for these very groups are mentioned in connection with the salvific work of God and the Lamb (5.9; 7.9). On the other hand, mention of these groups would remind the hearers that these very groups are those to whom John and the two prophetic witnesses are to prophesy (10.11; 11.9). The mention of these groups in 11.9 would be especially poignant, as they are the ones described as seeing the (dead) body of the two witnesses in the street of that great city. Perhaps the recurrence of these groups in 13.7 would be an ominous warning with regard to what lies ahead for the saints!

Verse 8 – The potency of the beast's authority is discovered in the next words encountered by the hearers, 'And all the inhabitants upon the earth will worship him'. Such a statement would not take the hearers by surprise for a couple of reasons. First, it follows that if the beast has 'authority over every tribe and people and tongue and nation', such authority would manifest itself in universal worship, an act already seen in 13.4. Second, the hearers' earlier encounters with the phrase, 'the inhabitants of the earth', would also prepare them for this statement. For 'the inhabitants of the earth' are the ones upon whom the great tribulation is about to come (3.10), the ones against whom the souls under the altar cry out for justice (6.10), the ones to whom the three woes are addressed by the eagle (8.13), and the ones who rejoiced at the death of the two witnesses because their witness had so tormented them (11.10). Thus, to find that all the inhabitants of the earth worshipped the beast, instead of God and the Lamb, would hardly come as a surprise, but rather would serve to confirm what was learned earlier (13.4). Neither would the comprehensive nature of the worship of the beast go unnoticed by the hearers, for this is the first and only occurrence of the word 'all' with this phrase in the Apocalypse.[49] A final significant aspect of these words is the fact that the primary verb, προσκυνήσουσιν ('will worship'), appears in the future tense rather than the past tense, as in the preceding verses, indicating that the time of such comprehensive worship lies at some point in the future.[50] The identity of those who worship the beast is made all the clearer in the words that follow, 'each one whose name was not written in the book of life of the Lamb who was slaughtered from the foundation of the world'. The shift from the plural, 'all', to the singular, 'each one', has the effect of refocusing attention upon the

---

[49] Aune, *Revelation 6-16*, p. 746.
[50] Smalley, *The Revelation to John*, p. 342.

fact that despite the universal way in which the beast will be worshipped by all the inhabitants of the earth, ultimately the worship of the beast is rendered by individuals who have rejected the Lamb's salvific provisions. For those who worship the beast are those who have not had their names inscribed in the Lamb's book of life. Mention of the Lamb's book of life would, no doubt, remind the hearers of its previous occurrence in 3.5, where the one who overcomes is promised by Jesus that his name will not be erased from it. That Jesus, the one who is alive, who is Life, has the authority to erase names from this book would surprise none of the hearers. The introduction of the book of life in 13.8 would carry with it the book's previous associations from 3.5, underscoring the fact that those who worship the beast are not alive, nor do they have the life brought by the one who is alive and is Life himself! Significantly, the book of life is explicitly identified with the Lamb, whose salvific work is underscored, emphasizing the close relationship that exists between the Lamb's death and the inscription of names in the book of life. The recurrence of the word ἐσφαγμένου ('slaughtered') in this verse would be a powerful reminder of the central role Jesus' death and shedding of blood play in the Apocalypse, a theme introduced as early as the book's prologue (1.5-6) and present consistently throughout to this point (5.6, 9; 7.14; 12.11). Clearly, those who have experienced the loosing of sins through his blood (1.5), who have been purchased in his blood (5.9), who have washed their garments in his blood (7.14), and who have overcome on account of the blood of the Lamb (12.11) are the very ones whose names have been written in the slaughtered Lamb's book of life. At the same time, emphasis placed upon the fact that the Lamb had been slaughtered would reveal the significant differences between the beast's slaughtered head, apparently received as a result of the ministry of the two prophetic witnesses, and the Lamb who had been slaughtered 'from the foundation of the world'. Such a claim with regard to the Lamb would rather clearly remind Johannine hearers of Jesus' words to the Father, 'you loved me before the foundation of the world' (Jn 17.24), a reference to their pre-temporal relationship when Jesus shared glory with the Father before the world began (17.5).[51] Though modern interpreters sometimes stumble at this

---

[51] O. Hofius, 'καταβολή', *EDNT*, II, p. 255.

idea,⁵² such a disclosure would be very much in keeping with the hearers' understanding of Jesus' pre-existence and relationship with the Father and the world. For when facing the prospect of all the inhabitants of the earth worshipping the beast, it would be important for the hearers to understand that such worshippers, unlike them, are tied to a transitory and passing figure.⁵³ And while the hearers are very well aware of the fact that it is possible for the Lamb to erase names from the book of life (Rev. 3.5), the fact that their names have been written in the slaughtered Lamb's book of life indicates that they will be able to withstand the temptation to worship the beast, owing to the basis of their salvation, which predates the world itself.

Verse 9 – Suddenly, without warning, the narrative about the beast is interrupted by words addressed directly to the hearers, words reminiscent of those heard previously, 'If anyone has an ear let that one hear'. Without question, such words would remind the hearers of the words of Jesus with which each of the seven prophetic messages conclude. It would also be remembered that Jesus' words were, at the same time, words the Spirit speaks to the churches. So while it is possible that the hearers would understand these words simply as John's own voice, owing to their earlier associations and the hearers' expectancy of additional divine assistance in their pneumatic discernment, it is likely that they would take these words as coming from the resurrected Jesus and/or the Spirit once again. As such, they would carry with them something of their meaning in chapters 2-3, where they call for response on the part of the churches (and hearers) to the words spoken by the resurrected Jesus, especially as they relate to those who overcome. Thus, as the hearers face the prospects of the future universal worship of the beast, 'the Spirit-inspired voice of prophecy' gives divine guidance as to how they as believers are to respond.⁵⁴ What the hearers do not know now, but will realize later, is that this pneumatic guidance

---

⁵² Cf., for example, the discussion in Aune, *Revelation 6-16*, pp. 746-47.

⁵³ Gause (*Revelation*, p. 182) astutely observes, 'Here is the irony of God's economy. This is the book of Life, but it is based on the death of the Lamb, and it is a death that was and is established from eternity. Eternal life is given for an eternally established death. The saints conquer the beast that conquers them. His conquest is temporal and physical. Theirs is eternal and spiritual'.

⁵⁴ Pattemore, *The People of God in the Apocalypse*, p. 171.

stands at the very center of John's words about the two beasts found in chapter 13.

Verse 10 – This familiar call to pneumatic discernment is actually the first line of a poetic section devoted to this topic, the first three lines of which all begin with the words εἴ τις ('if any'):

> If any one has ears let that one hear.
> If any one into captivity
> into captivity that one goes.
> If any one by the sword is to die
> he by the sword is to die.

If the hearers recognize that these prophetic words incorporate the prophetic words of Jer. 15.2 and 42.11 (50.11 LXX), they would perhaps also realize that while Jeremiah speaks of punishment upon those who disobey God, the words of Rev. 13.10 are not spoken to the beast and his followers but are addressed to believers,[55] both as encouragement and as warning. In the face of the impending universal reign and worship of the beast, the hearers learn what they might expect to encounter and how they are to respond. What they learn could be a bit daunting, for it appears that captivity and death by the sword are calamities potentially awaiting them. Yet, while such frightful fates could be a cause for drawing back and even capitulating to the power and purposes of the beast, they at the same time would remind the hearers of the similar fate of Jesus, Antipas, and the two prophetic witnesses. Such pneumatic discernment reveals that they are not to resist the fates marked out for them,[56] but rather accept them as somehow integral to their prophetic witness and as part of God's will and plan for the believing community. Perhaps the hearers would even detect in these words an echo of those spoken to the souls under the altar that they must wait until their number is completed by their fellow servants and brothers who are about to be killed (6.11). If so, perhaps the hearers further discern that they themselves might be part of those who must suffer and die. These Spirit inspired words of Jesus conclude with yet another call for pneumatic discernment, 'Here is the patient endurance and the faith of the saints'. This call, the first of four such calls

---

[55] Caird, *The Revelation of St. John*, p. 169.
[56] Ladd, *Revelation*, p. 182.

the hearers will encounter from this point in the Apocalypse (13.10, 18; 14.12; 17.9), places emphasis upon the saints' patient endurance and faith, with both terms being accompanied by the definite article in the Greek text.[57] For the hearers of the Apocalypse the mention of patient endurance would carry with it the previous nuances of the word encountered earlier in the book, where patient endurance is first mentioned by John, their brother in patient endurance (1.9), and comes to be used by the resurrected Jesus as a characteristic or work of the churches in Ephesus (2.2, 3), Thyatira (2.19), and Philadelphia (3.10). Such patient endurance is understood to be 'in Jesus' (1.9) and belonging to him (3.10) and would carry with it the idea of following Jesus in rendering one's witness even to the point of death. Similarly, mention of 'the faith of the saints' would remind the hearers of the way faith is used by the resurrected Jesus as a characteristic or work of the churches in Pergamum (2.13) and Thyatira (2.19). As with patient endurance, faith is closely associated with Jesus, as he speaks both of 'my faith' and 'my faithful witness Antipas' in 2.13. Such language would once again remind the hearers of their solidarity with Jesus' witness, being a call to the kind of faithfulness characteristic of an overcomer. Thus, in this call to pneumatic discernment, despite the impending universal reign and worship of the beast, they are called to faithful, patient endurance. For the time of the beast is limited, forty-two months, and they stand with Jesus, identifying and standing with him and his own faithful witness.[58]

Verse 11 – Without any words of transition, the narrative of the Apocalypse picks up where it left off before the call to pneumatic discernment was heard. At this point the hearers learn of yet another beast, 'And I saw another beast coming up out of the earth, and he had two horns as a lamb and he spoke as a dragon'. Each of the details revealed in this verse would be of significance for the hearers. First, they are now introduced, for the first time, to the third member of this triumvirate of evil, who comes alongside the dragon and the beast with seven heads to oppose God and make war upon his people. The beast's mere existence is enough to suggest to the hearers that the parody of God and the Lamb continues, only here

---

[57] Aune, *Revelation 6-16*, p. 751.
[58] Prigent, *L'Apocalypse de Saint Jean*, p. 318.

it appears that the parody extends beyond God and the Lamb to include the Spirit. Second, the fact that this beast's place of origin is identified as the earth makes clear to the hearers the comprehensive nature of this triumvirate's opposition, as they come from heaven (the dragon), the sea (the beast with seven heads), and the earth (the beast introduced here).[59] They might also see in this place of origin a fulfillment of the woe of warning spoken to the earth and sea from the great voice in heaven in 12.12. Third, the fact that the beast is described as having two horns like a lamb would be especially intriguing to the hearers, for they would know full well that lambs do not have horns![60] Thus, while reference to a lamb would no doubt remind them of the lamb language used for Jesus in the Apocalypse, at the same time, the emphasis here is placed not so much upon the lamb language, but upon the two horns, like those belonging to a lamb. While the hearers might possibly think of the ram with two horns in Dan. 8.3 as an analogy,[61] it is much more likely that the two horns (like those of a lamb) would be taken as a reference to the Lamb's two prophetic witnesses, in whom all prophetic abilities appear to converge Rev. 11.3-13.[62] Therefore, it would seem that in the triumvirate of evil, this beast would be a parody of the Spirit.[63] Fourth, the hearers learn that despite this beast's appearance, having two horns like a lamb, his speech indicates a more sinister relationship, for 'he speaks as a dragon'. While the beast with seven heads bears a physical resemblance to the dragon, this beast speaks as a dragon. Speaking as a dragon would remind the hearers that despite this beast's appearance, he is in league with the dragon, and his words are those of the dragon, just as the words of the Spirit, spoken through prophetic witnesses, are the words of God.

Verse 12 – Having learned of this beast's relationship to the dragon, the hearers now become aware of his relationship to the first beast, 'And he exercises (*lit.* 'does') all the authority of the first beast before him, and he makes the earth and those who are inhab-

---

[59] Kiddle, *The Revelation of Saint John*, p. 253.
[60] Aune, *Revelation 6-16*, p. 757.
[61] Aune, *Revelation 6-16*, p. 757.
[62] Sweet, *Revelation*, p. 215
[63] Gause, *Revelation*, p. 183.

itants in it worship the first beast, whose plague of death was healed'. The emphasis of this sentence is revealed by the first few words of the Greek text, translated somewhat literally as, 'and the authority of the first beast'. Thus, before attention is devoted to the second beast's activity, focus is already placed upon the authority of the first beast. The attentive hearers would hardly miss the fact that the authority exercised by this beast is the same authority originally derived by the first beast from the dragon himself (13.2, 4, 5, 7). While not stated explicitly, the hearers may suspect that this beast's exercising all the authority of the first beast may very well include the waging of war, as it is this specific attribute for which the first beast is praised by the whole earth (13.5). It might strike the hearers as significant that with the mention of this beast's activity the verb tense shifts from past to present, perhaps suggesting that the activity of this beast is an ongoing reality for John and his church. It should perhaps be noted that the verb found here is ποιεῖ ('he exercises' or 'he does'), the first of several occurrences of a form of this verb in the next six verses. Just as reference to the first beast's authority precedes the mention of this beast's activity, so reference to the first beast follows mention of this beast's activity, as the hearers learn that the exercising of this authority is done 'before him' or 'in his presence'. Thus, in the Greek sentence, references to the first beast form an inclusio around the mention of this beast, making clear the dependency of the latter upon the former. For the action of this beast to be described as ἐνώπιον αὐτοῦ ('before him') would be yet another way in which the hearers would detect a parody of God and his work, as to this point in the Apocalypse with few exceptions (2.14; 3.8, 9; 12.4) the term ἐνώπιον ('before') rather consistently occurs with reference to God (1.4; 3.2, 5; 4.5, 6, 10 [2x]; 7.9, 11, 15; 8.2, 3, 4; 9.13; 11.4, 16; 12.10) or Jesus (5.8; 7.9)! As such, it also reminds of those OT texts that use this language to denote 'serving before the Lord' as a faithful servant (1 Kgs 17.1; 18.15).[64] The parallel between this word to describe the relationship between this beast and the first beast, on the one hand, and to describe the relationship of the two lampstands (who are the two prophetic witnesses) and the Lord of the earth (Rev. 11.4), on the other hand, would be additional reason for the hearers to see in this beast

---

[64] Kiddle, *The Revelation of St. John*, p. 254.

a parody of the Spirit. However, the exercising of such authority, as the servant of the first beast, is not an end in itself. Rather this authority is exercised in order that the earth and those who are inhabitants in it might worship the first beast, a point which the second appearance of the verb ποιεῖ ('he makes') in this verse makes clear. Such information helps explain how it is that the whole earth comes to worship the dragon and the beast (12.4). Such worship is the result of the activity of this beast. Here the hearers learn that the implicit connection made earlier between the healing of the first beast's plague of death and his worship by the world (12.3, 4) is made explicit in this verse (13.12).[65]

Verse 13 – The words that follow begin to reveal the way this beast accomplishes his task, 'And he does great signs, in order that he even makes fire to come down unto the earth before men'. Owing to the Christologically conditioned nature of 'signs' within the Johannine community, the doing of great signs by this beast again underscores the way in which he continues to parody the activity of the Spirit. The extent of this beast's ability is demonstrated by the fact that he is even able to make 'fire fall from heaven unto the earth before men'. The mention of fire from heaven would no doubt remind the hearers especially of Elijah, whose sacrifice was consumed by fire that fell from the Lord (1 Kgs 18.38). Thus, this beast is able to do what the prophets of Baal could not,[66] in imitation of Elijah. At the same time, mention of fire could not help but remind the hearers of the two prophetic witnesses from whose mouth fire came to devour their enemies.[67] As such, the actions of this beast reveal his continued parody of the work of the Spirit. The attribution of many great signs to this beast also likely calls to the mind of the hearers the words of Deut. 13.1-5, which warn of a 'prophet' who performs signs or wonders and leads the people to worship other gods. These signs, especially the calling down of fire from heaven unto the earth, were specifically done 'before men'.

Verse 14 – The purpose of these great signs, and the fire falling from heaven in particular, is made explicit in the next words encountered by the hearers, 'and that he might deceive those who

---

[65] Allo, *L'Apocalypse*, p. 190.
[66] Beasley-Murray, *Book of Revelation*, p. 217.
[67] Osborne, *Revelation*, p. 513.

dwell upon the earth by means of the signs which had been given to him to do before the beast, saying to those who dwell upon the earth to make an icon/image to the beast, who has the plague of the sword and lived'. For Johannine hearers 'deceive' language reminds of those who would deceive themselves (Jn 7.47; 1 Jn 1.8; 2 Jn 7) or others (Jn 7.12; 1 Jn 2.26; 3.7), the false prophetess (called 'Jezebel' by Jesus), who 'teaches and deceives my servants to commit sexual immorality and to eat food sacrificed to idols' (Rev. 2.20), and most recently the agent of deception *par excellence*, the great dragon, the one who stands behind all the human agents of deception (Rev. 12.9). For the hearers to discover that this beast is also one of those who deceives others, makes clear to them his relationship, not only to the dragon, but also to the false prophetess 'Jezebel', and may even indicate that he himself should be considered the archetypal false prophet, a suspicion that will be confirmed later in the book (19.20). At any rate, the contrast between this beast and the two prophetic witnesses continues to become clear. The intended audience of these signs are 'those who dwell upon the earth', those earlier described as worshipping the first beast (13.8), explaining in part the reason for the first beast's worship. At the same time, it is made clear to the hearers that the signs which this beast performed was an ability given to him, presumably by means of the authority derived from the first beast (13.12). For these signs, like the exercising of authority, were done 'before the beast', a phrase that again parodies the relationship of God to his servants, especially the two prophetic witnesses (11.4). Part of this beast's activity of deception is his 'prophetic' words to those who are inhabitants upon the earth ποιῆσαι εἰκόνα ('to make an image') to the beast. It is significant that this beast seeks to encourage the worship of the first beast by instructing those who are inhabitants upon the earth to make an image of the beast themselves. Discerning hearers could not help but to find in this instruction a violation of the divine prohibition against the making of such images (Deut. 4.16). The fact that this beast does not make the image himself, but encourages the inhabitants of the earth to do so is indeed telling, for the hearers would likely understand such an act as constituting a tangible step on the part of the inhabitants upon the earth in the direction of worshipping the first beast. As observed earlier (13.3-4), there is a concrete connection between the worship of the first

Figure 12
Albrecht Dürer, *The Beasts*
(State Art Gallery in Karlsruhe, Germany)

beast and the fact that he had survived a mortal wound, as the beast is identified with the words, 'who has the plague of the sword and lived'. For the first time it is revealed that the plague, or wound, suffered by the beast, was inflicted by a sword. While it is possible that the hearers would take this detail as a subtle reference to the death of Nero, who took his own life with a dagger (Suetonius, *Nero* 49), it is possible that the reference to the sword would be taken as indicating the severity of the wound and the dangerous nature of the instrument that inflicted it. If this wound suffered by the beast is in any way to be identified with the activity of the two prophetic witnesses, it is possible that the hearers would understand in these words the irony of the fact that those destined to be put to death by the sword (13.10) may themselves inflict a mortal wound upon the beast, perhaps with the very sword which he wields. Their death by the sword would in reality be a wound inflicted upon the beast by that very sword. Again, the way in which the beast parodies the Lamb is seen by the fact that even though the beast suffered a mortal wound, 'he lived', just as Jesus lived after his death!

Verse 15 – The construction of the image is not an end in itself, for as the hearers discover, 'and it was given to him to give life to the image of the beast, in order that the image of the beast might even speak, and he acted in order that whoever did not worship the image of the beast might be killed'. Again, the hearers would be alert to the fact of the derived nature of this beast's authority by the way in which the passive ἐδόθη ('it was given') precedes the description of his activities. As noted before, there may be more than a slight chance that the passive form of this verb would underscore for the hearers the extent to which divine activity is being parodied by the evil triumvirate. The fact that this beast was given the authority to give πνεῦμα ('life' or 'spirit') to the image would convey at least two things to the hearers. First, they would perhaps be struck by the fact that this beast would be able to give life to the image of the first beast. While numerous examples from antiquity can be assembled with regard to the way in which statues and/or images could be made to appear alive, some with which the hearers may be familiar,[68] there is no indication in the text itself that this or

---

[68] Cf. Caird, *The Revelation of St. John*, p. 173.

other activities of this beast are achieved by trickery.[69] Second, the hearers would likely pick up on the fact that by means of his derived authority this beast gives the spirit of life, in a way that mimics God's gift of the Spirit of Life to the two witnesses earlier (11.11). Perhaps the discerning hearers would also understand this great sign as a parody of Ezekiel's prophetic activity where dead bones live (Ezekiel 37).[70] If so, the way in which this beast's prophetic activity rivals that of the two prophetic witnesses found in chapter 11 would continue to build. The activity of this living image even includes speaking, a detail that signifies much more than the effect of such a phenomenon, but would be understood as oracular in nature. In other words, the hearers would understand the speech that comes from the image of the beast to be the words of the first beast himself.[71] The result of such 'prophetic' speech is that all who do not worship the beast might be killed. It appears from the context that the oracular words coming from the beast's image insist both on the universal worship of the image of the beast, i.e. worship of the first beast himself, and the putting to death of anyone who does not participate in such worship.[72] Perhaps such oracular speech further defines for the hearers the great and blasphemous things the first beast is described earlier as having uttered (13.5-6). Thus, it here becomes clear that in the war waged by the dragon, the first beast, and now this second beast, those who withstand the onslaughts of this triumvirate face certain death. But, who are these who would oppose such universal worship of the beast and his image? These are the ones who keep the commands of God and have the testimony of Jesus (12.17), whose names are written in the book of life of the Lamb slaughtered from the foundation of the world (13.8), and who face captivity and sword (13.10). Could they be other than the souls under the altar, who had been slaughtered on account of the word of God and the witness which they had (6.9), or those coming out of the great tribulation who have washed their garments in the blood of the Lamb (7.14)? If the hearers have not

---

[69] Murphy, *Fallen Is Babylon*, p. 310.
[70] Sweet, *Revelation*, p. 214.
[71] Aune, *Revelation 6-16*, pp. 762-64. Lucian's account in *Alexander the False Prophet* (24) is perhaps the best-known example of this phenomenon and its oracular significance.
[72] Aune, *Revelation 6-16*, p. 765.

understood before, they certainly do now. The battle in which they will engage, and are already engaging, is one that requires a patient endurance that is faithful unto death (13.10). In this, they stand in solidarity with Jesus, Antipas, and the two prophetic witnesses. Perhaps they, better than modern hearers, understand how the present assaults of the dragon are very tightly connected to the assaults that loom in their future. Perhaps they understand that the war in which they now engage is the same war that lies still in the future. Perhaps they understand that their present responses are no less crucial than those they will make tomorrow. Perhaps they understand the way in which the present and future converge. For the lines of demarcation are clearly drawn; the hearers must either align fully with God or the dragon. There is no middle ground; there is no room for compromise.

Verse 16 – Additional oracular words from the image appear to follow in the next statement encountered by the hearers, 'And he makes all, the small and great, and the rich and the poor, and the free and the slaves, in order that there be given to them a mark upon their right hand or upon their forehead'. These words, amongst which the term ποιεῖ ('he makes') again appears, seem to reveal the means by which those who worship the image of the beast are to be identified. Conversely, this same means, the presence or absence of the beast's mark, would be the way in which those who do not worship the image of the beast could be identified as well. The intended audience is universal and, thus, the results inescapable.[73] The comprehensive list of categories makes clear the universal intent of this oracle. The hearers have earlier encountered a similar, though not identical, listing of humanity (6.15), suggesting that the meaning of this listing would not be lost on them. There is absolutely no one who can expect to be exempt from this demand. All, it seems, are expected to receive a mark in one of two prominent places on their bodies; either upon their right hand, the hand of honor, oaths, and business transactions, or upon their forehead, the place where religious articles were sometimes worn bearing the name of a particular deity indicating to which god or goddess one belonged. Clearly, the hearers would understand that the purpose of such a mark is identity, so that by this means, those who worship the image of the beast

---

[73] Kiddle, *The Revelation of St. John*, p. 258.

could be easily identified. What would the hearers make of such a specific command? How would they likely understand this particular χάραγμα ('mark' or 'brand')? It is possible that they would see in it a practice similar to that of the branding or tattooing of fugitive slaves, or the sign of a conquering people that was sometimes placed upon the vanquished (Plutarch, *Nicias*, 29), or a religious symbol branded upon a subject people (3 Macc. 2.28-30). While any or all of these ideas might be present as the hearers encounter these words, it would not be lost on any of them that the 144,000 have earlier been sealed by God upon their foreheads as a sign of his protection and ownership (7.3; 9.4). Consequently, it is hard to imagine that they would not see in this mark of the beast yet another parody of God and his people.[74] As the seal of God signifies ownership by him, so this beast's mark would signify ownership by the beast.[75] As God's seal signifies protection for his people against the events that accompany the sounding of the trumpets, so the beast's seal signifies protection for those who worship him from death inflicted by him. This mark, then, comes to represent the opposite of that represented by the seal of God. Thus, it becomes unquestionably clear to the hearers that the lines of demarcation between God and the dragon have been drawn absolutely and definitively. To bear the seal of God or the mark of the beast reveals the identity of the worshipper, as well as the identity of the one worshipped. Despite the temptations to the contrary, there is absolutely no middle ground. One either worships God or the beast. Therefore, the hearers' temptations to accommodate themselves to the beast and his system are not to be viewed as minor points of non-conformity to God and his Lamb, but carry in themselves the seeds of identification with the beast. They lead one to the worship of the beast and the receiving of his mark!

Verse 17 – But there is more, for the hearers learn that the image of the beast acts 'in order that no one might be able to buy or sell except the one who has the mark, the name of the beast, or the number of his name'. These words reveal that a close connection exists between the worship of the image of the beast, the bearing of his mark, and participation in commercial and economic life. One

---

[74] Resseguie, *The Revelation of John*, p. 188.
[75] Beale, *The Book of Revelation*, p. 716.

of the implications of such words is that the scope of the beast's authority, earlier described as extending over all human categories (13.7, 12), is now understood to encompass all economic categories as well. So much so that failure to worship the beast and bear his mark bars one from entry into the commercial and economic systems upon which life depends. Part of the implications of these words for the hearers would be that even if it were possible for one to refuse to receive the beast's mark, and somehow escape death at the moment of refusal, one can not escape death altogether. For one who does not bear the beast's mark would be excluded from the very agencies to which one normally looks in order to sustain physical life. Such a realization would affect the hearers in several ways. First, their understanding of the beast's authority and stature would be even higher than before, as they now understand that there is nothing or no one on earth beyond his control. Second, in the light of the relationship between worship of the beast's image and access to commercial and economic life, the hearers might now see the words of the resurrected Jesus with regard to eating food sacrificed to idols (2.14, 20) in a more comprehensive light. Perhaps such retrospective understanding would cause them to examine more carefully their own current involvement with commercial and economic entities, especially those connected to eating meat sacrificed to idols. Is it possible, they might wonder, that they could already be facing the temptation to worship the beast and bear his mark by the participation in various commercial and economic systems? Third, these ominous words of warning would reveal that too much attachment to and/or dependence upon a world order or its systems, that may be connected to the beast, is futile. Eventually, all who do not enter fully into participation and cooperation with the beast will be excluded from them and ultimately put to death. Thus, any temptation to compromise with this world and its systems is seen for the false choice that it is. Specifically, the beast and his system are to be viewed as in diametric opposition to those who keep the commands of God and the witness of Jesus. Not only do the hearers learn about the extent of the beast's authority in the commercial and economic realms, but they also discover more about the nature of the beast's mark for it is described as 'the mark, the name of the beast or the number of his name'. These enigmatic words serve both to inform, as well as intrigue, the hearers. On the one hand, if they earlier wondered as to the nature of the mark that those who worship the beast are to receive, they now know that by receiving it his worshippers bear his name, signifying that they belong to him. They are identified by the fact that they bear in their bodies his mark, his name, and/or the number of his name. On the other hand, they may be intrigued by the fact that the beast's name is not explicitly given as such, though they may be safe in assuming that it may be the same blasphemous name that appears upon his heads, but rather they seem to be given a kind of numerical punning.[76]

Verse 18 – As the hearers ponder such mixed hints, they are directly addressed in a way now familiar to them, as they encounter the formula 'Here is …' Specifically they are told, 'Here is wisdom. Let the one who has understanding calculate the number of the beast, for it is the number of man, and his number is 666'. The last time the hearers encountered the 'Here is …' formula, it followed words that appear to have come from the resurrected Jesus and/or the Spirit (13.10). Following the call, 'if any one has an ear let that one hear', prophetic words about captivity and sword are given and the following statement, 'Here is the patient endurance and faith of the saints' helps to unfold the mystery of the previous words. Owing to the close proximity of these words to those that occur in 13.18, it is likely that the reappearance of the formula, 'Here is …', would carry with it a similar sense of prophetic, pneumatic instruction as had those in 13.10. If so, these words may be yet another example of the pneumatic discernment to which the hearers have been called, time and again in the Apocalypse. The specific phrase, 'Here is wisdom', would be an especially potent one for the hearers, for to this point in the book wisdom has been ascribed only to the Lamb (5.12) and to God (7.12). Thus, it appears that the wisdom here invoked has divine associations and, consequently, is entirely appropriate in an appeal for pneumatic discernment.[77] Earlier the hearers had been instructed, 'If anyone has an ear let that one hear'. Now they are instructed, 'Let the one who has understanding calculate the number of the beast'. What would 'understanding' likely

---

[76] Sweet, *Revelation*, p. 217.

[77] Contra Aune (*Revelation 6-16*, p. 769), who sees no explicit mention of a need for divine help in order to understand.

mean to the hearers? Given its context, it could hardly have reference to mere human intellect. Rather, it would appear to be closely associated with 'wisdom', a suspicion that will be confirmed later in the book when both terms are used side by side in yet another 'Here is …' formula (17.9)! Owing to this close association, the hearers might well be wondering whether the term νοῦν ('understanding') would not carry with it a similar sense of divine endowment. Interestingly enough, a similar idea is found near the close of 1 John where the readers are assured that they 'have been given the ability to understand' (1 Jn 5.19). On that occasion, the Greek word διάνοιαν ('the ability to understand') occurs with reference to the process by which understanding comes, rather than to 'knowledge' or 'understanding' proper. As such, it bears a striking resemblance to the idea of 'the anointing', which the readers have received from him, an anointing that teaches them all things and makes the need for human teachers superfluous (2.20, 27).[78] Such an interpretation of 'understanding' fits nicely with the occurrence of νοῦν ('understanding') found in the call to pneumatic discernment in Rev. 13.18. Specifically, those who have such understanding are encouraged to 'calculate the number of the beast'. On one level, the hearers would be familiar with various ways by which the number of a person or thing could be calculated. And yet, the hearers would know full well that the calculation to which they are called is no mere parlor game, or a calculation that may be completed owing to one's own ingenuity. Rather, this calculation must take place in the Spirit! That is to say this calculation must be undertaken in the Spirit of pneumatic discernment.

To this point, then, the hearers understand that they must continue to follow the leads that the Spirit makes available to them. As it turns out, they do not have to wait for long before receiving their next bit of divine assistance, for of the beast's number it is said, 'and this is the number of man'. Such a statement must come as a bit startling to the hearers, for to this point there is little in the description of the beast that would have encouraged them to view the beast in human terms! In point of fact, most things said about the beast would seem to evoke animal like images, especially the graphic description of his physical appearance. And yet, as the hearers

---

[78] Thomas, *1 John, 2 John, 3 John*, p. 278.

reflect upon what has come before, perhaps these words bring a growing realization that the beast is more like a human than first thought. For example, the beast wears diadems (13.1), he receives and gives authority (13.2, 12), is wounded and healed (13.3), is worshipped owing to his abilities to make war (13.4), and even speaks (13.6). Thus, despite the beast's larger-than-life quality, the first part in the calculation of his number is to understand that it is 'the number of man'. Therefore, there is an explicit identification of the number and name of the beast with that of a 'man', though the anarthrous construction 'of a man' underscores the fact that the number is that of a human being, not necessarily that of a specific individual. But that is not the only assistance, for the hearers next learn the specific number of the beast, 'and his number is 666'. How would the hearers likely calculate this number? It seems reasonable to assume that, owing to the way in which other numbers in the Apocalypse function, this number too would be taken as having a symbolic or figurative quality.[79] That is to say that the number itself would generate echoes of various ideas and themes that converge in the intertext that is the number 666. So what the hearers are likely to discover is that the number of the beast generates a whole matrix of meaning, not a simple identification of a specific figure, and yet it may do that as well.

Perhaps the first thing to catch the attention of the hearers is the fact that this very number, 666, appears on at least one occasion in the OT, where it is used to designate the weight of gold talents that came to King Solomon on an annual basis (1 Kgs 10.14).[80] If such a detail was thought by the hearers to be echoed in the number of the beast it might suggest that such kingly associations reveal something of the kingly aspirations of the beast. At the same time, the implications of such monetary associations would not be lost on hearers who have recently learned that without the beast's mark or number, one is denied access to commercial and economic life. Such an intertextual detail would be enough to give the hearers pause before proceeding to their pneumatic calculations proper.

As they begin to calculate in the Spirit, perhaps the first clear hint given, that the beast's number is the number of man, alerts the

---

[79] Smalley, *The Revelation to John*, p. 352.
[80] A suggestion made by John Sweet to the author in private conversation.

hearers to the fact that despite the beast's mythological-like qualities he is to be calculated in human terms. In other words, the beast himself will be manifested in some way in human form, a realization that might cause the hearers to suspect that there are ways in which they already are encountering the beast in a variety of human forms around them, even as they await the kind of manifestation described in 11.7 and 13.1-18. Thus the realization that the number of the beast is the number of man speaks to genre, the kind of beast that the hearers are to calculate or discern. At the same time, it is very difficult to imagine that the call for pneumatic discernment to calculate the number of the beast would not bring the idea of gematria to the hearers' minds. For at the time in which the Apocalypse was written, letters in the Greek and Hebrew alphabets served a dual function as both letters and numbers. Specifically, Greek letters were assigned the following numerical values:

α′	=	1	ιβ′	=	12 etc.	σ′	=	200
β′	=	2	κ′	=	20	τ′	=	300
γ′	=	3	κα′	=	21 etc.	υ′	=	400
δ′	=	4	λ′	=	30	φ′	=	500
ε′	=	5	μ′	=	40	χ′	=	600
Ϝ′	=	6	ν′	=	50	ψ′	=	700
ζ′	=	7	ξ′	=	60	ω′	=	800
η′	=	8	ο′	=	70	ϡ′	=	900
θ′	=	9	π′	=	80	,α	=	1000
ι′	=	10	ϛ′	=	90	,β	=	2000
ια′	=	11	ρ′	=	100	,γ	=	3000 [81]

Therefore, it was possible to count up the numerical value of the Greek letters in any name or thing. The practice was popular and widespread even being found in graffiti written on the walls of various structures. Perhaps the most famous, and certainly most oft-cited, is the piece of graffiti found in Pompeii from sometime be-

---

[81] For a concise discussion of this use of the Greek alphabet cf. B.M. Metzger, *The Text of the New Testament: Its Transmission, Corruption, and Restoration* (3rd edition; Oxford: Oxford University Press, 1992), p. 190 n. 1.

fore 79 CE, which reads, 'I love her whose number is 545'.[82] The meaning of such a statement would be understandable to the person who wrote it and perhaps to the one 'whose number is 545', but probably not to too wide a circle. In addition to gematria, it was also possible at this time to create a pun out of the numerical value of the letters contained in certain words and names, a method known as isopsephism.[83] According to Suetonius (*Nero* 39), even the emperor Nero was subjected to such sport. One pun reads:

> Nero, Orestes, Alcmeon their mothers slew.
> A calculation new.
> Nero his mother slew.[84]

This isopsephism is based on two things. First, it is based on the well-known fact that Nero had killed his own mother. Second, the numerical value of the name Nero in Greek (1005) is, conveniently, or inconveniently enough, the equivalent to the numerical value of the Greek words translated 'the slayer of one's own mother'.

So, as the hearers begin to 'calculate', it would seem safe to assume that they would likely make use of gematia as they procede.[85] If so, and if some of the hearers are familiar with Hebrew, a possibility suggested by their earlier encounter with the name Abbadon (9.11), which is explicitly identified as a Hebrew name, then perhaps they discern their way to the fact that the numerical value of the Greek word θήριον ('beast') is 666 when transliterated into Hebrew characters.[86] The Hebrew letters were assigned the following numerical value:

---

[82] As cited in Deissmann, *Light from the Ancient East*, p. 277.

[83] Bauckham, *The Climax of Prophecy*, p. 386.

[84] Cited according to the translation of J.C. Rolfe, *Suetonius*, II (London: Heinemann, 1965), pp. 156-59.

[85] It should, of course, be apparent that it would be much easier to discern the practice of gematria if one starts with the name and arrives at the number, rather than beginning with the number and arriving at the name, for in the latter case, one would think the possibilities limitless, as they seem to be with 666!

[86] Cf. W. Hadorn, 'Die Zahl 666, ein Hinweis auf Trajan', *ZNW* 19 (1919-20), p. 23, who identifies the numerical value of the transliterated word תריון as ת = 400 + ר = 200 + י = 10 + ו = 6 + ן = 50 for a total of 666. [pp. 11-29]

א	=	1	ל	=	30
ב	=	2	מ	=	40
ג	=	3	נ	=	50
ד	=	4	ס	=	60
ה	=	5	ע	=	70
ו	=	6	פ	=	80
ז	=	7	צ	=	90
ח	=	8	ק	=	100
ט	=	9	ר	=	200
י	=	10	ש	=	300
כ	=	20	ת	=	400

Such a calculation would serve to confirm that the number of the beast, is indeed 666, as earlier stated, and that the hearers are calculating in the right way. But such an initial calculation would not likely exhaust their efforts on this score, for the call for pneumatic discernment in 13.18 seems to entail much more. Thus, it is likely that they would continue to calculate perhaps with the hope of identifying a specific individual, the number of whose name is 666. Following the calculations used in arriving at the conclusion that the Hebrew transliteration of the Greek word for beast calculates to 666, perhaps the hearers would discern that when the Greek name Νέρων Καίσαρ ('Nero Caesar') is transliterated into Hebrew, it too calculates to 666.[87] If the hearers' initial calculations point in the direction of Nero what would be the implications of such a pneumatic discerning? Perhaps that in the person of Nero, whose excesses were widely known and who seems to have embodied many of the characteristics of the beast, the hearers would be able to see how the larger-than-life beast could be manifested in human form. Thus, if for the hearers the beast now has a face, Nero appears to have sat for the portrait.[88] And if the beast has the face of

---

[87] Cf. Bauckham (*The Climax of* Prophecy, p. 387) who identifies the numerical value of the transliterated word נרון קסר as נ = 50 + ר = 200 + ו = 6 + ן = 50 + ק = 100 + ס = 60 + ר = 200 for a total of 666. It is significant that when the final 'n' is left off the Hebrew transliteration, following the Latin name rather than the Greek, the name calculates to 616, which might go some way toward explaining an early variant reading found in a few manuscripts of the New Testament that read 616 instead of 666 at this point.

[88] Koester, *Revelation and the End of All Things*, p. 130.

Nero, what are the implications for other details of the beast's description, for example, the fact that he has seven heads? Perhaps the hearers would begin to discern ways in which the beast and the empire were related (and this 'head' to the others?). At the same time it does not seem likely that the hearers would have equated the beast with Nero full stop and ceased their calculations, for there are several ways in which the image of the beast is at odds with what is known of Nero.[89] For one thing, there are differences in the way the death of both are described. One of the beast's heads is said to have suffered the plague of death by the sword, while Nero's own self-inflicted death was not a wound to the head with a sword but inflicted to his body with a dagger. There is also the fact that by the time of the Apocalypse Nero is surely dead, and despite arguments to the contrary, there is no evidence that the tradition of Nero's return included the idea of his death and resurrection, an idea that is clearly present in the description of the beast in Revelation 13.[90] Perhaps on this understanding, the hearers would think of their initial calculations of the beast, 'It is Nero all over again'.[91] Based on the calculation by means of gematria, it appears that, on the one hand, the hearers would likely see the face of Nero as intimately connected to the face of the beast, but, on the other hand, they would not likely confine the identity of the beast to Nero alone, for there would be still other means of calculation available to the hearers in their attempts at pneumatic discernment.

Specifically, discerning Johannine hearers' would likely be familiar with another form of calculation that involves 'triangular numbers', a knowledge that is illustrated in Jn 21.11 where reference is made to the catch of 153 fish. As early as the time of Augustine (*Homilies on the Gospel of John* 122.9), it was noted that 153 is the sum of every number from 1 to 17, indicating that it is a most important number indeed. Yet, in some ways its significance pales when it is compared to the number of the beast, 666, which is the sum of every number between 1 and 36. When arranged in order, as if placing

---

[89] In point of fact, it appears that by the time of Irenaeus, Nero was not even considered to be one of the possible solutions to the calculation, as he is not one of the three proposals suggested by Irenaeus (*Against Heresies* 5.30.3).

[90] Bauckham, *The Climax of Prophecy*, pp. 407-23.

[91] Koester, *Revelation and the End of All Things*, p. 133.

a corresponding number of beads from top to bottom, the number 666 would resemble a triangle. It can be illustrated in this way:

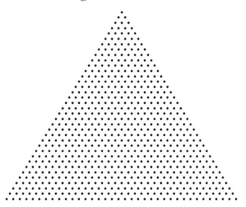

As can be observed, this illustrated version of 666 is perfectly symmetrical and complete in that fashion. What is more, 666 also has the added distinction of being a doubly triangular number, as 36, the last line of numbers, is itself a triangular number being the sum of the numbers from 1 to 8 as illustrated below:

Part of the significance of all this is the fact that doubly triangular numbers (triangular numbers that are built on another triangular number) are quite rare, with 666 being only the eighth such number to occur in the series 1, 6, 21, 55, 120, 231, 406, 666. The significance of the number becomes even more apparent when it is realized that 36 is the only number that is both triangular and square, which may be illustrated in the following way:

What is the significance of all this for the meaning of the number of the beast? Although the full implications of the hearer's calculations in this regard may not be realized until later in the book, owing to the significance of 36, which was especially honored among the ancients,[92] and the fact that 666 is the triangular number of that triangular number, it might not be going too far to see in the number of the beast, a number that would be understood as of cosmic proportions; perhaps a king amongst numbers![93] That is to say that this calculation of the number 666, along with the calculations by means of gematria, also reveals something of the identity of the beast, who not only exercises unrestrained authority on earth, but appears and acts as a king by the wearing of the ten diadems (13.1). Perhaps then in the number 666, the hearers discern a cosmic number, a king of a number for a beast who would himself be a divine king and control the cosmos! Thus, as a result of their calculations in the Spirit, the hearers would have discerned two primary things. First, by means of gematria, they have discovered something about his identity. Specifically, they have come to know that the number of the beast is indeed 666 and have gone so far as to peer into his face. And though his resemblance to Nero is remarkable, they know that he is not simply to be equated with Nero full stop, for Nero is dead, but the beast is not. Second, by means of calculations involving triangular numbers the hearers now have a better sense as to the kind of beast he is. Through their reflection on the number 666 they have discovered things about his aspirations, character, and power. He sees himself as enveloping in himself the cosmos (36) and even fancies himself as the divine king of all, traits consistent with the description of his actions encountered earlier in chapter 13. Consequently, the hearers' pneumatic calculations do not serve to satisfy a sense of curiosity to understand history written in advance, but rather they arm the hearers with discerning wis-

---

[92] Plutarch (*De Iside et Osiride* 75) notes that the number 36 was held to be particularly sacred by the Pythagoreans. 'The so-called *tetraktys*, namely thirty-six, was the greatest oath, as is well known, and was called the Cosmos (or 'and Cosmos was its name'); it was made up by the sum of the first four even (on the one hand) and (first four) uneven numbers (on the other hand)'. Cited according to the translation, with the addition of some Greek words, of J.G. Griffiths, *Plutarch's De Iside et Osiride* (Cambridge: University of Wales Press, 1970), p. 239. On this cf. F.H. Colson, 'Triangular Numbers in the New Testament', *JTS* 16 (1915), p. 70.

[93] Colson ('Triangular Numbers in the New Testament', pp. 70-71) observes, 'When we take into account the identity of what we call digits in 666, it seems likely that in Pythagorean or Nicomachean circles 666 would be a very king amongst numbers'.

dom to prepare them for their next encounter(s) with him, both now and in the future.

The Lamb and the 144,000, the Harvest and the Winepress (14.1-20)

Verse 1 – After a rather long discussion of the dragon, the beast from the sea, and the beast from the earth, and with the admonition to pneumatic discernment with regard to the name and number of the beast still being pondered, the hearers experience an abrupt transition as they encounter John's next words, 'And I saw, and behold the Lamb standing upon Mount Zion and with him 144,000 having his name and the name of the Father written upon their foreheads'. Such a sight is in diametric contrast to those of the dragon and the two beasts. Yet, if this triumvirate of evil stands ready to make war against the saints by every means necessary, so that every one that does not worship the image of the beast and receive his mark is to be killed, so the Lamb and those with him stand at the ready to enter into battle. The words, 'I saw, and behold', a now familiar formula, alert the hearers to the change of topic as a new aspect of the overall vision is now recounted. What John sees is another vision of the Lamb. Two aspects from the most recent mention of the Lamb (13.8), which made reference to 'the book of life of the Lamb slaughtered from the foundation of the world', would be carried forward to the description of the Lamb and his followers in 14.1. The first aspect is the close relationship that exists between the Lamb and those whose names are written in his book. As will be seen, the nature of their relationship is very close indeed. The second aspect is the emphasis once again placed upon the nature of the Lamb's death, for he is described as the one who had been slaughtered. Not only does this detail speak to the nature of the relationship between the Lamb and those with him, that their names are written in his book of life owing to his slaughter, but it also goes some way toward reminding the hearers of the nature of the war the Lamb and his followers are prepared to wage against the triumvirate of evil. Thus, the Lamb stands to oppose the dragon, the beast from the sea, and the beast from the earth. Neither is the location of the Lamb without significance, for the mention of Mount Zion at once conveys several things to the hearers. First, the phrase, 'And I saw ... upon Mount Zion' would continue the upward trajectory of the things John sees beginning in 13.1

from the sea (13.1), to the earth (13.11), and now to Mount Zion (14.1). Second, the description of the Lamb standing on Mount Zion would reaffirm the understanding of the Lamb as 'the Root of David' (5.5), owing to its close association with David, being known as the city of David (2 Sam. 5.7), therefore continuing a major emphasis of the book. Third, owing to its numerous OT associations as the place of God's residence (Pss. 9.11; 76.2; 132.13), the place where his anointed King overcomes the raging nations (Ps. 2.6), and as the eschatological place of protection and security for God's people (Isa. 24.23; 25.7-10), the Lamb's location here suggests that the eschatological promises are now seeing their fulfillment and that the hearers are not far from these eschatological events. Thus, the question whether Mount Zion is located on earth or heaven is a bit misplaced, as at this point in the book heaven and earth appear to be very close together for the hearers.[94] Given its numerous OT associations, it would not surprise the hearers that the Lamb has companions with him on Mount Zion, though the specific group of companions may indeed be unexpected, for there were with him 144,000. Despite the fact that there is no definite article standing before this number in the Greek text it is next to impossible to believe that the hearers would not think of the 144,000 sons of the tribes of Israel described earlier in Rev. 7.1-8 when encountering this number.[95] From their earlier description the hearers may well remember (1) that this number is perhaps based on Numbers 31, where Moses takes 12,000 men, one thousand from each of the twelve tribes of Israel, into battle with Midian; (2) the strong sense of connection that exists between their own community and the 144,000; (3) that the 144,000 would be thought of as a messianic group; (4) that this group would be seen as the heirs to what God has done through Israel; (5) that like the Johannine believers, this group is marked in part by its priestly identity; (6) the prophetic characteristics of this group and that they too share in

---

[94] Smalley, *The Revelation to John*, p. 354.

[95] On this point Beale (*The Book of Revelation*, pp. 733-34) notes, 'The lack of the article before "144,000" does not distinguish this group from the one in 7.4-9, where the article does occur. Throughout the Apocalypse images are repeated, sometimes without the article in later occurrences ... An article of previous reference is not needed here, since other features in the scene point clearly enough back to 7.4-9.'

this prophetic identity; (7) that this group is clearly one marked out as belonging to God and protected by him; and (8) that the innumerable crowd that follows is seen in some sense as growing out of the 144,000. Thus, when the 144,000 re-appears in 14.1, the hearers would hardly have forgotten that this image of the transformed Israel has itself been transformed in the light of the innumerable crowd, suggesting that for them the 144,000 are now forever identified with the innumerable crowd, not unlike the way in which the Root of David is now forever identified with the slaughtered Lamb. In that regard, it may not be insignificant that the 144,000 are here described as standing with the Lamb on Mount Zion, while the innumerable crowd was 'seen' as 'standing before the throne and the Lamb'! In 14.1, the 144,000 stand with the Lamb in opposition to the triumvirate of evil, ready to do battle. Earlier it was discovered that the 144,000 received the seal of God upon their foreheads (7.3). Now, the content of that seal is revealed, for the 144,000 bear the name of the Lamb and the name of his Father. In the light of the purpose of the seal God placed upon the sons of the tribes of Israel, and the purpose of the mark of the beast on those who worship his image, it is clear that the names that appear upon the 144,000 indicate possession, ownership, and protection.[96] The fact that they bear the name of the Lamb suggests a very close relationship between the Lamb and the 144,000. Specifically, it would call to mind the promise of the resurrected Jesus to the one who overcomes, 'and I will write upon him the name of my God' (3.12).[97] It suggests that they are like the one with whom they stand, the extent of which will become more explicit as the passage continues. Neither would the fact that the 144,000 bear the name of the Father be without significance for the hearers. For this mention of the Father would likely trigger a recollection of the previous associations this language has had to this point in the book.[98] Specifically, the hearers have been told that Jesus has made them 'a kingdom, priests to God and his Father' (1.6), that Jesus will give 'authority over the nations' to the one who overcomes just as he received from his Father (2.28-29), that Jesus will not erase the name of the one who

---

[96] Beale, *The Book of Revelation*, p. 734.
[97] Yarbro Collins, *Revelation*, p. 99.
[98] Smalley, *The Revelation to John*, p. 355.

overcomes 'out of the book of life and … will confess his name before my Father' (3.5), and that Jesus will give to the one who overcomes 'to sit with me on my throne even as I overcame and sat with my Father on his throne' (3.21). Therefore, for it to be revealed that the 144,000 bear the name of the Father suggests that these are they who are the heirs of these promises. As they stand with the Lamb, they are a kingdom; priests to God, who have authority over the nations. As they stand with the Lamb, they are those whose names are not only written in, but have not been erased from, the book of life of the Lamb who was slaughtered from the foundation of the world. As they stand with the Lamb they are those entitled to sit on the throne with Jesus, who sits on the throne of his Father. Thus, the 144,000 represent those who overcome, those who stand with the Lamb, those who stand ready to fight as he has fought. The explicit contrast between those who bear the mark of the beast, with his blasphemous name on their foreheads, and those who bear the name of the Lamb and the name of his Father on their foreheads would hardly be missed by the hearers!

Verse 2 – Suddenly the hearers detect a shift from what John saw to what he heard, 'And I heard out of heaven as a voice of many waters and as a voice of great thunder, and the voice which I heard was as harpists harping on their harps'. If the geographical location of Mount Zion is unclear in 14.1, with the move from what is seen to what is heard, the focus of attention now shifts to heaven, the location of the voice or sound. The hearers have come to know that there is a mysterious relationship between things seen and things heard, beginning with John's hearing a voice as a trumpet (1.10), but seeing one like the Son of Man in the midst of seven golden lampstands (1.12-13); hearing the Lion of the tribe of Judah and the Root of David (5.5), but seeing a Lamb looking as if it had been slaughtered (5.6); hearing the 144,000 sealed (7.4), but seeing an innumerable multitude (7.9). Later the hearers learn that sometimes what is heard precedes what is seen, as in the case with the silence in heaven (8.1) preceding the seeing of the seven angels who were given seven trumpets standing before the Lord (8.2). Therefore, when the focus of attention shifts from what John saw to what he heard in 14.2, the hearers are put on notice that they are about to learn something more about Jesus and the 144,000 standing on Mount Zion than they knew before. And what John hears both confirms the things they discerned earlier about the 144,000 (14.1) and yields additional knowledge to them. For the voice(s) that come from heaven concern the 144,000; their identity, their activities, and their character. Though the word φωνήν ('voice' or 'sound') can be understood broadly as 'sound', as will be seen here it appears best to take it as 'voice', as in most of its earlier occurrences in the book. The description of the voice out of heaven as a voice of many waters could not help but remind the hearers of the voice of Jesus, which was described this way in John's inaugural vision of Jesus (1.15). At the same time, the description of the voice as a voice of great thunder would remind them of the voice of one of the four living creatures crying 'Go' as the first seal is being opened by the Lamb (6.1). Thunder has also come to be closely associated with the activity of God, whether as part of the theophanic elements displayed in the inaugural vision of heaven (4.5) and at the end of the enumerated cycles of seven (8.5; 11.19) or the seven thunders that John was instructed to close up and not write down (10.3-4). Consequently, while the hearers may be unable to discern the exact identity of the voice at this point, they would no doubt take it as closely associated with the divine in one way or another. The other way in which this voice is described for the hearers is as 'harpists harping on their harps!' In this peculiar description the subject [κιθαρῳδῶν ('harpists'), verbal form [κιθαριζόντων ('harping')], and indirect object [κιθάραις ('harps')] are all part of the same word family, a construction that seems to place a great deal of emphasis upon this particular aspect of the voice's identity. The last time harps were mentioned they were again in the context of heaven, there in the hands of the twenty-four elders (5.8). As they accompany singing on that occasion, perhaps the hearers would expect that this sound from heaven in 14.1-2 would be accompanied by singing as well. Thus, this dramatic means of expression would likely be deemed by the hearers as an appropriate sound to come from heaven and one closely associated as coming from those very near the throne and the One who sits on it, the twenty-four elders![99] At the same time, this emphatic description goes some way toward

---

[99] As Sweet (*Revelation*, p. 222) says, 'Here the harping comes, by allusion, from the throne itself, and confirms the redemptive sense of John's vision'.

preparing the hearers for the possibility that this remarkable sound comes from a number of individuals rather than one, as the mental image is of numerous harpists harping on their harps!

Verse 3 – With this cacophony of sound in their ears the hearers now encounter words that bring some additional definition to those just encountered in 14.1-2, 'And they sing a new song before the throne and before the four living creatures and the twenty-four elders, and no one was able to learn the song except the 144,000, those who had been purchased from the earth'. One of the first things the hearers would likely note is the fact that just as in 5.8, so here, the mention of harps is accompanied by singing, only in this case it appears that the voice as harpists harping on their harps is actually the sound of numerous voices singing! Perhaps they would also be struck by the way in which this song stands in such stark contrast to the one sung by those enslaved to the beast (13.4).[100] Although there is some uncertainty with regard to the subject of the verb ᾄδουσιν ('they sing'), which could be another of the third person impersonal forms here translated as 'there was singing', it is likely that the hearers would take this third person plural verb as having reference to the 144,000.[101] For despite the way in which the whole of v. 2 separates the subject, given in v. 1, from the verb, given in v. 3,[102] the rest of v. 3 makes clear that the 144,000 are uniquely qualified to sing this song. Such a realization on the part of the hearers might cause them to discern the way the voice of the 144,000 resembles the voice of the Lamb, for if it is they who sing, both their voice and the voice of Jesus are depicted 'like the sound of many waters'.[103] In addition, the hearers may very well be appreciative of the fact that 'new song' language is holy war terminology, where a hymn of praise is offered for a new victory that a divine warrior wins over his foes (Pss. 98.1-3; 144.9-10; Isa. 42.10-13),[104] a fact that further underscores the military nature of this scene where the Lamb and the 144,000 stand ready to oppose the triumvirate of evil. The fact that this new song is sung 'before the throne and be-

---

[100] Allo, *L'Apocalypse*, p. 196.
[101] Despite the vehement protest of Aune, *Revelation 6-16*, p. 784.
[102] Pattemore, *The People of God in the Apocalypse*, p. 184.
[103] Pattemore, *The People of God in the Apocalypse*, p. 184.
[104] Bauckham, *The Climax of Prophecy*, p. 230.

fore the four living creatures and the elders' would undoubtedly remind the hearers of the last time a new song was sung in the Apocalypse (5.8-10). On that occasion the new song is sung before the Lamb and it appears to be sung by the twenty-four elders, who, as has been noted, bear a striking resemblance to the description of those who overcome in the seven prophetic messages spoken by the resurrected Jesus. These elders, who have harps and golden bowls full of incense, which are the prayers of the saints, sing of the worthiness of the Lamb to take the book and open its seals owing to his slaughter and his purchase for God individuals from every demographic segment of the world and making them a kingdom and priests to God who will reign upon the earth. The location of the song in 14.3 is the most appropriate place for it to be sung, as this is the redemptive center of the universe, for it is sung in the very presence of God! That the 144,000 are those who are to sing this song, if not those who already sing, is made clear in the following words that seem to restrict its singing to them alone, 'and no one was able to learn the song except the 144,000, those who had been purchased from the earth'. The first thing that might attract the attention of discerning Johannine hearers is the occurrence of the word μαθεῖν ('to learn'), which they know to have a special association with Jesus, who says in the FG, 'each one who hears from the Father and learns comes to me' (Jn 6.45). Interestingly, in Rev, 14.3 it is the ones who have the name of the Lamb and the name of his Father on their foreheads who are able to learn this new song. That the 144,000 are further identified as 'those who have been purchased from the earth' makes explicit the connection between this group and all the redeemed, as well as underscoring how it is that they have come to this place. For those purchased by the blood of the Lamb come out of every tribe and tongue and people and nation (5.9b), and the blood of Jesus is clearly the means by which this purchase is accomplished (5.9a). The passive voice of the participle οἱ ἠγορασμένοι ('the ones who have been purchased') further underscores the divine activity involved in this purchase.[105] The hearers could hardly forget that it is the blood of Jesus that has purchased them from the earth. And if it be asked why it is that this is the only song mentioned in the Apocalypse, the content of which is

---

[105] Gause, *Revelation*, p. 189.

not revealed, could it not be owing to the fact that the content of this 'new song' is the same as that revealed earlier in 5.8-10?[106] And if it be asked how these songs could be the same since the twenty-four elders sing it in 5.8-10, is it not owing to the fact that the twenty-four elders, who bear a striking resemblance to those who overcome, are themselves the representatives of all the redeemed?

Verses 4-5 – In the words that follow, the hearers discover even more about those who sing the new song, as they are told three additional things about the 144,000, with the pronoun οὗτοι ('these') standing at the beginning of each statement:

> These are the ones who have not been defiled by women, for they are virgins.
>
> These are the ones who follow the Lamb wherever he goes.
>
> These have been purchased from men as first fruits to God and the Lamb, and in their mouth is found no lie, for they are blameless.

In these chiastically structured statements it is revealed that several things the hearers may have suspected to be true of the 144,000 earlier are stated in more concrete form, even if the meaning of the statements are not immediately understandable. For here the nature of the imagery used is such that the hearers' skills in pneumatic discernment are put to the test. While it is possible that the hearers would take the first phrase, 'These are the ones who have not defiled themselves with women, for they are virgins', as an indication that the 144,000 are to be understood as an all-male, celibate community,[107] this interpretation ultimately fails to convince owing to several factors. First, there is nothing in the Johannine literature to suggest that women were thought of as a group to be avoided in social interaction, or to be avoided sexually within the bounds of marriage. In point of fact, every specific woman mentioned in the FG turns out to be a model of belief in Jesus, and in her own way, each serves as an exemplary witness as well. Second, to this point in the Apocalypse the only negative example of a woman is 'the woman called Jezebel', who is not condemned for her gender but for the fact that she is a false prophetess. That women are suddenly seen as

---

[106] Koester, *Revelation and the End of All Things*, p. 136.

[107] So Yarbro Collins, *Revelation*, p. 100. For early Christian writers who defend this position cf. ACCS 12, pp. 217-21.

a class of people to be avoided owing to their defiling nature would not seem to coincide with the experience of Johannine hearers. Third, neither would the hearers likely take these words as indicating an attitude suspicious of the defiling nature of sexual relations, as the positive light in which the wedding at Cana is presented appears to indicate otherwise (Jn 2.1-11). Fourth, though male imagery has been used to describe the 144,000, as both the sons of the tribes of Israel (7.4) and those who have not been defiled by women (14.4), the hearers have come to understand this group as one that ultimately encompasses all of the redeemed. Consequently, it is not likely that they would take the language in 14.4 in an overly restrictive way.[108] Thus, it would appear that the hearers would likely have to look elsewhere to discern the meaning of these words. If so, one of the things that would likely inform their interpretation of these words would be the 'holy war' context in which they occur. As the hearers would know, OT holy war regulations include stipulations with regard to sexual abstinence before battle (Deut. 23.9-10; 1 Sam. 21.5; 2 Sam. 11.11). Given the fact that the 144,000 appear ready to join the Lamb in battle against the triumvirate of evil and their sealing is reminiscent of a military roll call (7.4-8), the words they 'have not defiled themselves with women' would likely be taken as a sign of their dedication to and preparation for battle. At the same time, owing to the emphasis placed upon the language of 'fornication', 'eating food sacrificed to idols' (Rev. 2.14, 20), and 'committing adultery' (Rev. 2.22) to this point in the book, all of which are used in a religiously qualified sense, and the refusal of 'the rest of men' to repent for such activity (9.20-21),[109] it is likely that the idea of not being defiled would convey a sense of fidelity in witness and faith on the part of the 144,000 when faced with the temptation of such contamination.[110] Such an understanding is even more likely in the light of the fact that the previous occurrence of the word that appears here as ἐμολύνθησαν ('they had been defiled') in 3.4 describes those who had not defiled their clothing and whose names will not be erased from the book of life (3.5). The final statement of this first portion of this description of the

---

[108] Murphy, *Fallen Is Babylon*, p. 317.

[109] Pattemore, *The People of God in the Apocalypse*, pp. 186-87.

[110] Sweet, *Revelation*, p. 221.

144,000, 'for they are virgins', would then take on a rather thick meaning which combines the ideas of preparation, dedication, and purity unto the Lamb, an idea that would appear to anticipate the later description of the bride of the Lamb (19.7-8, 21.1-2).[111]

The second statement about the 144,000, marked out by the word οὗτοι ('these'), stands at the center of these three statements and is distinguished as well by the fact that unlike the first and third statements it does not contain a γάρ ('for') clause. Its location at the center of this chiastic section suggests that primary focus would be given here. Its strategic location is matched by its descriptive content with regard to the 144,000, 'These are the ones who follow the Lamb wherever he goes'. This phrase would have a very special meaning for Johannine hearers as the words οἱ ἀκολουθοῦντες ('the ones who follow') would evoke a number of images, for the language of 'following' is, in the Johannine community, discipleship language *par excellence*. This language is used by Jesus when he issues the invitation/command 'follow me' that appears near the beginning (Jn 1.43) and the end of the FG (21.19-20, 22), forming an inclusio of sorts around the entire gospel. As such, this invitation/command envelops the whole journey of discipleship. This verb not only appears in the invitation to discipleship in the FG, but is also used to describe the disciples' relationship to Jesus (1.37-38, 40). Following Jesus is the equivalent of walking in the Light (8.12) and is evidence that one hears and knows the voice of the Good Shepherd (10.4-5, 27). The FG reveals that such following is not easy, for despite Peter's protests to the contrary, which even includes a statement of his intent to die for Jesus, he is unable at that point 'to follow'. But in Jesus' final exchange with Peter, it becomes clear that following Jesus will lead to Peter's own death (21.19-22). It is this aspect of following that appears to be particularly in view in Rev. 14.4b, for it is the Lamb who has been slaughtered that the 144,000 follow. Thus, this imagery would be enough to convey the idea that the 144,000 follow Jesus even in death, but the phrase 'wherever he goes' drives this point home all the more. For Johannine hearers understand that this idea of going, with reference to Jesus, is unquestionably associated with his going to the Father (Jn 7.33; 8.14, 21-22; 13.3, 33; 16.5, 10, 17). At this point it is

---

[111] Pattemore, *The People of God in the Apocalypse*, p. 187.

not possible for the Jews or Jesus' disciples to follow him, or even know the way (13.36; 14.5), but Jesus expects them to know the way (14.4). Perhaps the most telling aspect of this verb for hearers of Rev. 14.4 is found in the story of the dialogue between Jesus and his disciples just before he goes to his friend Lazarus, who had just died. The disciples prophetically say, 'Rabbi, now the Jews are seeking to stone you, and again you go there?' In the FG, as in Rev. 14.4, where the Lamb goes inevitably involves suffering and death. Therefore, the meaning of this description of the 144,000 could hardly be missed by the hearers: they follow the Lamb wherever he goes, even to death,[112] which, as it turns out, is the means by which this war is waged against the dragon and his beasts. They, as their Lord, give the ultimate witness, as had Antipas and the two prophetic witnesses. Such a walk goes hand in glove with the first οὗτοι ('these') statement that makes clear the level of dedication and preparation on the part of the 144,000 for this battle.

The third statement with regard to the 144,000, also marked out by the word οὗτοι ('these'), forms a parallel to the first statement, 'These have been purchased from men as first fruits to God and the Lamb, and in their mouth is found no lie, for they are blameless'. As noted in 14.3, the 144,000 are those who have been purchased from the earth by means of the blood of the Lamb. This reality, in fact, is one of the components of the new song sung in 5.8-10 and it is to this characteristic of the 144,000 that the third statement returns. The fact that the 144,000 can be spoken of as first fruits would convey two things to the hearers. First, it indicates yet again that these have been dedicated to God and the Lamb in a special way. Earlier, the imagery of holy war and ritual purity was used to convey the idea that they are pure, not contaminating themselves with the religious adultery, sexual immorality, and idolatry with which they are confronted. Here, the imagery of first fruit offering further underscores their sacrificial identification as those dedicated to God and the Lamb. Second, first fruit imagery would also create within the hearers an expectancy that these are the first of many to join the Lamb in the great harvest that is to follow from the battle waged by the Lamb and the 144,000. In this way, the relationship of

---

[112] Eusebius (*EH* 5.1.10) cites this text in describing an early Christian martyr named Vettius Epagathus.

the 144,000 to the conversion of the nations stands in parallel to the relationship of the 144,000 to the innumerable crowd (7.1-17). Similarly, the 144,000 also stand in parallel to the two prophetic witnesses whose witness, including their death and resurrection, leads to the conversion of the vast majority of the universal city's inhabitants (11.3-13). Thus, such language could not help but encourage the hearers to expect a great harvest of belief to follow on from these first fruits.[113] These who are first fruits are further identified by the words, 'and in their mouth no lie was found, for they are blameless'. Unlike the mouth of the beast, that boasts great and blasphemous things, and in contrast to the Devil, who is the father of lies and speaks the language of lies (Jn 8.44), unlike those who claim to have fellowship with God but walk in darkness, who lie (1 Jn 1.6; cf. also 2.21, 27), and in contrast to those who make themselves to be apostles but are liars (Rev. 2.2), and to those who claim to be Jews but are lying (3.9), in the mouth of the 144,000 there is found no lie.[114] Rather, these bear a likeness to the Lamb, who speaks words of truth, words of the Spirit, words that are true and are not lies (1 Jn 2.21, 27). In this, they also bear a likeness to the remnant of Israel who speaks no lies (Zeph. 3.13b). The fact that they are truthful and do not lie would be of special significance owing to the temptations to compromise their witness to the Lamb in the face of persecution and even death![115] The γάρ ('for') phrase with which this section concludes reemphasizes what has been said earlier about the 144,000. The words, 'for they are blameless', both reinforces the imagery of sacrifice, known from various OT texts, and at the same time underscores the issue of moral purity. The 144,000 are not only ἄμωμοί ('blameless') as in a sacrifice without spot or defect, but they are also blameless with regard to moral purity.[116] In this as well, they resemble the Lamb with whom they stand.

Verse 6 – As the hearers reflect on the picture of the 144,000 that continues to emerge, most recently in 14.1-5, their attention is

---

[113] R. Bauckham, 'Revelation', *The Oxford Bible Commentary* (eds., J. Barton and J. Muddiman; Oxford: Oxford University Press, 2001), p. 1298.

[114] Michaels, *Revelation*, p. 172.

[115] Smalley, *The Revelation to John*, p. 360.

[116] Bauckham, *The Climax of Prophecy*, p. 232 and Smalley, *The Revelation to John*, p. 360.

yet again refocused as they hear the words, 'And I saw ...' Specifically they are told, 'And I saw another angel flying in mid-heaven, having an eternal gospel to preach unto those who are sitting upon the earth and unto every nation and tribe and tongue and people'. As the hearers have come to know, the occurrence of εἶδον ('I saw') normally designates a change of focus and, on this occasion, is the fourth in a series of appearances that continues the upward trajectory of the things John sees beginning in 13.1 from the sea (13.1), to the earth (13.11), to Mount Zion (14.1), and now to the mid-heavens (14.6). It might strike the hearers as somewhat odd that the angel here mentioned is described as 'another angel', for the last angel mentioned is Michael and his angels (12.7-9). However, such a description would perhaps cause the hearers to reflect back upon the last 'other angel' mentioned, the other mighty angel of 10.1-10. If so, they would perhaps take the mention of the angel who appears in 14.6 to be of particular importance, a suspicion that is bore out as this section unfolds. The location of this other angel, in mid-heaven, is identical to that of the eagle described earlier as also flying in mid-heaven, who pronounced with a great voice three coming woes (9.13). Such a location ensures that the angel could be seen and heard by everyone.[117] If the message of the eagle was important, the message of this angel is no less significant or dramatic, for while the eagle proclaimed the negative message of woes, this other angel, the first angel to be described in the Apocalypse as flying, proclaims a positive message, having an εὐαγγέλιον αἰώνιον εὐαγγελίσαι ('eternal gospel to preach').[118] The word play found in the Greek text would be easy to detect by the hearers, as would the emphasis of this phrase, the gospel, as both the direct object and the infinitive verb are forms of the same Greek word. Such an emphasis may be a bit surprising given the fact that this is the only occurrence of the term gospel in the Johannine literature, with only the verb form having appeared earlier. Significantly, in the only other reference to this Greek word in the Apocalypse God himself is said to have preached 'the mystery of God' to his own servants the prophets (10.7). Thus, while the content of the 'eternal gospel', which the other angel preaches, is not yet revealed, perhaps the

---

[117] Aune, *Revelation 6-16*, p. 824.
[118] Bauckham, 'Revelation', p. 1298.

hearers would see some connection between the eternal gospel this angel preaches and the mystery of God that he himself has preached. In any event, the eternal character of this gospel might very well be seen as quite fitting, coming as it does from the God who is earlier identified in the Apocalypse as 'the one who is and the one who was and the one who is coming' (1.4). At the same time, the hearers might also discern a contrast between this eternal gospel, and its offer of eternal life, with the transient message of the triumvirate of evil, and its offer of 'life' only for a brief time.[119] Whatever their initial impressions of this eternal gospel, the scope of its intended audience appears to be as wide as the gospel is eternal, for it is intended for all the inhabitants of the earth, described in the now familiar four-fold fashion, 'every nation and tribe and tongue and people'. Significantly, this is the sixth and final time this group of four demographic entities appears in the Apocalypse. Strikingly, they never appear in the same order twice! To this point, they have had reference to those groups out of whom the Lamb has purchased individuals with his blood (5.9), the innumerable crowd standing before the throne and the Lamb (7.9), those to whom John is to prophesy again (10.11), on which occasion the word 'kings' appears instead of 'tribes', those who saw the body of the two witnesses in the street for three days (11.9), and those over whom the beast from the sea is given authority by the dragon (13.7). From these occurrences three things are clear. First, these demographic groups are present in heaven and their presence there offers the hearers hope and encouragement with regard to the ultimate redemption of these groups. Second, these groups are under the influence of and side with the first beast over against God and his people in the present battle on earth. Third, these groups are those to whom God, the Lamb, and his church are to bear witness for the purpose of their conversion. The fact that the previous appearances of these groups convey such diverse ideas suggests that the hearers would find themselves facing those same tensions, between the hope of the conversion of the nations, the current reality of the nations' obstinate opposition to God and his people, and the unrelenting call to bear prophetic witness to these very groups at the cost of the witnesses' lives!

---

[119] Smalley, *The Revelation to John*, p. 361.

Verse 7 – Having learned something of the nature and scope of this eternal gospel, the angel and this message are further described, 'Saying with a great voice, "Fear God and give him glory, because the hour of his judgment has come, and worship the one who made the heaven and the earth and the sea and the springs of water"'. As had the eagle before him, who proclaimed the three woes to those who dwell upon the earth, this other angel speaks with a great voice, so that by means of both his location in the mid-heaven and the volume of his great voice all the intended audiences can hear his message. For the hearers, the message to fear God and give him glory would be an unmistakably clear call for repentance.[120] For, as they would recall, when the Spirit of Life of God entered into the two prophetic witnesses and stood them on their feet, great fear fell upon all who beheld this sight (11.11). Immediately after the ensuing earthquake, those who survived became fearful and gave glory to the God of heaven (11.13). The salvific nature of such fear is defined even more clearly when God is implored to 'give your reward to your servants, the prophets and to the saints and to those who fear your name' (11.18).[121] At the same time, the giving or ascribing of glory to God in the Apocalypse is consistently on the lips of believers (1.6; 4.9, 11; 5.12-13; 7.12; and 11.13). Thus, the other angel's message is one that calls for a conversion on the part of humankind, from fearing the beast and worshipping him to fearing God and giving glory unto him.[122] The urgency of this eternal gospel is revealed in the next phrase, 'because the hour of his judgment has come'.[123] This urgency is heightened by the fact that the certainty of the hour of judgment's arrival is spoken of as though it has already happened, with the past tense verb ἦλθεν ('has come') occurring instead of the present or future tense.[124] The words, 'the hour of his judgment', would likely be understood by the hearers as having reference to *the* final judgment,[125] the day of the Lord, when all those who bear the name of God and the Lamb on their fore-

---

[120] Osborne, *Revelation*, p. 535.

[121] Fear becomes even more closely associated with the saints in Rev. 15.4 and 19.5, where it will also appear in connection with giving glory.

[122] Yarbro Collins, *Revelation*, p. 102.

[123] Prigent, *L'Apocalypse*, p. 339.

[124] Smalley, *The Revelation to John*, p. 363.

[125] Aune, *Revelation 6-16*, p. 828.

heads will be saved and when all those who worship the image of the beast and bear his name will be destroyed. Thus, despite the obstinate refusal of these groups of humankind to repent and their continued worship of the image of the beast, the angel's proclamation of the eternal gospel reveals that though the hour of God's judgment is at hand, it is still not too late to repent![126] The language of judgment would convey two additional things to Johannine hearers. First, they would likely associate this judgment with the resurrection of the dead unto life for those who do good and unto judgment for those who do evil (Jn 5.29). Second, instead of dread, word of the hour of judgment would likely remind the hearers that for those in whom the love of God has been completed there is confidence in the day of judgment, for completed love casts out all fear of the judgment (1 Jn 4.17-18). Making clear the intent of his call to fear God and give him glory, this angel calls on those who hear his voice to 'worship the one who made the heaven and the earth and the sea and the springs of water'. The call to worship God as creator is not a new idea to the hearers of the Apocalypse (4.11; 10.6), but in this context they could hardly miss the contrast between the worship rendered to the dragon and the beast by the inhabitants of the earth and the true worship rendered to the creator of it all. One wonders if the hearers would not also see in the mention of 'the heaven and the earth and the sea' a reference to the places of origin of the dragon and the two beasts, indicating that though they are powerful foes, God is in fact the creator of everything.[127] Perhaps at this point, the hearers would also detect that the eternal gospel preached by this angel is none other than that spoken of in Ps. 96.2, a psalm in which the entire content of the angel's message could be found! If so, this is additional reason to understand the eternal gospel as God's unchanging message of salvation.[128]

Verse 8 – After hearing this angel preaching the eternal gospel, the hearers are told, 'And another second angel followed saying, "Fallen, fallen is Babylon the Great who out of the wine of the passion (wrath) of her sexual immorality she gave all the nations to

---

[126] Ladd, *Revelation*, p. 193.

[127] Koester, *Revelation and the End of All Things*, pp. 137-39.

[128] On this cf. Bauckham, *The Climax of Prophecy*, pp. 286-89, who suggests that Psalms 96-100 are all in view in the words of Rev. 14.8.

drink'". Though the expression 'another second angel' is somewhat peculiar, it might well remind the hearers of the seven angels with seven trumpets who were enumerated in chapters 8-9. At the least, they would understand this angel to be on the order of the other angel mentioned in 14.6-7, for the fact that he is described as following the first one mentioned would suggest that this angel too was flying in mid-heaven and preparing to proclaim a most important message on his own, perhaps an aspect of the eternal gospel itself. The emphasis of the angel's message would be easy for the hearers to detect for not only does it stand at the beginning of the sentence, a position of emphasis in Greek grammar, but it also appears in duplicate form.[129] The occurrence of the word ἔπεσεν ('fallen') in the aorist tense treats the fall of Babylon the Great, which is future, as though it has already taken place, so confident is he in the certainty of that which he speaks,[130] being yet another example of the prophetic perfect in the Apocalypse (6.17; 11.18).[131] It would, no doubt, be deemed as significant that the first mention of 'Babylon the Great' in the Apocalypse would come in a declaration of its utter and total demise! Perhaps the hearers would take this enigmatic mention of Babylon the Great as an indication that it, like the enigmatic mention of the beast in 11.7, will be taken up later in the book of this prophecy. To encounter the name Babylon the Great would, no doubt, generate a variety of associations on the part of the hearers, as Babylon would be remembered as a place of luxury and moral corruption.[132] It would also be known for its role in the destruction of Jerusalem in 586 BCE. Neither would the parallels between the ancient Babylon and the contemporary Rome, both as cities and empires, be missed by the hearers. At the same time, the description of her as 'great' might also remind the hearers of 'the great city' described in Revelation 11, the majority of which, though opposed to God and his servants, eventually give glory to God, in conformity to the command of the first other angel de-

---

[129] Wall, *Revelation*, p. 184.

[130] Tyconius (*Commentary on the Apocalypse*, 14.8 [ACCS 12, p. 225]) observes, 'This is a common way of speaking in the Scripture, which often refers to events as past when they are yet in the future, especially when he knows that what it predicts will inevitably be fulfilled'.

[131] Beale, *The Book of Revelation*, p. 754.

[132] Smalley, *The Revelation to John*, p. 264.

scribed in 14.7. Yet, at this point, Babylon the Great is defined simply as the one 'who out of the wine of the passion (wrath) of her sexual immorality she gave all the nations to drink'. This description would be significant in several ways. First, the four separate genitive constructions which make up the Greek phrase translated 'of the wine of the wrath of her sexual immorality' indicate that all of the constituent elements (wine, wrath, sexual immorality, and 'her') are closely connected. Perhaps when encountering the words τοῦ θυμοῦ ('of the passion' or 'wrath'), the hearers would pick up on the fact that this word, which can be translated as 'passion', also has the meaning of 'wrath', which the hearers have already encountered in the description of the dragon who, after his being cast down from heaven, had great θυμὸν ('wrath') (12.12). Thus, despite the clear contextual idea that her wine is wine of passion, borne of sexual immorality, it is at the same time a wine of wrath, akin to the wrath of the dragon. The objects of her 'affections' are, in words reminding the hearers of Jer 51.7-8, 'all the nations', indicating that those who drink of her wine are those to whom the first other angel has just preached the eternal gospel. The fact that her wine is the wine of sexual immorality might well remind the hearers that this sexual immorality language is the very language that was used to describe the activities of the woman called 'Jezebel' by Jesus (2.20-21). As such, its appearance here might well serve to suggest that in their encounter with the teaching of the Nicolaitans (2.14) and 'Jezebel', they are actually already encountering Babylon the Great, who, it should be remembered, is as good as fallen.

Verse 9 – With this the hearers encounter yet another angel, 'And another third angel followed them saying in a great voice, "If anyone worships the beast and his image and receives a mark upon his forehead or upon his hand, he himself will drink of the wine of the wrath of God, which has been mixed, though unmixed in the cup of his anger and that he will be tormented in fire and sulfur before the holy angels and before the Lamb"'. This angel, enumerated as the other third angel, and described as following the other two, would be taken as continuing in the work of his predecessors. He, too, would be understood as flying in mid-heaven and continuing the proclamation which the others have begun. As with the words of the second other angel, it would not surprise the hearers that the preaching of the eternal gospel includes the warnings of coming judgments for those who fail to heed this message and convert. This other third angel picks up on the very phenomenon of the universal worship of the beast, and the requisite receiving his mark, with which the hearers are all too familiar from the extended discussion of such in chapter 13. This reference back to the worship of the beast and the receiving of his mark makes clear the connection between drinking the wine of the passion of sexual immorality given by Babylon the Great and the worship of the beast and the receiving of his mark. Specifically, it is difficult to imagine that the hearers would not make the further equation that the beast (and those who stand with him), like Babylon the Great, already stands under the judgment of 'Fallen, Fallen' as well.

Verse 10 – One of the consequences for one who drinks the wine of the passion of sexual immorality given by Babylon the Great and worships the beast and receives his mark is that he will also drink of other wine, the wine of the wrath of God. The hearers could hardly miss the fact that the same word that appears with reference to the wine of Babylon the Great to describe its passionate character, τοῦ θυμοῦ ('of the passion'), appears here with the clear meaning of 'wrath'. Thus, through this word play they understand that drinking the wine of the passion of sexual immorality is in fact drinking from the wine of God's wrath. The one carries with it the other! While four genitive constructions occurred in the description of Babylon's wine, five occur in the description of God's wine! Perhaps most interesting to the hearers is the occurrence together of the words κεκερασμένου ἀκράτου ('mixed, unmixed'). This unusual combination conveys two aspects about God's wine of wrath at one and the same time. On the one hand, the former has reference to the practice of mixing wine with other substances to increase its strength, and owing to the fact that this form appears in the perfect tense suggests that it has been prepared at some point in the past for this very moment. On the other hand, the latter has reference to wine that has not been diluted by mixing it with water.[133] The meaning of this unusual combination for the hearers would be that this wine of God's wrath will be drunk at full potency. It has not been diluted, it is indeed at full strength! And if this is

---

[133] Smalley, *The Revelation to John*, p. 365.

not enough, God's wine is now described as 'the cup of his anger', which incorporates two additional potent images. On the one hand, reference to the word 'cup' carries with it a variety of OT associations with regard to God's judgment (Pss. 11.6; 75.9; Isa. 51.17, 22; Jer. 25.16, 27; 49.12; 51.7; Lam. 4.21; Ezek. 23.31-33; Hab. 2.15-16; Obad. 16; Zech. 12.2)[134] and for Johannine hearers would forever be associated with the fact that Jesus himself has drunk the cup of the Father (Jn 18.11), which led to death.[135] On the other hand, the occurrence of the word ὀργῆς ('anger' or 'rage') to describe the cup of his anger, would no doubt remind the hearers of its previous occurrences with reference to the anger or wrath of the Lamb (6.16, 17) and of God (6.17; 11.18). Therefore, in the hour of judgment, reference to the anger of God would be informed by its previous occurrences. Apparently, drinking from the cup of God's anger will involve being 'tormented in fire and sulfur before the holy angels and the Lamb'. The hearers would not be surprised to find that torment is a part of the punishment for those who fail to convert, as torment has appeared as part of the means that God uses in the Apocalypse in seeking to bring humankind to repentance (9.5; 11.10) and is even something the woman clothed with the sun experiences (12.2). In 14.10, the nature of the torment involves the incinerating effects of fire and sulfur, elements that appear in OT scenes of judgment (Job 18.15; Ps. 11.6; Isa. 30.33; 34.9), the best known of which is in the account of the destruction of Sodom and Gomorrah (Gen. 19.1-29), which becomes a notorious example (cf. Deut. 29.23).[136] However, it might surprise the hearers to find that this tormenting punishment takes place in the presence of 'the holy angels and the Lamb'.[137] Yet, if the reference to the holy angels is thought to include the three other angels described in this passage devoted to the eternal gospel, it follows that they would stand ready to serve as witnesses to the message they have proclaimed.[138] Similarly, since reference was earlier made to 'the wrath of the Lamb' (6.16-17) it would not be all that exceptional to find that the Lamb

---

[134] Aune, *Revelation 6-16*, p. 833.

[135] Smalley, *The Revelation to John*, p. 365.

[136] Smalley, *The Revelation to John*, p. 366.

[137] Aune (*Revelation 6-16*, p. 835) notes that such is without parallel in antiquity.

[138] Mounce, *The Book of Revelation*, p. 276.

himself is witness to the judgment of God that falls upon those who obstinately refuse to repent from their worship of the beast!

Verse 11 – The description of the punishment continues as the other third angel says, 'And the smoke of their torment goes up forever and ever, and they have no rest day and night, the ones who worship the beast and if any receive the mark of his name they have no rest day and night'. The image of smoke going up would be familiar to the hearers from the OT, where various cities are described in this manner (Gen. 19.28; Josh. 8.20; Judg. 20.40), serving as a sign of their complete and utter destruction. The fact that in Rev, 14.11 the smoke is described as going up forever and ever indicates that the nature of this divine torment is eternal, complete, and inescapable.[139] It would be clear to the hearers that the nature of this torment is very much the point as they stand in the position of emphasis at the beginning of this sentence. Such a description creates for the hearers a 'ghastly counterpart' to the description of the prayers of the saints that ascend to heaven like clouds of incense before the throne of God (5.8; 8.4; 14.11).[140] At the same time, the hearers could hardly help but notice that the phrase, 'they do not have rest day and night' is identical to one in 4.8, where these words describe the never ending praise of God offered by the four living creatures, creating the unforgettable contrast between unceasing worship and unending torment.[141] The final words of this other third angel makes clear that the recipients of such torment are none other than those who worship the beast and his image and whoever receive the mark of his name. Significantly, these words are the same as those with which the angel's words began in v. 9, indicating that they form an inclusio around the words about the nature of punishment that awaits those who refuse to repent, once again underscoring the importance of this dimension of the angel's words.

Verse 12 – At this point the hearers are addressed directly, 'Here is the patient endurance of the saints, those who keep the commands of God and the faith of Jesus'. Though these words might be thought to come from John, they would in any case likely be

---

[139] Beasley-Murray, *The Book of Revelation*, p. 226.

[140] Koester, *Revelation and the End of All Things*, p. 138.

[141] Aune, *Revelation 6-16*, p. 836.

taken as yet another call for pneumatic discernment, as they are so similar to such words that the hearers have earlier encountered in 13.10, 'Here is the patient endurance and the faith of the saints'. The call in 14.12, the third of four such calls the hearers encounter in the Apocalypse (13.10, 18; 14.12; 17.9), again places emphasis upon the saints' patient endurance, with 'patient endurance' being accompanied by the definite article in the Greek text. Again, the mention of patient endurance would carry with it the previous nuances of the word encountered earlier in the book, where patient endurance is first mentioned by John, their brother in patient endurance (1.9), and comes to be used by the resurrected Jesus as a characteristic or work of the churches in Ephesus (2.2, 3), Thyatira (2.19), and Philadelphia (3.10). Such patient endurance is understood to be 'in Jesus' (1.9) and belonging to him (3.10) and would carry with it the idea of following Jesus in rendering one's witness even to the point of death. Thus, though the previous section has focused on the preaching of the eternal gospel, which includes the sure promise of judgment and its requisite punishment, by means of this call to pneumatic discernment the hearers' attention would once again be focused upon the importance of their absolute commitment to the proclamation of the eternal gospel despite that which awaits them. For the definition of patient endurance here offered, 'those who keep the commands of God ...', would no doubt remind the hearers of the last occurrence of this phrase, where it appears synonymously with the rest of the woman's seed against whom the dragon makes war (12.18). The last words of this verse, 'and the faith of Jesus', also point to the call for pneumatic discernment in 13.10. The specific terminology, 'the faith of Jesus', would again remind the hearers of the way faith is used by the resurrected Jesus as a characteristic or work of the churches in Pergamum (2.13) and Thyatira (2.19). As with patient endurance, faith is closely associated with Jesus, as he speaks both of 'my faith' and 'my faithful witness Antipas' in 2.13. In 14.12, the phrase 'the faith of Jesus' would perhaps be taken as an objective genitive placing emphasis on faith *in* Jesus,[142] though in typically Johannine form, it might at the same time convey something about Jesus' faith, as an

---

[142] Ladd, *Revelation*, p. 197.

equivalent to Jesus' testimony.[143] Such language would once again focus the hearers' attention on their solidarity with Jesus' faith and witness, being a call to the kind of faithfulness characteristic of an overcomer. Thus, in this call to pneumatic discernment, the hearers are called to participate in the proclamation of the eternal gospel to a world that is drunk on the wine of the passion of Babylon the Great and that worships the beast and his image. Despite any hostile opposition they might encounter, the hearers are called to faithful, patient endurance in 'keeping the command of God and the faith of Jesus'.

Verse 13 – Following this call for pneumatic discernment are the words, 'And I heard a voice out of heaven saying, "Write; Blessed are the dead, those who die in the Lord from now on". "Yes", says the Spirit, "in order that they might rest from their labors, for their works follow after them".' Again an unidentified voice comes from heaven directing John to write. Owing to the number of times Jesus instructs John to write in the Apocalypse (1.19; 2.1, 8, 12, 18; 3.1, 7, 14), and that on one occasion a voice from heaven instructs John not to write what he saw (10.4), the hearers might well understand this instruction to write as coming from the resurrected Jesus himself. In any case, there would be no mistaking that such an instruction is a divine one. The instruction to write would also convey a sense of importance[144] and even urgency to the words that are to be written down. If the directive to write comes from the resurrected Jesus it is likely that the hearers would understand the content of what is to be written as coming from Jesus as well. Several aspects of these brief words would be of significance for the hearers. First, in these words, the second beatitude in the Apocalypse (14.13), they learn that while the death of those who worship the beast will be cursed, with unending torment, those who die in the Lord die a blessed death.[145] Second, these words clearly convey the sense that the death of the saints is inevitable, *ergo* the reason for this beatitude. Third, it would be clear that the construction ἐν κυρίῳ ('in the Lord') has reference to the sphere of the Lord as the place

---

[143] On this phrase as both objective and subjective genitive cf. Beale, *The Book of Revelation*, pp. 766-67.

[144] Smalley, *The Revelation to John*, p. 369.

[145] Gause, *Revelation*, p. 195.

where death occurs.¹⁴⁶ Finally, though they might be tempted to take the words ἀπ' ἄρτι ('from now') as suggesting that only from this moment are those who die in the Lord blessed, its other occurrences in the FG (Jn 13.19; 14.7) suggest that the idea is a bit more flexible (cf. also Rev. 12.10), focusing more on the eschatological and spiritual rather than the temporal and spatial.¹⁴⁷ These comforting words are not only spoken with the authority of the voice from heaven, they are affirmed and witnessed by the Spirit herself who says, 'Yes'! Owing to the numerous ways in which the Spirit has spoken to and communicated with the hearers throughout the Apocalypse, the numerous ways in which they have been challenged to engage in pneumatic discernment, and the numerous times that they have received divine assistance in such discernment, it would certainly not surprise the hearers to hear directly from the Spirit at this point. Here, the Spirit's words are not simply limited to the affirmative 'Yes', as important as that affirmation is, the Spirit adds to the blessing these words, 'in order that they might rest from their labor, for their works follow them'. Such pneumatic words would convey at least three things to the hearers. First, the fact that those who die in the Lord are said to rest from their labors would be heard in sharp contrast to those who worship the beast who have no rest day and night from their torment (14.11). Thus, this reveals one aspect of the blessing of dying in the Lord, rather than dying in obstinate opposition to him. Second, that they are to rest from their κόπων ('labors') would not be lost on the hearers, for in the message to the church in Ephesus the resurrected Jesus notes that they have not labored out in their labor (2.2-3)! Specifically, in this context their labor is seen as consisting of not bearing with evil ones and testing those who claim to be apostles but are not. Furthermore, they have exhibited patient endurance in the face of all these obstacles and have not labored out. The fact that this terminology also appears in Jesus' words about the harvest amongst the Samaritans (Jn 4.38) might be additional reason for the hearers to see a connection between their labor and the missiological nature of their labors.¹⁴⁸ Third, earlier it had been revealed that one of the charac-

---

[146] Smalley, *The Revelation to John*, p. 370.

[147] Smalley, *The Revelation to John*, p. 370.

[148] Sweet, *Revelation*, p. 231.

teristics of the 144,000 is they follow the Lamb wherever he goes. Here they learn that just as they follow the Lamb so their works follow them! This would not surprise the hearers, for they know that their works are known by the resurrected Jesus, that they indicate the condition of one's relationship with him, and that they are the basis of judgment by him (Rev. 2.23). That their works follow after them, even after their death, reveals the intimate connection that exists between one's person and one's works, and that, just as the Spirit's anointing upon the two prophetic witnesses did not cease with their death but extended beyond it, so too their works continue the witness given whilst they are alive, making clear yet another dimension of the blessing for the dead who die in the Lord.

Verse 14 – Though perhaps still mesmerized by the pneumatic words spoken with regard to the blessedness of those who die in the Lord, the hearers' attention is pointed in a new direction with the following, 'And I saw, and behold a white cloud, and upon the cloud sitting as a Son of Man, having upon his head a golden crown and in his hand a sharp sickle'. As the hearers have come to know, the occurrence of εἶδον ('I saw') normally designates a change of focus and, on this occasion, is the fifth in a series of appearances that continues the upward trajectory of the things John sees beginning in 13.1 from the sea (13.1), to the earth (13.11), to Mount Zion (14.1), to the mid-heaven (14.6), and now a white cloud (14.14). In this first and only encounter with a 'white' cloud in the Apocalypse the hearers would be prepared for a positive character or action on the part of the one described,[149] as to this point in the book white is uniformly associated with God and or the Lamb (1.14; 2.17; 3.4, 5, 18; 4.4; 6.2, 11; 7.9, 13). Several aspects of the figure next described reveal something about his identity. First, he is not described as another fourth angel, which the hearers might very well expect at this point, suggesting that he is distinct from them in some way. Second, unlike the 'mighty angel' who is clothed with a cloud (10.1) and the two prophetic witnesses who go up to heaven in a cloud (11.12), this figure is described as 'sitting upon the cloud', a description that likely reminds the hearers of the prophetic word with regard to Jesus that stands in the prologue of the book (1.7), 'Behold he comes with the clouds'. Third, the description of this figure,

---

[149] Smalley, *The Revelation to John*, p. 371.

ὅμοιον υἱὸν ἀνθρώπου ('as a Son of Man'), would make clear to the hearers the identity of this figure, as this identical phrase is used with reference to him in the inaugural vision of Jesus (1.13).[150] Clearly, this title would remind the hearers of Dan. 7.13, where reference to the Son of Man also appears. However, even such a powerful association would not exhaust this title's significance for Johannine hearers, as they would be familiar with its rich theological heritage from the FG as well. There, the Son of Man has special access to heaven (Jn 1.51; 3.13; 6.62), must be lifted up and glorified (3.14; 12.23, 34; 13.31), has been given authority to judge (5.27), and is the source of eternal life (6.27, 53) for those who believe in him (9.35). Such an understanding of Jesus as Son of Man in the Johannine tradition would hardly be lost on the hearers as they encounter this title in Rev. 14.14 and would seem to combine for them the elements of heavenly location, authority to judge, and the giving of eternal life to those who believe. It is difficult to avoid the conclusion that the hearers would take these words as having reference to the return of Jesus with the clouds.[151] Fourth, the golden crown that he has upon his head indicates that he himself is an overcomer (Rev. 2.10; 3.11; 4.4).[152] Fifth, reference to δρέπανον ὀξύ ('a sharp sickle') in his hand, would convey at least two things to the hearers. On the one hand, they would likely be reminded, by the adjective 'sharp', of the sharp sword that comes from the mouth of the resurrected Jesus (1.16), which can be an instrument of war (2.12) wielded against those who do not repent (2.15). On the other hand, mention of the sickle would no doubt carry with it the idea of harvest, perhaps even the final harvest of judgment of which Joel 3.13 speaks.

Verse 15 – With the stunning vision created by these words still in mind, the hearers learn more about the activities of this Son of Man in the words they next encounter, 'And another angel came out of the temple crying out with a great voice to the one sitting upon the cloud, "Send your sickle and harvest, because the hour to harvest has come, because the harvest of the earth has been ripened (dried up)"'. Several aspects of these words would be significant for

---

[150] Fee, *Revelation*, p. 203.

[151] Yarbro Collins, *The Apocalypse*, p. 105.

[152] Allo, *L'Apocalypse*, p. 222.

the hearers. The appearance of yet 'another angel' would remind them of the three other angels encountered previously in the words of 14.6-11 who announced the eternal gospel and its consequent warnings of judgment for those who refuse to repent. However, while each of those three other angels were located in mid-heaven, the other angel of 14.15 comes out of the temple! Such words would suggest that this angel came from the very presence of God, as the last reference to God's temple in heaven disclosed that it had been opened, revealing the ark of his covenant in his temple, which leads to a display of the theophanic elements that have reference to God's presence (11.19)! Thus, when the great voice of this other angel is heard it is understood to come from the very presence of God,[153] for all practical purposes being as good as the voice of God himself.[154] This divine command, issued to the one who sits on the cloud, focuses exclusively upon the activity of harvesting, with a form of the word 'harvest' appearing three times in the span of ten words in the Greek text, either in noun or verb form! The command makes clear the purpose of the sharp sickle in the Son of Man's hand. It is for the activity of harvesting and is to be sent forth to accomplish that task. For Johannine hearers the activity of harvesting would be conceived of in wholly positive terms, as the appearance of both the noun and verb forms in the missiological discussion of Jesus with his disciples in Jn 4.35-38 reveals. There the role of the disciples in reaping the fields white unto harvest is underscored with special reference to the Samaritan community. Such a missiological backdrop would make it altogether likely that the hearers would see in this command a reference to the salvific harvest by the Son of Man of those who respond to the proclamation of the eternal gospel (14.7).[155] While the first other angel speaks of this decisive moment as the arrival of 'the hour of judgment', this other angel conveys a similar idea by means of two different images. Like the first other angel, this angel too uses the imagery of 'the hour', only here it is the arrival of 'the hour to harvest' that is underscored. It too is spoken of in the past tense, indicating the certainty of its occurrence even though this activity still lies in the

---

[153] Gause, *Revelation*, p. 197.

[154] Allo (*L'Apocalypse*, p. 223) notes that it is divinity himself that speaks with Jesus.

[155] Bauckham, *The Climax of Prophecy*, p. 294.

future. In addition, this angel speaks of the harvest of the earth as ἐξηράνθη ('has been ripened' or 'dried up'). This Greek word carries with it the idea of something drying up, as branches that are cut off from the vine and cast into the fire (Jn 15.6), but when used in the context of harvest it indicates that the harvest has ripened to the point that it will spoil if not harvested.[156] In other words, the ripening of the harvest reveals that the hour of the harvest has arrived; it is the optimal moment for the harvest. The angel's words could not be any clearer, the final hour of harvest has arrived.

Verse 16 – No sooner was this divine command issued than it was carried out, 'And the one who sits upon the cloud cast his sickle out upon the earth and the earth was harvested'. While these words could be taken as simple redundancy, they do in point of fact contribute a couple of things to the hearers. First, these words make absolutely clear that it is the Son of Man, Jesus himself, who harvests the earth, reinforcing the idea that the depiction of the Son of Man in 14.14-16 has reference to the coming of Jesus with the clouds. The hearers might well detect here the fulfillment of Jesus' words found the FG, 'And if I go away and prepare a place for you, again I will come and receive you to myself, in order that where I am you will also be' (Jn 14.3). Second, the occurrence of the passive tense ἐθερίσθη ('was harvested'), the fourth appearance of a form from the same word family in two verses, continues to emphasize the centrality of the harvest as the primary activity of the Son of Man in these verses and its significance.

Verse 17 – Fast on the heels of the description of the harvesting of the world by the Son of Man the hearers learn, 'And another angel came out of the temple of the one in heaven also himself having a sharp sickle'. Like the other angel described in 14.15, this angel too is referred to simply as another angel, without enumeration. Like the previous other angel this other angel also comes out of the temple, only this time the temple is explicitly identified as 'the temple of the one in heaven' making even more explicit the connection between the activity of this angel and God himself. And like the Son of Man, the other angel of 14.17 also himself has a sharp sickle, indicating that he too is prepared to harvest, even though the earth has just been harvested!

---

[156] Aune, *Revelation 6-16*, pp. 789-90.

Verse 18 – But before any activities are attributed to him, the hearers are told, 'And another angel came out of the altar having authority over the fire, and he called with a great voice to the one having the sharp sickle saying, "Send your sharp sickle and gather the clusters of the vineyard of the earth, because his grapes are ripe"'. The emergence of this other angel from the altar would indicate to the hearers that he is very closely associated with the prayers of the souls under the altar (6.9) and the saints (8.3) for justice, as well as the activity of divine judgment (9.13), and the worshippers of God (11.1). In point of fact, this angel has authority over fire, which reminds the hearers of the other angel who casts fire from the altar onto the earth in 8.5, which is followed by a display of the theophanic elements, and the fire of judgment that accompanies the activity of the angels in 8.7-8 and 9.17-18. Thus, the hearers are likely to understand the location and authority of this angel as indicating a change in focus from the idea of harvesting, previously described, to that of judgment. This other angel, though not enumerated, is the sixth to be mentioned since 14.6 and calls out the divine command to the angel holding the sharp sickle to send his sickle and 'gather the clusters of the vineyard of the earth, because his grapes are ripe'. This divine command is reminiscent of the divine command given to the Son of Man, though this one focuses upon the gathering of clusters of grapes that are ripe for harvest. The introduction of grape and vineyard imagery could not help but remind the hearers of the wine imagery that has appeared earlier in this very context; specifically, the wine of the passion of sexual immorality of Babylon the Great, on the one hand, and the wine of the wrath of God, unmixed in the cup of his anger, on the other hand. Thus, the hearers may very well understand the divine command of 14.18 as being directly connected to the warning with regard to God's wine of wrath (14.10). The hearers would hardly miss the fact that two different Greek words for 'grapes' appear in this command, indicating in part that this imagery is of special significance.

Verse 19 – No sooner does the command go out than, 'The angel cast his sharp sickle into the earth and gathered the vineyard of the earth and it into the great winepress of the wrath of God'. Like the Son of Man before him this other angel casts or swings his sharp sickle into the earth, but unlike the Son of Man he does not harvest but rather gathers the vineyard of the earth. Here the imagery of Joel 3.13 is almost palpable as the activity of judgment can hardly be missed. For as wine comes out of the winepress when the grapes are crushed underfoot, so the wine of God's wrath is produced when the clusters of grapes gathered by this other angel are crushed underfoot in the great winepress of God's wrath! The description of this winepress as 'great' might be understood by the hearers as an intentional critique of the earlier description of Babylon as great. Owing to the broader context, the clear implication of the words in Rev. 14.19 would be that those who worship the image of the beast and receive his mark, who refuse to repent and give glory to God, will find themselves in the great winepress of God's wrath, experiencing this excruciating punishment under the divine foot itself!

Verse 20 – As might be expected, the great winepress of God's wrath produces wine of a great magnitude, 'And the winepress was trodden outside the city and blood came out of the winepress up to the bridles of the horses for 1,600 stadia'. A number of aspects of this remarkable verse would be of significance for the hearers. First, the passive voice verb ἐπατήθη ('was trodden') would suggest that it is God himself who does the treading. Second, the description of the activity of treading in the great winepress of God's wrath would stand in contrast to and in critique of the activity of the nations, earlier described as treading underfoot the outer court of the temple (11.2). Third, it may not be without significance that the great winepress of God's wrath is described as being outside of the city. On the one hand, such language may remind the hearers of the fact that the nations would trod under foot the court located outside of the temple (11.2). On the other hand, such language might very well remind the hearers that the place where Jesus was crucified was outside the city (Jn 19.20; cf. also Heb. 13.12 and Mt. 21.39).[157] On either understanding, it would appear that the punishment fits the crime.[158] Fourth, instead of the juice of the grapes coming out of the winepress, blood comes out of the great winepress of God's wrath, indicating something of the identity of the grapes and the

---

[157] Smalley, *The Revelation to John*, p. 377.
[158] Murphy, *Fallen Is Babylon*, p. 328. As Aune (*Revelation 6-16*, p. 847) observes, '… thus this judgment constitutes a kind of poetic justice'.

activity of treading! The mention of blood not only underscores the gruesome nature of the divine judgment (cf. also Rev. 8.7-8), but also stands in contrast to the way in which the blood of the Lamb and those who are faithful to him carries with it redemptive connotations. Fifth, the enormity of the extent of this judgment is conveyed in two ways. The blood that emerged from the winepress is first measured by depth or height, for it is as high as the bridle of horses, a height that is the rough equivalent to the stature of most of the individual hearers! If one were to experience such a horrendous sight, the blood would be of such a magnitude that it would cover practically all living beings! The blood is also measured in terms of length, as it covers 1,600 stadia. The fact that this distance is the rough equivalent of the length of Palestine would perhaps convey the idea that this judgment is universal and complete. At the same time, it is likely that by this point the hearers would expect the number 1,600 to convey a significance on its own, and not simply as a means of measuring geographical distance. If so, it is likely that they would note that this number is explicable by several means of calculation (4x400, 4x4x100, 4^2x100), carrying within itself the sacred number 40x40,[159] and reflecting the universal geography of the Apocalypse itself (4.6).[160] On any reckoning, the measurement of 1,600 stadia would convey the idea of universal and absolute judgment.[161]

---

[159] Allo, *L'Apocalypse*, p. 225.

[160] Prigent, *L'Apocalypse de Saint Jean*, p. 350.

[161] Resseguie, *The Revelation of John*, p. 202.

Seven Angels with Seven Bowls of Plagues (15.1-16.21)

Once again the hearers may be forgiven if they mistakenly think that they have come to the end of John's words, for the description of the dual activities of harvesting the faithful of the earth (14.14-16) and the gathering of grapes for the great winepress of the wrath of God (14.17-20) suggests just that. And yet, the vision continues to unfold ...

Another Great Sign in Heaven: The Seven Angels (15.1-8)
Verse 1 – For the hearers encounter still more words, 'And I saw another great and marvelous sign in the heaven, seven angels having the seven last plagues, because in them the wrath of God was completed'. These words would convey a number of things to the hearers. As they have come to know, the occurrence of εἶδον ('I saw') normally designates a change of focus and, on this occasion, is the sixth in a series of appearances that continues the upward trajectory of the things John sees beginning in 13.1 from the sea (13.1), to the earth (13.11), to Mount Zion (14.1), to the mid-heaven (14.6), to a white cloud (14.14), and now in heaven (15.1). The mention of 'another great and marvelous sign in heaven' could not help but remind the hearers of the great sign in heaven they encountered in 12.1.[1] With the encounter of this second 'great' sign, they now learn that chapters 12-14, which appear to reveal the contents of the unsealed scroll, is enveloped by reference to these two great signs, which form an inclusio around this section. Such a realization would indicate that not only is this previous section (Revelation 12-14) coming to an end, as the reference to the harvest and gathering of the grapes imply, but also may at the same time suggest that this section continues in some sense. Based on the nature of the first great sign and the fact that this other great sign is additionally described as marvelous, the hearers' level of expectancy with regard to the significance of this other great sign would be extraordinarily high. For if the first great sign introduces them to the woman clothed with the sun, who comes to combine within herself references to Eve, Israel, the mother of Jesus, and the Church, to what will this other great sign introduce them? If reference to this

---

[1] Contra Beasley-Murray [*Revelation*, p. 234] who explains the similarities as an accident of language.

'other great and marvelous sign' would cause the hearers to look back to the mention of the first great sign in 12.1, mention of 'seven angels with the seven last plagues' in 15.1 would likely cause them to look even further back to the seven angels with seven trumpets described in chapters 8.1-9.21 and 11.15-19. The similarities between these two sets of seven angels and the fact that the seven angels mentioned in 15.1 are said to have the seven last plagues serve to underscore the connection between these two sets of seven angels. As such, it would appear that the hearers would take the mention of the seven angels with the seven last plagues as in some way continuing the story line of the seven angels with the seven trumpets, not unlike the way in which the description of the seven angels with seven trumpets had earlier continued the story line of the opening of the seven seals. Thus, the identification of this other great and marvelous sign as 'the seven angels having the seven last plagues' almost certainly suggests that the hearers would see some connection between what has preceded in chapters 12-14 and that which follows. The fact that the angels are said to have the seven last plagues would clearly convey the idea of finality to the hearers, as well as call to mind yet additional reminders of the connection between the activities described and the plagues of Egypt. Not only does the occurrence of the word πληγὰς ('plagues' or 'bowls') suggest as much, but it is also possible that these seven angels with their plagues would be understood by the hearers as fulfilling the words of Lev. 26.21-24, which speak of the seven-fold punishment of plagues that awaits those who do not obey the law of the Lord.[2] But the hearers do not have to speculate long as to why these plagues are called the last ones, for they are explicitly told it is 'because in them the wrath of God has been completed'. Mere mention of the wrath of God would no doubt convey the idea of the completion of God's wrath, as his wrath most recently has reference to the wine of God's wrath (Rev. 14.10) and the great winepress of the wrath of God (14.19), both of which occur in contexts that suggest the end of all things. But here, his wrath is spoken of as already having been completed,[3] which the aorist passive ἐτελέσθη

---

[2] An interpretation prominent in the early church, for which cf. the discussions in ACCS 12, pp. 239-41.
[3] Gause, *Revelation*, p. 201.

('has been completed') indicates. As in 11.18 and 14.7, God's future actions are understood as so certain that they are spoken of as already accomplished,[4] with the divine passive suggesting that it is God himself who completes his wrath through these last seven plagues.

Verse 2 – Before being able to ponder the significance of 'the seven angels with the seven last plagues', the hearers' attention is directed to something else that John sees, 'And I saw as a glass sea mixed with fire and those who overcome [out of] the beast and [out of] his image and [out of] his number standing upon the glass sea having harps of God'. For the hearers, there is scarcely anything in these words that is not informed by words and/or images previously encountered. For mention of the glass sea would immediately take them back to the inaugural vision of heaven described in chapter 4, where stretching out before the throne is a sea of glass. Thus, there can hardly be any misunderstanding with regard to the location of the scene described in 15.2; it is in the very presence of God himself! In the description of the glass sea as mixed with fire, two significant ideas converge for the hearers. This description would likely remind them of the fact that the theophanic elements that come from the throne (4.5) appear to be reflected in the glass sea before the throne (4.6),[5] an indication that even those objects that have negative connotations, as does the 'sea' in antiquity, somehow reflect the glory of God. But the hearers have come to understand this enigmatic image in the light of the way both the opening of the seven seals and the trumpeting of the seven trumpets conclude with a display of the theophanic elements, which grow in intensity. Owing to the fact that both the seals and the trumpets are designed to lead humankind to repentance, the hearers would likely understand the reflection of the theophanic elements in the glass sea as pointing to God's redemptive judgments. Such an understanding appears to be confirmed by 15.2 where the glass sea is described as 'mixed with fire', for not only is fire closely associated with Jesus (1.14; 2.18; 3.18) and the Spirit (4.5), but it is also intimately connected with the prayers of the saints and the altar of God (8.5, 7) from which the fire of judgment comes (8.7, 8) with fire serving as a reg-

---

[4] Prigent, *L'Apocalypse de Saint Jean*, p. 354.
[5] S. Légasse, 'μείγνυμι, μειγνύω', *EDNT*, II, p. 402.

ular metaphor for God's judgment in the Apocalypse (9.17-18; 10.1; 11.5; 14.10, 18).[6] Thus, mention of this glass sea mixed with fire would be pregnant with meaning for the hearers, suggesting that even though the last seven plagues indicate the end of God's wrath, God's desire for the repentance of humankind has not yet come to an end. Yet, extraordinary as this description may be, the hearers are not allowed the luxury of pondering this sea for they immediately discover that standing ἐπὶ ('upon' or 'around') it are 'those who overcome the beast and his image and the number of his name'. For the hearers there could be little doubt that these individuals are identical to those described in 12.11, who have overcome the great dragon, the ancient serpent, the one called Devil and Satan, the deceiver of the entire inhabited world, and who are themselves heirs to the promises given by the resurrected Jesus to those who overcome in the seven prophetic messages to the seven churches in Revelation 2-3 (2.7, 11, 17, 26; 3.5,12, 21). Such associations would, no doubt, create within the hearers a heightened sense of expectancy that the eschatological promises are not far from fulfillment but are even at the door! The emphasis placed upon the one whom these overcome is made clear by the fact that reference is made to his identity in triplicate form, with various dimensions of his person being underscored with each reference. They overcome the beast, the one who made war against the offspring of the woman clothed with the sun; the image of the beast, which generates oracular speech and before whom all must worship; and the number of the beast, the mark that designates ownership by the beast, without which one cannot enter into commercial life and the refusal of which ultimately leads to death. Two additional observations should perhaps be made. First, the fact that τοὺς νικῶντας ('the ones who overcome') is a present participle may suggest that those upon/around the glass sea are even now in the act of overcoming. Second, the fact that each of the three references to an aspect of the beast's identity is preceded by ἐκ ('out of') may convey to the hearers something of the intensity of the faithful witnesses' conflict with the beast, perhaps suggesting that they have emerged from the midst of such intimate combat and danger. The description of the overcomers as ἑστῶτας ('standing') upon or around the glass sea

---

[6] Smalley, *The Revelation to John*, p. 384.

would be significant in a couple of different ways. First, this description would likely remind the hearers of the question raised by the inhabitants of the earth, 'Who is able to stand?' before the face of the One who sits on the throne and the wrath of the Lamb when the day of their wrath has come (6.16-17), which receives an answer in 7.9 where the innumerable crowd is 'standing before the throne and before the Lamb'. The description of the overcomers as standing in 15.2 would clearly provide a point of continuity between these two groups. Second, it is possible that the language of 'standing' in 15.2 might be an allusion to the first resurrection, which not only reflects the posture of those in 7.9 but also the Lamb that looked as though it had been slain who stands (5.6).[7] The further description of the overcomers as 'having harps of God' would also suggest to the hearers a certain continuity between these overcomers and the twenty four elders with harps around the throne in 5.8 and the 'harpists harping on their harps' who appear to be the 144,000 in 14.2.[8] While previous mentions of harps are located in heaven, in 15.2 their mention makes clear their divine origin as they are identified as God's harps, and thus would be understood as a divine gift or reward. Mention of the harps here would also create within the hearers an expectancy that singing could not be far away.

Verse 3 – This expectation is not left unfulfilled, for the hearers next encounter the words, 'And they sang the song of Moses the servant of God and the song of the Lamb saying …' Not only does the mention of harps prepare the hearers for these words with regard to singing, but the context does as well, for to this point in the Apocalypse explicit mention of the singing of songs has occurred only in the immediate presence of God (5.9; 14.3). These earlier associations between singing and the redeemed would further underscore the emerging continuity between these who overcome, the twenty-four elders, and the 144,000 before them. But unlike the songs of chapters 5 and 14, this song is not identified as a 'new' song but rather as 'the song of Moses the servant of God and the song of the Lamb'. The initial encounter with this phrase may suggest to the hearers that those who overcome sing two songs rather

---

[7] Smalley, *The Revelation to John*, p. 385.
[8] Caird, *The Revelation of St. John*, pp. 197-98.

than one, as a song seems to be attributed to both Moses and the Lamb. Mention of 'the song of Moses the servant of God' could not help but call attention to the place of Moses in Israel's redemptive history, which is without parallel, for not only is the descriptive title 'the servant of God' one used for Moses on numerous occasions in the OT (Exod. 14.31; Num. 12.7; Deut. 34.5; Josh. 1.1, 15; 8.31; 9.24; 1 Kgs 8.53, 56; 2 Kgs 18.12; 21.8; 2 Chron. 24.9; Neh. 1.8; Ps. 105[104].26; Mal. 4.4), but it also makes clear the fact that Moses himself is a prophet of God (cf. Rev. 10.7),[9] and a most important one at that! While this title would clearly emphasize Moses' prophetic and salvific identity, mention of the song of Moses could not help but remind the hearers of one specific moment in redemptive history, when the Song of Moses was sung in celebration of Israel's deliverance from Egypt, culminating in the crossing of the Red Sea (Exodus 15). Such associations would at the least suggest to the hearers a connection between those who overcome the beast, his image, and the number of his name and those who experienced the deliverance at the Red Sea, perhaps causing the hearers to pause with regard to the meaning and function of the glass sea. If so, there may at least be a visual connection between the crossing of the Red Sea and those who stand beside (have passed through) the Glass Sea.[10] The possible connection between these salvific acts is confirmed in part by the fact that not only is the Song of Moses described as being sung, but also the Song of the Lamb is said to be sung as well. If mention of the Song of Moses calls to mind the song recorded in Exodus 15, mention of the Song of the Lamb would at the least recall the new song of Rev. 5.9-14 in which the worthiness of the Lamb is extolled by the four living creatures, the twenty-four elders, a myriad of angels, and every creature in the universe owing to the Lamb's slaughter, his purchase out of all peoples, and his making kings and priests unto God. As the new song of Revelation 5 concludes, the praise of the Lamb is placed alongside that of the One who sits on the throne.

With this introduction the words of the song begin to make their way into the ears of the hearers.

---

[9] Bauckham, *Climax of Prophecy*, p. 300.
[10] Resseguie, *The Revelation of John*, p. 205.

> Great and marvelous are your works
> Lord, God, the All Powerful One;
>
> Righteous and true are your ways,
> the King of the nations;
>
> Who will not have feared you, Lord, and will glorify your name?
>
> For you alone are holy (pleasing to God),
> for all the nations will come and will worship before you,
> for your righteous acts have been manifested.

This song would speak to the hearers in a number of ways and at a variety of levels. Perhaps one of the first things to connect with the hearers would be the 'biblical feel' of this song, as it includes structural and linguist elements familiar to the hearers from the OT. Here they find Semitic parallelism revealed in the first four lines. They encounter at the center of the song an emphatic rhetorical question, reminiscent of those found in OT hymns (Exod. 15.11; Pss. 6.3; 15.1; Isa. 40.25; Mic. 7.18).[11] But this is not all, for they scarcely hear a word in the song itself that is not richly informed by its place in the OT. In point of fact, as the words of the song make their way into the ears of the hearers, it becomes evident that John describes not two songs but one. For in the words of this song the hearers encounter an incredible convergence of words and images from the OT as well as the Apocalypse and the FG, which go some way toward revealing the intriguing relationship between the Song of Moses and the Song of the Lamb. Perhaps such ponderings would lead the hearers to discern that the relationship between the Song of Moses and the Song of the Lamb is on the same order as the relationship between the Lion of the tribe of Judah and the Lamb that looked as though it had been slain in Revelation 5 or the 144,000 of the tribes of the sons of Israel and the innumerable crowd in Revelation 7. That is to say, the hearers may now begin to understand that the songs are to be understood in the light of one another and yet are, at one and the same time, one song![12]

---

[11] Smalley, *The Revelation to John*, p. 388.

[12] Cf. R. Meynet, 'Le cantique de Moïse et le cantique de l'Agneau (Ap 15 et Ex 15)', *Gregorianum* 73 (1992), p. 46 and J.N. Musvosi, 'The Song of Moses and the Song of the Lamb', *Journal of the Adventist Theological Society* 9.1-2 (1998), pp. 44-47.

The extraordinary nature of this song is revealed, in part, by its opening lines:

Great and marvelous are your works
Lord, God, the All Powerful One;

Righteous and true are your ways,
the King of the nations;

In these words, structured in familiar Hebraic parallelism, there is an incredible convergence of meaning for the hearers. The opening line would not only bring to mind the ways in which the mighty salvific works of God have been described in the OT (Exod. 15.11; Pss. 92.5; 98.1-2; 111.1-2; 118.1; 139.14; 1 Chron. 16.9), but also the fact that the activity of God and/or his agents are often spoken of as 'great' in the Apocalypse.[13] The convergence of such texts would serve to underscore the fact that God's activities throughout the Apocalypse have been designed to bring unrepentant humankind to repentance and true worship. Such an emphasis also fits nicely with the way in which the works of God are portrayed in the FG (Jn 4.34; 5.20, 36 (2x); 6.29; 7.3, 21; 9.3, 4; 10.25, 32 (2x), 33, 37, 38; 14.10, 11, 12; 15.24; 17.4), where his work is designed above all else to result in belief (6.29). At the same time it is unlikely that the hearers would not discern here a significant contrast between the great and marvelous works of God and the works of those who refuse to repent but continue in their worship of demons and idolatry in the face of the divine plagues sent upon the world (Rev. 9.20). Neither is it likely that the hearers would miss the explicit connection between 'the great and marvelous works' celebrated in this song and the 'other great and marvelous sign' with which this section begins, indicating the tight connection between the assessment of God's judgments as 'great and marvelous' and the seven angels with the seven last bowls of plagues (15.1). This opening line is followed by the invocation 'Lord, God, the All Powerful One', which is familiar to the hearers from its numerous appearances in the OT, where it occurs in prophetic oracles in which Yahweh warns of impending judgment (Amos 3.13; 4.13; 5.16, 27; 9.5; Nah. 3.5; Zech. 10.3), in texts that have reference to his work as creator (Amos 5.8;

---

[13] The term μέγας ('great') appears some forty-five times in the Apocalypse, many of which with reference to God, his activities, and/or his agents.

9.6), and in texts with reference to the promise of restoration (Hos. 12.5; Amos 5.14, 15; 9.15). The invocation is also familiar to them from its refrain-like occurrences in the Apocalypse, where it occurs in the prophetic words of God as a self-identification (Rev. 1.8) and in the songs sung to God around the throne where he is praised for his eternality (4.8; 11.17). Thus, its occurrence in the song of 15.3 would draw together the idea of God as creator – as unrivaled power in the universe – and as hopeful judge, elements that fit the context of Revelation 15 remarkably well. The next words the hearers encounter are no surprise for they form the second part of the Hebraic parallelism that stands in tandem with the song's opening. The words, 'Righteous and true are your ways, King of the Nations', are no less significant than their structural parallel. In hearing the ways of God described as 'righteous and true' a number of emphases would no doubt converge for the hearers. Not only would they know that God and his ways are spoken of in similar terms in the Torah (Deut. 32.4) and Psalter (145.17), but Johannine hearers would be especially aware of the close connection between Jesus (1 Jn 1.9; 2.1, 29; 3.7), his activity of righteous judgment (Jn 5.30; 7.24), and the righteous Father (17.25). Nor would Johannine hearers be unaware that in Johannine thought God is 'true God' (Jn 3.33; 7.28; 8.26; 17.3; 1 Jn 5.20) and that his Son is 'the Truth' (Jn 1.14, 17; 14.6; cf. also Rev. 3.7, 14). Thus, it comes as no surprise that God's ways are called 'righteous and true' in Rev. 15.3. However, even these remarkable associations may not exhaust the meaning of these words for the hearers, for it is altogether likely that in this line of the hymn in Rev. 15.3 the hearers would discern a partial response to the prayer of the saints for judgment and vindication in 6.10, where God is invoked with the words 'the holy and true Despot'. Perhaps the hearers would see in the words of those who sing this hymn in 15.3 the testimony of those who have been slain, that they are satisfied that the God whom they implored to act has indeed acted in his own ways and in his own time. If so, such testimony would ring in the ears of the hearers as assurance that despite the way in which a given earthly circumstance may create questions about God's sovereignty, care, and compassion, the testimony of those from the vantage point of heaven itself assure that the ways of God are indeed righteous and true. This line of thought is further borne out by the name attributed to God in this portion of the parallelism, 'the King of the nations'. The idea that God is the king of the nations or that he rules over them is one that has a rich heritage especially in the prophet Jeremiah and the Writings where it carries with it the idea of the absolute superiority of God over the nations and their gods (Jer. 10.7; Pss. 22.28; 47.8; 96.10; 99.2; 1 Chron. 16.31). But the significance of this title for the hearers would not be limited to its OT meanings for in it a whole range of meanings converges from the Apocalypse itself. Several layers of meaning would be present for the hearers in their encounter with the title 'King of the nations'. First, it would further underscore the unique and intimate relationship between God and Jesus made clear at various points throughout the book, given the fact that in the prologue Jesus himself has been called 'the Ruler of the kings of the earth' (1.5). Second, the title indicates that despite the rebellious actions of the kings of the earth (6.15), God is still their sovereign and his reign in contrast to theirs is an eternal one (11.15) that even now has begun (11.17-18). Third, at the same time, this title would serve to remind the hearers that despite the rebellious actions of the kings of the earth they continue to be the objects of God's prophetic call to repentance (10.11). Fourth, the mention of this title would also remind the hearers of the kingdom made for God by Jesus though his blood, kingdom members who have overcome and will join in the reign of God (1.6, 9; 5.10; 11.15-18; 12.10-12).

Verse 4 – At this point the hymn's parallelism gives way to a rhetorical question that forms the structural center and theological heart of this song:

Who will not have feared you, Lord, and will glorify your name?

Recognizable from the OT both in terms of its rhetorical form and its content (Exod. 15.11; Ps. 6.3; 15.1; Isa. 40.18, 25; Mic. 7.18), this question follows well upon the previous titles used for God in this hymn as 'Lord, God, All powerful One' and 'King of the nations', focusing upon and underscoring his incomparability. Thus, his role as cosmic deliverer, to whom none is worthy of comparison, serves to highlight further his unique role and person. While the words of many of these OT texts would no doubt converge in the mind of the hearers, none are likely to be as significant as those of Jer. 10.7 where the question with regard to his universal reverence is combined with the title 'King of the nations' and statements of his incomparability. But as important as these texts are, they would not be the only, or perhaps, the primary associations the words of the rhetorical question would have for the hearers. For it would be very difficult to imagine that this question would not be taken by the hearers as a direct response to and critique of the rhetorical question raised about the 'incomparability' of the beast, 'Who is like the beast and who is able to make war against him?' and the description of the universal worship of the dragon and the beast in 13.4 and 13.8, respectively.[14] It also seems likely that the rhetorical question of 15.4 would be taken by the hearers as in some way a response to the angelic proclamation of the Eternal Gospel in 14.6-7 to 'fear God and give him glory', perhaps suggesting the success of his message.[15] Such an interpretation is made all the more likely by the fact that both fear (11.11, 13, 18) and giving glory (1.6; 4.9, 11; 5.12-13; 7.12; 11.13) are viewed as closely connected with repentance and the worship of God, respectively. For the hearers, the glorification of God's name would convey the glorification of God himself, as his name is coterminous with his presence, which is coterminous with his person. At the same time this phrase might also be taken as an indication that the prophetic words of Mal. 1.11 are fulfilled, "'From the rising of the sun until its setting my name will have been glorified, and in every place where incense and a pure offering are offered; for my name is great among the nations", says the Lord God All Powerful'.[16] Thus, once again future realities are spoken of with such prophetic certainty that they are regarded as already having taken place, yet again underscoring the certainty of the conversion of the nations.

Following the hymn's rhetorical center is its conclusion that takes a threefold structure, each line beginning with the word ὅτι ('because' or 'for'):

> For you alone are holy,
> for all the nations will come and will worship before you,
> for your righteous acts have been manifested.

---

[14] Resseguie, *The Revelation of John*, p. 206.
[15] Caird, *The Revelation of St. John*, pp. 198-99.
[16] Gause, *Revelation*, pp. 204-205.

Accordingly, the lines of this stanza appear to build on the hymn's rhetorical center offering a series of justifications for its claims, which draw on and are informed by both the OT and that which precedes it in the hymn itself. Though God is previously called ἅγιος ('holy') in the Apocalypse (4.8; 6.10), this is the first of only two times he is referred to as ὅσιος ('holy') in the book (cf. 16.5, where the term also occurs in a hymn). This occurrence of the term, joined by the only occurrence of μόνος ('only') in the Apocalypse, might well suggest to the hearers a unique emphasis, underscoring the earlier praise of God's incomparability. Such an attribution might well bring to mind Deut. 32.4, where the Lord is described as ὅσιος ('holy') and Ps. 144.17 (LXX) where his works are described in this same fashion. As such, the hearers might well discern that while this line builds upon the hymn's rhetorical center it, at the same time, hearkens back to ideas found in the parallelism with which the song begins. Thus, this line offers an initial reason why all fear the Lord and will glorify his name – 'for he alone is holy'! The second line of this last stanza follows the lead of the first in three ways. It too begins with the word ὅτι ('because' or 'for'); it too builds upon the hymn's rhetorical center; and it too hearkens back to ideas found in the parallelism of the first stanza. Specifically, this line indicates that even the nations, which to this point in the book have often been depicted as having reference to the unbelieving world (10.11; 11.2, 9, 18; 14.8), will be drawn to the King of the Nations. These words, which echo those of certain eschatological promises found in the prophets (Isa. 2.2-4; Mal. 1.11), would continue to cultivate in the hearers the call to and hope for the conversion of the nations. Several ideas would converge for the hearers in discovering that such ones as these 'will worship before you'. First, it is likely that such language would convey the idea of vindication and righteous acknowledgment in that it would remind them of the virtually identical language used by the resurrected Jesus in his words to the church in Philadelphia about that which awaits those of the synagogue of Satan, ἥξουσιν καὶ προσκυνήσουσιν ἐνώπιον τῶν ποδῶν σου ('they will come and will worship before your feet'). Second, it would be difficult to imagine that the hearers would not take these words as an indication that the nations are joining with all other worshippers of the true God, described at various points throughout the book.[17] Third, neither is it likely that the hearers would fail to appreciate the contrast between these worshippers and those engaged in the illegitimate worship of the dragon and the beast (13.4, 8, 12, 15; 14.9, 11). The fact that there is surely some overlap between some who have been described as involved in illegitimate worship and those who will worship God would not likely be lost on the hearers but would serve to stoke the fire of their passion to work for the conversion of the nations. Thus, hope springs from such seeming incongruity. The third line of the third stanza is like the first two lines in that it too begins with the word ὅτι ('because' or 'for'), builds upon the hymn's rhetorical center, and hearkens back to ideas found in the parallelism of the first stanza. The words found in this line would convey at least three things to the hearers. First, they learn that the manifestation of God's righteous acts offers additional rationale for the truth of the rhetorical question standing at the hymn's center. Second, the Johannine hearers' encounter with ἐφανερώθησαν ('have been manifested') would likely be informed by its prominence in the FG where it often occurs in describing the manifestation of the work and glory of Jesus (Jn 1.31; 2.11; 3.21; 7.4; 21.1, 14) and that of his Father (3.21; 9.3; 17.6). In the vast preponderance of these texts there is a close connection between such manifestation and belief, thus providing another link between this line and the rhetorical center of the hymn. Third, the occurrence of τα δικαιώματα σου ('your righteous actions') at this point in the hymn would not only direct the hearers' attention back to the second part of the parallelism with which the hymn begins, where God's ways are described as δίκαιαι ('righteous') – giving the hymn a chiastic sense of structure, but it would also be additional explanation for the extraordinary response of humankind described in the hymn's rhetorical center. As such, it makes clear that God's acts of judgment are not random acts, but are indeed righteous acts designed to encourage true worship even amongst those who rebelliously worship the dragon, the beast, and the image of the beast.[18] Thus, the

---

[17] Contra Kiddle (*The Revelation of St. John*, p. 309) who caricatures such worship as having 'a turncoat flavor' to it.

[18] Prigent, *L'Apocalypse de Saint Jean*, p. 356.

hymn's closing line serves to tie up the song's major emphases in a way that would cause the hearers to marvel at the remarkably comprehensive nature of the salvation celebrated through the depth of this hymn's insightful lyrics.

Verse 5 – No sooner is this song sung than the hearers' attention is directed to another sight described by John, 'And after these things I saw, and the temple of the tabernacle of witness in heaven opened, and the seven angels having the seven plagues came out of the temple wearing clean, shining stone and being girded with golden sashes around their chests'. As they have come to know, the occurrence of εἶδον ('I saw') normally designates a change of focus and, combined with 'after these things' on this occasion, is the seventh in a series of appearances that continues the upward trajectory of the things John sees beginning in 13.1 from the sea (13.1), to the earth (13.11), to Mount Zion (14.1), to the mid-heaven (14.6), to a white cloud (14.14), to heaven itself (15.1), and now to the temple of the tabernacle of witness in heaven (15.5). This unique phrase, coming on the heels of the Song of Moses and the Song of the Lamb sung unto the Lord, God, the All Powerful One, draws the hearers even further into the divine presence than they have been to this point. No doubt still ringing in their ears are the words of 11.19 where 'the temple of God in heaven was opened and the ark of his covenant in the temple was opened'. The words of 15.5 would seem to invite them closer, to an even more intimate knowledge of God's presence, as 'the temple of the tabernacle of witness' is itself opened. It is difficult to imagine precisely how the hearers would envision such a description. It is possible they would take these words as an indication that the ark of the covenant, which was itself opened in 11.19, only now reveals its sacred contents, the two tablets of God's witness that signify his covenant faithfulness (Deut. 31.26; 1 Kgs 8.9). Or, perhaps the absence of an explicit mention of the ark of God's covenant in 15.5, paired with an explicit mention of the temple of the tabernacle of witness, would shift the focus of their attention from the tablets of witness to the faithful Witness himself, who sits on the throne with God,[19] and/or the witness to which those who overcome are called.[20] In

---

[19] Gause, *Revelation*, p. 206.
[20] Smalley, *The Revelation to John*, p. 390.

any case, there would be in these words an extraordinary convergence of ideas for the hearers that focus on the very presence of God, his tabernacle (and his tablets?) of witness, and his Faithful Witness; making clear that those things which follow come from the very presence of God himself.

Verse 6 – This convergence of ideas sets the stage for the next words the hearers encounter, 'and the seven angels having the seven plagues came out of the temple wearing clean, shining stone and being girded with golden sashes around their chests'. These words, coming on the heels of the song of Moses and the song of the Lamb, not only take the hearers back to the words of 15.1 where these seven angels were introduced, but also owing to the associations of 15.5 all the way back to 11.19, suggesting that the seven bowls pick up precisely where the seven trumpets leave off.[21] Thus, despite the cosmic interlude of chapters 12-14, the hearers are put on notice that the events associated with the seven bowls are intimately connected to those associated with the seven trumpets and the opening of the seven seals before them. The emergence of these seven angels having the seven plagues from the temple make clear that they come from the very presence of God and that their actions are his actions. Not only does their origin indicate their close relationship with the divine, but their appearance does as well. For there would be in their description a convergence of imageries for the hearers drawn from previous descriptions found within the Apocalypse. On the one hand, the somewhat odd expression ἐνδεδυμένοι λίθον καθαρὸν λαμπρὸν ('wearing clean, shining stone'), often thought by modern interpreters to make no sense whatsoever,[22] would in fact highlight the resemblance between the appearance of these angels and the appearance of the One who sits on the throne, whose own appearance resembles that of the stones jasper and sardius, stones that appear on the sacred breast piece worn by

---

[21] Michaels, *Revelation*, p. 184.

[22] Such is reflected in the almost universal preference for the reading λίνον ('linen') rather than λίθον ('stone') as the original reading at this point in the Greek text. The manuscript tradition, which is somewhat evenly divided amongst the several variants, is not conclusive. Though λίθον ('stone') is clearly the more difficult of the readings, many interpreters consider it to be too difficult. However, this reading, as indicated in the interpretation offered here, while being difficult is neither too difficult nor without meaning in the context of the Apocalypse. It does have the support of such manuscripts as A and C, among others.

the high priest. Hence, it is likely that this odd expression would convey to the hearers the way in which these seven angels resemble the God from whose temple they come. On the other hand, these angels are described as 'being girded with golden sashes around their chests', a description nearly identical to the description of the appearance of the risen Jesus in 1.13. Thus, the angels' very appearance indicates that their mission is a divinely sanctioned one and that they are the very agents of God and Jesus.

Verse 7 – But before the hearers are allowed to ponder these associations more fully they encounter words that add more to this amazing scene, 'and one of the four living creatures gave to the seven angels seven golden bowls being full of the wrath of God, the One who lives forever and ever'. Attentive hearers of the Apocalypse would not be altogether surprised that one of the four living creatures would reappear in the story line for they have not only been located in extraordinary proximity to the throne of God (4.6-9; 5.6, 8, 11, 14; 7.11-12; 14.3), but also have been instrumental in carrying out a variety of activities on his behalf (6.1, 3, 5, 6, 7). The appearance of one of the living creatures at this point further highlights the divine commission of the seven angels, as the living creature gives them the seven golden bowls. The mention of the seven golden bowls could not help but remind the hearers of the fact that the prayers of the saints had earlier been closely associated with golden bowls (5.8),[23] thus further underscoring the deep connection that exists in the Apocalypse between the prayers of the saints and the redemptive judgments that come from the hand of God (cf. 6.9-11; 8.3-5).[24] However, instead of the prayers of the saints, these golden bowls are literally full of the wrath of God.[25] Not only would this statement be a reminder that with these seven last plagues the wrath of God has been completed (15.1), but it would also continue to create within the hearers an expectancy of the end of all things, an end most recently anticipated by reference to the great wrath of God that will be manifested in the great winepress of God's wrath (14.19-20). Even the reference to God as 'the One who lives forever and ever' serves to heighten the hearers' sense of

---

[23] Ladd, *Revelation*, p. 207.
[24] Smalley, *The Revelation to John*, p. 391.
[25] Koester, *Revelation and the End of All Things*, p. 147.

access to the divine presence, as this title appears for the first time in the inaugural vision of the One who sits on the throne in chapter four, where God is twice described in precisely this manner as the four living creatures and the twenty-four elders render worship to him (4.9, 10), where his role as creator is praised. The close connection between this title and God's activity as creator would also be remembered from the activity of the angel with the opened scroll in his right hand who swears 'by the One who lives forever and ever, who created the heaven and the things in it and the earth and the things in it and the sea and the things in it'. Thus, it would be hard to imagine that the hearers would not understand such a title as here underscoring the fact that it is the God who is not limited by time or space, the creator of all things, whose wrath is full and will soon be poured out completely.

Verse 8 – Thought of the fullness of the bowls gives way to the fullness of the temple as the hearers next learn, 'And the temple was filled with smoke out of the glory of God and out of his power, and no one was able to enter into the temple until the seven plagues of the seven angels had been completed'. Such words describe a truly remarkable scene, thick with intertextual converges, pregnant with meaning for the hearers. The fact that the seven bowls are filled with God's wrath while the temple is filled with the smoke of his glory and power make clear the connection between the impending actions of the angels and his own person. The mention of the temple being full of his glory and power would also be informed for the hearers by those places in the OT where the glory of God comes down and fills the tabernacle (Exod. 40.34-35) and temple (2 Chron. 7.1-3), so much so that entry was impossible. At the same time, such language would remind them of the experience of the prophets (Isa. 6.1-4; Ezek. 44.4) who encounter the living God. Such associations would indicate to the hearers that God is fully present in majesty and glory to accomplish his purpose.[26] Thus, the hearers find themselves in the midst of the awesome presence of God. The fact that the smoke comes from his glory and power continues the integrated, holistic understanding of God as glorious and powerful. It might also be remembered that when the seventh seal was opened there had been silence in heaven for half

---

[26] Beasley-Murray, *Revelation*, p. 238.

an hour (8.1) before the seven trumpets were given to the seven angels, suggesting a connection between the silence and the trumpeting that follows. Now, no one is able to enter the temple until the seven plagues of the seven angels have been completed, owing to the smoke of God's glory and power, indicating the tight connection that exists between the smoke and the activity of the seven angels.[27] Neither is it likely to escape the hearers' notice that this section, which begins with a reference to 'the wrath of God being completed' concludes with a reference to 'the seven plagues of the seven angels having been completed', forming an inclusio around this entire section, further indicating the fact that in these words the hearers encounter the completion of God's wrath.[28]

The Pouring out of the Seven Bowls (16.1-21)

Verse 1 – It is with these expectations of the end that the hearers learn of the initiation of the completion of God's wrath, 'And I heard a great voice out of the temple saying to the seven angels, "Go (forth) and pour out the seven bowls of the wrath of God into the earth"'. Whose voice is it that comes from the temple at such a significant moment? The hearers would likely take this voice as the voice of God for at least a couple of reasons. First, this voice comes from the temple despite the fact that no one was able to enter into the temple because it was full of the smoke and power of God (15.8). Second, although the phrase 'a great voice' occurs some twenty times in the Apocalypse, only on this occasion does the adjective μεγάλης ('great') precede the noun φωνῆς ('voice'),[29] further underlining its importance. In fact, the hearers may well discern in these words the intertext of Isa. 66.6 where the sound of God's voice from heaven is placed within the context of the repayment of his enemies all they deserve to receive. Such ominous words are followed by the divine instructions given to the seven angels. When the seven angels are told ὑπάγετε ('Go [forth]'), the hearers understand this command to carry divine authority, as the term has had in two of its previous three occurrences in the book (10.8; 13.10. cf. also 14.4). Likewise, when the seven angels are told ἐκχέετε ('pour out'), the hearers learn that the angelic actions of

---

[27] Caird, *The Revelation of St. John*, p. 200.
[28] Aune, *Revelation 6-16*, p. 880.
[29] Aune, *Revelation 6-16*, p. 882.

pouring out the bowls of God's wrath into the earth is itself a liturgical act, as this term appears in the OT in cultic contexts (1 Sam. 7.6; Isa. 57.6), sometimes in the context of judgment (Jer. 7.20; 10.25; 14.16; Ezek. 9.8; 14.19; Ps. 78.3-6; Lam. 2.4).[30] Mention of the voice of God, along with his authoritative and liturgical commands, serves to make the reference to 'the seven bowls of the wrath of God' even more ominous, as the anticipation of the pouring out of his wrath has been building significantly over the course of the last two chapters (cf. 14.8, 10, 19; 15.1, 7). Now, the hearers discover that these bowls of God's wrath are to be poured out 'into the earth'.

Verse 2 – With breathtaking speed the angels waste no time in fulfilling the divine commands, 'And the first angel departed and poured out his bowl into the earth, and there came a bad and evil sore upon the men who have the mark of the beast and those who worship his image'. A number of aspects of these words would be of significance to the hearers. First, they are likely to be struck not only with the speed of the angel's response but also with the fact that he fulfills this command so literally. He is told to 'go forth and pour out his bowl into the earth' so he 'departs and pours out his bowl into the earth'. Such obedient exactitude would serve to reinforce the hearers' expectation of the certainty of the fulfillment of God's commands. Second, with the enumeration of this angelic being as 'the first angel' the hearers would understand this series of seven to be in some degree of continuity with the unsealing of the seven seals as well as the trumpeting of the seven trumpets by the seven angels, both of which are enumerated lists. It should perhaps also be noted that when the first trumpet was trumpeted various elements were cast unto the earth, specifically 'hail and fire mixed with blood'. Third, despite the fact that the bowl is poured into the earth, the effect of the bowl's contents does not seem to afflict the earth as such, but rather particular individuals upon it. Fourth, mention of the 'bad and evil sore', with which the specific objects of this bowl of God's wrath are afflicted, would be especially thick with meaning for the hearers. The severity of the sores is conveyed in part by the Greek grammatical construction that includes a combination of the adjectives κακὸν ('bad') and πονηρὸν ('evil') to de-

---

[30] Smalley, *The Revelation to John*, p. 400.

scribe the sores, a unique combination within the Apocalypse, underscoring the intensity of the suffering the sores inflicted. This image would also be informed by the fact that a plague of festering sores had been sent by God upon the Egyptians. In point of fact, the sores were so severe that the Egyptian magicians could not stand before Moses owing to their affliction. Neither would the result of this affliction be lost on the hearers, for God hardened Pharaoh's heart so that he would not listen to Moses and Aaron (Exod. 9.10-12). At the same time, the hearers might also recall that Job too was afflicted with sores by Satan, with God's consent (Job 2.1-10), but with a very different ending. Taken together, these texts converge to convey that the seven last bowls of plagues of God's wrath are in continuity with God's previous activity in the Exodus events and that such liturgical activity holds out the possibility of repentance on the part of those so afflicted.[31] Fifth, the fact that the affliction resulting from the pouring out of this bowl affects those who 'have the mark of the beast and those who worship his image' would be especially poignant for the hearers. For the objects of these sores are those who have trusted in the beast by receiving his mark of protection, avoiding death at his hands, and worshipping his image, choosing to obey its oracular commands instead of the voice of God. Thus, the hearers learn that in the pouring out of the first bowl of God's wrath that God directly confronts the idolatrous behavior advocated by the beast,[32] revealing the futility of such identification with the beast and the limits of his powers to protect those who so identify with him. The contrast, between the mark received from the beast and the sore (singular) sent by God, would hardly be missed by the discerning hearers. It would not be going too far to say that the beast's mark is replaced by God's sore on those who worship the beast.[33]

Verse 3 – No sooner are the actions of the first angel completed than the hearers encounter the activity of the second, 'And the second (angel) poured out his bowl into the sea, and it became blood as one dead, and every living soul died, the things in the sea'. Perhaps one of the first things the hearers would notice in these words

---

[31] Cf. the suggestive canonical comments of Wall, *Revelation*, pp. 196-97.

[32] Smalley, *The Revelation to John*, p. 400.

[33] Koester, *Revelation and the End of All Things*, p. 148.

is the fact that though the voice from the temple instructs the seven angels to pour their bowls of God's wrath into the earth, this second angel pours his bowl into the sea, perhaps suggesting that the earth is to be understood in a comprehensive fashion. The hearers would also appreciate the way in which the effects of the second trumpeting (Rev. 8.8-9) and the first plague sent upon the Egyptians (Exod. 7.14-24) inform these words.[34] For in both cases the water of the sea and that of the Nile River are turned into blood, respectively. The similarities shared by these three events reveal a certain amount of continuity amongst these divinely initiated acts, again suggesting that this liturgical activity holds out the possibility of repentance on the part of those so afflicted. Yet, while there are basic similarities amongst the first Egyptian plague, the second trumpet, and the bowl of the second angel, the events accompanying the pouring out of the second bowl reveal a comprehensiveness and intensity making clear the unparalleled nature of this bowl. Specifically, the description of the sea becoming blood ὡς νεκροῦ ('as one dead') is especially gruesome and repulsive as it conveys something of both the cause and effect of the scene.[35] At the same time, the effects of this bowl are unparalleled when compared to the effects of the plague upon the Egyptians and the effects of the second trumpet. For when the water of the Nile River was turned to blood all the fish died and the people could not drink the water, having to dig wells along the Nile for drinking water (Exodus 14-24) and when the second angel trumpeted his trumpet, a third of the sea was turned to blood resulting in the death of a third of the creatures in the sea and the destruction of a third of the ships on the sea (Rev. 8.8-9). However, when the second bowl is poured out in Rev. 16.3 the effects are comprehensive and complete, 'every living soul died, the things in the sea'. While it is possible that the hearers would take these words to mean all sea creatures, based upon Rev. 8.8-9, the appositional construction πᾶσα ψυχὴ ζωῆς ... τὰ ἐν τῇ θαλάσσῃ ('every living soul ... the things in the sea') would appear to include both human beings and aquatic life. Such comprehensive destruction would be indisputable evidence that the

---

[34] Beale, *The Book of Revelation*, pp. 814-15.

[35] Mounce (*The Book of Revelation*, p. 294) notes, 'The sea becomes like the blood of a dead person – that is coagulated and rotting'.

wrath of God is indeed being brought to completion in these seven last plagues. In this light, the hearers might be able to appreciate better the way in which the intensity of God's redemptive judgments have been building gradually throughout the book. From the opening of the fourth seal when a fourth of the inhabitants of the earth were slain (6.8), to the trumpeting of the seven trumpets when a third of the people or things afflicted were affected, to the death of every living soul, the things in the sea, when the first bowl is poured out, the hearers discern more clearly than before that the end is very near indeed!

Verse 4 – Yet the hearers are unable to reflect on the full extent of these words, they find that there is more, 'And the third (angel) poured out his bowl into the rivers and the fountains of water, and it became blood'. As the actions of the third angel unfold, their impact on their hearers would be felt in various ways. These words would convey the sense that there is absolutely no reprieve from the completion of God's wrath. For in one sense the effects of this bowl build upon that of the second bowl in that now it appears the water supply is completely contaminated, not just the water in the sea. Another aspect of this imagery is to convey something of the magnitude of the presence of blood upon the earth. For if it, in effect, replaces the entire water supply, the amount of blood is absolutely unfathomable. The hearers would also appreciate the way in which the effects of the third trumpeting (Rev. 8.10-11) and the first plague sent upon the Egyptians (Exod. 7.14-24) inform these words.[36] But as with the second bowl in relationship to the second trumpeting and first Egyptian plague, there is a greater intensity detected in this bowl's effects when compared to its counterparts. For while the Egyptians were apparently able to dig along the Nile River for drinking water (Exod. 7.24), and the third trumpeting affected a third of the rivers and fountains of water causing the death of a third of the people, the effects of the third bowl being poured out seems to be more intense and absolute.

Verse 5 – But before the hearers learn the effects of this devastating bowl upon the inhabitants of the earth, their attention is directed to something else John hears:

---

[36] Beale, *The Book of Revelation*, p. 816.

And I heard (the voice) of the angel of the waters saying,
'Righteous are you, the one who is and was, the Holy One
for you have judged these things
for blood of saints and prophets they have poured out
and blood you have given to them to drink,
(as) they are worthy'.

Though the hearers may expect to learn of the destruction the impact of the third bowl has, they instead encounter the voice of the angel of the waters. The hearers would likely understand this angel to be the third angel who has been responsible for pouring out the third bowl from which the rivers and fountains of water turn into blood.[37] The words of the angel are hymnic in nature and would be informed by numerous OT texts (Neh. 9.33; Pss. 7.11; 9.4; Jer. 46.28; Dan. 9.14) as well as the hymn found previously in Rev. 15.3-4.[38] The song of this angel not only celebrates God's person and work by means of various descriptive titles that each draw attention to some specific element of his being, but at the same time offers an insight into the true significance of the bowls.[39] The angelic words 'you are worthy' could not help but remind the hearers of a specific line in the song of Moses and the song of the Lamb where the ways of God are described as 'righteous'. Owing to this association they would immediately discern that the hymn of the third angel is directly related to the description of the pouring out of the bowls that precedes it. If the hearers are tempted to misunderstand these wrathful activities of God as too severe, they are immediately reassured that they come from the hand of a righteous God whose ways are 'true and righteous' (15.3). Neither would the hearers be unaware of the significance of the title that follows, 'the one who is and the one who was', as it conveys at least two things on this occasion. First, it carries with it all the weight of the threefold form that appears on three previous occasions in the Apocalypse, 'the one who is, and the one who was, and the one who is coming', providing a sense of continuity for the hearers. For the same God whom John describes in the prologue as sitting upon the throne (1.4), the same God who identifies himself with this title

---

[37] Mounce, *Revelation*, pp. 294-95. Contra Smalley, *The Revelation to John*, p. 402.
[38] Smalley, *The Revelation to John*, p. 402.
[39] Prigent, *L'Apocalypse de Saint Jean*, p. 361.

(1.8), the same God whom they know from the heavenly throne room vision (4.8), is now described as righteous. The one who transcends time, encompassing the beginning and the end, is the righteous God who sends these bowls of wrath. Second, the hearers would also recognize that the two-fold form of this title, first introduced in 11.17, 'the one who was and the one who is', underscores the reign of God as a present reality, the implication being that he is no longer the one who is to come for he has already come! The appearance of this two-fold title would be additional reason for the hearers to discern that they are indeed approaching the end of all things. This God, who is called righteous, as well as the one who was and the one who is, is now called ὁ ὅσιος ('the Holy One'). This title too takes the hearers back to the hymn in 15.2-4 where the words 'You alone are holy' are ascribed to God in a text that holds out hope for the conversion of the nations. On this occasion in 16.5 the title 'the Holy One' stands in continuity with its earlier reference (15.4) where the incomparability of God is emphasized. Neither is it without significance that this title appears in the context of the pouring out of the bowls of God's wrath. Coming as it does in 16.5, the hearers might very well discern the way in which 'the one who was and the one who is' are surrounded by the ascription that God is righteous and the title 'the Holy One', in itself offering some insight into the divine significance of the bowls of God's wrath. The second line of the hymn offers the justification for the lofty language of the opening line, 'for you have judged them', making explicit what the titles and ascription have implied. At least two aspects of this statement would be of significance for the hearers. First, the statement would be seen in some continuity with the cry of the souls under the altar, 'How long ... will you not judge?' (6.10) and the words of the twenty-four elders in still another hymn, 'the time has come to judge the dead' (11.17). Second, the intricate connection between the lofty titles and ascription given to God and the justification for them, following fast on the heels of the first pouring out of the first three bowls, indicates that the pouring out of the bowls of God's wrath are no capricious, one off acts of a ruthless and unethical tyrant, but are demanded by the very nature of this righteous and holy God, whose ways are righteous and true!

Verse 6 – The reason God is deemed righteous and holy in his judgment of these things, is made clear in the fourth and fifth lines of the hymn:

> for blood of saints and prophets they have poured out
> and blood to them you have given to drink.

Perhaps the first thing to strike the hearers is the way in which these lines stand in parallel to one another. Each of these lines focus on the word αἷμα ('blood'), which stands in an emphatic position at the beginning of both the fourth and fifth lines, each of them describes the pouring out or giving of blood, and each of them reveal who it is that acts in such ways. Reference to the blood of the saints and prophets being poured out is significant in at least two ways. First, this phrase comes to represent the cost of giving faithful witness to Jesus, an idea present in numerous places in the Apocalypse beginning with Jesus as Faithful Witness whose blood looses us from our sins (1.5), Antipas the faithful witness who is put to death in Pergamum (2.13), the souls under the altar who cry out for justice for their blood (6.10), the two prophetic witnesses who also die in the course of their faithful witness (11.7-12), those who are to die by the sword who would not worship the image of the beast (13.10, 15), the 144,000 who follow the Lamb wherever he goes (14.4), and those who have overcome the beast and his image and the number of his name (15.2-4). Second, reference to saints and prophets would perhaps be taken as a reference to the people of God as a whole and the prophetic witness to which they are called. Specifically, the saints are those whose prayers are always before the throne (5.8; 8.3, 4), are worthy to receive their reward (11.18), are made war against by the beast (13.7), and are the recipients of divine assistance for the task of pneumatic discernment (13.10; 14.12); while prophets are those who preach the mystery of God (10.7), whose death brings delight to the inhabitants of the earth (11.10), and are themselves worthy of their reward (11.18). Third, the fact that the verb ἐξέχεαν ('they poured out') occurs to describe the shedding of blood may indicate that their actions were, in effect, 'liturgical' activity offered in the worship of the beast. The term also provides a philological link between their activities of pouring out blood of saints and prophets, on the one hand, and the pouring out of the bowls of God's wrath, on the other hand. In fact it might not be going too far to say that God's righteous judgments are a direct response to their unrighteousness. They pour out blood of his saints and prophets, so he in turn pours out bowls of wrath. On its own, line four of the hymn would be enough to explain the significance of the pouring out of the bowls of God's wrath, but line five goes even further, 'and blood to them you gave to drink'. The parallel to line four describes the activity of God in such a way that it sits quite poetically with line four, on the one hand, while going further to explain why the second and third bowls of God's wrath have turned water into blood, on the other hand. In one sense, it is their own doing for they are being made to drink that which they have poured out. Of course, the hearers would likely pick up on the deeper irony present in these words. For the God who has given them blood to drink had earlier given them the blood of the Lamb for them to be loosed from their sins, but they have refused him, his Son, and his Spirit, by rejecting the faithful witness of his saints and prophets. The final line of the angelic hymn makes clear that these judgments are not capricious but righteous. For the giving of blood to drink is something of which 'they are worthy'. Not only do such words add a final testimony about the righteousness of God's judgments, but they also stand in direct contrast to those faithful in Sardis who have not stained their clothes, and as a result will walk with Jesus in white, 'for they are worthy' (3.4). The occurrence of the same words ἄξιοί εἰσιν ('they are worthy') to describe both groups would be virtually impossible to miss, driving home the sad but stark truth: those who pour out the blood of the saints and the prophets are as deserving of the bowls of God's wrath as the saints in Sardis are to walk with Jesus in white!

Verse 7 – While the hearers might expect the resumption of the account of the pouring out of the bowls of God's wrath to occur at this point, their attention is directed to yet another hymn, 'And I heard one from the altar saying, "Yes Lord, God, the All Powerful One, true and righteous are your judgments"'. In these words the hearers come to understand that standing alongside the testimony of the angel of the waters is another testimonial hymn. However, instead of coming from an angelic being this testimony comes from τοῦ θυσιαστηρίου (translated literally as 'one from the altar'). It is altogether likely that in these words the hearers would discern a reference back to the description of the opening of the fifth seal (6.10), where the souls under the altar who had been slaughtered cry out to God, 'How long, O Master, the Holy and True One, will you not judge and vindicate our blood on those who dwell upon the earth?'[40] The divine response to their cry for justice was to wait a little longer (6.11) until the number of their brothers who were about to be killed was full. In the intervening chapters there has been no direct mention of the souls under the altar, though reference to their prayers may appear in 8.3-4 and a partial response to their cry may be implied in the hymn in 15.3. Thus, in 16.7, where one of those under the altar speaks,[41] or the corporate voice of the martyrs is heard,[42] the hearers would be keen to discover the content of their words, for they have been waiting a very long time indeed! The first word in this testimonial hymn, Ναί ('Yes'), has occurred on two occasions in the Apocalypse to this point; once in response to the prophetic word about the resurrected Jesus in 1.7 and once from the Spirit in response to the beatitude spoken by the heavenly voice in 14.13. In keeping with those occurrences, its appearance in 16.7 indicates that it functions as an affirmation, an 'amen' if you will, to the words of the hymn spoken by the angel of the waters. Thus, the words that come from the one from the altar are understood as accepting of and building upon those that precede them. Specifically, this 'Yes!' affirms both the affirmation and titles of which the angel has spoken and, at the same time, affirms the truth of these statements with regard to the pouring out of the blood of saints and prophets, on the one hand, and the verdict that they are worthy to drink blood as a result, on the other hand. Following this weighty word of affirmation, the voice from the altar goes on to acknowledge God by the three-fold formula, 'Lord, God, the All Powerful One'. This combination of titles, which begins as a self-designation for God in a prophetic utterance (1.8), appears in contexts of worship (each time in a hymn) on the lips of the four living creatures (4.8), the twenty-four elders (11.17), and most recently those who have overcome the beast and his image

---

[40] Skaggs and Benham, *Revelation*, p. 162.
[41] Aune, *Revelation 6-16*, p. 888.
[42] Pattemore, *The People of God in the Apocalypse*, p. 100.

and the number of his name (15.3). As such its occurrence here would remind the hearers of God's incomparability, absolute power, and the fact that nothing is beyond his reach. In the declaration, 'true and righteous are your judgments', a number of things converge, for these words are intricately connected to both the cry from those under the altar and the words of the angel of the waters. The judgments of 'the Master, the holy and true One' (6.10) are 'true and righteous judgments' (16.7). The judgment resulting from the pouring out of the bowl that turns the waters into blood, which is brought upon those who pour out the blood of saints and prophets (16.4-6), is in direct correlation with the cry of the souls under the altar for God to 'judge and vindicate our blood' (6.10). The righteous God (16.5) is one whose judgments are themselves righteous (16.7). Thus, at this crucial moment in the unfolding of the Apocalypse, the hearers learn that the final word with regard to the righteousness of God and his judgments in these bowls is not left to an angelic being but to the martyrs[43] whose own testimony indicates that they themselves, who have suffered so much and waited so long, are satisfied that the ways of God are indeed true and righteous! Their testimony gives the hearers hope that they too will one day be in a position to make the same affirmation, to give the same testimony with regard to God's righteous and true acts!

Verse 8 – Following the hymns of the angel of the waters and the voice from the altar the hearers learn that the bowl sequence continues, 'And the fourth (angel) poured out his bowl upon the sun, and there was given to it to scorch men with fire'. Perhaps one of the first things to strike the hearers about these words would be their similarities with and differences from the trumpet sequence and Egyptian plague sequence. On the one hand, the similarities include the fact that, like the effects of this bowl, both the fourth trumpeting and the ninth Egyptian plague affect the sun (and/or other sources of light), and in the case of the ninth plague the effects could be felt. On the other hand, whereas the fourth bowl seems to intensify the sun's heat, the fourth trumpet and ninth plague affected the sun's ability to illuminate the earth. In point of fact, a third of the sun and moon were darkened after the fourth trumpeting, while the ninth plague brought darkness upon the

---

[43] Prigent, *L'Apocalypse de Saint Jean*, p. 362.

Egyptians that was so severe it could be felt! The hearers might very well be reminded of the way in which the results of this bowl stand in stark contrast to the eschatological promises given to those coming out of the great tribulation that 'the sun will not beat upon them nor any scorching heat' (7.16).[44] Significantly, the same root word appears in both 7.16 and 16.8. This contrast might also remind the hearers of the fact that though the Egyptians experienced darkness during this plague, the Israelites did not as they had light in the places where they lived (Exod. 10.23). The statement that men will be scorched 'with fire' would reinforce the idea that this is indeed a judgment of God, as fire has occurred in a variety of contexts in the Apocalypse with just that meaning (Rev. 8.5, 7, 8; 9.17, 18; 11.5; 14.10, 18).

Verse 9 – Whilst contemplating such rich intertextual associations the hearers are told more, 'And the men were scorched with great scorching heat and they blasphemed the name of God, the one having the authority over these plagues, and they did not repent to give him glory'. The extent of the suffering this bowl brings upon humankind is conveyed in part by the phrase ἐκαυματίσθησαν ... καῦμα μέγα ('scorched ... with great scorching'), a grammatical construction known as a cognate accusative, where the same root word appears as both the verb and the direct object. Just as the darkness of the ninth Egyptian plague could be 'felt', so the impact of the pouring out of this bowl could as well. At this point the testimony of the angel of the waters and the voice from those under the altar about the righteous nature of the bowl judgments is contrasted with the actions of those who are 'scorched with great scorching'. Instead of recognizing the justice of God's bowls of wrath – they blaspheme his name. Though these individuals rightly discern that these phenomena come from the hand of God,[45] who is described as the one who has authority over the plagues, they choose to blaspheme his name instead.[46] Inasmuch as the only

---

[44] Osborne, *Revelation*, p. 586. In thinking of the eschatological promise, it is even possible that the hearers would think of God's protection of Shadrach, Meshach, and Abednego. Cf. the comments of Sweet (*Revelation*, p. 245) who compares the promise of Rev. 7.16 with Dan. 3.22, 27 noting, '... the three who refused to worship Nebuchadnezzar's image were not even singed by the scorching furnace'.

[45] Ladd, *Revelation*, p. 211.

[46] Resseguie, *The Revelation of John*, p. 212.

character to blaspheme the name of God to this point in the Apocalypse is the beast, who not only has blasphemous names written upon his head (13.1) but also opens his mouth to blaspheme his name (13.5, 6), these individuals reveal their deep and intimate identification with the beast; they have wholly taken on the character of the one they worship.[47] The nature of their blasphemy is likely to be thought similar to that of the beast himself, which impinges in some way upon the identity and glory of God and his name. Such willful identification with the beast reveals the depth of their duplicitous relationship. Owing to the reference to the blasphemy of those who claim to be Jews but are not (2.9), the hearers are likely to understand blasphemy as having everything to do with the identity of God and those who honor him by embracing his identity and his name, which would be coterminous for the hearers. The plural 'plagues' may suggest that their response to God is based on the effects of all the plagues to this point.[48] Yet, despite recognizing the ultimate source of the plagues, they are unable to recognize the immediate cause, their unrepentant lives;[49] for despite their suffering at God's hand they refuse to repent and by that means give him glory![50] Not only would this refusal to repent be reminiscent of the consistent actions of Pharaoh when confronted with the plagues God sent on Egypt (Exod. 7.13, 22; 8.15, 19, 32; 9.7, 12, 34-35; 10.1, 20; 11.9-10; 14.4),[51] but also of the trumpet sequence in the Apocalypse where despite the effects of the six trumpet blasts the rest of the men still refuse to repent of the works of their hands, which includes the worship of demons and idols, and their murders, magic arts, sexual immorality, and thievery (9.20-21).[52] No doubt, the hearers would understand the need for repentance along these same lines. Not only this, but these humans explicitly reject the message of the angel in 14.7, who cries out with a great voice, 'Fear

---

[47] Caird, *The Revelation of St. John*, p. 202.

[48] Smalley, *The Revelation to John*, p. 405.

[49] Sweet, *Revelation*, p. 245.

[50] Primasius (*Commentary On the Apocalypse*, 16.9 cited in ACCS 12, p. 253) comments, 'It is the habit of blasphemers that they prefer to blame God for wickedness and iniquity rather than themselves, and therefore [they] do not seek penance after plagues but, even though tormented, continue to throw insults'.

[51] Aune, *Revelation 6-16*, p. 889.

[52] Beale, *The Book of Revelation*, p. 822.

God and give glory to him, because the hour of his judgment has come, and worship the one who made the heaven and the earth and the sea and the fountains of water'. Nearly every word of 14.7 is significant for that described in 16.9. Specifically, the hour of God's final judgment has come upon the earth (16.2), the sea (16.3), the fountains of water (16.4), and the heaven (16.8, 9). The maker of them all has sent his bowls of wrath upon them. And yet, these human beings refuse to repent, to give God glory, though based on 11.13 and 14.7, such was still possible even at this late hour. However, for those who reject such a proclamation, the judgment of God has come already.

Verse 10 – With these sobering words still ringing in their ears, the bowls continue to be poured out, 'And the fifth (angel) poured out his bowl upon the throne of the beast, and his kingdom became dark, and they were gnawing their tongues out of agony'. In the pouring out of the first bowl the hearers discover that the idolatry of those aligned with the beast are the targets of painful sores. With the pouring out of the fifth bowl, they learn that God's wrath is directed to the very center of the beast's power, his throne. As the hearers will know full well, the throne of the beast was a derived one. For it was given to him by the dragon, along with the dragon's power and authority (13.2). From this position of power he blasphemes God (13.5-6), makes war with the saints (13.7), and is worshipped by all the world's inhabitants except 'those whose names were written in the book of life of the Lamb who was slaughtered before the foundation of the world' (13.8).[53] The hearers would also know that apparently one manifestation of this throne is in Sardis, which incidentally is also connected to the blasphemy of those who claim to be Jews but are not. When this bowl is poured out the throne of the beast becomes dark, an occurrence that would again remind the hearers of the fourth trumpet and ninth Egyptian plague. Like the darkness the Egyptians experienced, this darkness appears to be felt as well, for the agony of those associated with the throne of the beast is so great that they were gnawing on their tongues, the verb ἐμασῶντο ('were gnawing'), an especially harsh

---

[53] Koester, *Revelation and the End of All Things*, p. 151.

term, being in the imperfect tense indicating that this gnawing was ongoing.[54]

Verse 11 – Yet, despite their intense agony the hearers learn, 'And they blasphemed the God of heaven out of their agony and out of their sores and they did not repent of their works'. Incredibly, the same tongues that were being gnawed, owing to their agony, are then used to blaspheme the God of heaven![55] Like those who blasphemed the name of God owing to being scorched with scorching heat, these too appear aware of the identity of the one who inflicts this suffering, but they also willfully reject the opportunity for repentance from their works, choosing to blaspheme God owing to their suffering. The words, 'out of their agony and their sores' suggests that the effects of the pouring out of the previous bowls are felt in a cumulative fashion, as the sores inflicted in 16.2 appear to be felt still.[56] The hearers would likely understand the works from which these refuse to repent as similar to those named in 9.20-21. It may not be insignificant that reference to 'sores' occurs in the two bowl accounts that deal directly with idolatry, further underscoring the relationship between the beast's mark and the sores inflicted by God.[57] In 16.2 the beast could offer no protection for his followers from the wrath of God; in 16.10-11 he can offer no protection for his own throne!

Verse 12 – The story continues, 'And the sixth (angel) poured out his bowl upon the great river the Euphrates, and its water was dried up, in order that the way of the kings from the rising of the sun (the east) might be prepared'. These words would be fraught with significance for the hearers for a variety of reasons. First, 'the great river, the Euphrates' is the object upon which this bowl is poured out. Yet unlike the preceding bowls that are directed to bodies or sources of water the purpose of this pouring out is not to turn the water into blood, but rather to dry the water up altogether! Owing to its great length, the largest river in southwest Asia, and its

---

[54] C. Schneider, 'μασάομαι', *TDNT*, IV, p. 514.

[55] Gause, *Revelation*, p. 213.

[56] Michaels, *Revelation*, p. 187.

[57] Aune observes (*Revelation 6-16*, p. 890), 'There is an inconsistency in the text in that there is no evident connection between darkness and the experience of pain and sores'. Perhaps this point of commonality between these bowls addresses one aspect of this 'inconsistency'.

abundance, the Euphrates was never known to have dried up.[58] For such to take place would indeed be owing to the hand of God. Second, it would be difficult to imagine that the hearers would not pick up on the way the drying up of this river stands in contrast to the drying up of the Red Sea (Exod. 14.21-22) and the Jordan River (Josh. 3.14-17) so that the people of God might pass through during the period of the Exodus and entry into the promised land, respectively. The significance of this juxtaposition of salvation and judgment would hardly be lost on the hearers. Third, neither would the hearers be unaware of the way in which the language of preparing the way for the kings of the east so closely parallels Isa. 11.15, which also speaks of the drying up of the Euphrates so that the remnant of God's people might return from exile, further developing the contrast between this drying up of the river for judgment and the drying up of the river for salvation.[59] Fourth, while it is not altogether certain how the hearers would understand the phrase 'the kings from the rising of the sun' or 'kings from the east', it appears that they would take this reference a) to stand in some continuity with the 'kings of the earth' that have appeared earlier in the Apocalypse (6.15), b) as a natural correlative to the drying up of the Euphrates, and c) as a representation of the ominous threats those from the east, especially the Parthians, were thought to pose to Rome.

Verse 13 – For the first time since 15.5, the hearers are told of something John saw, 'And I saw out of the mouth of the dragon and out of the mouth of the beast and out of the mouth of the false prophet three unclean spirits as frogs'. For the hearers the emphasis of these words would be clear as the phrase 'out of the mouth of' not only stands in a position of emphasis, but also occurs three times in this verse! Such an emphasis upon what comes from the mouths of this triumvirate of evil, mentioned here together for the first time in the book,[60] would no doubt remind the hearers of the things that have been said to come from their mouths previously, including the river which came from the mouth of the ancient serpent to drown the rest of the seed of the woman clothed with the

---

[58] Smalley, *The Revelation to John*, p. 407.

[59] Prompting Beasley-Murray (*Revelation*, p. 244) to conclude that this '… miracle of redemption has become an eschatological miracle of judgment'.

[60] Osborne, *Revelation*, p. 591.

sun (12.15) and the great and blasphemous things that come from the mouth of the beast (13.5-6). At the same time, these would likely be thought of in contrast to the double-edged sword that comes from the mouth of Jesus (1.16; 2.16), the fire and smoke of God that come from the mouths of the horses when the sixth angel trumpets (9.17-19), and the fire that comes from the mouth of the two witnesses (11.5).[61] But perhaps most poignantly they would be reminded of the fact that in the mouths of the 144,000 were found no lies (14.5). If the hearers earlier suspected that the beast from the earth functioned as a false prophet (13.11-16), their suspicions are confirmed in 16.13 for he is here explicitly identified as the 'false prophet'. In fact what comes from the mouths of these figures are 'unclean spirits, as frogs'. Both the words 'unclean spirits' and 'as frogs' would perhaps give the hearers pause when first encountered, for this is the first mention of 'unclean spirits' in the entire Johannine tradition, not to mention frogs! What would the hearers of the Apocalypse make of this unique phrase? The first hint is the adjective 'unclean', which will come to be identified with the sexual immorality of the Great Whore (17.4) and with the fallen Babylon (18.2). Whatever else they might be, these spirits are 'unclean' in the later Johannine sense. The second hint comes in the form of the somewhat enigmatic words that these unclean spirits came out of the mouths of this triumvirate 'as frogs'. On one level, this designation continues the juxtaposition of the previous verse in that whilst God sent a plague of frogs upon the Egyptians (8.15), here the enemies of God send the frogs. But at another level, it would be clear to the hearers that the phrase 'as frogs' too conveys that these spirits are unclean for frogs were deemed as unclean in the Torah (Lev. 11.9-12, 41-47), contact from which necessitating the need for ritual cleansing.[62] It is even possible that mention of the frogs would conjure up images of magicians and sorcerers.[63] This much is clear at this point, these unclean spirits are closely identified with the triumvirate of evil and as such would share their unclean nature.

---

[61] Sweet, *Revelation*, p. 249.
[62] Smalley, *The Revelation to John*, p. 409.
[63] So Prigent, *L'Apocalypse de Saint Jean*, p. 366.

Verse 14 – The hearers do not have to wait long to learn a bit more about these unclean spirits for they soon are told, 'For they are spirits of demons (demonic spirits) who do signs, which are sent out to the kings of the whole inhabited world to gather them together into the war of the great day of God the All Powerful One'. The identification of these unclean spirits as demonic spirits may assist the hearers in assessing the nature of the worship of demons that the rest of humankind refused to turn from and repent in 9.20-21. Though not stated as such on that occasion, it now becomes clear that their worship was closely associated with the dragon, the beast, and the false prophet. Such an understanding makes sense in a community where the only person to be accused of being demon possessed was Jesus (Jn 7.20; 8.48, 49, 52; 10.20, 21). In Rev. 16.14 these demonic spirits do signs, like the beast from the earth, the false prophet, did earlier to deceive the inhabitants of the earth (13.13-14), bearing a striking resemblance to the spirits that must be tested to determine whether they be from the Spirit of Truth or the spirit of deception (1 Jn 4.1-6).[64] A similar agenda seems to be at work here as well, as the signs performed by these demonic spirits appear to be linked to their ability to gather the kings together.[65] Ironically, the activity of the evil triumvirate takes place in tandem with the activity of God, for at the very time the sixth bowl of his wrath is being poured out, demonic spirits go forth from the triumvirate to gather together all the kings of the inhabited world for the war to end all wars, the war of the great day of God the All Powerful One! It appears that just as with other images previously, 'the kings from the east' have morphed into 'all the kings of the inhabited world', as the focus moves from a single compass point to that of the whole world.[66] With regard to the identity of this war, it apparently is well known to the hearers owing to the articular form of the word τὸν πόλεμον ('the war').[67] Could it be other than the final cataclysmic war to end all wars, the Day of the Lord, the day on which John writes?

---

[64] For the characteristics of such spirits in 1 Jn 4.1-6 cf. Thomas, *1 John, 2 John, 3 John*, pp. 197-214.
[65] Murphy, *Fallen Is Babylon*, p. 343.
[66] Smalley, *The Revelation to John*, p. 410.
[67] Aune, *Revelation 6-16*, p. 896.

Verse 15 – With such incredibly suggestive words bouncing around in their heads, and perhaps with a desire to learn of the fate of all these kings, the hearers may be stunned by the next words recounted, 'Behold, I come as a thief. Blessed is the one who watches and keeps his garments, in order that he not walk naked and they see his shame.' Like a lightning bolt these words of the resurrected Jesus break into the account of the bowls. On the one hand, his words may be seen as an intrusion into this account. On the other hand, none of the hearers would be surprised to hear the voice of the resurrected Jesus in the midst of a discussion of the Day of the Lord![68] If it is a familiar voice, it is because the hearers have encountered this voice already in the seven prophetic messages. It is as though that same voice breaks in here to ensure that the hearers understand the direct relevance of the events described in 16.12-14 to those given earlier,[69] to ensure that they do not become detached hearers at this point. Specifically, Jesus' words reveal that the war to end all wars is intimately connected with his return. The hearers have encountered references to the return of Jesus on various occasions in the Apocalypse (1.7; 3.11) along with other statements to the churches that he will come to them for judgment of those who refuse to repent (2.5, 16). While the latter two references sounded a bit less eschatological when first encountered, in the light of the context of his words in 16.15, the hearers may even begin to think of these earlier words as more eschatological than it first appeared. Earlier in the prophetic message to Sardis (3.3) the resurrected Jesus has issued a very similar warning, 'I come as a thief'. There, the suddenness is underscored to an even greater degree with the words, 'you will not know the hour when I come'. In 16.15, as with the threat/promise of Jesus' return to the church in Sardis, the promise is not conditional, predicated by whether or not they repent. Rather, the emphasis is upon the suddenness and certainty of his coming in salvation and judgment, and the warning not to be unprepared for it, and consequently unaware of its timing. This promise is followed by the third beatitude to appear in the Apocalypse (cf. 1.3; 14.13), which again is quite reminiscent of the promise/warning given to the church in Sardis. Specifically, the

---

[68] Michaels, *Revelation*, p. 188.
[69] Sweet, *Revelation*, p. 249.

term γρηγορῶν ('awake' or 'watchful') appears, conveying both the idea of wakefulness and watchfulness, combining the idea of vigilance with eschatological expectation. The one who is awake is the one who is aware, watchful, vigilate. In the prophetic message to Sardis (3.4) the imagery of clothing also appears, there with regard to those who have not soiled their clothes but walk with Jesus in white, for they are worthy. And in the prophetic message to Laodicea, they are warned about their nakedness and instructed to buy white garments to wear so that they can cover their nakedness and avoid exposure to shame (3.17-18). Clearly, the convergence of these terms and themes combine to underscore the gravity of this divine warning. The message for the hearers could not be clearer. Their vigilance with regard to their prophetic pneumatic witness necessitates lives whose works are praised and honored by Jesus himself. The language of 'walking about naked' and 'they will see their shame' confirms what has been stated earlier in the book, one's relationship to Jesus is visible, not only to Jesus, but to those around as well.[70] Especially in the light of the war to end all wars, vigilance is absolutely essential.

Verse 16 – Picking up where the account of the bowls left off before the intervening words of Jesus, the hearers next learn, 'And they gathered them into the place called in Hebrew, Harmagedon'. The first thing the hearers are likely to conclude from these words is that the demonic spirits had been successful in drawing together all the kings of the earth through the performance of signs! Such a result suggests that though the throne of the beast has been attacked, he, through his envoys, is still able to dominate, if not all the inhabitants of the earth, at least all the kings. Next, the hearers are hardly in doubt as to the reason for the kings' assembly, they have come for the great day of the war of God the All Powerful One, though they are apparently still unaware that it was God who initiated this gathering in the first place by the drying up of the Great Euphrates River. Perhaps the most difficult aspect of these words to discern for the hearers, as for many modern hearers, is the identity of 'the place called in Hebrew, Harmagedon'. Part of the complication for the modern interpreter is that a fair amount of uncertain-

---

[70] As Sweet (*Revelation*, p. 249) observes, 'Clothing signifies the righteousness and holiness which God will accept (cf. 19.8); nakedness signifies its lack'.

ty exists even with regard to the actual spelling of the name![71] What would these words likely convey to the hearers? First, they would know that the name Harmagedon is a Hebrew name. Second, they would also be aware that it is not an uncommon experience for them to encounter Hebrew names and terms in the vision. Third, they would know as well that such Hebrew terms can often have more meaning than their face value (2.14, 20; 9.11; 11.8; 14.8; 16.19).[72] In point of fact, on at least one occasion the Hebrew component was present even where no overt mention of it was made, as in the calculation of the number of the beast in 13.18. Fourth, they would also be well aware of the fact that 'in the Spirit' a number of elements converge to produce new and rich images and realities, such as, for example, the convergence in the vision of Jesus (1.9-20), the two prophetic witnesses (11.1-13), and the woman clothed with the sun (12.1-18). Thus, on this occasion they would likely suspect that the Hebrew name Harmagedon comes from two Hebrew words, הר (*har*, 'mountain') and מגדון (*megidon*, 'Megiddon'), a combination of Hebrew words that literally means 'Mountain of Megiddon'. Since there is no literal Mount Megiddon they would likely understand that as with a number of other names and terms in the book this one too is an image that emerges from the convergence of a variety of intertexts. How would the hearers discern their way forward? Perhaps the first hint would come from the fact that in the OT the city of Megiddo was associated with a number of significant battles including Deborah's victory over Sisera (Judg. 5.19), Azariah's escape from Jehu (2 Kgs 9.27), Josiah's defeat at the hands of the Pharaoh Neco (2 Kgs 23.29), as well as the eschatological weeping that will take place in Jerusalem like the weeping that took place in 'the valley of Megiddo' (Zech. 12.11). This battle imagery would be further enhanced by the fact that the Jezreel Valley stretches out before Megiddo where numerous battles have been fought, the vista of this site being particularly stunning from the vantage point of Mount Carmel some ten kilometers to the northwest. Thus, the Hebrew name Harmagedon would, at the least, carry with it associations of war, as perhaps no other location would. But such an understanding would not exhaust the significance of

---

[71] Metzger, *Breaking the Code*, p. 84.
[72] Koester, *Revelation and the End of All Things*, pp. 152-53.

this Hebrew word. For in the OT, mountains are tied to significant battles, even eschatological ones. Perhaps this would be enough for the hearers to recall the mountains of Israel (Ezekiel 38-39), important in one such eschatological context, and perhaps the possibility in the hearers' minds that if there is a valley of Megiddo where the nations shall mourn (Zech. 12.11) there must be a mountain of Megiddo as well.[73] It is even possible that the mountains mentioned in association with the destruction of Babylon in Isaiah 13 are at least in the back of the hearers' minds and go some way toward informing this name.[74] Thus, there is every likelihood that the Hebrew place name Harmagedon would be deemed by the hearers of the Apocalypse to be a most appropriate place for the war to end all wars to convene, with a variety of images converging at this point.[75] As the words of 16.16 conclude, the kings of the earth stand at the ready, gathered together for the war of the great day of God the All Powerful One!

Verse 17 – With anticipation of this great war running high, the description of the bowls sequence continues, 'And the seventh (angel) poured out his bowl upon the air, and a great voice came out of the temple from the throne saying, "It is done!"' One of the first things of significance about these words for the hearers would be the fact that the last seven plagues of God's wrath have actually been completed! With the words 'It is done' the hearers are closer than ever to the end of all things. Not only is there no more delay, but this last sequence of sevens has also been completed without an interlude or delay, as the previous two seals and trumpets sequences had been. With this seventh bowl the pouring out the bowls upon the earth has moved from the earth itself to the air, which surrounds it. Neither would there be any confusion with regard to the identity of the one who speaks. It is none other than the voice of

---

[73] On this whole question cf. esp. J. Day, 'The Origin of Armageddon', in *Crossing the Boundaries: Essays in Biblical Interpretation in Honour of Michael D. Goulder* (S.E. Porter, P. Joyce, D.E. Orton eds.; Leiden: Brill, 1994), pp. 315-26.

[74] On this possible identification cf. the work of M. Jauhiainen, 'The OT Background to Armageddon (Rev 16.16) Revisited', *NovT* 47.4 (2005), pp. 381-93.

[75] Schüssler Fiorenza (*Revelation*, p. 94) warns, 'The multivalence of the author's mythological-symbolic language cannot be reduced to a single one-dimensional definition! Such multivalence expresses the author's interest in giving prophetic interpretation rather than geographical-eschatological information'.

God! The hearing of his voice on this occasion at the end of the bowls sequence matches the sounding of his voice at the beginning of the sequence when God instructs the seven angels with the seven bowls to pour out their bowls, indicating that the entire bowls sequence is enveloped by the voice of God. His words indicate that their work has been accomplished and the end has arrived, the perfect tense γέγονεν ('It is done') indicating a past event the results of which are felt into the present. The fact that this bowl is said to come not just from the temple but also specifically from the throne would also remind the hearers of the way in which this, the longest portion of the vision, began, with a vision of the One who sits on the throne (4.1-5.14)! Thus, not only is the bowl sequence enveloped by God's voice, but this, the longest section of the Apocalypse (4.1-16.21) is also enveloped by reference to the throne of God.

Verse 18 – Then the seventh bowl was poured out, 'And there were lighting and sounds and thunder and there was a great earthquake, which had not been since before man had been upon the earth, so great was this earthquake'. In addition to the mention of the throne in 16.17, the display of the theophanic elements also points the hearers back to 4.5, where these elements are first recounted in the Apocalypse. The display of the theophanic elements also reminds the hearers of the way in which the sequence of seven bowls is connected to the opening of the seven seals and the trumpeting of the seven trumpets, for the display of theophanic elements accompanies the conclusion of each sequence with each sequence being more intense than the one that comes before. On this occasion the intensification comes initially by means of the reference to the earthquake of unparalleled magnitude. For the hearers of the Apocalypse who had perhaps experienced more than one earthquake in their lives, such a statement would carry great weight. This intensification amongst the theophanic elements serves both to remind the hearers of the direct connection between the One who sits on the throne and the pouring out of the seven bowls, on the one hand, and to provide a certain linear shape and movement to this section of the Apocalypse and the book as a whole, on the other hand. But the significance of this unparalleled earthquake would not be exhausted even by these associations, for the hearers would likely understand this earthquake in the light of the numerous OT texts where a great earthquake is part of the eschatological expectation (Isa. 13.13; Hag. 2.6-7; Zech. 14.4-5).[76] The piling up of synonyms in the description of the magnitude of this earthquake would do much to suggest its uniqueness to the hearers.

Verses 19-20 – With such momentous words still ringing in their ears the hearers now discover the effects of this extraordinary event, 'And the Great City came into three parts and the cities of the nations fell. And Babylon the Great was remembered before God to give to her the cup of the wine of the wrath of his anger'. The last mention of the Great City by this name came in 11.8-10, where it pneumatically is called 'Sodom' and 'Egypt', is identified as the place where their Lord was crucified, and has inhabitants from all over the world in its constituency who rejoice at the death of the two prophetic witnesses. Interestingly, this Great City is also struck by an earthquake, with ten percent of the population of 70,000 dying from the earthquake, while the surviving ninety percent feared and gave glory to the God of heaven. In 16.19 the Great City is literally broken apart, while the cities of the nations fall, suggesting that though the kings of the inhabited world had gathered together for the war with God the All Powerful One, rather than conquering him, their cities fell, perhaps including those seven cities in which the hearers lived![77] The expression that 'Babylon the Great was remembered by God' would be an ominous note with regard to the city's fate for not only is God righteous and true in his judgments, but he also has a memory! Nothing will go unrewarded; nothing will go without judgment. In this case this reality is conveyed to the hearers by a most emphatic phrase, 'the cup of the wine of the wrath of his anger', which according to the third angel of 14.9-10 awaits those 'who worship the beast and his image and receive his number'. The relationship between the beast and Babylon could not be clearer! But there is more, 'And every island fled and mountains could not be found'. Reminiscent of the events accompanying the opening of the sixth seal, the world comes undone![78]

Verse 21 – Unbelievably, the story continues, 'And great hail as a talent (ca. 100 pounds each) comes down out of heaven upon the

---

[76] Beasley-Murray, *Revelation*, p. 246.
[77] Michaels, *Revelation*, p. 191.
[78] Murphy, *Fallen is Babylon*, p. 347.

men, and the men blasphemed God owing to the plague of the hail, because her plague was extremely great'. After the breaking apart of the Great City, the falling of the cities of the nations, the fleeing of every island, and that mountains could no longer be found, the words of this verse might be a bit surprising to the hearers, especially the fact that any human beings are still around! But as with the catastrophic events that accompany the opening of the sixth seal, they are here nonetheless! These final words in the bowl sequence return to the theme of the theophanic elements that appear in 16.18. Reference to the great hail that weighed a talent at this point would convey several things to the hearers. First, they would perhaps recognize that the destruction of the Great City, cities of the nations, islands, and mountains are enveloped within the display of the theophanic elements the description of which began in 16.18. Second, this mention would complete their expectations for hail to occur, given the place of great hail in the theophanic display at the conclusion of the trumpet sequence (11.19). Third, neither would this reference be a surprise to the hearers owing to the fact that God not only sent great hail upon the Amorites in their battle with Israel (Josh. 10.11), but also will send hail upon Gog and Magog as part of the eschatological battle that is to come (Ezek. 38.22). Fourth, the weight of such great hail might well remind the hearers of the weight of the rocks used by the Roman army specifically of its conquest of Jerusalem (Josephus, *The Jewish Wars*, 5.270).[79] Finally, with the appearance of this great hail the hearers would likely understand that this portion of the Apocalypse has drawn to a close. Sadly, as with the results of the fourth and fifth bowls, this expression of God's righteous judgment does not result in repentance but with blasphemy, again revealing their identity with and worship of the beast. Thus, this last opportunity for repentance passes without the desired response.[80]

---

[79] Cf. Prigent, *L'Apocalypse de Saint Jean*, p. 368.

[80] Andrew of Caesarea (*Commentary on the Apocalypse*, 16.21 cited in ACCS 12, p. 264) writes, 'And so they will be like Pharaoh, or rather they will be even more intransigent than he was. For he at least to some extent was softened by the plagues sent from God and confessed his own ungodliness, but these persons will blaspheme even in the midst of being tormented'.

'In the Spirit' Carried to a Wilderness – Revelation 17.1-21.8

As the second and largest section of the Apocalypse comes to a close, the next major section begins with the occurrence of the third 'in the Spirit' phrase (17.3). This extended passage takes the hearers from the destruction of Babylon the Great City to the New Jerusalem descending from heaven. Thus, in this section the hearers encounter an accounting of the final things. Beginning with a detailed description of Babylon the Great City (17.1-18) the section moves to an extensive description of her destruction (18.1-24). Following this is an account of the great shouting in heaven that accompanies the marriage supper of the Lamb (19.1-10), the victory of the King of Kings and Lord of Lords over his enemies (19.11-21), the one thousand year reign of Jesus and those who overcome (20.1-6), Satan's final rebellion and defeat (20.7-10), the final judgment (20.11-15), and the initial description of the New Jerusalem descending from heaven (21.1-8).

The Woman on the Beast: Babylon the Whore (17.1-18)

Verse 1 – Once again the hearers may be forgiven if they are unprepared for the fact that the Apocalypse has not quite come to an end. For despite the fact that the last seven plagues of God's wrath have now been poured out, culminating in the destruction of the Great City and the fall of the cities of the nations, the narrative continues, 'And one of the seven angels having the seven bowls came and spoke with me saying, "Come, I will show to you the judgment of the Great Whore who sits upon many waters, with whom the kings of the earth have committed sexual immorality and the inhabitants of the earth have become drunk with the wine of her sexual immorality'". Though these words do not designate which of the seven angels is here in view, the hearers would likely understand this angelic figure to be the seventh angel who poured out the seventh bowl[1] that led to the destruction of the Great City, now described as the judgment of the Great Whore. The fact that this angel is one of those who poured out the seven last bowls of the plagues of God's wrath would also suggest to the hearers that the description of judgment to follow is closely connected to the pouring out of the bowls that precedes.[2] Perhaps the hearers would also appreciate the fact that although many angels have been described to this point in the book, this is the first time an angel addresses John directly. Such a dramatic encounter is made all the more significant by the specific words the angel speaks to John. While the very first word to come to John from the angel, Δεῦρο ('come'), could be taken as a simple command on the angel's part, Johannine hearers would likely recall that its only other occurrence in the whole of the Johannine tradition is in Jesus' command to Lazarus to 'come forth' from his tomb (Jn 11.43). Such an association would no doubt underscore the idea that in this angelic command John encounters a divine invitation. The significance of this invitation is further revealed by the next word from the angel, δείξω ('I will show'), as its meaning for Johannine hearers would include two specific aspects given its earlier occurrences within the Apocalypse and its usage in the broader Johannine tradition. First, the hearers have previously encountered this term in Rev. 1.1 and 4.1, where the term is closely associated with those things that must take place soon, suggesting that the judgment of the Great Whore must itself take place soon. Second, the term also has a rich history in the FG where it is often used to describe the divine revelation that comes from Jesus and or God (Jn 5.20; 10.32; 14.9; 20.20).[3] Thus, in Rev. 17.1 the term would strike the hearers as pregnant with divine revelatory meaning. Specifically, the angel promises to show John 'the judgment of the Great Whore who sits on many waters'. It is diffi-

---

[1] Smalley, *The Revelation to John*, p. 426.

[2] Prigent, *L'Apocalypse de Saint Jean*, p. 375 and Murphy, *Fallen Is Babylon*, p. 348.

[3] Schneider, 'δείκνυμι, δεικνύω', pp. 280-81.

cult to believe that the hearers would not see in the judgment of the Great Whore an answer to the prayer of the souls under the altar for God to judge those who shed their blood (6.10). Such an act of judgment would fit nicely with the fact that in the Apocalypse the time for judging the dead has already come (11.18; 14.7) and that the judgments of God are indeed deemed to be righteous (16.5, 7). Such connections would also suggest to the hearers that a description of the final judgment immediately awaits them. The occurrence of the word πόρνης ('whore') would both remind the hearers of its earlier occurrences, as well as introduce a word group in this context that will have near unrivaled prominence as the section unfolds. Earlier the hearers encountered the verbal form of this term in close association with eating food sacrificed to idols (2.14), specifically with reference to the activities of the woman who calls herself a prophet, but whom the resurrected Jesus calls 'Jezebel', who teaches the servants of God to commit sexual immorality and eat food sacrificed to idols (2.20). With regard to this woman the resurrected Jesus warns that judgment awaits her and her children if she does not repent of her sexual immorality (2.21-23). Perhaps it would not be going too far to suggest that the hearers would see in the judgment of the Great Whore in 17.2 an ultimate fulfillment of the warning the resurrected Jesus gives in his prophetic message to the church in Thyatira. At the same time, the hearers would not be unaware of the ways in which this term is often applied in the OT to Israel (Hos. 5.3) and a variety of cities including Jerusalem (Isa. 1.21; Ezek. 16.15; 23.1), Tyre (Isa. 23.16), and Nineveh (Nah. 3.4). But perhaps more than anything else the hearers would think of the words Jeremiah 51 speaks with regard to the destruction of Babylon.[4] The description of the Great Whore in Rev. 17.1 as 'sitting upon many waters' would not only remind the hearers of the description of Babylon in Jer. 51.13, as well as the physical qualities of historic Babylon through which the Euphrates ran and which was criss-crossed with canals,[5] but would also reveal something about the Great Whore's idolatrous ambitions as the hearers would likely

---

[4] Prigent, *L'Apocalypse de Saint Jean*, p. 375.
[5] Aune, *Revelation 17-22*, p. 929.

remember that it is Yahweh who is enthroned upon the flood (Ps. 29.10).[6]

Verse 2 – The words that follow this description make clear that the Great Whore is deserving of her title, for the Great πόρνης ('whore') is identified as the one with whom the Kings of the earth ἐπόρνευσαν ('have committed sexual immorality') and from whose wine of πορνείας ('sexual immorality') the inhabitants of the earth have become drunk.[7] Such a concentration of variations of the same Greek word in this sentence would serve to underscore her role in the seduction of others in her idolatrous activity. The fact that both 'the kings of the earth' and 'the inhabitants of the earth', a phrase that normally has negative associations in the book (3.10; 6.10; 8.13; 11.10; 13.8, 12, 14), are described as her active partners in sexually immoral activity indicate that her seduction to idolatrous activity has been universally successful, including both the world's leaders and its constituency. Mention of the wine of her sexual immorality would communicate at least two other things to the hearers. First, it would serve to heighten the context of judgment in which these words occur, given the hearers' earlier encounter with this phrase in 14.8 that occurs in the angelic words, 'Fallen, fallen is Babylon the Great'. Second, this association would be further encouragement for the hearers to make the connection between the Great Whore and Babylon the Great, a connection that will be made explicit in 17.5.

Verse 3 – While the hearers at this point may well be impressed by the many points of continuity between these first words of chapter 17 and those that have preceded, they quickly discover that they are standing at the beginning of the next major section of the Apocalypse as they hear the words, 'And he took me away into the wilderness in the Spirit'. For the third time, the hearers encounter the 'in the Spirit' phrase. From their earlier encounters with the phrase in 1.10 and 4.2 they would have come to expect that several things are significant about its appearance here in 17.3. First, since

---

[6] Smalley, *The Revelation to John*, p. 427.

[7] Unlike a courtesan, who would devote herself to one man of means and social standing the language πόρνης ('whore') indicates that the 'one who sits on many waters' is indeed a street prostitute who has many lovers. Cf. J.A. Glancy and S.D. Moore, 'How Typical a Roman Prostitute Is Revelation's "Great Whore"', *JBL* 130.3 (2011), pp. 551-69.

there is no hint in the text that John was no longer 'in the Spirit' as chapter 17 begins, the phrase's appearance here would convey a sense of continuity between John's experience in chapters 1-3, his experience in chapters 4-16, and his experience in chapter 17 and following. Second, owing to what the hearers learned from their last encounters with this phrase, they likely expect additional prophetic words from or about Jesus in what follows. Third, as the Apocalypse has unfolded they may now suspect that this phrase is central to the book's structure and further discern that the means by which the revelation is given is 'in the Spirit'. Fourth, there appears to be a connection between certain geographical locations and being 'in the Spirit'. In chapter one there was a connection between John being on the island of Patmos when 'in the Spirit' (1.9-10), while in Rev. 4.2, there appears to be a connection between John being 'in the Spirit' and being in heaven. This trend continues in Rev. 17.3 where John is transported to the wilderness whilst 'in the Spirit', no doubt reminding the hearers of Ezekiel's experience (Ezek. 3.12, 14; 8.3; 11.1, 24; 37.1; 43.5). While the location to which John is transported 'in the Spirit' might surprise contemporary hearers it is not likely to have surprised Johannine ones. For in the Johannine tradition the wilderness is a place where God is active in prophetic and redemptive ways. Not only is the wilderness the location of the prophetic work of John (the Baptist), who is likened to 'a voice crying in the wilderness' (Jn 1.23), but the redemptive sign of the serpent being lifted up also takes place in the wilderness (3.14).[8] In the bread of life discourse Jesus twice makes reference to the gracious provision of manna for Israel in the wilderness (6.31, 49). In addition to these associations the wilderness also functions as a place where Jesus and his disciples take refuge after the raising of Lazarus from the dead (11.54). From Rev. 12.6, 14 the hearers would know that the wilderness is a place prepared by God for the protection and sustenance of God's people. Thus, when John is transported to the wilderness 'in the Spirit' the hearers would, no doubt, discern that what awaits John will be no less filled with prophetic and salvific significance than other 'wilderness' events have been in the

---

[8] On the salvific dimension of this text cf. Thomas, *Spirit of the New Testament*, pp. 175-89.

Johannine tradition.[9] Such expectancy is not disappointed, for as soon as John has been so transported he immediately begins to see a number of things, 'And I saw a woman seated upon a scarlet beast, full of blasphemous names, having seven heads and ten horns'. In the Spirit John sees the Great Whore who sits upon many waters morph into a woman who sits upon a scarlet beast. Her presumptuous, idolatrous enthronement upon the waters, in the place of Yahweh, is revealed actually to be an enthronement upon an idolatrous beast. The hearers may not be altogether surprised that the woman is enthroned on this beast, for this beast's color is somewhat reminiscent of that of the Great Red Dragon,[10] while the physical appearance of this beast bears a striking resemblance to the beast that emerges from the sea in 13.1, who also has ten horns, seven heads, and blasphemous names.[11] If this woman is indeed enthroned on the scarlet beast, the hearers would have little doubt as to her character or intentions. Her power comes from the great red dragon who opposes the woman clothed with the sun, her child, and her other seed; the dragon who is cast down out of heaven. Eventually the great red dragon gives his authority to the beast from the sea, who is a parody of the Lamb, who worships the dragon, who is himself worshipped by the whole earth as invincible in battle, who blasphemes God and his dwelling, and who makes war upon the saints. The fact that this beast is described in 17.3 as being full of blasphemous names would not be difficult for the hearers to imagine, as such blasphemous names reveal his presumptuous and idolatrous actions and nature. If the woman is enthroned upon such a one, there can be absolutely no doubt as to her own presumptuous and idolatrous actions and nature.

Verse 4 – But before the hearers can ponder the relationship between the woman and the scarlet beast, their attention is directed to her attire, 'And the woman was clothed in purple and scarlet and covered with gold in gold and precious stones and pearls, having a gold cup in her hand full of abominations and the uncleanness of her sexual immorality'. The occurrence of the term περιβεβλημένη ('clothed') would likely draw the hearers' attention to the contrast

---

[9] Contra Aune, *Revelation 17-22*, p. 933 who suggests that wilderness here carries a negative connotation.

[10] Ladd, *Revelation*, p. 223.

[11] Murphy, *Fallen Is Babylon*, p. 335.

between how this woman is described and the last time this verb is used, where it describes the woman clothed with the sun (12.1). In fact to this point in the Apocalypse every occurrence of the verb περιβάλλω ('clothe') carries with it a positive connotation (3.5, 18; 4.4; 7.9, 13; 10.1; 11.3), suggesting that the contrast the hearers are to discern is not simply between these two women, as striking a contrast as that is, but also the contrast between this woman and all those clothed in white. Specifically, this woman is clothed in purple, a color that conveys at the very least pretensions to royalty,[12] but which to Johannine hearers would forever be associated with the mockery of Jesus by the soldiers during his passion, as they cloth and display him in a purple garment (Jn 19.2, 5) in the midst of which they mock him as 'the King of the Jews' (19.3). Thus, not only does her relationship with the beast reveal the presumptuous and idolatrous nature of this woman, but so also does the first article of clothing that she is described as wearing! The fact that she is also clothed in scarlet would make clear to the hearers not only that this woman is dependent upon the beast as the basis of her authority, but also that she actually shares in his nature.[13] The next detail of her appearance suggests that she is literally covered in gold, as the phrase κεχρυσωμένη χρυσίῳ ('covered with gold in gold') underscores the extraordinary amount of gold she wears, the same root word appearing in both verbal and noun forms to convey the point. As with the previous details, so this one reveals a contrast between all those individuals and things associated with gold to this point in the Apocalypse (Rev. 1.12, 13, 20; 2.1; 3.18; 4.4; 5.8; 8.3; 9.13, 20; 14.14; 15.6, 7) and this opulent portrayal.[14] Even the mention of the λίθῳ τιμίῳ ('precious stones') is not without significance as it would likely reinforce the presumptuous and idolatrous character of this woman for the hearers, as to this point only God and one of the angels have been described as wearing stones (4.3; 15.6) and to this point it is only to God and the Lamb that the related term τιμήν ('honor' or 'value') has been ascribed (4.9, 11; 5.12, 13; 17.12). Thus, the wearing of precious stones reveals something of the woman's nature. Given all these associations the hearers might well

---

[12] Aune, *Revelation 17-22*, p. 935.
[13] Gause, *Revelation*, p. 221.
[14] The only possible exception to this positive usage is found in 9.7.

expect mention of the pearls that the woman wears also to convey a similar message. However, at this point they are left to wonder, as they will have to wait until 21.21 to have their suspicions confirmed. Suffice it to say that in ways not always apparent to modern interpreters the attire of this woman reveals a great deal about her presumptuous and idolatrous nature and character. If the attire of the Great Whore reflects her character, even more is revealed by the golden cup in her hand. For in contrast to the golden bowl filled with the prayers of the saints (8.3), this golden cup is filled with abominations and the uncleanness of her sexual immorality.[15] The contents of the cup would be especially meaningful to the hearers for the phrase conveys several things to them. First, it may strike them as significant that both βδελυγμάτων ('abominations') and τὰ ἀκάθαρτα ('uncleanness') appear in the plural, underscoring the extent of her abominable and unclean activities. Second, while βδελυγμάτων ('abominations') might carry with it the general idea of that which is loathsome before God,[16] the hearers would likely discern a more concrete understanding of this term as in the Prophets (in the LXX) it often appears with reference to idols (Jer. 13.27; 39.35; 51.22; Ezek. 5.9, 11; 6.9).[17] Third, it would be difficult to imagine that the hearers would not see in the words τὰ ἀκάθαρτα τῆς πορνείας αὐτῆς ('the uncleanness of her sexual immorality') a reference to the unclean spirits of idolatry that come from the mouths of the dragon, the beast, and the false prophet in 16.13, who through demonic seduction gather the kings of the whole inhabited world together to make war with God (16.14).[18] Thus, it is clear that the appetites of this woman match her appearance. She constantly drinks in idolatrous abominations and the uncleanness of her own sexual immorality that characterizes her own idolatrous identity.

Verse 5 – If there is any confusion on the hearers' part as to this woman's identity, they are given additional divine assistance to help in their pneumatic discernment with the words, 'And upon her forehead a name had been written, mystery, "Babylon the Great,

---

[15] Wall, *Revelation*, p. 206.

[16] J. Zmijewski, 'βδέλυγμα', *EDNT*, I, pp. 209-10.

[17] Prigent, *L'Apocalypse de Saint Jean*, p. 377.

[18] Smalley, *The Revelation to John*, p. 431.

the Mother of whores and of all the abominations of the earth'". The very first words of this phrase would catch the attention of the hearers for they have come to know the significance that the forehead of an individual plays in the Apocalypse, for to this point it is the place where the seal of God (7.3; 9.4) and/or his name (14.1) has been placed upon those who identify with him and conversely the place where the mark of the beast has been placed upon those who identify with him (13.16; 14.9). Thus, mention of the woman's forehead would raise the level of the hearers' expectancy that they will soon have a clear indication of the woman's identity. Their expectations are not disappointed as they learn that a name has been written upon her forehead, a name written in the past that continues to be valid, as the perfect tense γεγραμμένον ('had been written') indicates. But there is more, as for a third time in the book the hearers encounter the word mystery. While it is possible that the hearers might take the word mystery as part of the woman's name, it is likely that the earlier occurrences of this term (1.20; 10.7), along with the other divine aids given to facilitate the hearers' pneumatic discernment, would put the hearers on notice that the name of the woman must be discerned, as many of the other names that have occurred in the book to this point (Balaam, Jezebel, Sodom, Egypt, the city where their Lord was crucified, the number of the beast, etc.).[19] Consequently, when the hearers learn that the name of the Great Whore is Babylon the Great, they understand that they must discern its meaning as they have discerned numerous other names, titles, and events throughout the Apocalypse. What exactly would the hearers discern in this regard? Perhaps the most obvious thing would be that this Babylon the Great is the same as the Babylon the Great of 14.8, whose fall was declared by the second other angel and out of whose wine of the wrath of her sexual immorality all the nations have drunk. Such reflection would go some way toward closing the gap between this figure and the description of the Great Whore with which this section begins, specifically the angelic words to John with regard to the judgment of the Great Whore in 17.1 and the fact that the inhabitants of the earth have become drunk from the wine of her sexual immorality. The hearers would also likely remember that the Babylon the Great named in 17.5 is the

---

[19] Aune, *Revelation 17-22*, p. 936.

same Babylon the Great who, in the context of judgment (16.17-21), was remembered before God to give her the cup of the wine of the wrath of his anger (16.19). Would the hearers also think of Babylon the Great who destroyed Jerusalem, exiled her inhabitants, was seated on the waters, and whose king eventually acknowledged the God of heaven (Dan. 4.34-37)? If so, perhaps they would discern that just as the beast continues to exist despite the death of Nero, so Babylon the Great continues to exist despite the destruction of Babylon of old![20] But the title 'Babylon the Great' does not stand alone for her name also includes the words 'the Mother of Whores and the Abominations of the Earth'.[21] Such words make clear that the Great Whore and Babylon the Great are indeed the same as this Great Whore is the source or origin, the Mother, of all whores, those who practice and advocate idolatrous activity. This Mother of all Whores stands in direct contrast to the Woman Clothed with the Sun who gives birth to the male child who is taken up into heaven (12.1-6) and the rest of her seed who are characterized by 'keeping the commands of God and having the witness of Jesus' (12.17).[22] In contrast, the Mother of all Whores brings forth those like the false prophetess 'Jezebel', who commits and advocates sexual immorality (2.20-21), just like her mother. The additional description of Babylon the Great as the mother of 'the abominations of the earth' makes doubly clear her relationship to the abominations of idolatry, for not only does she hold in her hand a gold cup filled with such abominations (17.4), she also produces children who both practice and actively propagate idolatrous activity.

---

[20] Cf. P.W. Cheung, 'The Mystery of Revelation 17.5 & 7: A Typological Entrance', *Jian Dao* 18 (2003) pp. 1-19, esp. 18.

[21] This graphic depiction of the Great Whore has led J.E. Bruns ['The Contrasted Women of Apoc 12 and 17', *CBQ* 26 (1964), pp. 459-63] to conclude that Valeria Messalina, the wife of the emperor Claudius (41-54 CE), sat for this portrait. Her exploits, as depicted by Juvenal (*Satire* 6.116-132), Tacitus (*Annals* 11.1, 2, 12 26-38) and Pliny (*Natural History* 11.171), suggest that 'Messalina was remembered ... as (1) a Roman Empress who (2) literally played the Harlot and (3) crowned her adulteries amid the luxurious surroundings of a drunken orgy'. According to Juvenal's description she literally bore an assumed name (on her forehead?) – 'Lycisca', 'The Wolf Girl'. Bruns suggests that her ignominious death parallels that of the Great Whore in Rev. 17.16. On the depiction of Babylon the Great as 'whore' rather than 'courtesan' cf. Glancy and Moore, 'How Typical a Roman Prostitute Is Revelation's "Great Whore"?'

[22] Smalley, *The Revelation to John*, p. 432.

Verse 6a – Despite these earlier descriptions of the Great Whore, her depiction becomes even more graphic with the next words the hearers encounter, 'And I saw the woman drunk out of the blood of the saints and out of the blood of the witnesses of Jesus'. The second occurrence of εἶδον ('I saw') in this passage confirms for the hearers that the woman John saw sitting upon a scarlet beast (17.3) is the same woman that he now sees drunk on the blood of the saints. Within this repulsive imagery a number of ideas converge. First, for the hearers there could hardly be any question that the blood of the saints and the blood of the witnesses of Jesus here emphasized is tightly connected to the blood of the souls under the altar (6.10) and the blood of the saints and the prophets (16.6). Such continuity reinforces the reality of persecution and death for those who would be faithful witnesses of Jesus. Second, mention of the blood of the saints and the blood of the witnesses of Jesus would serve once again to draw attention to the fact that Jesus' own faithful witness involved the shedding of his blood from which salvific consequences result and for which he is often praised. Thus, the hearers have yet another reminder that those who would follow the Lamb wherever he goes (14.4) must be prepared to follow him into death. Third, the hearers would also likely wonder whether there is not a connection between the blood from which this woman has become drunk and the gold cup in her hand that is full of abominations and sexual immorality. Though the contents of the cup do not morph into the blood of the saints and the blood of the witnesses of Jesus before the eyes (or ears) of the hearers, like the transformations that have taken place with a variety of other images in the Apocalypse to this point, the hearers are likely to discern a deep connection between the two. For as the Apocalypse has unfolded it has become quite clear that an increase in idolatrous activity upon the earth brings the death of the saints in its wake. This is learned in part from the way in which the great red dragon makes war against the saints (12.17) and the way in which the beast from the earth will allow no dissent from the first beast's universal worship (13.15). Those who remain faithful in their witness to Jesus and refuse to worship the beast, his image, his name, or his number inevitably face death. Thus, the contents of the gold cup and the blood from which the Great Whore becomes drunk share a deep connection.[23] The increase of the one entails the increase of the other. Fourth, the hearers might also discern a connection between the wine of her sexual immorality ἐκ ('out of') which the inhabitants of the earth have become drunk, the gold cup full of abominations and the uncleanness of her sexual immorality, and the blood of the saints and the blood of the witnesses of Jesus ἐκ ('out of') which the Great Whore has become drunk. Such a connection makes clear that the Great Whore is not alone in her culpability; it is shared by the kings of the earth who have committed sexual immorality with her (17.2) and the inhabitants of the earth who have become drunk from her wine, having worshipped the beast (13.8, 12, 14). Finally, the hearers might also wonder as to the relationship between the blood of the saints and the witnesses of Jesus from which she has become drunk and the blood that God has given his enemies to drink owing to the fact that they have poured out the blood of his saints and prophets (16.6). Whether or not the hearers would in retrospect see the blood with which God inundates the earth and its inhabitants with the pouring out of the last bowls of his wrath and the blood with which the Great Whore has become drunk, it is very difficult to imagine that they would not appreciate the deep connection that exists between the faithful witness of the saints, their blood that is shed, the prayers they offer, and God's ultimate judgment of the earth. If so, her drunken state resulting from the orgy of idolatrous activity that leads to the death of the saints and witnesses of Jesus reveals that the Great Whore has become intoxicated and unable to function in a clear headed fashion, having consumed the very witness that could have led to her salvation!

Verse 6b – Even the disturbing nature of the description of the Great Whore to this point might not prepare the hearers for the shock that comes from the next words they encounter, for John says, 'And I marveled seeing her a great marvel'. Several aspects of this sentence would be of significance for the hearers. Perhaps the first thing to strike them would be the grammatical structure, for the words 'seeing her' stand in the middle of the Greek sentence, surrounded by a cognate accusative where both the verb and the

---

[23] Smalley, *The Revelation to John*, p. 432.

direct object employ the same Greek root word, in this case ἐθαύμασα ('I marveled') ... θαῦμα μέγα ('a great marvel'). Thus, grammatically the sight of this woman is surrounded by John's marveling, underscoring that her appearance has generated such an effect. What would heighten the hearers' sense of concern is their memory that this very verb has appeared once before in the Apocalypse to describe the response of the whole world to the healing of the beast's wounded head (13.3), a response that results in the universal worship of the dragon and the beast (13.4)![24] Is it possible that John could here be susceptible to the same idolatrous seduction that has resulted in the worship of the dragon and the beast by the whole world?[25] Such a possibility would be an additional emphasis on the recurring theme of true and false worship. If John, who is 'in the Spirit' at the time, could be so tempted, could anyone be immune from such seduction? Such a possibility, in and of itself, would serve as a stark warning to the hearers about the vigilance required to withstand and not succumb to such temptation. At the same time, Johannine hearers would likely recall that this term is used to describe a response that often accompanies aspects of Jesus' teaching or actions that prove difficult to understand to various individuals in the FG (Jn 3.7; 4.27; 5.20, 28; 7.15, 21). So, in addition to heightening the significance of vigilance with regard to temptations to idolatrous worship, the hearers would perhaps also see in these words an indication of John's puzzlement in interpreting this detail of the vision.[26]

Verses 6b-7 – If the hearers are still concerned about John's response to the seductive power of the Great Whore, so it seems is the angel, as John recounts, 'And the angel said to me, "On account of what are you marveling? I will show you the mystery of the woman and the beast who bears her who has seven heads and ten horns"'. With these words the hearers learn that the angel addresses both aspects of their own reflection about John's response to the vision of the Great Whore. The angel begins with a question that can hardly be taken as anything other than a rebuke to John.[27] For

---

[24] Caird, *The Revelation of St. John*, p. 213.
[25] Schüssler Fiorenza, *Revelation*, p. 96.
[26] Aune, *Revelation 17-22*, p. 938.
[27] Gause, *Revelation*, p. 223.

the hearers the question would provide some space, however brief, for reflection upon John's response to the Great Whore. Perhaps it would also provoke the hearers to answer the same question themselves. Is there some seduction in this vision that could result in idolatrous activity on their part? Or to put it the other way round, what is it about this vision that proves seductive to them? The hearers learn various things from the rest of the words spoken to John. First, they are informed that they, like John, are to receive additional divine assistance in their pneumatic discernment when told that the angel will explain the mystery of the woman and the beast who bears her. Specifically, the hearers may well suspect that the meaning of the beast's seven heads and ten horns will be revealed by the angel, just as the resurrected Jesus revealed the mystery of the seven stars and the seven golden lampstands in 1.19-20. Second, the hearers learn of the close relationship that exists between the woman and the beast, as their mystery is to be explained together.[28] Third, in discovering that the woman is being borne by the beast (βαστάζοντος ['who bears']), the hearers would no doubt think of the contrast between this beast and what it bears and the church in Ephesus who was 'not able to bear (βαστάσαι) evil ones or things' (2.2), on the one hand, but who 'have patient endurance and bear (ἐβάστασας) on account of my name' (2.3), on the other hand.

Verse 8 – Perhaps contrary to the hearers' expectations, the angel begins his explanation of the mystery of the woman and the beast with attention focused on the beast, 'The beast which you saw was and is not and is about to come up out of the Abyss and go into destruction, and the inhabitants of the earth will have been made to marvel, those whose names have not been written upon the book of life from the foundation of the world, seeing the beast that was and is not and will be present'. The first thing to catch the attention of the hearers may well be the fact that the words 'the beast' stand first in the Greek sentence, as a point of emphasis, and is followed by the words ὅ εἶδες ('which you saw'), which becomes a literary marker that directs the hearers' attention to various details

---

[28] Ladd, *Revelation*, p. 226.

of the vision for which the angel now offers the interpretation.[29] While focusing attention upon the beast which John saw, the hearers learn that he is described with an appellation, 'was and is not

Figure 13
William Blake, *The Whore of Babyon*
(British Museum, London)

and is about to raise from the Abyss', which at one and the same time is a parody of both the One who sits on the throne and the Lamb. This three-fold appellation could not help but to bring to

---

[29] The phrase ὃ εἶδες ('that which you saw') will occur five times in 17.8-18 (vv. 8, 12, 15, 16, 18).

mind the three-fold description of God as 'the one who is and the one who was and the one who is coming' (1.4, 8; 4.8). By this appellation, the beast's idolatrous presumption would be seen for what it is and in keeping with that of the Great Whore. But the hearers might also discern that this appellation, as idolatrous as it may be, carries with it the testimony of the beast's destruction for they would hardly encounter it without remembering that the three-fold appellation for God has given way to the two-fold, 'the one who was and the one who is' (11.17), indicating that God is no longer described as the coming one for he has come! At the same time, the description of the beast as 'and was not' would no doubt be taken as having reference to the slaughter suffered by one of the beast's heads (13.3), which indicates that it is a parody of the Lamb, who himself was slaughtered (5.5). The description of the beast as 'about to come up from the Abyss and goes into destruction' reveals something of his character,[30] owing to his origin and end, and confirms for the hearers that this beast is identical to the one who makes war against and overcomes the two witnesses (11.7), as he too comes from the Abyss. Thus, their earlier suspicion that the beast who comes from the Abyss (11.7) and the beast who comes from the sea (13.1) are one and the same is confirmed. With such thoughts still in mind, attention is directed to the fact that 'the inhabitants of the earth are made to marvel', words that remind the hearers of the fact that the world's earlier astonishment at the healing of the beast's slaughtered head led to the universal worship of the dragon and the beast (13.3-4) and that John himself (and them with him?) has been made to be astonished at the sight of the Great Whore (17.6). For a second time in the book, the identity of the inhabitants of the earth, who are made to marvel by the beast, is made clearer by the description, 'whose names has not been written upon the book of life from the foundation of the world'. Earlier the book of life has been closely associated with the resurrected Jesus (3.5) and the Lamb slaughtered from before the foundation of the world (13.8). Here, despite the lack of exactitude in language, Johannine hearers would be reminded of the fact that those who are so taken with the beast have made a decision to identify with him

---

[30] Caird (*The Revelation of St. John*, p. 216) describes these as permanent qualities of the beast, not a description of one-off events; the beast is always arising from the Abyss and always heading for destruction.

disregarding the salvific provisions made by the slaughtered Lamb, salvific provisions which in fact predate the foundation of this world and are grounded in the pre-temporal relationship of the Father and the Son. Ultimately, they are reminded that such ones as these do not have their names written upon the book of life because they have chosen the one whose ways lead to destruction over the one who is life, in whose book their names do not appear. The amazement of the inhabitants of the earth, it is made clear, comes from 'seeing the beast that was and is not and is coming'. With these words perhaps it would dawn upon the hearers that the description of the inhabitants of the earth, who are astonished at the beast and whose names have not been written in the book of life, is bounded on either side by descriptions of the beast that consist of a three-fold appellation that underscores his presumptuous and idolatrous character. The intensity of the latter appellation is made even greater by the fact that it ends with the word παρέσται ('comes'), which not only is used exclusively for the activity of Jesus in the FG (Jn 7.6; 11.28), but is also the verb from which the noun παρουσία ('coming') is derived,[31] a term that is used on at least one occasion in the Johannine tradition for the return of Jesus (1 Jn 2.28). Thus the parody of the One who sits on the throne and the Lamb by the beast continues in the last word of Rev. 17.8.

Verse 9 – As the hearers reflect on such astonishing details they encounter words that once again encourage their pneumatic discernment, 'Here is the understanding, the one who has wisdom. The seven heads are seven mountains, where the woman sits upon them. And they are seven kings'. For the hearers it hardly matters whether this call is one to reflect back on the words of 17.8[32] or one that calls them forward into the explanation offered by the angel, for the words of 17.8 and those that follow are intricately connected to one another. The call to pneumatic discernment is quite reminiscent of a similar call in 13.18, where, following the words 'Here is Wisdom' a call is given for 'the one who has understanding' to calculate the number of the beast.[33] Significantly, the call in 17.9 combines the words 'understanding' with 'wisdom' and the verse is

---

[31] G. Schneider, 'πάρειμι', *EDNT*, III, p. 36.
[32] So Aune, *Revelation 17-22*, p. 941 and Smalley, *The Revelation to John*, p. 435.
[33] Murphy, *Fallen Is Babylon*, p. 359.

also concerned with spiritually discerning the aspects of the beast's identity, suggesting that the discernment called for in 13.18 and 17.9 are not unrelated activities. The first words to follow this call for pneumatic discernment assist the hearers in this task, for they reveal something about the identity of the beast's seven heads, just as Jesus had revealed the mystery of the stars and the seven lampstands earlier in the book (1.20). In 17.9 the angel reveals that the seven heads are seven mountains, an identification that might well prompt the hearers to think of the seven hills of Rome owing to such a description in numerous ancient authors (Vergil, *Geor.* 11.535; *Aen.* 6.783; Horace, *Carm* 7; Ovid, *Trist* 1.5.69; Martial, *Ep.* 4.64; Cicero, *ad Att* 6.5.).[34] Such an identification would also confirm the connection between the pneumatic discernment to which they had been called in 13.18 and the pneumatic discernment in 17.9 – just as there had been a resemblance between Nero and the beast in the former, so there is a resemblance between Rome and the beast in the latter. But just as the beast was not confined to the identification with Nero in the hearers' earlier pneumatic discernment, so it is not likely that the imagery of the seven mountains would be exhausted by the identification of Rome with the beast.[35] For, owing to the significance of the number seven throughout the Apocalypse it is difficult to believe that it would suddenly be reduced to conveying a literal and concrete meaning at this point. Rather, with the imagery of Rome in their minds, it is likely that the imagery of the seven hills would be taken to convey the idea of universal power,[36] not unlike the way in which mountains and hills were closely associated with political power in the OT (Jer. 51.25).[37] Such an identification would surely not come as a shock to the hearers owing to the universal power with which the beast rules in chapter 13. Neither does it come as a surprise that the Great Whore, Babylon the Great, sits upon them, for they are the seven heads of the beast! But before the hearers can fully take in such an interpretation, the image of the seven heads that has morphed into the seven hills, morphs into the image of seven kings. Though sometimes challenging to

---

[34] Caird, *The Revelation of St. John*, p. 216.
[35] Smalley, *The Revelation to John*, p. 435.
[36] Resseguie, *The Revelation of John*, pp. 220-21.
[37] Wall, *Revelation*, p. 207.

modern interpreters,[38] such a transformation confirms the hearers' initial discernment that the hills do indeed have reference to political powers, even universal political powers. Though not as overt as in the case of the seven hills, it is possible that the imagery of the seven kings would also remind the hearers of Rome, for in Roman and Etruscan histories (Tacitus, *Histories* 3.72; Pliny, *Natural History* 34.139) there were seven kings (Romulus, Numa Pompilius, Tullus Hostilius, Ancus Marcus, Tarquinius Priscus, Servius Tullius, and Tarquinius Superbus), with later historians going so far as identifying minor figures with major ones to preserve the number seven![39] At the same time, the imagery of seven kings would reinforce for the hearers the idea of universal or complete rule, which the seven hills first generate and the beast earlier exhibits in chapter 13.

Verse 10 – With the image of the seven kings now in mind, the hearers encounter additional words, 'And five have fallen, one is, another has not yet come, and when he comes it is necessary for him to remain a little while'. Several aspects of these enigmatic words would be significant for the hearers. First, it is clear that these words extend the description of and focus upon the imagery of the seven kings, as their corporate description now takes on a threefold shape. Second, this threefold shape is quite reminiscent of the threefold way of which the beast is spoken, 'was and is not and is coming' (17.8),[40] suggesting that the identity of the seven kings is to be understood as intimately connected to the identity of the beast. Third, the fact that 'five have fallen, one is, and one has not yet come' indicates that the hearers have already encountered the beast in the form of the 'five who have fallen', are currently facing the beast in the form of the one that is, and are sure to face him in the form of the one 'who has not yet come' but will reign for a little while. Fourth, the fact that 'five have fallen' and 'one (now) is' would suggest to the hearers that they indeed stand near the end of all things for they await the emergence of the one who brings the 'seven' to their completion.[41] Fifth, the words spoken of the sev-

---

[38] For example, Ladd (*Revelation*, p. 227) sees no connection between the seven hills and the seven kings, preferring to take the seven kings as representing seven kingdoms.
[39] Aune, *Revelation 17-22*, p. 948.
[40] Resseguie, *The Revelation of John*, p. 223.
[41] Beasley-Murray, *Revelation*, p. 257.

enth, that 'it is necessary for him to remain ὀλίγον ('a little'), might well remind the hearers of similar words spoken of the Devil, who knows that he has but ὀλίγον ('little') time (12.12), underscoring the connection between the Devil, the beast, and the seven kings all the more. Sixth, reference to 'remaining a little (while)' might even call to the hearer's mind the relatively short length of the beast's forty-two month reign (13.5), again pointing to the connection between the identity of the seven kings and the beast. Attempts to calculate the identity of these seven kings would be virtually impossible owing to the high number of variables involved, such as the starting point for the calculations (does one begin with Julius Caesar, Augustus, or even Tiberius?), the parameters that determine which kings are included and which are excluded (does one include all those who ruled, even the relatively minor figures Galba, Otho, Vitellius?), and the identity of the one who is (Galba, Otho, Vitellius, Vespasian, Titus, Domitian?).[42] While it is possible that little consensus would likely emerge even amongst the hearers as to the identity of the seven kings,[43] it is altogether likely that the close connection between the Devil, the beast, and the seven kings would be clear.[44]

Verse 11 – The relationship between the beast and the seven kings is made even clearer in the next words the hearers encounter, 'And the beast which was and is not and he is eighth and is of the seven, and he goes into destruction'. Perhaps one of the first things to strike the hearers when encountering these words is the way in which they, together with those in the last part of 17.8, serve as an inclusio around the mystery to which the hearers are called to discern in vv. 9-10. Thus, the beast and his identity are integrally intertwined with the seven hills that are the seven kings. The threefold formula, by which the beast has come to be known in a parody of both God and the Lamb,[45] is expanded in this verse drawing attention to elements of the beast's identity that to this point have not been made clear. Two aspects of this expansion are particularly noteworthy. First, in this verse the beast is identified as 'the eighth',

---

[42] For the various possibilities cf. the helpful overview by Aune, *Revelation 17-22*, pp. 945-50.
[43] For a similar point cf. Kiddle, *Revelation*, p. 350.
[44] For a similar conclusion cf. Murphy, *Fallen Is Babylon*, p. 358.
[45] Skaggs and Benham, *Revelation*, p. 175.

a somewhat startling detail owing to the fact that reference has been made only to seven kings to this point. Though it is conceivable that the hearers might be tempted to take these words to mean that the seven kings have morphed into an eighth king, such an interpretative option would not appear likely, owing in part to the prominence of the number seven throughout the book generally and its prominence with regard to the beast in particular. Rather, it would seem that this enigmatic detail would likely generate more reflection by the hearers upon the identity of the beast. Perhaps reference to the beast as 'eighth' would remind the hearers of the discerning reflection to which they were earlier called in calculating the name of the Beast and his number, 666. Among the many things discerned on that occasion about the number of the beast was the fact that the number 666 is a triangular number, the sum of every number from 1 to 36, and that triangular numbers are exceedingly rare. In point of fact, the number 666 is only the *eighth* such triangular number to occur (1, 6, 21, 55, 120, 231, 406, and 666).[46] At one level, then, the identification of the beast as 'eighth' in 17.11 would likely call the hearers' attention back to the calculations of the beast's number in 13.18, further revealing the connection between the seven kings and the beast. On this understanding the beast is not the eighth king after the seven, but is 'eighth' whose number is 666. Second, such an understanding would make clear for the hearers why it is said that the Beast is ἐκ ('out of') 'the seven', not one of the seven,[47] for his identity is coterminous with the seven as a whole, not as one of the seven individually. Thus it can be said that this eighth (666) is of the seven. Before leaving a discussion of v. 11 it should perhaps be noted that the words with which this verse concludes, 'and he goes into destruction', is a reminder that despite the Beast's relationship to the seven kings, he is ultimately doomed for destruction. It is characteristic of his identity, a detail he cannot escape!

Verses 12-13 – The hearers find that the description of the Beast continues with the next words, 'And the ten horns which you saw are ten kings, who have not yet received their kingship, but they will receive authority as king for one hour with the beast'. For

---

[46] Bauckham, *The Climax of Prophecy*, pp. 395-96.
[47] Mounce, *The Book of Revelation*, p. 316.

the second time in the description of the beast the hearers encounter the words ὃ εἶδως ('that which you saw') indicating that a new detail is being revealed about the mystery of the beast upon whom the Great Whore sits. Specifically, attention is now focused upon the beast's ten horns that are divinely revealed to be ten kings. As the hearers discover this detail a number of previous ideas would likely converge for them. For from this vantage point the connection between the ten days of suffering tribulation brought on by the Devil (2.10), the ten horns of the great red dragon (12.3), the ten horns and ten diadems of the beast (13.1), the number of the beast (666) which in Greek includes the word/number δέκα ('ten') in it, the ten horns of the beast upon whom the Great Whore sits (17.3, 7), and the ten kings which are the ten horns (17.12) are all intimately connected to the great Dragon, the ancient serpent, the one called the Devil and Satan, the one who deceives the entire inhabited world (12.9). In this regard, their work is one and the same. Thus, once again the work of the beast is concretized in human terms. While the identity of these ten kings is something of a mystery at this point, perhaps the hearers would see some continuity between them and the ten eschatological horns/kings of Dan. 7.24, on the one hand, and the kings from the east (Rev. 16.12) who appear to morph into all the kings of the whole inhabited world (16.14), on the other hand. The connection between the ten kings and all the kings of the inhabited world[48] would fit nicely with the way in which 'ten' is itself a number of completion in the Apocalypse. What would perhaps be clearer to the hearers at this point than their identity is the way in which the description of these ten kings that follows so parallels part of the description of the seven kings mentioned earlier. The description of the ten kings as 'not having received their kingship' and 'receiving authority as king for one hour' (17.12) stands in remarkable parallel to the previous description of the last of the seven kings described as 'the other has not yet come, and when he comes it is necessary for him to remain a little (time)' (17.10). Such similarities would at the least underscore the tight connection between these ten horns of the beast and one or more of the beast's seven heads. The short duration of the reign of these ten kings, one hour, stands in stark contrast to the forty-

---

[48] Beale, *The Book of Revelation*, p. 878.

two month reign of the beast (13.5), indicating that their reign is for only the shortest portion of his activity.[49] The derived nature of their authority is made clear by the fact that they have authority as kings 'with the beast'. The relationship of the ten kings to the Beast is made even clearer in the next words the hearers encounter, 'These have one purpose and their power and authority they will give to the beast'. The grammatical construction of this sentence suggests that their 'one' purpose is the giving of their power and authority to the beast, further underscoring the intimate connection that exists between these ten kings and the beast. When the hearers encounter one (the ten kings) they encounter the other (the beast)!

Verse 14 – The intensions of the ten kings are made clear in the next words, 'These will make war with the Lamb and the Lamb will overcome them, because he is Lord of Lords and King of Kings and those with him are called and chosen/elect and faithful'. In ways reminiscent of the demonic seduction of all the kings of the whole inhabited world who gather together at Harmagedon to make war (16.16), these ten kings will make war on the Lamb. At various points in the Apocalypse attention has been drawn to the ability of the beast (11.7) and the great red dragon (12.7, 17) to make war upon God's people. In fact, songs were even sung by the inhabitants upon the earth to the beast extolling his alleged invincibility in war (13.4). Despite such activities, 17.14 is the first text in which it is explicitly stated that war was made upon the Lamb! It probably does not surprise the hearers to learn that the efforts at war upon the Lamb by the ten kings (the ten horns of the beast) end in utter defeat, for this Lamb is uniquely connected with overcoming in the Apocalypse, as he has previously identified himself as one who has overcome (3.21), is described as having overcome as the Lion of the tribe of Judah (5.5), and his followers are said to overcome by the blood of the Lamb and the word of their testimony (12.11). It is this same Lamb, who earlier had promised to make war with the sword of his mouth upon those who refuse to repent at Pergamum (2.16), who proves victorious against (overcomes) the ten kings (of the beast). Whilst the hearers might be tempted to explore these rich associations further they are told explicitly why it is

---

[49] On the proportionality of the periods of time in the Apocalypse cf. Resseguie, *The Revelation of John*, p. 225.

that the Lamb overcomes, 'for he is Lord of Lords and King of Kings', an extraordinary attribution! To this point in the Apocalypse the term κύριος ('lord') has been frequently applied to 'the One who sits on the throne', 'the Lord, God, the all powerful One' (1.8; 4.8, 11; 11.4, 15, 17; 15.3, 4; 16.7), with the word used in reference to Jesus on only one occasion (11.8). The use of this title for the Lamb in 17.14 would, no doubt, impress upon the hearers the close relationship between God and the Lamb, on the one hand, and the superiority of Jesus over all the kings of the earth (the ten kings in particular), on the other hand. He is without rivals. The second part of the title would be especially significant to Johannine hearers for several reasons. First, Jesus' identification as king is a rich one in the Johannine tradition (Jn 1.49; 6.15; 12.13, 15; 18.33, 37, 39; 19.3, 12, 14, 15, 19, 21). Second, one of the first things the hearers learn about Jesus in the Apocalypse is that he is the ruler of the kings of the earth (Rev. 1.5). Third, the kings of the earth sometimes function in the Apocalypse either as those being at enmity with God and the Lamb (6.15; 16.12, 14) and/or as those to whom prophetic witness is to be given (10.11). Fourth, on occasion God himself is spoken of as king (15.3). Thus, for the Lamb here to be called the King of Kings underscores Jesus' inherent identity as king, as well as the fact that he is the ruler of all the kings of the earth, especially the ten kings who will seek to make war on him! In this he is also king over the beast, whose ten horns are these ten kings. Further, the hearers now learn that the Lamb does not stand alone, but, just as in 14.1-5 where he stands with the 144,000 who follow him wherever he goes, has certain ones with him. These are not described as participating in the war directly but simply referred to as those who are 'called and chosen and faithful'. This threefold designation underscores the character of those who stand with the Lamb, drawing upon the hearers' knowledge in a very subtle fashion. While the term κλητοί ('called') does not appear elsewhere in the Johannine literature, the verb form from which it is derived would likely inform its usage here. Johannine hearers would be aware of the way in which it is closely associated with discipleship, as it is used to describe the renaming of Simon as Cephas by Jesus (Jn 1.42), as well as functioning as a term of invitation for the disciples to the wedding at Cana (2.2), where they are described as believing in Jesus (2.11). At the same time, from the Apocalypse they would discern that this term is one that reveals the identity and even spiritual significance of places and/or individuals (Rev. 1.9; 11.8; 12.9; 16.16). In the light of these connections the hearers would likely understand the occurrence of κλητοί ('called') as indicating that those who stand with the Lamb are his disciples, who have been named or called by Jesus himself. The second term to appear in this threefold designation, ἐκλεκτοί ('chosen' or 'elect'), would also be of significance to Johannine hearers for this term of honor is used for either an individual or community in right standing with the Elder (2 Jn 1, 13). At the same time, when the verb form from which it is derived occurs in the Fourth Gospel it is always found on the lips of Jesus in contexts underscoring his own divine selection or choosing of his disciples (Jn 6.70; 13.18; and esp. 15.16). Thus, for those who stand with the Lamb to be called 'chosen' or 'elect' underscores the fact that their relationship with the Lamb rests upon divine initiative. The third term to appear in this threefold designation, πιστοί ('faithful'), would be immediately recognizable to the hearers for it has become the term *par excellence* for the faithful obedience unto death that exemplifies Jesus (Rev. 1.5; 3.14), those called upon to withstand the suffering inflicted by the Devil even unto death (2.10), and Antipas who was killed owing to his faithful witness (2.13). Thus, for those who stand with the Lamb to be called 'faithful' underscores the fact that such ones as these, like the 144,000 who follow the Lamb wherever he goes, are overcomers owing to their faithfulness even unto death![50]

Verse 15 – With these words of praise for those who stand with the Lamb still ringing in their ears, the hearers' attention is directed to still another dimension of this mystery, 'And he says to me, "The waters which you saw, upon which the Whore sits, are peoples and crowds and nations and tongues"'. The third occurrence of the words ὃ εἶδως ('that which you saw') in this angelic explanation guides the hearers to another aspect of that which John saw. It is a return to the Whore with whom this vision began, with specific reference made to the waters upon which she sat. Here the waters are identified as people by means of a, by now familiar, fourfold listing: peoples, crowds, nations, and tongues. For a seventh time in the

---

[50] It may be that these terms would be understood as building upon one another, as Prigent (*L'Apocalypse de Saint Jean*, p. 383) observes, 'Cette fidélité c'est la réponse de l'homme qui reconnaeît et accepte la vocations et l'élection'.

Apocalypse this fourfold formula appears (with slight variations), a formula that conveys a sense of universality.[51] By this point the hearers have come to understand the formula to designate all those who worship God and the Lamb (5.9; 7.9), those who are opposed to God and are under the authority of the beast (11.9; 13.7), those to whom John must prophesy a second time (10.11), and those to whom the everlasting Gospel must be preached (14.6). Not only would the hearers be struck yet again by the blasphemy of the Whore, who presumes to sit in the place of God (17.1), but would also understand even more fully than before that those to whom their pneumatic witness is to be directed find themselves under the oppressive authority of the Whore, just as they earlier were said to be under the authority of the beast (13.7).

Verse 16 – With such ideas about the peoples dominated by the Whore in their minds, the hearers' attention is directed to still another aspect of the vision with the words, 'And the ten horns which you saw and the beast will hate the Whore and will make her ruined/desolate and naked and will eat her flesh and will burn her in fire'. As had the three previous occurrences of the words ὃ εἶδως ('that which you saw'), so their fourth occurrence in this angelic explanation of the words alerts the hearers to the fact that yet another dimension of the vision is to be explained. Mention of the ten horns and the beast would serve to underscore for the hearers the solidarity of the actions of the ten kings and those of the beast. Amazingly enough, the beast (and his ten horns), who has to this point supported the Whore and her domination of the peoples of the world, turn upon her with a viciousness normally associated with the actions of wild animals![52] Their treatment of the Whore would likely generate a visceral response amongst the hearers as they encounter the language of hatred, desolation, nakedness, eating flesh, and burning with fire. Specifically, such graphic language would likely remind the hearers of the words of Ezekiel (23.1-49) in describing the divine judgments brought on by the actions of two whoring sisters, Oola (Samaria) and Ooliba (Jerusalem). Owing to their opulence and unrestrained adulteries and sexual immoralities, they are turned over to those who hate them, they are stripped na-

---

[51] Smalley, *The Revelation to John*, p. 440.
[52] Ladd, *Revelation*, p. 233.

ked, their flesh is mutilated, and their remnant burnt with fire![53] In addition to the message of divine judgment conveyed by the similarities to the Ezekiel passage the hearers would also likely pick up on a variety of other nuances in the text. The fact that the beast and the ten horns will hate the Whore might convey the idea that their actions are tied to God's judgment in some way, in as much as the resurrected Jesus himself has earlier claimed to 'hate' the works of the Nicolaitans (Rev. 2.6), perhaps suggesting a connection between their works and that of the Great Whore. Words of warning that the Whore will be ruined or made desolate are given in anticipation of that very event which is to follow (18.19). The fact that the Whore will be made naked would make clear the real nature of her spiritual state, as it had with the church in Laodicea (3.17), exposing her shame (16.15). Neither would the stark juxtaposition of her naked state with her earlier opulent attire be lost on the hearers. Perhaps they would wonder if there is not a deeper connection between the fact that the Whore's flesh is to be eaten and that her idolatrous sexual immoralities would no doubt have included the seduction to eat food sacrificed to idols, a temptation with which more than one of the seven churches struggled (2.14, 20). These gruesome words might also remind the readers of Jezebel's ultimate fate (2 Kgs 9.30-37).[54] Though the hearers would not realize it at this point, this description of the beast and his ten horns eating the flesh of the Whore serves as a harbinger of things to come (19.18). Owing to the close association between burning (8.7) and the display of fire as a near universal activity of God in the Apocalypse (the lone exception being 13.13), mention of her fiery fate could hardly be taken as anything other than divine judgment.

Verse 17 – If the previous verse leads the hearers to suspect the hand of God in the demise of the Whore the next words they encounter confirms that suspicion, 'For God gave into their hearts to do his purpose and to do one purpose and to give their kingship to the beast until the words of God might be fulfilled'. Now the hearers discover that even the one purpose of the ten kings, to give their authority to the beast as they go out to make war against the Lamb (vv. 13-14), is not beyond the activity of God. For just as the

---

[53] Murphy, *Fallen Is Babylon*, p. 364.
[54] Aune, *Revelation 17-22*, p. 957.

hearers had earlier learned that the pouring out of the sixth bowl had caused the Euphrates to dry up so that a way might be made for the kings of the east to invade (16.12), so now they learn that God himself has a hand in the cooperative venture of the ten kings and the beast! Their μίαν γνώμην ('one purpose') is in reality his μίαν γνώμην ('one purpose'). Such activities are part of the divine plan and will play a role in bringing to completion 'the words of God'.[55] The occurrence of the term τελεσθήσονται ('will have been completed') would be of special significance to Johannine hearers for not only is it the same verb that Jesus utters at the end of his life on the cross ('It is completed' – Jn 19.30), but it also functions in the Apocalypse to describe the completion of extraordinarily important things: the mystery of God (Rev. 10.7), the witness of the two prophetic witnesses (11.7), and the wrath of God (15.1, 8). Here it is difficult to believe that the hearers would not take these 'words of God' as coterminous with 'the words of this prophecy' (1.3; 22.7, 9, 10, 18, 19). Not only are the actions of these ten kings in accord with the divine will, but these actions are also being revealed in the book that John has written!

Verse 18 – At long last the angelic explanation returns to where it began with the words, 'And the woman which you saw is the great city which has the kingship over the kings of the earth'. The mystery of the woman, which the angel earlier promised to reveal (17.7), is now taken up directly again as she is identified with the great city. With these words a number of things converge for the hearers about the Woman's identity. The first mention of the great city in the Apocalypse described the city in which the body of the two prophetic witnesses would lie, a city called pneumatically Sodom, Egypt, the place where their Lord was crucified. They would likely recall that this universal city was a location, the identity of which could only be discerned by means of the Spirit (11.8). It is in conjunction with this city that the first mention of the Beast in the Apocalypse occurs (11.7), underscoring the close relationship between the two. Now in 17.18 they learn that this woman is identified with this 'great city', which is none other than Babylon the Great! With such words the hearers would be reminded that, de-

---

[55] As Gause (*Revelation*, p. 227) notes, 'Even in their sinful purposes, they are in actual fact fulfilling the will of God'.

spite her unrivaled power, this woman's fate is as certain as that of Babylon the Great who had earlier fallen!

The Destruction of Babylon (18.1-24)

Verse 1 – With the remarkable words about the mystery of the Great Whore still ringing in their ears, the hearers learn that even more is to be revealed as they encounter the next words from John, 'After these things I saw another angel coming down out of heaven having great authority, and the earth was enlightened out of his glory'. The combination of the words within this verse indicates that a new section[1] of this third major part of the vision is now about to unfold before their eyes and ears. Each component plays its part as the phrase 'after these things' often denotes a transition in thought in the Johannine literature, the word εἶδον ('and I saw') frequently indicates a new direction in the book's development, while the appearance of another angel suggests a change from or development of the previous scene. This introduction of still another angel would convey several things to the hearers. First, his introduction would remind them of the activity of the angel whom John encounters in chapter 17, who is clearly identified as one of the seven angels who has the seven bowls of plagues. Though not the same angel as the one described in the previous chapter,[2] it is unlikely that the hearers would not discern some similarities between their roles and functions, whether or not this angel too is initially thought to be one of the seven angels with the seven bowls of plagues. Second, the description of this angel as 'coming down out of heaven' would make clear that, as with other angelic figures in the Apocalypse, this angel comes from the very presence of God and as such his words will carry with them divine authority.[3] Third, the fact that this angel is deemed to have great authority would, no doubt, remind the hearers of the fact that the beast has earlier been described as receiving 'great authority' from the Dragon (13.2), a contrast between the origins of their respective great authority that would hardly be

---

[1] Resseguie, *The Revelation of John*, p. 228.
[2] Contra Beale (*Revelation*, p. 892) and Aune (*Revelation 17-22*, p. 985) who identify this angel with the previously mentioned one.
[3] Osborne, *Revelation*, p. 634.

missed by the discerning hearer. Fourth, the extraordinary characteristics of this angel could hardly help but to remind the hearers of the angels previously encountered in Revelation 5 and 10, who each convey a message of remarkable significance. Specifically, if the angel in Revelation 5 introduces the hearers to the slaughtered Lamb who is worthy to take the book and open its seals, while the colossal angel in Revelation 10 who reaches from earth to heaven is instrumental in John's commission to prophesy again 'to the peoples and nations and tongues and many kings' (10.11), the hearers might expect that this authoritative angelic figure may have a message of no less significance. Such expectations are not disappointed for the hearers immediately learn that 'the earth was enlightened out of his glory'. A number of aspects of these words would be significant for the hearers. First, they would, no doubt, be struck by the fact that this is the only angel to whom glory is attributed in the Apocalypse, an attribution made only to God (4.9, 11; 5.13; 7.12; 11.13; 14.7; 15.8; 16.9) and the Lamb (1.6; 5.12, 13) to this point in the book.[4] On this occasion the attribution of glory to the angel would likely be understood as being the result of the angel's origin from heaven having been in close spatial proximity to God. Second, the fact that the glory of the angel is said to enlighten the world would suggest a tight connection between the residual glory of the angel and his ability to enlighten the world, indicating that the enlightening of the earth comes from God via the angelic mission.[5] Third, the fact that the earth is itself enlightened underscores the global significance of this authoritative angel's mission.[6] Fourth, discerning Johannine hearers would also likely pick up on the soteriological implications of this statement as the term ἐφωτίσθη ('enlightened') would itself be understood in the light of the fact that this very verb appears in the prologue of the FG to describe the person and work of the Logos, 'He is the true Light, who enlightens every man coming into the world' (Jn 1.9). Thus, the soteriological role and function of this angel in Rev. 18.1 would hardly be missed and would be seen to

---

[4] Smalley, *The Revelation to John*, p. 443.

[5] As H.B. Swete (*The Apocalypse of St. John* [London: MacMillan, 1909], p. 226) nicely observes, 'So recently has he come from the Presence that in passing he flings a broad belt of light across the dark earth'.

[6] Gause, *Revelation*, p. 228.

stand in some continuity with the messages of the various angels in Rev. 14.6-20.

Verse 2 – With the description of this authoritative angel still in mind the hearers now encounter his words,

> And he cried with a strong voice saying,
> 'Fallen, fallen is Babylon the Great,
> and she has become a habitation of demons
> and a prison of every unclean spirit
> and a prison of every unclean and hateful bird'.

Owing to his previous description it perhaps does not surprise the hearers to learn that this is the first angel in the Apocalypse to cry with a 'strong' voice. The hearers might very well suspect that the strong voice of the angel would ensure that it is heard by (all?) the earth, in keeping with the way in which the angel's glory had enlightened it. His strong voice is certainly in keeping with his divine origin and the significance of his message.[7] The first words to come from this angel's mouth, 'Fallen, fallen is Babylon the Great', could not help but take the hearers back to Rev. 14.8 where this exact phrase occurs, when Babylon the Great is mentioned for the first time in the Apocalypse. It would also likely remind them of the fact that these same words were spoken about the Babylon the Great of old, as this same phrase is used to describe that previous event in Isa. 21.9, perhaps underscoring the fact that this Babylon the Great will fall under the judgment of God as surely as did that Babylon the Great. It is not insignificant that this future event is described with a past tense verb, underscoring the certainty of the future judgment, a grammatical technique sometimes known as the prophetic perfect.[8] The fallen state of Babylon the Great results in its transformation from a city of opulent splendor into a place of unclean creatures of every description. In point of fact, each of the three lines that describe Babylon the Great in her fallen state underscores the unclean nature of the place. The first line, 'she has become a habitation of demons', would convey at least two ideas to the hearers. This first and only appearance of the noun κατοικητήριον ('habitation') to this point in the Apocalypse would

---

[7] Smalley, *The Revelation to John*, p. 443.
[8] Aune, *Revelation 17-22*, p. 985.

remind the hearers of the numerous occurrences of the verb κατοικέω ('inhabit' or 'dwell') which has often appeared in the book in association with those who oppose God and or his people (3.10; 6.10; 8.13; 11.10; 13.8, 12, 14; 17.2, 8), especially those who enter into the idolatrous worship of the beast (13.8, 12, 14; 17.2, 8). Thus, the term 'habitation' would convey to the hearers the idea that Babylon the Great has become, as she was, a place of idolatrous worship. The fact that she is now called 'a habitation of demons' pushes this association further as in the Apocalypse demons have been intimately associated with the deception of false prophecy that leads to idolatrous worship (9.20; 16.13-14). Babylon the Great in her fallen-ness is what she was before, a place of demonic deception that leads to idolatrous worship. The second line, 'a prison of every unclean spirit', reinforces the first. While it is possible to take the term φυλακὴ ('prison') as 'haunt' or a general word for 'habitation' or 'domain' its use elsewhere in the Johannine literature (Jn 3.24) and the Apocalypse in particular (Rev. 2.10) suggests that it would likely be taken to mean 'prison' here rather than understood more generally as reference to domain.[9] The hearers would likely see in this term the idea that Babylon the Great, who has imprisoned many by her domination, 'sitting upon many waters', has now become a prison where every unclean spirit is captive. Neither would the discerning hearers be unaware that in the Johannine worldview unclean spirits are themselves closely associated with deception (1 Jn 4.1-6) and idolatrous worship (Rev. 16.13-14). The third line, 'and a prison of every unclean and hateful bird', not only continues the emphasis upon the unclean nature of Babylon the Great, but may also remind the hearers of Isaiah's words with regard to the fall of Edom and the unclean birds that take it over (Isa. 34.11-15). At the same time, the fact that these birds are described as μεμισημένου ('hateful') may suggest to the hearers that even these unclean birds may somehow be the instruments of God's activity, as to this point in the Apocalypse the term hate as been identified with the church in Ephesus who hates the works of the Nicolaitans (2.6), as does the resurrected Jesus himself, and identified with the ten kings who hate the whore, devour her flesh and burn it in fire, a purpose which God has put into their hearts (17.16-17).

---

[9] As, for example, Mounce (*The Book of Revelation*, p. 323) and others argue.

Perhaps the hearers would wonder if these birds too have a similar role to play?

Verse 3 – While the hearers ponder the remarkable transformation of Babylon the Great, a transformation in which her idolatrous unclean nature is left in tact, they next encounter angelic words that offer the rationale for this transformation,

> because out of the wine of her passion of her sexual immorality all nations have drunk
> and the kings of the earth have committed sexual immorality with her
> and the merchants of the earth out of the power of her extravagant luxury have become rich.

As had the previous words from the angel with regard to the transformation of the fallen Babylon the Great, so these words of rationale take triplicate form. The first line of this angel's words replicates exactly, along with the opening words of v. 2, the words of the second other angel associated with the eternal gospel heard already in 14.8. Thus, whereas the angel in 17.1 provides continuity with the seven bowls of plagues described in chapter 17, this other angel described in Revelation 18, provides continuity with the message of the second other angel described in Revelation 14, promising a more extensive description of this detail. As in 14.8 the hearers would be struck by the fact that the four separate genitive constructions that make up the Greek phrase translated 'of the wine of the wrath of her sexual immorality' indicate that all of the constituent elements (wine, wrath, sexual immorality, and 'her') are closely connected. When encountering the words τοῦ θυμοῦ ('of the passion' or 'wrath'), the hearers would perhaps pick up on the fact that this word, which can be translated as 'passion', also has the meaning of 'wrath',[10] which the hearers have already encountered in the description of the dragon who, after his being cast down from heaven, had great θυμὸν ('wrath') (12.12). Thus, despite the clear contextual idea that her wine is wine of passion, borne of sexual immorality, it is at the same time a wine of wrath, akin to the wrath of the dragon. Even more ominously, the hearers know that this wine of her passion has resulted in her being made to drink from the cup of

---

[10] Sweet, *Revelation*, p. 268.

the wrath of God's anger (16.19). Also, as in 14.8, the objects of her 'affections' are, in words reminding the hearers of Jer 51.7-8, 'all the nations', those to whom the first other angel in 14.6-7 had just preached the eternal gospel. In 18.3 the nations form the first of three groups described in the verse. The second line of v. 3 continues the emphasis upon sexual immorality, repeating in slightly different language the words of 17.2 where the kings of the earth are said to commit sexual immorality with the great whore. Such language would further underscore the fact that the Great Whore and Babylon the Great are identical entities, as well as reinforce the way in which she has been successful in the seduction of the leaders of the world into idolatrous activity. The emphasis upon the language of sexual immorality might well remind the hearers that this is the very language that was used to describe the activities of the woman called 'Jezebel' by Jesus (2.20-21). As such, its appearance in the first two lines in 18.3 might well serve to suggest that in their encounter with the teaching of the Nicolaitans (2.14) and 'Jezebel', they are actually already encountering Babylon the Great, who, it should be remembered, is as good as fallen.[11] The third line introduces yet another group that has felt the effects of Babylon the Great with the words 'and the merchants of the earth out of the power of her extravagant luxury have become rich'. The hearer's initial encounter with the word ἔμποροι ('merchants') would likely be colored by the negative connotations its associated term ἐμπόριον ('market' or 'emporium') has in the FG, where Jesus charges that the house of his father has been made into an emporium (Jn 2.16), perhaps implying that trade has replaced true worship in an idolatrous fashion. While the relationships of all the nations of the earth and the kings of the earth with Babylon the Great have been described by the language of sexual immorality, the relationship between these merchants and Babylon the Great is described in economic terms, for they are said to have become rich by means of τῆς δυνάμεως τοῦ στρήνους αὐτῆς ('the power of her extravagant luxury'). Such a statement would imply several things to the hearers. First, it would make more explicit the connection between idolatrous sexual immorality and the economics controlled by Babylon the Great, perhaps reminding them of the economic implica-

---

[11] Koester, *Revelation and the End of All Things*, p. 164.

tions of taking the mark of the beast. Second, such words would, no doubt, remind the hearers of the resurrected Jesus' prophetic words to the church in Laodicea with regard to their own claims to be rich (3.16), riches that he reveals to be poverty in contrast to his own riches. Perhaps such reflection would result in the realization that the riches acquired by the church in Laodicea were worthless owing to the fact that their origin was found in the extravagant luxury of Babylon the Great, a realization that would reveal the extent of their complicity with an idolatrous system. Third, if they have not earlier realized it, the grammatical construction τῆς δυνάμεως τοῦ στρήνους αὐτῆς ('the power of her extravagant luxury'), known as a genitive of source, makes clear that the power of Babylon the Great derives from its extravagant wealth.[12]

Verse 4 – If the previous words result in the hearers' contemplation of their own possible complicity with the luxurious wealth of Babylon the Great, such discerning reflection is confirmed by the next words they encounter,

> And I heard another voice out of heaven saying,
>
> 'Come out of her my people
> in order that you might not share in her sins
> and out of her plagues
> in order that you might not receive'.

The words of the angel with the strong voice now give way to another voice from heaven. Whether the voice of another angel or the divine voice itself, its origin from heaven makes clear to the hearers that it too comes from the very presence of God and thus its words are coterminous with the words of God.[13] The hearers' first encounter in the book with the words of direct address 'my people' would not only leave the impression that these words come directly from God himself, but would also convey an extraordinary sense of intimacy with God in contrast to his relationship with Babylon the Great who is as good as fallen. These first words from this voice from heaven are reminiscent of various expressions found throughout the OT, where God's people are warned to flee from a given location (Gen. 12.1; Num. 16.23; Isa. 48.20; 52.11; Jer. 50.8;

---

[12] Smalley, *The Revelation to John*, p. 445.
[13] Cf. Prigent, *L'Apocalypse de Saint Jean*, p. 389.

51.6, 45; Zech. 2.6-7).[14] Specifically, these words would call to mind those found in Jer. 51.45, which also include a declaration about the fall of the wall of Babylon. But how would the hearers understand this call for God's people to come out of Babylon the Great? Would they hear in it a call physically to depart from the city?[15] While such a possibility cannot be ruled out altogether, it does seem to stand at odds with the way in which faithful witness has been characterized throughout the book, perhaps most clearly in the example of the two prophetic witnesses in Rev. 11.3-13 who do not withdraw from the Great City but rather confront this city, known pneumatically as Sodom, Egypt, and the place where their Lord was crucified, with their pneumatically empowered faithful witness.[16] Their call is to a different kind of separation; from complicity with this city to resolute opposition to its injustice, murder, and idolatry.[17] The purpose of this instruction to come out of her is expressed by means of a double ἵνα ('because') clause that takes a chiastic form, with the word ἵνα ('because') standing at the beginning and end of the phrase. The first ἵνα ('because') makes clear the purpose of this call to come out, 'in order that you might not share in her sins', sins in which all the nations, kings of the earth, and merchants of the earth have participated; sins for which she and they will be judged. The second ἵνα ('because') clause 'in order that you not receive' follows the words 'out of her plagues' in the Greek text, making clear that those who do not separate themselves from Babylon the Great will find themselves victim of the plagues reserved for her, most recently depicted in chapters 16-17, for it is one of the seven angels having the seven bowls of plagues who shows John the mystery of the Great Whore (17.1-18).[18] Such a stark warning might again remind the hearers of the warning to the church at Laodicea, which too is described as rich.[19] Are her riches now understood to have come from complicity with Babylon the Great?

---

[14] Wall, *Revelation*, p. 214.

[15] A possibility raised by Wall, *Revelation*, p. 214.

[16] Sweet, *Revelation*, p. 226.

[17] Schüssler Fiorenza, *Revelation*, p. 100 and Resseguie, *The Revelation of John*, p. 229.

[18] Smalley, *The Revelation to John*, p. 446.

[19] Kiddle, *The Revelation of St. John*, p. 364.

Verse 5 – The reason for the command would become even clearer to the hearers as they encounter the next words from the voice from heaven, 'because her sins have piled up unto heaven and God remembered her unrighteous deeds'. This biblical image of the piling up of sins unto heaven (Jer. 51.9; Jon. 1.2; Ezra 9.6) conveys the idea that her sins are so high that they can no longer be ignored,[20] for they encroach upon heaven itself. Whether such an image would suggest to the hearers that Babylon's sins threaten the sovereignty of God,[21] it would at the least indicate that they can no longer be overlooked but at long last must be addressed. Neither would the remainder of v. 5 prove insignificant to the hearers for each word that follows would have special meaning for them. For the hearers know from the OT that when God remembers it is an indication that God has decided to act.[22] This detail, along with the fact that Babylon's sins are so great that they can no longer be ignored indicates that God's judgment upon her is imminent. The specific mention of her ἀδικήματα ('unrighteous acts') would no doubt remind the hearers that the God whose ways are δίκαιαι ('righteous') and true (15.3), who is δίκαιος ('righteous') (16.5), whose judgments are true and δίκαιαι ('righteous') (16.7), and whose δικαιώματά ('righteous deeds') have been manifested (15.4) is himself the one who remembers her ἀδικήματα ('unrighteous acts') and will judge them with righteous judgment (16.7). This emphatic language would make the warning to those called 'my people' all the more stark.

Verse 6 – With such emotionally charged language ringing in their ears, the hearers might be forgiven if they have failed to notice that if God's voice is the voice from heaven, in 18.5 he is spoken of in the third person, suggesting that these divine words are spoken by an angel or that there was an unidentified change of speaker between vv. 4 and 5. If such is the case, the hearers are not given long to ponder this transition, for in the next 'heavenly' words they encounter, commands are given to unidentified agents,

---

[20] Beasley-Murray, *Revelation*, p. 265

[21] Aune, *Revelation 17-22*, p. 992.

[22] Murphy, *Fallen Is Babylon*, p. 370.

Give to her even as she has given
and repay her double according to her works,
in the cup which she mixed, you mix for her double.

These words, full of mystery and emphasis, would raise a host of issues for the hearers to ponder, the first of which being, to whom are these commands addressed? On first encounter, these words would appear to be addressed directly to the hearers,[23] but the things that are commanded rather clearly require (almost) divine action and power. So unless it be understood that it is through their faithful witness that they accomplish these tasks,[24] it would appear likely that the commands would be taken as addressed to others. While it is possible that the hearers would understand these commands as directed to 'angels of destruction',[25] it would appear more likely that these commands would be understood in the light of the preceding narrative that describes the destruction of the Great Whore, where the hearers have learned that the ten kings and the beast will hate her and, ultimately, destroy her.[26] Thus, it would appear most likely that these commands would be taken as directed to the ten kings and the beast, into whose hearts God puts the destruction of the Great Whore. The commands themselves fall into the by now familiar triple form, with the first line, 'give to her even as she has given', calling to mind the *lex talionis* found at various places within the OT, indicating that the punishment she is to receive is just and that it fits her crime. The double use of the term ἀποδίδωμι ('give'), which stands at the beginning and the end of this first line in the Greek text, serves to underscore the connection between the acts of Babylon and the punishment that is to be dispensed further. The second line, 'repay her double according to her works', is no less powerful for if anything it heightens the emphasis upon the justice of Babylon's judgment by use of a phrase διπλώσατε τὰ διπλᾶ ('repay double'), a Greek construction that underscores the extent of the punishment by placing the same word in both verb and object form side by side, resulting in a literal meaning something like 'double pay her double according to her

---

[23] So Aune, *Revelation 17-22*, p. 994.
[24] So Michaels, *Revelation*, p. 204.
[25] A possibility raised by Smalley, *The Revelation to John*, p. 448.
[26] Wall, *Revelation*, p. 215.

works'. This thought, which conveys the idea of full and complete requital,[27] would no doubt be informed for the hearers by Jer. 16.18[28] where similar language is used to describe the double recompense destined for those who profane the land by evil works, sins, and abominations, some of the very language earlier used to describe the acts of Babylon the Great and the Great Whore. The third line, 'in the cup which she mixed, you mix for her double', not only underscores the emphasis of the first two, but goes beyond them in certain ways. First, it too contains a play on words with the terms ἐκέρασεν ('she mixed') and κεράσατε ('you mix') standing side by side in the Greek text, again underscoring the connection between the action of Babylon the Great and the act of punishment that is commanded. Second, the reappearance of the words 'cup' and 'double' in this line, not only connects this line with that which immediately precedes ('double'), but also with a very potent image of judgment ('cup') that awaits Babylon the Great and is even now imminent (14.10; 16.19; 17.4).

Verse 7 – If the hearers have forgotten why such punishment awaits Babylon the Great they are reminded in the next words they encounter, 'As much as she glorified herself and she lived opulently, so much give to her torment and mourning. Because in her heart she says, "I sit enthroned and I am not a widow and I will never see mourning"'. Here the hearers are reminded of the intimate connection between her idolatrous and self-indulgent lifestyle, on the one hand, and the torment and mourning with which she is judged, on the other hand. Her idolatrous activity is once again made clear by the fact that she has 'glorified' herself, an activity for which only one is worthy (15.4),[29] for aside from the residual glory of the angel who appears in 18.1, glory is only attributed to God (4.9, 11; 5.13; 7.12; 11.13; 14.7; 15.8; 16.9) and the Lamb (1.6; 5.12, 13) in the Apocalypse. In turn, this illegitimate glorification is now seen as closely related to her opulent lifestyle, an opulence out of which the merchants of the earth have been made rich (18.3). The connection between her lifestyle and judgments to follow would hardly be lost on the hearers as the terms ὅσα ... τοσοῦτον ('as much ... so

---

[27] Mounce, *Revelation*, p. 235.
[28] So Sweet, *Revelation*, p. 267 and Aune, *Revelation 17-22*, p. 992.
[29] Murphy, *Fallen Is Babylon*, p. 372.

much') would make such clear. Neither would it be ignored that the judgments which God has brought on a variety of individuals throughout the book who oppose him will now be visited upon Babylon the Great, torment (9.5; 11.10; 14.10, 11), with the added judgment of mourning. As if her culpability were not clear enough to the hearers, Babylon the Great's only words recorded in the book,[30] words that come from her heart, testify against her when she says, 'I sit enthroned and I am not a widow and I will never see mourning'. Each phrase in her triple boast reveals something of her idolatrous heart. Her claim to enthronement would remind the hearers of her being seated 'upon many waters' (17.1), who are 'the peoples and crowds and nations and tongues of the earth' (17.15), a position that belongs to God alone (Ps. 29.10). Her claim, 'I am not a widow', reveals something of her thoughts of invincibility, as widowhood was associated with vulnerability and being a victim of war;[31] ideas far removed from her self-assessment. At the same time, the claim would prove to be ironic to the hearers coming from one who is said to have had so many sexual partners, perhaps a not so subtle reminder of her adulterous activity. Her claim, 'I will never see mourning', may suggest to the hearers that in addition to her feelings of invincibility she harbors delusions of her own eternality.[32] Unbeknownst to her, mourning is on its way to her while these words are on the lips of her heart. If she thinks there is no God, or that she is divine, she is wrong!

Verse 8 – These extraordinary boasts give way to the words with which these 'heavenly words' about her judgment conclude, 'On account of this in one day her plagues will come, death and mourning and famine, and in fire she will be burned up, because strong is the Lord God, the one who judges her'. Clearly, her preceding boasts in Rev. 18.7, as well as her activities described in the previous verses of this chapter, become the basis for her judgment, as the terms διὰ τοῦτο ('on account of this') make clear. In contrast to her possible delusions about her own eternality, her judgment comes quickly, in one day! In fact, the speed with which her judgment will be accomplished is almost unbelievable in its velocity.

---

[30] Michaels, *Revelation*, p. 205.
[31] Mounce, *The Book of Revelation*, p. 326.
[32] Yarbro Collins, *The Apocalypse*, p. 127.

The great city, judged in one day! The judgment comes in the form of 'her plagues', plagues that the people of God have been warned that they can avoid only by coming out of her (v. 4). There can be little question in the hearers' minds as to the origin of such plagues, as throughout the Apocalypse plagues have come from God and/or his agents (9.18, 20; 11.6; 15.1, 6, 8; 16.9, 21; 18.4). On this occasion the plagues are identified in the now familiar triple form: death, mourning, and famine. The naming of such plagues would no doubt remind the hearers of the activities associated with the rider on the pale horse (6.7-8),[33] as well as the way such mourning stands in contrast to the boasts of Babylon the Great in 18.7. But the plagues are not completed with these three, for just as the ten kings and beasts will burn the Great Whore with fire (17.16), so Babylon the Great too will be burned up with fire,[34] further indicating that such activity on the part of the ten kings has been put into their hearts by God and is in effect the activity of God! It may not be lost on the hearers that burning is the fate of both Sodom (Gen. 19.28) and Edom (Isa. 34.10).[35] For despite all claims by this great kingdom to the contrary, 'strong is the Lord God, the one who judges her'. Such strength, attributed to God (7.12), the Lamb (5.12), and his messengers (5.2; 10.1; 18.2), stands in contrast to the lack of strength on the part of the great red dragon and his angels (12.8). The Lord God is strong to judge (cf. 6.10; 11.18; 14.7; 16.5, 7), he has no rival – not even Babylon the Great!

Verse 9 – Not all rejoice in the judgments of God upon her. In point of fact, the hearers learn that some mourn her destruction in dirge-like fashion, 'And they will cry and will lament over her, the kings of the earth, those who with her were sexually immoral and opulently wealthy, when they see the smoke of her fire'. The hearers might detect a certain emphasis upon the crying and lamenting that comes from these kings, as these terms stand first in this sentence in the Greek text. Not only would the word order underscore the significance of such crying, but the hearers would also remember that John himself is described as weeping at the news that no one in heaven or on earth or under the earth was found who could

---

[33] Smalley, *The Revelation to John*, p. 450.
[34] Murphy, *Fallen Is Babylon*, p. 371.
[35] Sweet, *Revelation*, p. 271.

break the seals of the scroll and look inside it (5.4), an activity prohibited by one of the elders (5.5), who directs his attention to the Lion of the tribe of Judah. Johannine hearers might also recall that elsewhere in the Johannine tradition this very verb, κλαίω ('cry'), occurs in the description of Mary crying at the death of her brother (Jn 11.31, 33), the disciples crying at the departure of Jesus (16.20), and Mary's crying at the tomb of Jesus (20.11, 13, 15). Perhaps the term's occurrence in Rev. 18.9 would convey something of the deep sense of loss experienced by the kings of the earth at the destruction of Babylon the Great, while standing in stark contrast with what would be deemed to be the proper crying of God's people. The mourning on the part of the kings of the earth would also strike the hearers as having a similar structural emphasis owing to its location in the sentence, while being deemed to have an equal sense of displacement, as the term has appeared earlier to describe the mourning all the tribes of the earth will experience at the appearing of Jesus with the clouds (1.7). Learning the identity of those who cry and mourn the destruction of the great city would explain the reason for such emotional responses, for the kings of the earth have committed sexual immorality with the great city (cf. 17.2) and with her enjoyed opulent wealth. The description of this intimate relationship reveals that it is one based upon idolatrous activity that results in economic advantage.[36] Further, their sexually immoral and idolatrous relationship is intimately connected to economic prosperity (cf. esp. 18.7). Specifically, the hearers learn that the crying and mourning results when the kings of the earth see the smoke of her fire – a sure sign of her destruction, a sign that all is lost as far as the great city is concerned!

Verse 10 – Much more is revealed about the response of these kings in the next words the hearers encounter, 'standing from afar, on account of the fear of her torment, saying, "Woe, woe, the great city, Babylon the strong, because in one hour your judgment came"'. First, their location, 'standing from afar', may suggest to the hearers a reverential distance for those suspected of being under divine judgment, as the appearance of μακρόθεν ('afar') here and in the LXX Ps. 37.12 (38.11) implies. Second, the explicit attribution of their reverential distance to 'the fear of her torment' would indicate

---

[36] Bauckham, *The Climax of Prophecy*, p. 372.

to the hearers that even the kings of the earth understood the great city to be under the judgment of God, as this word family is reserved for the activity of God and/or his agents in the Apocalypse (9.5; 11.10; 12.2; 14.10, 11; 18.7) and could hardly help but be understood as the direct result of the command given in 18.7 above. Third, the dirge, which they offer, reveals their continued infatuation with her, for even though her destruction is before their eyes she is still referred to by the kings as 'great', which reveals something of their own adulterous nature.[37] For the hearers, the irony of their misplaced fascination is made all the clearer when the kings of the earth refer to her as 'Babylon the mighty city', as ἰσχυρά ('mighty') is the very term used earlier to describe 'the Lord God who is mighty to judge her' (18.8)! The reason for this dirge, introduced by the double 'woe', is made clear in its final line, 'because in one hour your judgment came'. The occurrence of the second person pronoun 'your', rather than the more impersonal 'her', also reveals something of the kings' affections for her. At the same time, the fact that they reflect upon the suddenness of her judgment, expressed as 'in one hour' could hardly help but remind the hearers of the 'one hour' for which the ten kings will reign (17.12)[38] and the destruction of the Great Whore, which is part of their one purpose placed into their hearts by God (17.13, 16-17)!

Verse 11 – But before the words of this dirge are allowed to sink in, the hearers' attention is directed to yet another group who mourn the great city's destruction, 'And the merchants of the earth are crying and mourning about her, because their cargo no one buys any longer ...' Like the kings of the earth before them, the merchants of the earth were earlier tied to the great city in the words of the other angel coming down out of heaven, who cries out with a mighty voice (18.3). Specifically, the merchants were said to have become rich by the power of the great city's opulent wealth. At first, the description of the merchants of the earth differs from that of the kings of the earth in that the merchants stand first in the Greek sentence not their activities. Yet, they, like the kings of the earth, are at first described as crying, suggesting a deep sense of loss on their part. They too are described as mourning, but the word

---

[37] Smalley, *The Revelation to John*, p. 452.
[38] Caird, *The Revelation of St. John*, pp. 225-26.

used to describe this activity is πενθοῦσιν ('mourn' or 'grieve'), which earlier appears to describe the judgment that awaits the great city (18.7, 8) even while she denies that such grieving is a possibility for her (18.7). Thus, their grief would perhaps strike the hearers as being the direct result of the grief and mourning that God sends upon the great city as judgment, and in this way they experience the grief via her own grief. But whereas the kings of the earth seem to have cried and mourned owing to the intimate nature of their relationship with the great city, the merchants' crying and mourning turns out to be based on the loss of their means of sharing in the power of her wealth, 'because their cargo no one buys any longer'. Clearly, the hearers would understand that the basis of the relationship between the great city and the merchants was commercial, and that their interest in her was purely economical. At the same time, it might strike the hearers as ironic that while the beast, upon whom the great whore sits, appears to have the power to determine who can buy and can sell (13.17), ultimately such decisions reside with God for whom peoples are purchased through the blood of the Lamb (5.9; 14.3, 4) and from whom gold fired by fire may be purchased (3.18).

Verses 12-13 – The hearers are not given long to ponder this reality before they learn of the kinds of cargo that no one any longer buys, 'cargo of gold and of silver and of precious stone and of pearls and of linen garments and of purple clothing and of silk and of scarlet, and every kind of citron wood and every kind of object of ivory and every kind of product of precious wood and of brass and of iron and of marble, and cinnamon and amomum and incense and myrrh and frankincense and wine and oil and fine flour and grain and cattle and sheep, and horses and carriages and bodies, even souls of men'. Encountering such an extensive list would likely cause a number of ideas to float around in the hearers' minds. First, the hearers would note that each of the items are connected by the word καί ('and'), revealing their individual significance.[39] Second, they would perhaps be struck by the similarities between this list of cargoes and the extensive list (of 40 cargoes) found in Ezek. 27.12-24 that describes Tyre's trading partners. If so, they would likely note that while the Ezekiel list is structured around the various lo-

---

[39] Resseguie, *The Revelation of John*, p. 230.

cations of the trading partners, this list is structured around categories of cargo[40] and seems to move from most valuable to less valuable. Yet, this intertextual connection might well remind the hearers of the far reaching origins of the cargo here identified, origins that include the whole of the ancient known world spanning Spain, Morocco, North Africa, Asia Minor, Syria, India, and China, thus suggesting the vast reach and control of the great city. Third, the hearers could not help but notice the similarity between the beginning of this list of cargo in 18.12 and the description of the attire of the great whore in 17.4, where specific reference is made to purple, scarlet, gold, precious stones, and pearls, items with which the cargo list begins. Such details would go some way toward reinforcing the understanding that the great whore and the great city are one and the same and that it is she to whom the merchants come to sell their goods.[41] Fourth, neither would it be lost on the hearers that the majority of items in this list are luxury items[42] that by this time have become characteristic of opulent lifestyles that sometimes have been lived out in almost hyperbolic fashion.[43] The distance between those who consume such luxuries and the vast majority of the world's population would almost scream out to the hearers, further underscoring the opulent excesses of the great whore/city. Fifth, while it would be clear to the hearers that this list has a certain order, in that specific kinds of goods are listed together, its precise significance might be more difficult to discern. Would they find significance in the fact that there are twenty-eight items listed, owing to the significance of the numbers four and seven in the Apocalypse (for example, in contrast to the fact that the name Jesus occurs twenty-eight times)? Or would they discern a seven-fold division of these items into groups of 1) metals (gold and silver), 2) precious stones (including pearls), 3) cloth (fine linen, purple, silk,

---

[40] Bauckham, *The Climax of Prophecy*, pp. 350-51.

[41] Bauckham, *The Climax of Prophecy*, p. 369 and Smalley, *The Revelation to John*, p. 453.

[42] Koester, *Revelation and the End of All Things*, p. 165.

[43] Contra Ian Provain, 'Foul Spirits, Fornication and Finance: Revelation 18 from an Old Testament Perspective', *JSNT* 64 (1996), pp. 81-100, who argues that an economic critique is not the point of this passage. For examples of the way in which several of these items became the objects of excessive opulent indulgence cf. Mounce, *The Book of Revelation*, p. 329 and Aune, *Revelation 17-22*, pp. 998-1003.

scarlet), 4) costly articles (citron wood, ivory, precious wood, brass, iron, marble), 5) spices, fragrances, and food products (cinnamon, amomum, incense, myrrh, frankincense, wine, oil, fine flour, grain), 6) chattels (cattle, sheep, horses, carriages), and 7) humanity (slaves and souls).[44] Or would they perhaps discern a movement in this listing from most valuable to least valuable? Sixth, the way in which this listing ends would clearly not escape the attention of the hearers, for in some ways its final words offer a critique of the whole. For standing at the conclusion of this long list the hearers encounter the words καὶ σωμάτων ('and bodies'), 'the common term for slaves in the slave markets',[45] indicating that slaves are regarded as no more than chattel to the merchants who mourn the loss of their market. If, as it appears, this entire list is arranged in descending order of value,[46] the occurrence of slaves at the very end of the cargo list reveals a great deal about the values of the great city and the merchants. Perhaps such a place of low value would not take the hearers completely by surprise in an empire where it is thought that there were some 60,000,000 enslaved people.[47] But if they are tempted to share in such a view the next words they encounter καὶ ψυχὰς ἀνθρώπων ('even souls/lives of men') reminds them that despite their relatively low value on the commercial market, slaves are not simply animals to be bought and sold, but are themselves human beings. The final words of this list, 'even souls/lives of men', that stand in apposition to 'bodies', reveal the extent to which the values of the great city and of those with whom she does business are characterized by self indulgent opulence, for even human life is a commodity.[48] Such a critique suggests that the prosperity and luxury that characterizes her way of life, represented by this entire list of cargo, is condemned as a whole as being in diametric

---

[44] So Smalley, *The Revelation to John*, p. 454. Cf. Ladd, *Revelation*, p. 240 for a slightly different seven-fold division.

[45] Bauckham, *The Climax of Prophecy*, p. 371.

[46] Clarice J. Martin, 'Polishing the Cloudy Mirror: A Womanist Reading of Revelation 18.13', *From Every People and Nation: The Book of Revelation in Intercultural Perspective* (ed. David Rhoads; Minneapolis: Fortress, 2005), p. 99.

[47] Mounce, *The Book of Revelation*, p. 331.

[48] Martin, 'Polishing the Cloudy Mirror: A Womanist Reading of Revelation 18.13', pp. 89-90 suggests that the language καὶ ψυχὰς ἀνθρώπων ('even souls/lives of men') is an intentional critique of Aristotle's view of slaves as 'soulless bodies' or as possessing souls but not being 'ensouled'.

opposition to that to which John and his hearers are called, perhaps underscoring the vigilance required in discerning the extent to which they could be involved in the economic life in their locales.

Verse 14 – But before the implications of this long cargo list can be fully discerned the hearers encounter additional words, unidentified as to their origin:

> And the fruit of your soul/life's desire has departed from you
> and all the luxuries and the splendors have been destroyed/lost from you
> they will no longer find them.

The content and tone of these words would suggest to the hearers that they come from one of the heavenly voices encountered earlier in chapter 18. Coming fast on the heels of the cargo list these words, which take a tripartite form, are clearly informed by their context. Several aspects would be of note to the hearers. In the first line, reference to 'the fruit of your soul/life's desire' would no doubt be taken as intimately connected to the list of cargo that immediately precedes. Thus, the cargo and the fruit would be thought to be coterminous. For discerning Johannine hearers this phrase would also be informed by the fact that elsewhere in the Johannine tradition references to ἐπιθυμία ('desire' or 'lust') carry negative connotations, including references to the 'desires' or 'lusts' of 'your father' the Devil (Jn 8.44) and references to the 'desires' or 'lusts' of the world (1 Jn 2.16-17). Thus, the fruit of the desires of this great city would clearly be understood as in diametric opposition to the desires of God. Neither would it be lost on the hearers that often in the Apocalypse the appearance of the term ἀπέρχομαι ('depart') is closely associated with divine activity (Rev. 9.12; 11.14; 16.2), further underscoring the idea that the loss of the things that she desires is owing to God's own activity of judgment. The second line in this verse builds upon the first where the opulence of the great city, so well documented in the cargo list and other places is reenforced by reference to her luxuries, which have now been lost to her. In addition to underscoring her opulence, the occurrence of τὰ λαμπρὰ ('the splendors') would remind the hearers of her idolatrous desires/lusts for in its previous occurrence in 15.6 it describes the shining stone which the seven angels wore – and the term will be used to describe the appearance of the Bride (19.8), the water of the river of life (22.1), and the bright morning star (22.16). As with the first line, so the second concludes with allusions to the activity of God for her luxuries and splendors are described as being 'lost to her', as in Johannine thought ἀπόλλυμι ('lose' or 'destroy') often carries the idea of loss of eternal proportions (Jn 3.16; 6.12, 27, 39; 10.10, 28; 11.50; 12.25; 17.12; 18.2; 2 Jn 8).[49] The third line of these 'heavenly' words offers for the hearers a very emphatic conclusion as the Greek construction contains an unusual and somewhat grammatically awkward triple negative construction,[50] which emphatically states that 'these things' – the fruit of her soul's desires, the luxuries and splendors – have absolutely and decisively disappeared, not to be found any longer.[51]

Verse 15 – After a long interlude, which focuses upon the merchants' cargo that no one buys any longer and the divine words that describe the city's new situation, the hearers' attention is focused again upon these merchants with the words, 'These merchants, those who became rich from her, from afar stood on account of the fear of her torment, crying, and mourning'. As their attention is once again focused on these merchants the hearers are reminded of the merchants' relationship with the great city, they have become rich from her (cf. 18.3). And yet, despite the fact that they have become wealthy from her, from her they stand afar, with the construction ἀπ' αὐτῆς, ἀπὸ μακρόθεν ('from her, from afar') underscoring the contrast where the preposition ἀπὸ ('from') stands on either side of the pronoun 'her'. As with the kings of the earth, the location of the merchants ('standing from afar') may suggest to the hearers a reverential distance for those suspected of being under divine judgment, as the appearance of μακρόθεν ('afar') here and in the LXX Ps. 37.12 (38.11) implies. The explicit attribution of their reverential distance to 'the fear of her torment' would again indicate to the hearers that even these merchants understood the great city to be under the judgment of God, as this word family is reserved for the activity of God and/or his agents in the Apocalypse (9.5; 11.10; 12.2; 14.10, 11; 18.7) and could hardly help but be under-

---

[49] Cf. A Kretzer, 'ἀπόλλυμι', *EDNT*, I, p. 136.
[50] Aune, *Revelation 17-22*, p. 1003.
[51] Gause, *Revelation*, p. 234.

stood as the direct result of the command given in 18.7 above. As in 18.11, where the merchants are introduced to the hearers, so here they are referred to as crying and mourning, terms that suggest a deep sense of loss on the merchants' part as well as a recognition that their mourning is connected to the judgment that awaits the great city (18.7, 8), even while she denies that such grieving is a possibility for her (18.7). Thus, their grief would perhaps once again strike the hearers as being the direct result of the grief and mourning that God sends upon the great city as judgment, a grief they now experience via her own grief.

Verses 16-17a – Their grief is expressed first hand with the words,

> Woe, Woe, the Great City
> The one who wears fine linen
> and purple and scarlet
> and covered with gold in gold
> and precious stones and pearls,
> because in one hour such great wealth was laid waste.

As with the dirge offered by the kings of the earth, so this dirge begins with the double 'woe', perhaps suggesting again that the merchants view her destruction as divine in origin, owing to the way this expression of pain and lament often appears in the Apocalypse as intimately connected to the judgments of God (8.13; 9.12; 11.14). Again in continuity with the dirge of the kings of the earth, so this dirge reveals a continued infatuation with Babylon, for even though her destruction is before their eyes she is still referred to by the merchants as 'great'. But unlike the previous dirge, here the city is described in minute detail, a description that matches that of the Great Whore in near identical fashion (17.4), leaving no question that as far as the hearers are concerned Babylon the Great and the Great Whore are identical. The reason for this dirge is also made clear in its final line, which begins identically to the final line of the first dirge, 'because in one hour …' Yet, on this occasion instead of the words 'your judgment has come' the hearers encounter, 'such great wealth was laid waste'. This language clearly underscores for the hearers the commercial nature of the merchants' relationship with the city Babylon the Great. At the same time, the specific occurrence of the Greek term ἠρημώθη ('was laid waste') serves once again to connect the Great City with the Great Whore, as this term's only other appearance in the Apocalypse came in the description of the laying waste of the Great Whore by the ten kings and the Beast (17.16). Such vocabulary, combined with that which describes the suddenness of her judgment, expressed as 'in one hour', could hardly help but remind the hearers of the 'one hour' for which the ten kings will reign (17.12) and the destruction of the great whore, which is part of their one purpose, placed into their hearts by God (17.13, 16-17)!

Verses 17b-18 – Without any delay, attention is suddenly focused on another category of individuals, composed of four groups, standing alongside the kings of the earth and the merchants, who also mourn the loss of Babylon the Great, 'And every ship master and every one who sails for port and sailors and whoever works the sea, from afar they stand and are crying out seeing the smoke of the fire from her saying, "Who is like the great city?"'. Whether or not the fourfold division of this group of mourners would be taken by the hearers as having reference to four distinct groups of mariners in descending order of grade,[52] these four groups would at the least convey the idea of completeness to include all those who work the sea. Such a comprehensive understanding would go some way toward underscoring the image of Babylon the Great as the center of the commercial universe, with all ships and those who depend upon the sea for their livelihood as intimately connected to the commercial success of Babylon the Great. But as those mentioned before them, their infatuation with the city endures beyond her destruction, for even as they witness firsthand the smoke of the fire of her destruction, they were crying out, 'Who is like the Great City?' Instead of reminding the hearers of the lament offered about the manner of Tyre's destruction in Ezek. 27.32b, 'Who was ever destroyed like Tyre in the middle of the sea?', the words of the mariners in Rev. 18.18 are in keeping with those who worship the beast in 13.4, 'Who is like the beast and who is able to make war with him?'[53] Such similarity not only makes explicit the mariners' reverence for the Great City, suggesting that in some ways they consider

---

[52] As the text of Ezek. 37.32, to which Rev. 18.17 appears to have reference, may suggest so Prigent, *L'Apocalypse de Saint Jean*, pp. 394-95.
[53] Sweet, *Revelation*, p. 273.

the now destroyed city as an object worthy of worship, but also underscores the implicit connection between Babylon the Great (the Great Whore) and the beast.

Verse 19 – With these idolatrous words of worship on the lips of the mariners, more is revealed about their actions and words, 'and they were casting dust upon their heads and were crying out weeping and mourning saying,

> Woe, woe, the Great City
> in whom all those having ships in the sea were made rich
> out of her wealth
> because in one hour she was laid waste.'

Something of the intense pain felt by the mariners at the destruction of Babylon the Great is conveyed by their action of placing dust upon their heads, a sign of mourning throughout the near east[54] that occurs only here in the Apocalypse, adding to the intensity of the grief experienced by the mariners. They, as the merchants before them, are also described as 'weeping and mourning', terms that suggest a deep sense of loss on the mariners' part as well as a recognition that their mourning is connected to the judgment that awaits the great city (18.7, 8), even while she denies that such grieving is a possibility for her (18.7). Thus, their grief would perhaps once again strike the hearers as being the direct result of the grief and mourning that God sends upon the great city as judgment, a grief they now experience via her own grief. As with the dirge offered by the kings of the earth and the merchants before them, so this dirge proper begins with the double 'woe', perhaps suggesting that the mariners also view her destruction as divine in origin, owing to the way this expression of pain and lament often appears in the Apocalypse as intimately connected to the judgments of God (8.13; 9.12; 11.14). Again in continuity with the dirge of the kings of the earth and that of the merchants, so this dirge reveals their continued infatuation with Babylon, for even though her destruction is before their eyes she is still referred to by the merchants as 'great'. Such heartfelt grief is closely tied to the fact that her destruction affects all those who have boats upon the sea, who have been made rich out of the magnificence of the fullness of wealth. Thus, once

---

[54] A. Sand, 'χοῦς, χοός', *EDNT*, III, p. 471.

again the grief expressed for Babylon the Great in this chapter reveals a clear self interest on the part of the mourners, underscoring the economic nature of their relationship to the city. For a third time in this chapter the reason for mourning is revealed in a ὅτι ('because' or 'for') clause. The words of this third dirge would remind the hearers of that offered by the merchants for the first three words found in these two clauses are identical. But whereas the verb ἠρημώθη ('was laid waste') in 18.17 has reference to 'such great wealth', in 18.19 the verb clearly has reference to the city itself, 'in one hour she was laid waste'. It may at this point dawn on the hearers that the stated reasons for these three individual dirges stand in a chiastic structure with the middle phrase 'because in one hour such wealth was laid waste' (v. 17) standing between 'because in one hour your judgment came' (v. 10) and 'because in one hour she has been laid waste' (v. 19). Such an overarching structure would indicate that her being laid waste is indeed identical with the divine judgment executed upon her, and that these are coterminous with her opulent wealth being laid waste, suggesting that she and her opulent wealth are one and the same.

Verse 20 – But the hearers are not given much time to reflect on such implications for the next words they encounter reveal an abrupt unidentified change in speaker (and audience), reminiscent of the unidentified change in audience in 18.5 and 18.6, 'Rejoice over her, heaven and the saints and the apostles and the prophets, because God has judged your judgment upon her!' While a variety of individuals and groups have mourned the destruction of Babylon the Great, her demise is not met with grief on the part of everyone.[55] A number of ideas would converge for the hearers as they encounter the words of 18.20. First, though not identified as such, the hearers are likely to understand the imperative of 18.20 as coming from heaven, or at least as having its implicit authority. Second, when encountering the command, 'Rejoice over her', at least two things would come to the minds of the hearers. On the one hand, such language would perhaps remind them that this very verb was used earlier to describe the activity of the inhabitants of the earth when seeing the fate of the two prophetic witnesses whom the beast overcame and killed and left unburied in the streets so that all

---

[55] Murphy, *Fallen Is Babylon*, p. 237.

could witness their complete humiliation (11.10). On the other hand, it is difficult to imagine that the hearers would not be reminded of the other place in the Apocalypse where very similar language to that in 18.20 appears. For in the aftermath of the great red dragon's expulsion from heaven and the celebration of those who overcame him on account of the blood of the Lamb and the word of their witness (12.10-11), a great voice from heaven commands, 'On account of this rejoice heavens and those who dwell in them' (12.12). Such a close connection would suggest to the hearers that in the destruction of Babylon the Great they are witnessing the coming of the salvation, power, kingdom of our God, and authority of his Christ as well as the casting down of the accuser of the brothers (12.10). Third, the command for the heavens to rejoice would suggest that these words are not simply directed to a place but to all those within the heavens.[56] Such a command would not surprise the hearers for to this point the heavens have been teeming with those who praise God and the Lamb for a variety of things. These participants include the angels, the four living creatures, the twenty-four elders, and the innumerable multitude, to name but a few. Fourth, it is not altogether clear whether or not the hearers would differentiate between the three groups listed after the heavens which are instructed to rejoice; the saints and the apostles and the prophets. While the grammatical form of the list, where the article accompanies each of the nouns, might normally suggest that three distinct groups are here in view,[57] other considerations seem to suggest otherwise. For the hearers may recall that 'saints and prophets' have appeared together earlier in the Apocalypse (16.6) with apparent reference to the people of God as a whole and the prophetic witness to which they are called. Specifically, the saints are those whose prayers are always before the throne (5.8; 8.3, 4), are worthy to receive their reward (11.18), are made war against by the beast (13.7), are the recipients of divine assistance for the task of pneumatic discernment (13.10; 14.12), and whose blood has been poured out (16.6), out of which the Great Whore has become drunk (17.6); while prophets are those who preach the mystery of God (10.7), whose death brings delight to the inhabitants of the

---

[56] Michaels, *Revelation*, p. 207.
[57] Aune, *Revelation 17-22*, p. 1007.

earth (11.10), are themselves worthy of their reward (11.18), and whose blood (along with that of the saints) has been poured out (16.6). Both the contours of their theological characterization, generally, and the convergence of a variety of prophetic emphases in the description of the two prophetic witnesses in chapter 11, more specifically, suggest that the community may well have understood itself as a 'prophethood of all believers'.[58] From their earlier encounter with the term apostle (2.2) the hearers would be aware that the term apostle apparently conveys the idea of a divine sending, being informed by the extensive sending language in the FG and 1 John, suggesting that there are individuals whom God commissions for specific tasks, especially being sent to participate in the harvest of the world (Jn 4.38; 17.18; 20.21). The occurrence of sent language in the Apocalypse tends to deepen this understanding further as the term ἀποστέλλω ('send') appears on one occasion with reference to the Seven Spirits of God who are sent out into all the earth (5.6) and on two other occasions to describe the activity of God who sends his angel to make known to his servants all that is to happen quickly (1.1; 22.6). Such sent ones are likely special envoys[59] that God has sent into the global harvest to bear witness to the Lamb. The placement of 'the apostles' between 'the saints' and 'the prophets' would underscore the fact that the people of God, who have a prophetic vocation, are indeed 'the sent ones' of God himself. Thus, standing in the midst of saints and prophets in 18.20, the appearance of apostles would underscore all the more the idea that those who have shed their blood on behalf of the Lamb are now called upon to rejoice at the destruction of Babylon the Great, who had become drunk on their blood for she has now been judged. Fifth, the reason for such rejoicing is made explicit in the ὅτι ('because') clause with which the verse concludes, 'because God has judged your judgment upon her'. Several aspects of these words are likely to catch the attention of the hearers. Initially, they might well be struck by the fact that in the Greek text the word God is bounded on either side by words that speak of judgment, the verb 'has judged' and the object 'your judgment' making explicit the emphasis upon the divine nature of the judgment of Babylon the

---

[58] Cf. esp. Waddell, *The Spirit of the Book of Revelation*, pp. 176-77.
[59] So Prigent, *L'Apocalypse de Saint Jean*, p. 395.

Great. Neither would it be overlooked that the verb ἔκρινεν ('has judged') and the noun κρίμα ('judgment') are from the same Greek word family, further underscoring the idea of judgment. By means of this unusual phrase, 'God has judged your judgment upon her', the hearers learn that the judgment Babylon the Great has rendered upon these faithful witnesses, specifically 'the saints and the apostles and the prophets', has been brought upon her! Such a construction would no doubt remind the hearers of the words of the Torah where a false witness will have done to them what they have sought for the one falsely accused (Deut. 19.16-19).[60] She who was drunk on the blood of the saints has been given blood to drink. God has judged and vindicated the blood of the souls under the altar (6.10). As in the case of the two prophetic witnesses over whom the inhabitants of the earth rejoiced, there has been a divinely enacted inversion so that such ones as these, who gave their faithful witness and followed the Lamb wherever he goes, are now called upon to rejoice over their fallen enemy – for the time has come.

Verse 21 – With the call to rejoicing over the Great City's fall ringing in their ears the next words the hearers encounter begin to describe this very destruction before their mind's eye, 'And one strong angel took up a stone as a great millstone and cast it into the sea saying, "In the same way with wrath will be overthrown Babylon the Great City and will be found no longer"'. The appearance of this mighty angel and the actions attributed to him would be of significance to the hearers for a number of reasons. For as they may have come to realize this is the third angel in the Apocalypse to be described as ἰσχυρὸς ('mighty' or 'strong'). Owing to the significant roles played by each of the first two mighty angels, the first preaches the question in heaven, 'Who is worthy to open the book and to loose its seals?' (5.2), while the second is the agent of John's call to prophesy a second time (10.1), the hearers may well deduce that this mighty angel also fulfils a most significant role, if not a culminating one.[61] As it turns out, this angel is no less strong than the other two, for he takes up a stone as great as a mill stone,[62] and casts it into the sea! Such a superhuman feat would be enough to

---

[60] Sweet, *Revelation*, p. 275.
[61] Smalley, *The Revelation to John*, p. 462.
[62] Aune (*Revelation 17-22*, p. 1008) notes the mill stone would be the stone often pulled by a donkey.

garner the attention of the hearers, but their previous exposure to such angelic beings would likely lead them to expect more, as the actions of the other two mighty angels are accompanied by words. If so, their expectations are not disappointed for this mighty angel speaks a message that accompanies and explains his destructive actions, 'In the same way with wrath will be overthrown Babylon the Great City and will be found no longer'. The play on words describing the action of the angel, who ἔβαλεν ('cast' or 'threw') the great stone, and the action to be enacted upon Babylon the Great, βληθήσεται ('will be overthrown'), underscores the tight connection that exists between this angel's prophetic action and the prophetic judgment that accompanies this prophetic sign. Such a play on words would likely make it next to impossible for the hearers not to discern in this activity a deep intertextual connection between this prophetic activity and that of Jeremiah, who instructs Seraiah to take a book in which the prophet had written all the evil that would come upon Babylon, read all of its contents, bind it with a stone, cast it into the midst of the Euphrates, and say, 'Thus shall Babylon sink, to rise no more, because of the evil that I am bringing upon her' (Jer. 51.59-64). Such deep intertextual connections would underscore the continuity between this eschatological judgment of Babylon the Great written in the book of this prophecy and the casting down of this great mill stone with that spoken by Jeremiah long ago, going some way toward re-emphasizing once again the deep connection between this Babylon the Great and Babylon the Great of old. Neither would it escape the notice of the hearers that Babylon the Great Whore, who is oft described as wearing precious stones (17.4; 18.12, 16), would in the end be destroyed by a stone of judgment! Finally, the pronouncement of judgment upon the city is stated by means of the phrase καὶ οὐ μὴ εὑρεθῇ ἔτι ('and will be found no longer'), a phrase that will figure prominently in the words that follow.

Verses 22-23a – But before the hearers have opportunity to ponder the significance of the overthrow of Babylon the Great City they encounter five short vignettes from everyday life that illustrate the extent of Babylon's destruction,

> And a voice/sound of harpists and musicians and flutists and trumpeters
> will be heard in you no longer

> And every craftsman/artisan of every craft/art
> will be found in you no longer
>
> And a voice/sound of a mill
> will be heard in you no longer
>
> And a light of a lamp
> will shine in you no longer
>
> And a voice/sound of a bridegroom and bride
> will be heard in you no longer.

The first vignette focuses upon the voice or sound made by a cross section of musicians as well as perhaps those who sing. Clearly, the hearers would understand this vignette as emphasizing the fact that the normal musical sounds that mark the major events, transitions, and moments of life from celebration to mourning will simply be absent from Babylon the Great City, a large city in which such musical sounds of life would normally be heard on a daily basis. At the same time, it would be altogether likely that the hearers would discern deeper meaning in these rather straightforward words. For it would seem next to impossible for the hearers not to appreciate the irony of the fact that while the sound of harpists will be missing in the great city, they know that harpists are present in abundance before the throne of God and the Lamb (5.8), that harpists are harping on their harps as (or alongside) the 144,000 (14.2), and that those who overcome the beast and his image and his number are playing harps of God as they celebrate their victory (15.2), a reality that contrasts with the silence in the Great City in deafening tones. At the same time, the absence of the sound of the trumpeters could hardly help but to remind the hearers of the numerous trumpet-like sounds that accompany the activities of God in the Apocalypse (1.10; 4.1; 8.2, 6, 7, 8, 10, 12, 13; 9.1, 13, 14; 10.7; 11.15), including sounds of judgment that might now be welcome sounds, but no trumpeter is heard any longer. Significantly, in this verse is found the last mention of trumpet-like sounds in the Apocalypse, underscoring this ominous silence all the more! The portentous refrain 'will be heard in you no longer' adds to the foreboding sense of the vignette. The second vignette focuses upon the craftsmen and artisans normally plying their trades in any large city. In Rev. 18.22 the hearers would appreciate the complete absence of such normality in the Greek phrase πᾶς τεχνίτης πάσας τέχνης ('every craftsman of every craft'), which includes the double πᾶς ... πάσας ('every ... every'), suggesting that all craftsmen of every craft are here in view, as well as the play on words τεχνίτης ... τέχνης ('craftsman ... craft'), which further underscores this all inclusive understanding. These details, along with the refrain, 'will be found in you no longer' not only make clear the absolute absence of such craftsmen and crafts, but also reminds the hearers that just as Babylon the Great City 'will be found no longer' the same is true of normal craftsmen and their crafts. Similarly, the third vignette focuses upon the absence of a normal sound[63] – that of the mill stone at work grinding in the city to provide food for its inhabitants. Ironically, the stone like a great mill stone, which the mighty angel cast into the sea, has made the use of the ordinary mill stone unnecessary. The ominous refrain, 'will be heard in you no longer', makes clear the absolute absence of this normal (and essential) sound. The fourth vignette focuses upon an image familiar throughout antiquity, the light of the lamp, without which there is no illumination after the sun sets and darkness approaches. As such, the light of a lamp would be a common sign of life in any ancient community. Thus, the absence of such a common sight would be additional indication that life has been extinguished in the Great City. Although the hearers would no doubt be duly impressed with the image of a great city engulfed in darkness, discerning Johannine hearers might find even a deeper meaning in hearing these words. For in the Johannine literature φῶς ('light') is Christologically conditioned, having numerous explicit intimate connections to Jesus. For example, not only does the Prologue of the FG describe the Logos as the Light (Jn 1.4, 5, 7-9), but Jesus himself also explicitly claims to be the Light later in the gospel (8.12; 9.5; 12.46). Yet, Johannine hearers of Rev. 18.23 would be aware of even more, for they would know that in the FG, John (the Baptist), while not the Light, is explicitly called a lamp by Jesus himself (Jn 5.35), a lamp whose witness shines forth. Thus, it would seem altogether likely that in the ominous words, 'and will shine in you no longer', Johannine hearers would discern that the Light of the lamp's witness will

---

[63] In addition to its appearance here, φωνή ('sound' or 'voice') occurs in the first and fifth vignettes as well, forming a somewhat concentric structure.

no longer shine to bring her inhabitants to faith, or in the case of the Apocalypse, to repentance. The irony of this reality would be all the more potent owing to the fact that while the Light and the Light of John's witness continue to shine, the present tense verbs of Jn 1.5 and 5.35 indicating as much, the Light of witness will no longer shine in this Great City! The fifth vignette concludes this set of word pictures focusing on yet another normal activity in the life of a community and its members, the joyous occasion of a wedding. Here for a third time in the five vignettes the word φωνή ('voice' or 'sound') appears indicating a certain symmetry to the whole, as the term occurs in the first, third, and fifth vignettes. In Rev. 18.23 intertexts from Jeremiah again would be discerned by the hearers, as the imagery of silencing the voice or sound of the bridegroom and bride occurs on three occasions in connection with proclamations of judgment (Jer. 7.34; 16.9; 25.10). The fact that this vignette occurs last in the series suggests that it would likely be understood as the most important element in the group.[64] The hearers would well understand that if there are no wedding sounds found in the Great City, the city itself has no future, for without parents there are no children. Yet, as foreboding as these words are, Johannine hearers may discern deeper meaning in them as well. For not only is bridegroom language intimately associated with Jesus in the FG (Jn 3.29), but such language (Rev. 21.2, 9; 22.17) and other wedding imagery (Rev. 19.7, 9) will also figure prominently as the Apocalypse nears its conclusion, indicating that the absence of the sounds of weddings and marriage is not simply a temporal loss but an eschatological one as well.

Verses 23b-24 – Having viewed from all perspectives the ultimate judgment that awaits Babylon, the hearers now learn of the reason for such punishment, which is stated in three parts, two of which are governed by a ὅτι ('because'),[65] one of which is not:

> because your merchants were the great men of the earth,
>
> because with your enchantment all nations have been deceived
>
> and in you was found the blood of the prophets and saints
> and all those slaughtered upon the earth.

---

[64] So Ruben Zimmerman, 'Nuptial Imagery in the Revelation of John', *Biblica* 84.2 (2003), p. 161.

[65] Murphy, *Fallen Is Babylon*, p. 377.

The first reason offered for such silent devastation of Babylon the Great City takes the hearers back to a group who had earlier mourned her loss, the merchants. Mention of them would no doubt remind the hearers of the extent and scope of their trade, which was powerfully conveyed by the extensive, if not comprehensive, list of cargo found earlier in the chapter (18.12-13), as well as the merchants' intimate economic relationship that was wholly dependant on the Great City. It is these merchants who became rich from her opulent wealth (18.15) that were the great men of the earth. At least two things would likely strike the hearers as significant upon encountering the term οἱ μεγιστᾶνες ('the great men'). First, they might well remember that the great men of the earth have already appeared in the seven-fold list of humanity that opposes God, who beg the mountains and the stones to fall upon them and to hide them from the face of the One who sits upon the throne and the wrath of the Lamb (6.15-16). Thus, upon their encounter with this term in 18.23 the hearers would initially understand these great men as in opposition to God and the Lamb – an opposition not unexpected owing to their close association with the Great Whore. Second, a number of its occurrences in the OT would reveal to the hearers that the term οἱ μεγιστᾶνες ('the great men') often appears in contexts that reveal such individuals to be trusted companions, officials, and courtiers of the king and his family (2 Chron. 36.18; Isa. 34.12; Dan. 2.24; 4.33; 5.1, 2, 3, 9, 23; 6.17; Jon. 3.7), who normally have their position owing to God (Prov. 8.15-16). Such nuances would not be without significance for the hearers, underscoring the idea that the close economic relationship between the Great City and her merchants is what has elevated them to the status of 'the great men' of the earth, not their relationship with God. However, the somewhat straightforward meaning of these words takes on a darker tone in the light of the ὅτι ('because') that governs this clause, indicating that the destruction of the Great City is not unrelated to the economic relationship which makes of her merchants the great men of the earth, a relationship that now is shown to be a bankrupt one. The second reason for the silent devastation of Babylon the Great also comes in the form of a ὅτι ('because') clause, 'because with your sorcery all the nations have been deceived'. While at first glance it might appear that these two reasons have little to do with one another, further reflection would enable the hearers to discern their deeper connection, with the second building upon the first in a significant way. While the mention of φαρμακεια ('sorcery' or 'magic') might call to mind any number of ideas from magic to magic potions, incantations, or magic spells, the hearers might likely take its meaning here to be 'enchantment' as it is by this means that all the nations have been deceived. Such enchanting deception would be informed for the hearers by numerous specific examples in the Apocalypse including the deception of 'my servants' by the false prophetess whom Jesus calls 'Jezebel' (2.20), Satan's deception of the whole inhabited world (12.9), and the second beast's deception of those who dwell upon the earth so that they worship the first beast (13.14). In this context the enchantment that deceives would be closely tied to the deceptive power of the Great City's wealth and power that leads to an enchanted state for those caught up in such deception. The hearers would likely understand that such enchanting deception involves the false worship of idolatry,[66] an activity with which the Great Whore is intimately connected. The third reason for the Great City's silent devastation, while joined to the first two simply by the word καὶ ('and'), is clearly the culminating charge.[67] In an ironic twist the hearers learn of the close connection that exists between the things that will be found no longer, described in the five vignettes earlier, and the one thing that is (still?) found within her: blood![68] In explicit language they find that the blood of prophets and saints and all those slaughtered upon the earth is indeed the culminating charge. While the judgment inflicted upon the Great City owing to the blood of the saints and the prophets is by now familiar to the hearers, they know that God has indeed 'judged her with your judgment' (18.20), in 18.24 the hearers discover that the Great City's culpability expands to include the blood of 'all those slaughtered upon the earth', a charge that is both astonishing and enigmatic at one and the same time. Perhaps the hearers would understand such culpability as owing to the fact that the Great City is depicted as the ruling sovereign of the entire world and as such has

---

[66] Gause, *Revelation*, p. 236.
[67] Kiddle, *The Revelation of St. John*, p. 374.
[68] Smalley, *The Revelation to John*, p. 465.

a certain responsibility for all its inhabitants,[69] or that her guilt is so immense that it subsumes culpability for all shedding of blood.[70] But again, Johannine hearers might well discern a deeper interconnection between the Great City's opulent wealth and the power that comes from it, her self-deceptive arrogant idolatrous activity, and her political brutality.[71] The fact that the word that appears here to describe all those slaughtered upon the earth is the same word used to describe the slaughtered Lamb (5.6, 9, 12; 13.8) and the souls under the altar (6.9)[72] makes clear that while the blood of God's people is worthy of judgment and vindication, in the divine view all human life (blood) is sacred and its spilling does not go unnoticed, nor does it go unpunished!

---

[69] Mounce, *The Book of Revelation*, p. 335.

[70] Murphy, *Fallen Is Babylon*, p. 378.

[71] Cf. the penetrating observations of Koester, *Revelation and the End of All Things*, pp. 167-68.

[72] Prigent, *L'Apocalypse de Saint Jean*, p. 397.

From Babylon the Great to the New Jerusalem – From the Last Judgment to the New Creation (19.1-21.8)

At the mid point of the third major section of the Apocalypse marked by an ἐν πνεύματι ('in the Spirit') phrase, following the detailed description of Babylon the Great City (17.1-18) and the extensive description of her destruction (18.1-24), the hearers encounter a stretch of text which in many ways brings the story to its climax by narrating a number of final things, taking the hearers from the judgment of Babylon the Great to the New Jerusalem. Specifically, the hearers encounter the great rejoicing in heaven and on earth that accompanies the judgment of Babylon the Great and the invitation to the marriage supper of the Lamb (19.1-10), the appearance of the King of Kings and Lord of Lords (19.11-16), his victory over his enemies (19.17-21), the one thousand year reign of Jesus and those who overcome (20.1-6), Satan's final rebellion and defeat (20.7-10), the final judgment (20.11-15), and the initial description of the New Jerusalem descending from heaven (21.1-8).

Rejoicing in Heaven and on Earth and the Marriage Supper of the Lamb (19.1-10)

Verse 1 – With the vision of the long promised judgment upon the Great Whore still before their minds' eye, the hearers encounter words that build upon the preceding description, 'After these things I heard as a great voice of a great crowd in heaven saying, "Hallelujah, the salvation and the glory and the power of our God …"' The first words the hearers encounter in 19.1 would gain their immediate attention for this is the only time in the Apocalypse the words μετὰ ταῦτα ('after these things'), a phrase that often marks a transition in the narrative, is joined with ἤκουσα ('I heard').[1] This unique combination would not only mark a new transition in the storyline, but would also contrast nicely with the many things that 'will be heard no longer' (18.22, 23) in the Great City that lies in ruins. In point of fact, this contrast continues, for that which John hears is also a φωνήν ('a voice' or 'a sound'), a term that occurred three times in 18.22-23. In this case John hears a great voice or sound as of a large crowd in heaven. Such language would no doubt remind the hearers of another great crowd – which no one was able

---

[1] Aune, *Revelation 17-22*, p. 1024.

to count – standing before the throne and before the Lamb (7.9-10), as well as the great crowd in heaven which John heard after the great red dragon was cast down from heaven (12.10). These similarities would no doubt suggest to the hearers that this great crowd includes (if not made up exclusively of) the redeemed in heaven.[2] The first word that comes from the lips of this great crowd is appropriate and startling at one and the same time, for the word 'Hallelujah', a Greek transliteration of the Hebrew word הללויה ('praise Yahweh'), has not appeared elsewhere in the Apocalypse to this point, nor the whole of the NT for that matter. Its occurrence here would likely convey at least two things to the hearers. First, its somewhat unrivaled place in Israel's worship of Yahweh, where it introduces Palms 106, 111-113, 117, 135, 146-150, would alert the hearers to a sharp contrast in tone and mood from the previous passage that includes destruction and mourning.[3] Second, the appearance of this distinctive term of praise and rejoicing would likely indicate to the hearers that the command to the heavens, found in 18.20 to rejoice over the destruction of the Great City, is beginning to be fulfilled.[4] The specific words of praise, 'the salvation and the glory and the power of God', follow fast on the heels of the Hallelujah and are reminiscent of other worship scenes earlier encountered. Like its previous two occurrences (7.10; 12.10), the attribution of salvation to God in praise conveys a sense of finality, focusing upon salvation in its most comprehensive, eschatological sense. It stands first in this series owing to its foundational and fundamental role in the accomplishment of God's will in the world.[5] The attribution of glory to 'our God' would hardly surprise the hearers as this attribution has often been on the lips of those in heaven (4.9, 11; 5.12; 7.12) and earth (11.13; 14.7). Such an attribution by this heavenly crowd would also stand in sharp contrast to those who refuse to give God such praise and/or who, in the case of Babylon the Great (18.7), give glory to themselves, a most idolatrous act indeed, for in the Apocalypse glory is due only to God and the Lamb. Neither does the attribution of power surprise as God is constantly

---

[2] Caird, *The Revelation of St. John*, p. 232 and Prigent, *L'Apocalypse de Saint Jean*, p. 402.

[3] Smalley, *The Revelation to John*, p. 476.

[4] Beasley-Murray, *Revelation*, p. 270.

[5] Smalley, *The Revelation to John*, p. 477.

praised in such a manner in the Apocalypse (4.11; 7.12; 11.17; 12.10; 15.8). As with the attribution of glory so this attribution of power would stand in sharp contrast to the idolatrous use of power occasionally encountered in the book (13.2; 17.13; 18.3). Thus, not only does the voice of this heavenly crowd remind the hearers of other occasions of the praise of God in the Apocalypse, but the content of this praise also reinforces the similarity between this crowd and those whose praise precedes them (5.12-14; 7.9-10; 11.15; 12.10). As such, the words of praise found in 19.1 would convey something of a cumulative weight.

Verse 2 – As the words of the heavenly crowd continue the hearers discover the reason(s) for such extraordinary praise,

because true and righteous are his judgments
because he judged the great whore who corrupted the earth with her sexual immorality

and he avenged (gave justice to/vindicated) the blood of his servants out of her hand.

The explanation takes the now familiar triple form, with the first two reasons introduced by ὅτι ('because') clauses. In the first ὅτι ('because') clause the hearers learn the primary reason for such exalted praise by means of a phrase that sums up very well a dominant, if not the dominant, theme in the Apocalypse, 'true and righteous are his judgments'. Such a rationale for praise could hardly help but take the hearers back to the pleas of the souls under the altar to the holy and true God to judge and avenge/vindicate 'our blood' (6.10), to the words of the song of Moses and the Lamb (15.3), and finally to the words of affirmation and praise heard from the altar near the end of all the judgments (16.7), 'Yes, Lord, God, the All Powerful One, true and righteous are your judgments'. Owing to these similarities the hearers might very well conclude that some of the very voices heard earlier in the Apocalypse are to be found amongst this heavenly crowd as well and once again underscores these essential characteristics of God, that even though his judgments may seem to be delayed or absent altogether, they are true and they are righteous nevertheless. The second reason for such praise, which occurs in the second ὅτι ('because') clause, is closely connected to the first rationale offered and in some ways grows out of it. For God's true and righteous judgments have been seen most recently in his judgment of 'the great whore who corrupted the earth with her sexual immorality'. Not only is his judgment of the Great Whore the example *par excellence* of his true and faithful judgments, but the hearers are also reminded of the reason for her judgment,[6] for she is said to have 'corrupted the earth with her sexual immorality'. The imperfect verb form ἔφθειρεν ('corrupted' or 'ruined') would convey to the hearers something of the continuously corrupting influence of the Great Whore upon the world.[7] At the same time, the hearers might discern a deeper meaning here than simply the moral corruption of the earth brought on by her sexual immorality. For the meaning of the term φθείρω ('corrupt' or 'ruin') logically includes the idea of destruction,[8] a meaning that the related compound word διαφθείρω ('corrupt' or 'ruin') conveys in its three previous occurrences in the Apocalypse (8.9; 11.18). While both these texts speak of destruction brought through divine initiative, Rev. 11.18 explicitly states that the time has come 'to destroy the destroyers of the earth!' Thus, the hearers might well understand in the words of 19.2 that the destruction of the Great Whore is the result of her own destructive corruption of the earth![9] The third reason for the extraordinary rejoicing in heaven is closely related to the first two and is connected to them by the word καί ('and'). God's salvation and glory and power are celebrated with the Hallelujah owing to the fact that 'he avenged (gave justice to/vindicated) the blood of his servants out of her hand'. The occurrence of the verb ἐξεδίκησεν ('avenged' or 'vindicated'), which at its root is the word to judge, could not help but take the thoughts of the hearers, once again, back to the words of the souls under the altar, who specifically cry out to God with a great voice for him to judge and avenge/give justice to/vindicate their blood. As 19.2 and 6.10 are the only two places in the whole of the Apocalypse where the verb ἐκδικέω ('avenge' or 'vindicate') occurs, it is next to impossible to believe that the hearers would not understand this description of God's action as an indication that the prayers of

---

[6] Prigent, *L'Apocalypse de Saint Jean*, p. 403.

[7] Smalley, *The Revelation to John*, p. 477.

[8] F. Merkel, 'Destroy', *NIDNTT*, I, p. 469.

[9] Beasley-Murray (*Revelation*, p. 272) suggests that in corrupting the earth the Great Whore is undoing the work of creation.

the souls under the altar have been answered![10] His salvation and glory and power are praised for his judgments are indeed true and righteous, for he has vindicated the blood of the saints who died at the hands of the Great Whore, the blood with which she had become drunk (17.10). Clearly, for the hearers reference to 'the blood of his servants' would be a reminder that God's people are indeed his prophetic servants who bear faithful witness to him. But perhaps they would discern even more, for the words of this phrase match in a remarkable way the prophetic words spoken to Jehu in the LXX to avenge the blood of my servants the prophets and all the blood of the servants of the Lord from the hand of Jezebel (2 Kgs 9.7).[11] Such a close parallel would further underscore the prophetic identification of the servants in Rev. 19.2 for the hearers, as well as suggesting another connection between the Jezebel of old and the 'Jezebel' with whom the church in Thyatira contends (2.20-23).

Verse 3 – But before the hearers can reflect sufficiently upon the full implications of such climactic praise they encounter additional words, 'And a second time they said, "Hallelujah! And her smoke goes up forever and forever!"' Several aspects of the words of 19.3 would be of significance to the hearers. It would be clear that these words come from the same great voice of the great crowd in heaven that utters the first Hallelujah,[12] indicating that these words of praise issue forth from the previous ones. The second occurrence of the word Hallelujah in the span of two verses would raise the intensity of the praise and heighten the dramatic quality of the scene considerably for the hearers.[13] While it might at first appear that this second Hallelujah is offered simply as an affirmation of the words of praise and rationale that accompany the first Hallelujah, it soon becomes apparent that this Hallelujah stands in parallel to the first, as a word of praise, for it too is accompanied by words of explanation. The specific reason offered for the utterance of this Hallelujah is again closely connected to the destruction of the Great Whore, in this case a celebration of the

---

[10] Ladd, *Revelation*, p. 245.
[11] Aune, *Revelation 17-22*, p. 1025.
[12] Aune, *Revelation 17-22*, p. 1026.
[13] Mounce, *The Book of Revelation*, p. 338.

manner and permanence of her destruction. The mention of her smoke that rises forever and forever would remind the hearers of very similar words already spoken about her destruction (14.11; 17.16; 18.8, 9, 18), where the smoke of a city signifies its absolute destruction, indicating that this is no accident but the judgment of God.[14] These words would perhaps also remind the hearers of the similar fate experienced by Sodom of old (Gen. 19.28), revealing that this Babylon the Great has shown herself to be another Sodom, a name given pneumatically to the Great City in Rev. 11.18, and has shared in her fate.[15] At the same time, the rising of her smoke forever and forever would stand in ghastly contrast to the smoke of the incense which rises to God in heavenly worship mentioned at various points throughout the Apocalypse (5.8; 8.4; 14.11).[16] The extent and perpetuity of her destruction is conveyed by the phrase 'forever and forever'. Not only would this phrase leave the hearers in little doubt that her destruction is permanent, absolute, and irreversible, but it would take on even greater significance owing to the fact that the only other places this phrase occurs in the Apocalypse are in reference to the unending praise due and reign of the One who sits on the throne and to the Lamb (1.6; 5.13; 11.15). Thus, this second Hallelujah is offered owing to the sign that indicates that the Great Whore's destruction is absolute and eternal.[17]

Verse 4 – But even these words of praise do not conclude the worship here offered, for the hearers encounter even more, 'And the twenty-four elders and the four living creatures fell down and they worshipped the God who sits on the throne, saying, "Amen! Hallelujah!"' For the hearers to learn that the twenty-four elders and the four living creatures now join in this heavenly celebration would indicate that the praise of God for his righteous judgments is now complete, as the twenty-four elders appear to represent all the redeemed who overcome and the four living creatures appear to represent the entire created order.[18] Though it has been some time

---

[14] Prigent, *L'Apocalypse de Saint Jean*, p. 403.
[15] Beasley-Murray, *Revelation*, p. 272.
[16] Smalley, *The Revelation to John*, p. 278.
[17] Gause, *Revelation*, p. 239.
[18] Prigent, *L'Apocalypse de Saint Jean*, p. 403.

since they have encountered these heavenly characters (14.3), the hearers would not be taken completely aback by their appearance here owing to the fact that they were introduced during the inaugural vision of God (4.4, 7) and have punctuated the narrative with their praise and adoration of the One who sits on the throne at periodic intervals throughout. Their first appearance in the throne room scene and their last appearance here in 19.4 not only indicate that their praise of the One who sits on the throne surrounds the entire portion of the narrative given to the judgments of God,[19] but it also continues to underscore the fact that indeed God is sovereign! As is one of their defining characteristics, so here the twenty-four elders and four living creatures are described as falling down before the One who sits on the throne (4.10; 5.8, 14; 7.11; 11.16), a point emphasized by the fact that the word ἔπεσαν ('fell down') stands first in the Greek sentence. Such prostration appears to be the way in which God is to be worshipped in the Apocalypse, perhaps suggesting that it is an involuntary response to the divine presence. Significantly, although the hearers have long known the identity of the One who sits on the throne, here is one of the few places where he is explicitly identified as God in the title itself (cf. also 7.10; 11.16). The twenty-four elders and the four living creatures, who fall down and worship God, join their voices with the great voice of a great crowd that comes from heaven and say, 'Amen, Hallelujah!' Thus for a third time in the span of three verses the word Hallelujah occurs! Their word of Hallelujah takes its place alongside the other two Hallelujahs that punctuate this section of the Apocalypse, continuing to fulfill the command of 18.20 for the heavens to rejoice. At the same time, the hearers might also detect a certain sense of finality in the combination of these terms owing to the fact that these very words, 'Amen, Hallelujah', appear at the end of the fourth division of the Psalms in the Hebrew Bible (106.48) as an invitation to the hearers to respond to the book as a whole.[20] Thus, the words of the twenty-four elders and four living creatures would perhaps signal to the hearers a climax in the heavenly rejoic-

---

[19] Murphy, *Fallen Is Babylon*, p. 381.
[20] J. Goldingay, *Psalms Volume 3: Psalms 90-150* (BCOT; Grand Rapids: Baker, 2008), pp. 241-42.

ing prescribed in 18.20 and serve as an invitation for them to join in this Hallelujah as well!

Verse 5 – If the hearers do indeed suspect that the words of 19.4 serve as an invitation for them to join in the rejoicing, the words they next encounter confirms such suspicions, 'And a voice from the throne came out, saying, "Praise our God all his servants, those who fear him, the small and the great"'. Though at first the voice that comes from the throne might be thought to be the voice of God himself, the reference to 'our God' in the words of command suggest that it is that of one of the heavenly beings closest to the throne, perhaps one of the four living creatures.[21] But as the verb of origin ἐξῆλθεν ('came out of') makes clear, if this is not the voice of God himself the words that follow are the words of God, even if they come in mediated form.[22] These divine(ly authorized) words are quite reminiscent of numerous OT passages (LXX) where the people of God are instructed to praise God (e.g. Pss. 112.1, 3; 134.1, 3; 148; 150), by means of a term, αἰνέω ('praise'), that appears to be used exclusively in early Christian literature for the praise of God.[23] The command is directed to all those who are in right relationship with God, including his servants who enjoy an especially close relationship with God (1.1; 7.3), whose prophetic vocation is central to their identity (10.7; 11.18) and to whose blood has justice been given in the judgment of the Great Whore (19.2). These servants are identified as those who fear him, confirming a previous identification of God's people (11.18), indicating their obedience to the angelic command to 'fear God' (14.7). In addition to the mention of servants and those who fear him, the occurrence of the terms 'small and great' would convey at least three additional things to the hearers. First, such ones who are called upon to praise God stand in diametric opposition to those both small and great who worship the beast and receive his mark (13.15-16).[24] Second, these words would underscore the comprehensive nature of this command to praise; all, regardless of social standing, are commanded to praise God. Third, all these terms, appearing together here in

---

[21] Kiddle, *The Revelation of St John*, p. 378.

[22] Aune, *Revelation 17-22*, p. 1027.

[23] BAGD, p. 22.

[24] Sweet, *Revelation*, p. 279.

19.5, have earlier appeared together in 11.18 in a passage which both promises a reward to his servants the prophets and the saints and to those who fear his name both small and great, as well as speaks of a judgment of destruction upon those who have destroyed the earth! The relationship between the praise here proscribed and God's activity of rewarding and judging could hardly be more evident. Clearly, all the faithful (both past and present, the hearers may suspect) are the objects of this command.

Verse 6 – The hearers do not have to wait long for a response to this command, for it appears to be immediate, as John narrates, 'And I heard as a voice of a large crowd and as a voice of many waters and as a voice of strong thunder saying, "Hallelujah! Because our Lord God the All Powerful One reigns".' While the hearers have encountered the voice of a great crowd (19.1), the sound of many waters (1.15; 14.2), and the sound of thunder (6.1; 14.2) at various points in the Apocalypse, and even the combination of the latter two on one occasion (14.2), for the first time they encounter an extraordinary voice which reminds of the combination of three of the loudest sounds possible within their context. Not only does this unique combination of sounds distinguish this voice from the voice heard in 19.1, but the fact that the voice of 19.6 stands without the definite article, known in Greek as an anarthrous construction, also indicates that the two voices are not identical. Such a construction, as well as the unique combination encountered to describe the sound, would likely lead the hearers to understand that this voice, while standing in some continuity with the first, is both more extensive and may well even include the previous one. If so, what is envisioned comes very close to the scene already encountered by the hearers in chapter five, where it appears that every creature in the universe offers praise to the One who sits on the throne and to the Lamb![25] This voice would at the least include all those addressed in 19.5, the redeemed of all time, the universal church.[26] This deafening voice utters the fourth Hallelujah within this six-verse span. As such, it continues the explosive intensification of praise offered in this section, praise so great the hearers might well wonder if it is possible for them to participate in any-

---

[25] Smalley, *The Revelation to John*, p. 481.
[26] Allo, *Saint Jean: L'Apocalypse*, p. 275.

thing more grand or engaging. This fourth Hallelujah, like two of its predecessors, is accompanied by a rationale for such praise which takes the form of still another ὅτι ('because') clause. The reason for such universal praise is 'The Lord our God the All Powerful One reigns!' At least two aspects of this phrase would be of significance for the hearers. First, the verb with which this sentence begins in the Greek text, ἐβασίλευσεν ('reigns'), though often translated in the present tense actually stands in the aorist past tense. The hearers, as well as many modern scholars,[27] would no doubt pick up on the fact that this aorist form, known grammatically as an ingressive aorist, would here convey the idea that at some point in the past God's reign has begun and is now a recognizably present reality.[28] As such, the verb's meaning in 19.6 would likely remind the hearers of its occurrences in 11.15, 17, where it stands in both the future and aorist forms, testifying to something of the trans-temporal nature of this divine reign. Owing to the previous reasons given for the praise of God, the hearers might well be tempted to understand the beginning of this reign as being in some way connected to the judgment and destruction of the Great Whore. Second, the combination of titles for God in this verse, 'Lord, God, All Powerful One', has occurred five times before in the Apocalypse in contexts of praise (1.8; 4.8; 11.17; 15.3; 16.7), with the term παντοκράτωρ ('All Powerful One') underscoring the idea of God's unrivalled power (1.8; 16.14) and immense greatness.[29] This, the great God, whose current reign has already begun, is victorious over the Great Whore and is worthy of the praise of all.

Verse 7 – With the grandeur of such exalted praise in all its deafening intensity still ringing in their ears, the hearers encounter additional words of instruction, 'Let us rejoice and let us be glad and let us give glory to him, because the marriage of the Lamb has come and his bride has made herself ready!' While these words might at first appear to be little concerned with the past and wholly focused on the future, a careful reading of the verse reveals that this forward thrust is quite conscious of, if not rooted in, the past judgment of Babylon. One of the first things likely to strike the hearers

---

[27] Allo, *Saint Jean: L'Apocalypse*, p. 275.

[28] Murphy, *Fallen Is Babylon*, p. 382.

[29] G. Braumann, 'Strength', *NIDNNT*, III, p. 718.

about these words is that each of the commands takes the grammatical form of a hortatory subjunctive, a construction that on this occasion would serve to intensify the sense of eschatological joy as they combine in themselves both a recognition of the provisions of God's reign and the role those who hear are to play. The hearers are not simply called upon to appropriate what has been accomplished, but are called to active response. Each of the hortatory subjunctives serves to underscore a particular dimension of God's activity and deliverance in their active response. The first hortatory subjunctive would be full of meaning for discerning Johannine hearers. On the one hand, this verb often appears in what might be called eschatological contexts, such as: John the Baptist's language when he describes the rejoicing that takes place when the voice of the bridegroom is heard by the friend of the bridegroom (Jn 3.29); the rejoicing that takes place during the (eschatological?) harvest (4.36); Abraham's rejoicing when he saw Jesus' day (8.56); Jesus' rejoicing on account of his disciples who will soon see Lazarus raised from the dead (11.15); the rejoicing that Jesus asks of the disciples upon hearing 'I go and I come to you' (14.28); the disciples' promised future rejoicing after their mourning at Jesus' departure (16.22); as well as the disciples' rejoicing upon seeing the resurrected Jesus (20.20). Thus, this hortatory subjunctive to rejoice would be informed by a host of Christological and eschatological dimensions, which would contribute to making their eschatological rejoicing all the richer. On the other hand, this hortatory subjunctive would also be informed by the world's rejoicing while the disciples cry and mourn (16.20), as well as the rejoicing of the inhabitants of the earth over the death of the two prophetic witnesses (Rev. 11.10), tying their rejoicing specifically to the vindication of their blood by God! The second hortatory subjunctive, 'let us be glad' would also convey special meaning for discerning Johannine hearers as it too is informed by its place in the tradition of the FG. Not only is this verb used to describe the being glad that resulted from John the Baptist's shining lamp of testimony (Jn 5.35), but this verb is also found with the verb of the first hortatory subjunctive to describe the rejoicing and gladness that accompanied Abraham's seeing the day of Jesus (8.56). The third hortatory subjunctive would be no less significant for discerning Johannine hearers, as the giving of glory to God is quite important in the Apocalypse. They would know that the phrase has occurred earlier with reference to the activity of the four living creatures around the throne (Rev. 4.9), the reaction of the rest of the Great City that lives through the great earthquake having earlier witnessed the prophetic activity of the two witnesses (11.13), the evangelistic commandment given to the inhabitants of the earth by the angel flying in mid-heaven (14.7), and the refusal to give glory to God by those who refuse to repent (16.9). Clearly, the hearers would understand that by obeying the command of this third hortatory subjunctive they stand on the side of God and are invited to be active participants in this momentous activity. The rationale for this three-fold exhortation is made clear in the following words that appear almost abruptly in this context, 'because the marriage of the Lamb has come, and his bride has prepared herself'. With these words the hearers would discern a transition from a focus on the rejoicing that accompanies God's judgment of destruction upon those who destroyed the earth to rejoicing over the rewards that he now gives to his faithful servants. Although this wedding imagery might at first seem to come out of nowhere,[30] Johannine hearers would likely discern in it multifaceted meaning. First, they would no doubt be aware of the fact that on various occasions in the OT marriage/wedding imagery is used to describe the relationship between God and his bride, Israel (Hos. 2.5; Isa. 1.21; Jer. 2.2).[31] The fact that this imagery often appears in negative contexts depicting Israel's unfaithfulness seems to have led to an expectation that this ideal relationship would only be fulfilled in the future.[32] Second, Johannine hearers would be familiar already with the idea of Jesus as bridegroom from the words of John the Baptist in the FG where he speaks of himself as the friend of the bridegroom who rejoices at the sound of the bridegroom's voice (Jn 3.29), a voice that John hears in the ministry of Jesus. Third, owing to the fact that the voices of the bridegroom and bride will no longer be heard in the Great City as a result of its judgment (Rev. 18.23), the appearance of wedding imagery at this point in the Apocalypse would perhaps not take the hearers completely by surprise. In point of fact, the occurrence of such multifaceted imagery

---

[30] Prigent (*L'Apocalypse de Saint Jean*, p. 405) says that it appears brutally in this context.
[31] Caird, *The Revelation of St. John*, p. 234.
[32] Wall, *Revelation*, p. 222.

at this point in the Apocalypse would indicate to the hearers that the narrative is being pushed along to its dramatic conclusion.[33] Not only is the arrival of the marriage of the Lamb announced, but it is also noted that his bride (literally 'woman') has prepared herself. The hearers are likely to understand these words within the context of ancient Jewish two-stage weddings, where after the betrothal, at which point the couple is legally married, the bride continues to live in the house of her father where she prepares herself, as she awaits her husband's arrival, at a date in the future, to take her to his house.[34] It would be clear to the hearers that the bride of the Lamb is preparing herself for this extraordinary event, owing in part to the occurrence of ἑαυτήν ('herself') as the object of her preparations. At the same time, the specific vocabulary used to describe this preparation, ἡτοίμασεν ('prepared') would suggest a co-operative, if not reciprocal activity between the bride of the Lamb and God, as this verb's six previous occurrences in the Apocalypse (8.6; 9.7, 15; 12.6; 16.12) always describe the direct activity and intervention of God! As God's other preparations have not been altered nor retarded, so the hearers would understand that the bride's preparations will result in the plan of God being accomplished in her as well![35]

Verse 8 – The suspicions of the hearers with regard to the reciprocal relationship between God and the bride are confirmed and clarified somewhat by the next words the hearers encounter, 'and there was given to her in order that she might be clothed with fine linen, bright and pure'. In fact, both aspects of their reciprocal relationship appear in these words. On the one hand, the occurrence of the verb ἐδόθη ('there was given') in the passive voice (a form that appears throughout the Apocalypse) leaves the subject of the action unnamed, a grammatical form known as a divine passive, implying that God (or the Lamb) is the one who gives this garment of fine linen to the bride of the Lamb.[36] On the other hand, the purpose of this gift is made clear by the verb περιβάληται ('to be clothed'), the middle voice of which indicates that she is to clothe herself in this

---

[33] Metzger, *Cracking the Code*, p. 90.

[34] D.A. McIlraith, "'For the Fine Linen Is the Righteous Deeds of the Saints': Works and Wife in Revelation 19.8', *CBQ* 61.3 (July 1999), p. 524.

[35] Prigent, *L'Apocalypse de Saint Jean*, p. 406.

[36] Gause, *Revelation*, p. 242.

gift. Not only would the hearers be struck by the continued attention given to the reciprocal nature of the relationship shared by God and the bride of the Lamb, but they would also be struck by the description of the bride's attire itself. Its bright and pure characteristics would no doubt remind them of the bright and pure stones with which the seven angels that come from the temple of the tabernacle of witness in heaven with the seven plagues of God are clothed (15.6), suggesting that the bride too is in a very close relationship with God. At the same time the bride's 'fine linen, bright and pure', would stand in striking contrast to fine linen of the Great Whore, for while the latter's attire is the result of idolatrous opulence, the attire of the former is the result of an intimate relationship with the Lamb, perhaps underscoring his bride's sexual innocence in contrast to the sexual exploits of the Great Whore![37] The next words the hearers encounter serve to extend their discerning reflection about the relationship between God and the bride, as well as the contrast between her attire and that of the Great Whore, 'for the fine linen is the righteous deeds of the saints'. Several aspects of these words would be of significance for the hearers. First, it would be obvious that the fine linen here described is the same fine linen that was divinely given to the bride, the same with which she clothed herself. Second, despite the fact that this linen is a divine gift, it is here identified as τὰ δικαιώματα ('the righteous deeds') of the saints. This word would appear to be conditioned for Johannine hearers by their earlier encounter with this very term once before in the Apocalypse, where it has reference to the righteous deeds of God (15.4). There his righteous deeds of judgment are also described as great and marvelous works, as well as righteous and true ways. This occurrence, along with the fact that the root from which the 'righteous' family of words come have reference only to God in the Apocalypse,[38] indicates a close association between God and the saints. At the same time, this term would also be understood by the hearers in the light of the fact that the activities of Babylon, that God has remembered, are described as τὰ ἀδικήματα ('unrighteous deeds'), indicating that the contrast between the

---

[37] Allo [*Saint Jean: L'Apocalypse*, p. 276] refers to the bride's attire as 'vestments of innocence'.

[38] Aune, *Revelation 17-22*, p. 1031.

attire of the bride of the Lamb and the attire of the Great Whore has its basis in their diametrically opposed activities. Thus, the deeds that characterize the Great Whore are unrighteous, while the deeds that characterize God and the bride are righteous.[39] In addition to these philological and theological associations, it is difficult to imagine that the righteous deeds of the saints would be understood by Johannine hearers apart from the idea of works that has proven so important throughout the Apocalypse. The hearers would well remember that previously in the Apocalypse the word was used of good (2.2, 5, 19, 26; 3.1, 8, 15), bad (2.6), or incomplete (3.2) works; of works for which repentance should be, but is not always, offered (2.22; 9.20; 16.11); of works that are an extension of one's witness beyond death (14.13); of works that are the direct actions of God (15.3); and of works that are the basis of one's (future) judgment (18.6; cf. also 20.12, 13) and/or one's reward (2.23; cf, also 22.12). In this light the identity of the righteous deeds and the works of the saints could hardly be thought to be anything but coterminous. Specifically, such language is likely to bring to mind the activities of love, labor, patient endurance, keeping faith/keeping my (Jesus') word, faithful witness, service, moral purity, and discernment.[40] For the hearers, the fact that the fine linen given to the bride is at the same time the righteous deeds of the saints would well capture something of the divine human cooperation essential to a proper understanding of salvation in the Apocalypse.[41] In point of fact, the two-fold occurrence of the term τὰ δικαιώματα ('the righteous deeds') in the book captures this dialectic well indeed, for on the one hand it describes the righteous deeds of God carried out on behalf of the saints (15.4), while on the other hand it describes the righteous deeds of the saints carried out on behalf of God.[42] To

---

[39] McIlraith, "'For the Fine Linen Is the Righteous Deeds of the Saints'": Works and Wife in Revelation 19.8', pp. 526-27.

[40] On this whole question cf. the helpful discussion in McIlraith, "'For the Fine Linen Is the Righteous Deeds of the Saints'": Works and Wife in Revelation 19.8', pp. 512-29.

[41] Prigent (*L'Apocalypse de Saint Jean*, p. 399) calls the righteous deeds 'les manifestations humaines du salut, les signes terrestres du royaume ... les preuves evidentes de la puissance de Dieu', while Sweet (*Revelation*, p. 277) notes that her clothing is the sanctified lives of her members who have washed their robes in the blood of the Lamb (7.14).

[42] Smalley, *The Revelation to John*, p. 484.

put it still another way, their righteous deeds are consistent with his righteous deeds; their actions reflect the God who has given them salvation. Third, the identification of the fine linen with the righteous deeds of the saints confirms for the hearers that the bride of the Lamb is indeed identical to the saints.[43]

Verse 9 – With visions of the eschatological wedding of the Lamb and his bride capturing their imaginations, the hearers suddenly encounter still another voice, 'And he says to me, "Write: Blessed are those called to the marriage supper of the Lamb". And he says to me, "These are the true words of God".' It is not altogether clear that the hearers would initially understand the identity of the one who speaks to John for he is not immediately identified in the words they hear. As will be seen in v. 10, the one who speaks identifies himself as a fellow servant with John.[44] However the hearers would initially understand this speaker, the words that they encounter in 19.9 appear to have divine authorization. For the first time since 14.13 John is instructed to write, and on this occasion too the command is accompanied by a beatitude, the fourth such beatitude the hearers have encountered in the book (1.3; 14.13; 16.15). This beatitude, like its predecessors, conveys a blessing (and warning!) of eschatological proportions, 'Blessed are those called to the marriage supper of the Lamb'. Who are those called or invited to the marriage supper of the Lamb? It is quite likely that the first thing the hearers would think of is the fact that earlier (17.14) those who stand with the Lamb are referred to as the κλητοί ('called'), a term informed by the way in which the verb form from which it is derived, and occurs in 19.9, informs its usage here. Johannine hearers would recall that in the FG the verb καλέω ('call') is closely associated with discipleship (Jn 1.42), as well as functioning as a term

---

[43] Michaels, *Revelation*, p. 212.

[44] On the basis of a parallel to this passage occurring later in the book (22.8-9), where a fellow servant is explicitly identified as an angel, it is tempting to identify the one who speaks in 19.10 as an angel. But nowhere in 19.10 are the hearers told that this speaker is an angel. If the hearers discern that this speaker is indeed an angel, it is not altogether clear with which angelic figure they would identify him. On the one hand, the hearers might think him to be the last angel mentioned in the narrative, who both cast a boulder into the sea and spoke words of doom over the City (18.21-24) [so Smalley, *The Revelation to John*, p. 484]. On the other hand, they might well take this angel to be the one whom John encounters in 17.1, who shows John the mystery of the Great Whore [so Kiddle, *The Revelation of St John*, p. 380, amongst others].

of invitation for the disciples to the wedding at Cana (2.2), where they are described as believing in Jesus (2.11), and that in the Apocalypse it reveals the identity and even spiritual significance of places and/or individuals (Rev. 1.9; 11.8; 12.9; 16.16). There could be little doubt in the hearers' minds that those invited to the marriage supper of the Lamb are none other than those who follow the Lamb wherever he goes (14.4), who stand with him in battle (17.14). Oddly enough, those who are called to the supper are none other than the saints, the bride herself! Thus, once again, one image has morphed into another before the very eyes and ears of the hearers! The fact that οἱ ... κεκλημένοι ('those invited') is a perfect participle in 19.9 suggests that their call has been issued in the past and that this invitation is still valid. The idea of the marriage supper would not only alert the hearers to their own nearness to this eschatological event, but would also likely remind them of the eating imagery found already within the seven prophetic messages to the seven churches:[45] 'I will give to eat out of the tree of life' (2.7), 'I will give hidden manna' (2.17), 'I will dine with him and he with me' (3.20) and the theologically significant locations of the term supper in the FG (Jn 12.2; 13.2, 4; 21.20). The fact that the verb δειπνήσω ('dine' or 'sup') in Rev. 2.17 and the noun δεῖπνονη ('dinner' or 'supper') come from the same root would not likely be lost on the hearers. For a second time in this verse the hearers encounter the phrase, 'and he says to me'. On this occasion his words, "These are the true words of God'", convey a certain sense of finality and authority. Yet, there is a certain ambiguity in them as well, for they would perhaps strike the hearers as functioning equally well as an emphatic call to discerning obedience to the beatitude that immediately precedes (19.9), to all the words devoted to the mystery of the Great Whore (17.1-19.9),[46] and/or to all the words that precede it in the Apocalypse to this point (1.1-19.9).[47] Owing to such ambiguity perhaps the hearers would understand these words in a somewhat multivalent way. These are the true words of God spoken with regard to the marriage supper of the Lamb and those called to attend,

---

[45] Sweet, *Revelation*, p. 277.
[46] Beasley-Murray, *Revelation*, p. 275.
[47] Murphy, *Fallen Is Babylon*, p. 384.

with the implied warning it brings.[48] These are the true words of God spoken with regard to Babylon the Great, who despite her opulent wealth and the power that it brings will be judged as surely as there is a God; thus one must heed this warning. At the same time, these are the true words of God with regard to the revelation of Jesus Christ given to John, which must be heard and kept! This solemn pronouncement and call to discernment would give the hearers pause and perhaps a bit of time to reflect upon the significance of everything that precedes it in turn.

Verse 10 – With the enormity of these eschatological words weighing upon them, the hearers' attention is abruptly focused upon John and his quite shocking reaction to them, 'And I fell before his feet to worship him'. There could be no misunderstanding these words, for not only does John fall before the feet of this figure, an action that functions in the Apocalypse as one of the defining acts of worship (1.17; 4.10; 5.8, 14; 7.11; 11.16; 19.4), but he also uses the term προσκυνέω ('worship') to convey his intention to worship him, a term that has earlier been used for the worship of God (4.10; 5.14; 7.11; 11.1, 16; 14.7; 15.4; 19.4) and the Lamb (5.14), demons (9.20), the dragon (13.4), the beast (13.4, 8, 12; 14.9, 11), and the image of the beast (13.15; 14.9, 11; 16.2). Oddly enough, this is the first time in the book that the word is ever directly associated with John. Perhaps the hearers would understand John's actions as in part being the result of the ambiguity surrounding the identity of this speaker, thinking that if he speaks such divinely authorized words perhaps he shares in the divine power, and is himself divine.[49] But whereas John's earlier falling 'at the feet of Jesus as though dead' (1.17) appears to have been an involuntary reflex, his action here appears to be less involuntary and more intentional, somewhat reminiscent of the way in which he had marveled a great marvel at the appearance of the Great Whore (17.6), the kind of marveling that earlier led the inhabitants of the earth to worship the beast (13.3-4). If there are questions in the hearers' minds as to the appropriateness of John's actions they are quickly answered. For a third time in the span of two verses John hears the words, 'and he

---

[48] Sweet, *Revelation*, p. 280.
[49] K.E. Miller, 'The Nuptial Eschatology of Revelation 19-22', *CBQ* 60.2 (1998), p. 307.

says to me'. If John's earlier temptation to worship the Great Whore was met by an angelic rebuke (17.7), here his determination to worship the speaker is met with a more urgent and direct rebuke[50] in the form of a prohibition meaning something like, 'See that you do not do it!' The reason for this prohibition is underscored by the first word in the Greek sentence that follows the prohibition, σύνδουλός ('fellow servant'). The implications of John's intended worship would not need to be spelt out for the hearers, for they would know that what he intends amounts to idolatrous worship, owing to the fact that the one before whose feet he has bowed is not divine but a fellow servant! If John's temptation to worship the Great Whore earlier provided an opportunity for the hearers to examine their own hearts to determine the extent to which they themselves might be tempted to worship her as well, John's intention to worship this fellow servant would have no less of an impact. Here they discover that their stance against idolatrous worship, one of the dominant themes of this book, must be a comprehensively discerning one. For the temptation to idolatrous worship can infiltrate the church to the extent that the servants of God, rather than God, are worshipped![51] The next words the hearers encounter, 'I am your fellow servant and of your brothers who have the testimony of Jesus' would no doubt remind them of the only other place to this point in the book where nearly all of this vocabulary occurs together. When the fifth seal is opened, the souls under the altar, who have been slaughtered owing to the word of God and the testimony which they had, are told to wait until the number of their fellow servants and brothers who are about to be killed is full (6.9-11). Such remarkable similarities might suggest to the hearers that the speaker of these words is a fellow servant, one of the souls under the altar who has been killed to make the number of martyrs full.[52] As a representative of all the redeemed he steps out of the chorus of 19.6-8 and speaks individually to John, words of prophecy, true words of God, spoken prophetically on behalf of the holy and true Sovereign (6.10). On this view, the hearers might better understand John's intention to worship this speak-

---

[50] Michaels, *Revelation*, p. 213.
[51] Caird, *The Revelation of St. John*, p. 237.
[52] Contra Beale, *The Book of Revelation*, p. 946.

er, for if he is one of the souls slaughtered for his faithful witness and is an heir to a number of promises made to the one who overcomes, including reception of a new name that no one knows (2.17), authority to rule over the nations with an iron scepter and the morning star (2.26-28), and authority to sit on Jesus' throne with him (3.21), then perhaps in John's mind (and the minds of the hearers as well!) he is worthy of worship, for he would be thought to share extensively in Jesus' identity. But the speaker forbids such veneration for he is a fellow servant of John, as he is of John's brothers, those who have the testimony of Jesus. Owing to their faithful witness to the word of God and the testimony of Jesus they are John's fellow servants, they are his brothers in tribulation and kingdom and patient endurance (1.9). This fellow servant continues with what the hearers might take to be more 'true words of God' with the command, 'Worship God!' Not only is this message in conformity to that of the entire book, but it also redirects John's worship to its appropriate object. Only God is to be praised – not the dragon, nor the beast, nor the imagine of the beast, nor the Great Whore, not even those who have been slaughtered owing to the word of God and the testimony of Jesus – only God is to be praised! The call to worship God is in some ways justified by the following phrase, 'for the witness of Jesus is the Spirit of prophecy'. In this most intriguing verse a number of ideas would converge for the hearers. First, the hearers could not help but notice that the fellow servant's message to 'worship God' is connected to the following statement by the postpositive γὰρ ('for'), indicating a certain linkage between the two, suggesting that the worship of God is grounded in and supported by the witness of Jesus, the Spirit of Prophecy. Such linkage underscores the fact that since its beginning this Apocalypse has been concerned with the witness of Jesus, a witness intricately connected to the Spirit, and that this witness affirms and points again and again to the worship of God and the avoidance of idolatrous worship.[53] Second, while modern interpreters debate whether the phrase 'the witness of Jesus' is grammatically a subjective genitive or an objective genitive, whether Jesus' witness or the witness about Jesus is in view, it is unlikely that the hearers

---

[53] Koester, *Revelation and the End of All Things*, p. 170.

would make such a distinction at this point[54] for they have witnessed first hand how integrated these two dimensions of Jesus' witness are in the Apocalypse, for the witness about Jesus is indeed a message from Jesus.[55] The hearers are by now well aware of the fact that Jesus is the faithful witness *par excellence*, who is the first born of the dead, whose blood washed us from our sin and made us a kingdom, priests unto God (1.5-6; 3.4). Further they are aware of the fact that his own faithful witness is shared and/or emulated by his followers like John (1.2, 9), Antipas – my faithful witness (2.13), the souls under the altar (6.9-11), the two prophetic witnesses (11.3, 7), believers in general (12.11, 17; 17.6), as well as the 144,000 (14.4). In this, they are faithful unto death (3.10). It is also by this time abundantly clear to the hearers the extraordinarily close relationship that exists between Jesus and the Spirit. As the Apocalypse opens they are described together with the One who sits on the throne in the prologue (1.4-6). In the inaugural vision of Jesus, he stands in the midst of the seven lampstands. In the seven prophetic messages to the seven churches the words spoken by Jesus and the words spoken by the Spirit are coterminous (2.7, 11, 17, 29; 3.6, 13, 22), indicating that what Jesus says the Spirit says.[56] In the throne room scene, the intimate relationship between Jesus and the Spirit is conveyed by the fact that the Lamb has seven eyes, which are identified as the Seven Spirits of God that are sent out into all the earth (5.6).[57] The hearers also know that this same Spirit is closely associated with the life and ministry of Jesus' own faithful witness. Not only is this borne out in the example of the two prophetic witnesses who are given of Jesus' witness to prophesy, who are the two olive trees and lampstands that stand before the throne (11.3-4), and the apostles who are sent out in the power of the Seven Spirits before the throne (18.10), but also by the way in which the hearers are called to pneumatic discernment throughout (2.7, 11, 17, 29; 3.6, 13, 22; 11.8; 13.9-10, 18; 17.9-10). Thus, it should be abundantly clear that the witness of Jesus and the Spirit of Prophecy are intricately connected to one another and in the Apocalypse

---

[54] Murphy, *Fallen Is Babylon*, p. 385.

[55] Michaels, *Revelation*, p. 213.

[56] Mazzaferri, *The Genre of the Book of Revelation from a Source-Critical Perspective*, p. 310.

[57] Bauckham, *The Climax of Prophecy*, pp. 162-66.

cannot be understood apart from each other. That is to say that the witness of Jesus is quintessentially pneumatic, prophetic, dynamic, and active. The Spirit who goes out into all the world is the same Spirit that empowers the church's prophetic witness.[58] The same Spirit that speaks prophetically to the church is the same Spirit that speaks prophetically to the world, and in 19.10 these ideas are united. The hearers would not likely discern that this is simply a matter of a static equation between the witness of Jesus and the Spirit of Prophecy. For the community, participation in the faithful witness of Jesus is fueled by the Spirit of Prophecy.[59] It too is active and dynamic. It is the kind of pneumatic witness that is very much at home in a prophetic community, a community where the prophethood of all believers seems to be a basic understanding.[60] If the fellow servant who speaks in 19.9-10 is thought to be one of the souls under the altar, these words about the Spirit of Prophecy themselves come from this Spirit and are prophetic words spoken to a prophetic community! It is this Spirit that guarantees and underlies the truthfulness of their witness.[61]

The King of Kings and Lord of Lords: Victorious over All (19.11-21)

Verse 11 – But before the hearers can catch their collective breath, owing to the significance of the words of their fellow servant, their attention is directed to an event to which the entire book has been pointing, 'And I saw heaven opening, and behold a white horse, and the one who sat upon him was called faithful and true, and in righteousness he judges and makes war'. For the first time since 18.1 the hearers encounter the words 'I saw', indicating a new direction or the beginning of a new section in the book. As the hearers learn, the things that John saw are both old and new! In this remarkable narrative, the hearers have witnessed with John a number of heavenly revelations made possible by the opening of heaven to various degrees. They would well recall how it was by means of a

---

[58] Smalley, *The Revelation to John*, p. 478.

[59] Caird [*The Revelation of St. John*, p. 238] notes, 'It is the word spoken by God and attested by Jesus that the Spirit takes and puts into the mouth of the Christian prophet'.

[60] On this idea cf. Bauckham, *The Climax of Prophecy*, pp. 161-62 and Waddell, *The Spirit of the Book of Revelation*, pp. 189-91, 193-94.

[61] Miller, 'The Nuptial Eschatology of Revelation 19-22', p. 308.

door standing open in heaven that John gains access to the heavenly throne room scene after hearing the voice of Jesus invite him with the words, 'Come up here' (4.1); how, at the end of the seven trumpets announcing that the kingdom has come, the temple of God in heaven was opened revealing the ark of his covenant in his temple (11.19); and how the seven angels with the seven last plagues emerge from the opened temple of the tabernacle of witness in heaven (15.5)! But the opening of heaven in 19.11 suggests even greater access to the heavenly presence than any of these previous remarkable events, for coming from heaven will be the long awaited return of Jesus himself![62] The appearance of a white horse with the accompanying ἰδοὺ ('behold') would also be of significance for the hearers as they have earlier witnessed the emergence of a white horse (from heaven) that accompanied the breaking of the scroll's first seal by the Lamb (6.1). The appearance of the white horse in 19.11 could not help but cause the hearers to question whether or not these two white horses are one and the same. The previous white horse went out (from heaven) at the behest of one of the four living creatures with a στέφανος ('crown') on his head. He went out overcoming in order that he might overcome. His appearance, both his white color and his στέφανος ('crown'), appears to be in keeping with those who have ovecome to this point in the Apocalypse (2.10; 3.11; 4.4, 10) and it is for that purpose that he goes out, in order that he might overcome. Would the hearers not suspect that the white horse in 19.11 and its rider are also connected to such overcoming? Such a question would seem to receive an immediate answer when the one who sits upon the white horse of 19.11 is identified as the one called 'faithful and true'. Owing to the fact that Jesus is initially identified as the faithful witness in 1.5 and as the faithful and true witness in 3.14, there could be little confusion on the hearers' part as to the identity of this figure. For not only would the term faithful remind the hearers of Jesus' own faithfulness unto death and that of his followers, five of the eight occurrences of the term in the Apocalypse have reference to dying (1.5b; 2.10, 13; 3.14; 17.14), but the term true would also tie this rider to Jesus (3.7, 14) and to God who is true (6.10), as are his ways and

---

[62] McIlraith ['"For the Fine Linen Is the Righteous Deeds of the Saints"': Works and Wife in Revelation 19.8', p. 313] notes that heaven itself is now opened.

judgments (15.3; 16.7; 19.2, 9). As such, the very name of this rider reassures the hearers of the faithfulness and truthfulness of God and Jesus.[63] The hearers next learn that just as the rider of the first white horse went out to overcome, standing at the beginning of the judgments of God intended to bring humankind to repentance, so this rider goes out 'and in righteousness judges and makes war', executing the final judgment(s). Thus, the hearers might well discern that the recounting of the judgments of God in the Apocalypse are enveloped by white horses whose riders are intimately connected to executing the eschatological judgments of God! It might be difficult for the hearers to believe that the resemblance between these two horses and riders is fortuitous.[64] The fact that this rider's actions of judging and making war are grounded in righteousness underscores all the more the tight connection between this rider and God who is righteous both in his person (16.5) and ways (15.3; 16.7; 19.2), as well as emphasizing the relationship between the rider and the bride of the Lamb, who has been given a garment that consists of the righteous deeds of the saints.[65] Significantly, the verbs used to describe the actions of the rider, judging and making war, are both found in the present tense, perhaps suggesting to the hearers that these are ongoing characteristics of this rider.[66] The hearers might also remember that the making of war has earlier been attributed to the Lamb with regard to his church (2.16) as well as his enemies (17.14).[67] These actions would rather clearly include salvific acts on behalf of his people.[68]

Verse 12 – The description of this rider, unlike the description of the rider on the first white horse, continues in some detail in the next words the hearers encounter, 'His eyes as a flame of fire, and upon his head many diadems, having a name written which no one knew except him'. If the description of this rider as faithful and true

---

[63] T.B. Slater, *Christ and Community: A Socio-Historical Study of the Christology and Revelation* (JSNTS 178; Sheffield: Sheffield Academic Press, 1999), pp. 213-14.

[64] Prigent, *L'Apocalypse de Saint Jean*, pp. 415-16.

[65] McIlraith, '"For the Fine Linen Is the Righteous Deeds of the Saints": Works and Wife in Revelation 19.8', p. 314.

[66] Allo, *Saint Jean: L'Apocalypse*, p. 279.

[67] Sweet, *Revelation*, p. 282.

[68] M. Rissi, *Die Zukunft der Welt: Eine exegetische Studie über Johannesoffenbarung 19, 11 bis 22, 15* (Basel: Verlag Friedrich Reinhardt, 1966), p. 19.

indicates his identity for the hearers, the next words confirm it for some of these words have appeared before with reference to Jesus. The mention of 'his eyes as a flame of fire' would not only remind the hearers of the stunning vision of Jesus with which the revelation begins (1.14), but also of his prophetic message to the church in Thyatira (2.18). As in those previous passages, so in 19.12 this imagery would remind the hearers of his penetrating prophetic vision from which nothing is hidden.[69] Additionally, by this point the hearers may understand that his eyes as a flame of fire are intimately connected to the Seven Spirits before the throne of God (1.4), which in point of fact are the seven eyes of the Lamb that are sent out into all the earth (5.6). Thus, the description of this rider's eyes makes clear to the hearers that the rider here described is none other than the resurrected Jesus described in Revelation 1-3.[70] The fact that upon his head are many διαδήματα ('diadems') also holds significance for the hearers. In contrast to a στέφανος ('crown') that was normally given to one who overcomes, the διάδημα ('diadem') signified kingship over a particular kingdom or kingdoms, and unlike the laurel wreath of the crown, the diadem was, strictly speaking, a band worn around a tiara.[71] The hearers would likely remember that earlier the great red dragon was described as wearing seven diadems (12.3), a reference to his pretensions to absolute authority, and that the beast wore ten diadems, one for each king and their respective kingdoms (13.1). However, this rider is described as wearing many diadems, suggesting a number far greater than seven or ten,[72] indicating that his authority is unlimited and corresponds perfectly to the reality of one earlier called the Lord or lords and King of kings (17.14).[73] It is not altogether clear if the next phrase, 'having a name written which no one knows except he', would be taken by the hearers to mean that this name was written upon the diadems that the rider wears or upon the rider's head, as seems to be the case with the blasphemous names of the beast in 13.1. De-

---

[69] Kiddle, *The Revelation of St John*, p. 384 and Mounce, *The Book of Revelation*, p. 344.

[70] Slater, *Christ and Community: A Socio-Historical Study of the Christology and Revelation*, p. 222.

[71] C.J. Hemer, 'Crown, Scepter, Rod', *NIDNNT*, I, p. 405.

[72] Beasley-Murray, *Revelation*, p. 279.

[73] Prigent, *L'Apocalypse de Saint Jean*, p. 417 and Aune, *Revelation 17-22*, p. 1054.

spite the fact that the name is both written (for all to see) and at the same time unknown to all but the rider himself, it is likely that the hearers would be able to make their way through such an enigmatic paradox.[74] On the one hand, the name itself would be thought to have a special significance as 'written', owing to the way in which a variety of things written (and unwritten!) in the Apocalypse are of eschatological significance (1.3, 11, 19; 2.1, 8, 12, 17, 18; 3.1, 7, 12, 14; 5.1; 10.4; 13.8; 14.1, 13; 17.5, 8; 19.9). Not only do such written things often indicate one's spiritual identity in the book, but the written-ness of the Apocalypse itself would also underscore the extent to which this written name is part of the words of prophecy written in this book. On the other hand, the fact that this name is written implies that it is observable, at least to John, and in what follows will have some sort of testamentary function as it both reveals and conceals. The fact that no one knows the name except for the rider underscores its mysterious quality, indicating something of the unknown, even secret power of its bearer.[75] For if to know one's name implies that one can gain some knowledge and mastery over the one known, as was commonly thought, to have a secret name indicates something of the depth and superabundance of power that resides in its bearer; power that cannot be usurped.[76] It is difficult to believe that this imagery would not remind the hearers of the resurrected Jesus' promise to the one who overcomes, 'I will give to him a white stone and upon the stone a new name written which no one knows except the one who receives it' (2.17). The eschatological meaning of this promise would take on greater significance as the hearers now learn that the new name they will receive is the unknown name written upon the rider on the white horse. The fact that both he and they know this name would be yet another example of the way in which the followers of Jesus share in his identity and eschatological rewards, revealing that they too will have access to its power and depth. It is not insignificant that mention of the name that only he knows occurs before the final eschatological battle, implying that despite the fact that so much has been

---

[74] McIlraith, "'For the Fine Linen Is the Righteous Deeds of the Saints'": Works and Wife in Revelation 19.8', p. 313.

[75] Kiddle, *The Revelation of Saint John*, p. 385.

[76] Gause, *Revelation*, p. 244.

revealed about Jesus in this book there are deeper depths to him that remain unfathomable.

Verse 13 – The description of the rider continues with the words, 'and he was wearing a garment dipped in blood, and his name is called the Word of God'. While the description of the rider's garment as dipped in blood might very well remind the hearers of the judgments of God (8.7, 8; 11.6; 16.3, 4) and the Lamb's ability to make war (17.14), thus serving as an anticipation of the final battle that lies ahead,[77] it is next to impossible to believe that the hearers would not understand this mention of blood as somehow being informed by the numerous previous references to the death of Jesus and his saints (1.8; 5.9; 6.10; 7.14; 8.8; 12.11; 14.20; 16.6; 17.6; 18.24; 19.2). The rider who comes on this white horse, the rider who is called faithful and true, is the very one whose shed blood has loosed us from our sins and has purchased for God those out of every tribe and tongue and people and nation. The garment dipped in blood points to the nature of his victory or overcoming that enables him to confront all the nations of the earth, for he has been slaughtered for them, shedding his blood for them,[78] a past act to which this perfect passive participle points. Thus, the hearers would likely understand that the judging and making war he carries out are salvific acts based on his atoning life and death.[79] The imagery of the robe dipped in blood might even remind the hearers of the fact that this very verb is used by Jesus in the FG in his words that identify his betrayer, 'That is the one to whom I dip the morsel and I will give to him. Therefore, dipping the morsel he received and gave it to Judas Simon Iscariot' (Jn 13.26). Thus, even in this picture of the returning Jesus, who judges and makes war in righteousness, the hearers discover that the mention of his shed blood carries with it a reminder of his betrayal, a reality with which some of the hearers might be all too familiar. In addition to the description of his robe the hearers learn, 'and his name was called the Word of God'. Following fast on the heels of learning that this rider has a name written that only he knows, the hearers discover that he also has a name with which they are familiar but have not en-

---

[77] Ladd, *Revelation*, p. 254.

[78] Koester, *Revelation and the End of All Things*, p. 176.

[79] Origen (Com. Jo. vi.173) understands this detail as a symbol of Christ's incarnation and sacrifice. Cf. Kovacs and Rowland, *Revelation*, p. 196.

countered as a name before. It is difficult to imagine very many Johannine hearers for whom this name would not call to mind the prologue of the FG, where the Logos is described as existing before the creation of the world, as being in fellowship with God, as being God himself (Jn 1.1), as being the creator of the world (1.3), and as being the one through whom all might believe and have authority to become children of God (1.11-13). It is through this Logos who became flesh, who is full of grace and truth (1.14) that we have all received one grace after another (1.16), through whom the Father is revealed (1.18). The revelation that this rider on the white horse is the Word of God would especially resonate with Johannine hearers as they come to realize that the Logos through whom everything was created is the same Logos through whom the purpose of creation is fulfilled by means of his judging and making war in righteousness;[80] that the one who was not received by his own (1.11) will 'come with the clouds, and every eye will see him even those who pierced him, and all the tribes of the earth will mourn because of him' (Rev. 1.7). The perfect passive verb κέκληται ('was called') suggests that this name is one of long standing, given sometime in the past, continuing to remain valid. In this case, the past goes back all the way to eternity.

Verse 14 – Though such a revelation may leave the hearers filled with a desire to reflect more fully upon this recent discovery, they immediately learn that the rider on the white horse has companions, 'And the armies in heaven follow him upon white horses, wearing white, pure fine linen'. Perhaps the first thing the hearers would think of upon encountering these words is the only other mention of armies to this point in the Apocalypse (9.16-19), where an army of 200,000,000 riders and horses were involved in the destruction of a third of humankind. Dressed for battle, these horses and riders inflict punishment and death in order that the rest of humankind might repent. In the few words of 19.14 the hearers learn several things about the armies that accompany the rider on the white horse. First, these armies are said to be in heaven. While it is possible that such a detail might lead the hearers to conclude that these armies are comprised of myriads of angels, nothing in the text itself suggests such a conclusion other than the fact that they are located

---

[80] Beasley-Murray, *Revelation*, p. 280.

in heaven. Second, the hearers learn that these armies follow the rider on the white horse, no doubt reminding them of the 144,000 who follow the Lamb wherever he goes (14.4) and those called and elect and faithful who are with the Lamb who makes war (17.14), suggesting that these armies are comprised of those who are faithful witnesses to the Lamb.[81] Third, these armies like the rider are on white horses as well, indicating that they stand as one with the one who is faithful and true and that they too are overcomers and will overcome even as he.[82] Fourth, their clothing in white, pure fine linen reveals that instead of being dressed for battle, as the armies in 9.16-19, these armies are dressed for a joyous festival of celebration.[83] In point of fact, their attire is identical to that of the bride of the Lamb,[84] who is prepared for the marriage supper of the Lamb, indicating that just as the image of the saints has morphed from bride to wedding guest, so it now morphs into one of the heavenly armies who accompany the rider on the white horse. Such identification between the rider and his armies imply that they have overcome and been victorious in the same way, by way of their faithful witness even unto death.

Verse 15 – After a brief description of his companions, the hearers encounter additional words about the rider, 'And out of his mouth comes a sharp sword, in order that he might strike the nations and he will shepherd them with a rod of iron; and he tramples the wine press of the wine of the anger of the wrath of God the All Powerful One'. The hearers might well be struck by the fact that despite the presence of the armies that accompany this rider, he alone is described as being armed for battle! The only weapon mentioned is the sharp sword that comes from his mouth, a weapon with which the hearers would be well acquainted.[85] For in the stunning inaugural vision of the resurrected Jesus with which the book begins the hearers learn that a sharp two-edged sword comes from his mouth (1.16). This detail appears later as a mark of identification on the lips of Jesus as he speaks to the church in Pergamum,

---

[81] Sweet, *Revelation*, p. 283.
[82] Caird, *The Revelation of St. John*, p. 244.
[83] Koester, *Revelation and the End of All Things*, p. 177.
[84] McIlraith, "For the Fine Linen Is the Righteous Deeds of the Saints': Works and Wife in Revelation 19.8', p. 525.
[85] Metzger, *Breaking the Code*, p. 91.

indicating that the Jesus of the vision is the same one who speaks prophetically to this community (2.12), and this detail recurs in his words of warning to this same church that if they do not repent, 'I will come to you quickly, and I will make war with them with the sword of my mouth' (2.16). Thus, the sharp sword that emerges from the rider's mouth would remind the hearers of the power of his prophetic pronouncements as well as his ability to make war with the word of his mouth. But the hearers are not left to wonder as to the purpose of the sharp sword that comes from his mouth but are informed of its purpose by the ἵνα ('in order that') clause that follows. The purpose of this weaponry is 'in order that he might strike the nations'. The imagery of striking would be familiar to the hearers from the authority of the two prophetic witnesses to strike the earth with every kind of plague (11.6) and suggests that the nations will finally receive their due punishment. But this making of war by the sword of his mouth is not an end in itself, for 'he will shepherd them with a rod of iron'. By this point the hearers will have come to understand the messianic imagery of shepherding with an iron rod (Isa. 49.2) as having reference to the Lamb who has the authority to perform this task (Rev. 7.17; 12.5), as well as to give this authority to the one who overcomes (2.27). The idea appears to be wide enough to include kind and gentle tending of the flock, on the one hand, to strong and dominating action that is sometimes required, on the other hand. In the context of 19.15 the fact that such shepherding is mentioned after the action of striking may be taken as a hopeful sign by the hearers, suggesting that even in the context of the return of Jesus, who judges and makes war in righteousness, hope for the conversion of the nations has not been completely lost nor forgotten![86] To the imagery of the sharp sword for striking and the iron rod for shepherding are added, 'and he tramples the wine press of the wine of the anger of the wrath of God the All Powerful One'. Reference to the rider's action of trampling would no doubt remind the hearers of the fact the holy city has previously been described as being trampled for forty-two months by the nations/gentiles (11.1-2). Would such associations suggest to them that the nations, who had earlier trampled the holy city, are now themselves to be trampled by the rider on the white

---

[86] Sweet, *Revelation*, p. 283.

horse? In any case, the hearers would no doubt remember that the winepress of the wrath of the great God has earlier been encountered and that the effects of the trampling of this wine press is the production of blood up to the bridles of the horses (14.19-20). They might also recall a previous mention of 'the cup of the wine of the anger of his wrath' that Babylon the Great was given owing to the fact that God remembered her (16.19).[87] It appears that a variety of ideas would converge for the hearers in a phrase that is the longest string of words in the genitive case in the whole of the Apocalypse,[88] the wine press 'of the wine of the anger of the wrath of God the All Powerful One', where ten consecutive words in the Greek text appear in the genitive case. In this construction the wine press of God's judgment and the displeasure of God with unrepentant humanity combine with the twofold name of God, which includes the name that underscores his unrivaled power in the universe. Thus, the eschatological judgment of God culminates in the activity of the rider on the white horse, who judges and makes war in righteousness.

Verse 16 – Perhaps somewhat overwhelmed by this description of the rider on the white horse, the hearers learn even more about him in the words that follow, 'And he has upon his garment/robe and upon his thigh a name written: King of kings and Lord of lords'. Earlier the hearers learned that the rider on the white horse had a name written (upon the bands of the diadems?) that no one knows except he, now they learn that he has a name that is not only prominently displayed but one with which they are familiar. The importance of the location of this name is underscored by the fact that the locations where the name is written stand first in the Greek sentence. Apparently the rider bears these names upon his garment and in his person, indicating the extent to which this name is connected to and representative of his person. The fact that the thigh is normally the place where one's sword was worn may even underscore for the hearers the significance of the rider's sword all the more.[89] The hearers have encountered the name King of kings and Lord of lords, in the reverse order, already in 17.14, which con-

---

[87] Smalley, *The Revelation to John*, p. 494.
[88] Aune, *Revelation 17-22*, p. 1062.
[89] Smalley, *The Revelation to John*, p. 495.

veyed several aspects of meaning with regard to this identification. For Jesus here to be identified as King of kings draws upon the rich Johannine tradition about his kingship (Jn 1.49; 6.15; 12.13, 15; 18.33, 37, 39; 19.3, 12, 14, 15, 19, 21), the fact that one of the first things the hearers learn about Jesus in the Apocalypse is that he is the ruler of the kings of the earth (Rev. 1.5), the fact that the kings of the earth sometimes function in the Apocalypse either as those being at enmity with God and the Lamb (6.15; 16.12, 14) and/or as those to whom prophetic witness is to be given (10.11), and that on occasion God himself is spoken of as king (15.3). Thus, for the Lamb here to be called the King of kings underscores Jesus' inherent identity as king, indicating that his power is unrivaled! The second part of this extraordinary attribution would remind the hearers that to this point in the Apocalypse the term κύριος ('lord') has been frequently applied to 'the One who sits on the throne', 'the Lord, God, the All Powerful One' (1.8; 4.8, 11; 11.4, 15, 17; 15.3, 4; 16.7), with the word used with reference to Jesus on only one occasion (11.8). Thus, the use of this title for the Lamb in 17.14 would, no doubt, impress further upon the hearers the close relationship between God and the Lamb, on the one hand, and the superiority of Jesus over all the kings of the earth, on the other hand. Together, these titles make his absolute sovereignty clear.[90] He is quite simply without any rivals. Perhaps such language, 'King of kings and Lord of lords', unrivaled in Jewish messianic expectation,[91] would reinforce for the hearers that only the rider on the white horse is armed for battle, not his armies, and that he alone, the King of kings and Lord of lords, will fight it.[92] And with this extraordinary title the description of the rider is complete.

Verses 17-18 – With such a stunning description of the rider upon the white horse ringing in their ears, the hearers' attention is now directed to one of the angels, 'And I saw one angel standing in

---

[90] P.W. Skehan ['King of Kings, Lord of Lords', *CBQ* 10.4 (1948), p. 398] argues that 'the combination "King of Kings, Lord of Lords", in Aramaic מלך מלכין מרא מרון adds up to 777', though the fact that the word 'and' must be omitted in order to arrive at this numerical value makes its significance less certain.

[91] Slater, *Christ and Community: A Socio-Historical Study of the Christology and Revelation*, p. 219.

[92] Beasley-Murray, *Revelation*, p. 281.

Figure 14
Christ the Conqueror
Beatus at Osma (Burgo de Osma, Archivo de la catedral)

the sun, and he cried with a great voice to all the birds that were flying in the mid heavens, "Come, gather into the great supper of God, in order that you might eat flesh of kings and flesh of captains and flesh of mighty and flesh of horses and those sitting upon them and flesh of all free and slave and small and great'". For the first time since the description of the rider on the white horse began (19.11) the hearers encounter another 'I saw', indicating that a new subject or slightly new direction is being introduced into the story. Attention is focused upon an angel whose prominent position on or in the sun ensures a universal hearing,[93] reminding of the eagle that flies in the mid heaven who announces the three woes that are to come upon the earth (8.13) and the other angel who flies in mid-heaven who proclaims an eternal gospel to those upon the earth – 'to fear God and give him glory and worship the maker of heaven and earth' (14.6-7).[94] The hearers may well suspect that the message of this angel will be no less significant and that it too may be connected to the judgments of God. The angel of 19.17, like his predecessors, speaks with a great voice, so great it appears that all the birds flying in the mid-heavens can hear it. The fact that birds have once before been encountered in the book (18.2) may lead the hearers to wonder as to their function here. The angel's message for them to 'come' is filled with urgency, like the invitation of the Samaritan woman to the villagers to 'come see a man ...' (Jn 4.29), as is the command to 'gather together', which the hearers would know in the Johannine tradition can appear with both positive (Jn 4.36; 6.12, 13; 11.52; 18.2) and negative connotations (11.47; 15.6), but never without theological significance. They would also know that in the Apocalypse this term is used to describe the gathering together of the kings of the whole earth for the war of the great day of God the All Powerful One (Rev. 16.14), at a place named Harmegedon (16.16).[95] As the hearers will discover the invitation to the birds of the air to gather together is not unrelated to these previously described gatherings for war! Specifically, these birds are invited to 'the great feast of God'. Upon first encounter the hearers might well be tempted to think that this supper is the same supper

---

[93] Smalley, *The Revelation to John*, p. 479.
[94] Schussler-Fiorenza, *Revelation*, p. 106.
[95] Sweet, *Revelation*, p. 285.

mentioned earlier, the marriage supper of the Lamb, for it too would seem to qualify as a great supper of God. But as the hearers take in the words that follow, they discover that this great supper stands as a ghastly counterpart to the marriage supper of the Lamb![96] The purpose of the invitation is made clear by the appearance of a ἵνα ('in order that') clause that follows. The birds of the air are invited, in order that they might eat the flesh of all humans (and horses too!). The list which follows is a remarkable one and would remind the hearers of a similar list in 6.15, where humankind that opposes God is divided into seven divisions comprised of the kings of the earth and the great men and the captains and the rich and the strong and each slave and free. While similar to the previous list, five of the same groups reappear in the list of 19.18, this latter list is distinctive in several ways. First, in the list of 19.18 the hearers encounter the word σάρκας ('flesh') five times, making clear the all flesh menu that awaits the birds of the air. The hearers might well recall that the only previous occurrence of 'flesh' in the Apocalypse has reference to the flesh of the Great Whore, which is also to be eaten by the ten kings and the beast they serve (17.16). Such an ominous association would heighten the sense of drama for them in 19.18. It is possible that the five-fold mention of flesh might even be understood by the hearers to provide a basic structure revealing the five groups into which all humanity might be divided. Second, the fact that nine different groups are actually named in this verse reveals a sense of growing intensity, perhaps suggesting that this list is an even more comprehensive list than the one previously encountered in 6.15. Third, this list includes the flesh of horses, perhaps indicating that the flesh that is to be eaten by the birds will be the result of war. Fourth, significantly this invitation for the birds of the air to gather together is issued even before these enemies are described as assembled, underscoring for the hearers God's absolute sense of sovereignty.[97] For if God is in control in advance of this rebellion, as the hearers may well think, he would not be unaware of the threatening circumstances that face the Johannine church. The extraordinarily graphic nature of this verse, along with the contrasting marriage supper of the Lamb,

---

[96] Beasley-Murray, *Revelation*, p. 282.
[97] Beale, *The Book of Revelation*, p. 965.

would offer a stark warning (and promise) to hearers who might be tempted to settle for the complacency of accommodation to the beast and Babylon the Great rather than to maintain their faithful witness.[98] The message is very clear. Absolutely no one will be exempt from the judgment inherent for those who stand in opposition to the rider on the white horse. No one will escape. No favoritism will be shown.[99]

Verse 19 – This graphic account is followed by additional words, 'And I saw the beast and the kings of the earth with their armies gathered together to make war with the one who sits upon the horse and with his army'. For a third time in the span of nine verses the hearers encounter the words 'I saw', again indicating a slightly new direction in the story line. The new focus of attention is upon those who have now gathered together for battle. As the hearers encounter these words they likely are reminded of at least two things. First, this gathering of powers in opposition to the rider on the white horse is very reminiscent of those who have been gathered together by the demonic spirits to the war of the great day of God (16.14), the battle of Harmagedon (16.16).[100] The similarities would no doubt suggest to the hearers that the battle of Harmagedon has finally arrived![101] Second, the hearers may well recall that the last mention of the beast was in the context of the destruction of the Great Whore (17.17),[102] where ironically the beast's actions is part of the completion of the words of God. Thus, the battle lines are drawn with the beast and the kings of the earth and their armies on one side and the one who sits upon the white horse and his army on the other side. The hearers might well believe that the culmination of their numerous expectations with regard to the end is at hand. The destruction of the Great Whore has been documented (17.1-18.24); could the destruction of the beast be far behind? The appearance of the rider on the white horse, the one called faithful and true, results in united opposition to him by those

---

[98] Koester, *Revelation and the End of All Things*, pp. 178-79.
[99] Slater, *Christ and Community: A Socio-Historical Study of the Christology and Revelation*, p. 228.
[100] Smalley, *The Revelation to John*, p. 497.
[101] Ladd, *Revelation*, p. 257.
[102] Prigent, *L'Apocalypse de Saint Jean*, p. 423.

who remain unrepentant, despite all the opportunities given to repent and worship God.[103]

Verse 20 – The expectations of the hearers that they are not far from the demise of the beast are not disappointed for they next learn, 'And the beast was seized and with him the false prophet, the one who did signs before him, with which he deceived those who received the mark of the beast and those who worshipped his image'. After the extensive description of the destruction of Babylon the Great and the dramatic build up to the confrontation of the beast and the rider on the white horse, the hearers might well be surprised that this battle is not described in any great detail. In point of fact, the battle is not really described at all, only its results! If the hearers had any questions as to the involvement of the army dressed in white, pure fine linen that accompanies the rider, they discover that they are not involved in the combat at all – for the rider on the white horse does all the fighting.[104] Beginning with the first word [after 'and'] in the Greek text this understanding is conveyed, as the term ἐπιάσθη ('was seized') takes the form of a divine passive, where the subject of the action is left unstated, the implication being that such action is the activity of God, in this case the rider on the white horse. Though the only occurrence of the term 'seize' in the Apocalypse, Johannine hearers would be quite familiar with it as it often occurs in Johannine thought to describe the intentions of Jesus' opponents to seize or arrest him (Jn 7.30, 32, 44; 8.20; 10.39; 11.57) and even occurs to describe the catching of fish (21.3, 10).[105] Clearly for the hearers, the appearance of this word would set the tone for what follows in this verse. That which is seized is none other than the beast himself and with him the false prophet. No struggle ensues, no battle rages. The beast and the false prophet are completely outmatched. They are not equal to the King of kings and Lord of lords! Significantly, the false prophet is described in considerable detail, a description that would encourage the hearers to reflect on his person and activity all the more. Called 'the false prophet' for only the second time in the book (16.13), the description of his activities that follow reveal that he is none other

---

[103] J.W. Mealy, *After the Thousand Years: Resurrection and Judgment in Revelation 20* (JSNTS 70; Sheffield: JSOT Press, 1992), p. 91.

[104] Aune, *Revelation 17-22*, p. 1065.

[105] Allo, *Saint Jean: L'Apocalypse*, p. 282.

than the other beast who comes from the earth and, though he looks like a lamb, he speaks as a dragon (13.11). Specifically, the hearers are reminded of the signs that the false prophet performed 'before the beast', a phrase that conveys the idea of worship, and the role these signs played in deceiving those who ultimately received the mark of the beast and who worship his image.[106] If the testimony of Jesus is the Spirit of prophecy (19.10) – a testimony and prophetic work in which the hearers share – in the false prophet they encounter the diametric opposite, one who deceives rather than leads to the truth, one who leads to and promotes idolatrous worship instead of one who leads to the true worship of God. Not only did the false prophet's work result in the deception of the inhabitants of the world to receive the mark of the beast (the idea of receiving underscoring the active nature of the participation of those so deceived)[107] and worship his image, but it also results in the death of all those who would not join in his deception and engage in the idolatrous worship he promotes (13.15-17). The words the hearers encounter in 19.20 reveal that not only are the origins of the beast and the false prophet intimately connected (13.1-18) but their end is intimately connected as well.[108] In point of fact, the next words the hearers encounter make this all the clearer, 'The two were cast living into the lake of fire kept burning with sulfur'. The order of the Greek text, which literally reads something like, 'Living were cast the two into the lake …', emphasizes the nature of their punishment, perhaps recalling the fate of the rebels in Num. 16.20,[109] with the first word ζῶντες ('living') underscoring the fierceness of the punishment. Such language may suggest something more than annihilation to the hearers,[110] especially given the fact that this term is often used of Jesus (Rev. 1.18; 2.8) and God (7.2), underscoring the eternality of the latter (4.9, 10; 10.6; 15.7)! The place where the beast and false prophet are cast would also be of significance for the hearers. First, they might well recall the

---

[106] Murphy, *Fallen Is Babylon*, p. 349.

[107] Resseguie, *The Revelation of John*, p. 241. Christopher C. Rowland, 'The Book of Revelation, Introduction, Commentary, and Reflections', in *The New Interpreter's Bible* 12 (ed. L.E. Keck; Nashville: Abingdon, 1998), p. 700.

[108] Michaels, *Revelation*, p. 219.

[109] Sweet, *Revelation*, p. 286.

[110] Smalley, *The Revelation to John*, p. 499.

words of the angel who warned that those who worship the beast and receive his mark would suffer this very punishment (14.9-10)! Thus, the beast and the false prophet are now seen to suffer the very punishment that their deceptive idolatry led others toward. Second, the contents of this lake – ongoing fire and noxious sulfur – would indicate that this lake is an abode of death not life, the imagery even suggesting an on-going death.[111] Thus, despite the claims of the beast and the false prophet to determine who lives and who dies (13.7, 15), they themselves inherit a place of ongoing death! Third, the individual elements found in the lake would have significance for the hearers as well. For example, it might well be recalled that one of the signs that the false prophet performed in order to deceive the inhabitants of the earth was to call down fire from heaven. Ironically, the false prophet now meets his demise in the lake of the burning fire of God's judgment. While the mention of sulfur might well remind the hearers of the punishment of Sodom and Gomorrah (Gen. 19.24),[112] at the same time the hearers might now come to understand that their earlier encounters with the sulfur that came from the mouths of the instruments of God's redemptive judgments in 9.17-18 were actually gracious invitations to those who witnessed such to avoid as their destiny a lake of sulfur, of which these earlier appearances stood as anticipations! Thus, in one verse the hearers learn of the dispatch of the beast and the false prophet at the hands of the rider on the white horse.

Verse 21 – Perhaps with their heads spinning from the pace of this account the hearers quickly learn of the battle's conclusion, 'And the rest were killed with the sword of the one who sits upon the horse that comes out of his mouth, and all the birds gorged themselves out of their flesh'. The rest of those involved in the battle would obviously be thought to include the kings of the earth and their armies (19.19),[113] which would no doubt include captains, strong men, horses, cavalrymen, free, slave, small, and great – all those who have assembled to make war with the rider on the white horse. As with the seizure of the beast and the false prophet and their subsequent casting into the lake of fire, so the battle between

---

[111] Sweet, *Revelation*, p. 285 and Prigent, *L'Apocalypse de Saint Jean*, p. 424.

[112] Mounce, *The Book of Revelation*, p. 349.

[113] Aune, *Revelation 17-22*, p. 1067.

the rest and the rider on the white horse is short and to the point. Again, only the rider on the white horse is involved in the fighting,[114] as the rest are all put to death by the sword that comes out of his mouth. In the Greek text reference to 'the one who sits upon the horse' is surrounded by reference to his weapon as the words 'with the sword' standing before it and the words 'that comes out of his mouth' following it, underscoring both the one who acts and the weapon that comes from his mouth. The fact that all the birds gorge themselves on their flesh reveals several things to the hearers. First, it underscores the fact that the victory by the one who rides the white horse is a one-sided one, again demonstrating that this King of kings and Lord of lords has no rivals. His victory over the kings and their armies makes clear that he is indeed the ruler of all the kings of the earth (1.5)! Second, the fact that the victims of this war are eaten by the birds of the air indicates that they have been denied a proper burial, a humiliation that might be thought by the hearers to be an avenging judgment for the similar treatment of the two prophetic witnesses earlier in the book (11.8-10).[115] Third, the fact that the birds now gorge themselves on the flesh of the fallen fulfils the purpose of their angelic call to gather together for the great supper of God (19.17), with which this section begins, forming an inclusio around the action of 19.17-21. In retrospect, these verses appear to take on the following structure:

> The birds are invited to the great supper of God (19.17)
>> The armies are described (19.18)
>>> The beast gathers his armies (19.19)
>>>> The beast and the false prophet are captured and thrown into the lake of fire (19.20)
>> The armies are killed by the sword of his mouth (19.21)
> The birds feast on the flesh of the slain (19.21).[116]

In gruesome contrast to the imagery of the marriage supper of the Lamb and the fullness that resulted from Jesus' feeding the 5,000 in the FG, where the word χορτάζω ('eating one's fill') is also found

---

[114] Gause, *Revelation*, p. 250.
[115] Kiddle, *The Revelation of St John*, p. 389.
[116] Michaels, *Revelation*, p. 218.

(Jn 6.24), the sight of the birds gorging themselves graphically drives home the point to the hearers that compromise with the beast and the Great Whore leads to absolute desolation, death, and humiliation! And with this, the vindication of the saints appears to be complete, for those who have opposed God and his people have now met their ultimate fate.[117]

The Thousand-Year Reign (20.1-10)

Verse 1 – The hearers are allowed very little time to reflect upon the truly extraordinary eschatological events described in chapter 19 for their attention is immediately directed to yet another aspect of John's vision, 'And I saw an angel coming down out of heaven having the key of the Abyss and a great chain in his hand'. The words 'and I saw' indicates to the hearers that John's visionary experience continues with attention now given to a new detail, a detail that stands in continuity with the previous frequent occurrences of the phrase 'and I saw' beginning in 19.11 and continuing in strategic locations throughout this section of the Apocalypse (19.11, 17, 19). Despite contemporary claims to the contrary, it is difficult to imagine that Johannnine hearers would not take these words in continuity with what precedes and in some sense of chronological development. It might strike the hearers as a bit odd that after the detailed description of the rider on the white horse and his disposing of the beast, the false prophet, and all those who stood with them in opposition to this rider, that attention is suddenly shifted to an angel. Such a shift in focus, in and of itself, would create within the hearers a great sense of expectancy, for not only does this angel remind them of other significant angelic figures who have appeared throughout the book doing the work of God, but the physical description of what this angel bears is quite intriguing on its own. The origin of this angel, 'coming down out of heaven', indicates that he comes with divine authority and a sense of divine commission, which the instruments in his hands reveal. The fact that he has the key to the Abyss would remind the hearers of the star that was given the key to the shaft of the Abyss at the time the fifth angel trumpeted (9.1), whose actions released an army of locusts who torment the inhabitants of the earth. In fact, the hearers might well

---

[117] Slater, *Christ and Community: A Socio-Historical Study of the Christology and Revelation*, p. 229.

believe that the angel introduced in 20.1 is the same angel as the one described as the angel of the Abyss mentioned in 9.11, where he is given the names Destruction and Destroyer, in Hebrew and Greek respectively, names reminiscent of the Destroyer of Exod. 12.23. If so, the hearers would recognize the instruments in his hands as indicating his authority over the Abyss, on the one hand, and his ability to subdue any opponent with the great chain he possesses, on the other hand. While in the Apocalypse the Abyss is the place of origin of the tormenting locusts (9.1, 2, 11) and the beast (11.7; 17.8), it is clear that God himself controls the Abyss and that God himself has authority over it. Owing to the fact that the rider on the white horse has apparently destroyed all his opponents but one, perhaps the hearers anticipate that the appearance of this angel is connected to the judgment of the final cosmic opponent, the Dragon.

Verse 2 – If so, the hearers would not be surprised by the next words they encounter, 'And he seized the dragon, the ancient serpent, who is Devil and Satan, and he bound him for a thousand years'. For a second time in the Apocalypse the dragon's full identity occurs with the names, the dragon, the ancient serpent, Devil and Satan standing together. In 20.2, as in 12.9, the occurrence of these names together underscores his identity in all its intensity. The appearance of the name the dragon would remind the hearers of his role as the persecutor of the woman clothed with the sun (12.3), his attempt to kill her child 12.4, the loss of his place in heaven (12.7-9), his persecution of the rest of the woman's seed (12.13), his giving power to the beast (13.2), receiving idolatrous worship (13.4), and out of whom unclean spirits emerge (16.13). Mention of the ancient serpent, as in 12.9 would remind the hearers of the Genesis story (Gen. 3.1-7), where the serpent tempts Adam and Eve with eating from the forbidden fruit of the Tree of the Knowledge of Good and Evil. Thus, the serpent of which the hearers would think when hearing the words 'the ancient serpent' would likely be the serpent of Genesis 3. Nor would the correlation between the dragon's intention to devour the woman's child at birth and the enmity between the serpent and Eve's seed be lost on the hearers (12.14). He is the ancient serpent, the liar and murderer from of old. With the mention of the name Devil, Johannine hearers would be reminded that he is a murderer from the beginning and one of whom it is said, lying is his native tongue (Jn 8.44). They would also be reminded that 'the one who commits sin is of the Devil, for the Devil sins from the beginning' (1 Jn 3.8) and that the Son of God was manifested in order that he might destroy the works of the latter (1 Jn 3.9). Earlier in the Apocalypse (Rev. 2.10) they learned that '… the Devil is about to cast some of you into prison in order that he might test you. Be faithful unto death and I will give you the crown of life'. Joined to the name Devil in 20.2 is the name Satan, with whom Johannine hearers would be well acquainted owing to the fact that in the FG Satan entered Judas just before this disciple goes out into the night (Jn 13.27). In the Apocalypse, this sinister figure is especially associated with Jewish opposition to the church, the synagogue of Satan (Rev. 2.9; 3.9), the powerful presence of Satan (2.13), and the ominous nature of his 'deep things' (2.24). For the great dragon to be identified as identical to Satan concretizes further for the hearers the nature of the dragon's activity and power. But in 20.2, as in 12.9, the remarkable convergence of this impressive cacophony of titles and names does not overwhelm the hearers, for they remember that this very creature, this very opponent has earlier been 'cast down'. In 20.2, the hearers learn that this very creature, with pretensions to deity, is not seized and bound by God directly, but by an unnamed angelic creature![118] In point of fact, the authority of this unnamed angel in 20.2 becomes clear to the hearers, not only by his actions, but also from the structure of this sentence in the Greek text, for in ways reminiscent of his description in 12.9, the Dragon's full identity is surrounded by verbs that describe his impotence. In 12.9 his full identity was surrounded by the words, 'was cast down', whereas in 20.2 his identity is surrounded by the words, 'seized' and 'bound'. This angel seized him and bound him (apparently with the great chain in his hand). Neither would the length of this binding be without significance for the hearers, for the dragon is bound for a thousand years, an extraordinarily long period of time. Though numerous periods of time have been encountered throughout the Apocalypse, nothing to this point compares with the thousand years of binding. The hearers might well be impressed by the fact that this period of binding dwarfs all other periods of binding and persecution of the saints in the book.

---

[118] Gause, *Revelation*, p. 251.

All such times of persecution would now appear different to the hearers in the light of this monumental binding. For while Satan may indeed throw some of the saints in Smyrna into prison for ten days (2.10), Satan himself is to be bound for a thousand years – a ratio of one hundred years of being bound for each day he has imprisoned the saints. While the temple will be trampled underfoot and the beast will speak blasphemy for forty-two months (11.2; 13.5, respectively), the dragon will be bound for a thousand years – a ratio of some two hundred eighty years of binding for each year of persecution. While the bodies of the two prophetic witnesses will lie in the streets of the Great City for all the world to see for three and a half days (11.9), Satan will be bound a thousand years – a ratio of some two hundred eighty years of binding per day of humiliation. While the ten kings who serve the beast will rule for one hour (17.12), Satan will be bound for a thousand years – a ratio of a thousand years of being bound for each hour of reign. Whilst such mathematical ratios may mean little to modern interpreters, their meaning for discerning Johannine hearers would be hard to overestimate. For in the light of this binding of Satan, the saints' periods of persecution, imprisonment, and humiliation lose some of their potency and are seen from a different perspective. For the saints may indeed suffer unto death, but Satan will be bound a thousand years!

Verse 3 – But the hearers are not allowed to reflect further on this detail for the actions of this unnamed angel continue at almost breakneck speed, 'And he cast him into the Abyss and he shut/locked it and sealed over it in order that he might not deceive the nations until the thousand years are completed: after these things it is necessary for him to be loosed for a short time'. The next action of the angel is reminiscent of Michael's action (12.9), for on this occasion as well the dragon is cast down. The hearers might well detect progression in this cosmic story for whereas Michael's activity resulted in the dragon being cast down out of heaven unto the earth, the unnamed angel's activity results in the dragon being cast down (from the earth?) into the Abyss.[119] And whereas the earth and sea were warned about the great wrath of the devil, who has little time to carry out his persecution of the rest of the

---

[119] Resseguie, *The Revelation of John*, p. 244.

596 *The Apocalypse*

Woman's offspring, the unnamed angel binds and imprisons the dragon for a thousand years, after which he is to be loosed a short time. No doubt the hearers would find poetic justice in the fact that

Figure 15
Albrecht Dürer, *Satan Cast into the Abyss*
(State Art Gallery in Karlsruhe, Germany)

the Devil, who would cast some of those in the church in Smyrna into jail for ten days (2.10), is now being cast into the Abyss, a place in the Apocalypse over which God and his agents have authority and from which some of his redemptive agents arise (9.1, 2, 11), as well as one of the enemies of God and his people, the beast (11.7; 17.8). The hearers next learn more about the unnamed angel's authority over the dragon, when the unnamed angel both shuts/locks and places a seal upon the Abyss, where the dragon has been cast. The hearers might well discern in the shutting and/or locking of the Abyss by the angel the same kind of divine activity they encountered in Jesus' words to the church in Philadelphia, 'I have the key of David, the One who opens and no one can close, and closes and no one can open' (3.7), and the prophetic powers of the two witnesses who have the authority to shut the heavens (11.6). Thus, the shutting and/or locking of the Abyss would be understood as divine activity on the angel's part. The hearers would also understand that when the angel seals over the Abyss he not only ensures that the prisoner cannot escape unobserved,[120] but also that this action is in keeping with the previous sealing vocabulary in the Apocalypse (7.3, 4, 5, 8; 10.4 and 5.1, 2, 5, 9; 6.1, 3, 5, 7, 9, 12; 7.2; 8.1; 9.4; cf. also Jn 3.33; 6.27); indicating divine authorization of this action, ensuring that God's will is to be done in the matter, and serving as an authentication that this activity is indeed God's doing. It is not insignificant that to this point in the Apocalypse all sealing takes place through divine initiative; this sealing would be no different. The purpose of this angelic activity is expressed by means of a ἵνα ('in order that') clause, 'in order that he might not deceive the nations until the thousand years have been completed'. Several aspects of these words would be of significance to the hearers. First, the relationship between deception and the dragon would surprise none of the hearers, for as they learned in Rev. 12.9, he is 'the one who deceives the whole inhabited world'. In point of fact, the dragon is the one who stands behind all human agents of deception (Jn 7.12, 47; 1 Jn 1.8; 2.26; 3.7; Rev. 2.20), as well as the false prophet (13.14; 19.20) and Babylon (18.23).[121] However, unlike the current situation where the church faces daily the deceiver and his agents, when the dragon is locked in the Abyss, there will be a thousand year period in which the nations will not be subjected to his deception! Second, the hearers might well be startled to learn that those who are to be

---

[120] Beasley-Murray, *Revelation*, p. 285.
[121] Prigent, *L'Apocalypse de Saint Jean*, p. 436.

protected from the dragon's deceptive activity are the nations, for apparently all opponents of the Rider on the White Horse were slain by the sword of his mouth in the preceding passage (19.21). Thus, the hearers might well wonder as to the identity and origin of these nations mentioned in 20.3. Would they be understood as the remnants of the nations as a whole that opposed God, but for some reason were not completely destroyed?[122] Or would they be thought of as representative of the nations?[123] Or would they be thought of as nations that did not join in the war of opposition against the Rider on the White Horse? Or would they be thought to be the ghosts of the nations that had earlier been described as slain by the Rider?[124] While it is possible that any number of these ideas might be rumbling around in the minds of the hearers, their previous pneumatic discernment might lead them to suspect that just as a variety of things in the Apocalypse have disappeared only to reappear later, in ways that push beyond mere cyclical repetition to suggest a certain linear progression, so the (re)appearance of the nations serves a similar function, suggesting that there is even more to the linear development of the nations. At the same time, the major theme of the conversion of the nations, one of the things in the Apocalypse to which the witness of the pneumatic church is called, continues in a somewhat unexpected way. For despite the fact that the nations have apparently been completely destroyed by the Rider on the White Horse, they (re)appear here, and in a context suggesting that at long last they may be able to respond to the witness of the church without the deceptive influence of the dragon. Just as the detail about the iron rod with which the Rider would shepherd the nations (19.15) suggests a role for the nations still, so their (re)appearance here confirms that they have not yet been completely forgotten! Third, a second mention of the thousand years, in the span of two verses, would reinforce the fact for the hearers that this extraordinary period of time, during which the dragon is to be bound, serves a specific function. It is a period in which the nations

---

[122] Mounce, *The Book of Revelation*, p. 353. Caird, *The Revelation of St. John*, p. 251.
[123] Ladd, *Revelation*, p. 263.
[124] Rissi, *Die Zukunft der Welt*, pp. 34-36 and Mealy, *After the Thousand Years*, pp. 181-86.

are not to be deceived by the dragon[125] and a period of time that must run its course for the divine will to be accomplished, as the theologically significant Johannine word τελεσθῇ ('has been completed') indicates (Jn 19.28, 30; Rev. 10.7; 11.7; 15.1, 8; 17.17). The hearers quickly learn that just as the thousand years fulfills a divine function so does its conclusion, for 'after these things it is necessary for him to be loosed for a short time'. The word δεῖ ('it is necessary') would not only convey to the hearers the idea that the conclusion of the period serves a divine necessity,[126] but also indicates that Satan's release is no escape but is itself part of the divine plan.[127] As incredulous as this detail might at first appear, after all who would release the dragon after he has been captured, perhaps the hearers would suspect that if the nations are being given an opportunity to respond to the witness of the church without the deceptive influence of Satan during this thousand year period, then perhaps they would not be surprised that any such positive response on the nations' part must of necessity be tested by the deception of the dragon.

Verse 4 – As the hearers ponder such a remarkable turn of events, they encounter even more astounding words, 'And I saw thrones, and they were seated upon them, and judgment was given to them, and the souls of those beheaded on account of the witness of Jesus and on account of the word of God, and those who did not worship the Beast nor his image and did not receive his mark upon their forehead and upon their hand. And they came to life and they reigned with Christ a thousand years'. The words 'and I saw' would alert the hearers to the fact that new details of the various visionary reports are to be revealed. On this occasion John sees thrones, a detail that would perhaps speak to the hearers at a couple of different levels. For, on the one hand, they would by this point be quite familiar with the throne of God (and the one who sits upon it), owing to the frequent reference made to it throughout the book (1.4; 3.21; 4.2, 3, 4, 5, 6, 9, 10; 5.1, 6, 7, 11, 13; 6.16; 7.9, 10, 11, 15, 17; 8.3; 12.5; 14.3; 16.17; 19.4, 5). They would also by this point be aware of the throne of Jesus that he will share with believ-

---

[125] Gause, *Revelation*, p. 252.
[126] Sweet, *Revelation*, p. 288.
[127] Gause, *Revelation*, p. 252.

ers (3.21) and the thrones of 24 elders (4.4; 11.16). On the other hand, the hearers would have encountered reference to the throne of Satan (2.13), as well as the throne of the beast (13.2; 16.10). While the throne of God and those of the twenty-four elders are located in heaven, the throne of Satan and the beast appear to be contextualized on earth. Owing to the earthly orientation beginning in 19.11 and extending through 20.10, the hearers might well suspect at this point that the throne of Satan and the beast have given way to other thrones, perhaps in keeping with the promise of Jesus to those who overcome (3.21), an idea supported by the fact that the verb καθίζω ('sit') occurs only in 3.21, where the promise is made, and here in 20.4 in the entire book. As the vision progresses it may become clear to the hearers that the things seen (by John and described to them) take on a kaleidoscopic form with a variety of images described one after the other, images that appear to converge as they pile one on top of the other. For in addition to the thrones, the hearers learn that there were those seated upon them, yet another somewhat ambiguous individual detail that could set the hearers' minds to wondering as to the identity of such throne sitters, perhaps the twenty-four elders or the overcomers themselves? But before they can contemplate this aspect of the vision in any detail they encounter yet another somewhat ambiguous individual detail, 'and judgment was given to them'. While it is possible that the hearers might take these words to imply that those who sit on the thrones are involved in the dispensing of judgment,[128] owing in part to the meaning of the term κρίμα ('judgment') in its other occurrences in the Apocalypse (17.1; 18.20; cf. also Jn 9.39) it is more likely that the hearers would understand that those who sit on the thrones have received judgment in the sense of vindication.[129] But again, before they can devote much reflection to this aspect of the vision yet another somewhat ambiguous individual detail is encountered, 'and the souls of those beheaded on account of the witness of Jesus and on account of the word of God'. Reference to 'the souls of those beheaded' would be both familiar and unfamiliar to the hearers at one and the same time. For on the one hand, men-

---

[128] Mealy, *After the Thousand Years*, p. 109.
[129] Pattemore, *The People of God in the Apocalypse*, p. 108 and Smalley, *The Revelation to John*, p. 506.

tion of 'the souls' could hardly help but remind them of the souls under the altar who had been slaughtered owing to the word of God and the testimony which they have, who cry out to God for him to judge and vindicate their blood (6.9). It appears that it is they who have now been given judgment. On the other hand, the hearers may be quite unprepared to discover that these are the souls of those who have been beheaded as here for the first (and only) time (in the whole of Scripture) they encounter the verb πελεκί-ζομαι ('behead'). While it is not altogether clear exactly how the hearers would understand this unexpected detail it is clear that if reference to the souls in 20.4 is taken in continuity with reference to the souls under the altar of those slaughtered, then the manner of death by beheading stands in direct continuity with the previous description of their death as slaughtered. It would also be clear that the death of these respective souls is owing to their relationship with the witness of Jesus and the word of God. The hearers of course would be well aware by this time of the close relationship that exists between the witness of Jesus and death, not only for Jesus, the faithful witness, but for all those who would follow the Lamb wherever he goes (14.4), a point emphasized as recently as 19.10. The fact that the death of these souls is also directly tied to the word of God would not only remind the hearers of John's own suffering owing to the prophetic activity of God (1.9), but would perhaps by now be seen to reinforce the tie to Jesus himself who has recently been called 'the Word of God'. The connection between the death of these souls and the person of Jesus would be difficult to miss. But the question remains, what would the idea of beheading convey to the hearers? The word itself is a perfect participle indicating that their beheading had taken place in the past but its effects are still felt. It would seem to be self evident that reference to this graphic manner of execution would intensify the visceral nature of the description of their death from the more generic slaughtered (a visceral term itself!) to the more specific beheaded. But the hearers might discern even more in the introduction of this detail at this point. Coming fast on the heels of the observation that those who were seated on the throne had received judgment, perhaps the hearers would be reminded of the contrast between the fate of these beheaded ones, on the one hand, and that of the beast who had suffered a mortal wound to one of his heads, the healing of which resulted in his near universal worship, on the other hand. That is to say, while both the beast and these souls suffered mortal head wounds, the latter being much more severe as the head itself has been removed, it is they and not he who in fact have received the judgment of life! And with this, yet another somewhat ambiguous detail is encountered, 'and those who did not worship the beast nor his image and did not receive his mark upon their forehead and upon their hand'. While the previous phrase seems to have reference to the martyrs exclusively, the latter phrase appears to be inclusive enough to include all those who offer faithful witness to Jesus by worshipping God not the beast in any form, whether their faithful witness results in a martyr's death or not. However, the paradoxical ambiguity of these phrases, standing side by side, reinforces to the hearers yet again the importance of being faithful unto death.[130] It is only with the next words that the seemingly disparate individual somewhat ambiguous pieces of this verse converge for the hearers, 'And they came to life and reigned with Christ a thousand years'. With these words the hearers discover that the souls of the beheaded ones, those who did not worship the beast in any form, to whom the verdict of judgment was given, who are seated upon the thrones themselves experience resurrection, just as had their Lord (1.18; 2.8) and the two prophetic witnesses (11.11),[131] reign with Christ in accord with his promises to those who overcome (2.26; 3.21; 5.10) for a thousand years.[132] How would Johannine hearers understand such words about these overcomers coming to life? While ambiguities abound, it would appear to be certain that the hearers would understand this coming to life as similar to and standing in continuity with the coming to life of Jesus, owing in part to the fact that the same word found here appeared earlier in the Apocalypse to describe the resurrection of Jesus (2.8). Such an understanding would be at home with the idea found in 1 Jn 3.2 that despite the fact that the nature of such a resurrected existence is not yet evident, it is enough to know that 'we shall be like him, because we will see him as he is', and would be at home with the descriptions of the resurrected Jesus in John 20 and 21. Thus, while

---

[130] Mealy, *After the Thousand Years*, pp. 109-19.
[131] Sweet, *Revelation*, p. 289.
[132] Ladd, *Revelation*, p. 264.

modern interpreters may be fascinated with the idea that this coming to life is not a physical resurrection, but a spiritual one,[133] such an idea would likely be quite foreign to Johannine hearers. Rather, this is the moment at which the souls of those who had been beheaded, those who have not worshipped the beast, are resurrected in bodily form, as had been their Lord. Thus, the judgment that is rendered to them is integrally connected to their being brought to life. For in their being brought to life in resurrected form they experience more fully the eternal life with which Johannine hearers are quite familiar and share more immediately in their identification with God who is often described in the Apocalypse as the One who lives forever and ever (4.9, 10; 7.2; 10.6; 15.7). Not only do such ones come to life, but they also reign with Christ for a thousand years. The sheer temporal magnitude of this period of reigning would serve to dwarf all other reigns mentioned in the Apocalypse to this point, whether it be the forty-two month reign of the beast (13.5) or the one-hour reign of the ten kings (17.12). The thousand-year reign of these overcomers simply cannot be compared to any reign of the enemies of God upon the earth. Thus, the hearers learn that the entire time that the dragon is bound in the Abyss, those who have been faithful witnesses experience a different reality altogether – they reign with Christ. It might strike the hearers as remarkable that after the numerous Old Testament intertexts they have encountered throughout the book, at this point there is a stark absence of Old Testament references, despite the fact that so many appropriate intertexts could be included and perhaps are in the minds of the hearers! Yet, the depiction of this thousand-year reign is extraordinarily restrained and sparse in its description. In point of fact, the hearers discover that the focus of attention is placed not upon a description of its contents or other characteristics but upon the relational nature of the thousand-year period.[134] Specifically, they will be with Christ for the thousand years. Thus, not only will the deceptive influence of Satan be absent during this period, the overcomers will be with Christ for this entire period; they will be with the same resurrected Lord that they experience even now via

---

[133] P. Gaechter, 'The Original Sequence of Apocalypse 20-22', *Theological Studies* 10 (1949), p. 491.

[134] Koester, *Revelation and the End of All Things*, pp. 184-85.

the Spirit's prophetic witness. The resurrected Lord whom they know in their worship and faithful witness, whom they follow wherever he goes, whose return is imminent, is the same Lord with whom they will reign. All that Christ is as redeemer, they will now be as redeemed.[135] These resurrected overcomers will be with their resurrected Lord for longer than any of the hearers could imagine or fathom – for a thousand years(!) – the exact amount of time for which Satan is bound in the Abyss. Owing to the relational nature of this reign the issue about over whom or over what they reign with Christ would not appear to be of primary concern for the hearers. However, if reflection were devoted to this issue it is likely that the hearers would suspect that two things may be involved. Owing to the fact that Satan is unable to deceive the nations during this period, perhaps their reign would be connected to the nations in some way. If one of the purposes of this extraordinarily long period is to give the nations yet another chance to respond in faith, perhaps their reign involves a continuation of bearing their prophetic, faithful witness, not unlike that bore by the two witnesses whom the Spirit of life from God raised up (11.11-14)! At the same time, the idyllic conditions of this thousand year reign might well remind the hearers of the conditions at the beginning in the Garden of Eden, where the human being was given charge over the creation and creatures within it (Gen. 1.26-28).[136] On this view, the thousand-year reign with Christ would be designed in part to be a visible sign of the redemption of creation itself, with resurrected human agents reigning with Christ in a way that fulfills that initial command and commission.

Verse 5 – The hearers' attention continues to be focused upon resurrection as they encounter the next words, 'The rest of the dead did not come to life until the thousand years were complete. This is the first resurrection'. If the faithful witnesses who overcome come to life and reign with Christ for a thousand years then the rest of the dead would likely be thought to consist of the opponents of the Rider on the White Horse (19.21),[137] as well as all those who do not

---

[135] Gause, *Revelation*, p. 254.
[136] Mealy, *After the Thousands Years*, p. 116.
[137] Mealy, *After the Thousand Years*, p. 115.

believe in him.¹³⁸ Again, owing in part to the vocabulary, a physical resurrection of the dead appears to be in view.¹³⁹ While modern interpreters are sometimes troubled by the idea of two separate resurrections, it does not appear that discerning Johannine hearers would have the same concerns, for they might well understand these two resurrections as in accord with the teaching of Jesus himself who says, 'Do not be astonished at this, because an hour comes in which all those who are in their graves will hear his voice and will come out, the ones who have done good into resurrection of life, but the ones who practice evil into resurrection of judgment' (Jn 5.28-29). But unlike those overcomers who come to life and reign with Christ for a thousand years, the rest of the dead do not come to life until after the thousand years. Rather, they are in their graves for this entire period, just as Satan is bound in the Abyss for the period the overcomers reign with Christ. The theologically significant term τελεσθῇ ('were complete') might well convey to the hearers the idea that just as the binding of Satan in the Abyss until the thousand years is complete is theologically significant, so it is with those who are not resurrected until the thousand years is complete. Mention of the extraordinarily long thousand year period, the fourth such mention in a five verse span, again underscores the magnitude of the loss for the rest of the dead who lie in their graves while the overcomers reign with Christ. The next words encountered, 'This is the first resurrection', appear to direct the hearers' attention back to the description of those who came to life and reign with Christ for the thousand years. It is these who experience the first resurrection! Clearly in this context, the first resurrection is so named owing to its chronological and theological precedence over the resurrection of the rest of the dead. Though a 'second resurrection' is nowhere named as such in the Johannine literature,¹⁴⁰ the fact that the first resurrection identifies the resurrection of the overcomers who reign with Christ a thousand years and precedes the resurrection of the rest of the dead, confirm that the hearers would understand that two resurrections, separated by a thousand years, are indeed here

---

¹³⁸ Ladd, *Revelation*, p. 265.

¹³⁹ Aune, *Revelation 17-22*, p. 1090.

¹⁴⁰ Wall, *Revelation*, p. 239 and Prigent, *L'Apocalypse de Saint Jean*, p. 429.

described,[141] and would be in keeping with the teaching of Jesus as well (Jn 5.28-29).

Verse 6 – The hearers' reflection upon the significance of this first resurrection is reinforced by the next words they encounter, 'Blessed and holy is the one who has a part in the first resurrection; over these the second death has no authority, but they will be priests of God and of Christ, and they will reign with him a thousand years'. For a fifth time in the book the hearers encounter a beatitude and for the first time the beatitude contains a compound predicate, for to the characteristic 'blessed' is added 'and holy'.[142] Not only would the beatitude speak directly to the hearers owing to its form, as have the preceding ones (1.3; 14.13; 16.15; 19.9), but the unique addition of 'holy' would also have special significance, for it reinforces the idea of those who overcome as faithful witnesses who have stayed awake and kept their garments, not walking around naked (16.15), and have been deemed worthy of invitation to the marriage supper of the Lamb, having prepared themselves through righteous acts (19.8-9). At the same time, the hearers would know that the word here translated as holy, ἅγιος ('holy'), is the same Greek word for saint, perhaps reinforcing for them that all the saints will have part in the first resurrection. Discerning Johannine hearers would not only be sensitive to the significance of the beatitude form, but would also pick up on the theologically significant word μέρος ('share' or 'part'), which in Jn 13.8 is closely identified with eternal life, solidarity with Jesus' destiny, mission, martyrdom, and resurrection.[143] Thus, the vocabulary itself emphasizes the depth of identification and solidarity between Jesus the faithful witness and the faithful witnesses that participate in the first resurrection. In point of fact, 'over these the second death has no authority!' Such words would no doubt remind the hearers of the promise of the resurrected Jesus to the church in Smyrna, 'the one who overcomes will not be harmed at all by the second death' (Rev. 2.11), making even clearer that the one who participates in the first resurrection has no fear of the second death, a death that has not yet been fully identified in the text but which the hearers might at

---

[141] Aune, *Revelation 17-22*, p. 1091.
[142] Murphy, *Fallen Is Babylon*, p. 399.
[143] Thomas, *Footwashing in John 13 and the Johannine Community*, pp. 92-95.

this point suspect is tied to some form of eternal death. However, rather than being susceptible to the second death, those who participate in the first resurrection will be in the very presence of God and Christ, serving as priests[144] and reigning with Christ for the thousand years. The mention of the word priests would no doubt remind the hearers of the fact that it is through Jesus, the one with whom they will reign for a thousand years, that they have been made into a kingdom – priests to God (1.6; 5.10). It is by his death that they gain admission to the divine presence[145] and minister to God and Christ. Such language may well suggest to the hearers that the overcomers have an active role to play still in the conversion of the nations and that their reigning with Christ may well involve such a priestly dimension as they continue to act as faithful witnesses to the witness of Jesus and the Word of God – for a thousand years![146] The fifth mention of the thousand years in the span of five verses would not likely be taken by the hearers as insignificant repetition, but rather would underscore for them the fact that they shall serve as priests to God and Christ and reign with Christ for an unimaginably long period of time, unquestionably longer than their time of persecution.[147] It will be a reign in which they may enjoy their time with Christ, seek the conversion of the nations, and fulfill the command given to Adam and Eve in the Garden. They will reign with him for a thousand years – a thousand years indeed!

Verse 7 – No sooner than these words about the activity of the thousand years are spoken do the hearers encounter words about its completion, 'And when the thousand years were completed, Satan will be loosed out of his prison'. Several aspects of these words would be of significance for the hearers. First, the theologically significant term τελεσθῇ ('were completed') would not only indicate that the thousand years (and its purposes) have now come to completion,[148] but the occurrence of the verb in the passive form would also remind the hearers that this period did not come to an end on its own but was brought to its completion by God himself. Second,

---

[144] Smalley, *The Revelation to John*, p. 510.
[145] Gause, *Revelation*, p. 254.
[146] Caird, *The Revelation of St. John*, pp. 255-56.
[147] Metzger, *Cracking the Code*, p. 93.
[148] Gause, *Revelation*, p. 255.

Satan's confinement in the Abyss is now revealed to have been an imprisonment for after the thousand years he will be loosed from his prison. Third, the passive form λυθήσεται ('will be loosed'), indicates that just as God is active in bringing the thousand years to completion, so the loosing of Satan is no escape but is in accord with the divine purpose and is indeed God's own activity.

Verse 8 – If the hearers have been wondering as to Satan's plans upon his release from the Abyss they find out in the next words they encounter, 'And he will go out to deceive the nations those in the four corners of the earth, Gog and Magog, to gather them together into war, the number of them being as the sand of the sea'. The first words of this verse reveal immediately that the Satan who was bound for a thousand years so he could no longer deceive the nations in 20.3 is the same Satan who emerges from his prison to deceive the nations in 20.8. For the first word the hearers encounter in this verse after 'and', ἐξελεύσεται ('he will go out') would be known to discerning Johannine hearers as a term closely associated with deception and betrayal, as it appears to describe Judas' departure to betray Jesus in Jn 13.30 and is used to describe the missionary activity of the many deceivers who have gone out into the world in 2 Jn 7.[149] Thus, even before the hearers are told explicitly that Satan goes out to deceive, they would well suspect that such activity is his intention. But there is no mistake about it, for despite his long imprisonment in the Abyss, Satan emerges as ready as ever to deceive the nations and is prepared to do so in as comprehensive a fashion as possible.[150] The extent of his intended deception is conveyed to the hearers in two ways. First, they learn that Satan goes out to deceive the nations who are at the four corners of the earth, the proverbial furthest points of the earth. Second, these nations are also called by the names Gog and Magog. Gog would be known to the hearers as the chief prince of Meshech and Tubal (Ezek. 38.2), while Magog would be known as the son of Japheth (Gen. 10.2) and becomes identified as the territory located in the uttermost parts of north (Ezek. 38.6).[151] As with other names in the book, the hearers would likely suspect that these two names have a

---

[149] Thomas, *1 John, 2 John, 3 John*, p. 45 and Smalley, *The Revelation to John*, p. 511.

[150] Koester, *Revelation and the End of All Things*, p. 187.

[151] Mounce, *The Book of Revelation*, p. 362.

deeper meaning still as it appears that by this point these names would be thought of as the eschatological enemies of the North[152] that attack the people of God after a period of peace.[153] The purpose of Satan's going out to deceive is 'to gather them together into war', a phrase similar to one encountered earlier by the hearers in Rev. 16.14.[154] Such similarity would remind the hearers not only of similar hostile intentions of the nations, but also of their ultimate demise on that occasion as well. The success of Satan's deception is revealed by the fact that the nations gathered together for war are numbered as the sand of the sea, a phrase that not only indicates something of the overwhelming success of his deceptive work, but one that also would draw upon the ominous associations this phrase has from its earlier appearance, where the dragon stands upon the sand of the sea looking for the emergence of the beast (12.18).[155] This detail too would perhaps encourage the hearers with regard to the outcome of this looming conflict as they reflect on the outcome of the conflict championed by the beast that emerges from the sea. Such language stands in stark contrast to the promise given to Abraham with regard to the number of his descendants,[156] indicating something of the diametric opposition of the purposes of God and those of Satan. If the hearers had wondered as to the outcome of this final opportunity for the nations to convert, the words of this verse suggests that despite the thousand year period in which Satan is kept from deceiving the nations and despite the fact that Christ himself reigns with those who are faithful to him, the nations are as susceptible as ever to the deception of Satan and, despite these ideal circumstances, refuse to repent and worship God and the Lamb.[157]

Verse 9 – Little space stands between the description of Satan's desires and their effects as the next words reveal, 'and they went up upon the breadth of the earth and circled the camp of the saints and the beloved city'. The actions of these deceived nations, whose

---

[152] Allo, *Saint Jean L'Apocalypse*, p. 288.

[153] Caird, *The Revelation of St. John*, p. 257.

[154] Aune, *Revelation 17-22*, p. 1095.

[155] Sweet, *Revelation*, p. 292.

[156] Aune, *Revelation 17-22*, p. 1096.

[157] Cf. the esp. perceptive comments of Mealy, *After the Thousand Years*, pp. 186 and 189.

number is as the sand of the sea, is no less significant than their numbers, for they traverse the face of the earth, and encircle their intended targets, a strategy well known in ancient warfare, where cities are circled to cut their inhabitants off from the outside world. While the hearers know that the nations have been deceived by Satan to gather together for war, and while they may suspect that Christ and those who reign with him are the intended targets, they learn that the nations intend to make war upon 'the camp of the saints' and 'the beloved city'. Mention of the camp of the saints would not only reveal the intended target of the nations' planned attack as consisting of the saints, those holy ones who have a part in the first resurrection and reign with Christ for a thousand years, but it would also remind the hearers yet again of the tight connection that exists between the Johannine believers and the heritage of Israel, especially in a book where they have already been described as part of a transformed Israel (cf. esp. 7.1-8). Specifically, the phrase 'the camp of the saints' would remind the hearers of Israel's dependency upon God as he led them through the wilderness via a cloud by day and a pillar of fire by night (Exod. 13.17-22),[158] imagery that would likely remind Johannine hearers of the pneumatic activity that is an essential part of their life together. At the same time, mention of 'the beloved city' would have special significance for the hearers, for it would call up memories of Yahweh's special love for Zion, the city of Jerusalem (Pss. 87.2; 132.13; cf. also Jer. 11.15; 12.7), the place where Yahweh chose to dwell,[159] and as such could well be taken as an anticipation of the New Jerusalem that the hearers know is to come down out of heaven (Rev. 3.12), thus, affirming the continuity that exists between the people of God at the end of the thousand years and the New Jerusalem that is to come. To learn that even at the end of the thousand years the people of God face attacks inspired by Satan would also remind the hearers that they are from start to finish always dependent upon God for their protection, security, and defense. But at the very moment of attack the hearers learn, 'and fire came down out of heaven and consumed them'. Despite the fact that the hearers might be poised for details of a great battle, a final battle if you will, as with previous war

---

[158] Sweet, *Revelation*, p. 292.
[159] Sweet, *Revelation*, p. 292.

scenes no battle takes place.[160] Rather, the fire of judgment comes from heaven and consumes the nations gathered together for war, reminiscent of the way fire comes from the mouths of the two witnesses and consumes their enemies (11.5). The fact that the fire comes from heaven makes the origin of this victory unmistakable,[161] and reminds of the fire of judgment that falls upon Gog (Ezek. 38.22) and Magog (Ezek. 39.6).[162] Yet again, the people of God stand vindicated. They will be as secure at the end as they are during the present times of distress.

Verse 10 – If the vindication of the saints were not enough, the hearers learn even more, 'And Satan, the one who deceives them, was cast into the lake of fire and sulfur, where both the beast and the false prophet (were cast), and they will be tormented day and night for ever and ever'. Now, at long last, the archenemy of God and his people receives his final judgment. Several things are said about Satan in this verse that would be of significance to the hearers. First, he is identified as 'the one who deceives them', reminding the hearers of 12.9 where he is called 'the one who deceives the whole inhabited world'. This description would tie his fate directly to his activity of deceiving the nations. Second, this marks the third occasion in the book where Satan is described as ἐβλήθη ('was cast down'). This occasion joins his full description in 12.9 where the word stands on either side of his names and the description of the action of the unnamed angel in 20.3 who cast Satan down into the Abyss. This most recent reference to Satan being cast down in 20.10 would remind the hearers that despite his power and opposition he is from start to finish one who has been cast down. But whereas Satan had earlier been cast down to earth (12.9) and into the Abyss (20.3), he is now described as having been cast into the lake of fire and sulfur! The hearers would know that this place of judgment and death is the same place into which the Rider on the White Horse cast living the beast and the false prophet (19.20) and would understand this as the most ominous of places. Third, if the hearers have not already made this association they learn that Satan goes to the same place to which his accomplices, the beast and the

---

[160] Ladd, *Revelation*, p. 270.
[161] Gause, *Revelation*, p. 257.
[162] Mounce, *The Book of Revelation*, p. 363.

false prophet, have preceded him.¹⁶³ Not only would this reveal the final destiny of this triumvirate of evil to the hearers, but their appearance together here makes very clear that all opponents and opposition to God, his Lamb, his Spirit, and his people have no future but judgment and eternal punishment, regardless of the strength they may currently exhibit in their persecution of the faithful witnesses of the prophetic community. They are doomed to judgment! Fourth, the hearers learn that just as they had acted together to deceive the nations and the inhabitants of the whole earth, so they are judged together and are to be tormented together. The appearance of the passive verb βασανισθήσονται ('they will be tormented') would indicate to the hearers that the torment that awaits comes from the hand of God, as the appearance of the divine passive often indicates in the Apocalypse. The third person plural form of the verb also makes clear that the torment that awaits includes all three opponents: Satan, the beast, and the false prophet. This verb also confirms to the hearers the fact that the time that awaits the triumvirate in the lake of fire and sulfur is not only a time of confinement, but a time of punishment in the form of torment as well. Fifth, the time of their torment is unfathomably constant and long, a detail the hearers learn from the two temporal indicators with which these words conclude. The constancy of torment is conveyed by the phrase 'day and night',¹⁶⁴ indicating something of the unrelenting nature of the torment that awaits. Perhaps the hearers would understand such constancy of torment to be an appropriate judgment for 'the one who accuses the brothers day and night before our God' (12.10). At the same time, it is difficult to believe that the hearers would not pick up on the contrast between the torment of this triumvirate of evil and the four living creatures who do not cease praising God day and night (4.8) and those who are coming out of the great tribulation who are before the throne of God serving him day and night (7.15). The duration of their torment is conveyed by the words 'for ever and ever'. Perhaps the first thing the hearers would think of when encountering this temporal designation is how small the thousand year period seems next to 'for ever

---

¹⁶³ Beasley-Murray, *Revelation*, p. 298.
¹⁶⁴ Smalley labels these words a hendiadys generating the meaning 'without interruption', *The Revelation to John*, p. 515.

and ever'. But as with the phrase 'day and night' it is likely that the hearers would pick up other details in the narrative to this point. On the one hand, they may well see some continuity between the smoke of destruction of God's enemies that goes up forever and ever (14.11; 19.3) and the torment of this triumvirate. On the other hand, the hearers may well think of the reign of God that lasts forever and ever (11.15) and the worship rendered to God and/or the Lamb by every creature in the universe (5.13) and the angels and four living creatures and twenty-four elders (7.11-12). It would be quite clear to the hearers that both the constancy of the torment and its duration point to an eternal death for Satan, the beast, and the false prophet rather than to their annihilation.[165]

The Final Judgment (20.11-15)

Verse 11 – With what appears to be the end of the cosmic battle ringing in their ears, the hearers may be surprised at the words that follow, 'And I saw a great white throne and the one sitting upon it, from whose face the earth and heaven fled, and a place was not found for them'. With the words 'and I saw' the hearers would be alerted to the fact that a new development in this visionary experience is about to be revealed. The appearance of a great white throne would be an extraordinarily stunning aspect of this vision, for while they have just witnessed the description of a number of thrones in 20.4, here they encounter a great white throne. Its description as great would serve to emphasize its magnitude, owing to the fact that it alone is described this way in the Apocalypse, and thereby would draw additional attention to its judicial function. It is the throne of judgment. Its description as white would remind the hearers that in the Apocalypse white is the color of Jesus (1.14; 14.14; 19.11), the angels (4.4), the stone (2.17), as well as the dress of faithful believers (3.4-5, 18; 6.11; 7.9, 13-14; 19.14), conveying in 20.11 the qualities of holiness and vindication.[166] While the hearers might well have had an expectation that the Lamb would sit upon the throne of judgment,[167] the vast preponderance of references to God as the One who sits upon the throne throughout the book makes it likely that the hearers would take the reference to 'the One

---

[165] Murphy, *Fallen Is Babylon*, p. 403.
[166] Smalley, *The Revelation to John*, p. 516.
[167] Gause, *Revelation*, p. 258 and Aune, *Revelation 17-22*, p. 1101.

who sits upon it' in 20.11 as alluding to God. But perhaps even more remarkable than the stunning appearance of this great white throne is the response of the earth and heaven to it! For at the appearance of the face of the One who sits upon the throne both the earth and heaven fled. While such language could simply convey their disappearance, the hearers might well take the verb ἔφυγεν ('fled') as conveying a somewhat more aggressive meaning than an involuntary response.[168] If so, it would appear that the fleeing of the earth and heaven has to do with the character of the One who sits upon the throne, on the one hand, and the character of the earth and heaven, on the other hand, a contrast not unlike the cry of humanity for the mountains and rocks to fall upon them and hide them from the face of the One who sits upon the throne (6.16). Perhaps the hearers would understand them to flee owing to the moral grandeur of God or the glory of his presence.[169] Or owing to the judicial significance of this throne perhaps they would understand that judgment itself begins with the known elements of the world, the earth and heaven.[170] Or perhaps they would understand this to be the physical disillusionment of the universe in the direct presence of God and his throne.[171] What would be clear is that the earth and heaven have no more use and as such find no place for existence. Their time has expired. Their usefulness has run their course.[172] The boundaries of the old order no longer exist.[173] All that remains is the great white throne and the One who sits upon it, suspended in space by God's own power. Nothing any longer separates God from humanity.[174] A most awesome sight indeed!

Verse 12 – This awe inspiring sight gives way to additional extraordinary details that John saw, 'And I saw the dead, the great and the small, standing before the throne, and books were opened; and another book was opened, which is the book of life; and the dead were judged out of the things written in the books according to their works'. The hearers learn that John saw the dead, apparently

---

[168] Caird, *The Revelation of St. John*, p. 258.
[169] Ladd, *Revelation*, p. 271 and Metzger, *Breaking the Code*, p. 95.
[170] Michaels, *Revelation*, p. 229.
[171] Mounce, *The Book of Revelation*, pp. 365-66.
[172] Murphy, *Fallen Is Babylon*, p. 404.
[173] Sweet, *Revelation*, p. 294.
[174] Resseguie, *The Revelation of John*, p. 248.

all those who had come to life in the resurrection(s). The qualifications of this group as both 'the great and the small' suggest that all of the dead are present, as the hearers would be familiar with the phrase 'the great and small' for it has appeared earlier in the book as a designation of universality (11.18; 13.16; 19.5, 18). However, normally the phrase appears in the inverse order of its appearance here, with the progression from small to great. The fact that in 20.12 the order is 'the great and the small' may suggest to the hearers that absolutely no one, beginning with the great people of the earth and going to the least, is absent or exempted.[175] No one is too important or unimportant.[176] All claims to privilege are given up.[177] All the dead are seen, joining the great white throne and the One who sits upon it as the only things visible since earth and heaven have fled. The discovery that the dead are standing before the throne would perhaps remind the hearers of those earlier described as standing before the throne (5.6; 7.15)[178] and those who had cried for the mountains and rocks to fall upon them who ask, 'for the great day of their wrath has come and who is able to stand' (6.17), the latter text suggesting that standing before the throne is inevitable, a fate from which nothing or no one is able to deliver. Neither would it surprise the hearers that 'books were opened' on this occasion, as books of judgment normally accompany judgment scenes (cf. esp. Dan. 7.10). Owing to this close association, this phrase might even convey the meaning 'and judgment was rendered'. But the hearers quickly learn that these, as yet unidentified, books are joined by another book that has been opened, which is identified. It is the book of life, a book that the hearers have encountered already on several occasions. Specifically, to this point they know the name of the one who overcomes will never be erased from it, but rather this one's name will be confessed by the resurrected Jesus before the Father and his angels (3.5). They know that this book of life belongs to the Lamb who has been slaughtered from before the foundation of the world (13.8). They know that those whose names are written in the book of life are opposed to the worship of the

---

[175] Metzger, *Breaking the Code*, p. 95.
[176] Mounce, *The Book of Revelation*, p. 365.
[177] Kiddle, *The Revelation of St John*, p. 404.
[178] Smalley, *The Revelation to John*, p. 517.

Beast (17.8). Thus, when the hearers learn that one of the books opened at the great white throne event is the book of life, they would understand that redemption is not absent and that for those who overcome, and whose names have been written in the book of life owing to their faithful witness, Jesus himself stands ready to confess their names before the Father and his angels. At this point the suspicions of the hearers, that these other opened books signify judgment, are confirmed, for 'the dead were judged out of the things written in the books according to their works'. In the light of these words, these books would be understood to provide the evidence for judgment written by the lives of every human being.[179] At the same time, the appearance of these open books for judgment would insure for the hearers that the judgment that comes from the great white throne is not capricious but accurate[180] and indisputable![181] Nor would the hearers be unaware of the importance of works and their eternal destiny, for in point of fact they here find that such works form the basis of their judgment, explaining the continuous emphasis upon works found throughout the Apocalypse (2.2, 5, 6, 19, 22, 23; 3.1, 2, 8, 15; 9.20; 14.13; 15.3; 16.11; 18.6)!

Verse 13 – As is consistent with other places in the book, the words of v. 12 anticipate those that follow in v. 13,[182] 'and the sea gave up the dead in it, and Death and Hades gave up the dead in them, and each one was judged according to their works'. The hearers are likely to understand that the scene described in v. 12 is now explained in v. 13. The sea is specifically mentioned as one of the places that gave up their dead, who stand before the great white throne. Death at sea held a special horror in the ancient world, in part owing to the fact that a proper burial was impossible for its victims.[183] But the words the hearers here encounter reveal that even those who seem to have disappeared into nothingness are remembered by God[184] and that the manner and place of death make

---

[179] Mounce, *The Book of Revelation*, p. 365.
[180] Smalley, *The Revelation to John*, p. 517.
[181] Mealy, *After the Thousand Years*, p. 171.
[182] Allo, *Saint Jean L'Apocalypse*, p. 304.
[183] Caird, *The Revelation of St. John*, p. 260.
[184] Prigent, *L'Apocalypse de Saint Jean*, p. 447 and Smalley, *The Revelation to John*, p. 519.

no difference.[185] Even those lost at sea stand before the great white throne. Perhaps even more astounding is the fact that Death and Hades give up the dead in them! To this point the hearers know that the resurrected Jesus has the keys of Death and Hades (1.18), indicating his absolute power and authority over them, and they know that Death and Hades are companions when the fourth seal is opened, as they are given authority over a fourth of the earth to kill with the sword and with famine and with death and authority over the beasts of the earth (6.8). Therefore, all the dead from the sea and from Death and Hades stand before the great white throne. For a second time in the span of two verses the hearers are told that each one was judged according to their works, again underscoring the tight connection that exists between one's final destiny and the works of one's life only, on this occasion the specificity of each one's works is emphasized even more than before.

Verse 14 – But there is more, 'And Death and Hades were cast into the lake of fire. This is the second death, the lake of fire'. The hearers now learn that Death and Hades suffer a similar fate to the dragon, the beast, and the false prophet, for Death and Hades are cast into the lake of fire. The fact that Hades is never mentioned except as a companion of Death and the fact that Death is always mentioned first before Hades suggests that in some way Death rules over or has authority over Hades.[186] To discover that these final foes now meet their eternal fate reveals that the horrors of both are now banished forever.[187] It is hard to overestimate the significance of the demise of Death and Hades for the hearers, for the death of death would be terribly encouraging to those who face death daily owing to their faithful witness to Jesus.[188] The hearers have long known that the one who overcomes cannot be harmed by the second death at all (2.11) and that for those who have a part in the first resurrection the second death has no authority over them at all (20.6). They also know that the lake of fire is the place of eternal punishment into which the beast and the false prophet (19.20) and Satan (20.10) have been cast eternally. Now they learn

---

[185] Metzger, *Breaking the Code*, p. 96.
[186] Aune, *Revelation 17-22*, p. 1103.
[187] Kiddle, *The Revelation of St John*, p. 408.
[188] Smalley, *The Revelation to John*, p. 519.

that their earlier suspicions are confirmed, that the lake of fire is the second death. They learn that while those who experience physical death will be brought to life again, those who experience the second death experience eternal death from which it is now impossible to escape! If Satan, the beast, the false prophet, Death, and Hades are all cast into this eternal death the nature of the lake of fire could hardly be more ominous! It is unmitigated death, complete separation from God.[189]

Verse 15 – But before this passage concludes the hearers learn the fate of the dead, 'And if any were not found written in the book of life that one was cast into the lake of fire'. After two warnings with regard to judgment based upon one's works and a description of the fate of Death and Hades, stern words appear yet again about the judgment. However, on this occasion the emphasis is slightly different for instead of underscoring the importance of works, the focus of attention is upon whether or not one is found written in the book of life. Specifically, if anyone is not found written in the book of life they too are cast into the lake of fire. The implications could not be clearer. If one identifies with Satan and the beast and the false prophet in this life, they will suffer eternal death with them owing to the fact that they have not repented and offered faithful witness to Jesus. At the same time, despite the ominous scene of the great white throne and the judgment that accompanies it, the hearers would be assured that they have no need to fear, not even a list of evil works in one or more of the opened books, for they are written in the book of life and have overcome, having offered faithful witness to Jesus.[190]

The Descent of the New Jerusalem (21.1-8)

Verse 1 – The extraordinary accounts found in chapter 20 might well lead the hearers to conclude that they have encountered the end of all things, but as the following words reveal much more awaits them, 'And I saw a new heaven and a new earth; for the first heaven and the first earth had departed, and there is no more sea'. The familiar 'and I saw' indicates to the hearers that a new aspect of the vision now comes into focus. The discovery of a new heaven and a new earth would be a breathtaking prospect, though, while at

---

[189] Metzger, *Breaking the Code*, p. 97.
[190] Gause, *Revelation*, p. 262.

the same time, a not altogether unexpected development, for the heaven and earth have earlier fled from the presence of the One who sits on the great white throne. Perhaps the first aspect of this discovery on which the hearers would pick up is the word that describes the newness of this heaven and earth, for καινὸν ('new') is a term that designates something new in kind not just a new thing of the same kind;[191] it is a newness hitherto unknown.[192] Such newness would be startling especially as the hearers contemplate a new heaven. For the heaven that has been described throughout the Apocalypse has itself been difficult enough to fathom, as it is the dwelling place of God, the One who sits on the throne, the place from which his righteous and holy judgments come, the place where those who have been martyred reside, the place of praise and thanksgiving, and the place of divine self revelation. If this extraordinary place, which the hearers would no doubt long to share with God, the Lamb, and the Seven Spirits before the throne, stretches the bounds of the imagination and as such would represent more than could be hoped for on the part of the hearers, what could possibly await in the new heaven! Perhaps they would understand that many of the promises to those who overcome would find their ultimate fulfillment in this new heaven. At the same time, thoughts of a new earth would in many ways be just as perplexing and engaging. For while the thousand year reign with Christ that awaits those who overcome (20.1-10) might provide a sampling of what ideal life in the future might look like, a new earth would convey that this existence is even more radically different than anything that could be imagined! But before the hearers are allowed to linger long on the possible implications of this new creation, they are reminded of its necessity by means of reference to the departure of the first heaven and first earth, which was earlier described as fleeing from the face of the One who sits upon the great white throne and that there was no place found for them (20.11). This explicit reference would perhaps remind the hearers of the fact that their fleeing was a part of the last judgment, that the first heaven and first earth had served their purpose. While the language of first heaven and first earth may suggest some continuity between them and the new heaven and

---

[191] Sweet, *Revelation*, p. 297.
[192] Smalley, *The Revelation to John*, p. 524.

new earth, the disappearance of the former and the radical newness of the latter would lead the hearers to put pride of place on the latter. Whatever other thoughts such words might generate amongst the hearers, they find that this new creation, this new heaven and new earth, stands in remarkable discontinuity in at least one specific respect, for 'there was no more sea'.[193] Such a discovery might well come as a bit of a shock, for the hearers know that both in the first heaven (4.6) and the first earth (12.12; 13.1) reference is made to the sea. The explicit mention that there is no more sea in the new creation would likely lead the hearers to conclude that just as the first heaven and first earth had served their purpose, so the sea had served its purpose and that as part of the last judgment, its place too has been exhausted. The numerous associations of the sea with evil in the Apocalypse, as well as the broader biblical tradition, would likely be taken as evidence that evil itself has no place in the new creation.[194] Just as the hearers had learned in the first reference to the sea in the Apocalypse (4.6) that the glory of God is reflected even in those objects that have negative associations, so now in the last reference to the sea in the Apocalypse they learn that the purpose of this mixed image has passed.[195] There is no more sea, for there is no more evil.[196] And more, these words may even suggest to the hearers that there is no longer any need for the glory of God to be reflected or mediated, perhaps leading them to suspect that in this new heaven and new earth, the glory of God is experienced more immediately and directly.[197]

Verse 2 – Without delay the hearers' attention is directed to a particular sight, 'And the holy city New Jerusalem I saw coming down out of heaven from God, prepared as a bride adorned for her husband'. Additional details are now revealed to the hearers as once again they encounter the words καὶ εἶδον ('and I saw'), though for the first and only time in the Apocalypse here the conjunction and

---

[193] Beasley-Murray, *Revelation*, p. 307.

[194] Schüssler Fiorenza, *Revelation*, p. 110.

[195] Fee, *Revelation*, p. 291.

[196] P. Lee, *The New Jerusalem in the Book of Revelation: A Study of Revelation 21-22 in the Light of its Background in Jewish Tradition* (WUNT 129; Berlin: Mohr Siebeck, 2001), p. 269.

[197] Kiddle, *The Revelation of St John*, p. 411.

verb are separated by the direct object,[198] a construction that adds further emphasis to and focus upon the object, 'the holy city New Jerusalem'. How would the hearers understand this holy city, this New Jerusalem? Perhaps the first hint comes early in the book where the people of God have metaphorically been called the holy city (11.2), who were to be trampled for forty-two months. Thus, perhaps they would immediately see some degree of continuity between this holy city and the people of God here in 21.2. At the same time, the hearers would also be aware that this is the second time that they have encountered the name New Jerusalem in the Apocalypse, with the first occurrence coming in the prophetic message to the church in Philadelphia in the form of a promise from the resurrected Jesus to the one who overcomes – 'I will write upon him the name of my God and the name of the city of my God, the New Jerusalem' (3.12),[199] thus further underscoring the identity of the city as closely connected if not identical to the people of God. As in its first mention in the book, so too here New Jerusalem is identified as 'coming down out of heaven from God', words that make clear to the hearers that New Jerusalem is, unlike the Jerusalem of old, an entity that is of divine origin, coming from God himself. It would be difficult to imagine that the hearers would not pick up on the fact that this two-fold attribution makes clear the divine origin of this holy city. The fact that in both references to this point in the Apocalypse New Jerusalem is identified as 'coming down out of heaven from God' might well lead the hearers to understand this phrase as a defining attribute of the city, underscoring its ongoing divine origin. If the hearers have suspicions that this holy city New Jerusalem is closely identified with the people of God, the last phrase in 21.2 makes such a connection clear, for she is 'prepared as a bride adorned for her husband'. Such language would be significant to the hearers for at least two reasons. First, the description of New Jerusalem as a bride would remind them of the radical difference between this city, described as a bride, with fallen Babylon in which the voice (or sound) of the bride will be heard no longer (18.23), contrasting yet again the impotency of the Great Whore with the promise of the Bride. Second, the language of 21.2 could

---

[198] Aune, *Revelation 17-22*, p. 1120.
[199] Mounce, *The Book of Revelation*, p. 370.

not help but call to mind the marriage supper of the Lamb and his bride, γυνὴ ('woman') in this instance, who has prepared herself for her marriage by means of her righteous acts (19.7-8). Thus, it would be difficult for the hearers not to take the holy city New Jerusalem as the bride of the Lamb,[200] perhaps indicating that the marriage supper of the Lamb has indeed come at last.[201] If so, her preparations, which consist of her righteous acts, might be understood further in the light of her designation as the holy city. Her preparations are coterminous with her having adorned herself for her husband, an activity that is now past, the effects of which are still felt, as the perfect κεκοσμημένεν ('adorned') indicates, standing in stark contrast to the adornment of the Great Whore in 17-18. Finally, the hearers might additionally discern that the kind of discontinuity that exists between the first heaven/first earth and the New Heaven/New Earth would likely also exist between the Jerusalem of old and the holy city New Jerusalem. For this is not another Jerusalem of the same kind as the first, rather it is a New Jerusalem. The hearers might well wonder, since some of the eschatological promises found earlier in the Apocalypse appear to be fulfilled in the New Heaven and New Earth, is it not possible that the eschatological promises with regard to eschatological Jerusalem, scattered throughout the biblical tradition, would be fulfilled in New Jerusalem?[202]

Verse 3 – Whatever reflection these words generate within the hearers, it is interrupted by even more extraordinary words, 'And I heard a great voice out of the throne saying, "Behold the dwelling of God is with men, and he will dwell with them, and they will be his peoples, and God himself will be with them"'. A number of aspects of these words would be significant for the hearers. First, while they will have by this time encountered a number of voices from heaven, and even a voice from the throne (19.5), this is the first great voice from the throne that they have encountered. The combination of the adjective 'great' with the fact that this voice originates from the throne would heighten the dramatic quality of the narration and lead the hearers to expect that the words to be

---

[200] Zimmermann, 'Nuptial Imagery in the Revelation of John', p. 169.
[201] Ladd, *Revelation*, p. 277.
[202] Smalley, *The Revelation to John*, p. 535.

heard are indeed significant and of great eschatological consequence.[203] As these divine words from the throne are made known, once again they take on third person form, being words spoken about God. Second, the first words from the throne, 'Behold the dwelling of God is with men', serve to confirm the hearers' earlier suspicions that the nature of the relationship between God and his people in the New Creation will be more direct and unhindered.[204] These words would be of great significance for the hearers, as a number of OT texts would appear to converge before their eyes and ears at this point. The language of dwelling could hardly help but point to the presence of God in the tabernacle amongst Israel during her wilderness wanderings (Lev. 26.11-12), once again echoing the continuity between God's past salvific activity with what lies ahead.[205] At the same time, discerning Johannine hearers would be well aware of the fact that in the life and ministry of Jesus the presence of God amongst them was made even more immediate, for 'the Word became flesh and dwelt among us, and we beheld his glory, the glory of the unique Son of God' (Jn 1.14). They would also likely be quite impressed by the fact that the dwelling of God, previously encountered in heaven (Rev. 15.5), is now amongst human beings, confirming that divine access is now more immediate and direct. Third, the fact that the dwelling of God is said to be 'with men' would perhaps remind the hearers yet again of the wideness in God's mercy, for despite the fact that significant numbers of 'men' have perished earlier in the Apocalypse (8.11, 9.15, 18), the dwelling of God 'with men' at this point would appear to give additional hope amongst the hearers for the conversion of the nations.[206] Fourth, the next line, 'and he will dwell with them', also echoes numerous OT texts and reinforces the words of the previous line, with the verb σκηνώσει ('will dwell') appearing here, where the noun σκηνή ('dwelling') had earlier appeared. In the Apocalypse the hearers would know that such language points to the fulfillment of the eschatological promises for those who come out of the great tribulation where the One who sits upon the throne

---

[203] Smalley, *The Revelation to John*, p. 537.

[204] Beasley-Murray, *Revelation*, p. 311.

[205] Gause, *Revelation*, p. 265.

[206] D. Mathewson, 'The Destiny of the Nations in Revelation 21.1-22.5: A Reconsideration', *TynB* 53.1 (2002), p. 128.

'will dwell upon them' (7.15). Such linguistic repetition leaves no doubt that the nature of God's relationship to the faithful is immediate and unveiled. It is on a new level and order. Fifth, the next line, 'and they will be his peoples', drives the point home even further, again underscoring the fulfillment of the eschatological promises of many OT texts, while at the same time again affirming the large scope of the soteriological reality.[207] Among other things the hearers might well pick up on the fact that here the term 'peoples' is plural, rather than singular as in Lev. 26.12 and Jer. 24.7, perhaps suggesting to the readers that the eschatological people of God, Israel, has expanded to include all peoples,[208] in accord with John's earlier vision of the crowd from every tribe and tongue and people and nation around the throne (Rev. 5.9), and the innumerable crowd out of all nations and tribes and peoples and tongues who are coming out of the great tribulation (7.9).[209] Sixth, the emphasis upon the intimate relationship between God and his peoples continues to be made clear in the final line of v. 3, where it is emphatically stated that 'God himself will be with them', the emphatic construction αὐτὸς ὁ θεὸς ('God himself') occurring here alone in the whole of the Apocalypse.[210] It is difficult to imagine how the personal eschatological presence of God amongst his peoples could be conveyed more powerfully. It is he of the dwelling of God, he who will dwell with them, he whose peoples they are; it is this very God himself who will be with them!

Verse 4 – Perhaps overwhelmed by the overpowering reality of the intimate eschatological relationship between God and his people, the hearers next learn of the fulfillment of certain eschatological promises, 'And he will wipe away every tear from their eyes, and death is no more, neither is there any longer mourning nor crying nor pain; because the first things have departed'. Similar to the way in which the New Creation was described in part by what is missing, 'there is no more sea', these words describe the intimate relationship with God in the New Creation by what is missing. In fact, at this point the hearers may realize that the things that are missing

---

[207] Bauckham, *Climax of Prophecy: Studies on the Book of Revelation*, pp. 311-13.

[208] Pattemore, *The People of God in the Apocalypse*, p. 201.

[209] R.H. Gundry, 'The New Jerusalem: People as Place, not Place for People', *NovT* 29 (1987), p. 257.

[210] Smalley, *The Revelation to John*, p. 538.

in the New Creation stand in chiastic parallel to one another, further defining the lack of a sea as an indication that the sea stands in continuity with the trouble, evil, and suffering of the first heaven and first earth.[211] The specific elements encountered by the hearers in 21.4 are very similar to those earlier found in 7.16-17, where the eschatological promises to those who are coming out of the great tribulation are given. The shedding of tears will be wiped away by the one who will not wipe away (erase) the name of the one who overcomes from the book of life (3.5). The assurance of such eschatological comfort would surely convey to the hearers the sense that healing from the assorted afflictions and persecutions endured during the course of their faithful witness is an ongoing part of the intimate relationship shared with God in the New Creation. The fact that death is no more, not only reminds the hearers of the fact that death itself experiences eternal death in the lake of fire and sulfur, but also again underscores the contrast between New Jerusalem, where death is found no longer, and fallen Babylon, where all signs of joy and life are found no longer (18.21-23).[212] Closely connected with the absence of death is the absence of its close associates: mourning, crying, and pain. For as surely as death continually experiences eternal death, so mourning, crying, and pain are found no more – for they are characteristics of the first things, the first heaven and first earth,[213] that have now departed. These experiences, which would be all too well known by the hearers, find no place in the New Creation where the presence of God is experienced in such an intimate manner. As these initial words associated with the great voice from the throne come to a close, the hearers might well notice how they are enveloped by references to the passing of first things, underscoring the radical difference between the New Creation and the old that has now passed.

Verse 5 – While the divinely authorized words continue, the speaker appears to change in that which follows, 'And the One who sits upon the throne said, "Behold I make all things new". And he says, "Write, because these words are faithful and true".' Not since the direct words spoken by God in 1.8, 'I Am the Alpha and Ome-

---

[211] D. Mathewson, 'New Exodus as a Background for 'the sea was no more' in Revelation 21.1c', *Trinity Journal* 24 (2003), p. 245.

[212] Sweet, *Revelation*, p. 299.

[213] Aune, *Revelation 17-22*, p. 1124.

ga', and those in 16.17, have the hearers encountered words explicitly identified as coming from him identified in 21.5 as the One who sits on the throne.[214] Such a startling announcement would alert the hearers to the fact that what follows is as important as anything in the book, perhaps even more important than anything that precedes. These divinely spoken words stand in close continuity with what has preceded in 21.4 for while the hearers have been told of a New Heaven and New Earth, they now hear the One who sits on the throne say, 'Behold I make all things new'. The emphasis of this sentence in the Greek text is on the newness of all things, as καινά ('new') stands first in the sentence immediately after 'behold'. The fact that this is the same word that occurs earlier to describe the radical newness of the New Heaven and the New Earth makes clear that the 'all things' made new are not new things of a previous kind but new things that are hitherto unknown. These words also imply that it is the One who sits on the throne that is the one who creates the New Heaven and New Earth, New Jerusalem, and all things associated with it.[215] The present tense verb 'make' suggests that God is even now making all things new, that he continues to be active in his work of New Creation. His words continue with the command for John to write. Although John has received such instructions from the resurrected Jesus (1.11, 19; 2.1, 8, 12, 18; 3.1, 7) and a voice from heaven (14.13) earlier in the Apocalypse, this is the first and only time that this instruction comes from the One who sits on the throne! This command not only stands in continuity with the previous instructions received by John, but also serves to validate their divine origin, underscoring the value and authority of the words of the book of this prophecy. The words that are to be written, 'these words are faithful and true', are a divine authorization of the trustworthiness of the words spoken by the One who sits on the throne in this context, but by extension, authorization of all the words found in this book. These words are guaranteed by the authority of the one who speaks them![216] As before in the Apocalypse, the combination of the words 'faithful and true' would remind the hearers of the same words used earlier to describe the

---

[214] Caird, *The Revelation of St. John*, p. 265.
[215] Smalley, *The Revelation to John*, p. 540.
[216] Beasley-Murray, *Revelation*, p. 312.

resurrected Jesus (3.14), the Rider on the White Horse (19.11).[217] The declaration of the words spoken by the One who sits on the throne as faithful and true would once again draw attention to the way in which God and the Lamb stand in such a close and intimate relationship to one another.

Verse 6 – These divine words continue, 'And he said to me, "They are completed, I Am the Alpha and the Omega, the Beginning and the End. I will give to the one who is thirsty a gift out of the fountain of living water"'. These words could not help but remind the hearers of those spoken in 16.17, where a great voice coming out of the temple from the throne says Γέγονεν ('It is done').[218] They would perhaps recall that on that occasion this Greek term had reference to the completion of the seven bowls of the judgments of God that lead to the destruction of Babylon the Great (16.18-21). They would also perhaps recall that this utterance stands just before the conclusion of the second major section of the Apocalypse (4.1-16.21), which gives way to the third section of the book that examines more closely the destruction of Babylon the Great and the emergence of the New Jerusalem (17.1-21.8). The appearance of Γέγοναν ('They are done') in 21.6 would be understood to stand in parallel with its counterpart in 16.17, only here the term is a third person plural form and may have reference to the completion of God's words that are faithful and true, God's words that stand behind the New Creation. Owing to the placement of this term the hearers might also suspect that it signals the end of the book's third major section and anticipates a fourth next major section of the Apocalypse, where the New Jerusalem will be examined in more detail.[219] For a second time in the book the hearers encounter a prophetic utterance from God himself, the words of which are identical and quite familiar to Johannine hearers. For ἐγώ εἰμι ('I Am'), the words with which this prophetic utterance begins, are words often on the lips of Jesus in the FG. In Rev. 21.6, as in Rev. 1.8, the predicate to the 'I Am' statement is 'Alpha and Omega', which has reference again to God himself. If, upon the hearers' first encounter with this divine self-identification, they had anticipated

---

[217] Prigent, *L'Apocalypse de Saint Jean*, p. 462.
[218] Murphy, *Fallen Is Babylon*, p. 412.
[219] Bauckham, *The Climax of Prophecy*, p. 7.

what this title might mean, now, standing near the end of the Apocalypse, the hearers are able to understand better just what an extraordinary claim this is. For all of creation, the first heaven and first earth, as well as the New Heaven and New Earth, stand within his purview and are enveloped by his presence and power![220] If the hearers are in any doubt with regard to the meaning of the title, Alpha and Omega, its meaning is made even more explicit by the fact that standing alongside it is the additional title, 'the First and the Last', which would be well known to the hearers from Isa. 44.6, where God's claim to exclusivity as the only God is made clear. These two identifications, standing side by side, convey the idea that God is indeed the beginning and the ending, the first and the last, he is the all in all. Nothing exists outside of him! Perhaps this combination of titles would even suggest to the hearers that the end is not an event but a person.[221] It is this very unrivaled God who promises to the thirsty a gift out of the well of living water. Such words could well be almost too much for the hearers to comprehend, for in them a number of eschatological promises converge including the promise of Yahweh to Judah (Isa. 55.1), Jesus' offer of salvation to those who would believe in him (Jn 4.7-15), and the reward that comes to those who come out of the great tribulation (Rev. 7.16-17).[222] The language, which draws on past longings, present experience, and eschatological hope, would not only encourage the hearers to remain faithful so that they might experience such eschatological provision, but would also reassure them that the eternal life which they experience even now, stands in great continuity with that which awaits in the very presence of God. The sources of this well are deep and never ending![223]

Verse 7 – Still the divine words from the throne continue, 'The one who overcomes will inherit these things and I will be to him God and he will be to me son'. The language of overcoming would no doubt remind the hearers of the eschatological promises to those who overcome found in the seven prophetic messages spoken by the resurrected Jesus to the seven churches of Asia (2.7, 11,

---

[220] Beale, *The Book of Revelation*, p. 1055.
[221] Caird, *The Revelation of St. John*, p. 266.
[222] Sweet, *Revelation*, p. 299.
[223] Smalley, *The Revelation to John*, p. 541.

17, 26-27; 3.5, 12, 21).²²⁴ The fact that the one who overcomes will inherit all these things would not only include these seven promises, but also the eschatological promises of 21.3-4,²²⁵ which seem to culminate in the words, 'I will be to him God and he will be to me son'. It would be difficult to overestimate the impact of these words upon the hearers for at least a couple of reasons. First, owing to the fact that these words echo the divine promise given to David with regard to his seed (2 Sam. 7.14), it is likely that the hearers would understand that this Davidic promise is inherited by those who overcome, offering further support for the understanding that Johannine believers are indeed part of the transformed Israel represented in the 144,000 who are sealed by God (7.1-8). Second, discerning Johannine hearers would also be aware of a most significant detail in this verse. On the one hand, unlike in the promise of 2 Sam. 7.14, the One who sits on the throne is referred to as God rather than Father, perhaps reminding the hearers that on only one occasion in the Johannine literature is God referred to as the Father of believers (Jn 20.17).²²⁶ On the other hand, in the rest of the promise the hearers discover something that would be most astounding and exhilarating all at the same time. For they would well know that the Johannine tradition in which they have been formed is very careful to make a clear distinction between Jesus as Son of God and believers as children of God. In point of fact, the term υἱός ('son') is never used in the FG or 1-3 John to describe believers as sons of God. This term is reserved to describe the unique Son of God, Jesus. And yet here in Rev. 21.7, the hearers learn that the eschatological promise of God to the one who overcomes is that such a one will be υἱός ('son') of God! It is difficult to know what kind of impact such an unexpected and startling discovery would have on the hearers. It would be clear that the fierce monotheism found within the Apocalypse would rule out the idea that any created being is to be considered divine or worshipped, an idolatrous idea that the words of this prophecy condemns all the way through. But, part of the implications of this extraordinary statement would, no doubt, cause the hearers to reexamine the var-

---

²²⁴ Mounce, *The Book of Revelation*, p. 375.
²²⁵ Beasley-Murray, *Revelation*, p. 313.
²²⁶ Prigent, *L'Apocalypse de Saint Jean*, p. 465.

ious eschatological promises for the one who overcomes encountered earlier, in order to discern more deeply other nuances of these promises. Specifically, eating from the tree of life in the paradise of God (2.7), not being harmed by the second death (2.11), receiving the hidden manna and a white stone with a new name (2.17), receiving authority over the nations to shepherd them with a rod of iron – receiving the morning star (2.28), walking in garments of white with Jesus – having his or her name confessed by Jesus before God and his angels (3.5), being made a pillar in the temple of God – having the name of God and the New Jerusalem written upon him or her (3.12), and receiving the authority to sit on the throne of Jesus even as he sits on the throne of his Father (3.21), all of these sound a bit different in the light of the fact that the one who overcomes will be to God υἱός ('son'). At the same time, this discovery may have implications for the close and intimate relationship between Jesus and the believer. What else the overcomer will share with Jesus, aside from his throne, is difficult to discern. Would this encourage the hearers to think in terms of an embryonic theosis, or some other form of sharing in the divine nature? Whatever the full implications of this discovery, it is clear that it would at the least indicate that the close relationship that exists between God and the overcomer is even more intimate than the hearers could have anticipated to this point, a further illustration of the immediacy between God and his people that characterizes the New Jerusalem. To be called υἱός ('son'), now that is really something!

Verse 8 – If these are the promises to the one who overcomes, the hearers next encounter words from the throne about those who do not overcome, 'and to the cowardly and unfaithful and those who commit abominations and murderers and sexually immoral and magicians and idolaters and all liars their part will be in the lake of burning fire and sulfur, which is the second death'. As the hearers make their way through these words it would perhaps become apparent that this is no ordinary list of sinners, but that each of the categories found here appears to represent groups of believers who have succumbed to temptations that kept them from being faithful until the end as overcomers,[227] for almost all of these categories

---

[227] Gundry, 'The New Jerusalem: People as Place, not Place for People', p. 258.

have a special meaning that derives from the Apocalypse itself.[228] Thus, this list has the effect of a warning to Johannine believers not to lose their way and stop short in their faithful witness.[229] The term cowardly, which would be taken as the antonym of overcomer in this context,[230] would have less to do with one's general disposition and more to do with the lack of courage to offer faithful witness in following the Lamb wherever he might go, specifically to death. By saving one's life before the threats of the beast and his false prophet, these cowardly in point of fact lose their lives. Giving in to the fear of suffering and death, they are unable to join those in Smyrna (2.10) and Pergamum (2.13-15) in offering faithful witness.[231] The term unfaithful or unbelieving stands with the first in identifying those Christians who, owing to their fear of the beast and/or the seduction of the Great Whore, are unable to offer the faithful witness that is reflective of their Lord and his followers.[232] Johannine hearers might well recall the words of Jesus to his disciple Thomas, who was in danger of losing his way, no longer to be unbelieving but believing (20.27). There could be no mistaking the meaning of the next category, for the term translated 'those who commit abominations' would be defined by the fact that in the Apocalypse abominations are wholly associated with the activity of the Great Whore (17.4), who is in point of fact identified as the mother of the abominations of the earth (17.5).[233] By succumbing to the seduction of the Great Whore and participating in her abominations, these individuals now share in the punishment that awaits rather than sharing in the eschatological promises to the one who overcomes. Those who commit murder would, as the preceding category, be understood in the light of its meaning in the Apocalypse, where amongst the works of their hands for which the rest of men refuse to repent are murders (9.21).[234] And though a different word is used to de-

---

[228] Murphy, *Fallen Is Babylon*, p. 415.

[229] G.D. Cloete, '"And I saw a New Heaven and a New Earth, for the First ... Were Passed Away" (Revelation 21.1-8)', *Journal of Theology for South Africa* 81 (December, 1992), pp. 58-59.

[230] Aune, *Revelation 17-22*, p. 1131.

[231] Sweet, *Revelation*, p. 300.

[232] Michaels, *Revelation*, p. 239.

[233] Prigent, *L'Apocalypse de Saint Jean*, p. 466.

[234] Ladd, *Revelation*, p. 279.

scribe their murderous activities, discerning Johannine hearers would not be unaware of Jesus' words that Satan is a murderer from the beginning (Jn 8.44), nor would they be unaware that in the Apocalypse refusal to worship the Beast results in death for such offenders (13.15). Thus, this category would suggest that those who identify with the Beast are complicitous in his murderous activity of those whose names are written in the Lamb's book of life.[235] Joining these other categories are the sexually immoral. This word and its word family in the Apocalypse is also very closely identified with the activity of the Great Whore (17.1, 2, 4, 5) whose idolatrous charms result in the sexual immorality of the kings of the earth (18.3, 9), a temptation with which even the church must contend (2.14, 20).[236] For this activity the Great Whore is judged (17.16; 19.2), as are all those who are sexually immoral owing to their economic and idolatrous relationship with her. Next are mentioned the magicians. This activity too is described as a work of their hands for which the rest of 'men' did not offer repentance (9.21), as well as being the means by which the Great Whore had deceived all the nations (18.23). Such an understanding might well lead the hearers to conclude that those who have been enchanted by her magic themselves share in this activity and will suffer a similar fate to the Great Whore. Closely associated with the previous two categories are idolaters. The hearers would know that in the Apocalypse such activity is closely associated with sexual immorality and eating meat sacrificed to idols (2.14, 20), an activity that implies corruption by participation in the economic system that is in collusion with the beast and the Great Whore. Ultimately, those who worship the beast and/or join in the idolatrous activity of the Great Whore, even those who worship the servants of God, commit idolatry. Only God is to be glorified – all who engage in idolatrous activity betray him and forsake true worship. The hearers reach the end of this list when they encounter all liars, a designation that would be rich in meaning for them. By this time they know that when the devil lies he speaks his native tongue (Jn 8.44), that the one who lies is diametrically opposed to the truth (1 Jn 2.21, 27), and that there are those who claim to be apostles or Jews but are not for they lie

---

[235] Mounce, *The Book of Revelation*, p. 375.
[236] Pattemore, *The People of God in the Apocalypse*, p. 211.

(Rev. 2.2; 3.9). Perhaps the hearers would also understand this category to include those who have believed the lie of the beast and the Great Whore and by their participation with them have perpetuated that lie.[237] At the least, they would likely be struck by the difference between those who lie and those followers of the Lamb in whose mouths no lie is found (14.5)! Owing to the close association with the beast and the Great Whore, all such ones as these (cowardly, unfaithful, those who commit abominations, murderers, sexually immoral, magicians, idolaters, and all liars) have a share or portion in the same eternal punishment that awaits the dragon, the beast, and the false prophet (19.20; 20.10). The message could not be any clearer; those who identify with and/or are seduced by the beast and the Great Whore choose to share in their destiny rather than in that which awaits the overcomers.[238] Instead of being called υἱός ('son') by God, and experiencing the fellowship this title portends, these individuals who have not offered faithful witness unto death now experience eternal death – the second death – a death that holds no power over the overcomers. The hearers would well understand that such warnings at this point are clearly intended for the church.[239]

---

[237] Beasley-Murray, *Revelation*, p. 314.
[238] Caird, *The Revelation of St. John*, p. 268.
[239] Sweet, *Revelation*, p. 300.

'IN THE SPIRIT' ON A MOUNTAIN – REVELATION 21.9-22.5

The final major section of Revelation is introduced by the fourth and final 'in the Spirit' phrase (21.10). A detailed description is given of the New Jerusalem noting its appearance (21.9-21), the role of God and the Lamb as temple and light (21.22-27), and the tree of life and the direct immediacy of the presence of God and the Lamb (22.1-5).

Verse 9 – As the hearers ponder the dire warning found in the words of 21.8, their attention is directed once again to an angel, 'And one of the seven angels having the seven bowls, full of the seven last plagues, came and was speaking with me saying, "Come, I will show you the bride, the wife of the Lamb"'. The hearers would no doubt be immediately struck by the fact that the first twelve words in the Greek text of 21.9 are exactly like those with which 17.1 begins. On that occasion the angel invites John to see the judgment of the Great Whore who sits upon many waters. Whether the same angel now reappears in 21.9 or not, the *verbatim* repetition of 17.1 in 21.9 would make certain to the hearers that a contrast is intended between the judgment of the Great Whore and the marriage of the bride of the Lamb.[1] The reappearance of one of the angels having the seven bowls, following closely on the heels of the list of those who do not inherit the eschatological promises of God, would be a not so subtle reminder that the God who rewards is also the God who punishes, continuing the implicit warning to the community to avoid contamination from the seductions of the Great Whore and to offer a faithful witness to God and the Lamb

---

[1] Mounce, *The Book of Revelation*, p. 377.

to the end. This identical opening statement is qualified somewhat in 21.9 where it is noted that these seven bowls were filled with the seven last plagues, both reinforcing the way in which the previous words serve as a warning to the hearers, while also perhaps underscoring the transition from the judgment of the Great Whore to a vision of the bride of the Lamb. The hearers learn that the angel who speaks with John uses identical words to those in 17.1 in issuing the invitation, 'Come, I will show to you'. Johannine hearers would know well from its appearance in 17.1 that in the word Δεῦρο ('come') John is encountering a divine invitation, not unlike the one Jesus issues to Lazarus in the FG (Jn 11.43). As in 17.1 the significance of this invitation is further revealed by the next word from the angel, δείξω ('I will show'), as Johannine hearers would know it to be the term closely associated in the Apocalypse (Rev. 1.1; 4.1) with those things that must take place soon, and a word with a rich history in the FG where it is often used to describe the divine revelation that comes from Jesus and or God (Jn 5.20; 10.32; 14.9; 20.20).[2] Thus, in Rev. 21.9, as in 17.1, the term would strike the hearers as pregnant with divine revelatory meaning. What is to be shown to John on this occasion, in contrast to the judgment of the Great Whore, is 'the bride the wife of the Lamb'. As with the first reference made to the bride of the Lamb in 21.2, this mention would remind the hearers of the radical difference between this city, described as a bride, and fallen Babylon, in which the voice (or sound) of the bride will be heard no longer (18.23), contrasting yet again the impotency of the Great Whore with the promise of the bride. This mention of the bride would again likely resurface for the hearers the expectation of the marriage supper of the Lamb that was announced earlier in 19.7-8. It might strike the hearers as significant that the words τὴν νύμφην ('the bride') and τὴν γυναῖκα ('the wife') stand side by side in the Greek text. While this construction could be taken as superfluous duplication, in point of fact it serves to inform the hearers in a couple of ways. First, this construction makes clear that the bride of the Lamb is identical to the wife of the Lamb, whose bright shining linen garment is defined as the righteous acts of the saints (19.7-8), indicating that the bride and the church are coterminous. Second, the occurrence of these

---

[2] Schneider, 'δείκνυμι, δεικνύω', pp. 280-81.

two nouns side by side might also convey something more about her theological identity, with the term bride pointing to virginal purity,[3] newness, and intimacy and the word wife to covenant fidelity, intimacy, and fruitfulness.[4]

Verse 10 – No sooner is the invitation delivered to John than he is on his way with the angel, 'And he carried me in the Spirit unto a great and high mountain, and showed me the holy city Jerusalem coming down out of heaven from God, having the glory of God'. For the fourth time, the hearers encounter the 'in the Spirit' phrase. From their earlier encounters with the phrase in 1.10, 4.2, and 17.3 they would come to expect that several things are significant about its appearance here in 21.10. First, since there is no hint in the text that John was no longer 'in the Spirit' as this section begins, the phrase's appearance here would convey a sense of continuity between John's experience in chapters 1-3, his experience in chapters 4-16, and his experience in 17.1-21.8. Second, owing to what the hearers learn from their last encounters with this phrase, they likely expect additional prophetic words from or about Jesus in what follows. Third, as the Apocalypse has unfolded they would now understand that this phrase is central to the book's structure and further discern that the means by which the revelation is given is 'in the Spirit'. Fourth, the hearers might well expect the connection between certain geographical locations and being 'in the Spirit' to continue. They would recall that in chapter one there was a connection between John being on the island of Patmos when 'in the Spirit' (1.9-10), in Rev. 4.2 there appears to be a connection between John being 'in the Spirit' and being in heaven, and in Rev. 17.3 John is transported to the wilderness 'in the Spirit'. The hearers learn that as in 17.3, John is again transported 'in the Spirit', only in 21.10 he is not taken to the theologically rich wilderness but to a great and high mountain. This particular site would also be significant for the hearers for a variety of reasons. First, in the OT, mountains function as a place of the divine presence (Gen. 22.2; Exod. 17.9-10; 1 Kgs 18.42), communication and revelation (Exodus 19), as well as prophetic activity (Judg. 9.7; 1 Kgs 18.20-46), and eschatological

---

[3] Allo, *Saint Jean: L'Apocalypse*, p. 316.
[4] Celia Deutsch, 'Transformation of Symbols: The New Jerusalem in Rv 21.1-22.5', *ZNW* 78 (1987), pp. 112-13; and Smalley, *The Revelation to John*, p. 545.

expectation (Isa. 2.2-4; Mic. 4.1-3).[5] Second, the hearers would likely be familiar with the way in which the mountain functioned as a place of solitude and refuge for Jesus in the FG (Jn 6.3, 15). Third, the hearers would no doubt be aware of the similarity between John's experience in Rev. 21.10 and that of Ezekiel who was also set upon a high mountain to see the cleansed and rebuilt Jerusalem (Ezek. 40.1-2).[6] The high level of expectancy on the hearers' part owing to these associations would not be disappointed for the mountain in Rev. 21.10 is described as great and high, which might well be taken as an indication of its supernatural size.[7] But rather than simply being a high vantage point from which to view the New Jerusalem, it appears that John is taken to this enormous mountain owing to the fact that it is the location of the city that he sees. Though the angel promises to show John the bride of the Lamb what John is shown is 'the holy city Jerusalem coming down out of heaven from God'. By now the hearers are familiar with such morphing of images from one into another. In this particular case, the shift from bride to the holy city Jerusalem would be reminiscent of the interplay between the description of the destruction of the Great Whore that morphs into the destruction of Babylon the Great, a similarity that would once again serve to underscore the contrast between these two women and cities. It might not be insignificant that in 21.2 the holy city New Jerusalem is described as a bride adorned for her husband, whereas in 21.9-10 the bride of the Lamb is described as the holy city Jerusalem. What John is shown in 21.10 is identical to what he saw in 21.2, with the exception that in 21.10 Jerusalem is not explicitly referred to as New Jerusalem, though there could hardly be any doubt in the hearers' minds that these cities are one and the same. The hearers would also pick up on the fact that just as the destruction of Babylon the Great was introduced in 16.19 before its more detailed description in 17.1-19.2, so the New Jerusalem, which was introduced in 21.1-2, here in 21.10 begins to be described in greater detail. As noted in 21.2, the hearers would be inclined to discern the close connection between this holy city and the people of God, who themselves are the holy

---

[5] C. Brown, 'ὄρος', *NIDNTT*, III, pp. 1009-1010.
[6] Sweet, *Revelation*, p. 303.
[7] Smalley, *The Revelation to John*, p. 456.

ones. In like fashion they would pick up on the fact that the divine origin of the city is once again underscored in a twofold fashion, as this city continues to be described as 'coming down out of heaven' and as 'from God'. But as the hearers discover, this city does not only originate with God, it bears the glory of God, a phenomenon that would not take the hearers entirely by surprise owing to what has been learned about the direct and immediate nature of God's relationship to his people in New Jerusalem. For if his dwelling is indeed with them, his shekinah would be certain to shine forth, not unlike the way in which Moses' face shone with the glory of God after being in his presence on Mt Sinai (Exod. 34.29-35).[8] If the unmediated eschatological presence of God shines forth with nothing to obstruct it in all its intensity,[9] it is met among his people, his sons, who continue to give him glory in the praise and adoration they offer.

Verse 11 – The nature of God's glory shining forth in the holy city is revealed in the words that follow, 'Her radiance is as a precious stone, as a stone of translucent jasper'. The comparison of the unbelievable brilliance of the city to that of a precious stone would no doubt remind the hearers of the precious stones with which the Great Whore sought to glorify herself and give the impression that such adornment was an accurate indication of her person and worth (17.4; 18.12, 16). In stark contrast, it is not the precious stones that give this city its value or impressiveness. Rather, the value and beauty of a precious stone can only be used in comparison to the radiance of God's glory with which the city is characterized. Specifically, this brilliance is compared to a particular precious stone, translucent jasper. The hearers would not likely be surprised by this comparison for they quickly learned in their journey through the Apocalypse that this very stone is closely connected to the appearance of the One who sits on the throne (4.3) and accordingly is the final stone found upon the breastplate of the High Priest (Exod. 28.17-21), an appearance that further testifies to the close connection between this precious stone and God. The fact that this stone is described as κρυσταλλίζοντι ('clear', 'translucent', or 'clear as

---

[8] Murphy, *Fallen Is Babylon*, p. 418.
[9] Prigent, *L'Apocalypse de Saint Jean*, p. 451.

crystal') may convey something of its purity and value[10] and indicate that it, as the holy city, is especially formed and suited to reflect the glory of God, a characteristic also attributed to the crystal sea before the throne of God (4.6)! Significantly, the two occurrences of this root word in the Apocalypse both are closely associated with reflecting the glory of God.

Verse 12 – The description of the holy city continues for the hearers, 'having a wall great and high, having twelve gates, and upon these gates twelve angels, and names have been written which are of the twelve tribes of the sons of Israel; from the east three gates and from the north three gates and from the south three gates and from the west three gates'. With these words the hearers begin to learn of the physical attributes of the holy city. Several details would be of significance for them. First, the hearers discover that the city John sees is described exactly like the mountain to which he is taken, as great and high, suggesting that the wall is in keeping with the mountain upon which the city apparently sits. As the description continues the hearers could not help but be impressed by the various combinations of the number twelve that they encounter, each occurrence which would remind them of the theologically significant ways in which they have encountered the multiples of the number twelve previously (4.4, 10; 5.8; 7.4-8, 11; 11.16; 12.1; 14.1, 3; 19.4). This theologically significant number is in some ways indistinguishable from the city itself, for it is deeply embedded in its very essence and being. Such emphasis would likely suggest to the hearers perfection in all details. In this case the wall of the city has the perfect number of (twelve) gates, attended by the perfect number of (twelve) angels, with the names of the perfect number of the (twelve) tribes of the sons of Israel! The twelve gates suggest perfect access,[11] while the twelve angels convey the idea of divinely appointed perfect oversight of access. The names that have been written on the gates include all the names of those encountered earlier when the 144,000 of the tribes of the sons of Israel were divinely sealed (Rev. 7.4-8). As the hearers ponder these names perhaps they would remember the strong connection between their own community and the 144,000, the messianic character of this group; that

---

[10] Aune, *Revelation 17-22*, p. 1154.
[11] Lee, *The New Jerusalem in the Book of Revelation*, p. 281.

these are the heirs to what God has done through Israel, owing in part to the presence of the historically important tribes; that this group is marked in part by its priestly identity; that this group has a prophetic identity; and that this group is clearly one marked out as belonging to God and protected by him. Thus, twelve gates, each of which bears the name of one of the tribes of the sons of Israel, would testify to the way in which God's people and the holy city are identical.[12]

Verse 13 – The gates, the hearers discover, are symmetrically distributed around the city with three gates on each side, but in the peculiar geographical order – East, North, South, and West.[13] At the least, the enumeration of these twelve gates that open in all directions would suggest universal access,[14] as no corner of existence stands without three entrances to the holy city.[15] However, it is not altogether clear what the hearers would make of the peculiar order found here, as normally such a description would follow a North, East, South, West direction (e.g. Ezek. 48.30-35). What might such an order suggest to the hearers? Perhaps it would not be overlooked that the place of prominence is given to the East and that it is in this direction that the door of the Jerusalem temple faced.[16] Would such a theological-geographical detail suggest to the hearers that this city, which the wall encloses, is itself a temple, owing to the brilliant radiance of the glory of God present in it and its eastern orientation? Would the hearers also remember that when the sixth bowl was poured out a way was prepared for the kings of the east to make their way to the war of the great day of God the All Powerful One (16.12-16)? If so, would the three gates on the East wall of the holy city suggest to the hearers that there is even hope for these kings from the East, kings who violently opposed God, to enter the holy city? When thinking of the gates on the North would the hearers think of the ways in which Gog and Magog, the traditional enemies from the North (Ezek. 38.6), gathered together to make war with the camp of the saints, God's beloved city (Rev.

---

[12] Gause, *Revelation*, p. 271.

[13] Sweet, *Revelation*, p. 304.

[14] Smalley, *The Revelation to John*, p. 548.

[15] Resseguie, *The Revelation of John*, p. 254.

[16] Yet another observation for which I am indebted to my colleague L.R. Martin.

20.8)? If so, would they be inclined to think that these gates are opened to them and all others from the four points of the earth (20.8) that have opposed God? When contemplating the gates on the South side of the wall, would they be reminded of the city pneumatically called Sodom and Egypt that humiliates the two Spirit inspired prophets (11.8)? Is it possible that there exists access to the holy city even for these? And would thoughts of the three gates on the West remind them of the great sea, which is no more? Is there hope even for those that are in its grip? While it is impossible to know what the hearers would make of the peculiar geographical orientation of the description of these gates, it is almost certain that these details would not be passed over without discerning reflection.

Though the hearers learn that a name of each of the tribes of the sons of Israel appear on each of the holy city's gates, they are not told which names appear on which gates. While there is a sense in which the names of the twelve tribes of the sons of Israel would function as a unified theological reality at this point in the book with little significance attached to the details of which gates bear the names of a given tribe, owing to the fact that the hearers have previously encountered the names of the twelve tribes of the sons of Israel in 7.5-8, perhaps they would wonder about the distribution of these names. If so, perhaps they would understand that the names of the tribes would occur one after the other in order of their occurrence in 7.5-8 and that these names would be attached to the twelve gates in the order in which the gates are named, from East to North to South to West. If so, then perhaps they would envision something like the following:

	Manasseh	Naphtali	Asher	
Benjamin				Gad
Joseph				Reuben
Zebulun				Judah
	Issachar	Levi	Simeon	

When previously encountering these names in 7.5-8 the hearers would have noted a number of things about the list, not least of which was the chiastic way in which the tribes from which the kings of Israel originate (Judah and Benjamin) envelop the entire list, the way in which Reuben and Joseph stand in chiastic parallel, the way in which some of the historically important tribes (Simeon, Levi, Issachar, Zebulun) follow the tribes that come from the handmaid of Leah (Zilpah – Gad and Asher) and Rachel (Bilhah – Naphtali), tribes that often come near the end of various OT lists, as well as the elevation of one grandson (Manassah), the son of Joseph, into this list. If the arrangement proposed above is anything close to their own reflections then perhaps the hearers would notice the way in which the kingly tribes stand across from one another diagonally, the way Reuben and Joseph stand directly across from one another, and how that each of the handmaiden tribes, along with the grandson tribe, stand either directly or diagonally across from one of the historically important tribes including the following pairs: Gad and Zebulun, Asher and Simeon, Naphtali and Levi, and Manassah and Isssachar. Such visualization might well aid the hearers in understanding in even greater detail more about the complex nature of this transformed Israel and its relationship to the holy city coming down from heaven from God.

Verse 14 – The description of the city's wall continues for the hearers, 'And the wall of the city having twelve foundations and upon them twelve names of the twelve apostles of the Lamb'. At this point the hearers' attention is directed to what stands under the wall; its supports and remarkably there are twelve foundations signifying a perfect foundation. Apparently these foundations are visible,[17] as some of the foundations of ancient Jerusalem, so that the names of the twelve apostles of the Lamb are revealed. Such a notation would likely take the hearers somewhat by surprise for a couple of reasons. First, they would well know that this is the first time this phrase has occurred in the Johannine literature, for while 'the Twelve' appears on three occasions in the FG (Jn 6.67, 70, 71), the Twelve are never named as such in the FG, only nine seem to be specifically mentioned (Andrew, Simon Peter, Philip, Nathaniel, Judas Ischariot, Thomas, Judas not Ischariot, Sons of Zebedee), ten if one includes the Beloved Disciple who does not seem to make an apostolic claim for himself. Second, the phrase, the twelve apostles of the Lamb, would be further complicated for the hearers by the

---

[17] Allo, *Saint Jean: L'Apocalypse*, p. 318.

fact that the term apostle never appears in the FG or 1-3 John outside of one proverbial use (Jn 13.14). Nor has the term appeared in the technical sense of the twelve apostles earlier in the Apocalypse (Rev. 2.2; 18.20). From its previous occurrences in the book of prophecy the hearers would be aware that the term apostle conveys the idea of a divine sending, being informed by the extensive sending language in the FG and 1 John, suggesting that there are individuals whom God commissions for specific tasks, especially being sent to participate in the harvest of the world (Jn 4.38; 17.18; 20.21). The occurrence of 'sent' language in the Apocalypse deepens this understanding further as the term ἀποστέλλω ('send') appears on one occasion with reference to the Seven Spirits of God who are sent out into all the earth (Rev. 5.6) and on two other occasions to describe the activity of God who sends his angel to make known to his servants all that is to happen quickly (1.1; 22.6). Such sent ones are likely thought of as special envoys[18] that God has sent into the global harvest to bear witness to the Lamb. The placement of 'the apostles' between 'the saints' and 'the prophets' in 18.20 underscores the fact that the people of God, who have a prophetic vocation, are indeed 'the sent ones' of God himself. The first and only reference to the twelve apostles of the Lamb in 21.14 seems to combine the idea of the Twelve from the FG with that of the special envoys sent by God into the world harvest and their close association with the Lamb. Their relationship to the Lamb, whose mention would remind the hearers of his death,[19] may suggest, along with the appearance of the term apostles in 18.20, that they too have followed the Lamb even unto death. At the same time, the hearers would likely be struck by the foundational role they play in the holy city. Such a foundational role for the twelve apostles of the Lamb fits well with the way in which the hearers seem to have understood the term generally, but here it appears to be used in a more technical way. The fact that the names of the twelve apostles appear along with the names of the twelve tribes of the sons of Israel would invite reflection, perhaps alerting the hearers to the way in which both the twelve tribes of the sons of Israel and the twelve apostles of the Lamb are foundational for the redemptive commu-

---

[18] So Prigent, *L'Apocalypse de Saint Jean*, p. 395.
[19] Aune, *Revelation 17-22*, p. 1157.

nity, a reality to which the twenty four elders may point as they themselves appear to stand for all the redeemed.[20] In addition to their contribution to the overall image of perfection in the holy city, owing to their respective numbers, the corporate image of these two groups of twelve would convey to the hearers a sense of the perfection of God's people in the holy city.[21]

Verse 15 – With these details of the wall of the city in their minds the attention of the hearers is directed back to the angel, 'And the one speaking with me has a measuring rod of gold in order that he might measure the city and her gates and her wall'. Attention back upon the angel who is speaking with John would create within the hearers an expectancy that they, with John, will be shown even more about the holy city. These expectations are not diminished by the fact that this angel has a measuring rod of gold. The mention of such an instrument would well remind the hearers of the fact that John himself had earlier measured the temple of God and the altar and those who worshipped in it, a measurement that on that occasion conveys protection to the things measured (11.1). But in 21.15 it is not John who measures but the angel, who is in a position to show John and the hearers even more about the holy city. If John's measuring signified protection for the temple, altar, and worshippers for forty-two months, perhaps this angelic measurement of the holy city would signify eternal protection and/or security for the people of God. The fact that the measuring rod is made of gold would convey to the hearers something about the importance and value of that which is being measured[22] and would perhaps be thought as altogether suitable for measuring a holy city that descends from heaven from God,[23] as to this point gold seems to be valued as the purest of metals and it has regularly been associated with heaven and heavenly objects (4.4; 5.8; 8.3; 9.13; 14.14; 15.6, 7). Such a valuable measuring rod could not help but create a sense of expectancy and excitement as to what awaits John and his hearers in the unfolding description of the holy city.

---

[20] Beasley-Murray, *Revelation*, p. 321.

[21] Gause, *Revelation*, p. 271.

[22] Smalley, *The Revelation to John*, p. 550.

[23] Aune, *Revelation 17-22*, p. 1159.

Verse 16 – As the angel measures the holy city the hearers are informed as to its dimensions and shape, 'And the city lies as a square and her length is as the breadth. And he measured the city with the rod upon twelve thousand stadia; the length and the breadth and the height of her is equal'. What the hearers now learn continues to push their imaginative abilities beyond their boundaries![24] Like the temple that Ezekiel (45.2) sees, this city lies square, a point made explicit when the hearers are told that its length is equal to its breadth. The square itself seems to be a shape associated with perfection.[25] But the size of the holy city that the angel measures dwarfs Ezekiel's city (48.8-9, 30-35) on an almost one thousand to one scale,[26] for when the angel measured the city he found that it measured 144,000 stadia! The first thing to strike the hearers may well be the fact that the size of the city is identical to the number of those sealed from the twelve tribes of the sons of Israel introduced in Rev. 7.5-8, the 144,000 who appear with the Lamb who have his name and the name of his Father written upon their foreheads (14.1-4), still another clue that the holy city and the holy people are one and the same. A second thing that would impress itself upon the hearers is the enormous, almost supernatural size of the holy city,[27] for each of its sides measure 144,000 stadia. If a stadion contains about 400 cubits, which measures to about 214 yards, then the size of this city is about 1,500 miles on each side![28] Such a city has never been seen, for even Babylon of old measured only 120 stadia per side (Herodotus 1.178), which was itself an enormous size.[29] The holy city would stretch across the known world and into the heavens itself, perhaps indicating that the New Heaven and New Earth unite in the New Jerusalem![30] This city is not only supernaturally enormous, but its dimensions also reveal that it is the perfect home for the people of God who number 144,000 and even the

---

[24] Caird, *The Revelation of St. John*, p. 272.

[25] Kiddle, *The Revelation of St John*, p. 429.

[26] Koester, *Revelation and the End of All Things*, p. 196.

[27] Smalley, *The Revelation to John*, p. 551.

[28] O.R. Sellers, 'Weights and Measures', *The Interpreter's Dictionary of the Bible* (ed. G.A. Buttrick; Nashville, TN: Abingdon, 1962), 4, p. 838.

[29] Sweet, *Revelation*, p. 305.

[30] Bealsey-Murray, *Revelation*, p. 322.

innumerable crowd as well![31] Finally, when the hearers learn that this city not only sits as a square, but its length and width and height are also equal, they would realize that the holy city actually takes the form of a cube. Not only would this shape imply perfection, but the hearers would also be hard pressed not to remember that the shape of the holy of holies in the temple takes the form of a cube as well, which was twenty cubits long, wide, and high (1 Kgs 6.20).[32] Such a discovery would make clear that the holy city is itself a temple; indeed, the entire city is a holy of holies! Such a reality would fit well with the immediacy and direct access believers have to God in New Jerusalem (Rev. 21.1-8), for the city is itself a temple, and this realization might even go some ways toward explaining the peculiar geographical direction of the description of the city gates, where prominence is given to the East, the direction which the Jerusalem temple faced.

Verse 17 – As the measurement continues, even more is revealed about the wall of the city, 'And he measured her wall being 144 cubits, a measure of man, which is of an angel'. Once again a multiple of twelve appears in the description of the holy city and its wall, with the measurement of the wall being 144 cubits. Such a measurement would no doubt continue the idea of perfection present throughout the description of the holy city, in this case suggesting that the wall itself is a perfect fit for the city, fulfilling its function perfectly.[33] But it is not altogether clear what the hearers would take its function to be, in part owing to the fact that while 144 cubits is not an insignificant measurement for a wall, in comparison to the size of the city itself this measurement is almost ludicrously small.[34] For if the length of the various walls are 144,000 stadia (ca. 1,500 miles), the wall itself is measured at 144 cubits (ca. 218 feet). Such a comparatively small wall would surely generate a certain amount of reflection amongst the hearers. In the first place, it is not altogether clear whether the 144 cubit measurement describes the height or breadth of the city's wall. It is possible that the wall's breadth is here in view, serving as a graphic boundary of de-

---

[31] Michaels, *Revelation*, p. 242.
[32] Mounce, *The Book of Revelation*, p. 380.
[33] Gause, *Revelation*, p. 271.
[34] Sweet, *Revelation*, p. 305.

marcation.³⁵ Yet, owing to the fact that the wall has earlier been described as great and high (21.12), like the mountain to which John was transported, perhaps the hearers would take the wall to be 144 cubits high, a good height for a wall, to which only a few on earth would compare. Or perhaps the hearers would understand the measurement to have reference to both the height and breadth of the wall, in keeping with the symmetrical dimensions of the city itself. While the wall would well strike the hearers as comparatively small, perhaps they would be more impressed by the way in which the wall's dimensions would accentuate the unbelievable enormity of the holy city that lies behind these walls! What would the hearers understand the purpose of this wall to be? On first encounter they might assume that this wall designates protection and security as city walls in the ancient world normally would and it is likely that they would be unable to imagine any foe, even if they existed at this point in the narrative, being able to penetrate such a great and perfect wall. At the same time, perhaps the comparatively small size of the wall would draw attention to the fact that God's ability to protect and secure the holy city is not dependent upon walls or other fortifications.³⁶ But there is one more aspect of these words about the measurement of the city's wall that would likely give the hearers pause and perhaps encourage even more pneumatic discernment on their part, for the measurement is described as 'a measure of a man, which is of an angel'. On one level the hearers would understand these words as indicating that the measurement of the wall is given in terms of the human measurement of cubits but is actually measured by an angel,³⁷ suggesting that such a task (the measuring of the entire city which is also given in human measurements) would seem to be well beyond the abilities of any human! But such an understanding might not exhaust the meaning of these words for the hearers. Perhaps this somewhat odd notation, as well as the comparatively small wall, would spur the hearers to discern on the order of earlier discernment with regard to the number of the beast, which is the number of man, 666. For interestingly enough, when the Greek word ἄγγελος ('angel') is written in Hebrew characters

---

³⁵ Sweet, *Revelation*, p. 305.
³⁶ Beasley-Murray, *Revelation*, p. 323.
³⁷ Ladd, *Revelation*, p. 282.

its numerical value is 144.[38] Such a realization would perhaps serve to contrast for the hearers humanity debased to the level of the beast (666), with humanity exalted to the level of the angels (144), surrounded by the square of 12.[39]

Verse 18 – If the hearers are engaged in pneumatic discernment with regard to the number of the angel their attention is quickly directed from numbers to materials, 'And the material of her wall is jasper, and the city is pure gold as pure glass'. The hearers might well be impressed by the fact that the material of the wall is jasper, for this very stone earlier describes the One who sits on the throne (4.3)[40] as well as the radiance of the holy city Jerusalem through which the glory of God shines. Thus, like God and his city, the wall is characterized by the glory of God, so that the walls of this holy of holies shine forth the glory of God rather than hides it.[41] Not surprisingly, the material out of which the holy city is made is transparent gold, clear as glass or crystal, which itself reflects all the more the glory of God that is within the city. The gold out of which the city is constructed underscores the value of the city, for gold is the most valuable of metals,[42] and demonstrates the way in which this holy city far transcends any of its earthly rivals, even the earthly temple in which jasper and gold were used in its construction (1 Kings 6-7). The spectacular splendor of the holy city shines forth the glory of God in ways that stagger the imagination.[43]

Verses 19-20 – For the hearers the description continues, 'The foundations of the wall of the city were adorned with every precious stone; the first foundation jasper, the second sapphire, the third chalcedony, the fourth emerald, the fifth sardonyx, the sixth carnelian, the seventh chrysolite, the eighth beryl, the ninth topaz, the tenth chrysoprase, the eleventh jacinth, and the twelfth amethyst'. As the hearers reflect upon these words a number of things

---

[38] א = 1 + נ = 50 + ג = 3 + ל = 30 + ס = 60 = 144. On this cf. Bauckham, *The Climax of Prophecy*, p. 298.

[39] Bauckham (*The Climax of Prophecy*, p. 300) concludes, 'Thus whereas humanity debased to the level of the beast bears the triangular number 666, humanity raised to the level of the angels in the new Jerusalem is surrounded by the square of 12'.

[40] Sweet, *Revelation*, p. 305.

[41] Mealy, *After the Thousand Years*, p. 198 n. 1.

[42] Prigent, *L'Apocalypse de Saint Jean*, p. 474.

[43] Gause, *Revelation*, p. 272.

would be significant for them. First, they would no doubt see the connection between the bride κεκοσμημένην ('adorned') for her husband (21.2) and the foundations that are κεκοσμημένοι ('adorned') with these precious stones (21.19), further underscoring the relationship between the bride and the city. Second, the richness and value of the holy city made of gold would be further emphasized owing to such elaborate foundations. Third, perhaps the hearers would remember that great and costly stones were used as a foundation for the house of God that Solomon built (1 Kgs 5.17).[44] Fourth, such a vision would also likely remind of the promise that Yahweh will lay foundations of sapphire in the ideal days to come (Isa. 54.11).[45] Fifth, perhaps the hearers would recall in Ezekiel's lamentation to the King of Tyre the list of precious stones in the Eden of God, where several of these very stones appear (Ezek. 28.13).[46] Sixth, owing to the fact that the holy city takes the shape of a temple, it is likely that the hearers would recall the description of the breastplate of the high priest on which were twelve precious stones in four rows of three,[47] where several of the stones the hearers encounter in Rev. 21.19-20 appear. Such a convergence of intertexts could hardly help but convey that in the foundations of the holy city Jerusalem a number of OT prophecies and ideas are fulfilled. Owing to the fact that these stones are so intimately connected to God, it would be difficult for the hearers to escape the conclusion that all the foundations point to the special presence of God in the holy city that descends from heaven from God! But such associations would not exhaust the significance of these foundations for the hearers as they would well recall that in the inaugural vision of heaven, the One who sits on the throne has the appearance of jasper and carnelian, with a rainbow around the throne that resembles emerald (4.3). As each of these stones has a prominent place in the twelve foundations, the relationship of the foundations with the special presence of God would be reinforced all the more. Neither are they likely to forget that each of the foundations has written upon it a name of one of the twelve apostles of

---

[44] Sweet, *Revelation*, p. 306.
[45] Beasley-Murray, *Revelation*, p. 324.
[46] Kiddle, *The Revelation of St John*, p. 433.
[47] Aune, *Revelation 17-22*, p. 1165.

the Lamb, though the hearers are not told which names appear on which foundations. But here the enumeration of the respective foundations, makes even clearer the fact that each foundation is made of a specific precious stone, perhaps conveying the idea of the foundations laying on top of one another.[48] This aspect of the stunning vision of the holy city would add to the overall splendor therein contained. For as the hearers reflect on this extraordinary convergence of colors[49] perhaps they would be struck by the way in which not only are various shades of the primary colors of green (jasper, chalcedony, emerald, beryl, chrysoprase), blue (sapphire, jacinth), and red (sardonyx, carnelian) prominent, but also that there are present other colors, yellow (chrysolite, topaz) and purple (amethyst), created by the combination of primary colors. Thus, even the foundations of the holy city are found to be perfectly suited to it![50]

Verse 21 – Hardly allowed to catch their collective breath the hearers are told even more about the holy city, 'And the twelve gates are twelve pearls, each one of the gates was out of one pearl. And the street of the city was pure gold as clear as glass or crystal'. If the hearers found the description of the twelve foundations of the holy city staggering to comprehend, they would experience no less bewildering amazement at the words of 21.21. For while they might well be prepared to think of the gates of the city as inlaid with pearl, what they are in fact told is that each of the gates is indeed one pearl! While the descriptions of other parts of the holy city might prepare them for such an incredibly extraordinary obser-

---

[48] Smalley, *The Revelation to John*, p. 545.

[49] For the relationship between these precious stones and their respective colors cf. Mounce, *The Book of Revelation*, p. 382.

[50] An intriguing Christological interpretation of the specific order of the precious stones that adorn the foundations comes from M. Wojciechowski ('Apocalypse 21.19-20: titres christologiques cachés dans la liste des pierres précieuses', *NTS* 33 (1987), p. 154) who points out that the first letter of each stone produces the following combination of sacred names and titles IC XC CC X B T X Υ A which stand for 'Jesus, Christ, Savior, Christ, King and Telos, Christ, Son of Man'. This configuration underscores the title of Christ, presenting his eschatological mission as the realization of the prophets about the king messiah and about the Son of Man. While it is not altogether clear that the hearers would arrive at such a result via their pneumatic discernment, one of the things in favor of such a possibility is the fact that all of these names and titles would be familiar to Johannine hearers.

vation, this detail could not help but push their imaginative abilities to their limits.[51] But perhaps such an amazing detail would, as other amazing details have earlier, push the hearers to engage in more pneumatic discernment as to the meaning of this astounding detail. If so, then perhaps this mention of these gates of pearls would remind them of the only other times they have encountered the word pearl in the Apocalypse to this point. Interestingly enough, the word pearl has been exclusively associated with the Great Whore (17.4), Babylon the Great (18.16), and her merchants (18.12). In each case, the mention of pearls underscores the opulent wealth of the Great Whore, as she is bedecked in pearls and in this regard appears to have no rivals! But just as her judgment and destruction reveals the impotency of her claims and the illegitimacy of her way of life, so now it is revealed that the woman with whom she is compared, the bride of the Lamb, is adorned to such an unbelievable extent that the Great Whore's claims to wealth are revealed to be almost laughable. For if she makes claims by wearing pearls around her neck and upon her clothing, the bride of the Lamb has (wears?) whole gates that are composed of single pearls – a most staggering comparison indeed. The bride of the Lamb outshines the Great Whore in incomparable ways! But there is more, for not only do gates of pearls stand as entrances to this rich city, but once inside those who enter also walk on a street of gold. While it is not altogether clear if the hearers would understand ἡ πλατεῖα τῆς πόλεως ('the street of the city') as having reference to the central street of the city, to the plaza of the city, or as a collective having reference to all the streets of the city,[52] it would appear that such a reference would be significant to the hearers for at least two reasons. First, the mention the street of gold could hardly help but remind the hearers that just as the priests of the OT ministered on a floor inlaid with gold (1 Kgs 6.30), those who enter the holy city walk on a street of gold that is not just covered with gold but is made of solid gold that is clear as glass,[53] thus continuing to remind them of the fact that the holy city is itself a temple. Second, at the same time the words might hearken the hearers back to the only

---

[51] Metzger, *Breaking the Code*, p. 101.
[52] Aune, *Revelation 17-22*, p. 1166.
[53] Mounce, *The Book of Revelation*, p. 383.

other time they have encountered the similar phrase, 'the street of the great city', where the body of the two prophetic witnesses lay for three days in utter humiliation (Rev. 11.8). The hearers would no doubt be struck by the contrast between the shame the saints experienced in the street of the great city and the eternal glory that awaits in the holy city![54]

Verse 22 – After hearing numerous details about the description of the holy city the hearers now learn about what is not seen in the city, 'And a temple I did not see in it, for the Lord God the All Powerful One and the Lamb is the temple'. For the hearers these words might be the most surprising discovery about the holy city yet, for the following reasons. First, the grammatical construction of the Greek text suggests that John expected to see a temple in the holy city.[55] Second, the hearers have encountered sufficient temple language in the book to this point to lead them to believe that a temple does indeed exist in heaven (7.15; 11.19; 14.14, 17; 15.5, 6, 8; 16.1, 17),[56] an understanding that might lead them to conclude that they expected to learn of a temple in the holy city as well. Third, Ezekiel devotes seven chapters (Ezekiel 40-46) to his description of the eschatological temple and its activities,[57] which might also lend credence to the idea that the hearers would expect a temple alongside John. Yet, while the hearers might well be surprised along with John that a temple he did not see in the city, they might not be completely surprised to learn that the Lord God the All Powerful One and the Lamb is the temple, for in this discovery several things would converge for them. For as their attention is directed to this aspect of the holy city its shape as a cube – like the holy of holies (Rev. 21.16), the eastern orientation of its twelve gates (21.13), the fact that the overcomer is promised to be made a pillar in the temple of my God (3.12), the unmediated presence of God in the New Jerusalem (21.1-8),[58] the priestly language scattered throughout the book (1.6; 5.10; 7.15; 20.6), and the fact that Jesus' body is spoken of as a temple in the Johannine literature (Jn 2.19,

---

[54] Wall, *Revelation*, pp. 254-55.
[55] Smalley, *The Revelation to John*, p. 556.
[56] Murphy, *Fallen Is Babylon*, p. 423.
[57] Mounce, *The Book of Revelation*, p. 383.
[58] Of which this is another sign, Resseguie, *The Revelation of John*, p. 256.

20)[59] all come together in a new and comprehensible fashion. The relationship between God and his people in the holy city Jerusalem represents complete integration of God with his people, with the mention of the Lamb underscoring the means by which salvation itself is accomplished.[60]

Verse 23 – The hearers learn of still other things that are not in the city, 'And the city has no need of the sun nor the moon in order that they might enlighten it, for the glory of God lightens it and his lamp is the Lamb'. For several reasons, these words would be filled with significance for Johannine hearers. First, taken together they could hardly help but remind the hearers of Isaiah's near identical wording with regard to the future that awaits God's people (Isa. 60.19-20),[61] suggesting yet another way in which OT prophecy is fulfilled in the holy city Jerusalem. Second, the fact that the city has no need of the sun or moon would no doubt be taken as closely connected to the fact that there is no temple in the city, owing to the radiance of God's direct presence. Third, the fact that the sun (and moon) has functioned as the standard by which to judge illumination in the book indicates something of the comparative power of the glory of God to illuminate, for if the sun previously is a point of reference for comparison (Rev. 1.16; 10.1; 12.1; 19.17), now even it is outdistanced in its ability to illuminate. Fourth, the hearers are acquainted with the fact the holy city radiates with the glory of God (21.11), but now learn that the holy city is enlightened by the glory of God, a glory so powerful that it makes redundant the need for the sun or the moon! Nor would it likely escape the hearers' attention that the word ἐφώτισεν ('enlightened') carries with it soteriological associations as it is the same term used to describe the Logos shining in the darkness and the darkness' inability to comprehend or extinguish it (Jn 1.5). Thus, the way in which the glory of God enlightens the holy city carries with it salvific overtones; its light does not simply enable physical sight, but soteriological sight as well! Not only does the glory of God act in such a way but so too does the Lamb who reflects the glory of God in an especially impressive way, for the Lamb is the lamp for the holy city through

---

[59] Aune, *Revelation 17-22*, p. 1168.
[60] Gause, *Revelation*, p. 273.
[61] Prigent, *L'Apocalypse de Saint Jean*, p. 478.

whom the glory of God shines forth in its comprehensive salvific fashion. Unlike the judged city Babylon the Great, where the light of a lamp no longer enlightens it (Rev. 18.23), this holy city is enlightened by the Lamb himself!

Verse 24 – The hearers next learn, 'And the nations will walk by means of its light, and the kings of the earth bring their glory into it'. The hearers would find these words significant for the following reasons. First, the words' content could not help but remind the hearers of yet another Isaianic promise with regard to the ideal age to come, where once again near identical wording occurs (Isa. 60.3). Second, there could be little doubt that the hearers would understand this language to mean that the nations who walk in its light are those who have experienced his salvation, owing in part to the fact that in Johannine thought the word περιπατέω ('walk') functions metaphorically as a description of one's relationship or fellowship with God, Jesus, and/or the Light (Jn 6.66; 8.12; 11.9-10; 12.35; 1 Jn 1.6-7; 2.6, 11; 2 Jn 4, 6; 3 Jn 3, 4) and this very word has been encountered earlier in the Apocalypse to describe fellowship with the resurrected Jesus (Rev. 2.1), eschatological reward (3.4), and ethical conduct (16.15). Third, in some ways the words of 21.24 follow on quite naturally from the optimistic impression left by the perfect and universal access to the holy city conveyed by the twelve gates that open in all directions (21.13). The hearers would well recall from that context the questions raised with regard to the possible conversion of the enemies of God and his people from the East (the kings from the east), the North (Gog and Magog, traditional enemies from the north), the South (the great city pneumatically known as Sodom and Egypt), and the West (the sea that is no more). Thus, it appears that the hearers would discern a further reason to believe that the rebellious nations will find a place in God's salvific light that fills the holy city, fulfilling their previous expectations based upon descriptions of the nations in precisely these terms (5.9; 7.9; 11.9-13; 15.3-4); nations that are the specific objects of faithful witness and prophecy (10.11; 11.9-13; 14.6). Fourth, at the same time, the hearers would know full well that the nations have been previously spoken of as being opposed to God and his people (11.9-13, 18), as being under the authority of the beast (13.7), as being intoxicated with the wine of the Great Whore's sexual immorality (14.8; 18.3) – under her domination (17.15) – deceived by her magic (18.23), being deceived by Satan (20.3, 8), and as being judged by God and the Rider on the white horse (16.17; 19.15). The fact that the nations, perhaps these very nations, are spoken of as walking in the light of the holy city – the very glory of God – would stretch the imaginative abilities of the hearers to their limits as they are forced to hold these dialectical possibilities together, the possible implication being that God is even more gracious and longsuffering than they could have ever imagined! These first words of 21.24 would clearly suggest to the hearers that the nations who walk in the light of the holy city are indeed converted, but would go further, being pregnant with meaning, causing them to reflect on the incongruities of these two ends of the dialectic – that perhaps those who have expressed such open hostility and opposition to God and his people somehow experience his salvific light! If the hearers are uneasy and reluctant to consider such possibilities, the rest of the words in 21.24 almost demand that they give them serious reflection as the hearers to continue to engage in pneumatic discernment, for not only are the nations said to walk in the light of the holy city, but it is also said that 'the kings of the earth bring their glory into it'! These words, as those that precede, would be significant to the hearers. First, as with the previous words in this verse, these that follow could not help but remind the hearers of the same Isaianic promise with regard to the ideal age to come, where near identical wording occurs (Isa. 60.3). Second, it is clear that the kings of the earth in this verse are seen not only as entering the holy city, but also as bringing their glory into it, a word that in the Apocalypse is closely associated with worship (Rev. 1.6; 4.9, 11; 5.12, 13; 7.12; 11.13; 14.7; 16.9; 19.1, 7),[62] indicating that the kings of the earth too are engaged in the worship of the God whose own glory enlightens the entire city. Third, in some ways these words would appear to be even more challenging to the hearers than those with regard to the nations, for aside from the first reference to the kings of the earth, where Jesus is referred to as the ruler of the kings of the earth (1.5), there is no other place in the whole of the Apocalypse where the kings of the earth do not function as

---

[62] Matthewson, 'The Destiny of the Nations in Revelation 21.1-22.5: A Reconsideration', p. 130.

the enemies of God (6.15; 17.2, 18; 18.3, 9; 19.19) save in 21.24,[63] but in point of fact appear to have been destroyed by the Rider on the white horse! And yet, here they are spoken of as bringing their own objects of worship into the holy city.[64] Would not such an inversion suggest that a remarkable conversion takes place amongst the kings of the earth whose idolatrous greed and self serving pursuit of power, whose opposition to God and his people have been transformed so that they now worship God with the very things they had formally sought for themselves?[65] As with the nations, it would be clear to the hearers that these kings of the earth have indeed been converted as a result of the faithful witness of God's people, but would the absolute polarities and incongruities encountered in the text not push the hearers to contemplate a greater wideness in God's mercy than they have hitherto been prepared to explore or for which even to hope?[66] If so, would not such a marvelous optimism serve to encourage their faithful pneumatic witness all the more[67] – that the conversion of the nations and their kings might possibly include even greater numbers than the hearers are able to see or have heard in the words of this prophecy and that, therefore, they cannot begin to calculate its importance? If so, the significant fact that the two positive references to the kings of the earth in the Apocalypse envelop the negative references would not be lost on the hearers.[68]

Verses 25-26 – The perfect access to the holy city is made even clearer in the words the hearers next encounter, 'And its gates are never closed by day, for night is not there, and they will bring the glory and honor of the nations into it'. Not only do the twelve gates provide perfect access to the holy city from all directions, but they also provide immediate access, for unlike the city gates of the an-

---

[63] Aune, *Revelation 17-22*, p. 1171.

[64] Caird, *The Revelation of St. John*, p. 279.

[65] Beasley-Murray, *Revelation*, p. 328; Sweet, *Revelation*, p. 308; and Bauckham, *The Climax of Prophecy*, p. 315.

[66] Pattemore, *The People of God in the Apocalypse*, p. 202.

[67] As R. Herms [*An Apocalypse for the Church and the World: The Narrative Function of Universal Language in the Book of Revelation* (BZNW 143; Berlin: Walter de Gruyter, 2006), p. 260] notes, '… universal language does not necessarily presuppose universal salvation; rather, it serves to vindicate the faithful community, and validate their present circumstances in light of a future reversal'.

[68] Herms, *An Apocalypse for the Church and the World*, p. 211.

cient world, where gates would close for security purposes especially at night, these gates never close during the day owing to the fact that the angelic sentries and God himself ensure its security. In point of fact, these gates would appear to provide around the clock access to the holy city, in accord with the Isaianic promises of the ideal days to come (Isa. 60.11),[69] for there is no night there! These words would likely convey at least two things to the hearers. First, they would no doubt take these words to indicate that the radiance of the glory of God means that darkness is never manifested in the holy city, which is enlightened at all times. Confirming this interpretation is the fact that whenever the words day and night occur in close proximity in the Apocalypse (Rev. 4.8; 7.15; 12.10; 14.11; 20.10), with one exception (8.12), the meaning conveys the idea of around the clock activity or access. Second, discerning Johannine hearers might well detect here a still deeper meaning owing to how in Johannine thought both night (Jn 3.2; 9.4; 11.10; 13.30; 19.39) and darkness (1.5; 6.17; 8.12; 12.35, 46; 1 Jn 1.5; 2.8, 9, 11) often have ominous spiritual connotations. If the hearers pick up on these associations in Rev. 21.25 it would be further proof that there is no place in the holy city for the unbelief and doubt of night and/or darkness – for all is light in it.[70] Thus, this around the clock, immediate access to the holy city means that the kings of the earth will have ample opportunity to bring into it the glory and honor of the nations. The combination of the words glory and honor would well remind the hearers of that particular combination in 4.9, 11 and 5.12-13 where they combine to describe the worship given to the One who sits on the throne and to the Lamb,[71] indicating once again that the kings and nations offer genuine worship to God as they enter into the holy city. Perhaps the hearers would also see here a contrast between the earthly kings who brought their glory into the Babylon of old,[72] and is yet another sign of the conversion of the nations, and the kings of the earth that bring in their glory in accord with the eschatological hopes found in various places in the OT (Isa. 45.20, 22, 24; Zech. 2.11; 8.23; Dan. 7.14). Such a contrast

---

[69] Beasley-Murray, *Revelation*, p. 329.
[70] Smalley, *The Revelation to John*, p. 560.
[71] Smalley, *The Revelation to John*, p. 558.
[72] Sweet, *Revelation*, p. 310.

would further reinforce the dialectical relationship confronting the hearers between the conversion of the nations and the judgment of those who fail to repent,[73] who appear to be punished in the lake of burning sulfur (Rev. 20.15).

Verse 27 – If the hope for the conversion of the nations is nurtured in the hearers by the words found in 21.24-26, the other end of the dialectic is underscored in the very next words they encounter, 'And every impure thing and the one who engages in abominations and falsehood will never enter into it, except those who have been written in the Lamb's book of life'. While the previous verses have made clear that the nations and the kings of the earth will be present in the holy city, they do not make explicit at what point these entities convert nor do they explain how these opponents of God, who apparently are punished by God in the lake of burning sulfur, are transformed into those worthy to gain admission to the holy city. Without resolving such tensions for hearers, the words of 21.27 reveal that however such a transformation comes about, those who enter the holy city, including the nations and the kings of the earth, will not enter it as impure entities or as those who are characterized by abominations, like the Great Whore (17.4-5; 21.8), or falsehood, like the beast (21.8). Rather, just like all others who overcome, they too must of necessity have their names written in the Lamb's book of life (3.5; 13.8; 17.8; 20.12, 15),[74] an indication that they too have experienced the salvation offered by the Lamb who had been slaughtered (5.6) and whose blood has loosed them from their sin (1.5; 5.9), and thus have rejected the Beast and joined in offering faithful witness to the Lamb!

Chapter 22, Verses 1-2a – The attention of John and his hearers is next directed to yet another incredibly significant sight, 'And he showed to me a river of living water clear as crystal, coming out of the throne of God and of the Lamb in the middle of the street'. As with so many images encountered in the Apocalypse in this one a number of ideas converge. For in this river the hearers no doubt are made to think of the original river that came out of the Garden of Eden feeding four fountainheads (Gen. 2.10), the river Ezekiel describes that brings life to all things it encounters (Ezek. 47.1-12),

---

[73] Aune, *Revelation 17-22*, p. 1173.
[74] Michaels, *Revelation*, p. 246.

and the river of living water of which Jesus speaks in the FG, the most recent reference which the hearers may remember is in Rev. 21.6 in which past longings, present experience, and eschatological hope combine indicating something of the deep and never ending soteriological resources that come from God and the Lamb. In 22.1, emphasis is placed upon the image of this river of living water as a central one, conveying something of its strategic salvific importance in the holy city, clear as crystal like other aspects of heaven and the New Jerusalem (Rev. 4.6; 21.11). The flow of this river through the city underscores its immediate and ready access to all those who inhabit New Jerusalem. Johannine hearers would likely be struck by the way in which the pneumatological promises known from the FG find their ultimate fulfillment and consummation in the holy city. The divine origin of this river of living water is made clear by the fact that it flows from the very throne of God and the Lamb, a more explicit depiction of the river's divine origin that would be hard to imagine for in some ways the throne of God and the Lamb is an unrivalled image of the presence of God in New Jerusalem. This river is God's river; it is the Lamb's river. It is their salvific gift to all those who believe in and offer faithful witness to them; a complete gift that provides abundantly for all soteriological needs. The hearers would likely be impressed by the fact that there is but one throne, not two, shared by God and the Lamb[75] in accordance with the words of the resurrected Jesus to the church in Laodicea (3.21).[76] This incredible image would underscore for the hearers yet again the extraordinarily intimate nature of the relationship of God and the Lamb and would also continue to nurture the theme of the unbelievably immediate and direct access God's 'sons' have to his presence and that of the Lamb in the holy city. At the same time, mention of the Lamb would remind the hearers once more of his own faithful witness offered unto God that is the basis of the redemption of all those who believe in him. The strategic location of the river is revealed in part by the fact that it flows prominently down the city's street,[77] suggesting that all who inhabit

---

[75] Murphy, *Fallen Is Babylon*, p. 428.
[76] Ladd, *Revelation*, p. 286.
[77] Smalley, *The Revelation to John*, p. 562.

the holy city surround and have access to this soteriological provision.

Verse 2b – The hearers learn more about this river and its effects in the next words they encounter, 'and on either side of the river a tree of life bearing twelve fruits, each month giving its fruit, and the leaves of the tree for healing of the nations'. The potency of the river of living water is underscored by the fact that it is surrounded by plantings of the tree of life on either side of the river.[78] Mention of the tree of life, in conjunction with the river of living water, could not help but remind the hearers of the tree of life found in the Garden of Eden. They would well remember how human access to the fruit of this tree was prohibited after Adam and Eve ate the fruit of the tree of the knowledge of good and evil, lest they take the fruit of the tree of life and live forever (Gen. 3.22-24), with Cherubim placed at the entrance of the Garden with a flaming sword to protect this tree of life. But the appearance of the tree of life in Rev. 22.2 would not take the hearers completely by surprise for in the very first prophetic message given by the resurrected Jesus to the seven churches the hearers learn that the one who overcomes will be given to eat of the tree of life in the paradise of God (2.7)![79] Therefore, the anticipation created by this initial eschatological promise of life, given by the resurrected living one (!), is finally fulfilled. The presence of this tree signals the reversal of the curse brought on by the disobedience of Adam and Eve while again making clear the immediate and direct access the overcomers have to God, for this tree is a sign that the previous separation and enmity between God and humankind is now completely removed.[80] Thus, the fruit of the tree of life that had been prohibited for human consumption by divine initiative is now freely available to those who inhabit the New Jerusalem. At the same time, owing to the close association between the tree of life and the paradise of God, the hearers would perhaps suspect that this holy city bears the characteristics of a garden. Something of the inexhaustible supply of eternal life in this New Jerusalem is exhibited by the fact that the tree of life brings forth a staggering amount of fruit, far exceeding

---

[78] Gause, *Revelation*, p. 276. The Greek expression ξύλον ζωῆς ('tree of life') is a collective, standing for this whole genus of trees.

[79] Kiddle, *The Revelation of St John*, pp. 441-42.

[80] Mayo, *'Those Who Call Themselves Jews'*, p. 196.

even that described in Ezekiel's vision (Ezek. 47.12).[81] For in keeping with the other characteristics of the holy city, the tree produces the perfect amount of eternal sustenance – as it generates twelve crops, with these twelve crops of fruit given not just once or even twice a year, but every month – twelve times a year! This supply of eternal life, like that of the river, is more than enough and never ending. But in some ways perhaps the most surprising detail about this remarkable part of this vision are the words, 'and the leaves of the tree are for the healing of the nations'. Several aspects of this statement would be of significance for the hearers. First, it would be clear that the leaves of this tree of life, a tree that stands on both sides of the river of life, are closely associated with eternal life and, consequently, are signs of its bestowal. Second, these words stand with the other statements in the description of New Jerusalem that underscore a view of a wideness in God's mercy that includes the conversion of the nations (21.3, 12-13, 24-26).[82] Third, discerning Johannine hearers would also likely find a deeper soteriological significance in these words, for in the FG there is an almost indistinguishable connection between signs of healing and salvation, i.e. belief in Jesus. In point of fact, each physical healing described in the FG is directly connected to the experience of eternal life based in the atoning life and death of Jesus (Jn 4.46-54; 5.1-18; 9.1-41; 11.1-57).[83] Thus, when the hearers learn that the leaves of the tree are for the healing of the nations, they would likely understand healing in its most holistic and comprehensive fashion, encompassing both physical and spiritual healing for both are part of the salvific work of Jesus.[84] Fourth, owing to this comprehensive understanding of the healing of the nations, the hearers might well discern in these words some additional insight into the conversion of the nations, for while they still are not told exactly when and how such a conversion takes place, they now learn that provision is indeed made for such and is part of the very fabric of the New Jerusalem! Perhaps they would understand this healing to include the healing of the wounds of the nations incurred in their rebellion

---

[81] Aune, *Revelation 17-22*, p. 1178.

[82] Matthewson, 'The Destiny of the Nations in Revelation 21.1-22.5: A Reconsideration', p. 139.

[83] Cf. Thomas, *Spirit of the New Testament*, pp. 175-89.

[84] Resseguie, *The Revelation of John*, p. 258.

against God and the Lamb.[85] Thus, not only is the eternal life that flows in this river and is available in the fruit of the tree of life inexhaustible, but it is also comprehensive for all who will respond to its offer.

Verses 3-4 – This focus appears to continue in the next words the hearers encounter, 'And there is no curse any longer. And the throne of God and the Lamb is there, and his servants serve (worship) him and they will see his face and his name will be upon their foreheads'. Owing to the thoughts about the tree of life in the Garden of Eden generated by reference to the tree of life on either side of the river of life in the New Jerusalem and the implications of the mention of the leaves of the tree for the conversion of the nations, the first words in 22.3 'and there is no curse any longer' would likely have at least a double meaning for the hearers. On the one hand, it is very difficult to imagine that the lifting of the restriction to the fruit of the tree of life and its immediate availability in the New Jerusalem could be seen as anything other than the removal of the curse incurred by humanity via the disobedience of Adam and Eve.[86] On the other hand, the recent emphasis upon the healing of the nations would likely suggest that reference to the absence of a curse in 22.3 would convey to the hearers the sense that the nations are also in mind, specifically, that the ban of destruction placed upon the enemies of God has now been lifted (Zech. 14.11).[87] No curse remains upon humanity or the nations in New Jerusalem, for eternal life is available to all there.

Again the hearers' attention is directed to the throne of God and the Lamb, from which the river of living water originates. As such, the hearers are not only reminded of the throne's presence in New Jerusalem, but the way in which its presence stands in some contrast to the curse's absence there. Significantly, the throne is identified, as in 22.1, as that of God and the Lamb. But remarkably, in what follows singular pronouns are used to describe God and the Lamb![88] His servants worship 'him'; they shall see 'his' face; and it is 'his' name that is written upon their foreheads! Once again it ap-

---

[85] Sweet, *Revelation*, p. 311.

[86] Murphy, *Fallen Is Babylon*, p. 429.

[87] Matthewson, 'The Destiny of the Nations in Revelation 21.1-22.5: A Reconsideration', pp. 139-41.

[88] Sweet, *Revelation*, p. 312.

pears that normal Greek grammar is insufficient to convey the theological realities of the unique relationship and solidarity between God and the Lamb. This theological reality breaks apart the grammar! Each of these statements reveals that the relationship of God and the Lamb with his people is unprecedented, reaching an unrivaled crescendo. As his servants who λατρεύσουσιν ('minister') to him, his people fulfill their priestly function in the very presence of God, a function and status that have been anticipated at various points throughout the book (1.6; 3.12; 5.10; 7.15; 20.6). What's more, in contrast to those who seek to hide or flee from his face (6.16; 20.11), the hearers learn that such ones as these 'will see his face'. While it is clear that in one sense these words would convey the idea of being admitted into the immediate presence of God,[89] this statement would nonetheless stretch the hearers' imaginative abilities to the breaking point for they would well know that no human can see God's face and live! Moses himself was told as much and only allowed to see the back parts of God as his glory passed before Moses (Exod. 33.20). Johannine hearers would also be aware of the fact that no one has seen the Father at any time except for his Son who has made him known (Jn 1.18; 6.46; 1 Jn 4.12). And yet the longing to see God, even to see his face, continued to be expressed amongst his people (Pss. 11.7; 17.15; 42.2),[90] showing up in modified form in the Johannine tradition (1 Jn 3.2). To see the face of God is to be in perfect and complete harmony with God. It is the beatific vision. It is transformative to the extent that the one who sees his face is made unto his likeness (1 Jn 3.2). For if the holy one is at the center of the holy city, those admitted into it – those who see his face – experience in an even greater way the extraordinarily holy and transformative power of his presence. Absolutely nothing stands in the way of such incredible intimacy that awaits in New Jerusalem.[91] Such communion is the end for which humanity is created, for which it is intended, for which it longs! Such ones as these are those who bear the name of God and the Lamb upon their forehead – who belong wholly to him (Rev. 3.12). They are those who have been sealed by him (7.3; 9.4; 14.1).

---

[89] Metzger, *Cracking the Code*, p. 103.
[90] Michaels, *Revelation*, p. 248.
[91] Resseguie, *The Revelation of John*, p. 258.

They are those whom he protects. They are his. They bear his name for they bear his nature.[92] Just like the high priest, they bear the name of God upon their foreheads; these servants who serve before his throne, who see his face![93] Overwhelmed by such unimaginable splendor, perhaps the hearers may be forgiven if they have nearly forgotten the mark, name, and number that the beast seeks to place upon them, for what he has to offer compares in no way to that which awaits in New Jerusalem.

Figure 16
The River of Life
Bamberg Apocalypse (Bamberg, Staatsbibliothek, 140 [olim A ii 42, f. 57r.])

Verse 5 – With their heads spinning from such unbelievable details about the holy city, the hearers encounter words that would sound very familiar, 'And night is not there and they have no need for a light of a lamp and a light of the sun, because the Lord God

---

[92] Caird, *The Revelation of St. John*, pp. 280-81.
[93] Koester, *Revelation and the End of All Things*, p. 200.

shines upon them and they will reign for ever and ever'. In some ways these words, which the hearers might at first be inclined to take as just so much repetition, sum up all that has preceded from 21.9 to this point, for they remind the hearers of the fundamental characteristics of the holy city. First, in the words 'there is no night there', the hearers would be reminded of the words' previous occurrence in 21.25 where they learn that there is no spiritual night or darkness of unbelief (in the Johannine sense), nor is access to the holy city ever closed off. All evil is absent; access to the holy city is always available. Second, the words that deny the need for sources of light in the city, whether the artificial light of a lamp or the more permanent light of the sun, also echo words the hearers have previously encountered in 21.24-25. Not only do such words reveal that the incomparable glory of God makes the need for other forms of illumination unnecessary, but they also remind the hearers that such divine illumination is salvific, making it possible for the nations to walk in it as well as the kings of the earth to bring their glories into the holy city. Finally, New Jerusalem is characterized by the fact that along with God and the Lamb its inhabitants will reign forever and ever! Such a statement would not only remind the hearers of the eternal reign described earlier in the Apocalypse (5.10; 11.15, 17), but would also underscore the relationship between God's people and the God who lives forever and ever (4.9, 10; 7.2; 10.6; 15.7). At the same time, just as the thousand year reign dwarfed the forty-two month reign of the beast (13.5) and the one-hour reign of the ten kings (17.12), so now the prospect of a reign that lasts forever and ever even dwarfs the unbelievably long thousand year reign! This reign is eternal and perfect, in complete continuity with the other characteristics of the unmediated presence of God and the Lamb and the believers' identification with him in New Jerusalem. Not only are they in his presence, they share his reign; dare one say, they sit on his throne which he shares with the Lamb.

CONCLUSION AND EPILOGUE – REVELATION 22.6-22.21

Verse 6 – As the hearers encounter the next words it becomes clear that they find themselves in both the conclusion of the fourth major section and in the book's epilogue, for the concerns of both are detectable as there is considerable overlap between the two in 22.6-9. The words that next occur would be somewhat familiar to the hearers, 'And he said, "These words are faithful and true, and the Lord, the God of the S/spirits of the prophets, sent his angel to show his servants that which is necessary to take place quickly"'. Several aspects of this verse would be of significance for the hearers. First, the hearers would, no doubt, pick up on the fact that the phrase 'these words are faithful and true' has recently been encountered near the end of the third major section of the Apocalypse (21.5) devoted to the fall of Babylon the Great Whore and the emergence of New Jerusalem coming down from heaven. There the phrase testifies both to the trustworthiness of the words of this specific portion of the vision as well as the contents of the book itself. On that occasion, the trustworthiness is affirmed by the One who sits on the throne. In 22.6, this phrase stands near the conclusion of the fourth major section of the book, affirming the trustworthy nature of the vision about New Jerusalem (21.9-22.5) as well as the contents of the book itself. Encountering this phrase at two such strategic locations would serve once again as a way of comparing and contrasting the two women/cities to which these two major sections have been devoted. Second, the fact that these words were first spoken by the One who sits on the throne (21.5) might lead the hearers to believe that their occurrence on this occasion (22.6) have a similar origin. Yet here, the Lord God is spoken of in the third person, perhaps suggesting that the speaker on this occasion is the Lamb. Third, the identification of the Lord as the God of the S/spirits of the prophets might on the surface of things be taken as having reference to individual human spirits of the individual prophets in the community, i.e. the psychic power of the prophets.[1] However, discerning Johannine hearers would perhaps understand these words as conveying more than this initial impression might suggest. For, they would well know the ways in which the community is called upon to test the spirits that inspire the prophetic activity within the community (1 Jn 4.1, 2) to determine whether the prophetic activity is inspired by the Spirit of Truth or is inspired by the spirit of deception (1 Jn 4.6).[2] At the same time, by this point the hearers of the Apocalypse have come to understand the tight connection between the Seven Spirits of God (Rev. 1.4; 4.5; 5.6) and the prophetic activity of the Spirit anointed community in the world. Thus, it would seem likely that this phrase both underscores the origin of the community prophets' inspiration as well as the fact that such inspiration is closely connected to the One who sits on the throne before whom the Seven Spirits appear (1.4; 4.5) and the Lamb who bears seven eyes that are the Seven Spirits of God sent out into all the earth (5.6). Fifth, the mention of the mission of God's angel in 22.6 would not only take the hearers back to his initial mention in 1.1 but also to the ways in which he has 'shown' his servant John (and God's other servants) that which is necessary to take place soon, words that also echo the book's opening in 1.1, an additional indication to the hearers that they are now standing near the book's close. By this point, the hearers realize that they could scarcely have imagined the many spiritually significant things that John, and they through him, would be shown! They would also now realize the many ways in which they themselves have been called upon to engage in pneumatic discernment, an activity dependent upon the prophetic activity of the Spirit in their midst. As they draw near the end of the book the hearers are reminded yet again of the nearness to them of the things described – 'it is necessary for them to take place soon or quickly!' The hearers' existential experience of the things described to this point would go some way

---

[1] Aune, *Revelation 17-22*, p. 1182.
[2] On this whole matter cf. Thomas, *1 John, 2 John, 3 John*, pp. 197-214.

toward closing the gap between their description and their occurrence, while increasing the longing for their fulfillment all the more. Perhaps the hearers would now realize that they are already experiencing some of the things that must take place quickly in the course of their daily activity – experiences the significance of which are far deeper than they appear on the surface – for they are connected to eschatological events and activity!

Verse 7 – As the hearers attempt to tease out the meaning of these somewhat familiar words they discover others that add to the dramatic tone of the book while reminding them of those which they have encountered earlier, 'And behold I am coming quickly. Blessed is the one who keeps the words of the prophecy of this book.' If there was some question as to the speaker's identity in 22.6, there is no mistaking it in 22.7, as the words 'Behold I come quickly' could hardly come from anyone but Jesus! It would be difficult to imagine that the hearers would miss the connection between the things that must take place ἐν τάχει ('quickly') and Jesus' description of his return as taking place ταχύ ('quickly'), underscoring the fact that among the things that must soon take place is his own coming. They would also be aware of the fact that twice before in the Apocalypse these words of Jesus occur. Their first occurrence describes his coming to the church in Pergamum to make war with the sword of his mouth upon those who fail to repent (2.16), while their second occurrence serves as a warning to the church in Philadelphia not to allow anyone to take their crown (3.11). When encountering these words for a third time in the book, their previous meanings would likely converge for the hearers, tying present and future together, indicating that this Jesus who comes quickly can come in judgment at any moment and will surely come quickly at the consummation as well. Just as the hearers already experience in their daily activities eschatological realities in the things that must take place quickly, so they experience the coming of Jesus here and now in their community worship and activities, a coming that is tied to the eschatological reality of his return in the consummation. Immediately after these words the hearers encounter a sixth beatitude, one that takes them back to the book's very first one (1.3), framing the contents of the book between these similar beatitudes.³ For in this beatitude the hearers are reminded of the importance of keeping, in the sense of obeying, the words written herein. The command contained in this beatitude is fortified by the fact that here, in ways similar to 1.3, the words that are to be kept are referred to as 'the words of the prophecy of this book', underscoring all the more the authority and significance of the book's contents. How would the hearers understand this command? How could they keep the words of the prophecy? Primarily, such obedience would be understood as maintaining one's faithful witness to God and the Lamb through a Spirit empowered prophetic life that offers one's witness to a hostile world with a view toward the conversion of the nations. Such obedience entails pneumatic discernment in one's daily activities in order that such a witness might not be compromised owing to the seductions of the beast, the false prophet, and/or the Great Whore. Keeping the words of this prophecy is a call to pneumatic discernment, whether such seductions are encountered in the church or in the world; a call to offer the same faithful witness as did the slaughtered Lamb; a call to follow the Lamb wherever he goes; a call to engage in the eschatological harvest of the conversion of the nations. Such a call is no passive affair or a resignation to circumstances, but an active participation in the pneumatically empowered witness of the church. This beatitude is spoken to hearers who must respond to the words of this prophecy as a warning not to be deceived by the seductions of the beast and his accomplices, on the one hand, and as an encouragement to follow the Lamb in the company of all the saints who offer a faithful witness, on the other hand.

Verse 8 – Whilst contemplating the words of the resurrected Jesus the hearers' attention is directed back to John, 'Even I John am the one who hears and sees these things. And when I heard and I saw, I fell to worship before the feet of the angel who is showing these things to me'. For the first time since 1.9 the hearers encounter the author's name, John,⁴ perhaps an indication to them that they are now standing near the end of the book, with John's name framing the entire work. Standing alongside Jesus' declaration of the integrity and authority of these words (22.6), John's words

---

³ Murphy, *Fallen Is Babylon*, p. 436.
⁴ Michaels, *Revelation*, p. 250.

about that which he hears and sees reveal to the hearers the content of the witness which he bears to those things shown to him by the angel; a witness to which he refers at the book's opening as well (1.2). Thus, he offers his own words with regard to the book's integrity and authority. The hearers might be surprised to learn that the cumulative effect of this revelation upon John, as he confesses, was to cause him to fall before the feet of the angel who shows all these things to him. For the hearers may well recall that on two previous occasions John has been tempted or attempts to worship someone other than God. Their first encounter with such activity is when John marvels a great marvel upon seeing the Great Whore (17.6-7), a marveling akin to that of the world upon seeing the healing of the mortal wound inflicted upon the beast, which leads to his worship by the whole world (13.3-4). Their second encounter with such activity is when John falls to the feet and attempts to worship his fellow servant and brother who speaks divinely authorized words (19.10). Owing to the similarities between this figure and the souls under the altar who have been killed to make the number of martyrs full (6.9-11), it appears that John's temptation to worship him is based upon his identity as one of the souls slaughtered for his faithful witness who is heir to the numerous promises made to the one who overcomes, including reception of a new name that no one knows (2.17), authority to rule over the nations with an iron scepter and the morning star (2.26-28), and authority to sit on Jesus' throne with him (3.21). But John finds that even this redeemed one is not to be worshipped; God alone is deserving of such. Significantly, this event takes place just after a divine affirmation that the words of this prophecy are the true words of God (19.9), just as John's falling before the angel in 22.9 follows similar words of Jesus in 22.6. John's action of falling at the feet of the angel extends the theme of legitimate worship further, for surely the one who is showing him all these things is worthy of veneration, for he is sent by God for this specific revelatory purpose and indeed even speaks for God![5] Whether John's hearers are themselves tempted to worship such heavenly emissaries, they no doubt anxiously await the angel's response and John's next words.

---

[5] Beasley-Murray, *Revelation*, p. 336.

Verse 9 – In keeping with previous descriptions of John's attempts at worship the hearers learn, 'And he says to me, "See that you do not do it! I am the fellow servant of you and your brothers the prophets and of those who keep the words of this book. Worship God!"' Just as one of the souls under the altar forbids John's attempt at worship, so does the angel in 22.9, using the same words as his counterpart in 19.10 – Ὅρα μή ('See that you do not do it'), making absolutely clear to the hearers that such intended veneration is completely unacceptable. Rather than being a divine being worthy of worship, the angel uses words similar to those spoken by his counterpart in 19.10, underscoring the fact that he, like John and his brothers, is on the creaturely divide between Creator and Creation. Earlier his counterpart identifies himself as a co-worker of John and his brothers who have the testimony of Jesus (19.10), while here the angel underscores his solidarity with John and his brothers the prophets, as well as those who keep the words of this book. The description of John's brothers the prophets would likely convey at least two things to the hearers. First, it would underscore the relationship this angel shares with John and his brothers the prophets in the revelatory experience of the Apocalypse, suggesting that they along with John have a role in its reception and/or interpretation in the community. At the least, it would suggest an active role for them in the pneumatic discernment to which the hearers are called. Second, along with the mention of the S/spirits of the prophets in 22.6, mention of John's brothers the prophets would continue to drive home the point that this is a prophetic community, perhaps even one that includes an understanding of the prophethood of all believers. The mention of those who keep the words of this book would go some way toward identifying the hearers as amongst those who heed the beatitude of 22.7. The message of the fellow servant continues and is identical to that of his counterpart in 19.10, 'Worship God!' As such, these words reinforce the overriding message of the book as a whole. Only God (and the Lamb) is worthy of worship. Any other form of worship is idolatrous, whether that worship be offered to the beast, the Great Whore, one who overcomes via faithful witness, or a revelatory angel of the Apocalypse itself![6] Perhaps at this point it dawns on the

---

[6] Bauckham, *The Climax of Prophecy*, p. 136.

hearers that the words of 22.6-9 function as a conclusion to the previous section, devoted to the bride of Christ just as those of 19.9-10 function as a conclusion to the section devoted to the Great Whore.[7] The hearers might also discern at this point the way in which these verses form a transition to the epilogue of the book proper.[8]

Verse 10 – In addition to the angelic prohibition and instruction with regard to worship, the next words reveal an additional directive given to John, 'And he says to me, "Do not seal up the words of the prophecy of this book, for the time is near"'. Though the speaker's identity may not be altogether clear at this point, the hearers may well discern the voice of the resurrected Jesus here, or at the least his words through the revelatory angel. Unlike the command that Daniel received to seal up the words of his prophecy (Dan. 12.4)[9] and the command that John himself earlier received from a voice out of heaven not to write but to seal up what he heard in the seven thunders (Rev. 10.4),[10] here in 22.10 John is clearly directed not to seal up the words of the prophecy of this book. This instruction stands in continuity with the commands he earlier receives to write what he sees and hears (1.11, 19), indicating that these words are to be read and heard very soon indeed. The reason for such urgency is revealed in the words, 'for the time is near', a phrase that takes the hearers back to the book's opening when near identical wording occurs with regard to those who read, hear, and keep the words written in this book (1.3).[11] Thus, the hearers discover that the revelation encountered in the words of the prophecy of this book are enfolded by words underscoring their urgency in the light of their eschatological context.

Verse 11 – It is within this context that John and his hearers next encounter words that take the form of a proverb, 'The one who does evil let that one do evil still, and the filthy let that one be

---

[7] Bauckham, *The Climax of Prophecy*, p. 133.

[8] On this cf. B.W. Longenecker, '"Linked Like a Chain": Rev 22.6-9 in Light of Ancient Translation Technique', *NTS* 47.1 (2001), pp. 105-17 who argues that this passage is a carefully linked transition similar to those found in 3.21-22; 8.1-5; 15.1-4.

[9] Schüssler Fiorenza, *Revelation*, p. 115.

[10] Smalley, *The Revelation to John*, p. 570.

[11] Michaels, *Revelation*, p. 251.

filthy still, and the righteous let that one do righteousness still, and the holy one let that one be holy still'. Though the significance of these words might not be immediately clear, the hearers would be able to discern a number of things in them. The proverbial form itself would be a call to the hearers to reflect carefully upon the observational truth contained therein. But in this case such observational truth has the authority of the resurrected Jesus himself! The hearers would also quickly pick up on the fact that they have encountered nearly all the words contained in this verse elsewhere in the book and that the convergence of these words here is significant. Neither would the structure of these words be without significance as four kinds of individuals and activities are identified, with the two negative examples standing first and the two positive examples standing last. Interestingly enough, the first term the hearers encounter, ἀδικέω ('do evil' or 'harm'), is normally used of divine commands and activity or that of God's agents in the Apocalypse (6.6; 7.2, 3; 9.4, 10, 19) or his protection against such (2.11). However, the meaning of this phrase for the hearers would likely be shaped by 11.5 where the term occurs twice to describe those who seek to harm or do evil to the two prophetic witnesses. Thus, the hearers would understand the first part of this verse to focus on those who seek to oppose God and his people by seeking to do them harm. Though the term used to describe the second category of individuals in 22.11, ῥυπαρός ('filthy'), has not been encountered in the Apocalypse to this point, perhaps the hearers would be reminded of the contrast between the one whose filthy garments are taken away, being replaced by clean ones in Zech. 3.3-7, and those described here. Such language would also no doubt bring to their minds the admonitions in the Apocalypse to keep one's garments clean and dress appropriately, avoiding nakedness (Rev. 3.4; 16.15). Those who are filthy clearly stand alongside those who seek to persecute the people of God as displeasing to him. It would be difficult to imagine that the hearers would not appreciate the contrast between these first two groups and those that are next described, for the hearers would know that in the Apocalypse the language of righteous and righteousness is closely associated with God and the Lamb (15.3; 16.5, 7; 19.2, 11), indicating that the righteous here described bear a characteristic resemblance to God and the Lamb and as such belong to him. If such connections are true of the righteous they are even more so with regard to the language of ἅγιος ('holy' or 'saint') that describes the last group, language that is intimately connected to God, the Lamb, and his people throughout the book. Thus, the hearers would have little doubt about the proverb's content, but what of its meaning? Would they understand it to mean that things are as they are and that the time for repentance is past[12] – that the words of God's prophecy are firm and fixed despite the response of humanity?[13] Would they take these words as making explicit the reality that there are two basic responses to God's prophetic words and that these two responses will no doubt accompany the words of this prophecy?[14] Given the eschatological context, the continuous invitations for repentance in the book, even for those who do evil (11.3-13), perhaps these words would be understood as conveying the ominous message that indeed the end of all things is near and that while it is possible that the words of this prophecy will not be kept by those who hear them, they will be ignored to one's own peril. The stark reality is that one's response to the words of this prophecy is revealed by the life of the one who hears them;[15] a response that will be clear to all.

Verse 12 – With such ominous statements ringing in their collective ears, the hearers encounter additional ones from the resurrected Jesus, 'Behold I come quickly, and my reward is with me to give to each according to his/her work'. The hearers would quickly realize that this is the second time in the book's conclusion (cf. 22.7) that the phrase 'Behold, I come quickly' occurs and that such language would clearly underscore all the more the importance of keeping the words of this prophecy, for the hearers' eternal destiny is dependent upon their response. Perhaps at this point they would recognize that this has been the clarion message they have heard from the beginning of the book. At the same time, the second occurrence of this phrase within a span of six verses would reiterate the nearness of the hearers to the end for if Jesus comes quickly the time is indeed near! As before, these words would tie present and future together, reminding the hearers that this Jesus who comes

---

[12] Gause, *Revelation*, p. 280.
[13] Wall, *Revelation*, p. 265.
[14] Michaels, *Revelation*, p. 252.
[15] Prigent, *L'Apocalypse de Saint Jean*, p. 492.

quickly can come in judgment at any moment and will surely come quickly at the consummation as well. On this occasion, Jesus' words about his soon return are accompanied by words of judgment, 'and my reward is with me to give to each according to his work'. Such a statement would not likely surprise the hearers, although it would certainly get their attention, for works have been part of the theological landscape throughout. For not only does Jesus know the works of the churches he addresses in the seven prophetic messages to the seven churches (2.2, 19; 3.1, 8, 15), but works also form the basis of divine judgment both now (2.23) and at the final judgment (20.12-13). The reward that he bears in 22.12 could hardly help but convey to the hearers that the end of all things is near, the time for judging the dead to give his reward to his servants the prophets and to the holy ones and to those who fear his name, as 11.18 foretells. The ominous nature of these words is made even more so by the fact that emphasis is placed upon the specificity of the reward that is given to each one according to one's individual works, thus reinforcing the dualistic warning of 22.11![16]

Verse 13 – Not having time to ponder these words in any degree of detail the hearers immediately discover that the authority by which Jesus speaks, by which he comes, and by which he judges[17] in the bringing of his reward is grounded in his own person and being, 'I Am the Alpha and the Omega, the First and the Last, the Beginning and the End'. Perhaps the first thing to catch the attention of the hearers in these words is the fact that Jesus' identity is conveyed by means of three titles that appear together only here in the whole of the Apocalypse,[18] a combination that underscores his absolute power and authority. The fact that each of these titles is formed by a combination of two antithetical terms reveals that the person who bears them encompasses both ends of the extremes.[19] The extraordinary titles here claimed by Jesus would be made all the more extraordinary to the hearers owing to the fact that two of them have been used exclusively for God to this point in the book! They could hardly help but recall that the self-designation of the titles 'the Al-

---

[16] Michaels, *Revelation*, p. 253.
[17] Ladd, *Revelation*, p. 293.
[18] Smalley, *The Revelation to John*, p. 573.
[19] Aune, *Revelation 17-22*, p. 1219.

pha and the Omega' and 'the Beginning and the End' by God (1.8; 21.6) conveys the claim that all of creation, the first heaven and first earth, as well as the New Heaven and New Earth, stand within his purview and are enveloped by his presence and power! These two identifications, standing side by side, convey the idea that God is indeed the beginning and the ending, he is the all in all. Nothing exists outside of him! Astonishingly enough, these titles, which have previously been claimed by God for himself, in what appears to be a somewhat exclusive fashion, are now claimed by Jesus as well, further underscoring the intimate relationship between God and Jesus that emerges in the book. Significantly, the other title, 'the First and the Last', which has been used exclusively for Jesus in the Apocalypse (1.17; 2.8), stands between the titles earlier used by God as a self-identification, emphasizing all the more the extraordinary unity and intimacy between God and Jesus. This title, 'the First and the Last', might also remind the hearers of Isa. 44.6, where God's claim to exclusivity as the only God is made clear, a claim that is now shared by Jesus! The hearers could hardly miss the fact that not only does Jesus share these titles with God, but he shares his throne as well! Perhaps this extraordinary combination of titles would also make clear to the hearers that the end is not so much an event but a person,[20] and that it is this person who has authority to come with his reward with him.

Verse 14 – Following Jesus' self-identification, by means of these three titles, are words of a beatitude, 'Blessed are those who wash their robes, in order that they might have their authority to the tree of life and through the gates they might enter into the city'. A number of aspects of this beatitude would be of significance to the hearers. First, this is the seventh (and final) beatitude the hearers will have encountered in this point, no doubt reminding them of the blessings pronounced previously. Second, they might also pick up on the fact that as with the beatitudes found in 14.13 and 19.9 the plural form Μακάριοι ('Blessed') appears here as well.[21] Third, neither would the hearers be ignorant of the way in which this pronouncement of blessing by the resurrected Jesus himself continues the theme of warning that characterizes the epilogue, by use of lan-

---

[20] Sweet, *Revelation*, p. 316.
[21] Aune, *Revelation 17-22*, p. 1219.

guage and imagery familiar to the hearers. Fourth, the fact that this blessing is pronounced upon those who wash their robes could hardly help but call the hearers' attention back to the way in which clothing has functioned in the book to this point. If so, they would recall the way in which the resurrected Jesus praises some of those in Sardis whose garments have not been soiled and the beatitude found in 16.15 where blessing is pronounced upon those who are awake and keep their clothes with them, not walking in nakedness allowing their shame to be seen. But, more specifically, the hearers would, no doubt, recall the description of those who come out of the great tribulation who 'have washed their robes and made them white in the blood of the Lamb' (7.14), owing to the remarkable similarity of vocabulary between these words. However, in 7.14 an aorist past tense verb occurs, ἔπλυναν ('have washed'), indicating that they have washed their robes in the blood of the Lamb at a particular point in the past, while in the beatitude of 22.14 a present participle, οἱ πλύνοντες ('those who wash'), occurs indicating that these are they who continually wash their robes.[22] In these words of warning, such continuous action conveys the idea that only those who are vigilant about their lives of purity and continue to wash their robes in the blood of the Lamb will be heirs to the promises of this beatitude. The idea of such ongoing cleansing would be at home in Johannine thought (cf. esp. 1 Jn 1.5-2.2; 3.4-10, 19-24; 5.14-17), perhaps reminding the hearers of one of the community practices that embodies this very phenomenon, the rendering and receiving of footwashing.[23] Such active participation would not be interpreted as mere self-improvement on their part but rather would be seen as the saving and purifying effect of the blood of the Lamb.[24] Fifth, those upon whom this beatitude is pronounced are promised access to the tree of life and to the (holy) city itself. The hearers would be well aware of these eschatological rewards, having encountered both items in the previous description of New Jerusalem (21.9-22.5). Perhaps they would also remember that the prom-

---

[22] Smalley, *The Revelation to John*, p. 573 and Resseguie, *The Revelation of John*, p. 259.

[23] For this suggestion cf. Mounce, *The Book of Revelation*, p. 393. For the sacramental significance of footwashing in the Johannine community cf. Thomas, *Footwashing in John 13 and the Johannine Community*.

[24] Metzger, *Cracking the Code*, p. 105.

ise to eat of the tree of life was the first given to the one who overcomes in the very first prophetic message to the church in Ephesus (2.7). Both images convey the promise of eternal life in the holy city, recalling the abundance of the fruit of the tree of life, in the former, and the richness and beauty of the Bride of Christ, in contrast to that feigned by the Great Whore, in the latter. It almost goes without saying that admission into and enjoyment of the holy city is contingent upon the continual washing of one's robes, the purifying of one's life, in the blood of the Lamb.

Verse 15 – But Jesus' return does not simply have implications for those who keep the words of the prophecy of this book, but also for those who refuse to keep them,[25] 'Outside are the dogs and the magicians and the sexually immoral and the murderers and the idolaters and everyone who loves and makes a lie'. This warning would remind the hearers very much of a similar warning encountered in 21.8, with many of the same terms occurring in both lists. In the earlier passage, the hearers encountered no ordinary list of sinners, but rather categories that appear to represent groups of believers who have succumbed to temptations that kept them from being faithful until the end as overcomers, for almost all of these categories have a special meaning that derives from the Apocalypse itself. While in 21.8 the list functioned as a warning to Johannine believers not to lose their way and stop short in their faithful witness, the list the hearers encounter in 22.15 is a specific warning as to the consequences of not keeping the words of the prophecy of this book. Again, most, if not all, the terms in this list have special meaning derived from the Apocalypse itself. If those who keep the words of the prophecy of this book, who continuously wash their robes, have access to the tree of life and to enter the holy city, those who are 'outside' are those excluded from access, not those in close proximity to the city.[26] It is not altogether clear how the hearers would understand the first category in this list of those who do not keep the words of the prophecy of this book, for οἱ κύνες ('the dogs') appears only here in the Apocalypse. While it might be safe to assume that the hearers would likely know of the reputation of dogs as the scavengers of the ancient world who come to represent

---

[25] Ladd, *Revelation*, p. 293.
[26] Metzger, *Cracking the Code*, p. 105.

the extremes of base behavior,[27] and consequently would be unclean and deemed unfit to gain admission to the holy city,[28] perhaps there would be more to this identification for them. For example, they might think of the ways in which dogs function in the Psalter (22.16, 20), where the term has reference to malicious people who oppose and persecute God's anointed.[29] At the same time, the hearers would likely remember that in the Torah the word 'dog' is a metaphor having reference to a male prostitute, whose person and money are deemed unclean and, therefore, cannot be brought into the house of the 'Lord your God' (Deut. 23.17-18).[30] Owing to the reference to abominations in this same passage in the Torah, it is possible that the hearers might even consider the word dog to be a synonym for one who commits abominations, paralleled in the list of Rev. 21.8 and the reference in 21.27.[31] Thus, such biblical associations would suggest to the hearers that the dogs are those who persecute the people of God, having sold themselves into the sexual immorality of the Great Whore. Such ones as these are clearly outside the holy city. Listed next are the magicians. In contrast to the participial form in the list of 21.8, here the hearers encounter the noun form, as with most of the entries in this latter list. As before they would remember that such activity is described as a work of their hands for which the rest of men did not offer repentance (9.21), as well as being the means by which the Great Whore had deceived all the nations (18.23). As in 21.8, such an understanding might well lead the hearers to conclude that those who have been enchanted by her magic themselves share in this activity and will suffer a similar fate to the Great Whore. Joining these first two categories are the sexually immoral. Again the hearers would know that this noun and its word family in the Apocalypse are very close-

---

[27] S. Pederson, 'κύων', 'κυνός', *EDNT*, II, p. 332.

[28] M. Philonenko, '"Dehors les Chiens" (Apocalypse 22.16 et 4QMMT B 58-62)', *NTS* 43.3 (1997), pp. 445-50, who connects this passage to the numerous references to 'outside the camp' in Numbers and Leviticus, as having to do with issues of purity. Citing a text from Qumran, where dogs are prohibited from the camp owing to the danger they pose to eating the bones from the sanctuary, Philonenko argues that the term 'dogs' in Rev. 22.15 is given a spiritual interpretation on the order of the spiritual interpretation given to the New Jerusalem.

[29] Ladd, *Revelation*, p. 293.

[30] Aune, *Revelation 17-22*, p. 1222.

[31] Smalley, *The Revelation to John*, p. 575.

ly identified with the activity of the Great Whore (17.1, 2, 4, 5) whose idolatrous charms result in the sexual immorality of the kings of the earth (18.3, 9), a temptation with which even the church must contend (Rev. 2.14, 20).[32] For this activity the Great Whore is judged (17.16; 19.2), as are all those who are sexually immoral owing to their economic and idolatrous relationship with her. Murderers would also be understood in the light of its meaning in the Apocalypse, where amongst the works of their hands for which the rest of men refuse to repent are found murders (9.21).[33] And though a different word is used to describe their murderous activities, discerning Johannine hearers would not be unaware of Jesus' words that Satan is a murderer from the beginning (Jn 8.44), nor would they be unaware that in the Apocalypse refusal to worship the Beast results in death for such offenders (Rev. 13.15). Thus, this category would suggest that those who identify with the Beast are complicitous in his murderous activity of those whose names are written in the Lamb's book of life.[34] Closely associated with the previous categories are the idolaters. The hearers would know that in the Apocalypse such activity is closely associated with sexual immorality and eating meat sacrificed to idols (2.14, 20), activities that imply corruption by participation in the economic system that is in collusion with the beast and the Great Whore. Ultimately, those who worship the beast and/or join in the idolatrous activity of the Great Whore, even those who worship the servants of God, commit idolatry. Only God is to be glorified – all who engage in idolatrous activity betray him and forsake true worship. The hearers reach the end of this list when they encounter each one who loves and does a lie. By this time they know that when the devil lies he speaks his native tongue (Jn 8.44), that the one who lies is diametrically opposed to the truth (1 Jn 2.21, 27), that there are those who claim to be apostles or Jews but are not for they lie (Rev. 2.2; 3.9), and that all liars will have their part in the lake of burning sulfur (21.8). Perhaps the hearers would also understand this category to include those who have believed the lie of the beast and the Great Whore and by their participation with them have perpetuated that

---

[32] Pattemore, *The People of God in the Apocalypse*, p. 211.
[33] Ladd, *Revelation*, p. 279.
[34] Mounce, *The Book of Revelation*, p. 375.

lie.³⁵ At the least, they would again be struck by the difference between those who lie and those followers of the Lamb in whose mouths no lie is found (14.5)! Owing to the close association with the beast and the Great Whore, all such ones as these (the dogs, the magicians, the sexually immoral, the murderers, the idolaters, and each one who loves and does a lie) are 'outside', excluded from access to the holy city. As such, the hearers are reminded once again of the dire consequences of not keeping the words of the prophecy of this book!

Verse 16 – Though the words of this startling warning appear to come to an end, the words of Jesus continue, 'I Jesus sent my angel to witness to you these things to the churches. I Am the root and offspring of David, the bright morning star'. For the first and only time in the Apocalypse Jesus refers to himself by name,³⁶ underscoring the authority of the words he speaks all the more. While the hearers have known from the book's beginning of God's role in the sending of the angel who makes this revelation known (1.1-2), Jesus himself makes clear that he too has a role in the sending of the angel, which is now referred to as 'my angel', emphasizing the connection between Jesus and his revelation that his angel makes known. Just as John has witnessed, and those in the community have borne witness, so now the angel of Jesus is said to have witnessed the things found in this book to 'you'. Such shared witness would underscore the fact that this angel is truly a fellow servant with John and his brothers the prophets in offering witness to Jesus. It is not altogether clear how the hearers would understand the plural 'you' as the recipients of this witness since the plural, 'the churches', stands in close proximity. It would appear that they would either take the plural 'you' as having reference either to John and his brothers the prophets in the community³⁷ or to the angels of the churches to which the seven prophetic messages are directed.³⁸ In either case attention is once again drawn to the chain of revelation by which this revelation of Jesus Christ comes: from Jesus to his angel to his servants (either prophetic or angelic or both) to the

---

³⁵ Beasley-Murray, *Revelation*, p. 314.

³⁶ Michaels, *Revelation*, p. 255.

³⁷ G. Biguzzi, 'The Chaos of Rev 22,6-21 and Prophecy in Asia', *Biblica* 83.2 (2002), p. 197.

³⁸ Smalley, *The Revelation to John*, pp. 575-76.

churches, a chain of revelation reminiscent of that found at the book's beginning (1.1-2). Such an inclusio would again indicate to the hearers that they are finally approaching the book's conclusion. Not only does Jesus refer to himself by name in 22.16, but also by means of two titles; titles that are preceded by the theologically significant 'I Am', underscoring further Jesus' shared identity with God, who also appropriates this title for himself (1.8; cf. 1.17; 2.23 for earlier occasions where Jesus uses this title), as well as underscoring his divine authority. Both titles would be familiar to the hearers from their earlier occurrences in the book. The first title, the root and offspring of David, would remind the hearers of the fact that the resurrected Jesus claims to hold the key of David (3.7) and that he is identified by John as the Lion of the tribe of Judah, the root of David (5.3). Here, the combination of ἡ ῥίζα ('the root') and τὸ γένος ('the offspring' or 'the shoot') of David would appear to underscore the fact that Jesus is indeed the Alpha and Omega, the First and the Last, the Beginning and the End for he is both the origin of Davidic kingship and its culmination! He is that from which it comes and that to which it leads! Such an extraordinary claim would offer additional rationale to the hearers for the indispensable role of the Jewish heritage found in the book. The second title, 'the bright morning star', would also be familiar to the hearers for the morning star is promised to the one who overcomes in 2.28. Discerning hearers might well find in this title reference to yet another messianic title via Num. 24.17, which speaks of a star that will come forth from Jacob.[39] In the context of Rev. 22.16, they would be hard pressed to miss the messianic character of this title, underscoring all the more the importance of the Jewish heritage for both Jesus and the church. For not only is he the origin and culmination of Davidic kingship, but he is also the star that comes from the patriarch Jacob. He is the fulfillment of all the messianic promises and longings, for as the Johannine hearers know, he is even greater than 'our father Jacob' (Jn 4.12).

Verse 17 – With these authoritative words of the resurrected Jesus in their ears, the hearers encounter still more, 'And the Spirit and the Bride say "Come". And the one who hears, let that one say "Come". And the one who is thirsty, let that one come, the one

---

[39] Bauckham, *The Climax of Prophecy*, pp. 323-25.

who desires to receive living water without cost'. It is not altogether clear how the hearers would take these words, for their meaning in part would be determined by the identity of the speaker, about which there is some question. While it is possible that the hearers would think that these are the words of John who narrates the events he is shown, to this point there is no compelling reason to suggest that the identity of the speaker changes in 22.12-20 but rather are the words of the resurrected Jesus himself.[40] As such, these three phrases would be construed as a series of invitations to 'come' offered by the subject found in each phrase. Therefore, the first invitation comes from the Spirit and the Bride, whose identities would hardly be mistaken. For it is clear that by this point the hearers would have come to know the strategic and indispensable role the Spirit plays in the pneumatic witness offered to the kings and nations of the earth.[41] For it is the Spirit who is before the throne of God (1.4; 4.5), who resides within the churches (1.19-20), whose words are coterminous with those of Jesus (2.7, 11, 17, 29; 3.6, 13, 22), who are the seven eyes of the Lamb that go out into all the earth (5.6), who anoints the prophetic faithful witness of the church (11.3-13; 22.6), who is coterminous with the witness of Jesus (19.10), and by whom John receives this revelation (1.10; 17.3; 21.10). It is this same Spirit who now says 'come' to those who have ears to hear and those who do not, for it is this Spirit who speaks both to the churches and to those beyond them. Again pneumatic discernment would appear to be very much to the point as the Spirit issues this pneumatic invitation. Neither would the identity of the Bride be a mystery to hearers, for they have come to know that the Bride and the saints are identical (19.7-8), having discerned by this point the continuity that exists between the Bride and the churches of which they are a part.[42] Their prophetic pneumatically inspired message is identical to the message that comes from the Spirit. For it is the Spirit that empowers their own faithful witness, which is offered to a hostile and unbelieving world. The Bride offers this invitation for she knows that somehow her faithful witness is intimately connected to the conversion of the nations, a

---

[40] Michaels, *Revelation*, p. 256.
[41] Smalley, *The Revelation to John*, p. 578.
[42] Smalley, *The Revelation to John*, p. 578.

result that will exceed her wildest dreams! The words the hearers encounter in the second phrase, 'The one who hears, let that one say, "Come"', contains a twofold invitation. In keeping with the numerous calls for pneumatic discernment found throughout the book, in this verse the resurrected Jesus calls for pneumatic discernment and obedience to the words of this prophecy on the part of the one who has ears to hear. A positive response would manifest itself by the one who hears joining in the proclamation of the Spirit and the Bride, which in turn would result in the issue of the invitation to the kings and nations of the earth to 'Come'. The hearers might be forgiven if they also discern in these first two invitations the longing of the Spirit, the Bride, and the one who hears for the soon coming of Jesus. Owing to the broader context this secondary meaning of the invitation to 'come' would likely be present in their thinking. In the verse's third phrase, the invitations of the Spirit and the Bride and the one who hears are joined by an invitation by the resurrected Jesus himself to the one who is thirsty to come, the one who desires to receive the water of life without cost, a call Johannine hearers would well remember from the call of Jesus in the FG (Jn. 7.37-39). Not only are the previous invitations clarified by this one – the invitation to come and drink of the water of life – but it also would make clearer to the hearers the connection between the availability of this water of life in the present and in the holy city.[43] One's response to these invitations has eternal consequences. At the same time, the hearers might also understand this invitation to be part of the call of Jesus to keep the words of the prophecy of this book and as such an example of the continuous washing of one's robes upon which a blessing is pronounced.[44]

Verses 18-19 – As the book draws to a close the words of Jesus continue in a most ominous fashion, 'I witness to each who hears the words of the prophecy of this book; if anyone adds unto them, God will add unto him the plagues written in this book; and if anyone takes away from the words of the book of this prophecy, God will take away his/her part from the tree of life and out of the holy city, written in this book'. As these words continue, the hearers find

---

[43] Bauckham, *The Climax of Prophecy*, p. 168.
[44] Wall, *Revelation*, p. 267.

themselves addressed directly by the resurrected Jesus.[45] The faithful witness bears the witness of warning to them with regard to keeping the words of the prophecy of this book, underscoring the fact that in order to keep, and thus obey, the words of the prophecy of this book they must embrace it in its entirety, not giving in to the temptation of compromising it by addition or diluting its message by deletion. Such a witness of warning might well remind the hearers of the stern admonition given to Moses and Israel with regard to obedience to God's Torah (Deut. 12.32).[46] In addition to underscoring the importance of individual obedience, these words would also serve as a warning to the prophets and others within the community who may be entrusted with the reading of the words of the prophecy of this book, who, owing to the words' uncompromising and unrelenting nature, might be tempted to soften or make them more palatable to the churches to which they are read.[47] Specifically, for those tempted to add to these words God will add to the plagues contained herein. While the hearers would again likely think of the warning of Deuteronomy 29[48] as well as the manifestations that accompany the opening of the seven seals or the trumpeting by the seven angels earlier in the Apocalypse, they would no doubt be reminded of the seven plagues poured out upon the earth described in Revelation 15-16. While it might be warning enough for the hearers to reflect on the fact that these unimaginable plagues will be added to, the warning would be all the more ominous owing to the fact that these seven plagues are spoken of as the last plagues of God! Such plagues will be visited upon them, for in the failure to keep the words of the prophecy of this book they will have demonstrated that they have sided with those who reject God, refusing to repent for the works of their hands, entering into the sexual immorality of idolatrous activity.[49] Those tempted to take away from these words God will take away from them their share. Johannine hearers will know that to lose one's μέρος ('part' or 'share') means

---

[45] Michaels, *Revelation*, p. 257.
[46] Michaels, *Revelation*, p. 258.
[47] Beasley-Murray, *Revelation*, p. 346.
[48] R.M. Royalty, Jr., 'Don't Touch This Book!: Revelation 22.18-19 and the Rhetoric of Reading (in) the Apocalypse of John', *Biblical Interpretation* 12.3 (2004), pp. 282-99.
[49] Sweet, *Revelation*, p. 319.

to loss one's relationship with Jesus by disobedience, as Peter learned in the account of the footwashing (Jn 13.8).[50] In Rev. 22.19 this share is spoken of in terms very similar to those found in the seventh and final beatitude of 22.14, access to the tree of life and entrance into the holy city. Clearly, failure to keep the prophecy in its entirety disqualifies one from the eternal life that awaits in New Jerusalem. For the hearers, it would be difficult to imagine a more disheartening and horrifying fate. The seriousness with which the resurrected Jesus treats the words of this prophecy is indicated in part by the fact that four times reference is made to what is written in this book within the span of two verses. There could be no mistaking that one's response to the words of the prophecy of this book are of eternal consequence, a reality that would remind the hearers of the book's initial beatitude with regard to those who read, hear, and keep the words of this prophecy (1.3).

Verse 20 – As the book draws to a close the hearers encounter the final words of Jesus, in tandem with the words of John, 'The one who witnesses says these things, "Yes, I am coming quickly". "Amen, come, Lord Jesus".' On this occasion Jesus is identified as 'the one who witnesses (or testifies to) these things', which appears to have reference to the entire book but could not help but be understood as part of the authoritative way in which the Apocalypse draws to a close. For the one who bears witness (ὁ μαρτυρῶν) here in 22.20 is the same one who bears witness of warning (μαρτυρῶ) in 22.18. And for a third time in the epilogue the hearers encounter Jesus' promise, 'I am coming quickly'.[51] On this occasion these words of promise are preceded by an emphatic 'Yes!' in the place of 'Behold', which accompanies its first two occurrences (22.7, 12), acting as an affirmation of both that which precedes in the epilogue as well as all the words of the prophecy of this book. This third occurrence of 'I am coming quickly' in the span of fourteen verses could not help but to underscore and reinforce the fact that the revelation of Jesus Christ which John and his hearers experience is oriented by this extraordinary promise. This emphatic promise clearly picks up on the words of warning by the resurrected Jesus that he will come in judgment to those churches who do not hear

---

[50] Thomas, *Footwashing in John 13 and the Johannine Community*, pp. 92-95.
[51] Caird, *The Revelation of St. John*, p. 288.

(and keep) what the Spirit is saying to them in the seven prophetic messages and the words of the prophecy as a whole. At the same time, these words also emphasize all the more the way in which the consummation of this promise is the consummation of all the eschatological promises, of all prophetic words – for in a very real way the return of Jesus is indeed the climax of prophecy, even history itself! The convergence in this promise of the extraordinary images, texts, visions, sights, sounds, smells, touches, and tastes experienced in the Apocalypse, would perhaps be overwhelming for John and his hearers – for their minds would be filled with all that has preceded in one moment. Such an extraordinarily rich convergence of eschatological ideas could hardly help but generate a response from John and his hearers, as John adds his own affirmation and prayer 'Amen, come, Lord Jesus'. In his uttering the word Amen, the hearers might well recall the word's initial occurrences in the book as an affirmation of Jesus' redemptive work (1.6) and as a conclusion to the word of prophecy with which the book commences (1.7). Not only is the Amen Christologically conditioned in these verses, but 'the Amen' is also a self-designation used by the resurrected Jesus in addressing the church in Laodicea (3.14). In addition, the hearers would be aware of the fact that the term also occurs in contexts of worship as a final affirmation especially on the lips of the twenty-four elders (5.14; 7.12; 19.4). When John utters this Amen his hearers would not only be aware of its Christological significance, but also of the fact that it is normally offered in contexts of worship. The current context of worship in which the Amen is offered is made even clearer by the fact that John next voices his own eschatological prayer for the Lord Jesus to come (quickly). This prayer would indicate that John has heard and is keeping the words of this prophecy. John's prayer for Jesus to come quickly would be an invitation for the resurrected Jesus who stands at the door and knocks to come into the church (3.20) to fulfill his promises and warnings, and for Jesus to come quickly in all his eschatological power and glory – to make possible the unmediated spectacular intimacy that awaits in New Jerusalem. John's prayer, as his earlier falling at the feet of Jesus as though dead (1.17), would be an invitation for his hearers to join him in this final act of worship described within the words of the prophecy of this book! 'Amen, Come, Lord Jesus'.

Verse 21 – Finally, the hearers encounter the last words found within this book, 'May the grace of the Lord Jesus be upon all'. While often seen as a somewhat ill-fitted conclusion by modern interpreters, these final words are likely to be of significance for the hearers in several ways. First, they would no doubt be struck by the fact that this circular letter ends with a benediction, which is most unusual for an epistle.[52] However, the meaning of such unusual concluding words of blessing would not be lost on the hearers, for their appearance would extend the context of worship in which they experience the book. Second, neither would the significance of the word grace be missed. For the hearers would well remember that the only other occurrence of the term in the entire book stands at its beginning and is also part of John's words (1.4), indicating that despite the ominous contents of this book of prophecy the entire book is enfolded by grace. Johannine hearers might discern even greater depth in the occurrence of the word here for they would no doubt remember that it is the Word made flesh who is full of grace and truth, and that it is out of his fullness we have all received one grace after another (Jn 1.14-16). Thus, owing to the fact that the Apocalypse is a revelation of Jesus Christ, it is possible that the hearers would now appreciate the way in which its unfolding is indeed the revelation of one grace after another as Jesus Christ is more fully revealed than ever before, further underscoring the fact that this book, despite its ominous contents, is actually a means of grace! This extraordinary grace is pronounced upon all those in the community who heed its call to pneumatic discernment that manifests itself in prophetic faithful witness to a hostile world with the goal of the conversion of the nations – for indeed Jesus is coming quickly!

---

[52] Mounce, *The Book of Revelation*, p. 396.

Bibliography

Allo, E-B., *Saint Jean: L'Apocalypse* (Paris: J. Gabalda, 1921).
Apocalyptic Spirituality: Treatises and Letters of Lactantius, Adso of Montier-en-Der, Joichim of Fiore, The Franciscan Spirituals, Savonarola (New York: Paulist Press, 1979).
Archer, M.L., '"And the Seventh Angel Trumpeted": A Literary Analysis of Revelation 11:15-19' (ThM Thesis, Columbia Theological Seminary, 2006).
Aune, D.E., *Revelation 1-5* (WBC 52a; Dallas: Word, 1997).
—*Revelation 6-16* (WBC 52b; Nashville: Nelson, 1998).
—*Revelation 17-22* (WBC 52c; Nashville: Nelson, 1998).
Bacchiocchi, A., *From Sabbath to Sunday: An Historical Investigation into the Rise of Sunday Observance in Early Christianity* (Rome: Pontifical Gregoriam University Press, 1977).
Ball, D., *'I Am' in John's Gospel: Literary Function, Background and Theological Implications* (JSNTS 124; Sheffield: JSOT Press, 1996).
Barr, D.L., 'The Apocalypse of John as Oral Enactment', *Int* 40 (1986), pp. 243-56.
Bauckham, R., *Jesus and the God of Israel: God Crucified and Other Studies on the New Testament's Christology of Divine Identity* (Grand Rapids, MI: Eerdmans, 2008).
—'Monotheism and Christology in the Gospel of John', in Richard N. Longenecker (ed.), *Contours of Christology in the New Testament* (Grand Rapids, MI: Eerdmans, 2005), pp. 148-68.
—*The Climax of Prophecy: Studies on the Book of Revelation* (Edinburgh: T&T Clark, 1993).
—*The Theology of the Book of Revelation* (Cambridge: Cambridge University Press, 1993).
Beale, G.K., *The Book of Revelation: A Commentary on the Greek Text* (NIGNT; Grand Rapids: Eerdmans, 1999).
Beasley-Murray, G.R., *Revelation* (Grand Rapids: Eerdmans, 1981).
Bede (The Venerable Beda): *The Explanation of the Apocalypse* (trans. E. Marshall; Oxford and London: James Parker and Co., 1878).
Benson, E.W., *The Apocalypse: An Introductory Study of the Revelation of St John the Divine* (New York: Macmillan, 1900).
Biguzzi, G., 'The Chaos of Rev 22,6-21 and Prophecy in Asia', *Biblica* 83.2 (2002), pp. 193-210.
Bloom, H., *Blake's Apocalypse: A Study in Poetic Argument* (Garden City: Doubleday, 1963).
Boesak, A.A., *Comfort and Protest: Reflections on the Apocalypse of John on Patmos* (Edinburgh: The Saint Andrew Press, 1987).
Bowman, J.W., 'The Revelation to John: Its Dramatic Structure and Message', *Int* 9 (1955), pp. 436-53.

Brewer, R.R., 'The Influence of Greek Drama on the Apocalypse of John', *ATR* 18 (1935-36), pp. 74-92.
Brown, R.E., *The Epistles of John* (AB 30; Garden City, NY: Doubleday, 1982).
Bruns, J.E., 'The Contrasted Women of Apoc 12 and 17', *CBQ* 26 (1964), pp. 459-63.
Bugliosi, V., (with C. Gentry), *Helter Skelter: The True Story of the Manson Murders* (New York: Norton and Company, 1974 [1994]).
Caird, G.B., *A Commentary on the Revelation of Saint John the Divine* (London: A & C Black, 1966).
Callahan, A.D., 'The Language of the Apocalypse', *HTR* 88 (1995), pp. 453-70.
Charette, B.B., *The Theme of Recompense in Matthew's Gospel* (JSNTS 79; Sheffield: JSOT Press, 1992).
Charles, J.D., 'The Apocalyptic Tribute to the Lamb (Rev 5:1-14)', *JETS* 34 (1991), pp. 461-73.
Charles, R.H., *The Revelation of St. John,* I (ICC; Edinburgh: T. & T. Clark, 1920).
Cheung, P.W., 'The Mystery of Revelation 17:5 & 7: A Typological Entrance', *Jian Dao* 18 (2003), pp. 1-19.
Cloete, G.D., '"And I saw a New Heaven and a New Earth, for the First ... Were Passed Away" (Revelation 21:1-8)', *Journal of Theology for South Africa* 81 (December, 1992), pp. 55-65.
Collins, A. Yarbro, *The Apocalypse* (NTM 22; Collegeville, MN: Michael Glazier Press, 1979).
Collins, J.J., 'Toward the Morphology of a Genre', *Semeia* 14 (1979), pp. 1-20.
Colson, F.H., 'Triangular Numbers in the New Testament', *JTS* 16 (1915), pp. 67-76.
Court, J., *The Book of Revelation and the Johannine Apocalyptic Tradition* (JSNTS 190; Sheffield: Sheffield Academic Press, 2000).
Dansk, E., *The Drama of the Apocalypse* (London: T. Fisher Unwin, 1894).
Day, J., 'The Origin of Armageddon', in *Crossing the Boundaries: Essays in Biblical Interpretation in Honour of Michael D. Goulder* (S.E. Porter, P. Joyce, D.E. Orton eds.; Leiden: Brill, 1994), pp. 315-26.
Deppermann, K., *Melchior Hoffman: Social Unrest and Apocalyptic Visions in the Age of Reformation* (trans. M. Wren; ed. B. Drewery; Edinburgh: T. & T. Clark, 1987).
Deutsch, C., 'Transformation of Symbols: The New Jerusalem in Rv 21:1-22:5', *ZNW* 78 (1987), pp. 106-26.
Draper, J.A., 'The Heavenly Feast of Tabernacles: Revelation 7:1-17', *JSNT* 19 (1983), pp. 133-47.
Eusebius: The Ecclesiastical History I (trans. K. Lake. London: Heinemann, 1926).
Eusebius: The Ecclesiastical History II (trans. II K. Lake. London: Heinemann, 1932).
Farrer, A.M., *The Revelation of St. John the Divine* (Oxford: Clarendon, 1964).
Fee, G.D., *Revelation* (NCCS; Eugene, OR: Cascade Books, 2011).
Feuillet, A., 'Les Martyrs de l'humanité et l'Agneau égorgé: Une interprétation nouvelle de la prière des Égorgé en *Ap* 6:9-11', *NRT* 99 (1977), pp. 189-207.
Frey, J., 'Erwägungen zum Verhältnis der Johannesapokalypse zu den übrigen Schriften des Corpus Johanneum', in M. Hengel, *Die johanneische Frage*, pp. 326-429.

Gaechter, P., 'The Original Sequence of Apocalypse 20-22', *Theological Studies* 10 (1949), pp. 485-521.
Giblin, C.H., 'Revelation 11:1-13: Its Form, Function, and Textual Integration', *NTS* 30 (1984), pp. 433-59.
Glancy J.A. and S.D. Moore, 'How Typical a Roman Prostitute Is Revelation's "Great Whore" ?' *JBL* 130.3 (2011), pp. 551-69.
Griffiths, J.G., *Plutarch's De Iside et Osiride* (Cambridge: University of Wales Press, 1970).
Gundry, R.H., 'The New Jerusalem: People as Place, not Place for People', *NovT* 29 (1987), pp. 254-64.
Hadorn, W., 'Die Zahl 666, ein Hinweis auf Trajan', *ZNW* 19 (1919-20), pp. 11-29.
Hauret, C., 'Éve transfigurée: de la Genèse à l'Apocalypse', *Revue d'histoire et de philosophie religieuses*, 59 (1979), pp. 327-39.
Hemer, C.J., 'Seven Cities of Asia Minor', in R.K. Harrison (ed.), *Major Cities of the Biblical World* (Nashville, TN: Nelson, 1985), p. 236.
—*The Letters to the Seven Churches of Asia in their Local Settings* (JSNTS 11; Sheffield: JSOT Press, 1986).
Hengel, M., *Die johanneische Frage: Ein Lösungsversuch* (Tübingen: J.C.B. Mohr [Paul Siebeck], 1993).
—*The Johannine Question* (London; Philadelphia: SCM Press; Trinity Press International, 1989).
—*Studies in the Gospel of Mark* (trans. J. Bowden; Philadelphia: Fortress Press, 1985).
Herms, R., *An Apocalypse for the Church and the World: The Narrative Function of Universal Language in the Book of Revelation* (BZNW 143; Berlin: Walter de Gruyter, 2006).
Heschel, A.J., *The Prophets* 2 vols (Peabody, MA: Hendrickson, 2003).
Hill, D., *New Testament Prophecy* (Atlanta: John Knox Press, 1979).
Hillyer, N., '"The Lamb" in the Apocalypse', *EQ* 39 (1967), pp. 228-36.
Holwerda, D.E., 'The Church and the Little Scroll (Revelation 10,11)', *CTJ* 34 (1999), pp. 148-61.
Hort, F.J.A., *The Apocalypse of St. John* I (London: Macmillan, 1908).
Hurtado, L., *Lord Jesus: Devotion to Jesus in Earliest Christianity* (Grand Rapids, MI: Eerdmans, 2005).
Irenaeus, 'Adversus Haereses', in *The Apostolic Fathers: Justin Martyr and Irenaeus* (Rev. A. Cleveland Cox, ANF, Vol. 1, ed. Alexander Roberts and J. Donaldson; Peabody, MA: Hendrickson, 1984), 3.17.2.
Jauhiainen, M., 'The Measuring of the Sanctuary Reconsidered (Rev 11:1-2)', *Biblica* 83 (2002), pp. 507-26.
—'The OT Background to Armageddon (Rev 16:16) Revisited', *NovT* 47.4 (2005), pp. 381-93.
Joachim of Fiore, *Expositio in Apocalypsim* (Frankfurt am Main: Minerva, 1964).
Johns, L.L., *The Lamb Christology of the Apocalypse of John* (WUNT 2 Reihe 167; Tübingen: Mohr Siebeck, 2002).

Koester, C.R., 'God's Purposes and Christ's Saving Work according to Hebrews', in Jan G. van der Watt (ed.), *Salvation in the New Testament: Perspectives on Soteriology* (Leiden: Brill, 2005), pp. 361-88.
—*Revelation and the End of All Things* (Grand Rapids: Eerdmans, 2001).
—'The Message to Laodicea and the Problem of its Local Context: A Study of the Imagery in Rev 3:14-22', *NTS* 49 (2003), pp. 407-24.
Kovacs, J. and C. Rowland, *Revelation* (Oxford: Blackwell, 2003).
Kretschmar, G., *Die Offenbarung des Johannes: Die Geschichte ihrer Auslegung im 1. Jahrtausend* (CTM 9; Stuttgart: Calwer, 1985).
Ladd, G.E., *Gospel of the Kingdom: Scripture Studies in the Kingdom of God* (Grand Rapids, MI: Eerdmans, 1959).
—*A Theology of the New Testament* (Grand Rapids, MI: Eerdmans, 1993).
Lee, P., *The New Jerusalem in the Book of Revelation: A Study of Revelation 21-22 in the Light of its Background in Jewish Tradition* (WUNT 129; Berlin: Mohr Siebeck, 2001).
Linton, G., 'Reading the Apocalypse as an Apocalypse', *SBL Seminar Papers* (Atlanta: Scholars Press, 1991), pp. 161-86.
Lohse, E., *Die Offenbarung des Johannes* (NTD; Göttingen: Vandenhoeck und Ruprecht, 1960).
Longenecker, B.W., '"Linked Like a Chain": Rev 22:6-9 in Light of Ancient Translation Technique', *NTS* 47.1 (2001), pp. 105-17.
MacKenzie, R.K., *The Author of the Apocalypse: A Review of the Prevailing Hypothesis of Jewish-Christian Authorship* (MBPS 51; Lewiston, NY: Edwin Mellon Press, 1997).
Martin, C.J., 'Polishing the Cloudy Mirror: A Womanist Reading of Revelation 18:13', in David Rhoads (ed.), *From Every People and Nation: The Book of Revelation in Intercultural Perspective* (Minneapolis: Fortress, 2005), pp. 82-109.
Martin, L.R., *The Unheard Voice of God: A Pentecostal Hearing of the Book of Judges* (JPTSup 32; Blandford Forum: Deo, 2008).
Mathewson, D., 'New Exodus as a Background for "the sea was no more" in Revelation 21:1c', *Trinity Journal* 24 (2003), pp. 243-58.
—'The Destiny of the Nations in Revelation 21:1-22:5: A Reconsideration', *TynB* 53.1 (2002), pp. 121-42.
Mayo, P.L., *'Those Who Call Themselves Jews': The Church and Judaism in the Apocalypse of John* (PTMS; Eugene, OR: Pickwick Pub, 2006).
Mazzaferri, F.D., *The Genre of the Book of Revelation from a Source-Critical Perspective* (Berlin: Walter de Gruyter, 1989).
McIlraith, D.A., '"For the Fine Linen Is the Righteous Deeds of the Saints": Works and Wife in Revelation 19:8', *CBQ* 61.3 (July 1999), pp. 512-29.
Mealy, J.W., *After the Thousand Years: Resurrection and Judgment in Revelation 20* (JSNTS 70; Sheffield: JSOT Press, 1992).
Melito of Sardis: On Pascha and Fragments (ed. & trans. S.G. Hall; Oxford: Clarendon Press, 1979).
Metzger, B.M., *Breaking the Code* (Nashville: Abingdon, 1993).
—*The Canon of the New Testament: Its Origin, Development, and Significance* (Oxford: Clarendon Press, 1987).

Meynet, R., 'Le cantique de Moïse et le cantique de l'Agneau (Ap 15 et Ex 15)', *Gregorianum* 73 (1992), pp. 19-55.
Michaels, J.R., *Interpreting the Book of Revelation* (Grand Rapids: Baker, 1992).
—*Revelation* (IVPNTC; Downers Grove, IL: IVP, 1997).
Miles, B., *Paul McCartney: Many Years from Now* (New York: Henry Holt and Co., 1997).
Miller, K.E., 'The Nuptial Eschatology of Revelation 19-22', *CBQ* 60.2 (1998), pp. 301-18.
Moore, R.D., 'Joel', *The Book of the Twelve* (ed. J.C. Thomas; Blandford Forum: Deo, forthcoming).
—*The Spirit of the Old Testament* (JPTSup 35; Blandford Forum: Deo Publishing, 2011).
Morton, R., 'Glory to God and the Lamb: John's Use of Jewish and Hellenistic/Roman Themes in Formatting his Theology in Revelation 4-5', *JSNT* 83 (2001), pp. 89-109.
Mounce, R.H., *The Book of Revelation* (Grand Rapids, MI: Eerdmans, 1977).
Moyise, S., *The Old Testament in the Book of Revelation* (JSNTS 115; Sheffield: Sheffield Academic Press, 1995).
Murphy, F.J., *Fallen Is Babylon: The Revelation to John* (Harrisburg, PA: Trinity Press International, 1998).
Musvosi, J.N., 'The Song of Moses and the Song of the Lamb', *Journal of the Adventist Theological Society* 9.1-2 (1998), pp. 44-47.
Newport, K.G.C., *Apocalypse & Millennium: Studies in Biblical Eisegesis* (Cambridge: Cambridge University Press, 2000).
Osborne, G.R., *Revelation* (ECNT; Grand Rapids: Baker, 2002).
Ozanne, C.G., 'The Language of the Apocalypse', *TynB* 16 (1965), pp. 3-9.
Pattemore, S., *The People of God in the Apocalypse: Discourse, Structure and Exegesis* (SNTSMS 128; Cambridge: Cambridge University Press, 2004).
Philonenko, M., '"Dehors les Chiens" (Apocalypse 22:16 et 4QMMT B 58-62)', *NTS* 43.3 (1997), pp. 445-50.
Poirier, J.C., 'The First Rider: A Response to Michael Bachmann', *NTS* 45 (1999), pp. 257-62.
Poucouta, P., 'La mission prophétique de l'Église dans l'Apocalypse johannique', *NRT* 110 (1988), pp. 38-57.
Prigent, P., *L'Apocalypse de Saint Jean* (CNT 14; Geneve: Labor et Fides, 2000).
Provain, I., 'Foul Spirits, Fornication and Finance: Revelation 18 from an Old Testament Perspective', *JSNT* 64 (1996), pp. 81-100.
Putter, A., *An Introduction to the* Gawain-*Poet* (London: Longman, 1996).
Ramsay, W., *The Seven Letters to the Seven Churches of Asia and their Place in the Plan of the Apocalypse* (London: Hodder & Stoughton, 1904).
Resseguie, J.L., *The Revelation of John: A Narrative Commentary* (Grand Rapids: Baker, 2009).
Rissi, M., *Die Zukunft der Welt: Eine exegetische Studie über Johannesoffenbarung 19, 11 bis 22, 15* (Basel: Verlag Friedrich Reinhardt, 1966).
Rowland, C.C., 'The Book of Revelation, Introduction, Commentary, and Reflections', in L.E. Keck (ed.), *The New Interpreter's Bible* 12 (Nashville: Abingdon, 1998), pp. 501-743.

Royalty, Jr., R.M., 'Don't Touch This Book!: Revelation 22:18-19 and the Rhetoric of Reading (in) the Apocalypse of John', *Biblical Interpretation* 12.3 (2004), pp. 282-99.

Ruiz, J.-P., *Ezekiel in the Apocalypse: The Transformation of Prophetic Language in Revelation 16,17-19,10* (EUSST 23; Frankfurt am Main: Lang, 1989).

Schimanowski, G., *Die himmlische Liturgie in der Apokalypse des Johannes: Die frühjüdischen Traditionen in Offenbarung 4-5 unter Einschluß der Hekhalotliteratur* (WUNT 2 Reihe 154; Tübingen: Mohr Siebeck, 2002).

Schroder, J.A., 'Revelation 12: Female Figures and Figures of Evil', *Word and Witness* 15 (1995), pp. 175-81.

Schüssler Fiorenza, E., *Revelation: Justice and Judgment* (Philadelphia: Fortress, 1985).

—*Revelation: Vision of a Just World* (Minneapolis: Fortress, 1991).

Sellers, O.R., 'Weights and Measures', in G.A. Buttrick (ed.), *The Interpreter's Dictionary of the Bible* (Nashville, TN: Abingdon, 1962), 4, pp. 828-39.

Simoens, Y., *Apocalypse de Jean: Apocalypse de Jésus Christ* (Paris: Éditions Facultés Jésuites de Paris, 2008).

Skaggs, R. and P. Benham, *Revelation* (PCS: Blandford Forum: Deo, 2009).

Skehan, P.W., 'King of Kings, Lord of Lords', *CBQ* 10.4 (1948), p. 398.

Slater, T.B., *Christ and Community: A Socio-Historical Study of the Christology and Revelation* (JSNTS 178; Sheffield: Sheffield Academic Press, 1999).

Smalley, S.S., *The Revelation to John* (Downers Grove, IL: IVP, 2005).

—*Thunder and Love: John's Revelation and John's Community* (Milton Keynes, UK: Word, 1994).

Smith, C.R., 'The Portrayal of the Church as the New Israel in the Names and Order of the Tribes in Revelation 7:5-8', *JSNT* 39 (1990), pp. 111-18.

Stevenson, J., *The Catacombs: Life and Death in Early Christianity* (Nashville, TN: Thomas Nelson, 1985).

Suetonius II (trans. J.C. Rolfe; London: Heinemann, 1965).

Sweet, J., *Revelation* (London: SCM Press, 1990).

Swete, H.B., *The Apocalypse of St. John* (London: MacMillan, 1909).

Tacitus IV (trans. J. Jackson; London: Heinemann, 1962).

The Ante-Nicene Fathers I, VII (eds. A. Roberts and J. Donaldson; Grand Rapids: Eerdmans, 1989).

The Apostolic Fathers: Greek Texts and English Translations (ed. Michael W. Holmes. Grand Rapids: Baker, 1992).

The Cambridge Companion to Handel (ed. D. Borrows; Cambridge: Cambridge University Press, 1997).

The Complete Poetry and Prose of William Blake (ed. D.V. Erdman; New York: Doubleday, 1988).

The Methodist Hymn-Book (London: Wesleyan Conference Office, 1904).

The Pearl (trans. & ed. S. Deford, *et al.*; New York: Appleton-Century-Croft, 1967).

The Oxford Bible Commentary (eds. J. Barton and J. Muddiman; Oxford: Oxford University Press, 2001).

The Writings of Tertullian I (eds. A. Roberts and J. Donaldson; Edinburgh: T. & T. Clark, 1869).

Thomas, J.C., *Footwashing in John 13 and the Johannine Community* (JSNTS 61; Sheffield: JSOT Press, 1991).
—*1 John, 2 John, 3 John* (London: T & T Clark International, 2004).
—*The Devil, Disease, and Deliverance: Origins of Illness in New Testament Thought* (Cleveland, TN: CPT Press, 2011).
—*The Spirit of the New Testament* (Leiderdorp, The Netherlands: Deo Publishing, 2004).
Thayer, J.H., *Greek-English Lexicon of the New Testament* (Grand Rapids: Zondervan, 1973).
Tobin, J., *Handel at Work* (New York: St. Martin's Press, 1964).
van der Meer, F., *Apocalypse: Visions from the Book of Revelation in Western Art* (New York: Alpine Fine Arts, 1978).
Waddell, R.C., *The Spirit of the Book of Revelation* (JPTSup 30; Blandford Forum: Deo Publishing, 2006).
Wainwright, A.W., *Mysterious Apocalypse* (Nashville: Abingdon, 1993).
Wall, R.W., *Revelation* (NIBC, NTS 18; Peabody, MA: Hendrickson, 1991).
Wall, R.W. and E.E. Lemcio, *The New Testament as Canon: A Reader in Canonical Criticism* (JSNTS 76; Sheffield: JSOT Press, 1992).
Walsh, R., 'On Finding a Non-American Revelation: *End of Days* and the Book of Revelation' in G. Aichele and R. Walsh (eds.), *Screening Scripture: Intertextual Connections Between Scripture and Film* (Harrisburg, PA: Trinity Press International, 2002), pp. 1-23.
Whealey, A., 'The Apocryphal Apocalypse of John. A Byzantine Apocalypse from the Early Islamic Period', *JTS* 53 (2002), pp. 533-40.
Williams, G.H., *The Radical Reformation* (Philadelphia: Westminster, 1962).
Williams, J., *The Illustrated Beatus: A Corpus of the Illustrations of the Commentary on the Apocalypse*, 5 vols (London: Harvey Miller Publishers, 1994-2003).
Wojciechowski, M., 'Apocalypse 21:19-20: titres christologiques cachés dans la liste des pierres précieuses', *NTS* 33 (1987), pp. 153-54.
Zimmerman, R., 'Nuptial Imagery in the Revelation of John', *Biblica* 84.2 (2003), pp. 153-83.

INDEX OF BIBLICAL AND OTHER ANCIENT REFERENCES

Old Testament

Genesis
1.10	312
1.26-28	604
2.9	124
2.10	658
3	367, 593
3.1-7	367, 593
3.15-16	358
3.15	354, 359, 380
3.16	354, 386
3.22-24	660
3.22	124
3.23-24	124
4.15	261
12.1	524
16.10	309
19.1-29	436
19.24	283, 590
19.28	437, 530, 557
22.2	636
22.11-18	309
24.7	309
31.11-13	309
49.8-12	223
49.8	223

Exodus
1.22	378
3.2-12	309
3.17-22	610
7.14-24	468, 469
7.17	332
7.20-21	286
7.20	288
7.22	477
7.23	477
7.24	470
8.15	477
8.19	477
8.32	477
9.7	477
9.10-12	467
9.12	477
9.22-26	286
9.34-35	477
10.1	477
10.4-20	294
10.20	477
10.21-23	290
10.23	476
11.9-10	477
12	261
12.23	300, 593
14-24	468
14-15	378
14.14	477
14.19	309
14.21-22	480
14.31	453
15	453
15.11-12	388
15.11	454, 455, 457
15.22-17.7	362
15.25	290
16	141
17.9-10	636
19	636
19.4	376
19.16	208
20.13	307
20.14-15	307
21.24	350
22.18	307
25.31-40	209
28	205
28.17-21	205, 638
28.36-38	183
32.31-33	168
33.20	257, 663
34.29-35	638
40.4	209
40.24-25	209
40.34-35	464

Leviticus
11.9-12	481
11.41-47	481
24.20	350
26.8	296
26.11-12	623
26.12	624
26.21-24	449

Numbers
11.1	302
12.7	453
16.23	524
16.31-33	379
22-24	137
24.17	158, 682
25.1-2	137
25.2	138
31	262
31.16	137
35.30	328

Deuteronomy
3.24	388
4.19	353
12.32	685
13.1-5	400
17.3	353
17.6	328
19.15	328
19.16-19	544
19.21	350
23.9-10	425
23.17-18	679
28.42	294
29	685
29.23	436
31.26	461
32.4	456, 459
32.11-12	376
32.23-25	241
34.5	453

Joshua
1.1	453
1.15	453
3.14-17	480
5.12	141
8.20	437
8.31	453
9.24	453
10.11	489
18.30-31	265

Judges
1.7	350
2.1	309
5.19	485
5.31	103
6.22	309
9.7	636
13.20-22	30
15.11	350
16.13-22	298
20.40	437

1 Samuel
4.8	332
7.6	466
21.5	425

2 Samuel
5.7	418
7.14	629
8.2	323
11.11	425
14.25-26	298

1 Kings
1.10	283
1.12	283
1.14	283
5.17	649
6.20	646
6.30	651
8.9	461
8.37	294
8.53	453
8.56	453
10.14	410
12.25-33	265
16.31-32	146
17.1	332, 399
18.3	363
18.15	399
18.20-46	636
18.38	400
18.42	636
19.1-18	362
19.18	341

2 Kings
1.10	331
9.7	556
9.22	147
9.27	485
9.30-37	516
10.1-11	151-52
18.12	453

19.4	260	75.9	436	**Isaiah**		49.10	275
19.16	260	76.2	418	1.4	292	50.3	254
21.8	453	77.18	208	1.21	563	51.3	125
21.13	323	78.3-6	466	1.21	492	51.17	436
23.5	353	78.46	294	2.2-4	459, 637	51.22	436
23.29	485	79 (LXX 78)	250	2.10	256	52.11	524
1 Chronicles		79.5	250	2.19	256	53.7 (LXX)	225
16.9	455	82.2	250	2.21	256	54.1	355
16.31	457	86.8	388	5.8-22	292	54.11	649
24.4-6	207	87.2	610	6.1-4	464	55.1-3	191
2 Chronicles		88.11	299	6.3	213	55.1	628
7.1-3	464	89.8	388	6.13	341	57.6	466
24.9	453	90.13	250	10.5	292	60.1-22	176-77
36.16	549	92.5	455	11.1-10	223	60.3	654, 655
Ezra		94.3	250	11.4	224	60.11	657
9.6	526	96.1	230	11.6-8	224	60.19-20	653
Nehemiah		96.2	432	11.10	224	62.6	184
1.8	453	96.10	457	11.15	480	66.6	465
9.33	470	98.1-3	422	13	486	66.7-9	355
Job		98.1-2	455	13.13	254, 488	66.7	359
1.16	283	98.1	230	21.9	520	**Jeremiah**	
2.1-10	467	98.5	229	21.17	241	1.2-3	41
18.15	436	99.2	457	22.12	329	1.2	89
26.6	299	105.26	453	22.22	172	1.4	89
28.22	299	106	553	23.16	492	1.11	89
31.12	299	106.48	558	24.23	418	2.2	563
31.26	353	111-113	553	25.7-10	418	4.8	329
Psalms		111.1-2	455	25.8	277	4.11-12	258
2.6	418	112.1(LXX)	559	26.16-17	355	4.24	254
2.8-9	157	112.3(LXX)	559	27.1	355	5.14	331
6.3	454, 457	113.5	388	28.16-17	323	7.20	466
7.10	153	115.3-8	307	29.10	493	7.34	548
7.11	470	117	553	30.33	436	8.2	353
7.14-16	350	118.1	455	32.12(LXX)	531	9.15	289
9.4	470	119.103	320	34.4	254	10	307
9.11	418	132.13	418, 610	34.9	436	10.7	457, 457
11.6	283, 436	134.1(LXX)	559	34.10	530	10.25	466
11.7	663	134.3(LXX)	559	34.11-15	521	11.15	610
13.1	250	135	553	34.11	323	11.20	152
13.2	250	139.14	455	34.12	549	12.7	610
15.1	454, 457	144.9-10	422	37.12(LXX)	537	13.27	497
17.15	663	144.9	230	40.18-20	307	14.16	466
18.31	388	144.17	459	40.18	457	15.2	396
22.16	679	145.17	456	40.25-26	388	16.8	528
22.20	679	146-150	553	40.25	454, 457	16.9	548
22.28	457	147.7	229	40.31	376	17.10	152
29.10	529	148	559	41.6-7	307	20.12	152
32.2	229	149.1	230	42.10-13	422	23.1	292
33.3	230	150	559	42.20	230	23.15	289
40.4	230	**Proverbs**		43.3-4	177	24.7	624
42.2	663	3.12	195	44.6	628, 676	25.10	548
47.8	457	8.15-16	549	44.7	388	25.16	436
68	303	15.11	299	44.9-20	307	25.27	436
68.17	303	30.27	299	45.14	177	31.38	323
69.9 (LXX)	195	**Song**		45.20	657	39.35	497
74.10	250	5.2	196	45.22	657	42.11	396
74.14	355			45.24	657	46.28	470
				48.20	524	49.12	436
				49.2	103		

49.36	258	37.32	539	2.5	563	1.15	302
50.8	524	38.6	640	2.14-15	362	2.6-7	488
50.29	241	38.22	489, 611	5.3	492	2.6	254
51.1-2	258	39.6	611	7.13	292	**Zechariah**	
51.3	241	40-46	652	11.10	312	1.1	41
51.6	525	40-48	33	12.5	456	1.6	323
51.7-8	434, 523	40.1-2	637	**Joel**		1.7	302
51.7	436	43.5	494	1.1	89	240	
51.9	526	44.4	464	1.3	41	2.1-2	323
51.13	492	45.2	645	1.4-7	298	2.6-7	525
51.22	497	47.1-12	658	2.1-11	298	2.11	657
51.25	507	47.12	661	2.10	254	2.13	278
51.34	355, 358	48.8-9	645	2.31	254	166	
51.45	525	48.30-35	640, 64	3.13	446	3.3-7	673
51.59-64	545	**Daniel**		**Amos**		166	
Lamentations		1.14	131	1.1	41	4	330
2.4	466	2.24	549	3.8	312	92, 103	
2.8	323	3.6	103	3.13	455	4.1-14	209
4.21	436	3.22	476	4.13	455	4.6	330
Ezekiel		3.27	476	5.3	341	4.10	226
1.4-28	211	4.33	549	5.8	455	4.14	330
1.13	208, 284	4.34-37	499	5.14	456	6.2-6	240
1.24	103	5.1	549	5.15	456	6.5	259
2.3	41	5.2	549	5.16	455	8.23	657
2.8-3.2	319	5.3	549	5.18	291	10.3	455
3.12	494	5.9	549	5.27	455	12.2	436
3.14	494	5.23	549	7.7-9	323	12.3	326
5.9	497	6.17	549	9.5	455	12.10-12	95
5.11	497	7	334, 383,	9.6	456	12.11	485, 486,
5.12	258		388	9.15	456	13.8-9	287
5.16-17	241	7.7-23	334	**Obadiah**		14.4-5	488
6.9	497	7.7	356	16	436	14.11	662
8.3	494	7.9	103, 207	**Jonah**		**Malachi**	
9.1-11	261	7.10	615	1.2	526	1.11	458, 459
9.8	466	7.13	95, 103,	3.6-8	329	3.2	257
9.11	103		442	3.7	549	4.4	453
10.2-8	283	7.14	657	**Micah**		**New Testament**	
11.1	494	7.20	388, 389	1.1	41	**Matthew**	
11.24	494	7.21	334, 384	2.5	323	11.15	122
14.19	466	7.23	384	4.1-3	637	13.9	122
15.1	466	7.24	511	4.9-10	355	13.43	122
15.7	466	7.25	326, 377,	7.18	388, 454,	21.39	446
16.15	492		390, 392		457	24-25	19
23.1-49	515	8	357	**Nahum**		24.43	164
23.1	492	8.3	398	257		**Mark**	
23.31-33	436	8.10	357	3.4	492	4.9	122
24.6	292	8.11-14	326	3.5	455	4.23	122
27.12-24	533	9.14	470	**Habakkuk**		10.39	49
27.32	539	10.4-6	103	2.15-16	436	13	19
28.13	125, 649	10.8-17	321	2.20	278	13.26	95
29.3	355	10.13	364	**Zephaniah**		**Luke**	
31.8-9	125	10.21	364	1.1	41	8.8	122
32.3-16	355	12.1-2	273	1.7	278	9.1	33
37	404	12.1	364	5.13b	428	12.39	164
37.1	494	12.4	672	**Haggai**		14.35	122
37.3	272	12.7	326	41		21	19
37.5	339	**Hosea**				22.14	33
37.10	339	1.1	41, 89				

John		2.20	653	5.24	90, 113	6.70	33, 514,
1.1-18	89	2.23	339	5.25	90, 143		642
1.1	187, 579	3.2	147, 657	5.27	442	6.71	33, 642
1.2-3	218	3.7	502	5.28-29	605, 606	7.3	455
1.3	187, 579	3.10	263	5.28	90, 502	7.4	460
1.4	104, 124,	3.13	442	5.29	432	7.6	506
	547	3.14	162, 362,	5.30	113, 456	7.12	368, 401,
1.5	547, 548,		442, 494	5.35	547, 548,		597
	653, 657	3.16-18	143		562	7.14	147, 324
1.6	113	3.16	93, 116,	5.36	113, 317,	7.15	386, 502
1.7-9	547		537		455	7.16	113
1.9	172, 519	3.17	113	5.37	113	7.18	113, 215
1.11-13	579	3.20	121	5.38	113	7.20	306, 482
1.11	579	3.21	460	5.45	371	7.21	386, 455,
1.12	115	3.24	130, 521	6	124		502
1.14-16	688	3.28	113	6.2	339	7.24	456
1.14	91, 214,	3.29	162, 548,	6.3	637	7.28	113, 147,
	275, 361,		562, 563	6.5	231		324, 456
	374, 391,	3.33	261, 456,	6.6	180, 654	7.29	113
	456, 579,		597	6.12	537, 585	7.30	165, 588
	623	3.34	113	6.13	585	7.32	588
1.16	91, 579	3.35	143	6.15	360, 513,	7.33	113, 426
1.17	91, 381,	3.36	257		583, 637	7.35	147
	456	4	270	6.17	288, 657	7.37-39	275, 684
1.18	88, 143,	4.6	289	6.19-20	104, 129	7.38	276, 290
	579, 663	4.7-15	628	6.19	288, 339	7.44	588
1.19-34	129	4.8	231	6.21-23	288	7.47	368, 401,
1.20	135, 169	4.12	682	6.24	592		597
1.23	362, 494	4.13-15	275	6.25	147	8.12	426, 547,
1.29	19, 46,	4.14	276, 277,	6.27	261, 442,		654, 657
	93, 225		289, 290		537, 597	8.14	426
1.31	263, 460	4.19	339	6.29	113, 141,	8.16	113, 172
1.33	113	4.20-24	178, 325		455	8.18	113
1.34	143	4.22	270	6.31	141, 362,	8.20	147, 165,
1.35-39	129	4.23	214, 325		494		324, 588
1.37	90	4.27	386, 502	6.32	172	8.21-22	426
1.37-38	426	4.29	585	6.33	141	8.24	162
1.38	147	4.31	147	6.35	141, 275	8.26	113, 456
1.40	90, 426	4.34	113, 317,	6.38-40	218	8.28	88, 147
1.42	142, 513,		455	6.38	113	8.29	113
	567		443	6.39	113, 537	8.42	113
		4.35-38	348, 562,	6.40	339	8.44	114, 128,
1.43	426	4.36	585	6.44	113		130, 176,
1.47-51	129		113, 440,	6.45	147, 423		307, 358,
1.47	93, 263	4.38	543, 643	6.46	663		368, 428,
1.49	93, 143,		90, 270	6.49	141, 362,		536, 594,
	147, 263,	4.42	215		494		632, 680
	513, 583	4.44	661	6.50-51	141	8.47	90
1.51	442	4.46-54	661	6.53	442	8.48-49	306, 482
2.1-11	425	5.1-18	299	6.53-58	141	8.50-54	215
2.1-12	360	5.2	129, 150,	6.53-56	93	8.51-55	90, 163
2.2	513, 568	5.14	324	6.57	113	8.52	306, 482
2.4	165		375	6.59	147	8.56	562
2.11	214, 460,	5.16	386, 455,	6.61-66	137	8.59	324
	513, 568	5.20	491, 502,	6.62	442	9.1-41	191, 661
2.14-15	324		635	6.66	166	9.2	147
2.16	523			6.67	33, 642	9.3	150, 460
2.17	319	5.23	113	6.69	171	9.3-4	455
2.19-20	324	5.28	386			9.4	113, 657
2.19	652	5.24-28	197				

The Apocalypse

9.5	547	11.54	362, 494	14.6	104, 124,	16.24	115, 162
9.6	194	11.56	324		171, 456	16.26	115
9.22	169	11.57	588	14.7	440	16.33	98, 126,
9.34-38	326	12.2	145, 198,	14.9	491, 635		198, 223,
9.35	442		568	14.10	88		272
9.38	178	12.6	164, 308	14.10-12	455	17.1	165
9.39	600	12.13	263, 269,	14.13	115	17.2	157
10.1-21	276		513, 583	14.14	115	17.3	113, 172,
10.1	164, 308,	12.15	513, 583	14.15	174, 381		456
	326	12.20	178	14.15-24	90, 163	17.4	317, 455
10.3-5	197	12.23	165, 442	14.17	171, 339	17.5	214, 235,
10.3	90	12.25	121, 145,	14.19	339		394
10.4-5	426		373, 537	14.21	381	17.6	90, 163,
10.7-10	173, 174	12.26	145	14.23-24	174		179, 460
10.7	172	12.29	313	14.24	113	17.8	88, 113
10.8	90, 164	12.31	367	14.26	113, 115,	17.11-15	90, 163
10.10	164, 308,	12.31-32	165		147	17.11	171, 213
	537	12.33	88, 353	14.27	91	17.12	162, 537
10.11	248	12.34	442	14.28	90, 562	17.13	162
10.11-17	373	12.35	654, 657	14.30	344	17.14-15	179
10.12	360	12.38	162	14.31	381	17.14	88, 121
10.14-18	381	12.42	169	15.1	172	17.17	171
10.15	248	12.43	215	15.2	146	17.18	113, 543,
10.16	90, 197,	12.44	113	15.6	444, 585		643
	326	12.45	113, 339	15.7	333	17.19	171
10.17	248	12.46	547, 657	15.10	90, 163,	17.21	113
10.20-21	306, 482	12.49-50	88		174, 381	17.23	93, 113
10.23	324	12.49	113	15.11	162	17.24	248, 339,
10.25	455	12.50	381	15.12	381		394
10.27	90, 197,	13.1	93, 117,	15.13	248, 373	17.25	113, 456
	426		165	15.15	88, 90	18.2	537, 585
10.28	537	13.2	130, 198,	15.16	115, 514	18.9	162
10.28-29	360		568	15.18-16.4	123	18.11	436
10.32	491, 635	13.3	426	15.18-19	121	18.12	301
10.32-33	455	13.4	198	15.18	121	18.14	191
10.36	113, 143,	13.8	606, 686	15.20	90, 163,	18.15	326
	171	13.13-14	147		375-76	18.20	147, 324
10.37-38	455	13.14	643	15.21	113, 115	18.24	301
10.39	588	13.16	113	15.23-25	121	18.25	135
11.1-57	661	13.18	162, 514	15.23-24	121	18.29	371
11.4	143, 150,	13.19	440	15.24	455	18.32	88, 162,
	214	13.20	113	15.25	162		353
11.8	147	13.26	578	15.26	113, 171	18.33	513, 583
11.9-10	654	13.27	368, 594	16.1-4	46	18.36	344
11.10	657	13.29	231	16.1	137	18.37	197, 513,
11.15	562	13.30	608, 657	16.5	113, 426		583
11.27	143	13.31	442	16.7	113	18.39	513, 583
11.28	147, 506	13.33	426	16.8-11	195, 227	19.2	496
11.31	221, 531	13.34	118, 381	16.10	426	19.3	496, 513,
11.33	221, 531	13.35	118, 144	16.11	123, 344,		583
11.35	277	13.36	427		367	19.5	496
11.40	214	13.37	248, 373	16.13-15	122	19.7	143
11.43	491, 635	13.38	135, 248,	16.13	171, 276,	19.12	513, 583
11.44	301		373		588	19.13	299
11.42	113			16.17	426	19.14-15	513
11.47	585	14.2-3	248, 362	16.20	338, 531	19.14	583
11.48	146	14.3	444	16.21	98, 126,	19.15	583
11.50	537	14.4	427		272, 562	19.17	299
11.52	585	14.5	427	16.23	115	19.19	513, 583

Index of References   701

19.20	299, 446	21.18	207	1.1-2	681-82		431, 457, 458, 519, 528, 557, 607, 652, 655, 663, 687
19.21	513, 583	**1 Corinthians**		1.1-3	6, 105		
19.24	162, 301	10.25-30	138	1.1-8	5, 80, 87-96		
19.24b-27	129	14.6	87				
19.25-27	360, 380	14.19	296	1.1-3.22	81		
19.28	599	**Ephesians**		1.1-19.9	568		
19.30	317, 517, 599	6.21	10	1.2	42, 89-90, 92, 102, 249, 328, 372, 572, 670	1.6-7	186, 237, 271
19.31	225	**Colossians**				1.7	67-68, 95, 103, 119, 177, 251, 309, 340, 441, 474, 483, 531, 579, 687
19.33-34	46	4.13	21				
19.34	93	4.16	10, 21				
19.26	162	**1 Thessalonians**		1.3	2, 7, 11, 42, 89, 90-91, 101, 122, 156, 163, 175, 203, 279, 328, 375, 483, 517, 567, 577, 606, 668-69, 672, 686		
19.31-37	335	4.17	95				
19.37	95	5.2	164				
19.39	657	**2 Thessalonians**				1.7-8	40, 94-96
20.11	221, 531	5.27	10			1.8	12, 96, 104, 152, 214, 346, 456, 471, 474, 505, 513, 561, 578, 583, 625, 627, 676, 682
20.13	221, 531	**1 Timothy**					
20.14	102, 339	4.14	207				
20.15	221, 531	5.17-19	207				
20.16	147	**Titus**					
20.17	629	1.5	207				
20.19	91	**Philemon**		1.4	3, 10-11, 41, 119, 122, 157, 159, 198, 204, 209, 214, 346, 399, 430, 470, 505, 576, 599, 667, 683, 688		
20.20	491, 562, 635	2	10			1.9	41, 44, 89, 94, 97-99, 115, 126, 130, 145, 150, 179, 249, 253, 272, 372, 397, 438, 457, 514, 568, 571, 572, 601, 669
20.21	113, 543, 643	**Hebrews**					
20.22	163	13.12	446				
20.24	33	**James**					
20.26	91	5.8	162				
20.27	131	5.17	332				
20.31	115, 143, 352	**1 Peter**					
21.1	460	5.1	207				
		5.13	33				
21.3	288, 588	**2 Peter**		1.4-5a	91-93		
21.6	288	2.1	250	1.4-6	572		
21.7	191	3.10	164	1.5	25, 66, 93, 117, 131, 136, 156, 179, 186, 187, 195, 198, 227, 232, 249, 255, 274, 328, 371, 372, 394, 457, 472, 513, 514, 574, 583, 591, 655, 658		
21.9	548	**1 John**					
21.10	588	1.5	97			1.9-10	204, 494, 636
21.11	414	**3 John**				1.9-20	5, 42, 97-107, 329, 485
21.14	460	1-15	117				
21.19	88, 353	**Jude**					
21.19-20	426	4	250			1.9-3.22	5, 80, 97-200, 201
21.19-22	426	**Revelation**					
21.20	198, 568	1	111				
21.22	426	1-3	72, 203, 494, 576, 636			1.10	3, 39-40, 56-57, 100-01, 122, 159, 203, 209, 225, 250, 280, 291, 420, 493, 546, 636, 683
21.23	97						
Acts		1-8	80		574		
11.28	88	1.1	41, 87-89, 203, 253, 262, 310, 318, 322, 349, 491, 543, 559, 635, 643, 667	1.5b			
11.30	206			1.5-6	394, 572		
14.23	207			1.5b-6	93-94, 98, 143, 183, 207, 237, 266, 275, 325, 370, 419,		
15.2	207			1.6			
15.4	207						
15.6	207						
15.22-23	207					1.10-11	100-02
15.28-29	154					1.11	10-11, 42, 105, 221,
16.4	207						
20.17-38	207						

	313-14, 321, 577, 626, 672	2-3	336, 496, 498, 507 11, 20, 26, 29,	2.5b 2.6	139 30, 111, 112, 116, 120-21,	2.12	673, 683 6, 132-33, 142, 158, 170, 185,
1.12	102-03, 192, 224		31, 37, 80, 108,		139, 140, 516, 521,		439, 442, 577, 581,
1.12-13	281, 420, 496		110, 121, 124, 209,	2.7	566, 616 24, 26,	2.12-17	626 132-42
1.12-16	105		210, 222,		121-25,	2.13	26, 27,
1.12-20	40, 101, 202, 204, 335		226, 267, 322, 371, 372, 395,		141, 158, 197, 240, 334, 371,		46, 115, 128, 131, 133-37,
1.13	111, 192, 240, 442, 463	2.1	451 109-11,		451, 568, 572, 628, 630, 660,		144, 161, 175, 179, 198, 204,
1.13-16	103		125, 132,		678, 683		227, 246,
1.14	6, 91, 142, 166, 167, 193, 252, 441, 450, 576, 613		134, 142, 158, 160, 170, 181, 185, 192, 281, 439, 496, 577, 626, 654	2.8	125-26, 131, 132, 142, 158, 161, 170, 185, 225, 439, 577, 589, 602,		249, 307, 328, 368, 372, 384, 397, 438, 472, 514, 572, 574, 594, 600
1.15	309, 421, 560	2.1-7	109-25		626, 676	2.13-15	111, 631
1.16	6, 91, 111, 133, 160, 247, 309, 332, 384, 442, 481, 580, 653	2.1-3.22 2.2	3, 5, 12, 97, 108-200 30, 33, 49, 111-15, 120, 127, 128,	2.8-10 2.8-11 2.9	26 125-32 27, 29, 126-29, 133, 147, 150, 153,	2.13-17 2.14	133 116, 136-39, 147, 153, 165, 308, 399, 407, 425,
1.17	91, 104, 129, 201, 216, 229, 270, 569, 676, 682, 687		133, 144, 145, 147, 160, 176, 180, 428, 503, 543, 566, 568,	2.9-10	161, 176, 190, 234, 263, 368, 383, 477, 594 46, 98,	2.14-15 2.15	434, 485, 492, 516, 523, 680 30 139, 147, 442
1.17-18	103-05		616, 633,		272, 391	2.16	6, 118,
1.17-3.22	122		643, 675,	2.10	27, 29,		119, 139-
1.18	104, 124, 125-26, 131, 161, 172, 173, 225, 293, 297, 589, 602, 617	2.2-3 2.2-6 2.3	680 98, 116, 179, 397, 438, 440 112, 116 26, 46, 112, 115,		114, 129-32, 150, 155, 179, 180, 181, 208, 227, 240, 298, 354, 368,		40, 149, 155, 181, 305, 332, 334, 343, 364, 481, 483, 512, 575, 581, 668
1.19	42, 102, 105, 130, 203, 246, 292, 313-14, 321, 439, 577, 626, 672	2.4	134, 145, 161, 175, 503 116-17, 120, 126, 136, 144, 165	2.10-11 2.11	373, 442, 511, 514, 521, 574, 594, 595, 596, 631 246 24, 26,	2.17	24, 26, 123, 135, 140-42, 158, 161, 167, 175, 185, 198, 240, 334,
1.19-20	503, 683	2.4-5	146		123, 132,		371, 441,
1.20	24, 105-07, 111, 120, 121, 160, 192, 272, 281, 317, 330,	2.5	107, 111, 117-20, 149, 155, 166, 181, 305, 483, 566, 616		162, 240, 297, 334, 371, 451, 568, 572, 606, 617, 628, 630,		451, 568, 571, 572, 577, 613, 629, 630, 670

Index of References   703

2.18	6, 142-44, 152, 158, 159, 170, 171, 185, 439, 450, 576, 577, 626	2.26	123, 131, 163, 240, 334, 370, 371, 381, 385, 451, 566, 602	3.6	615, 625, 629, 630, 658	3.14	683 6, 131, 181, 185-88, 238, 249, 263, 271, 372, 439, 456, 514, 574, 577, 627, 687
		2.26-27	6, 629	3.7	24, 170, 193, 572, 683		
2.18-29	142-158	2.26-28	26, 155-		170-73,		
2.19	98, 111, 144-46, 151, 155, 156, 160, 162, 179, 397, 438, 566, 616, 675		58, 571, 670		185, 197, 213, 223, 230, 250, 282, 293, 332, 439, 456, 574, 577, 597, 626, 682		
		2.27	157, 276, 359, 409, 581			3.14-15	121
						3.14-22	185-200
		2.28	143, 157, 290, 630, 682			3.15	111, 181, 190, 566, 616, 675
				3.7-13	170-85	3.15-16	188-89
2.20	12, 24, 42, 116, 138, 139, 146-48, 153, 161, 165, 262, 292, 318, 368, 401, 407, 409, 425, 485, 492, 516, 550, 597, 632, 680	2.28-29	419	3.8	26, 111, 115, 173-76, 178, 185, 202, 381, 384, 399, 566, 616, 675	3.16	292, 524
		2.29	24, 572, 683			3.17	189-91, 194, 234, 516
		3.1	111, 158-62, 168, 169, 170, 171, 185, 209, 210, 223, 229, 439, 566, 577, 616, 626, 675			3.17-18	126, 484
						3.18	142, 167, 190, 191, 194, 195, 231, 240, 252, 441, 450, 496, 613
				3.9	27, 29, 117, 128, 173, 175-78, 195, 263, 307, 368, 387, 399, 428, 594, 633, 680		
						3.19	118, 195-96, 200, 305
2.20-21	434, 499, 523	3.1-2	161				
		3.1-6	158-70				
		3.2	111, 162-65, 292, 399, 566, 616			3.20	189, 196-98, 568, 687
2.20-23	353, 556						
2.20-25	30			3.10	98, 114, 134, 145, 178-81, 251, 292, 337, 381, 393, 397, 438, 493, 521, 572		
2.21	12, 118, 139, 148-49, 297, 308					3.21	26, 123, 143, 157, 160, 198-200, 206, 208, 223, 229, 240, 276, 334, 361, 371, 372, 420, 451, 512, 571, 599, 600, 602, 629, 630, 659, 670, 672
		3.3	118, 122, 163-65, 179, 181, 305, 308, 381, 483				
2.21-22	305						
2.21-23	492						
2.22	111, 118, 126, 149-51, 176, 425, 566, 616	3.4	111, 142, 165-67, 168, 193, 217, 425, 473, 484, 572, 654, 673	3.11	111, 119, 132, 181-82, 208, 240, 298, 343, 354, 442, 483, 574, 668		
2.22-25	149, 153, 154						
2.23	111, 151-53, 156, 158, 246, 348, 441, 566, 616, 675, 682	3.4-5	182, 240, 252, 273, 441, 613	3.12	26, 115, 123, 142, 173, 182-85, 240, 274, 324, 334, 371, 419, 451, 577, 610, 621, 629, 652, 663	3.21-22	
		3.5	26, 123, 142, 143, 160, 163, 167-69, 208, 240, 334, 371, 394, 395, 399, 420, 425, 451, 496, 505,			3.22	24, 272, 385, 572, 683
2.24	27, 128, 153-55, 368, 594					4	203, 316, 450
2.25	111, 131, 155, 176, 181, 348					4-5	61, 206, 239, 346, 374
				3.13	24, 181, 185, 572,	4-16	494, 636
2.25-27	233						

Ref	Pages	Ref	Pages	Ref	Pages	Ref	Pages
4.1	77, 80, 88, 101, 201-03, 280, 322, 340, 491, 546, 574, 635			5.3-4	561, 583, 612, 657		275, 325, 370, 457, 602, 607, 652, 663, 665
		4.8c	213-14	5.4	221		
		4.9	94, 214-15, 217, 234, 235, 237, 271, 342, 431, 458, 496, 519, 528, 553, 563, 655, 657		167, 221-22, 531		
				5.5	123, 173, 222-24, 225, 240, 334, 418, 420, 505, 512, 531, 597		303, 463, 599
						5.11	233-35, 270, 344
4.1-5.14	5, 201-38, 487					5.11-12	
4.1-7.17	80					5.12	84, 167, 237, 250, 251, 271, 292, 342, 366, 370, 384, 408, 530, 551, 553
4.1-8.1	81						
4.1-11.19	346, 351			5.6	19, 46, 94, 129, 160, 224-27, 229, 231, 251, 276, 394, 420, 452, 463, 543, 551, 572, 576, 599, 615, 643, 658, 667, 683		
4.1-16.21	5, 7, 201-489, 487, 627	4.9-10	204, 215, 260, 464, 589, 599, 603, 665				
4.2	3, 156, 209, 493, 494, 636	4.10	103, 117, 132, 177, 215-17, 229, 240, 270, 298, 307, 325, 345, 354, 387, 399, 558, 569, 574, 639			5.12-13	65-66, 387, 431, 458, 496, 519, 528, 655, 657
4.2-3	203-06, 599						
4.3	309, 351, 496, 638, 648, 649					5.12-14	554
4.4	132, 167, 192, 206-08, 240, 252, 273, 281, 284, 298, 354, 441, 442, 496, 558, 574, 599, 600, 613, 639, 644			5.7	204, 228, 309, 599	5.13	85, 204, 212, 215, 235-37, 271, 342, 519, 528, 557, 599, 613
		4.11	167, 213, 215, 217-19, 220, 221, 230, 231, 233, 234, 235, 316, 342, 347, 370, 384, 387, 431, 432, 458, 496, 513, 519, 528, 553, 554, 583, 655, 657	5.8	103, 117, 192, 228-30, 270, 281, 282, 345, 399, 421, 422, 437, 452, 463, 496, 542, 546, 557, 558, 569, 639, 644		
						5.14	66, 103, 118, 177, 237-38, 270, 271, 307, 325, 345, 387, 463, 558, 569, 687
4.5	7, 239, 284, 288, 313, 330, 351, 399, 421, 450, 487, 599, 667, 683						
				5.8-9	229		
				5.8-10	423-24, 427	6	77, 81, 268, 291
4.5-6a	208-10	5	80, 219, 230, 267, 312, 319, 321, 452-54, 519	5.9	94, 142, 167, 234, 249, 268, 274, 322, 372, 392, 394, 430, 452, 515, 533, 551, 578, 597, 624, 654, 658		310
4.6	72, 399, 447, 450, 599, 620, 639, 659					6-9	239, 421, 463, 560, 574, 597
						6.1	247
						6.1-8	
4.6-9	463	5.1	204, 219, 260, 309, 312, 577, 597, 599			6.1-17	5, 238-58
4.6b-8b	210-13					6.1-8.5	3, 5, 201, 238-85
4.7	291, 298, 304, 376, 558					6.2	123, 132, 167, 240-41, 243, 257, 259, 298, 334, 441
		5.2	93, 167, 220-21, 234, 250, 292, 309, 318, 366, 530, 544, 597	5.9a	423		
4.8	96, 213, 230, 237, 282, 346, 347, 371, 387, 437, 456, 459, 471, 474, 505, 513,			5.9b	423		
				5.9-10	94, 230-33, 234, 387	6.3	463, 597
						6.3-4	241-43
				5.9-14	453		
		5.2-8	231	5.9b-14	213	6.4	249, 356
		5.3	221, 682	5.10	94, 266,	6.5	463, 597

Index of References

6.5-6	243-45		204, 297,		369, 387,	8.1-9.21	449
6.6	246, 463, 673		341, 347, 599, 614,		553, 558, 599	8.1-11.18 8.2	80 61, 101,
6.7	245, 463, 597	6.16-17	663 46, 436,	7.10-12 7.11	213 103, 118,		279-81, 399, 420,
6.7-8	530		452		177, 307,		546
6.8	105, 151, 245-47, 256, 287, 294, 297, 305, 385, 469, 617	6.17 7	259, 347, 356, 433, 615 52, 81, 270, 342,	7.11-12	325, 344, 345, 346, 387, 399, 558, 569, 599, 639 270-71, 463, 613	8.2-5 8.2-11.18 8.2-11.19 8.3	285 81 3-4, 201, 238 149, 192, 281-82, 300, 325,
6.9	89, 247-49, 300, 325, 372, 404, 445, 551, 597, 601	7.1 7.1-3	454 111, 212, 258-59, 260, 284, 301 280, 295	7.12	215, 218, 234, 235, 342, 346, 347, 366, 370, 384,	8.3-4 8.3-5	399, 445, 496, 497, 599, 644 474, 542 463
6.9-10	85	7.1-8	418, 610,		387, 408,	8.4	282, 399,
6.9-11	26, 269, 274, 281, 316, 463, 570, 572, 670	7.1-17 7.2	629 4-5, 238, 258-78, 428 259-60,		431, 458, 519, 528, 530, 553, 554, 655, 687	8.5	437, 557 7, 209, 281, 282-85, 286, 313, 351,
6.10	134, 172, 180, 249-52, 281, 286, 292, 338, 355, 393, 456, 459, 471, 472, 474, 475, 492, 493, 500, 521, 530, 544, 554, 555, 570, 574, 578	7.2-3 7.3 7.3-8 7.4	292, 316, 355, 589, 597, 603, 665 673 183, 260-62, 284, 318, 406, 419, 498, 559, 597, 663 295 262-64, 303, 420,	7.13 7.13-14 7.13-17 7.14 7.14-17 7.15	142, 167, 441, 496 271-74, 613 68-69 98, 126, 142, 166, 273, 324, 356, 372, 394, 404, 578, 677 26 204, 274-75, 371,	8.6 8.6-11 8.6-9.21 8.6-11.19 8.7 8.7-8	421, 445, 450, 476 101, 285, 302, 546, 564 331 5 5, 285-351 286-87, 351, 450, 476, 516, 546 445, 447,
6.11	98, 142, 167, 252-53, 273, 281, 292, 396, 441, 474, 613	7.4-8 7.4-9 7.5 7.5-8	425, 597 207, 354, 425, 639 418 597 263-67,	7.16	374, 391, 399, 599, 612, 615, 624, 652, 657, 663 118, 476	8.7-12 8.7-9.21 8.8	450, 578 212 286-308 101, 356, 476, 546, 578
6.12	286, 341, 353, 597	7.8	641, 645 597	7.16-17	275-78, 625, 628	8.8-9	287-88, 468
6.12-13	290, 356	7.9	142, 167,	7.17	289, 359,	8.9	555
6.12-14	78, 253-55		232, 274, 297, 322,		581, 599	8.10	101, 118, 289, 293,
6.13	118		392, 399,	8	81		356, 546
6.14	120, 256		420, 430,	8-9	433	8.10-11	288-90,
6.15	126, 234, 405, 457, 480, 513, 583, 586, 656	7.9-10	441, 452, 496, 515, 599, 613, 624, 654 267-70,	8.1 8.1-2 8.1-5	80, 278-79, 284, 420, 465, 597 3 5, 8, 238,	8.11 8.12 8.12-13 8.13	293, 469 623 290-91, 353, 657 101, 546 101, 134,
6.15-16	549		553, 554		278-85,		180, 212,
6.15-17	255-58	7.10	204, 271,		672		291-92,
6.16	118, 150,		292, 355,				

	293, 300, 302, 320, 338, 342, 374, 376, 393, 493, 521, 538, 540, 585	9.18 9.19 9.20	481 530, 623 357, 385, 673 80, 111, 118, 138, 149, 177, 192, 305-	10.9-10 10.10 10.11	361 320-21 42, 232, 318, 321- 23, 328, 337, 349, 393, 430, 457, 459,	11.7-12 11.8	512, 517, 572, 593, 597, 599 472 24, 335- 36, 356, 367, 373, 485, 513,
9 9-14 9.1	53 80 101, 118, 292-93, 546, 592		07, 342, 387, 455, 496, 521, 530, 566,		513, 515, 519, 583, 654		514, 517, 568, 572, 583, 641, 652
9.1-2 9.2 9.2-3 9.3 9.4	593, 597 356 293-95 385 262, 295, 406, 498, 597, 663, 673	9.20-21 9.21	569, 616 286, 308, 343, 425, 477, 479, 482 118, 139, 149, 307- 08, 631, 632, 679,	11 11.1	32-33, 42, 72, 76-77, 318, 323, 370, 404, 433, 543 31, 177, 323-25, 326, 387, 445, 569,	11.8-10 11.9 11.9-13 11.10	488, 591 232, 336- 37, 338, 372, 393, 430, 459, 515, 595 654 13, 134, 180, 318,
9.5	299, 338, 355, 436, 529, 532, 537	10	680 42, 318, 353, 519	11.1-2 11.1-13	644 327, 331, 350, 581 26, 27,		337-38, 355, 374, 393, 436, 472, 493,
9.5-6 9.7	295-97 132, 140, 192, 302, 334, 362, 564	10.1	220, 234, 308-10, 366 441, 451, 496, 530, 544,	11.2	485 318, 325- 27, 328, 329, 332, 389, 446,	11.11	521, 529, 532, 537, 542, 543, 562 338-40,
9.7-11 9.8 9.9 9.10 9.11 9.12 9.13 9.13-14 9.13-21 9.14 9.15 9.16 9.16-19 9.17 9.17-18 9.17-19	297-300 212, 304 140, 334 305, 357, 385, 673 258, 325, 412, 485, 593, 597 292, 300, 342, 374, 536, 538, 540 101, 192, 325, 399, 429, 445, 496, 644 300-01, 546 343 93, 101, 356 93, 179, 302, 362, 564, 623 302-03 579, 580 212 445, 451, 476, 590 303-05,	10.1-2 10.1-10 10.1-11.13 10.1-11.14 10.2 10.3 10.3-4 10.4 10.5 10.5-6 10.6 10.7 10.8 10.8-10 10.9	653 353 429 342 4-5, 308-43 310-12 212, 312- 13, 355 3, 421 313-15, 318, 343, 439, 577, 597, 672 382 315-16 432, 589, 603, 665 13, 24, 101, 105, 316-18, 349, 429, 453, 472, 498, 517, 542, 546, 559, 599 42, 318- 19, 465 321 319-20	11.3 11.3-4 11.3-13 11.4 11.5 11.6 11.7	459, 595, 621 327-29, 363, 377, 496, 572 572 227, 373, 382, 398, 428, 525, 674, 683 329-31, 399, 401, 513, 583 319, 331- 32, 361, 451, 476, 481, 611, 673 332-33, 385, 386, 530, 578, 581, 597 26, 123, 140, 293, 320, 333- 35, 380, 382, 385, 392, 411, 433, 505,	11.11-13 11.11-14 11.12 11.13 11.14 11.15 11.15-18	342, 356, 404, 431, 458, 602 26 604 340-41, 344, 441 118, 179, 215, 235, 341-42, 356, 431, 458, 478, 519, 528, 553, 563, 655 292, 342- 43, 374, 536, 538, 540 65, 101, 343-45, 346, 347, 369, 370, 387, 457, 513, 546, 554, 557, 561, 583, 613, 665 213, 457

Index of References 707

11.15-19	3, 5, 343-51, 449	12.1-13	499 27		512, 572, 578	13.3-4	502, 505 30, 401, 505, 569, 670
11.16	103, 118, 177, 204, 325, 345-46, 387, 399, 558, 569, 600, 639	12.1-18 12.1-14.20 12.1-15.4 12.2	5, 352-82, 485 5, 351-447 201 354-55, 436, 532, 537	12.12 12.13	27, 338, 373-75, 382, 387, 391, 398, 434, 509, 522, 542, 620 355, 375-76, 593	13.4	27, 140, 177, 213, 216, 334, 355, 387-88, 389, 392, 393, 399, 410,
11.16-18	346						422, 458,
11.17	96, 215, 218, 346-47, 370, 384, 392, 456, 471, 474, 505, 513, 554, 561, 583, 665	12.3 12.3-4 12.4 12.5	130, 355-57, 366, 511, 576, 593 355, 400 319, 357-58, 399, 400, 593 157, 276, 358-61,	12.13-17 12.14 12.15 12.15-16 12.16 12.17	363 212, 376-78, 494, 593 378, 481 289 355, 379 26, 89, 140, 334,	13.5	460, 502, 512, 539, 569, 593 127, 327, 329, 388-89, 392, 399, 509, 512, 595, 603, 665
11.17-18	387, 457		367, 581,		347, 355,	13.5-6	404, 477,
11.18	13, 43, 80, 250, 257, 288, 318, 340, 347-50, 379, 431, 433, 436, 450, 458, 459, 472, 492, 530, 542, 543, 555, 557, 559-60, 615, 654, 675	12.6 12.7 12.7-8 12.7-9 12.7-12 12.8 12.8-12	599 302, 329, 361-63, 376, 377, 494, 564 140, 334, 355, 380, 512 363-66 374, 429, 593 27, 375 530 365	12.18 13 13.1	379-81, 404, 499, 500, 512, 572 381-82, 438, 609 31, 54-55, 77, 392, 396, 414, 416, 435, 507, 508 8, 27, 127, 130,	13.6 13.7 13.8	478, 481 127, 374, 390-91, 410 123, 140, 232, 334, 391-93, 399, 407, 430, 478, 515, 542, 590, 654 134, 169, 177, 180,
11.19	4, 7, 209, 286, 313, 324, 350-51, 352, 356, 421, 443, 461, 462, 489, 574, 652	12.9	27, 128, 148, 180, 355, 366-69, 378, 401, 511, 514, 550, 568, 593, 594, 595,		210, 374, 382-83, 389, 410, 416, 417-18, 429, 441, 448, 461, 477, 495, 505, 511, 576,		216, 393-95, 401, 404, 417, 458, 460, 478, 493, 501, 505, 521, 551, 569, 577, 615, 658
11.19-14.20	81		597, 611		620	13.9	395-96
11.19-15.8	80	12.10	94, 218,	13.1-18	5, 382-	13.9-10	12, 24,
12	25, 75, 82, 242, 352, 354, 360, 362, 370, 382		269, 369-71, 384, 385, 399, 440, 542, 553, 554,	13.1-15.2 13.2	417, 589 7 27, 134, 212, 218, 355, 383-	13.10	572 98, 145, 396-97, 403, 404, 405, 408,
12-14	3-4, 7, 382, 448, 449, 462	12.10-11	612, 657 367, 375, 542		85, 389, 399, 410, 478, 518,		438, 465, 471, 472, 542
12.1	7, 132, 298, 352-54, 448, 449, 496, 639, 653	12.10-12 12.11	213, 369, 387, 457 123, 131, 371-73, 374, 381,	13.3	554, 593, 600 27, 33, 385-87, 389, 410,	13.11	8, 27, 355, 375, 397-98, 418, 429, 441, 448,
12.1-6	364, 375,		394, 451,				

708   The Apocalypse

13.11-15	461, 589, 28	14.2	229, 420-22, 452, 546, 560		445, 449, 451, 466, 476, 528	15.2	89 8, 27, 123, 229, 382, 450-52, 546
13.11-16	481						
13.11-17	27	14.3	142, 232, 422-24,	14.10-11	304, 529, 532, 537		
13.12	33, 134, 177, 180, 216, 398-400, 401, 407, 410, 460, 493, 501, 521, 569		427, 452, 463, 533, 558, 599, 639	14.11	177, 216, 437, 440, 460, 557, 569, 613, 657	15.2-4	471
						15.3	96, 111, 452-57, 470, 474, 475, 513, 526, 554, 561, 566, 575, 583, 616, 673
		14.4	25, 26, 67, 166, 232, 465, 471, 500, 533, 568, 572, 580, 601, 644	14.12	26, 98, 145, 397, 437-39, 472, 542		
13.13	400, 516						
13.13-14	482			14.13	7, 12, 26, 90, 111, 439-41, 474, 483, 566, 567, 577, 606, 616, 626, 676	15.3-4	213, 470, 513, 583, 654
13.14	28, 134, 148, 180, 400-03, 493, 501, 521, 550, 597					15.4	177, 340, 342, 359, 431, 457-61, 471, 526, 528, 565, 566, 569
		14.4b	426				
		14.4-5	424-28				
		14.5	481, 633, 681				
13.15	177, 216, 403-05, 460, 471, 500, 590, 632, 680	14.6	8, 232, 318, 428-30, 441, 445, 448, 461, 515, 654				
				14.14	8, 132, 142, 167, 192, 298, 441-42, 448, 461, 496, 613, 652	15.5	461-62, 480, 574, 623
13.15-16	559						
13.15-17	589	14.6-7	433, 458, 523, 585			15.5-6	324, 652
13.16	126, 234, 256, 262, 349, 405-06, 498, 615					15.6	192, 462-63, 496, 530, 536, 565
		14.6-11	443				
		14.6-20	520	14.14-16	444, 448		
		14.7	177, 179, 212, 215, 235, 250, 289, 340, 342, 431-32, 434, 443, 450, 477, 478, 492, 519, 528, 530, 553, 559, 563, 569, 655	14.15	179, 324, 442-44		
13.16-17	28			14.16	444	15.6-7	496, 644
13.17	232, 406-08, 533			14.17	324, 444, 652	15.7	192, 463-64, 466, 589, 603, 665
13.18	24, 27, 234, 397, 408-17, 438, 485, 506, 507, 510, 572			14.17-20	448		
				14.18	258, 325, 445, 451, 476	15.8	131, 215, 218, 235, 324, 464-65, 517, 519, 528, 530, 554, 599, 652
				14.19	445-46, 449, 466		
				14.19-20	463, 582		
14	52, 61, 452, 522			14.20	446-47, 560, 578		
		14.8	118, 139, 359, 432-34, 459, 466, 485, 493, 498, 520, 522, 523, 654	15	456	15.8-16.4	123
14.1	8, 115, 143, 183, 185, 261, 262, 417-20, 421, 422, 429, 441, 448, 461, 498, 577, 639, 663			15-16	685	16	77
				15-22	80	16-17	525
				15.1	3-4, 7, 8, 280, 352, 448-50, 455, 461, 462, 463, 466, 517, 530, 599	16-21	322
						16.1-21	5, 80, 280, 465-89
		14.9	177, 216, 262, 434-35, 437, 460, 498, 569			16.1	324, 465-66, 652
14.1-2	213, 421, 422			15.1-4	8, 672	16.2	27, 177, 216, 466-67, 478, 479, 536, 569
		14.9-10	488, 590	15.1-8	5, 448-65		
14.1-4	645	14.9-11	27	15.1-16.17	81		
14.1-5	513	14.10	257, 347, 435-37,	15.1-16.21	3-5, 201, 352, 448-		
14.1-20	5, 417-47						

Ref	Pages	Ref	Pages	Ref	Pages	Ref	Pages	Ref	Pages
16.2-9	212		180, 334, 482, 497, 511, 513, 561, 583, 585, 587, 609	17.1-18.24	587	17.9-10	509, 572
16.3	467-69, 478			17.1-18.25	80	17.9-11	29, 31
16.3-4	578			17.1-19.2	637	17.10	118, 191, 508-09, 511, 556
16.4	289, 469, 478			17.1-19.9	568		
16.4-6	475	16.15	7, 12, 26, 90, 119, 164, 181, 191, 256, 308, 483-84, 516, 567, 606, 654, 673, 677	17.1-21.8	4-5, 7, 490-633, 636	17.10-11	78-79
16.5	250, 258, 459, 469-71, 475, 492, 526, 530, 575, 673			17.2	134, 139, 180, 255, 492, 493, 501, 521, 523, 531, 632, 656	17.11	28, 509-10
						17.11-14	28
						17.12	130, 496, 504, 511, 532, 539, 595, 603, 665
16.5-7	213			17.3	3-4, 27, 127, 130, 204, 490, 493-95, 500, 511, 636, 683	17.12-13	510-12
16.6	13, 26, 43, 167, 318, 349, 471-73, 500, 501, 542, 543, 578	16.16	484-86, 512, 514, 568, 585, 587			17.13	218, 532, 539, 554
		16.17	7, 324, 486-87, 599, 626, 627, 652, 655	17.4	28, 139, 140, 192, 481, 495-97, 499, 528, 534, 538, 545, 631, 632, 638, 651	17.14	123, 131, 199, 334, 512-14, 567, 568, 574, 575, 576, 578, 580, 582, 583
16.7	96, 250, 325, 473-75, 492, 513, 526, 530, 554, 561, 575, 583, 673	16.17-21	499			17.15	139, 232, 504, 514-15, 529, 654
		16.18	209, 313, 487-88, 489	17.4-5	308, 658, 680		
16.8	475-76	16.18-21	7, 627	17.5	24, 28, 105, 139, 262, 493, 497-99, 577, 631, 632	17.15-16	308
16.8-9	478	16.18-19.21	81			17.16	121, 130, 139, 499, 504, 515-16, 530, 539, 557, 586, 632, 680
16.9	118, 127, 149, 215, 235, 342, 476-78, 519, 528, 530, 563, 655	16.19	118, 257, 335, 347, 485, 499, 523, 528, 582, 637				
		16.19-20	488	17.6	26, 30, 505, 542, 569, 572, 578	17.16-17	28, 521, 532, 539
16.10	27, 134, 478-79, 600	16.21	127, 286, 488-89, 530				
				17.6a	500-01	17.17	89, 131, 516-17, 587, 599
16.10-11	479	17	27, 28, 32, 54, 88, 493, 494, 518, 522	17.6b	501-02		
16.11	111, 118, 123, 127, 149, 479, 566, 616			17.6b-7	502-03		
				17.6-7	30, 670	17.18	255, 335, 504, 517-18, 656
				17.7	24, 27, 105, 112, 130, 511, 517, 570		
16.12	289, 302, 479-80, 511, 513, 517, 564, 583	17-18	25, 75, 622			18	28-29, 77, 522, 536
		17.1	4, 88, 139, 490-93, 498, 515, 522, 529, 600, 632, 634-35	17.8	28, 134, 169, 180, 503-06, 508, 509, 521, 577, 593, 597, 616, 658	18.1	255, 518-20, 528, 573
16.12-14	483					18.1-24	5, 490, 518-51, 552
16.12-16	640						
16.13	27, 28, 42, 355, 480-81, 497, 588, 593	17.1-2	308, 680	17.8-18	504	18.1-19.8	13
		17.1-3	4	17.9	24, 78, 234, 397, 409, 438, 506-08	18.2	234, 256, 306, 481, 520-22, 530, 585
		17.1-18	5, 490-518, 525, 552				
16.13-14	306, 521						
16.14	96, 140,						

18.2-3	118		234, 288,		622		256, 516,	
18.3	28, 126,		292, 335,	19.6	65, 96,		586, 591,	
	139, 218,		516, 540-		234, 256,		615	
	234, 308,		41		560-61	19.19	28, 140,	
	359, 522-	18.20	13, 213,	19.6-8	570		334, 587-	
	24, 528,		250, 318,	19.7	215, 235,		88, 590,	
	532, 537,		338, 541-		302, 548,		591, 592,	
	554, 632,		44, 550,		561-64,		656	
	654, 656,		553, 558-		655	19.20	28, 42,	
	680		59, 600,	19.7-8	426, 622,		148, 177,	
18.4	524-25,		643		635, 683		216, 304,	
	530	18.21	234, 256,	19.8	349, 537,		401, 588-	
18.4-5	526		335, 544-		564-67		90, 591,	
18.5	526, 541		45	19.8-9	606		597, 611,	
18.6	111, 526-	18.21-23	625	19.9	7, 89, 90,		617, 633	
	28, 541,	18.21-24	567		141, 198,	19.21	140, 590-	
	566, 616	18.22-23	552		548, 567-		92, 598,	
18.7	152, 528-	18.22-23a	545-48		69, 575,		604	
	29, 530,	18.23	148, 256,		577, 606,	20	618	
	531, 532,		307, 359,		670, 676	20.1	80, 293,	
	537-38,		563, 597,	19.9-10	573, 672		592-93	
	539, 540,		621, 632,	19.10	42, 98,	20.1-6	79, 490,	
	553		635, 654,		118, 177,		552	
18.7-8	533, 538,		655, 679		216, 227,	20.1-10	6, 81,	
	540	18.23b-24	548-51		567, 569-		592-613,	
18.8	234, 250,	18.24	13, 26,		73, 589,		619	
	256, 529-		43, 318,		601, 670,	20.2	27, 111,	
	30, 532,		336, 349,		671, 683		301, 355,	
	557		578	19.10a	89		593-95	
18.9	255, 304,	19	25, 592	19.10b	89	20.3	27, 93,	
	308, 530-	19.1	215, 218,	19.11	131, 140,		131, 148,	
	31, 557,		235, 255,		142, 167,		293, 595-	
	632, 656,		269, 552-		250, 334,		99, 608,	
	680		54, 560,		573-75,		611, 655	
18.10	179, 234,		655		585, 592,	20.4	28, 89,	
	250, 256,	19.1-8	213		600, 613,		166, 177,	
	292, 335,	19.1-10	6, 490,		627, 673		262, 599-	
	531-32,		552-73	19.11-16	6, 108,		604, 613	
	541, 572	19.1-21.8	5, 552-		241, 552	20.4-6	26	
18.11	232, 532-		633	19.11-21	6, 490,	20.5	81, 131,	
	33, 538	19.1-22.21	80		573-92		604-06	
18.12	192, 545,	19.2	26, 139,	19.12	575-78	20.5-6	339	
	638, 651		250, 251,	19.13	89, 115,	20.6	7, 73, 90,	
18.12-13	533-36,		308, 554-		578-79		94, 132,	
	549		56, 559,	19.14	142, 167,		162, 325,	
18.14	536-37		575, 578,		579-80,		606-07,	
18.15	126, 234,		632, 673,		613		617, 652,	
	537-38,		680	19.15	96, 140,		663	
	549	19.3	304, 556-		257, 276,	20.7	75, 93,	
18.16	179, 192,		57, 613		347, 580-		131, 607-	
	292, 335,	19.4	104, 118,		82, 598,		08	
	545, 638,		177, 204,		655	20.7-8	27	
	651		557-59,	19.16	65, 115,	20.7-10	490, 552	
18.16-17a	538-39		569, 599,		582-83	20.7-20	27	
18.17	234, 541		639, 687	19.17-21	552, 591	20.8	140, 148,	
18.17b-18	539-40	19.5	157, 340,	19.17-18	198, 583-		212, 334,	
18.18	304, 335,		349, 431,		87, 591,		608-09,	
	557		559-60,		592, 653		640-41,	
18.19	126, 179,		599, 615,	19.18	234, 255,		655	

Reference	Pages
20.9	319, 609-11
20.10	28, 42, 131, 148, 304, 600, 611-13, 617, 633, 657
20.11	142, 167, 613-14, 619, 663
20.11-15	6, 490, 552, 613-18
20.11-22.21	81
20.12	59, 169, 349, 614-16, 658
20.12-13	111, 250, 566, 675
20.13	616-17
20.13-14	105, 246
20.14	132, 162, 304, 617-18
20.15	169, 618, 658
21	81
21-22	72
21.1	72, 142, 210, 618-20
21.1-2	426, 637
21.1-8	6, 490, 552, 618-33, 646, 652
21.2	142, 184, 302, 548, 620-22, 635, 637, 649
21.3	374, 391, 622-24, 661
21.3-4	629
21.4	277, 624-25, 626
21.5	131, 142, 204, 625-28, 666
21.6	7, 187, 276, 289, 627, 659, 676
21.7	123, 628-30
21.8	132, 138, 139, 162, 304, 307, 630-33, 634, 658, 678, 679, 680
21.9	4, 88, 548, 634-36, 665
21.9-10	4, 637
21.9-21	634
21.9-22.5	6, 634-65, 666, 677
21.9-22.9	4, 7,
21.10	3-4, 88, 184, 204, 326, 634, 636-38, 683
21.11	215, 235, 638-39, 653, 659
21.12	639-40, 647
21.12-13	354, 661
21.12-14	207
21.13	640-42, 652, 654
21.14	31, 33, 642-44
21.15	192, 644
21.15-16	323
21.16	645-46, 652
21.17	646-48
21.18	192, 648
21.19	206
21.19-20	648-50
21.19-21	205
21.21	192, 497, 650-52
21.22	96, 324, 345, 652-53
21.22-27	634
21.23	215, 235, 653-54
21.24	93, 111, 166, 174, 178, 256, 654-56
21.24-25	665
21.24-26	658, 661
21.25	665
21.25-26	656-58
21.27	168, 169, 658, 679
22.1	88, 537,
22.1-2	659, 662
22.1-2a	65, 289
22.1-5	658-660
22.2	634
22.2b	660
22.3-4	660-62
22.4	662-64
22.5	183, 185, 262
22.6	664-65
22.6-7	13, 43, 88, 131, 318, 543, 643, 666-68, 669, 670, 671, 683
22.6-9	6
22.6-11	666, 672
22.6-21	8
22.7	4, 6, 666-688
22.7-20	7, 90, 95, 119, 181, 343, 517, 668-69, 671, 674, 686
22.8	12
22.8-9	11, 41, 88, 104, 118, 177, 216, 669-70
22.9	567
22.9-10	12, 43, 98, 177, 318, 670, 671-72
22.10	517
22.11	12, 91, 375, 672
22.12	672-74, 675
22.12-20	95, 119, 181, 343, 348, 674-75, 686
22.13	187, 675-76
22.14	7, 90, 676-78, 686
22.15	138, 139, 307, 678-81
22.16	10, 158, 173, 537, 679, 681-82
22.17	239, 548, 682-84
22.18	686
22.18-19	12, 43, 517, 684-86
22.20	67, 95, 119, 181, 239, 343, 679, 686-87
22.21	11, 688

OTHER ANCIENT REFERENCES

Pseudepigrapha
3 Maccabees
| 2.28-30 | 406 |

Josephus
War
| 5.270 | 489 |

Early Jewish and Christian Authors

Andrew of Caesarea
Com Apoc
| 13.2 | 384 |
| 16.21 | 489 |

ApocJohnChry
1-4	56
5-10	56
8-19	56
20-51	56

Clement of Alexandria
Who Is the Rich Man that Is Saved
| 42 | 38, 48 |

CopApocJohn
2	58
3	58
7	58
13	58
14	58
18	58

Didache
| 14.1 | 39 |

Eusebius
EH
3.23.5-6	38
3.34.2	50
3.39.8-17	50
4.26.9-10	36
5.1.10	427

5.24.3	44	Origen		24	57	Pliny	
7.25.1-27	48	*Com on John*		25	57	*Letters*	
7.25.1-2	48	6.173	578	26	57	10.46, 47	36
7.25.7-8a	48	10.35	40	27	57	*Natural History*	
7.25.8b-11	48	Primasius		35	57	34.139	508
7.25.17-24	48	*Com Apoc*		Tyconius		Plutarch	
7.25.26	48	16.9	478	*Com Apoc*		*De Iside et Osiride*	
7.25.17	48	*Second Apoc John*		14.8	433	75	416
Gos. Pet.		1	55	**Classical References**		*Nicias*	
35	39	2-3	56	Cicero		29	406
50	39	7	56	*Ad Att*		Suetonius	
Hippolytus		8	56	6.5	507	*Nero*	
De Antichristo		10-11	56	Herodotus		16.2	35
18	48	17	56	*Hist.*		39	412
36-42	48	18-19	56	1.178	645	49	403
Ignatius		20	56	Horace		Strabo	
Magn.		24	56	*Carm.*		*Geography*	
9.1	39	27	56	7	507	13.4.14	189
Irenaeus		*Sibylline Oracles*		Lucian		Tacitus	
Against Heresies		5.343	35	*Alexander False Prophet*		*Annals*	
1.26.3	48	Tertullian		24	404	3.37	133
2.22.5	38	*Against Marcion*		Martial		3.72	508
3.3.4	38	3.14.3	48	4.64	507	4.30	98-99
3.11.11	212	3.14.4	48	Ovid		15.44	34
4.14.2	48	*Apology*		*Trist*		Vergil	
4.20.11	48	5.4	36	1.5.69	507	*Aenid*	
5.26.1	48	*Third ApocJohn*		Philostratus		6.783	507
5.30.3	39	1	57	*Vit. Apoll.*		*Geor.*	
Justin Martyr		2-10	57	4.20	147	11.535	507
Dialogue with Trypho		11-35	57	4.38	35		
81.4	37, 47	23-27	57				
		23	57				

NAME INDEX

Alcmean 412
Allo, E.-B. 87, 222, 261, 283, 330, 356, 385, 400, 422, 442-443, 447, 560, 561, 565, 575, 588, 609, 616, 636, 642
Ancus Marcus 508
Andrew of Caesarea 384, 489
Andrew of Crete 57
Antiochus the Great 159, 165
Antipas 25-27, 131, 135, 136, 179, 187, 227, 249, 307, 328, 335, 396, 397, 405, 427, 438, 472, 514, 572
Archer, M.L. 345-346, 350
Augustus 32, 133, 134, 509
Aune, D.E. 2, 31, 34, 39, 92, 112, 120, 122, 125, 134, 151, 158, 167, 186, 189-190, 208, 217, 221-222, 225, 228, 242, 244, 246, 248, 250, 254, 268, 280, 289, 296, 312, 314-315, 321, 331, 335, 340, 342, 348, 354, 363, 367, 390, 393, 395, 397-398, 404, 408, 422, 429, 431, 436-437, 444, 446, 465, 474, 477, 479, 482, 492, 495-496, 498, 502, 506, 508-509, 516, 518, 520, 526-528, 534, 537, 542, 544, 552, 556, 559, 565, 576, 582, 588, 590, 605-606, 609, 613, 617, 621, 625, 631, 639, 643-644, 649, 651, 653, 653,
656, 658, 661, 667, 675-676, 679
Bacchiocchi, A. 40, 101
Ball, D. 96
Balz, H. 169, 180, 221, 292
Barr, D.L. 8-9
Barton, J. 428
Bauckham, R. 2, 10, 13, 15-16, 29, 33, 43, 92, 156, 206, 209, 212, 214, 223, 226, 227, 229, 232, 235, 262, 279, 284, 309-310, 312, 315, 323, 329, 337, 342, 345, 367, 412-414, 422, 428-429, 432, 443, 453, 510, 531, 534-535, 572-573, 624, 627, 648, 656, 671-672, 682, 684
Bauer, J.B. 359
Beale, G.K. 16, 33, 39, 47, 88, 91, 93, 105, 142, 152, 177, 193, 196, 209, 215, 239, 245, 251, 273, 281, 289, 300, 309, 322, 331, 354, 361, 406, 418-419, 433, 439, 468-469, 477, 511, 518, 570, 586, 628
Beasley-Murray, G.R. 87, 135, 303, 331, 335, 339, 389, 400, 437, 448, 464, 480, 488, 508, 526, 553, 555, 557, 568, 576, 579, 583, 586, 597, 612, 620, 623, 626, 629, 633, 644, 645, 647, 649, 656-657, 670, 681, 685
Beatus 62, 584
Bede 80-81
Benham, P. 101, 157, 314, 474, 509
Benson, E.W. 9
Beyer, H. 145, 383
Biguzzi, G. 681
Bloom, H. 72
Bocher, O. 293
Bockelson, J. 52
Boesak, A.A. 83-86, 252
Bowman, J.W. 9
Braumann, G. 561
Brewer, R.R. 9
Brown, C. 637
Brown, R.E. 22
Bruns, J.E. 499
Budge, E.W. 58
Bugliosi, V. 53
Burrows, D. 66
Caird, G.B. 47, 159, 184, 206, 210, 224, 259, 262, 336, 342, 372, 396, 403, 452, 458, 465, 477, 502, 505, 507, 532, 553, 563, 570, 573, 580, 598, 607, 609, 614, 616, 626, 628, 633, 645, 656, 664, 686
Callahan, A.D. 47
Charette, B.B. 348
Charles, J.D. 229
Charles, R.H. 46, 143, 176
Cheung, P.W. 499
Cicero 244, 507
Claudius 32, 499
Clement of Alexandria 38, 48
Cloete, G.D. 631
Collins, J.J. 14
Collins, A. Yarbro 160, 164. 173. 187, 202, 244. 248, 308, 322, 419, 424, 431, 442, 529
Colson, F.H. 416

Constantius 82
Court, J. 55-58
Cyprian 57
Cyril 38
Cyrus 159, 165
Dansk, E. 9
Day, J. 486
DeCaro, S. 110
Deford, S. 72
Deissmann, A. 412
Deppermann, K. 52
Deutch, C. 636
Domitian, 30, 32, 35, 36, 38, 39, 79, 83, 84, 509
Donaldson, J. 36, 38
Draper, J.A. 275
Drewery, B. 52
Eusebius 35, 36, 38, 44, 48-49, 80, 427
Farrer, A.M. 315
Fee, G.D. 50, 118, 158, 206, 212, 269, 442, 620
Feuillet, A. 249
Folger, A. 53
Frey, J. 23, 46
Frykowski, V. 53
Gaechter, P. 603
Gaius 32
Galba 32, 79, 84, 509
Gause, R.H. 128, 278, 303, 310, 327, 356-357, 376, 384, 387, 390, 395, 398, 423, 439, 443, 449, 458, 461, 476, 479, 496, 502, 517, 519, 537, 550, 557, 564, 577, 591, 594, 599, 604, 607, 611, 613, 618, 623, 640, 644, 646, 648, 653, 660, 674
Giblin, C.H. 332
Giesen, H. 165
Glancy, J.A. 493, 499
de Goedt, M. 129
Goldingay, J. 558
Gregory 38, 62
Griffiths, J.G. 416
Grubb, N. 61
Gundry, R.H. 624, 630
Hadorn, W. 412
Hall, R.G. 211

Handel 65-66, 70
Harrison, R.K. 110
Hartman, L. 390
Hauret, C. 356, 381
Hemer, C.J. 37, 110, 125, 133, 576
Hengel, M. 23, 44
Herms, R. 656
Herod 32, 82
Herodotus, 645
Heschel, A.J. 13
Hicks, A. 66
Hill, D. 24, 88
Hillyer, N. 225
Hippolytus 38, 48
Hoffman, M. 51-52
Hofius, O. 394
Holmes, M.W. 38
Holwerda, D.E. 322
Horace 507
Hort, F.J.A. 46
Howell, V.W. 54
Hurtado, 206, 208
Irenaeus 38, 48, 62, 212, 414
Jackson, J. 35
Jauhiainen, M. 328, 486
Joachim 81-83, 357
Johns, L.L. 223, 227
Josephus 498
Joyce, P. 486
Julius Caesar 32, 509
Justin Martyr 37, 47
Juvenal 499
Keynes, M. 9
Kiddle, M. 168, 203, 221, 228, 237, 246, 262, 301, 336, 378, 385, 398, 399, 405, 460, 509, 525, 550, 559, 567, 576-577, 591, 615, 617, 620, 645, 649, 660
Koester, C.R. 70, 110, 171, 188, 189, 202, 212, 216, 237, 321, 323, 329, 335, 341, 364, 413-414, 424, 432, 437, 463, 467, 478, 485, 523, 534, 551, 571, 578, 580, 587, 603, 608, 645, 664
Koresh, D. 54-55

Kovacs, J. 83, 241, 328, 357, 578?
Kretschmar, G. 81
Kretzer, A. 537
LaBianca, L. 53
LaBianca, R. 53
Ladd, G.E. 224, 280, 356, 396, 432, 438, 463, 476, 495, 503, 508, 515, 535, 556, 578, 587, 598, 602, 605, 611, 614, 622, 631, 647, 659, 675, 678-680
LaHaye, T. 77
Lake, K. 36, 38, 48, 49
Lampe, P. 262
Lee, P. 620, 639
Légasse, S. 450
Lemcio, E.E. 17, 20
Linton, G. 14
Litchenberger, H. 280
Livia 159
Lohse, E. 220
Longennecker, B.W. 672
Lucian 404
MacKenzie, R.K. 44
Manson, C. 53-54
Marshal, E. 80
Martial 507
Martin, C.J. 535
Martin, L.R. 90, 210, 350, 640
Mathewson, D. 623, 625, 655, 661, 662
Mayo, P.L. 127, 128, 177, 660
Mazzaferri, F.D. 2, 13, 42, 572
McIlraith, D.A. 564, 566, 574-575, 577, 580
Mealy, J.W. 588, 598, 600, 602, 604, 609, 616, 648
Melito of Sardis 21, 35-36
Merkel, F. 555
Mesomoth 82
Methodius 38
Metzger, B.M. 18, 212, 226, 230, 259, 287, 336, 411, 485, 564, 580, 607, 614-615, 617-618, 651, 663, 677-678
Meynet, R. 454

Author Index 715

Michaels, J.R.   21, 224, 228, 237, 282-283, 287, 291, 304, 346, 386, 428, 462, 479, 483, 488, 527, 529, 542, 567, 570, 572, 589, 591, 614, 631, 646, 658, 663, 669, 672, 674-675, 681, 683, 685
Miles, B.   54
Miller, K.E.   569, 573
Mohammed   82
Monachus, G.   49
Moore, R.D.   13, 16, 41, 47
Moore, S.D.   493
Morton, R.   213
Mounce, R.H.   133, 139, 159, 171, 182, 197, 220, 245, 260, 271, 282, 299, 314, 320, 383, 436, 468, 470, 510, 521, 528-529, 534-535, 551, 556, 567, 576, 590, 598, 608, 611, 614-616, 621, 629, 632, 634, 646, 650-652, 677, 680, 688
Moyise, S.   17, 45, 110
Muddiman, J.   428
Murphy, F.J.   17, 31, 125, 141, 143, 149, 155 158, 176, 187, 188, 224, 230, 251, 272-273, 277-278, 281, 283, 285, 301, 307, 347, 350, 354, 380, 404, 425, 446, 482, 488, 491, 495, 506, 509, 516, 526, 528, 530, 541, 548, 551, 558, 561, 568, 572, 589, 606, 613-614, 627, 631, 638, 652, 659, 662, 669
Musvosi, J.N.   454
Nero   29-36, 79, 82, 84, 403, 412, 413-414, 416, 499, 507
Nerva   32, 79
Newport, K.   54, 66
Numa Pompilius   508
Nutzel, J.M.   178

Orestes   412
Origen   40, 261, 578
Orton, D.E.   486
Osborne, G.R.   47, 88, 96, 102-103, 105, 107, 112, 114, 119, 126, 128, 148, 191, 197, 202, 205, 209, 215, 218, 222, 257, 275, 293, 297, 305, 307, 328, 335, 384, 400, 432, 476, 480, 518
Otho   32, 79, 509
Ovid   507
Ozanne, C.G.   46
Painter, J.   18
Parent, S.E.   53
Pattemore, S.   249, 250, 251, 253, 258, 270, 275, 336, 391, 395, 422, 425, 426, 474, 600, 624, 632, 656, 680
Pederson, S.   679
Philonenko, M.   679
Philostratus   35
Pilate   34, 197, 335, 371
Pliny   36, 37, 499, 508
Plutarch   406, 416
Poirier, J.C.   242, 247
Polanski, S.T.   53
Poldermann, C.   52
Porter, J.E.   486
Poucouta, P.   24
Primasius   477
Prigent, P.   2, 23 131, 135, 144, 161, 177, 188, 199, 225-226, 228, 271, 280, 298, 303, 323, 334, 354, 358, 388, 397, 431, 447, 450, 460, 470, 475, 481, 489, 491492, 497, 514, 524, 539, 543, 551, 553, 555, 557, 563, 564, 566, 575-576, 587, 590, 597, 605, 616, 627, 629, 631, 638, 643, 648, 653, 674
Provain, I.   534
Putter, A.   70
Radl, W.   291
Ramsay, W.   21, 109-110

Resseguie, J.L.   4, 47, 87, 89, 92, 125, 158, 161, 182, 197, 211, 217, 219, 227, 234, 245, 255, 258, 261, 267, 269, 280, 283, 287, 293, 296, 305, 312, 315, 328-329, 334, 336, 380, 382-384, 406, 447, 453, 458, 476, 507-508, 512, 518, 525, 533, 589, 595, 614, 640, 652, 661, 663, 677
Rissi, M.   575, 598
Roberts, A.   36, 38
Robinson, J.A.T.   84
Rolfe, J.C.   35, 412
Romulus   508
Rowland, C.C.   83, 241, 328, 357, 578, 589
Royalty, Jr., R.M.   685
Ruiz, J.P.   10, 24, 46
Saladin   82
Sand, A.   288, 540
Sanger, D.   200
Schneider, C.   479
Schneider, G.   88, 491, 506, 635
Schimanowski, G.   224
Schwenckfield, C.   52
Schroder, J.A.   359
Schussler, F.E.   14-16, 210, 252, 269, 282, 486, 502, 525, 585, 620, 672
Schwarzenegger, A.   74-75
Seabring, J.   53
Sellers, O.R.   645
Shepherd of Hermas   15
Servius Tullius   508
Siebeck, P.   22
Simoens, Y.   23, 91, 108, 155, 207, 209, 211
Skaggs, R.   101, 157, 314, 474, 509
Skehan, P.W.   583
Slater, T.B.   575-576, 583, 587, 592
Smalley, S.S.   9, 23, 88-90, 98-99, 102, 105, 109, 151-152, 166-168, 173-174, 177, 186, 196,

198, 202-203, 205, 215, 217, 219-220, 222, 225, 244-245, 249, 257-258, 263-264, 266-267, 276, 280-281, 289-291, 294, 298, 300, 317, 321-322, 328, 334, 344, 349, 363, 371, 388-389, 393, 410, 418, 419, 428, 430-431, 433, 435-436, 439-440-441, 446, 451-452, 454, 461, 463, 466, 467, 470, 477, 480-482, 491, 493, 497, 499, 501, 506-507, 515, 519-520, 524, 525, 527, 530, 532, 534, 535, 544, 550, 553, 555, 557, 560, 566, 573, 582, 585, 587, 589, 590, 600, 607, 608, 612, 613, 615, 616-617, 619, 622-624, 626, 628, 636-637, 640, 644-645, 650, 652, 657, 659, 672, 675, 677, 679, 681, 683
Smith, C.R. 265
Smith, E. 65
Stenger, W. 296
Stevenson, J. 59-60
Strabo 189
Suetonius II 35, 403, 412

Sweet, J. 14, 19, 165, 179, 198, 231, 244, 259, 290, 298, 305, 313, 332, 385-386, 398, 404, 408, 410, 421, 425, 440, 476-477, 481, 483-484, 522, 525, 528, 530, 539, 544, 559, 566, 568-569, 575, 580-581, 585, 589590, 599, 602, 609-610, 614, 619, 625, 628, 631-633, 637, 640, 645-649, 656-657, 662, 676, 685
Swete, H.B. 519
Tacitus IV 34-35, 98, 133, 499, 508
Tarquinius Priscus 508
Tarquinius Superbus 508
Tertullian 36, 48
Thayer, J.H. 304
Thomas, J.C. 16, 19, 22, 49-50, 113-114, 150, 156, 166, 171, 193, 409, 482, 494, 606, 608, 661, 667, 677, 686
Tiberius 32, 34, 170, 509
Titus, 32, 79, 509
Tobin, J. 65-66
Trajan, 32, 36, 38, 412
Trummer 217
Tulla Hostilius 508
Tyconius 62, 80, 81, 83, 433

Untergassmair, G. 149
Unwin, T.F. 9
Valeria Messalina 499
Van der Meer, F. 61-62, 65, 246
Vergil 507
Vespasian 32, 79, 170, 509
Vettius 427
Victorinus 43, 77-80, 241
Vitellius 32, 79, 509
Waddell, R.C. 19, 44, 310, 326, 329, 331, 336, 543, 573
Wainwright, A.W. 52, 83
Wall, R.W. 11, 17, 18, 20, 142, 206, 239, 244, 283, 297, 301, 320, 333, 338, 433, 467, 497, 507, 525, 527, 563, 605, 652, 674, 684
Wallis, R.E. 77-79
Walsh, R. 76
Webster, J.S. 124
Weiser, A. 145
Wesley, C. 66-67, 70
Wesley, J. 66
Whealey, A. 55
Williams, G.H. 52
Williams, J. 62
Wojciechowski, M. 650
Wren, M. 52
York, M. 76
Zimmerman, R. 548, 622
Zmijewski, J. 497